ULTIMATE TEAM PRO PACK INCLUDING BARRY SANDERS

Go to www.PrimaGames.com/MUTProPack and enter the code below*

ULTIMATE TEAM PRO PACK WITH BARRY SANDERS

Enter your code:

dzmj-jdpv-zxkx-hjfx

Once you get your FREE Pro Pack with Barry Sanders...

Go the the Ultimate Team section of the guide

to find out more about this free-to-play game mode that combines player trading items with on-the-field Madden NFL action. Along the way, you can earn, buy, auction, and trade players to build your ultimate team of football legends past and present. In Ultimate Team mode you put together a team that fits any style or mold you want and then compete against other players!

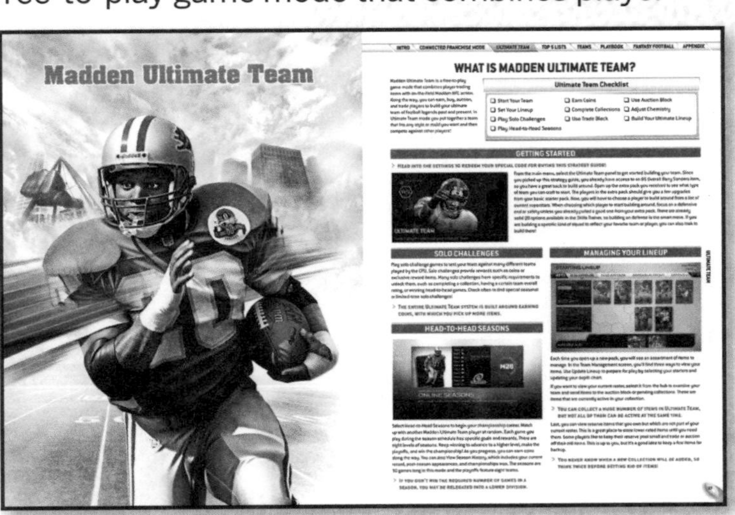

*GOOD ONLY FOR NEW PURCHASES OF THE PRIMA MADDEN NFL 25 OFFICIAL G

EA SPORTS
MADDEN
NFL
1989
25
2014

Glossary 4

New Features 8

HOW WE ADVANCED THE GUIDE 8
WHAT'S NEW IN *MADDEN NFL 25* 8

Connected Franchise Walkthrough 13

BUILDING A POWERHOUSE FRANCHISE IN NFL 25: TIPS, TRICKS, AND STRATEGIES 14
GETTING STARTED 14
TOP 5 OFFENSIVE CREATE-A-PLAYER POSITION TYPES 16
TOP 5 DEFENSIVE CREATE-A-PLAYER POSITION TYPES 17
TOP 5 WIN NOW TEAMS 18
TOP 5 TEAMS FOR THE FUTURE 19
TOP 5 TEAMS FOR REBUILDING 20
TOP 5 SLEEPER TEAMS 21
TOP 5 FANTASY DRAFT TIPS 22
ON THE JOB 24
OWNER DUTIES 27
MOVING YOUR TEAM 30
SCOUTING 32
POSTSEASON 34
OFF SEASON 34
NFL DRAFT 35
START SEASON 2! 35

Madden Ultimate Team 36

WHAT IS MADDEN ULTIMATE TEAM? 37
TOP 5 BEST OVERALL PLAYERS 41
TOP 5 OFFENSIVE STARTER CAPTAINS 42
TOP 5 DEFENSIVE STARTER PLAYERS 43
TOP 5 COLLECTION TYPES 44
TOP 5 COIN-COLLECTING TIPS 45

Top 5 Lists 46

THE TOP 25 PLAYS IN *MADDEN NFL 25*! 48

TOP 5 NEW GAMEPLAY TIPS 50
NEW GAMEPLAY MECHANICS 50
NEW RUN GAME TIPS 51
NEW GAMEPLAY CONTROLS 52
NEW HOT ROUTES 53
PRECISION MODIFIER MOVES 54
TOP 5 MADDEN SHARE TIPS 55

TOP 5 BEGINNER TIPS 56
HOW TO PLAY OFFENSE 56
HOW TO PLAY DEFENSE 58
HOW TO PLAY SPECIAL TEAMS 60
CHOOSING A PLAYBOOK 62
SETTING YOUR LINEUP 63
HOW TO SET YOUR OFFENSIVE AUDIBLES 64
HOW TO SET YOUR DEFENSIVE AUDIBLES 65
HOW TO STOP THE RUN 66
TOP 5 GAME PLAN TIPS 67

TOP 5 EXPERT TIPS 68
COMMONLY ASKED QUESTIONS 68
TOP 5 OFFENSIVE FORMATIONS 70
DEFENSIVE FORMATIONS 71
OPTION REQUIREMENTS 72
WAYS TO DEFEND THE OPTION 73
WAYS TO USE PRACTICE MODE 74
WAYS TO READ DEFENSIVE COVERAGES 75
WAYS TO STOP SCRAMBLING QBS 76
WAYS TO DEFEND TIGHT ENDS 77
WAYS TO DEFEND SCREEN PASSES 78
WAYS TO STOP SLOT WRS 79
WAYS TO DEFEND THE RED ZONE 80
WAYS TO DEFEND A NO-HUDDLE ATTACK 81
WAYS TO SET UP BLITZES 82

TOP 5 DEVELOPER TIPS 83
NEW THINGS TO LOOK OUT FOR WITH REX DICKSON 83
NEW PLAYBOOKS WITH ANTHONY WHITE 84
BLOCKING TIPS WITH CLINT OLDENBURG 85
OFFENSIVE RATINGS WITH DONNY MOORE 86
DEFENSIVE RATINGS WITH DONNY MOORE 87
TOP 5 PLAYERS 88
QUARTERBACKS 89
HALFBACKS 90
WIDE RECEIVERS 91
TIGHT ENDS 92
DEFENSIVE ENDS 93
DEFENSIVE TACKLES 94
LINEBACKERS 95
CORNERBACKS 96
SAFETIES 97

TOP 5 TEAMS 98
ONLINE RANKED GAME TEAMS 98
RUSHING TEAMS 99
PASSING TEAMS 100
DEFENSIVE TEAMS 101
SLEEPER TEAMS 102

Teams 103

OVERVIEW 104

HOW TO USE THE TEAMS CHAPTER: OFFENSIVE PLAYS 104
HOW TO USE THE TEAMS CHAPTER: DEFENSIVE PLAYS 105
CHICAGO BEARS 106
CINCINNATI BENGALS 112
BUFFALO BILLS 118
DENVER BRONCOS 124
CLEVELAND BROWNS 130
TAMPA BAY BUCCANEERS 136
ARIZONA CARDINALS 142
SAN DIEGO CHARGERS 148
KANSAS CITY CHIEFS 154
INDIANAPOLIS COLTS 160
DALLAS COWBOYS 166
MIAMI DOLPHINS 172
PHILADELPHIA EAGLES 178
ATLANTA FALCONS 184
SAN FRANCISCO 49ERS 190
NEW YORK GIANTS 196
JACKSONVILLE JAGUARS 202
NEW YORK JETS 208
DETROIT LIONS 214
GREEN BAY PACKERS 220
CAROLINA PANTHERS 226
NEW ENGLAND PATRIOTS 232
OAKLAND RAIDERS 238
ST. LOUIS RAMS 244
BALTIMORE RAVENS 250
WASHINGTON REDSKINS 256
NEW ORLEANS SAINTS 262
SEATTLE SEAHAWKS 268
PITTSBURGH STEELERS 274
HOUSTON TEXANS 280
TENNESSEE TITANS 286
MINNESOTA VIKINGS 292

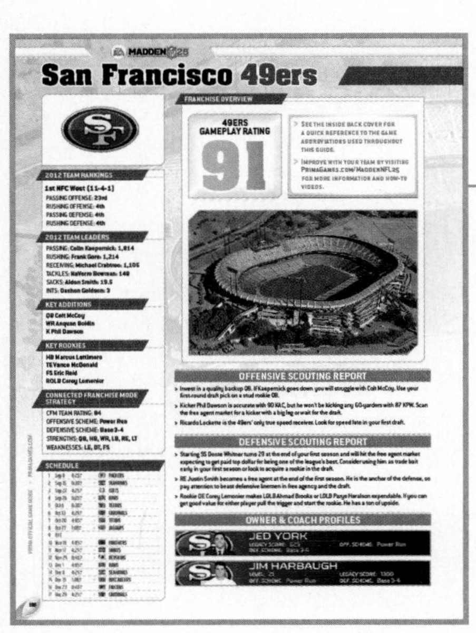

Playbook 298

MINNESOTA VIKINGS OFFENSIVE TOURNAMENT GUIDE 299

WITH US, WINNING IS EASY 299
FORMATIONS AND PLAYS 300
TEAM SELECTION 300
TOP 5 TEAMS TO USE 301
GUN EMPTY BUNCH 302
GUN TREY OPEN 304
GUN TRIPS TE 306
SINGLEBACK BUNCH 308
FULL HOUSE NORMAL WIDE 310
GOAL LINE 312

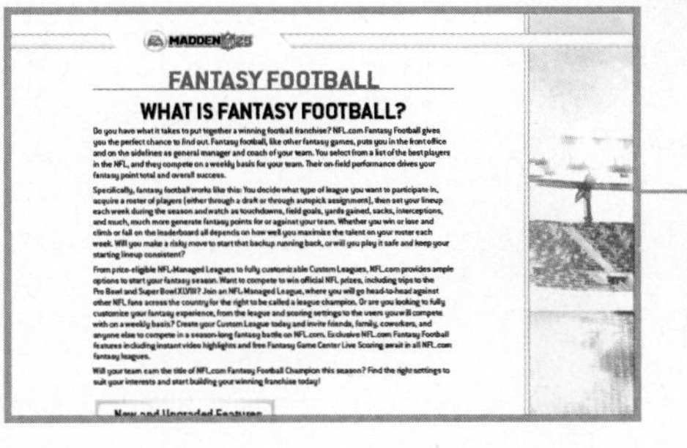

Fantasy Football 314

FOREWORD BY MICHAEL FABIANO 315

FANTASY FOOTBALL 316

WHAT IS FANTASY FOOTBALL? 316
WHY CHOOSE NFL.COM FANTASY? 316
SCORING SETTINGS (NFL-MANAGED) 317
HEAD-TO-HEAD SCORING FORMAT 317
LEAGUE SETTINGS 317
NFL-MANAGED DRAFT TYPES 317

FANTASY FOOTBALL EXPERT TIPS WITH NFL.COM'S MICHAEL FABIANO 318

TOP 5 MUST-HAVE PLAYERS 318
TOP 5 SLEEPERS 319
TOP 5 OVERRATED PLAYERS 320
TOP 5 ROOKIES 321
TOP 5 WAIVER SECRETS 322
TOP 5 DRAFT DAY TIPS 323
TOP 5 AUCTION DRAFT TIPS 324

Appendix 327

GLOSSARY

Here are some common football terms that are used in the *Madden NFL 25* guide. This section will give you a reference point to check if you aren't understanding a specific term. With so much information packed into the main sections of the guide, we often overlook some key terms that newer players may not understand yet. There is also a manual inside *Madden NFL 25* that includes full controls that can further help with questions you may encounter playing the game. Feel free to email us at ZFarls@maddentips.com or SGibs@maddentips.com if you have any additional questions.

A gap — The gap in the offensive line between the center and the guards is the A gap. There is one to the right and one to the left. This is the fastest way to the QB since it's right up the middle.

Audible/Audibling — The act of coming to the line and then changing your play. If you call something in the huddle and get to the line of scrimmage and realize the defense is doing something different than you expected, you want to call an audible. This will allow you to change your play to something you think will work better. You can set up to five audibles before the game to make sure you are ready for any situation.

Blitz — On offense, the defense may look to blitz you by bringing more defenders towards your QB than you can block. On defense, you blitz by rushing more players at the QB than your opponent can block. This leaves your coverage vulnerable, but you may force the offense into a bad decision or get a sack.

Block an HB — Blocking an HB is done by putting a player behind the line into a blocking hot route. This will help if you sense a blitz coming at your offense and want him to stay in and block.

Blue Route — This is a "block-and-release" route, which tells your offensive player (whose route is blue) to help block before releasing out on his route for a pass.

The Box — The area on defense before the snap where the defensive line and LBs line up. Looking at "the box" can help you decide if the defense is defending a run and has "eight defenders in the box" or not.

Bunch Set — Three players stacked tightly together on one-half of the field makes a bunch set. A bunch is great for flooding certain areas of the field. An example is Singleback Bunch.

Check Down — To dump off a short pass to the halfback or last option on a play, especially after seeing that your other options are covered.

Clicking onto a Player — This is the act of switching your player mid-play to control someone close to the action. "I clicked onto the WR and tried to make the catch."

Depth Chart — The area of the game where you can set your lineup. Access this by pressing the pause menu and you can set which players play where.

Draw — This is a run play that makes believe the offense is passing. The QB drops back and the receivers start to run routes. Once the defense is fooled, the QB hands off to the RB, who looks for open running lanes.

Dropping a Lineman — Placing a defender on the line of scrimmage into a zone assignment. This is most common with a zone blitz play.

Empty Set — A common formation with an empty set is Shotgun Empty. The backfield is "empty" because there are five WRs in on the play.

Flat — The area of the field near the sideline in line with the line of scrimmage. The most common term is a "pass to the flat," which means a short pass to the HB who is running towards the sideline from out of the backfield.

Flood — When you send more receivers into a certain area of the field than the opponent has coverage. One example is Four Verticals against a Cover 3 defense. You have four receivers downfield and the opponent only has three defenders deep — therefore one must be open.

Horizontal Passing Concepts — Attacking the field with a short to medium passing game that uses safe throws to keep the chains moving. This offense lacks the big plays of a vertical passing game but should yield a higher percentage of completed throws. The mesh concept is a horizontal passing concept.

Hot Route — Before the snap, you can change any of your players' route assignments to one of eight pre-set routes based on his position. If you read that the defense is weak in a certain area, look to call a hot route or use multiple hot routes to create a new play on the fly.

Hurry-Up Offense — After a play you can call your players back to the line of scrimmage without going back to the Play Call screen. The last play you called will be selected and the defense won't be able to substitute. This up-tempo offense can be used to tire out the defense and keep them off balance. It is also known as a no-huddle offense.

Juke — Use the right stick to have your offensive player make a move to fake out the defender.

Line of Scrimmage — A horizontal plane where the ball is spotted right before it's snapped. This is where the linemen blocking the defense take their places.

Motion a WR — Before the snap, you can highlight an offensive player (WR, TE, or HB) and have him move to a new position. When the blue circle is underneath him, use the D-pad to move him to a new position. This can create new formations and forces the defense to watch where you move your player.

Option Run — A play where the QB can either hand off the ball to his teammate or keep it for himself depending on what he sees with the defense. Also known as Read Option.

Press Coverage — When press coverage is called, your defensive back will stand close to the WR and play physical at the snap. This will force the receiver to use his hands to get off the jam at the line and can throw off timing with the QB. The danger is that if the WR can get free, he will often get good separation from the defender. This is also known as bump-n-run coverage.

Packaging — Using packages at the Play Call screen with the right stick can sub specific players into the game for special situations. For example, the Dual HB package will take out the FB and place another HB into the game at his position.

Pistol — This is a unique formation where the QB takes a shotgun snap but the HB still lines up behind him. You'll find the Pistol in the Redskins playbook, for example.

Play-Action Pass — Play action involves faking a handoff to the back to try to fool the defense into thinking it's a run. The QB still has the ball and looks to throw.

Quick Audible — Before the snap, you can quickly audible to another play if you read that the defense is weak against something. You can call a quick pass, deep pass, play-action pass, or run from any formation by using the right stick in a specific direction.

Read Option — An option run in which the QB either hands the ball off to his HB or keeps it. The QB must "read" the defender and make a quick decision!

Screen Pass — Screen passes are most often used when facing an aggressive defense. They look to hit the HB near the flat and try to get the offensive linemen out in front to block.

Shotgun Snap — Any formation where the QB lines up 4–5 yards behind the center, who snaps the ball to the QB in the air. This increases chances for bad snaps and most commonly is used with formations that lean heavily towards the pass. The QB catches the snap and doesn't have to backpedal, so he is all set up to throw.

Slide Protection — Before the snap, you can tell your linemen to slide left, right, or pinch into the middle. This will help them pick up blitzers if you sense them coming from a specific area.

Strafe — On defense, strafing will square your hips to the line of scrimmage and give you better control of your player. You will not be able to move as fast when strafing.

Swat — Having your defender try to knock the ball down rather than go for the interception. He looks to knock away the pass, which gives him more range and can be safer than trying for an interception.

Tight Set — Tight sets bring your receivers into the middle of the field rather than out wide as in most formations. This will create a lot of action in the middle of the field and force the defense to bump into each other as they try to cram into a tight area. Shotgun Tight Flex is a tight set.

Trips Set — These formations place three WRs onto one side of the field. This forces your opponents to shift their attention towards that side since there are more players on that side of the field. Trips sets are great for flooding zone coverages. Shotgun Trips is one example.

Truck — A move by the ball carrier where he tries to run over the defender. Trucking is most commong with power backs, especiall near the goal line.

Under Center — Any formation where the QB lines up directly behind the center and takes a handoff directly from him. This is the opposite of a shotgun snap.

Usering/User Control — When you actively control a player during a play. Whatever player you use on defense is who you are "usering." The best players believe they can make more plays than if the computer was controlling the same player.

User Catch — The act of clicking onto a WR and holding the Catch button to go after a pass.

Verticals Passing Concept — This passing concept looks to stretch the field aggressively towards your opponent's end zone. Most often the deep pass audible, by flicking the right stick right, will give you this style of play. The most common way to attack the defense is with Four Verticals, which looks to flood coverage deep by sending all four receivers deep downfield.

Zone Blitz — The art of bringing pressure from one area of the field while dropping defenders into another. This is a tactic used to confuse the offense.

DEFENSIVE PLAYMAKER ADJUSTMENTS

Blitz — You can make any selected player blitz by using this hot route command, a.k.a. a blitz straight down since the players' rush angle will appear straight down on the screen.

Buzz Zone — The "curl to flat" zone defender will drop 8–10 yards deep and defend the curl; if there is no route threatening that area, he will move to the flat. A buzz zone is also known as a purple zone because of the zone color.

Deep Zone — This dark blue zone will drop back and play deep assignments.

Flat Zone — This light blue zone will drop down and play the flat. It is great for guarding short throwing offenses and players who like to dump off passes to the HB.

Hook Zone — This yellow zone will guard a 3- to 5-yard radius around wherever it is assigned. It is great for covering the middle of the field.

QB Contain — This hot route will make sure your defender watches the QB if he looks to run outside the pocket. It is a great way to stop scrambling QBs who try to run outside the defense.

QB Spy or QB Spies — A QB spy tells your defender to watch the QB and attack him if he runs past the line of scrimmage. This is a great way to stop scrambling QBs. This route also helps stop short throws right over the middle.

DEFENSIVE COVERAGE ADJUSTMENTS

Back Off — If you want to play bend-but-don't-break defense, use Back Off coverage. This literally moves your defenders farther away from the line of scrimmage and puts them in a "prevent" defensive position.

Base Align — This allows defenses to align their defenders in the general settings of the formation. As offensive formations change they can alter how a formation looks and plays. To prevent that from happening we use Base Align.

Press — This will jam receivers at the line of scrimmage. Pressing slows down offenses and allows blitzes more time to get after the quarterback.

Safeties In — When your opponent attacks the deep middle of the field you can adjust the coverage of your deep safeties by using Safeties In. This will make them take away anything directly over the middle of the field.

Safeties Out — If your opponent is attacking the sideline, use this coverage adjustment. It will make the safeties protect the sidelines.

Shift Left — If the left side of the field is being attacked, use Shift Left to make your safeties shade the left side of the field.

Shift Right — If the right side of the field is being attacked, use Shift Right to make your safeties shade the right side of the field.

Show Blitz — A great way to load the box up with defenders is to utilize Show Blitz. Most formations in the game will create a Bear front, which is great for stopping the run and blitzing your opponent.

OFFENSIVE HOT ROUTES

> FOR ALL THE NEW HOT ROUTES IN *MADDEN NFL 25*, CHECK OUT THE "TOP 5 NEW HOT ROUTES" SECTION IN THE "TOP 5" CHAPTER.

Block-and-Release — This blue route tells your back to help block before releasing to the flat.

Comeback — A new route for outside WRs that runs around 15 yards downfield before turning around.

Curl — The WR starts out on a straight pattern and turns around sharply after 8–10 yards.

Drag — A drag runs straight across the field after a 2-yard move forward.

Fade — This route starts the WR moving a few steps towards the sideline and then runs straight downfield.

Flat — A short route by the HB that runs to the flat and gives the QB a short option near the sideline.

Hitch — Similar to the curl route but runs shorter and is only available on the inside.

In — The receiver runs straight for 8 yards before cutting 90 degrees towards the middle of the field. This is the opposite of an out route.

Option — A route by the HB that gives the player the option to sit underneath zone or continue towards the sideline against man-to-man.

Out — The receiver runs straight for 8 yards before cutting 90 degrees towards the sideline. This is the opposite of an in route.

Slant — This route starts like a streak for a few steps and then breaks sharply at an angle across the field.

Smart Route — By pressing RB or R1, you can tell your WR to run his route to the first down marker. This is great for third-and-long plays where the standard route won't run far enough downfield.

Smoke — The WR on the outside turns towards the QB to quickly catch the pass and get upfield. This route is best against defenses that are playing far back off the receiver.

Streak — This route runs straight downfield (a.k.a. a "go" or "9" route).

Wheel — This route starts like a flat route but cuts upfield on a streak once it reaches the sideline.

Zig — A zig appears to start like a slant route, but the receiver pivots and cuts back to the outside towards the sideline.

POSITIONS

OFFENSE

Quarterback (QB) — The player who takes the snap from the lineman and either hands off, passes, or runs the ball.

Halfback (HB) — The player who usually lines up behind the QB and takes handoffs on run plays (a.k.a. RB — running back). On pass plays he can either run a route and become a receiver or stay in to help block.

Fullback (FB) — Lines up in front of the HB and looks to block players trying to tackle the HB. Can also catch and block on pass plays.

Wide Receiver (WR) — Receivers line up outside the linemen and look to get open downfield on pass plays. The QB looks to throw them the ball and they can run after they catch it.

Tight End (TE) — Most commonly lines up outside the linemen and can either block on run plays or go out on pass plays.

Slot Receiver — This receiver lines up outside the tackles and is a receiver but lines up inside the farthest WR. These players most often run routes over the middle of the field or look to use their speed to get deep.

Offensive Linemen (OL) — These players block for the QB and HB. The center is in the middle and snaps the ball to the QB on every play.

DEFENSE

Defensive End (DE) — The defensive end matches up against the other team's lineman on the outside and is most known for trying to sack the QB on passing plays. You have two DEs on the field in most situations (3-4 and 4-3 defenses).

Defensive Tackle (DT) — The DT plays in the middle of the defensive line usually closest to the center. He is mostly known for plugging up the middle and is usually one of the biggest players on the team (there's one DT in a 3-4, two in a 4-3 defense).

Outside Linebacker (OLB) — These LBs line up outside and can cover receivers or blitz on pass plays. They must tackle anything that gets past the line on a run play. You have two OLBs on the field in a 3-4 and a 4-3 defense.

Middle Linebacker (MLB) — This player controls the middle of the field for the defense. He stands behind the defensive tackle and must tackle everything that comes through the middle. You have two MLBs in 3-4 and one in a 4-3 defense.

Cornerback (CB) — These players play outside and must cover the WRs on passing plays.

Free Safety (FS) — This player backs up the cornerbacks and helps give them support in the passing game.

Strong Safety (SS) — This player helps in the passing game but can also be brought towards the line of scrimmage to help in the run game as well.

PLAYER RATINGS

After playing *Madden NFL 25* for many seasons, here is our breakdown of exactly what each rating does in the game. Some of these descriptions are based on what we feel with out hands on the controller, while others have been tested like a science experiment in practice mode!

Overall (OVR) — This rating provides a great snapshot of a player's attributes. Although you need to dig deeper to find out exactly what type of player you have, this will allow you to make quick decisions about who to start.

Key Position: All players

Speed (SPD) — How fast a player runs.

Key Position: All players excluding offensive linemen

Strength (STR) — How strong a player is and how well he can stand his ground or get pushed during a line battle.

Key Position: Offensive and defensive lines

Agility (AGI) — How quickly and tightly a player is able to cut.

Key Position: HB, WR, CB

Acceleration (ACC) — How quickly a player gets to top speed.

Key Position: HB, WR, DE, OLB, CB

Awareness (AWR) — How smart a player is on the field; a good Awareness rating is great for CPU-controlled players.

Key Position: All positions

Break Tackle (BTK) — How well a ball carrier can break tackles against a defender.

Key Position: QB, HB, FB, WR

Trucking (TRK) — How good a player is at using power moves to run over defenders. Trucking is more common in power backs.

Key Position: HB, FB, QB

Elusiveness (ELU) — How good a player is at using elusive moves to get away from defenders. Elusiveness is more common in speed backs.

Key Position: HB, WR, QB

Ball Carrier Vision (BCV) — How well a CPU-controlled player can find holes in the defense and use moves.

Key Position: HB, WR, QB

Stiff Arm (SFA) — How good a ball carrier is at using his free hand to ward off tacklers.

Key Position: HB, WR, QB

Spin Move (SPM) — How well a ball carrier can use a spin style move to get away from defenders. The rating can affect the tightness of the spin radius.

Key Position: HB, WR, QB

Juke Move (JKM) — How well a player can use a fake step juke move to get away from defenders. The rating can affect the tightness of the move and the amount of ground covered when juking.

Key Position: HB, WR, QB

Carrying (AR) — How well a ball carrier holds onto the ball; a higher number means a lower chance of a fumble.

Key Position: HB, FB, QB, WR

Catch (CTH) — How well a receiver can catch and hold onto the ball; a higher number means fewer dropped passes.

Key Position: WR, TE, HB

Route Running (RTE) — How well a receiver can run sharp routes that can get him space from the defender.

Key Position: WR, TE, HB

Catch in Traffic (CIT) — How well a receiver is able to catch and hold onto a ball in traffic. A higher number means a better chance of hanging onto the ball when being tackled by a defender.

Key Position: TE, WR, HB

Spectacular Catch (SPC) — How well a receiver is able to go up and make jumping or unique catches. A higher number means a better chance of amazing catches over defenders.

Key Position: WR, TE

Release (RLS) — How good a receiver is at getting off of press coverage. The higher the rating, the better chance he has to beat press coverage.

Key Position: WR

Jumping (JMP) — How high a player can jump.

Key Position: WR, TE, CB

Throwing Power (THP) — How fast and far a QB can throw the ball. A higher number means better downfield throws.

Key Position: QB

Throwing Accuracy (THA) — How accurate a QB is when throwing the ball. A higher number means more consistent throws downfield.

Key Position: QB

Short Throw Accuracy (SAC) — How accurate a QB is when throwing the ball to short areas of the field.

Key Position: QB

Medium Throw Accuracy (MAC) — How accurate a QB is when making medium-range throws downfield.

Key Position: QB

Deep Throw Accuracy (DAC) — How accurate a QB is when throwing the ball deep downfield.

Key Position: QB

Throw on the Run (RUN) — How well a QB can throw while rolling out of the pocket or on the move.

Key Position: QB

Play Action (PAC) — How good a QB is at using play action fakes. A higher rating will increase chance of faking out the defense.

Key Position: QB

Tackle (TAK) — How well a defensive player can tackle a ball carrier. A higher number means a lower chance of broken tackles.

Key Position: OLB, MLB, FS, SS

Hit Power (POW) — How hard a defensive player can tackle a ball carrier. A higher number means more hit stick and fumble chances.

Key Position: OLB, MLB, FS, SS

Power Move (PMV) — How good a player rushing the QB is at using a power-style move to get off blocks. An example is a rip move.

Key Position: DE, DT, OLB

Finesse Move (FMV) — How good a player rushing the QB is at using a finesse move to get off blocks. An example is a swim move.

Key Position: DE, DT, OLB

Block Shedding (BSH) — How good a player is at getting off a block while trying to defending the run.

Key Position: DE, DT, OLB

Pursuit (PUR) — How good a player is at taking proper angles to track down a ball carrier.

Key Position: OLB, MLB, FS, SS

Play Recognition (PRC) — How quickly a defensive player identifies what type of play the offense is running. A higher rating means less of a chance to be fooled on play action and the quicker the player will attack the line on run plays.

Key Position: OLB, MLB, FS, SS

Man Coverage (MCV) — How well a player can stick with his receiver while he is running his route. The higher the number, the closer he will play his assignment.

Key Position: CB, FS, SS

Zone Coverage (ZCV) — How well a player will track his receiver in zone coverage. The higher the number, the more he will be able to cover a play in his zone during a pass play.

Key Position: OLB, MLB, CB, FS, SS

Press (PRS) — How good a defender is at lining up in front of a WR and not letting him off the line of scrimmage. The higher the number, the better the defender will be at playing bump-n-run coverage.

Key Position: CB, FS, SS

Pass Blocking (PBK) — How well an offensive lineman is at blocking a defender who is rushing the QB on a passing play.

Key Position: Offensive line

Run Blocking (RBK) — How good an offensive lineman is at blocking a defender on a rushing play.

Key Position: Offensive line, FB, TE

Impact Blocking (IBK) — How good a player is at making blocks in the open field. The higher the rating, the bigger the chance for a big block that can knock an opponent off his feet. These are more common in the special teams return game.

Key Position: Offensive linemen, FB, TE

Run Block Strength (RBS) — How strong a lineman is at pushing back his defender in the run game.

Key Position: Offensive linemen

Run Block Footwork (RBF) — How well an offensive lineman moves his feet when run blocking.

Key Position: Offensive linemen

Pass Block Strength (PBS) — How strong a lineman is at pushing back his defender in the pass game.

Key Position: Offensive linemen

Pass Block Footwork (PBF) — How well an offensive lineman moves his feet when pass blocking.

Key Position: Offensive linemen

Kick Power (KPW) — How far a player can kick a field goal, punt the ball, or kick off.

Key Position: K, P

Kick Accuracy (KAC) — How accurate a player is when kicking a field goal, punting the ball, or kicking off.

Key Position: K, P

Return (RET) — How good a player is at running with the ball on special teams.

Key Position: KR, PR

Stamina (STA) — This affects how long a player can stay in the game before becoming tired. The higher the rating, the more snaps a player will have before having to rest.

Key Position: All positions

Injury (INJ) — How good a player is at staying healthy. The higher the rating, the less of a chance a player will get injured during the game and over the course of a season.

Key Position: All Positions

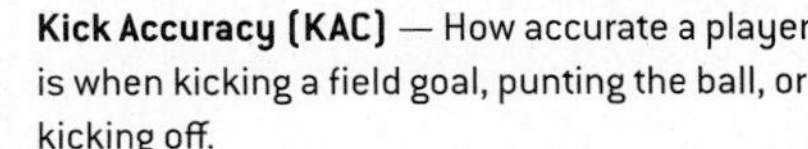

New Features

We've already spent hundreds of hours playing *Madden NFL 25* this season, and in this section we let you know what to look out for!

HOW WE ADVANCED THE GUIDE

In the past, guides have been too much like textbooks that you needed to continually reference and study. There was a good compilation of information, but it was often too hard to access, especially when you were facing a big third and 3. Football is a complex game, but by answering the questions we get most often from *Madden NFL* gamers and making the information easy to find and understand, we believe we have a found a great formula.

The format of the guide this year reflects our feedback from the fans, who quickly understood and used the Top 5 lists and team flow charts sections from last year. We updated all the lists to reflect everything new in *Madden NFL 25,* and we focused more on separating the information for beginners and experts. We made the guide something you can look at in the middle of the game thanks to its quick access to valuable information. If you hop online and compete against someone running the option, you can find useful tips for stopping them instead of needing to pause and read a chapter on "gap assignments"! This guide is easier to use, faster to understand, and fits our main goal, which is to get you more wins!

> **MAKE SURE TO BRING A MARKER AND SOME STICKY NOTES—THIS IS YOUR PLAYBOOK!**

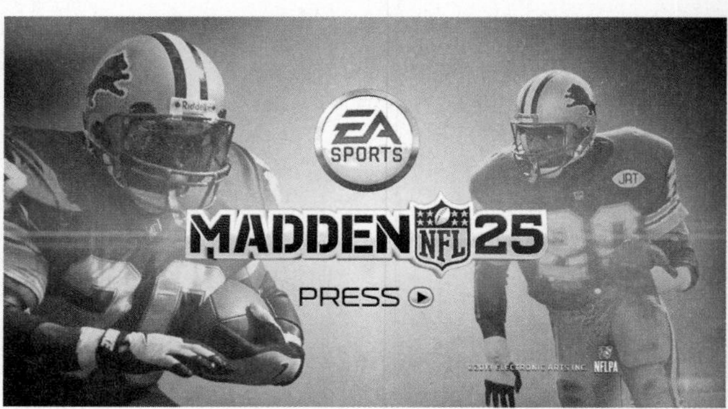

WHAT'S NEW IN *MADDEN NFL 25*

Every year the team at EA SPORTS adds new features to the game that make it more authentic. Understanding the different areas of the game is key to finding what's new and learning how these changes will affect you on the gridiron!

CONNECTED FRANCHISE MODE

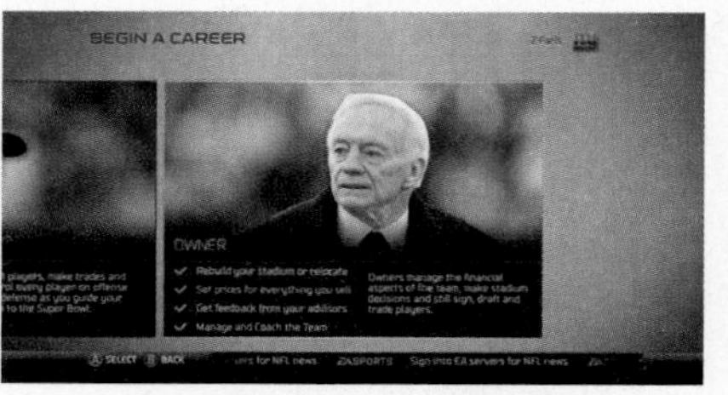

Last season, Connected Career Mode was added as a brand-new experience that combined Superstar and Franchise modes. This mode was both an online and offline experience that gave gamers a new way to experience the game. By starting as a player or coach last year, you started your career and attempted to leave a legacy on the way to Canton and the Hall of Fame! This season, *Madden NFL 25* features Connected Franchise Mode, and so much has changed that we are covering all the updates in the dedicated "Connected Franchise Mode" chapter of this guide. The team has brought back some old favorites, too, like the ability to import your draft class from *NCAA Football 14*!

OWNER MODE

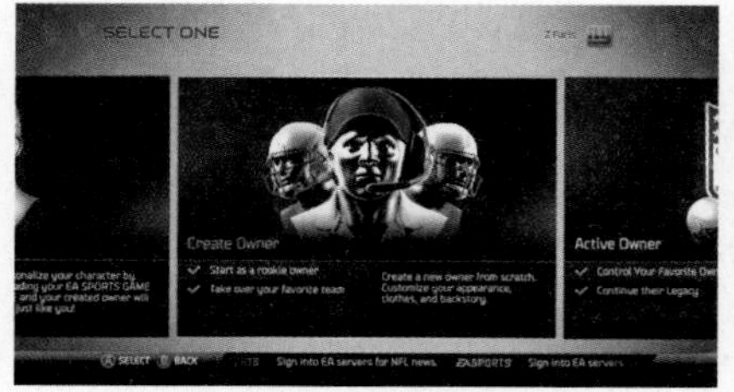

Inside of Connected Franchise Mode is the brand-new Owner Mode. This allows you to take over a team of your choosing and control every aspect of your franchise. You're required to talk with the media, set prices, and even possibly move your team! Choosing a new location is a great way to add new life to a stale franchise. This mode leaves gamers with so many options for their experience. You can play as any current owner or create your own likeness, using EA SPORTS' Game Face for an owner who looks just like you! We will dig further into this experience later in the guide!

MADDEN ULTIMATE TEAM (MUT)

This mode has been extremely popular in the *Madden NFL* franchise over the last few seasons, and it received some great new features for *Madden NFL 25*. Ultimate Team allows gamers to collect, trade, and buy items to build their ultimate team of NFL stars, past and present. Gamers can then set lineups and compete against other players online or take on the computer in solo challenges. We will cover everything you need to create a dominant team in Madden Ultimate Team in a later section in the guide, including brand-new chemistry!

HEAD-TO-HEAD SEASONS

Within Ultimate Team mode is the ability to play head-to-head seasons. This online mode allows you to play a 10-game season that could end in a playoff berth if you are successful. This mode makes each of your online games with your MUT team mean something special. How many divisions can you climb up, or will you need a stronger team to get to the top? Don't worry; if the competition gets too tough, you can be relegated to a lower division that matches up with your current skill level. This is a great way to pack tons of action into a short amount of time.

PRESENTATION

How is presentation going to factor into wins? This season, presentation goes beyond all the usual upgrades to sights and sounds usually found in the *Madden NFL* series. The game features enhanced commentary by Jim Nantz and Phil Simms, who got back in the booth together to bring even more conversation to the game. The standard camera for gameplay will also be moved back to make sure those pass-heavy players can see the whole field without needing to zoom out. This view looks more like the coach cam and should also help players who like to make multiple adjustments. Other available cameras in this year's game include broadcast, zoomed, legacy, and wide!

> Madden NFL 25 introduces a brand new member to the Madden broadcast commentary team. Sideline Reporter Danielle Bellini joins Jim Nantz and Phil Simms to describe the action from the field including key matchups, injuries, updates and many other stories from the sideline.

> Madden NFL includes 19 authentic NFL Quarterback cadences recorded by NFL Films during the 2012 – 2013 NFL Season.

> Madden NFL 25 adds depth with an additional 80 hours of Jim Nantz and Phil Simms commentary from the broadcast booth.

> Building on the newly composed Madden NFL theme, Madden NFL 25 includes a new high end broadcast score and soundtrack composed by award winning composer Christopher Lennertz.

> Madden NFL 25 adds an all new layer of on the field player chatter adding to the Madden sound experience.

ATMOSPHERE

There are great new aerial stadium shots to view before the game and in-game TD celebrations to look out for in *Madden NFL 25!* The crowd reacts better to those big third down plays and may even have you feeling nervous.

> **OUR FAVORITE NEW CELEBRATION IS EITHER VICTOR CRUZ'S TD DANCE OR COLIN KAEPERNICKS "KAEPERNICKING"**

SIDELINE REPORTER

Danielle Bellini has joined the virtual sidelines in *Madden NFL 25* to bring you all the stories that take place during the game. By utilizing the information she reports on the field, you can put yourself in a better position to win more games.

> **MAKE SURE TO LISTEN IN FOR KEY INFORMATION LIKE INJURY UPDATES!**

GAMEPLAY

Madden NFL has made huge changes this season that will impact the action on the field. These are a few areas that received big overhauls. There are also more subtle changes that we cover later in the guide.

RUN FREE

Last season, the mobile QB dominated the NFL, and we saw new schemes take over the league and wow the fans. Now, any player who is running with the ball will have more than 30 moves at their disposal to fake out potential tacklers. These moves include combo and precision moves and can be dominant in the hands of the right gamer. Great new blocking in the game this year will pave open holes and allow you more control in the ground game. Acceleration burst is back and will let your player get up to top speed quickly!

> **A PLAYER NEEDS A 90-PLUS RATING IN A MOVE CATEGORY TO PULL OFF A PRECISION MOVE. FOR EXAMPLE, A PRECISION HURDLE REQUIRES A 90-PLUS JUMP RATING.**

INFINITY ENGINE 2

Physics were a great addition to *Madden NFL 13,* and they are back and better than ever. The new Infinity Engine 2 will give the defense a counter to all the new Run Free action this year. Defenders can now unleash Heat Seeker, which will help track the ball carrier and deliver crushing tackles and hit sticks. The offense can also use the new Force Impact system to deliver stiff arms that can drive defenders back. This just scratches the surface of in-game changes, and we will cover the rest in the "Top 5" section!

> **YOU CAN NOW HOLD DOWN THE TACKLE BUTTON AND USE THE LEFT STICK TO STEER YOUR PLAYER IN FOR THE HIT.**

AUDIBLES

Players who like to set audibles will notice a big change in *Madden NFL 25*. Gone are the five formation audibles you could access before the snap, and in is a newer, more authentic system. Now, gamers can audible to any formation that matches the current personnel they are lined up in. This means that if you come out in a four-wide-receiver set, you will no longer be able to audible down to a power run set like goal line. What makes this new system better is the ability to set *all* of your "quick audibles" for every formation. For example, if you have five formations that use "22 personnel" (2 RB, 2 TE, and 1 WR), you can audible to 20 different plays, all from the line of scrimmage!

> **YOU CAN NOW SET YOUR AUDIBLES FOR ALL 32 TEAMS WITH JUST ONE PROFILE, WHICH IS GREAT FOR GAMERS WHO LIKE TO SWITCH IT UP.**

> **ALL OF THE OTHER CHANGES TO GAMEPLAY THAT AFFECT THE WAY YOU PLAY ON THE FIELD HAVE BEEN COVERED IN THE "NEW GAMEPLAY TIPS" SECTION OF THE "TOP 5" CHAPTER.**

SKILLS TRAINER

The Skills Trainer in *Madden NFL 25* is a great way to learn both the new controls and old controls in the game. For newer players, the number one way to get better is to learn the buttons, and the Skills Trainer will quickly teach you and then challenge you on what you learned. For veteran gamers, it is smart to check out the Skills Trainer to learn any new commands and to test yourself to make sure you really are as good as you thought! Another great reason to check out the Skills Trainer is that you earn items in MUT as rewards for getting gold in the drills!

Skills Trainer to Do List

Watch Video

Complete Skills Tutorial

Complete Skills Drill

Earn Item Reward

SKILLS TRAINER LESSONS

RUNNING

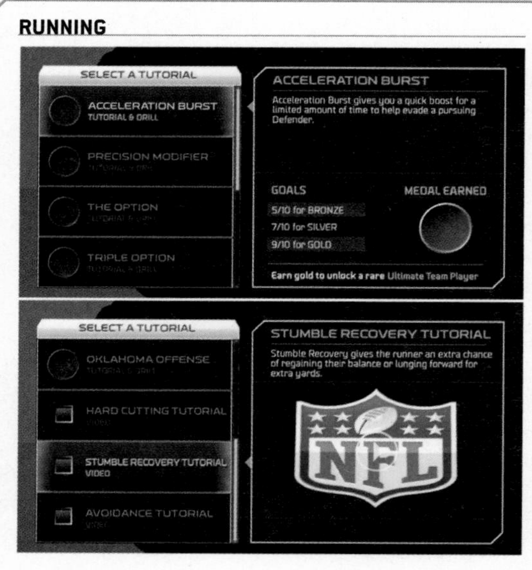

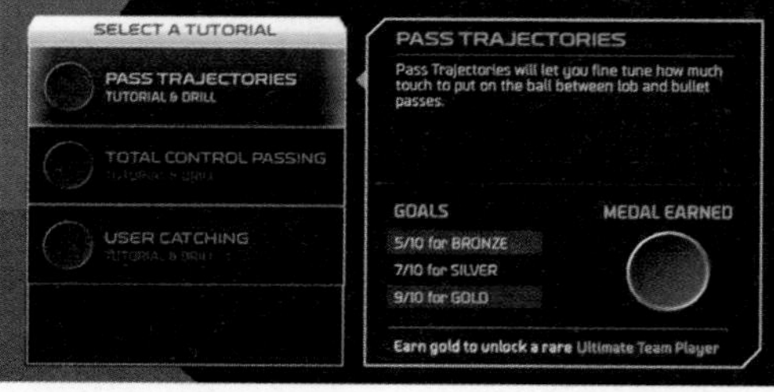

PASSING

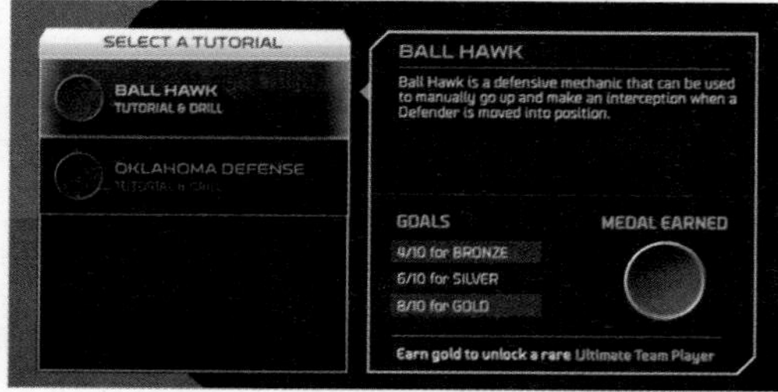

DEFENSE

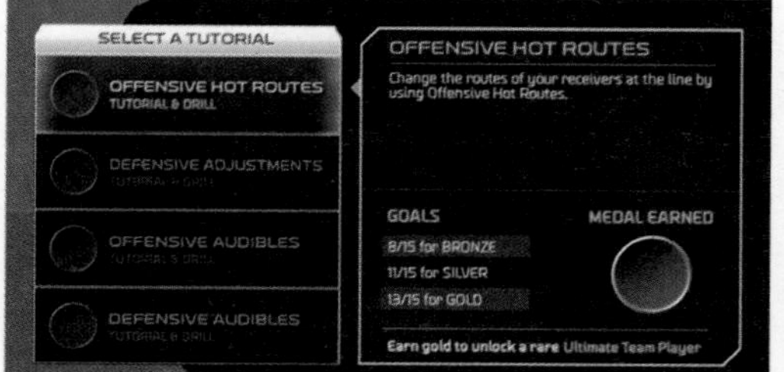

PRE-PLAY

VIDEO HELP

When you select a drill, you will watch a video that gives you an idea of how to perform the upcoming tutorial. This is a great way to learn how to play the game, even if you aren't looking to earn the Ultimate Team rewards!

SKILLS TUTORIAL

Tutorials allow you a controlled environment for practicing for your upcoming drill. These teach you the required buttons and proper situations for each action. They require you to pass a certain number of attempts to move on to the drill. If you are having trouble later in a drill, always remember that you can go back and do the tutorial again.

> **MAKE SURE TO FOLLOW INSTRUCTIONS; YOU NEED TO PERFORM THE CORRECT MOVES TO GET CREDIT FOR THE REP!**

SKILLS DRILL

The drill gives you 10 chances to practice everything you just learned in the tutorial in a game-style situation. The events will be random, so don't expect a specific pattern as in the tutorial. Each drill has a certain number of points needed to earn medals. If you get an average score, which is usually around a 50 percent rate, you will receive bronze. Silver is the next level and is usually around the 70 percent rate. Gold is the final tier and is earned on most drills by completing 90 percent of your attempts. After you complete the drill, you will get a summary of your successful and failed attempts.

> **EARNING GOLD IN A SKILLS DRILL UNLOCKS AN ITEM TO USE IN MADDEN ULTIMATE TEAM!**

EARNING GOLD IN THE FIVE TOUGHEST DRILLS

5 PRECISION MODIFIER
4 OFFENSIVE AUDIBLES
3 TOTAL CONTROL PASSING
2 DEFENSIVE AUDIBLES
1 OKLAHOMA DRILL DEFENSE

5 PRECISION MODIFIER

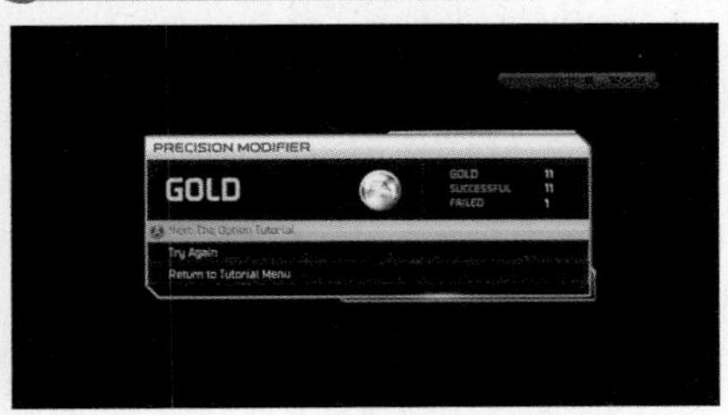

The key to beating this drill is to pay attention and use the actual move to score a TD. Scoring a TD but using a stiff arm when you were supposed to spin won't earn a positive result. Make sure you learn the timing of each move; a well-timed truck will give you a better chance to break a tackle and score.

> THE ACCELERATION BURST DRILL IS ALSO A CHALLENGE, BUT WITH ENOUGH TRIALS, YOU SHOULD BE ABLE TO PASS IT.

4 OFFENSIVE AUDIBLES

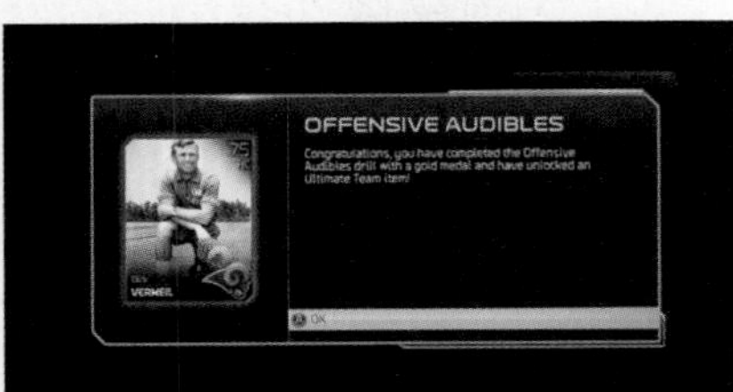

This is a great drill to show off how to audible using the new system in *Madden NFL 25*. Remember that right stick up is quick pass, right stick down is run, right stick left is play action, and right stick right is deep pass. These will give you quick calls and allow you a few more seconds to add some audibles in at the line of scrimmage!

> STAY IN BEHIND YOUR BLOCKERS ON THE RUN AUDIBLE—THESE SHOULD BE SIMPLE CONVERSIONS.

3 TOTAL CONTROL PASSING

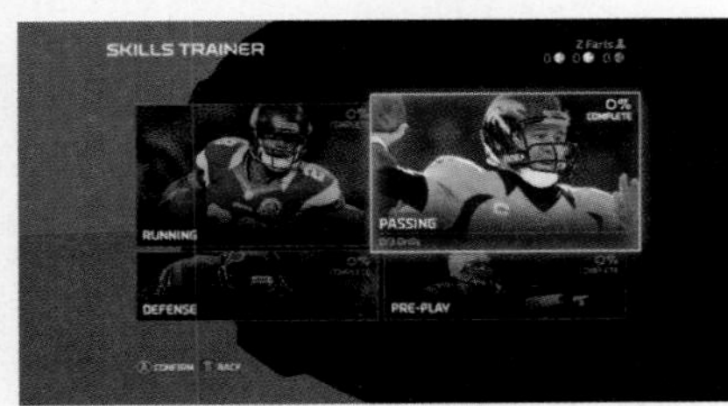

The Total Control Passing drill requires 10 out of 10 for a gold medal. The key is to really exaggerate the motion on the left stick to make sure your pass gets counted. There are three very tough throws to make: a deep pass in the seam, the comeback route on the right, and the in route by the TE over the middle. If you can get a setup that only has these passes being run once, you should have a good chance. The low passes to the outside and lead passes over the middle are very consistent, so they will be easy. You should see the same coverages with each route, so just be patient and learn how to make each throw.

> IF YOU CAN CLICK ON TO THESE RECEIVERS TO HELP MAKE USER PLAYS, YOU WILL PASS THIS SOONER!

2 DEFENSIVE AUDIBLES

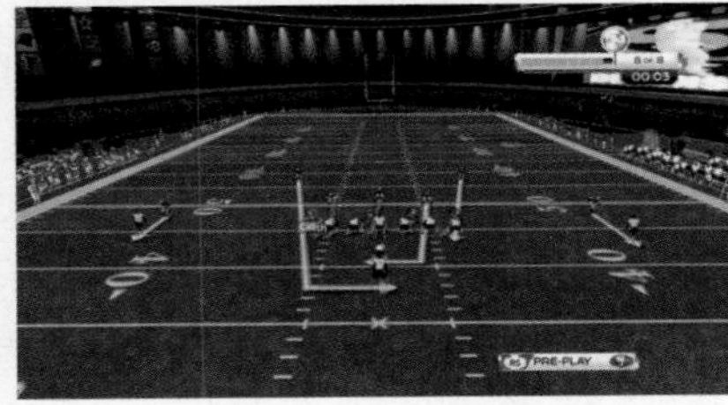

This is a challenging drill because you need eight out of eight to complete it. There are some keys to making it easier. Any time you see Cover 2, you know it is a pass. Blitz both your OLBs and user-control the yellow zone in the middle of the field on the TE. Any time you see Cover 3, it is either a pass or a toss to the right side of the field. Shift your LBs and bring your defensive end from the left to the right side of the field. If it turns out to be a pass, drop towards the deep middle of the field. Any time it is man-to-man, the threat is the slot WR on the right. Quickly blitz the LB covering him and then user-control the defender on the HB. The HB never leaves the backfield, so follow the uncovered TE across the middle and you will get a sack. Last is the play where you blitz; this is either a run left or a toss left. Blitz every player and shift your line and LBs to the left. This should earn you a gold in no time!

> YOU RUN THROUGH EACH AUDIBLE TWICE, SO MAKE SURE TO REMEMBER WHAT WORKS FOR EACH ONE.

1 OKLAHOMA DRILL (DEFENSE)

The hardest drill, in our opinion, is the Oklahoma Drill on defense. This took some time to achieve but we stuck with it because it was the last gold that we needed to complete the Skills Trainer. The key with the defensive tackle is to always go right and to not hit stick. You need to use the right stick to get off the block, but press the Tackle button instead once you are squared up. If you fail one rep, restart. After you get three in a row with the DT, you move back to the LB, where you need to get seven in a row. The back will now go either left or right, and you must read the play and make the tackle. Look out for the line battle going on in front of you, as it can sometimes block you off from the back. Wait to see what direction the handoff goes before attacking downhill. Most of the time just go for the tackle unless you have the back lined up. If you have him at a good angle, go for the hit stick. Your last chance is to ride the back out of bounds, which works well. There is no pattern to which direction the run goes, and although your LB sometimes looks to have an idea with his steps before the snap, you need to wait to see the handoff! Set aside some time for this drill. Good luck going 10 out of 10—it *is* possible!

ULTIMATE TEAM GOLD DRILL REWARDS

> All Skills Trainer item rewards have a 75 Overall rating!

BALL HAWK

DEION SANDERS (COWBOYS)

This is the only reward item that will help your secondary, so beat this easy drill quickly!

TOTAL CONTROL PASSING

DAN MARINO (DOLPHINS)

See our tips for the Total Control Passing drill—you don't want to miss out on a legend item.

PASS TRAJECTORIES

PEYTON MANNING (BRONCOS)

Peyton Manning's popularity will make him a valuable item to trade on the market.

ACCELERATION BURST

CHRIS JOHNSON (TITANS)

This drill is challenging, but getting a speedy back like Johnson is well worth the investment.

TRIPLE OPTION

COLIN KAEPERNICK (49ERS)

Kaepernick is a nice option for players who want to work with the Pistol playbook.

RUNNING THE OPTION

RANDALL CUNNINGHAM

Cunningham is a great reward for the gamer who prefers a versatile player at the QB position.

USER CATCHING

LYNN SWANN (STEELERS)

Swann is one of the greatest at making spectacular catches.

OFFENSIVE HOT ROUTES

AARON RODGERS (PACKERS)

This is a pretty nice reward for a drill that is easily beatable for the patient player.

DEFENSIVE HOT ROUTES

DERRICK THOMAS (CHIEFS)

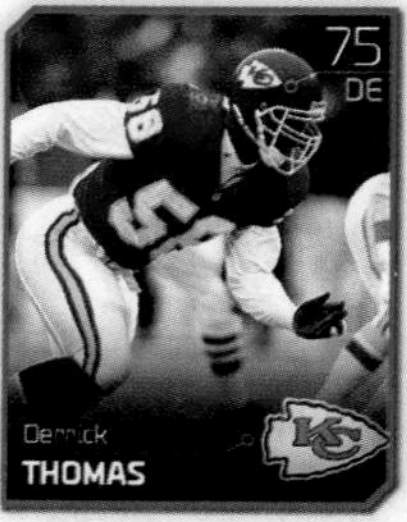

Thomas is a great early player who can sack the QB with almost any style of rush.

OFFENSIVE AUDIBLES

DICK VERMEIL (RAMS)

Calling some hot routes after you audible makes this drill much easier.

DEFENSIVE AUDIBLES

TOM LANDRY (COWBOYS)

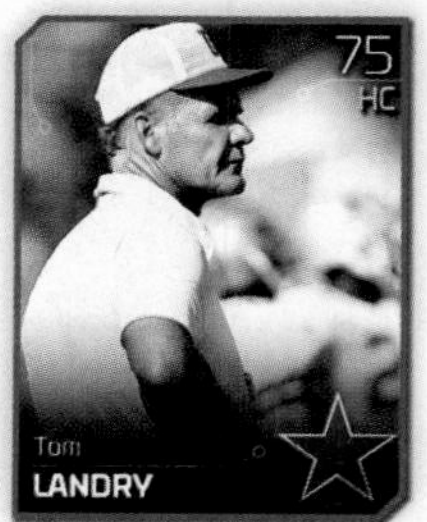

Landry is a great legend item; be sure to follow our tips for this tough drill.

OKLAHOMA DRILL (OFFENSE)

ADRIAN PETERSON (VIKINGS)

This early version of A.P. is solid, but there will be better ones out there.

OKLAHOMA DRILL (DEFENSE)

NDAMUKONG SUH (LIONS)

Suh is a great force for the middle of your defense, but this is a very challenging drill.

PRECISION MODIFIER

WALTER PAYTON (BEARS)

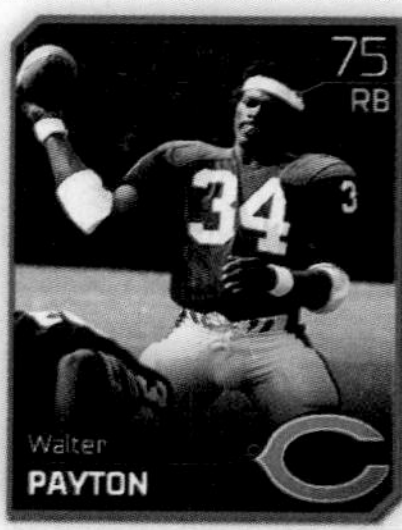

Payton is a great legend back to earn for your Madden Ultimate Team.

Connected Franchise Walkthrough

BUILDING A POWERHOUSE FRANCHISE IN NFL 25: TIPS, TRICKS, AND STRATEGIES

Connected Franchise Mode (CFM) is the deepest mode in the history of the Madden NFL series. This mode was rebuilt from the ground up for *Madden NFL 13* and has only continued to add more and more depth ever since. Each year, the EA SPORTS team gives you more options to customize your play experience and create your own unique football universe. Whether you play offline against the computer or online with friends, CFM gives everyone a chance to build a franchise that will be viewed as a dynasty.

This section fully breaks down CFM, shows off new features of *Madden NFL 25,* and gives tips to beginners and experts alike. Those willing to invest time learning the ins and outs of CFM will soon have an in-depth gaming experience at their fingertips.

GETTING STARTED

Connected Franchise Mode Checklist

- ❑ Start CFM
- ❑ Choose Online, Offline, Create, or Join League
- ❑ Choose Default Roster or Import Custom Roster
- ❑ Choose Existing Player/Coach/Owner or Create New!
- ❑ Select Team
- ❑ Select Options
- ❑ Fantasy Draft Optional
- ❑ Start Season
- ❑ View Trade Block
- ❑ Set Depth Chart
- ❑ Cut Players
- ❑ Practice
- ❑ Talk to Media
- ❑ Start Regular Season
- ❑ Check Free Agent Wire
- ❑ Upgrade Players
- ❑ Scout for NFL Draft
- ❑ Playoffs
- ❑ Free Agency
- ❑ NFL Draft
- ❑ Start Season 2!

OPTIONS FOR STARTING A CFM

OWNER

PLAYER	COACH	OWNER
• Choose to be a player and build your legacy on your way to the Hall of Fame. ✔ Choose team to play on ✔ Earn XP and upgrade ratings ✔ Compare your legacy to others ✔ Control just your player	• Draft players, make trades, and control every player on offense and defense as you guide your team to the Super Bowl. ✔ Sign, trade, and draft players ✔ Control offense and defense ✔ Earn XP and upgrade your coach ✔ Progress and develop players	• Owners manage the financial aspects of the team, make stadium decisions, and still sign, draft, and trade players. ✔ Rebuild your stadium or relocate ✔ Set prices for everything you sell ✔ Get feedback from your advisors ✔ Manage and coach the team
IMPORT GAME FACE • Personalize your character by uploading your EA SPORTS GAME FACE and your created player will look just like you. ✔ Your player looks like you	**IMPORT GAME FACE** • Personalize your character by uploading your EA SPORTS GAME FACE and your created coach will look just like you. ✔ Your player looks like you	**IMPORT GAME FACE** • Personalize your character by uploading your EA SPORTS GAME FACE and your created owner will look just like you. ✔ Your player looks like you
CREATE PLAYER • Create a new character from scratch. Customize your appearance, gear, and backstory. ✔ Start as a rookie ✔ Choose your position ✔ Choose your player type ✔ Choose your backstory	**CREATE COACH** • Create a new coach from scratch. Customize your appearance, clothes, and backstory. ✔ Start as a rookie coach ✔ Coach your favorite team ✘ Start with very few traits	**CREATE OWNER** • Create a new coach from scratch. Customize your appearance, clothes, and backstory. ✔ Start as a rookie owner ✔ Take over your favorite team
CONTROL ACTIVE PLAYER • Take over the career of any active NFL player and continue to build his legacy. ✔ Control your favorite player ✘ Retire after 15 years	**CONTROL ACTIVE COACH** • Play as a rookie version of an all-time great. Can you re-create his historic career? ✔ Control your favorite coach ✔ Inherit their default traits	**CONTROL ACTIVE OWNER** • Take over the career of any actice NFL owner and continue to build his legacy. ✔ Control your favorite owner ✔ Continue their legacy
CONTROL NFL LEGEND • Play as a rookie version of an all-time great. Can you re-create his historic career? ✔ Choose from dozens of legends ✘ Ratings will be lower as a rookie	**CONTROL NFL LEGEND** • Play as a rookie version of an all-time great. Can you re-create his historic career? ✔ Choose from several legends ✘ Can't change your backstory	**CONTROL NFL LEGEND** • Play as a rookie version of an all-time great. Can you re-create his historic career? ✔ Choose from several legends ✘ Can't change your backstory

In the Main menu, simply scroll down and select Connected Franchise Mode. From here, you can choose to start an online franchise or play offline. If you have friends who have started an online league or you would like to search for a random league, use the "Join a League" tile. There are great communities online that welcome players of all different skill levels and gameplay styles. Playing online with other humans adds a unique competitive element to CFM, so we highly recommend giving it a chance!

> ADDING THE HUMAN ELEMENT VIA AN ONLINE CFM CAN REALLY INCREASE THE COMPETITIVE NATURE OF A FRANCHISE!

CREATION BACKSTORY

Player	Coach	Owner
Early Draft Pick	Motivator	Former Player
Late Round Pick	Strategist	Lifelong Fan
Undrafted	Team Builder	Financial Mogul

PLAYER	COACH	OWNER
EARLY DRAFT PICK • Being a first-round pick doesn't guarantee you anything but high expectations. ✔ Good initial ratings ✖ High expectations ✖ Normal Development trait	**MOTIVATOR** • This backstory gives you a discount on Motivational packages. ✔ FA packages discount ✔ Retire packages discount	**FORMER PLAYER** • This backstory gives you an advantage when it comes to team popularity. ✔ 500 legacy score ✔ Roster happiness + ✖ Start with $0 funds ✖ $ happiness –
LATE ROUND PICK • This backstory has slightly lower ratings but gives you the quick development trait. ✔ Decent initial ratings ✔ Decent expectations ✔ Quick Development trait	**STRATEGIST** • This backstory gives you a discount on Strategy traits. ✔ XP Boost discount ✔ Trade package discount ✔ Progression package discount	**LIFELONG FAN** • This backstory gives you an advantage with fan happiness. ✔ Fan happiness boost ✔ Success happiness + ✖ Start with $0 funds ✖ Pop. happiness –
UNDRAFTED • This backstory has lower ratings but gives you the Super Star Development trait. ✔ Lower initial ratings ✔ Low expectations ✔ Super Star Development trait	**TEAM BUILDER** • This backstory gives you a discount on Progression traits. ✔ Scouting discount ✔ Contract discount	**FINANCIAL MOGUL** • This backstory gives you an advantage financially. ✔ Start with $10M ✔ $$ happiness + ✖ No legacy score ✖ Player happiness –

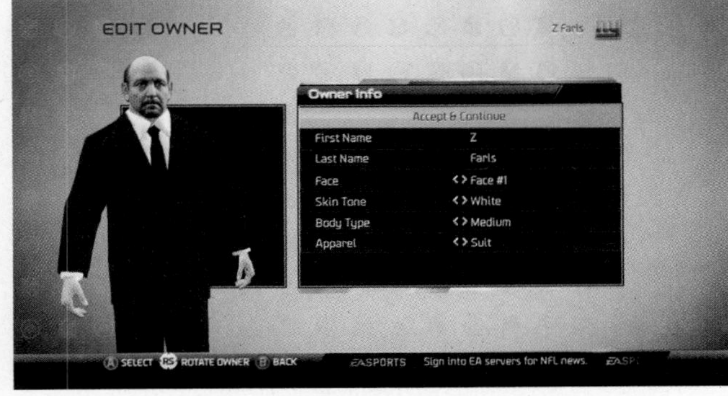

Once you select a league, the real fun begins. Now you must choose to be a player, coach, or owner! Owner mode is brand-new in *Madden NFL 25*, so it will likely be a popular option. We highly recommend that you create your own character—you'll be more attached to it because you can add your face and select a backstory. Your created character will feel like an RPG (role-playing-game) character that you are building up. For this walkthrough, we create an owner that is true to the author's likeness. If you have a favorite character, however, feel free to use it!

GENERAL STARTING TIPS

Creating a Player: Think about what type of position you want to play and how the team you join may affect your playing time!

Creating a Coach: Consider what type of scheme you want to run before selecting a team and look into who has the personnel to fit it!

Creating an Owner: If you are looking to move your team, consider starting with a team that is struggling with their stadium, finances, or fan base; otherwise it may be tough to leave!

> USING AN OWNER WILL GIVE YOU ALL THE CONTROL OF A COACH AND MORE, INCLUDING THE ABILITY TO SET PRICES!

We are going to select the New York Giants, as they fit our style of a balanced offensive scheme and an attacking 4-3 defense. They have a some nice young talent to develop on both sides of the ball while having veterans who are ready to win now! The Giants also have the most important thing in *Madden NFL 25* and that is solid QB play.

CHOOSING A TEAM

Selecting a franchise to build into a powerhouse forces you to consider many factors. Do you want to start from the bottom and spend a few seasons building your team? Are you looking to win right away and want to take over a stacked squad? Perhaps you have a favorite childhood team or want to use a player from your alma mater? With hundreds of players and 32 owners and coaches to choose from, you have many options in *Madden NFL 25*. Here are some teams to check out, depending on your goals.

TOP 5 OFFENSIVE CREATE-A-PLAYER POSITION TYPES

5 STRONG ARM QB
4 VERTICAL THREAT TE
3 RED ZONE THREAT WR
2 ONE CUT HB
1 MOBILE QB

Choosing which position to play when starting a career in Connected Franchise Mode can be a daunting task. There are more than 50 choices combined on offense and defense. The real key is to figure out which position you want to play and from there choose a style of player. Think about your favorite player in the league and model yourself after him? Perhaps you currently or used to play a specific position, maybe go with that? You can always create a new player and try another position if things aren't working out.

OFFENSIVE PLAYER POSITION TYPES

QB	HB	WR	TE
Balanced	Balanced	Balanced	Balanced
Pocket Passer	Speed	Speed	Receiving
Strong Arm	Power Back	Route Runner	Vertical Threat
Mobile	One Cut	Red Zone Threat	
West Coast	Receiving	Possession	

5 STRONG ARM QB

- ✔ Great Arm Strength
- ✔ Good Deep Accuracy
- ✖ Poor Short Accuracy
- ✖ Poor Medium Accuracy
- ✖ Decent Awareness

> PLAYER EXAMPLE: RYAN MALLETT, PATRIOTS

> **MAKE YOUR SHORT THROWS EASY BY USING SCREEN PASSES TO YOUR HB AND WR UNTIL YOU CAN UPGRADE YOUR PLAYER!**

One of the most valuable assets for a QB is the ability to throw downfield. If defenses know the deep ball can't beat them, they will be more likely to pack defenders in, which can clog up running and passing lanes. By starting with a QB who has a big arm, you can be confident you can make the toughest throws and later work on getting your consistency and accuracy up. This QB will need a good offensive line that gives him time to set up in the pocket and throw the ball, so consider that when choosing a team.

4 VERTICAL THREAT TE

- ✔ Good Speed
- ✔ Good Agility
- ✔ Good Acceleration
- ✔ Good Spectacular Catch
- ✖ Poor Blocking
- ✖ OK Route Running
- ✖ Decent Catching

> PLAYER EXAMPLE: VERNON DAVIS, 49ERS

> **OPPONENTS WILL BE LOOKING FOR QUICK THROWS TO THE TE THIS SEASON!**

Although TEs are required to run-block on some snaps, they are a huge asset in the passing game. Some TEs are bigger guys that are more reliable than explosive. Other TEs are much better pass catchers and can almost be thought of as an extra WR. As a vertical threat TE, you can be sure you will get plenty of chances to make big plays downfield. These players are versatile and extremely athletic players who can get into the seam against the defense. Consider going to a team that likes to throw the ball downfield to really maximize your chances!

3 RED ZONE THREAT WR

- ✔ Good Catch in Traffic
- ✔ Good Jumping
- ✔ Good Spectacular Catch
- ✖ Decent Speed
- ✖ Decent Catching
- ✖ Decent Agility

> PLAYER EXAMPLE: RAMSES BARDEN, GIANTS

> **WORK ON UPGRADING THE CATCH IN TRAFFIC RATING SO YOUR PLAYER CAN HANG ONTO THE BALL IF HE TAKES A HIT.**

If you want to play as a big athletic type, the red-zone threat WR is a great choice. These players already have the valuable rating to catch in traffic, which means you can spend your XP in other areas. If your favorite team is a run-heavy squad, try this and look to give your team a way to convert in the air. You won't get as many chances as on a team that likes to air it out, but your catches will often score your team points.

2 ONE CUT HB

- ✔ Good Ball Carrier Vision
- ✔ Decent Trucking
- ✔ Decent Agility
- ✖ Decent Speed
- ✖ Decent Acceleration
- ✖ Poor Elusiveness

> PLAYER EXAMPLE: ARIAN FOSTER, TEXANS

> **USE THE NEW ACCELERATION BURST TO GET BACK UP TO SPEED AFTER A CUT.**

With all of the new run-blocking in the game this year, playing as a one-cut HB is a great option. Gamers may think that a one-cut back is very shifty, but the key is to run with power! Start slow towards the hole, and once you make your decision, really use the acceleration burst to get through it. If you choose this style, you will be more of a power back who must learn to read blocks and be very decisive. While you may not break many long runs, you will fatigue the defense and move the chains all game long!

1 MOBILE QB

- ✔ Good Awareness
- ✔ Good Short Accuracy
- ✔ Decent Medium Accuracy
- ✖ OK Arm Strength
- ✖ Poor Deep Accuracy
- ✖ Poor Agility

Mobile QB

> PLAYER EXAMPLE: CAM NEWTON, PANTHERS

> **USE YOUR MOBILITY AS A SECONDARY OPTION—DON'T FORGET TO SET YOUR FEET!**

Playing as a mobile QB who can break down defenses with either his arm or the legs is extremely fun. Make sure you don't rely on your legs for every snap, because if you force the action it can be frustrating. Instead, look to make quick reads and throws all over the field. If the play starts to break down or all your reads are covered, then you can take off. By sticking to your strengths in the passing game and looking to develop your down-the-field throwing, playing as a mobile QB is one of the best experiences in *Madden NFL 25*!

TOP 5 DEFENSIVE CREATE-A-PLAYER POSITION TYPES

5 SPEED RUSH RE
4 MAN-TO-MAN CB
3 3-4 PASS RUSHER ROLB
2 PROTOTYPE MLB
1 RUN SUPPORT FS

Another great way to choose a player is to consider your play style. If you are a pass-heavy player, you will probably enjoy QB more than the HB position. On defense, do you tend to go for the big hit, or are you all about the interception? Asking yourself these questions can make it easier when looking through all the options! Here are our recommended defensive choices when creating a player in CFM.

DEFENSIVE PLAYER POSITION TYPES					
DEFENSIVE END	DT	MLB	OLB	CB	SAFETY
Balanced	Balanced	Balanced	Balanced LOLB	Balanced	Balanced
Speed Rush	Pass Rushing	3-4 Tackler	3-4 Pass Rusher LOLB	Man-to-Man	Playmaker
	Prototype	Prototype	Prototype LOLB	Prototype	Prototype
		Cover 2	Cover 2 LOLB	Press Run Support	Run Support
				Zone	

5 SPEED RUSH RE

- ✔ OK Finesse Moves
- ✔ Good Acceleration
- ✔ Good Pursuit
- ✘ Poor Strength
- ✘ Poor Tackling
- ✘ Poor Power Moves

> PLAYER EXAMPLE: OSI UMENYIORA, FALCONS

> A GREAT SPEED RUSHER CAN ALSO HELP CONTAIN THOSE PESKY MOBILE QBS!

Chasing down the QB and getting a game-sealing sack is something that every defensive end dreams about. By choosing a speed-rushing DE, you will have the physical attributes to work your way around the corner and force the QB out of his comfort zone. Work on timing the snap to use your great acceleration to your advantage. Another great reason to choose speed over power is that you will have an easier time dropping off into coverage on zone blitzes and surprising the QB.

4 MAN-TO-MAN CB

- ✔ Good Man Coverage
- ✔ Good Speed
- ✔ Good Pursuit
- ✘ Poor Zone Coverage
- ✘ Decent Tackling

> PLAYER EXAMPLE: PATRICK PETERSON, CARDINALS

> IF YOU HOLD DOWN THE SWAT BUTTON AT THE SNAP OF THE BALL, YOU CAN MANUALLY PRESS YOUR ASSIGNMENT.

With the addition of ballhawk last season, many gamers started to gain confidence that they could get interceptions if they clicked onto a defender down the field when the ball went in the air. This mind-set is great, because going up and getting a user interception is a great feeling. As a true lockdown CB, you can take the opponent's best WR out of the game and really frustrate the offense. This will be a tough position, but choosing a team with a solid pass rush can make life easier.

3 3-4 PASS RUSHER ROLB

- ✔ Good Finesse Moves
- ✔ Good Acceleration
- ✔ Good Pursuit
- ✘ Poor Strength
- ✘ Poor Tackling
- ✘ Poor Zone Coverage

> PLAYER EXAMPLE: CLAY MATTHEWS, PACKERS

> DON'T FORGET TO TRY OUT THE RIP AND SWIM STYLE MOVES TO GET AWAY FROM YOUR BLOCKER.

As an edge rusher in a 3-4 defense, your main goal will be to get after the QB! Since you start plays as a stand-up rusher, you will have a solid chance at getting around the blocker and putting pressure on the QB. Since you will be out on the edge, you must also look out for pulling linemen on run plays, who will want to try to seal you away from the ball carrier. Lining up in a pure pass-rushing situation as a 3-4 rusher and going one-on-one with a lineman is a great experience!

2 PROTOTYPE MLB

- ✔ Good Speed
- ✔ Good Acceleration
- ✔ Good Hit Power
- ✘ Poor Awareness
- ✘ Poor Tackling
- ✘ Poor Pursuit
- ✘ Poor Play Recognition

> PLAYER EXAMPLE: PATRICK WILLIS, 49ERS

> IF YOU SEE A BLOCKER BETWEEN YOURSELF AND THE BALL CARRIER, TRY TAPPING THE TACKLE BUTTON TO DIVE THROUGH.

If you are the type of gamer who likes to be in the middle of the action, playing as an MLB is the way to go. A prototypical MLB has solid physical skills that can make enough plays to continue upgrading ratings like Pursuit and Play Recognition. By being in the middle of the defense, you will have to defend the run and the pass, which will keep you involved and entertained.

1 RUN SUPPORT FS

- ✔ Good Tackling
- ✔ Good Hit Power
- ✘ Poor Awareness
- ✘ Poor Zone Coverage
- ✘ Poor Man Coverage

Run Support FS

> PLAYER EXAMPLE: ANTREL ROLLE, GIANTS

> PLAYERS WHO CAN WRAP UP CONSISTENTLY IN THE OPEN FIELD ARE VALUABLE AGAINST THE RUN GAME THIS YEAR!

Playing as a free safety can be a great way to learn more about defense, since you will be forced to cover more ground. This is a fun way to play because your assignments will switch from zone coverage to man-to-man to blitzing depending on the play called. You'll be required to cover multiple areas of the field. One of the best feelings in the game is to lay a crushing tackle on the opponent that knocks the ball loose; by choosing the run support safety, you will already have a solid rating that will increase your odds! If you can focus on spending your XP to help your skills in pass coverage, you will be on your way to a solid career!

TOP 5 WIN NOW TEAMS

5 NEW YORK GIANTS
4 DENVER BRONCOS
3 NEW ENGLAND PATRIOTS
2 GREEN BAY PACKERS
1 SAN FRANCISCO 49ERS

HONORABLE MENTION: **TEXANS, STEELERS, SAINTS**

Winning isn't everything, but for some it is the only thing. The teams on this list are fully loaded and ready to win right away. Depending on your play style, choosing one of these teams will have you not only in the conference title race, but also looking to play for a Super Bowl. If you're competing in an online CFM, these teams should be quite popular, so make sure to grab them right away!

5 NEW YORK GIANTS

The Giants are a great passing team that can finish off games with their defense.

OFF SCHEME: **Balanced**
DEF SCHEME: **Attacking 4-3**
CFM OVERALL: **79**

The Giants still have the main pieces responsible for their two recent championships in QB Eli Manning and their defensive line. With young talent at WR, you can extend their window if you can find a way to manage the cap. Look to develop their young HB to make sure you don't get too pass happy.

4 DENVER BRONCOS

Denver has a great pass rush that can help force turnovers in big spots.

OFF SCHEME: **Spread**
DEF SCHEME: **Attacking 4-3**
CFM OVERALL: **76**

Denver has one of the best QBs ever to play—Peyton Manning. By signing WR Wes Welker to work the middle of the field, this team should be a top contender in the AFC once again. With a well-balanced defense, Denver has a nice window to win early in CFM.

3 NEW ENGLAND PATRIOTS

The Patriots are able to attract great free agents due to their recent winning history.

OFF STYLE: **Spread**
DEF STYLE: **Hybrid Multiple Front**
CFM OVERALL: **82**

The Patriots have an offense that is capable of bringing in a championship early in your franchise. Look to develop a backup QB who can keep winning games. Make sure to spend points on your defense to round out this team and keep them winning.

2 GREEN BAY PACKERS

Make sure to find ways to get your rookie HBs plenty of touches and focus your XP on them.

OFF SCHEME: **West Coast**
DEF SCHEME: **Attacking 3-4**
CFM OVERALL: **82**

Green Bay is the perfect team for the pass-happy player who can make quick reads. For the gamer who knows how to stress defenses with a mobile QB, QB Aaron Rodgers can convert huge third downs. Make sure to draft along your offensive and defensive line to take control of the line of scrimmage. Look to extend the career of QB Aaron Rodgers by protecting him and paying good money at the LT position.

1 SAN FRANCISCO 49ERS

The 49ers' defense has so much talent that setting your depth chart is a challenge.

OFF SCHEME: **Power Run**
DEF SCHEME: **Base 3-4**
CFM OVERALL: **84**

The San Francisco 49ers have been in control of the NFC for the last few seasons and are a great team for the defensive-minded player. Defense wins championships, and their lineup will have you forcing turnovers. You also have a young star QB—Colin Kaepernick—who will outlast the rest of the players on this list!

TOP 5 TEAMS FOR THE FUTURE

5 CINCINNATI BENGALS
4 ATLANTA FALCONS
3 INDIANAPOLIS COLTS
2 WASHINGTON REDSKINS
1 SEATTLE SEAHAWKS

HONORABLE MENTION: **RAVENS, FALCONS, PANTHERS**

All of the teams on this list have some great pieces in place to win. Whether it is a great QB who can lead them into the playoffs or a strong defense, you will be set up to win over the long-term. As a coach or owner, you have the ability to mix in a few of the right pieces, which could result in a championship! However, make sure to manage your salary cap, as young players provide great value early but turn into expensive stars in the future!

5 CINCINNATI BENGALS

The Bengals in the playoffs is becoming a more consistent sight with QB Andy Dalton!

OFF SCHEME: **Balanced**
DEF SCHEME: **Base 4-3**
CFM OVERALL: **73**

The Bengals' offense starts with star WR A.J. Green and QB Andy Dalton. This combo will determine just how far the Bengals can make it each season. Thankfully, Cincinnati gave them great help in the draft by picking up some talent on offense. On defense, the Bengals have fantastic team speed and one of the most under-the-radar defenses in the game.

4 ATLANTA FALCONS

Make sure to have a backup plan for TE, as Tony Gonzalez is an amazing star approaching the end of his career.

OFF SCHEME: **Balanced**
DEF SCHEME: **Attacking 4-3**
CFM OVERALL: **75**

The Falcons have a dynamic passing game with QB Matt Ryan and star WRs Roddy White and Julio Jones. Atlanta really handed the offense over to Ryan last season, and he commanded a great passing game that led them all the way to the NFC Championship game. Ryan will be around and make this team relevant for years to come, but look into the HB and TE positions to give him support. On defense, finding a star LB may speed up how fast you get to the big game.

3 INDIANAPOLIS COLTS

The Colts drafting Andrew Luck secured their spot on this list for years to come.

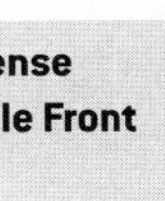

OFF STYLE: **Balanced Offense**
DEF STYLE: **Hybrid Multiple Front**
CFM OVERALL: **68**

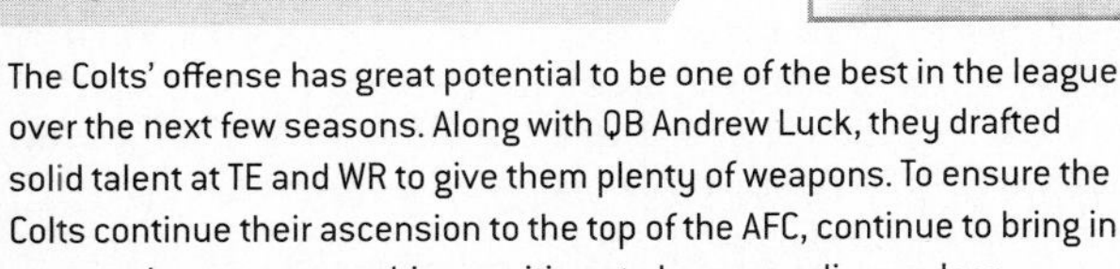

The Colts' offense has great potential to be one of the best in the league over the next few seasons. Along with QB Andrew Luck, they drafted solid talent at TE and WR to give them plenty of weapons. To ensure the Colts continue their ascension to the top of the AFC, continue to bring in young talent at pass-rushing positions to keep your lineup deep.

2 WASHINGTON REDSKINS

Make sure to protect RGIII, as he is the key for the Redskins' future.

OFF SCHEME: **Power Run**
DEF SCHEME: **Base 3-4**
CFM OVERALL: **77**

The Redskins' offensive scheme is great for players who like to run a pistol-style offense that relies on a great power back like Alfred Morris. By forcing your opponents to stop the run, you will open up the quick passing game and gash the defense. The Redskins' defense is solid but needs young talent injected in the lineup to be ready for a long-term run.

1 SEATTLE SEAHAWKS

Seattle is a solid team that just added some quality off-season additions to make the top of this list.

OFF SCHEME: **Power Run**
DEF SCHEME: **Base 4-3**
CFM OVERALL: **75**

The Seattle Seahawks have been battling with the 49ers for NFC West supremacy, and both have tremendous talent. By building around QB Russell Wilson, Seattle will have a scheme that the defenses will have to focus building their team around to stop! Seattle has done a solid job of building up a great secondary that can stop some of the other pass-happy opponents they will face on their way to a title.

TOP 5 TEAMS FOR REBUILDING

5 ARIZONA CARDINALS
4 BUFFALO BILLS
3 OAKLAND RAIDERS
2 CLEVELAND BROWNS
1 JACKSONVILLE JAGUARS

HONORABLE MENTION: **JETS, CHARGERS, RAMS**

All of the teams on this list need long-term vision to help them get back to the top. These teams have a few parts to build around and some flexibility, which will be important as you look to turn them around. In Owner mode, you also have the ability to move your franchise if things aren't working out; this could help rejuvenate a struggling team too!

5 ARIZONA CARDINALS

Finding someone to get WR Larry Fitzgerald the ball is crucial when taking over the Cardinals!

OFF SCHEME: **Balanced**
DEF SCHEME: **Attacking 3-4**
CFM OVERALL: **68**

Arizona has put together a solid defense over the last few seasons, and you should keep building it by focusing on lockdown corner Patrick Peterson. On offense, focus on finding some players to build around WR Larry Fitzgerald, or look to move him to get multiple picks to build in the draft. This is a cheaper alternative and can be a great idea for players who are into their team for the long-term. If you can't bring enough fans to the game, consider taking your talents to Los Angeles or Mexico City, which have huge markets.

4 BUFFALO BILLS

The Buffalo Bills youth on offense makes them one of our favorite sleeper teams in *Madden NFL 25*.

OFF SCHEME: **Balanced**
DEF SCHEME: **Hybrid Multiple Front**
CFM OVERALL: **67**

Buffalo has made some early season noise the last few seasons but has been unable to turn it into a playoff appearance. They have some talent in the backfield but will need to develop a franchise QB before being considered a contender. After drafting QB E. J. Manuel in the first round, gamers will have a nice player to start developing into the QB of the future. Buffalo has spent big money on their defense and has a solid pass rush that will help them get after the top team in their division in New England. If you can't turn around the Bills, consider moving them to Toronto in Owner mode to keep the revenue positive.

3 OAKLAND RAIDERS

The Raiders have always been a big player in free agency. Is it time to change up that style?

OFF STYLE: **Vertical**
DEF STYLE: **Base 4-3**
CFM OVERALL: **67**

With a solid backfield combo of Taiwan Jones and Darren McFadden, Oakland is a team that can play a running style. While the Raiders are known for attacking downfield, gamers will need to use QB Terrelle Pryor to his strength, which is in the shorter passing game. On defense, the Raiders have lost some of their big-name players but have plenty of depth that can be upgraded and kept for great value. If the Raiders can't steal headlines from the 49ers in the Bay Area, perhaps move them north to Sacramento, California?

2 CLEVELAND BROWNS

In the slot WR position is a great speed weapon in Josh Gordon.

OFF SCHEME: **Balanced**
DEF SCHEME: **Attacking 4-3**
CFM OVERALL: **67**

Cleveland has started to put the talent together to make a playoff run, but playing in a tough division has been challenging. Focus on building around HB Trent Richardson and determine what to do at the QB position, depending on what type of scheme you want to run. On defense, the Browns have some good youth along the line and brought in some capable players in free agency. By using XP on their new pass-rushing combo of Barkevious Mingo and Paul Kruger, the Browns can build up a core of rushers like their division rival—the Steelers!

1 JACKSONVILLE JAGUARS

Look to feed Maurice Jones-Drew the ball during your early seasons, as he can carry the load.

OFF SCHEME: **Balanced**
DEF SCHEME: **Base 4-3**
CFM OVERALL: **65**

The Jaguars are a team with a star in the backfield; however, they will need a few more stars to be considered a contender. If you are struggling to make revenue with them, consider trying a new location like Orlando, Florida, to generate some buzz. On defense, the Jags face pretty balanced teams in their division, so look to keep your scheme balanced.

TOP 5 SLEEPER TEAMS

5 MIAMI DOLPHINS
4 TENNESSEE TITANS
3 MINNESOTA VIKINGS
2 KANSAS CITY CHIEFS
1 DETROIT LIONS

HONORABLE MENTION: **BEARS, COWBOYS, BUCS**

All of the teams on this list wouldn't be your first choice to win right away, but all are capable of being successful for the right type of player! By using a specific style with these teams, you can turn around their championship drafts and bring a title home! Build around your elite players, and you can be assured these teams can jump into the top 10 by year two of your CFM.

5 MIAMI DOLPHINS

Continue to develop QB Ryan Tannehill and make him your franchise QB!

OFF SCHEME: **West Coast**
DEF SCHEME: **Base 4-3**
CFM OVERALL: **68**

The Dolphins picked up a speedy WR in Mike Wallace. His ability to go deep should take some pressure off the offense. Build up your young HB Lamar Miller, who has some talent but needs XP to round out his skill set. Pass rusher Cameron Wake is the key on the defensive side of the ball; you should build around him for the future!

4 TENNESSEE TITANS

HB Chris Johnson is one of the fastest in the game and can make defenses who overlook him pay.

OFF SCHEME: **Balanced**
DEF SCHEME: **Base 4-3**
CFM OVERALL: **70**

With the new Run Free controls in *Madden NFL 25*, a dominant ground game is extremely important. Having a talented back like Chris Johnson to carry the ball 20+ times per game is very important and can help give your team an identity. If you can develop QB Jake Locker, you will have a solid tandem for the future. On defense, look to free agency to get a veteran presence on your defense right away.

3 MINNESOTA VIKINGS

Signing WR Greg Jennings in the off-season will help fill the void left by trading Percy Harvin to Seattle.

OFF STYLE: **Power Run**
DEF STYLE: **4-3 Tampa 2**
CFM OVERALL: **73**

The Vikings will run their offense through Adrian Peterson; this is a great choice, as he is the top back in the game. This strategy led them to the playoffs last season, but Minnesota needs to keep building on this success to stay relevant in a tough NFC North division. On defense, Jared Allen is the man to unleash on third downs to get your defense off the field.

2 KANSAS CITY CHIEFS

Bringing in QB Alex Smith gives KC a fresh start at QB. Play to his strengths and you will benefit.

OFF SCHEME: **West Coast**
DEF SCHEME: **Base 3-4**
CFM OVERALL: **78**

Jamaal Charles is a dynamic back who is capable of breaking long runs on any play. This will be a great weapon for new coach Andy Reid to work with this season. Kansas City also has a solid defense, with some big players in the secondary who will be able to match up against all the physical WRs in the division! For a gamer who likes a run-first approach, the Chiefs will be a great team available in many leagues.

1 DETROIT LIONS

To improve the Lions, focus on signing a dominant defensive player who can control the middle of the defense.

OFF SCHEME: **Vertical**
DEF SCHEME: **Base 4-3**
CFM OVERALL: **70**

The Lions have the best WR—Calvin Johnson. QB Matt Stafford has a big arm and should target Johnson all game long; however, this can lead to tight throws into double coverage. Work on developing a second and third receiving option to clear out some space downfield. New HB Reggie Bush can also be a threat underneath in the passing game. On defense, look to control the defensive line with your talented line and get after the QB to close out wins.

TOP 5 FANTASY DRAFT TIPS

5 CPU VS. HUMAN
4 DRAFT ORDER
3 LONG-TERM VALUE
2 POSITION VALUE
1 TEAM SCHEME

Gamers who are looking for even more roster customization can also start a CFM with a "Fantasy Draft." This puts every player in the league into a pool and starts a 32-team draft. This is a great way to switch up rosters with friends and build the team of your dreams. You will see this option as an item under the Actions tab right before you press Start Season!

5 CPU VS. HUMAN

When doing a fantasy draft, it is important to know who you are going up against. The CPU has a more conservative style of choosing players while a 32-user draft can be all over the place. Players with certain elite skills like speed will likely be drafted early in a User vs. User draft. If you are playing with a friend, think about the type of player they like to use on their favorite team and if they might draft them to their team. This can be a great way to disrupt another player's strategy. If you have a mix of users and computer players, think about the draft!

> **ALWAYS REMEMBER TO SORT BY A RATINGS CATEGORY IF YOU'RE LOOKING FOR A GEM PLAYER!**

4 DRAFT ORDER

Some users like to draft early to make sure they get a key building block, and some players would rather draft 32nd so they get back-to-back picks and can select two solid players instead. Knowing when your next pick will be is key to making sure you don't miss out on a "run" of players before you get a chance to select. Kickers, punters, and tight ends usually come off the board in waves, so don't miss out by taking a position where you already have depth.

> **CHOOSING FIRST OVERALL IS GREAT, BUT YOU WON'T GET TO PICK UNTIL 60+ PICKS LATER DUE TO THE SERPENTINE STYLE.**

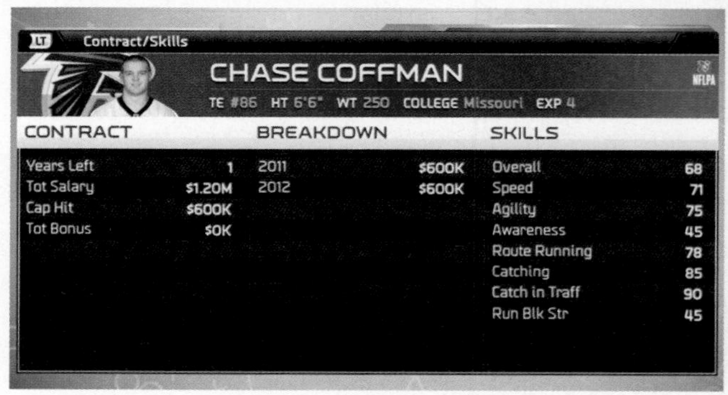

3 LONG-TERM VALUE

Looking for young talent to develop into stars is a great way to build your team. Strike a balance between high-rated veteran leadership and young players who can take over when those players retire. If you plan on playing multiple seasons in your CFM, it is wise to build around young inexpensive players who will be the foundation of your franchise.

> **WHILE VETERANS ARE GREAT DUE TO THEIR HIGH RATINGS, THEIR CAREERS ARE OFTEN SHORTER AND THEY CAN COST MORE THAN YOUNG PLAYERS.**

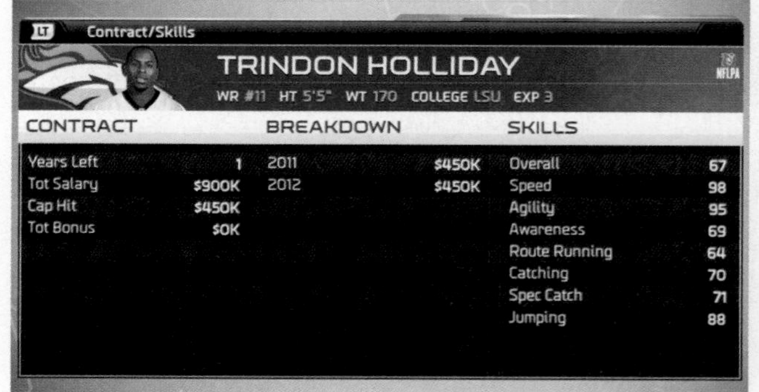

2 POSITION VALUE

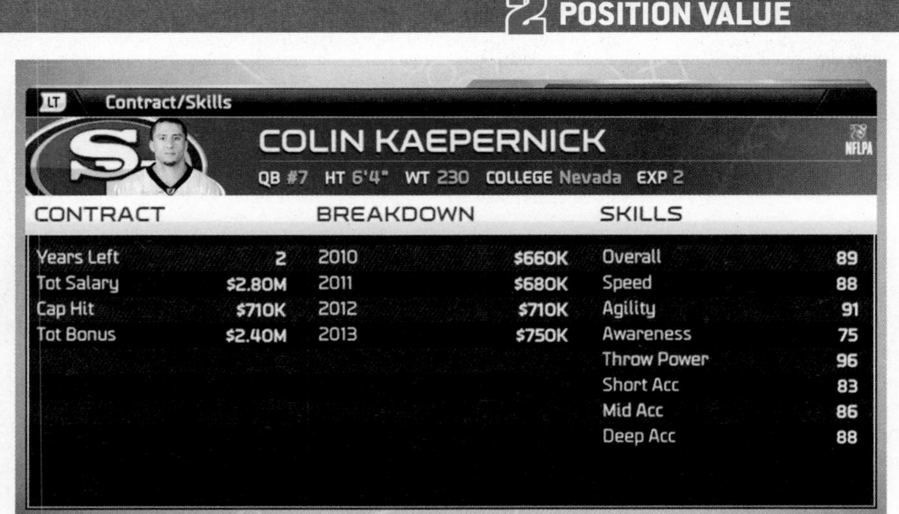

Getting a good QB is key to developing a winning team in CFM. If you select a pocket passer in an early round, back him up with a mobile QB who can run different schemes and be valuable in the red zone. Players should look for fast safeties who can slide to CB if needed and DEs who can move inside to tackle on third downs to rush the passer. Knowing which positions are valued by the CPU can allow you to jump in early and grab the players you want.

> **Bringing in flexible players like TEs who can take snaps at a WR is a great way to maximize your selections.**

1 TEAM SCHEME

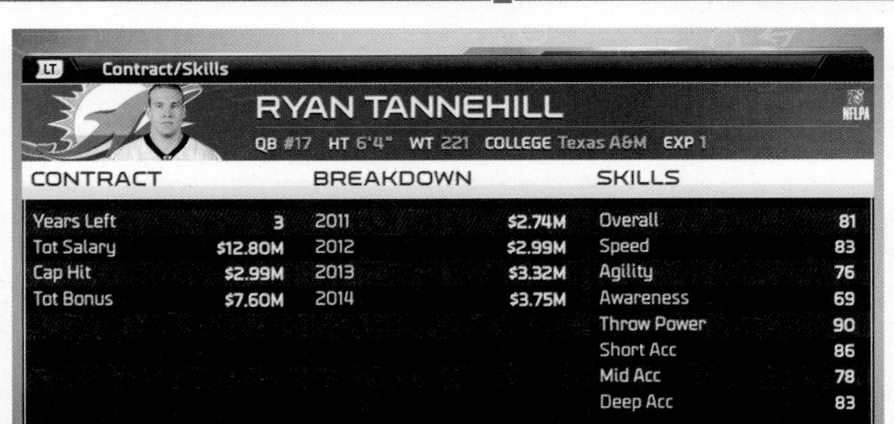

Schemes matter in Connected Franchise Mode. For example, if you are going to play a 4-3 style, don't draft a 3-4 DE! Decide what type of offensive and defensive scheme and playbook you want to use and build around those positions. If you need three WRs and one HB for your main package, don't draft a second HB until you have picked all your WRs! Many players overlook this and take the best available player rather than the best fit for their scheme!

> **Plan what type of personnel you want on the field before you draft!**

FANTASY DRAFT SLEEPERS

OFFENSE				DEFENSE			
QB	HB	WR	TE	DE	LB	CB	SAFETY
Terrelle Pryor	Taiwan Jones	Devin Hester	Chase Coffman	Margus Hunt	Sergio Kindle	DeMarcus Van Dyke	Antwon Blake
Ryan Tannehill	Jeff Demps	Trindon Holliday	Scott Chandler	Stephen Paea	Korey Toomer	Onterio McCalebb	Jerron McMillian
Brock Osweiler	Da'Rel Scott	Ramses Barden	Gavin Escobar	Al Woods	Mychal Kendricks	Chris Greenwood	Eric Reid
Geno Smith	LeGarrette Blount	Marquise Goodwin	Luke Willson	Dontay Moch	Mario Harvey	Marcus Sherels	Mike Mitchell
Mike Glennon	Jonathan Dwyer	Brandon Banks	James Hanna	Terrence Cody	Corey Lemonier	Tommie Campbell	Nate Ebner

ON THE JOB

STARTING YOUR LEAGUE

The beauty of CFM mode is the ability to create your own universe, reflecting your football dreams. There are many options to tweak and toggle to create the experience you desire in your league. The most popular are turning on and off the salary cap, how often to progress players, and what type of trades to allow. New to the Options menu this year are relocation settings, which can be on regular, open to everyone, or disabled completely.

You can now begin your league and get into the main hub. If you are playing alone, head over to the Actions tab on the top and select Start Your League. If you are waiting for friends to join or your commissioner hasn't started yet, you can still control your team. Head over to the Team tab at the top and get ready for the season by setting your depth chart, reviewing salaries, and checking with your advisors.

> **You can also play as more than one user in a dynasty if you want to control everything. Use RS/R3 in game to switch teams!**

PRESEASON

You now enter a four-week period before the start of the regular season. During this time, you have a few jobs to do. Learn what players you want to keep on your team and how they are most effective. You will need to evaluate all of your talent here, as the wins and losses don't matter at the end of the season.

DEPTH CHART

Setting your lineup is an important way to get one final look at your team before the season starts. Make sure to review your star players, depth positions, special teams, and strengths and weaknesses.

> **Check out our "Top 5 Beginner Tips" article "Setting Your Lineup" to get more tips on setting the perfect depth chart.**

> **Setting your depth chart is especially important if you are going to simulate any of your games.**

NEWS

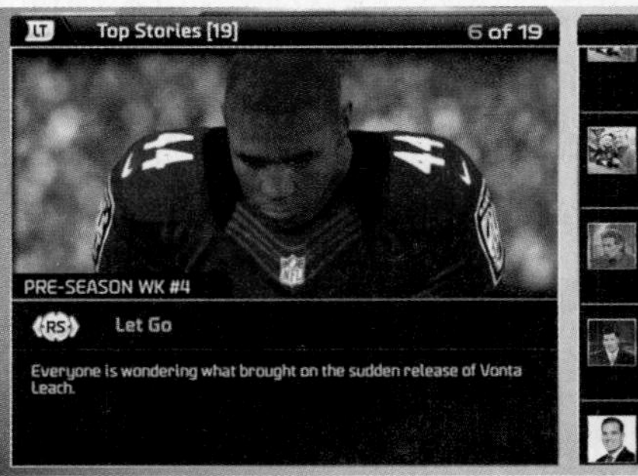

The News tab inside your CFM will refresh every week with all the latest stories from your universive. You can sort these by Top Stories, My Stories, Draft Stories, and All Stories to help keep you organized. These stories are key to pay attention to—see what is being said about you and about your opponents. Make sure to look for the latest information on players in the upcoming NFL draft, as their story lines will change over the course of a season. Currently in this CFM, a HB named Ben Bones is tearing up college football, but there are rumors that he may play baseball instead, so we are keeping a close eye on the situation.

> **You can also view a full log of every transaction in your CFM to make sure your opponents don't fly under the radar.**

TWITTER

On the same News tab is the in-game Twitter feed made up of fake tweets from real football pundits from around the league. Each personality keeps their tone in the tweets and can help you out in certain areas. Chris Mortensen will deliver information on moves around the league while Skip Bayless will make harsh remarks about your team if they struggle. There are many great personalities, so pay attention. One of our favorites is Todd McShay, whose tweets are packed with draft knowledge.

> **Use the Twitter feed to track rumors about your opponents and their possible upcoming moves.**

SCHEDULE

Go over to the Action tabs to see your upcoming items for the week. These will vary during the season, and it is always wise to check this tab every week rather than just play your game straight from the home screen!

> **You can simulate or dismiss any item from the Actions tab by pressing Ⓧ on the 360 or ■ on PS3.**

CUT DAY

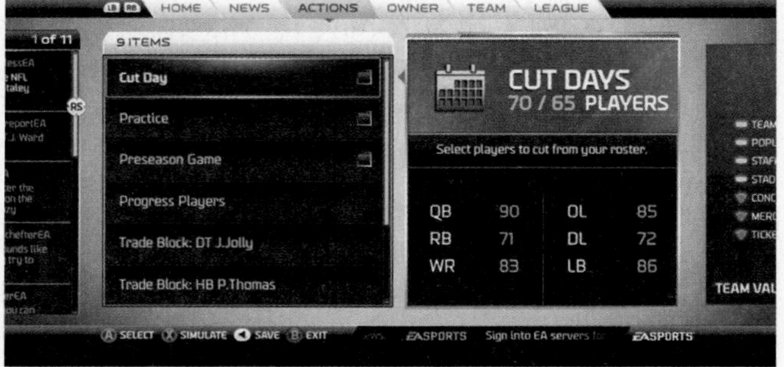

Your first task during the preseason is Cut Day, which will take course over the whole preseason. Going into each position and seeing your depth makes it much easier to make a decision on your roster. The game will also let you know if cutting a specific player will make you take a salary cap penalty. This cost can make deciding between similar players easier, as not every player costs and some free up space.

- **Week 1:** Down to 70 players
- **Week 2:** Down to 65 players
- **Week 3:** Down to 59 players
- **Week 4:** Down to 53 players

> **Cutting lower-rated rookies is easier in the short-term, but sometimes you have to cut declining veteran players and rebuild.**

PRACTICE

Practice is such an important area of CFM. It requires you to select from several different scenarios to prepare for the upcoming game and earn XP. Rewards vary based on the difficulty of the scenario. You can always restart a practice scenario without penalty, so don't fear going for the challenging ones. Depending on how much time you want to spend in practice, it can be a valuable place to grind and get XP. You will earn more XP this season, so it really is a valuable area to spend time in, and you will get a look at your next opponent's scheme!

> **PRACTICE SCENARIOS NO LONGER REQUIRE YOU TO WIN TO GET XP; YOU WILL NOW GET SOME CREDIT JUST FOR PLAYING!**

TRADE BLOCK

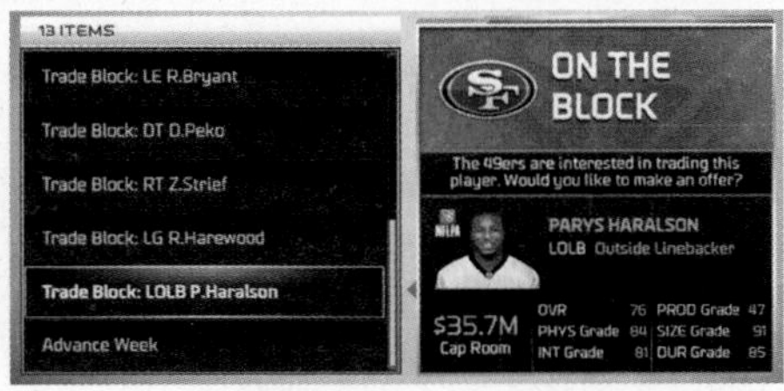

One item you will see is players around the league who are available in trades. You can click in and make an offer with either players or draft picks from your team. Here we see a solid LB in Parys Haralson, who is expendable due to the 49ers having great depth at LB. After looking through our roster, we have an expendable DT in Cullen Jenkins, who is around similar value ratings-wise. We add him to the list and submit the trade.

We can now wait and will get an answer after doing another task or advancing the week. We miss out on Haralson, as the 49ers accept another offer. In the future, we will have to offer what the 49ers are looking for in return to maximize their potential of accepting. You also want to make sure the player is a match for your scheme. The 49ers are a 3-4 team, and we currently are using a 4-3, which could cause a slight ratings decline. You will also receive offers from other teams; you can delegate them to the CPU or handle them.

> **THE IN-GAME TWITTER FEED IS A GREAT PLACE TO HEAR WHAT IS BEING SAID ABOUT YOUR ORGANIZATION. WILL YOU IGNORE IT OR LET IT INFLUENCE YOU?**

PLAY PRESEASON GAME

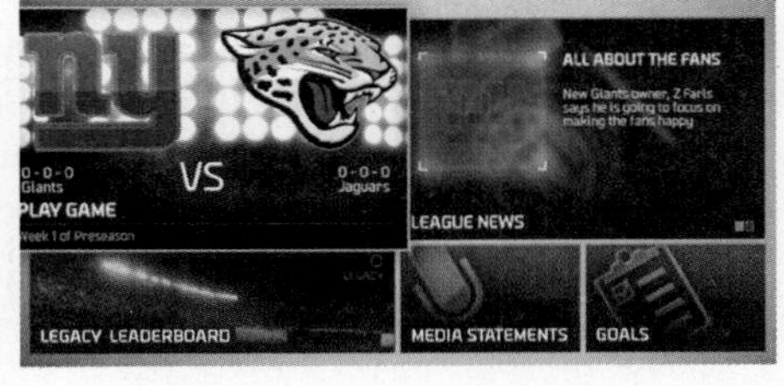

You may be very eager to start the regular season at this point but playing the Preseason is a great way to learn about your talent in some stress-free games. Your team will automatically sub in the backups so you can get a proper look at their skills. Try out all your players and run as many plays as possible. You can even experiment with different offensive and defensive playbooks at the Team Select screen by pressing Advanced Options. This can be an excellent way to find some great new plays in games where the win/loss result isn't super important.

> **KEEPING A NOTEPAD HANDY AND MARKING DOWN WHO PLAYS WELL WILL MAKE IT EASIER ON CUT DAY!**

PROGRESS PLAYERS

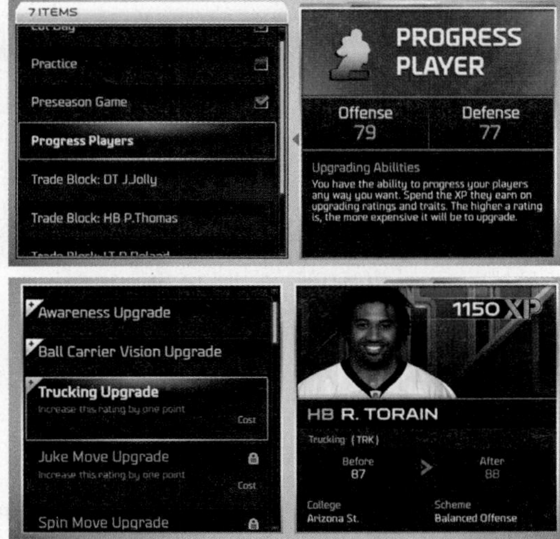

The XP you earn during practice and games is one of the ways to progress your players during the season. Each week, you will get a pool of XP to spend on individual players. The points don't expire, so you can save them up and build toward a more expensive upgrade. Anything you can unlock will be at the top, and anything that is too expensive will have a lock icon. Think about the type of team you are creating and what the players' roles will be. Check the glossary to learn what each rating does and which ratings are good buys. You can also access this menu by choosing "Upgrade Players" from the Team tab.

OFFENSE

BEST VALUE	QB	HB	WR	TE	OL
1	Deep Accuracy	Trucking/ Elusive*	Catching	Catch In Traffic	Run Block
2	Throw Power	Catching	Catch in Traffic	Impact Blocking	Pass Block
3	Medium Accuracy	Catch In Traffic	Route Running Upgrade	Speed	Impact Block
LOWER VALUE	**QB**	**HB**	**WR**	**TE**	**OL**
1	Ball Carrier Vision	Toughness	Spectacular Catch	Release	Stamina
2	Speed Upgrade	Agility	Jump	Ball Carrier Vision	Injury
3	Injury Upgrade	Kick Return	Speed	Toughness	Toughness

*Look to raise either stat depending on player type/scheme—only focus on one!

> **AWR IS MORE IMPORTANT IF YOU PLAN ON SIMULATING GAMES.**

DEFENSE

BEST VALUE	DE	DT	OLB	MLB	CB	SAFETY
1	Finesse/ Power Move*	Block Shed	Man/Zone Coverage	Hit Power	Man/Zone Coverage	Man/Zone Coverage
2	Acceleration	Strength	Finesse/ Power Move*	Pursuit	Speed	Hit Power
3	Speed	Finesse/ Power Move*	Hit Power	Tackle	Press Coverage	Catching
LOWER VALUE	**DE**	**DT**	**OLB**	**MLB**	**CB**	**SAFETY**
1	Play Recognition	Tackle	Pursuit	Block Shedding	Stiff Arm	Injury
2	Toughness	Hit Power	Toughness	Strength	Carrying	Elusiveness
3	Agility	Play Recognition	Play Ball Trait	Jumping	Kick Return	Juke

*Look to raise either stat depending on player type/scheme—only focus on one!

> **YOU CAN CHOOSE TO MANUALLY PROGRESS YOUR PLAYERS OR HAVE IT DONE AUTOMATICALLY.**

GOALS

When looking to earn XP for your players, it is important to check in on their goals for the upcoming season. Completing these are essential to maximizing the amount of XP you earn and will make a big difference in how your players progress. There are three main types of goals to check on for each of your players, and they will be affected by the role of the player and scheme.

WEEKLY GOALS

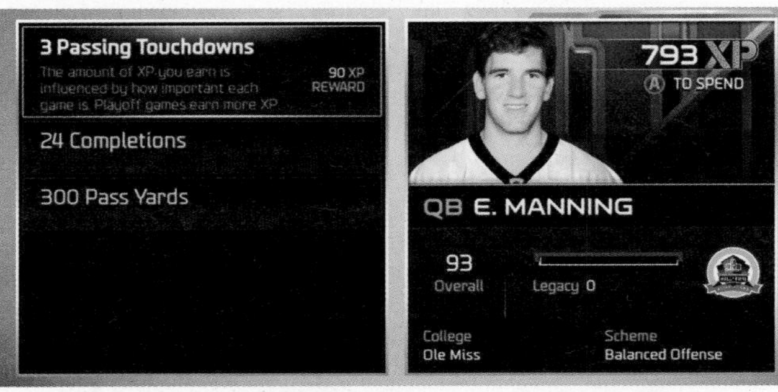

During the season, you will have weekly goals to complete that will give you bonus XP. These are based on the player positions and should be kept in mind during the game. If you are getting close to a goal during the game, try and earn the reward but never put a win in jeopardy to earn XP! For example, a weekly goal for Eli Manning is passing TDs with 300 yards and 24 completions. Each one of these will give a separate reward!

> **YOU WILL EARN MORE XP IN IMPORTANT GAMES, SO REALLY FOCUS DURING THE PLAYOFFS TO GET BIG REWARDS!**

SEASON GOALS

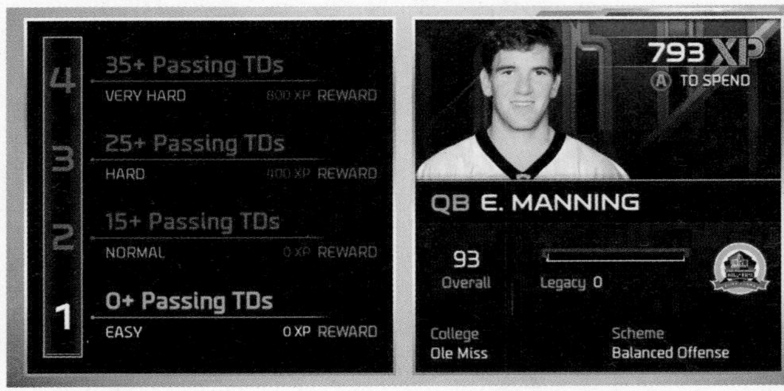

Check in at the start of the season to view your goals. Again, these are based on position and you have four different levels (easy, normal, hard, and very hard); each brings different bonuses. If you can at least get to the Hard Level 3 goal, that will be a nice bonus for your player!

> **CHECK BACK EVERY FEW WEEKS DURING THE SEASON TO VIEW YOUR PROGRESS!**

MILESTONE GOALS

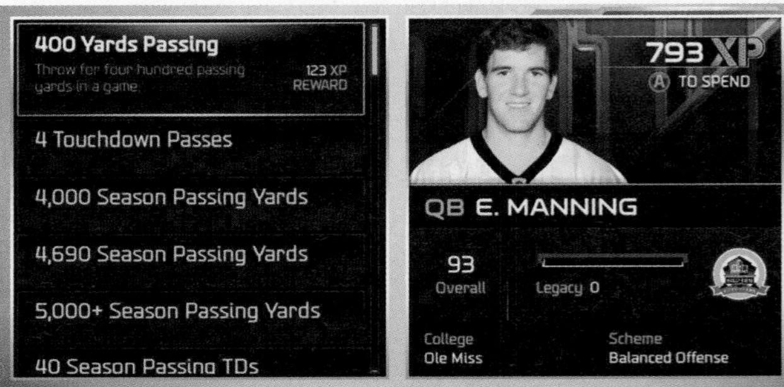

Milestone Goals provide solid rewards but will be tough to earn. Meet them in individual games by having huge performances like 400+ yards passing. You can also earn them during a season by throwing for 4,000 or 5,000 yards passing and unlocking a reward at each level. If you can earn career milestones, you will also be able to get more XP rewards, but these are less frequent. Check out those career stats to see where you stand!

STATS AND AWARDS

If you are waiting for your league to advance or want to dive even deeper, make sure to look into the Stats and Awards pages. There are Weekly, Yearly, and Pro Bowl to check out under Awards. Stats are very deep, with season and career stats for each player and in-depth team stats for all 32 squads. You can also view stats for your coach and all the NFL records, from individual performances to career records. Can you take down a legendary record like all-time passing TDs?

INJURY REPORT

If a player goes down with an injury during the season, access the Team tab to view their status. It will let you know how many weeks they will be out, and you can perform a few actions and see if you can get them back on the field faster. If they are going to be out for an extended period of time, look to place them on injured reserve.

> **YOU CAN SEE INJURED PLAYERS FOR ALL 32 TEAMS. CHECK YOUR UPCOMING OPPONENT BEFORE THE GAME!**

OWNER DUTIES

OWNER
- Rebuild your stadium or relocate
- Set prices for everything you sell
- Get feedback from your advisors
- Manage and Coach the Team

Owners manage the financial aspects of the team, make stadium decisions and still sign, draft and trade players.

As an owner, here are some areas you need to keep under control to ensure the success of your franchise! Depending on your backstory and goals as an owner, success in these categories can mean different things. Head over to the Owner tab in CFM to get a handle on your finances and get reports from all your advisors.

FINANCES

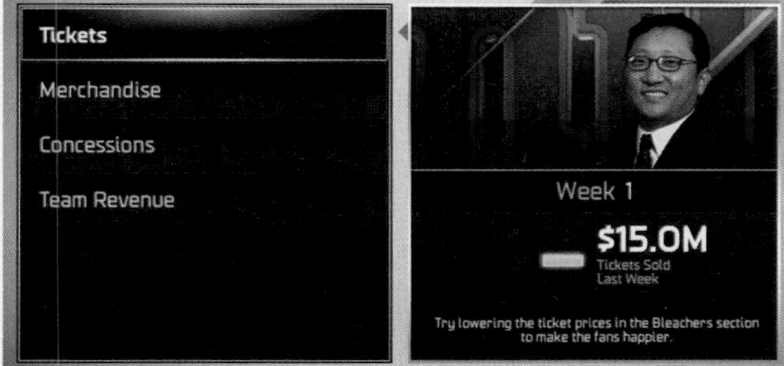

The finances section of Owner mode is important for the owner who is big on profits. If you are a financial mogul type of owner, study this area carefully. Even if you are an owner who cares about his fans, it is hard to operate a franchise if you aren't making any money.

> **For owners who want to win on the field, having some extra cash in your pocket can help bring in more talent.**

TICKETS

Tickets are a huge source of revenue for your team and should be monitored and adjusted due to demand. Depending on your stadium, there are different areas of tickets to sell. The most expensive is the suite area, which also has the lowest capacity. These areas are a great way to bring in big value to your team even though your most hardcore fans probably can't afford them. For regular seats, there are lower-, middle-, and upper-level tickets available. You can change the prices on any of these areas, but be careful, as your fans will give you feedback and let you know if the prices get too high.

A great time to check your tickets is the week after a home game; you can see how many tickets you sold the week before and how much money you made. Look at the capacity of the section and do some math to determine if lowering/raising prices or filling up your stadium will be more valuable. If you make a playoff run or have a win streak going on, you can raise prices to capitalize on the demand!

> **Suites are a great way to bring in money from ticket sales. Look into upgrading older stadiums to add more capacity!**

MERCHANDISE

Selling team gear so fans can represent your franchise is another great way to make money. There are three different types of items you can sell: team apparel, jerseys, and memorabilia. You can set prices of each item in this menu. The apparel is going to be the least expensive, with jerseys of your fans' favorite players costing more. Memorabilia is the most expensive of the items but doesn't have quite the demand of items like T-shirts. There is an average price listed that is a good guideline of how to set your prices. You can increase it, but that could drive down the amount of fans who will buy the items. Check back every few weeks to see what is selling and whether you need to put something on sale to drive some purchases.

> **If you make a Super Bowl run, you can capitalize on all the extra gear you will unlock and can sell to your fans!**

CONCESSIONS

Fans who attend your games don't just buy tickets and gear; they want to buy food and drinks too! If you can offer great items at good value, your fans will open their wallets and you will have opened another revenue stream. There are five levels of concessions in CFM: Basic, 2 Star, 3 Star, 4 Star, and 5 Star. The most common and inexpensive are items like chips, fries, and soda. These are available no matter what team is used. As you head into the more expensive items, you will see stadium-specific items like NY pizza for the Giants. These items have a higher average cost, and you can always raise or lower the price.

> **Your advisor will give you some tips on what the fans are saying or what items you should change the price on!**

TEAM REVENUE

Team Revenue is a great area to see how you are doing with your income versus expenses. On the income side, it will show you the total amount of money you are bringing in. The expenses side has all of your player and staff salaries, along with any stadium lease and maintenance information. Your stadium can pull away some of your profits, so make sure you will get good return on your investment over the long-term with any money you put in! This will add up over time and leave you with an available pool of funds to work with. You can put these back into your team on the field or perhaps lower prices to give back to the fans if you have extra.

STADIUM

Your stadium is a huge factor in how much money you can make. It affects everything from the amount of tickets you can sell to what you can offer at the concession stands. If your team has a lower rated stadium, you will want to invest in some upgrades over the long haul or even consider building a new one. However, this is a massive project and must be something you plan out. If you can't afford a new stadium, perhaps consider moving to a new city that will give you money to support building a new location. You can upgrade your stadium in different areas, such as seating, concessions, bathrooms, fan zone, team store, and parking! A higher rating in each category will open up new items, and you will want to work your way toward Level 5 in each category to maximize what you can sell and ultimately maximize your profits!

> **IF YOU BUILD A BRAND-NEW STADIUM, KEEP SOME MONEY ASIDE FOR RENOVATIONS TO KEEP YOUR STADIUM IN TOP SHAPE AS THE YEARS PASS!**

MARKETING

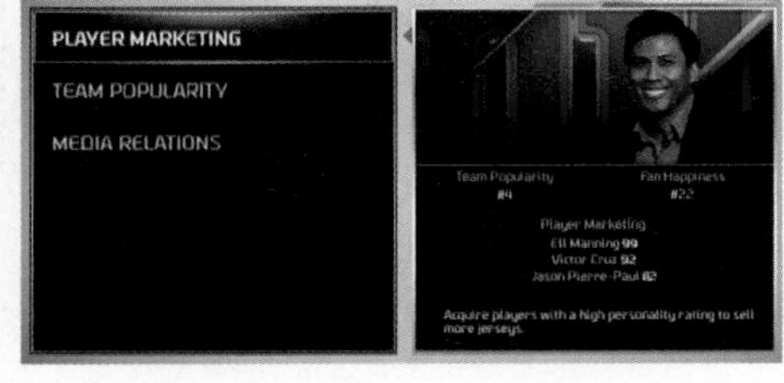

Marketing your team is a great way to bring in more revenue and increase your popularity! Your advisor will have great information on how you are currently doing and how you can improve your situation. You can market your individual players along with your team. Check in with the fans and see if they are receptive, since they are a main revenue source for your franchise!

> **ACQUIRE PLAYERS WITH A HIGH PERSONALITY RATING TO SELL MORE JERSEYS.**

PLAYER MARKETING

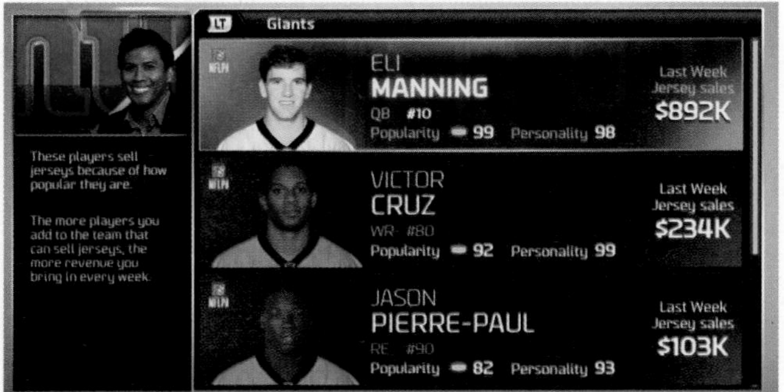

Your most popular players will be eligible as marketing options, and depending on their personality and popularity, they can bring in big money from jersey sales! If you don't have the star power you need in this area, consider picking up a popular player; however, make sure they fit into your team or scheme, or it may cost you more in the long run.

> **HERE YOU CAN VIEW THE TOP 10 JERSEY SELLERS IN THE LEAGUE ALONG WITH THE POPULARITY AND PERSONALITY RATINGS!**

TEAM POPULARITY

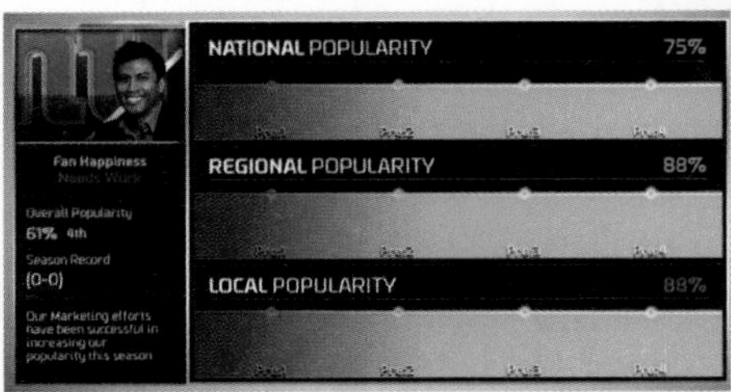

Your team has three main areas of popularity: national, regional, and local. These are updated each week, and winning is a big factor in their trend. Depending on your location and how well you market, you can increase these numbers, which will bring in more money over the long-term. Keep in mind your fan happiness and monitor your overall popularity percentage to see how it is trending.

> **IF YOU'RE A SMALL MARKET TEAM, FOCUS ON YOUR LOCAL POPULARITY!**

MEDIA RELATIONS

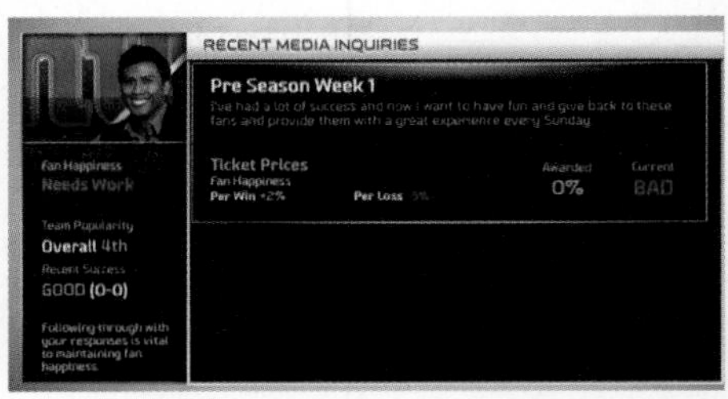

Here you can get a recap of your statements to the media and how it affected your situation. In our first exchange, we put pressure on our team to get a win and if we had, we would have gotten a +2% boost, but we lost and got a -5% penalty. We can see our fan happiness is still at an okay level and will want to monitor that and consider it before speaking with the media again!

FAN HAPPINESS

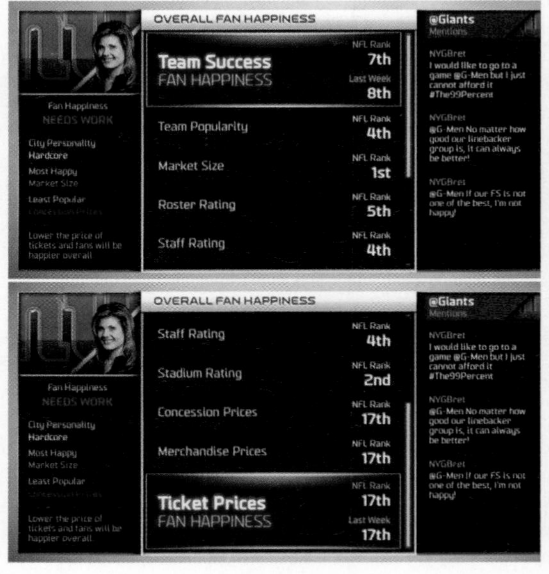

This is the area where you get great information on how to increase your happiness with your fans and where you currently rank around the league. On the left side of this screen, you can learn more about your franchise from your city personality; discover what the fans are most happy about and what they would like to see changed. By adjusting prices in certain areas, you can change your rank and bring up your fan happiness. Things that are harder to change are items like market size and stadium rating, but if these are low, you could always consider moving! If your staff isn't pleasing the fans, you can always bring in another group too!

> **SOME RANKS LIKE TICKET PRICES CAN CHANGE QUICKLY, BUT TEAM SUCCESS CAN TAKE LONGER TO IMPROVE!**

STAFF

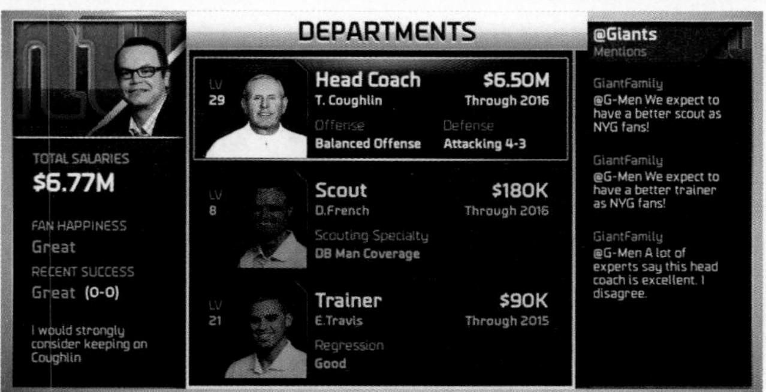

Having a great staff will give your fans confidence that the franchise is heading in the right direction. There are three key areas of your staff: coach, scout, and trainer. First is the coach, who will give your team an identity with their scheme on both offense and defense. They will have a level as well, so the higher it is, usually the bigger the contract! You can replace your coach after the season if he isn't getting the wins out of the talent on your roster.

Scouting is the next area to focus on so you can locate great players in the draft. Each scout has a specialty and will give you an advantage when looking for certain types of players.

The last area of staff is the trainer, who is very important for keeping players on the field and for getting injured players back on the field. Trainers also have skills, such as being able to slow the rate of your players' regression!

> **IF YOU NEED A NEW COACH, CONSIDER BRINGING A LEGEND OUT OF RETIREMENT.**

STAFF PACKAGES

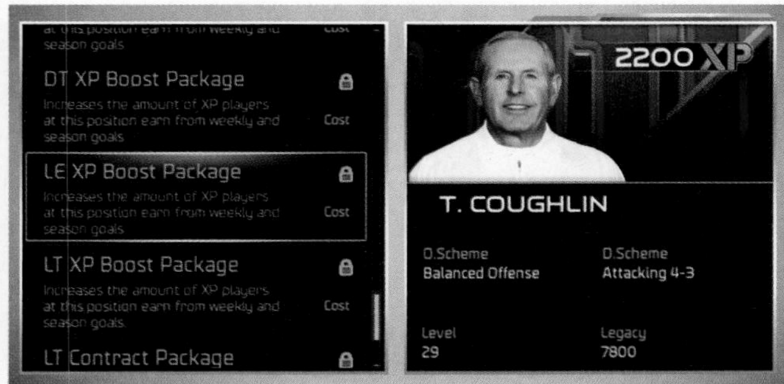

If you want to increase your coach, scout, or trainer skills, upgrade packages to give them new skills. If you have an area of need like a defensive line, upgrade your coach's negotiation for that position to give an advantage when talking to free agents. If you have an older QB, upgrade your coach's package to help him talk the player out of retiring. Think ahead to your team needs for the upcoming off season and use your coach XP accordingly!

> **COACHES CAN RETIRE AT THE END OF THE SEASON, SO ALWAYS MONITOR YOUR SITUATION!**

TEAM SUCCESS

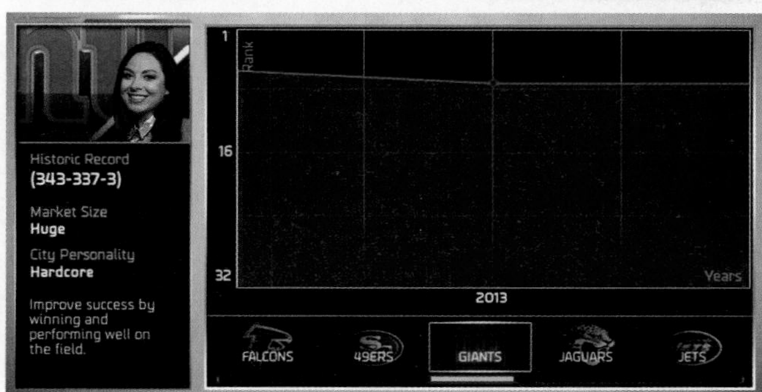

Winning on the field takes cares of most problems with your franchise. Even a team in a small market can draw in fans if they make a few title runs! Here you can see your city personality and where you rank in success, both historic and recent. Recent will show you a graph with a weekly timeline, while historic will focus more on years. There is really only one way to improve this rank—by winning!

> **YOU CAN VIEW GRAPHS FOR ALL 32 NFL TEAMS' SUCCESS IN THIS AREA TOO!**

MEDIA INQUIRY

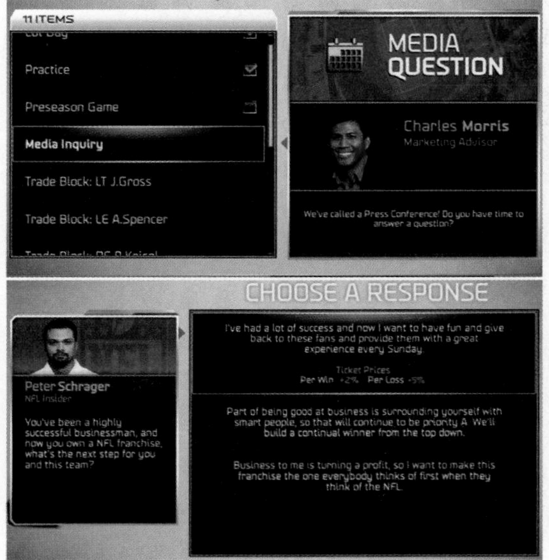

Now that you are an NFL owner, it is your job to talk with the media. They want to learn your plans for the franchise and will give you some option on how to respond. Here is a sample question: *You've been a highly successful businessman, and now you own an NFL franchise. What's the next step for you and this team?* Your three answers give you different results. The first will get the fans on your side, the second will let your team know you are serious about winning, and the third will let everyone know you are in this for the profit. There will be multiple questions that will start to shape your tendencies as an owner, so take a second to consider what your answer says about your style! Here, we give the fans some love in our answer and it affects our ticket prices +2% for a win and -5% for a loss.

> **THINK ABOUT THE FANS, YOUR TEAM, AND YOUR FINANCES DURING MEDIA INQUIRIES. WHAT IS MOST IMPORTANT TO YOU?**

MOVING YOUR TEAM

Moving Your Team Checklist Box

- ❑ Select Location
- ❑ Select Uniforms
- ❑ Select Nickname
- ❑ Select Stadium

If your team has a stadium rating below 20, you will be able to move your team to one of 16 locations. You can also stay put and build a new stadium if your rating is below 40. To move your team, enter Owner mode and select Stadium. It will take a few weeks to pull together a list of candidates, but you will soon see an action item to move cities!

> **TURNING RELOCATION SETTINGS TO "EVERYONE" IN THE CAREER SETTINGS OPTIONS WILL ALLOW EVERYONE TO RELOCATE.**

LOCATIONS!

Here are your cities to choose from in *Madden NFL 25*! Keep in mind the market size, fan interest, and how much funding they are offering toward your stadium. All of these will be factors in determining how much money you will be able to make in the future!

CFM RELOCATION CITIES
 Austin, Texas
 Brooklyn, New York
 Columbus, Ohio
 Chicago, Illinois
 Dublin, Ireland
 London, England
 Los Angeles, California
 Memphis, Tennessee

CFM RELOCATION CITIES
 Mexico City, Mexico
 Oklahoma City, Oklahoma
 Orlando, Florida
 Portland, Oregon
 Sacramento, California
 San Antonio, Texas
 Salt Lake City, Utah
 Toronto, Canada

NICKNAME

Once you select a city, you will have to choose a nickname. Each team has three choices per city that are all unique to the history. You also have the option of sticking with the original franchise name. Each nickname will give you different support from the fans, so choose carefully!

Chargers

Hounds

Egyptians

Steamers

UNIFORMS

Once you select your nickname, you will get three options for uniform schemes. There are classic, modern, and traditional uniforms for each team. You can go with your favorite, listen to the fans, or go with whichever won the popularity poll.

STADIUM

The last order of business when moving is to select what type of stadium you want to build! There are eight different types of stadiums with a basic and deluxe version of each. They all cost a certain amount to build; this will be reflected in your weekly expenses, so be prepared to pay! You will also learn information about the capacity, number of suites, and percentage of stadium funding you receive here!

Basic Canopy Stadium

Deluxe Canopy Stadium

The eight different types of stadiums are:

Canopy	**Euro**	**Glass**	**Sphere**
Classic	**Futuristic**	**Hybrid**	**Traditional**

REGULAR SEASON

Now is the time when all your work in the preseason pays off, as these regular season games matter. You will make your playoff push over the next 17 weeks. You will now have another key area to check out to make sure you are ready for the upcoming NFL draft after the season.

> **BETWEEN THE PRESEASON AND REGULAR SEASON IS THE TIME TO IMPORT AN NCAA'14 DRAFT CLASS FROM *NCAA FOOTBALL 14* IF YOU SAVED ONE.**

SCOUTING

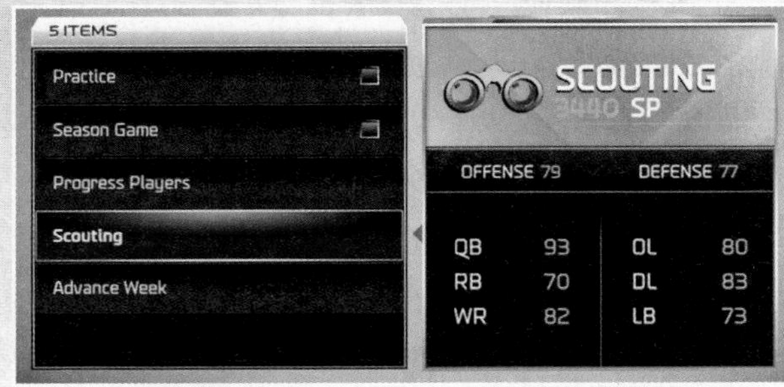

TOP 5 SCOUTING CATEGORIES

5 SCHEME/PLAYER TYPE
4 PHYSICAL
3 BEST POSITION XP TRAIT
2 DEVELOPMENT
1 OVERALL

Scouting is extremely important to building a successful long-term franchise. This is where you start to create your list of players to target for the upcoming NFL draft. By spending XP, you will learn more about each player and what skills they have. Just think, by studying the incoming class, you can find a late round talent like QB Tom Brady!

5 SCHEME/PLAYER TYPE

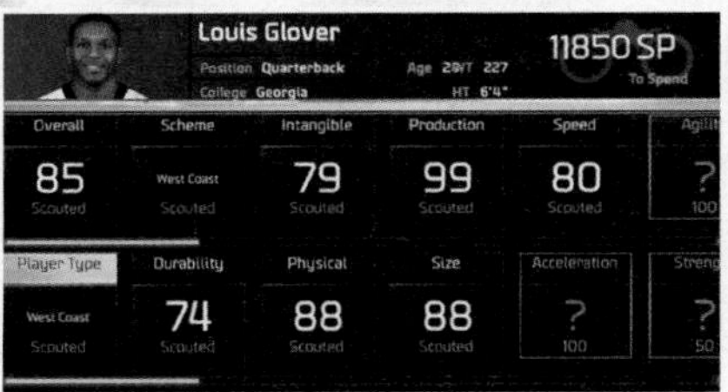

By looking into the scheme your player will fit into, you can eliminate players from your board who don't fit your style. If you run a 4-3 scheme, you won't need a 3-4 edge rusher. The player type fits along with scheme and should reflect it pretty closely. These are two very important categories that are very inexpensive and can eliminate a bunch of players quickly to leave you with a shorter list where you can really start spending points!

> **YOUR SCOUTING XP IS A SEPARATE POOL THAT HAS TO BE DIVIDED OVER EVERY PLAYER YOU CHOOSE TO BREAK DOWN.**

4 PHYSICAL

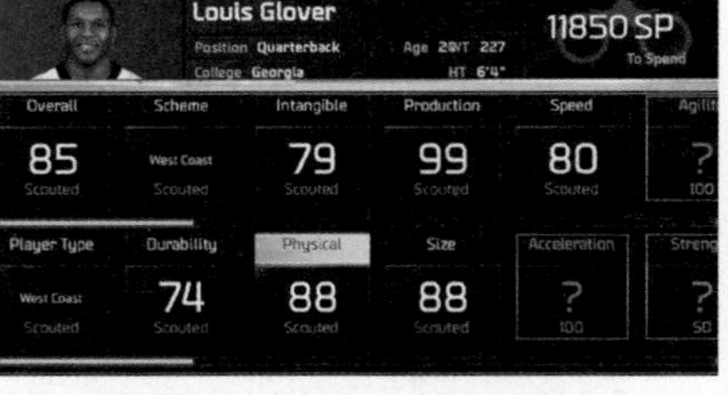

Rather than going after multiple physical skills like speed and acceleration, this category will give you more of a snapshot of a player's abilities. A great physical talent will be athletic in key ratings for their positions. This will allow you to save on multiple categories by using this one physical snapshot.

> **SORT BY PROJECTED DRAFT ROUND AND DRAFT PICK TO FIND THE CONSENSUS TALENT.**

3 BEST POSITION XP TRAIT

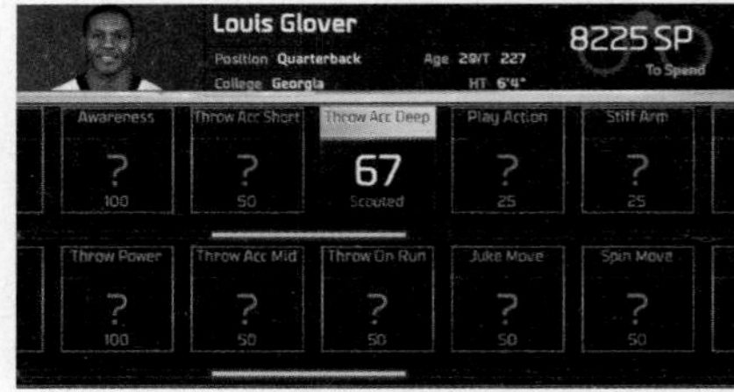

Depending on the position of your player, you will need to upgrade them with key ratings later in their career. By looking into Trucking/Elusive for an HB or Finesse/Power for a DE, you will know how far you have to go to round out your players' skills. Only scout one of these two categories and base it off the type of player. Speed players are more Elusive/Finesse while strong players are more Truck/Power.

> **MAKE SURE TO STAY TUNED TO THE NEWS TO FOLLOW SOME OF THESE PLAYERS' STORIES AND LEARN MORE ABOUT THEIR HISTORY.**

2 DEVELOPMENT

The development trait is another expensive one but can be important for the long-term success of your player. If you are able to uncover a star trait, you can be sure this player will progress at a high rate. Even if your player ends up with a lower rating overall, he can develop over the course of a career. This could be the difference between a decent late round player and a gem!

> **PLAYERS CAN CHANGE DEPENDING ON BRANCHING STORY LINES, SO DON'T EXPECT TO GET THE SAME PLAYER EVERY TIME.**

1 OVERALL

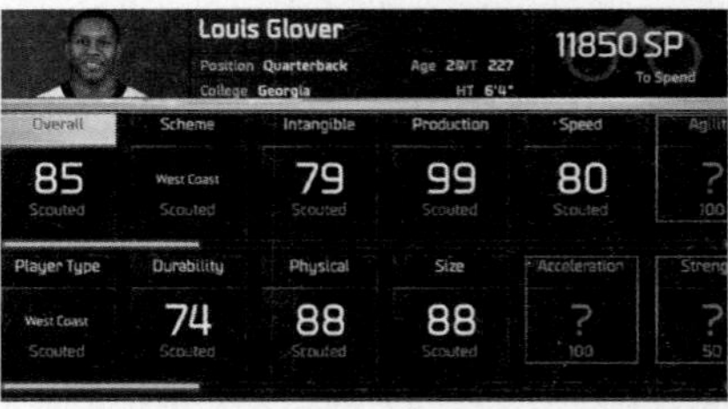

Investigating a player's overall rating can be very expensive. If you are looking at a 3-7th rounder, perhaps don't spend the money to see the number and just look at the grade. If you are doing research on your first or early second rounder, though, go the extra distance and find out their overall! You will build your franchise around this player, so it is worth it to be certain they are the right player.

> **MAKE SURE TO FOCUS ON SCOUTING PLAYERS IN POSITIONS OF NEED.**

TOP 5 CFM SCOUTING RATINGS

Connected Franchise Mode has its own ratings that are unique to *Madden NFL 25*. These five categories take into account a player's rating in multiple areas to give you a quick idea of what to expect. This can be a great way to scout and also helps you understand why you may see different ratings in certain areas of the game. Here are what those ratings mean and why they are important!

5 DURABILITY
4 INTANGIBLE
3 SIZE
2 PRODUCTION
1 PHYSICAL

5 DURABILITY

Your durability rating is built upon a player's injury, stamina, and toughness ratings. Stamina is a big factor in *Madden* and is crucial for players who like to play fast. There are plenty of players in the draft story that could be stars if they stay healthy. Are you willing to take the risk?

> YOU MIGHT NOT THINK INJURIES ARE IMPORTANT UNTIL YOU NEED YOUR STAR PLAYER ON THE FIELD IN A BIG MOMENT.

4 INTANGIBLE

The intangible ratings are based off a specific player's positional skill ratings. So for an HB, it factors in items like ball carrier vision and running moves. A QB's rating is more focused off of throwing ratings like Accuracy and Power. These are those key ratings you will have to upgrade later to improve your player, so starting high will save you XP in the future!

> THE LINEMEN UP FRONT WILL GET THEIR INTANGIBLE RATING FROM THINGS LIKE RUN AND PASS BLOCK.

3 SIZE

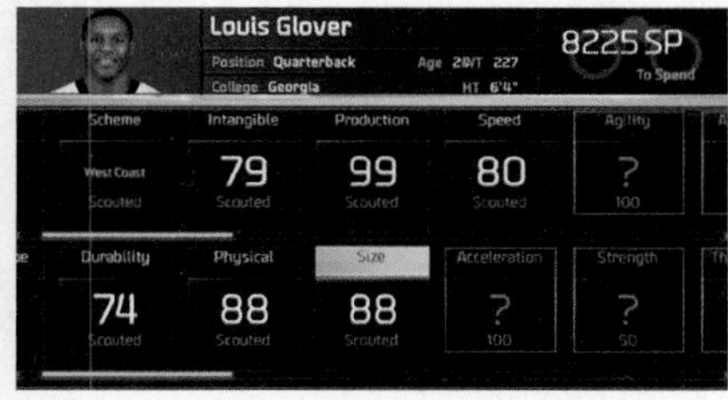

This rating takes into account the height and weight of a player along with his position. While you can get most of this information from the top bar, remember what type of player you are looking at and how that will change his player type. There aren't many 6'6" WRs who are speedy; they tend to be more possession type. You also can't coach height, and with physics, weight matters more than ever!

> SMALLER HBS AND WRS TEND TO DEVELOP INTO SPEEDY OR ELUSIVE TYPE PLAYERS.

2 PRODUCTION

Production ratings reflect the stats a player has put up during his career. A rookie will always enter the league with a production rating of 0. This is not an error and it will continue to improve as he puts together a few seasons and builds a legacy. A player like RGIII has great physical skills but hasn't produced over a long window yet; when he does, his overall rating will continue to improve.

> A GREAT PRODUCTION GRADE FOR A PROSPECT MEANS THEY ARE A PROVEN PRODUCER WHO PUT UP BIG NUMBERS IN COLLEGE.

1 PHYSICAL

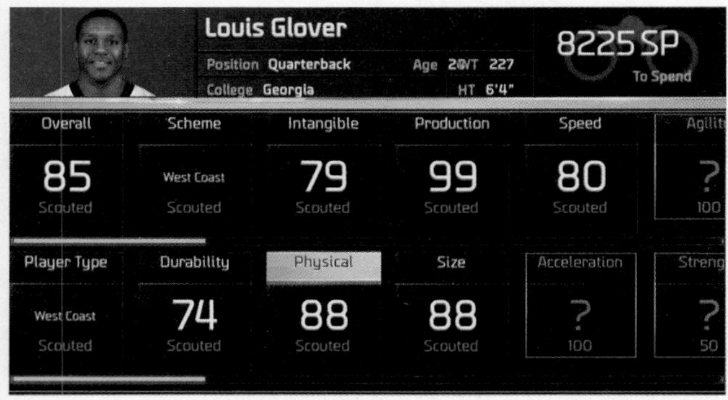

> THIS IS THE ATHLETIC GRADE FOR PLAYERS. FOR PLAYERS WHO NEED SPEED, ACCELERATION, AND AGILITY LIKE CBS AND WRS, THIS IS A GREAT CATEGORY. A PLAYER IS GENERALLY NOT GOING TO GET MORE ATHLETIC AS HIS CAREER WEARS ON, SO THE HIGHER RATING YOU CAN FIND, THE MORE YOU CAN BUILD THIS PLAYER IN HIS OTHER SKILL CATEGORIES. FINDING A RAW ATHLETIC TALENT TO MOLD INTO A SKILLED STAR IS VERY EXCITING.

> PAYING THE XP PRICE FOR ALL THE PHYSICAL UPGRADES CAN GET EXPENSIVE, SO FIND PLAYERS WITH GREAT RATINGS IN THIS CATEGORY.

POSTSEASON

Watch that playoff race under Standings to see where you are as you near the end of the season. If you are one of the top teams in your division or can grab a wildcard spot, you will earn a berth in the playoffs. If you don't qualify, you can start making your off-season plans and you may even see some teams fire their coaches. If you play in a competitive league, this is when the action really heats up!

STAFF NEGOTIATIONS

If your staff contracts are up, you can offer them a new deal during staff resigning. We don't have a head coach, so we wait until the Staff Hiring process and can look into the candidates! Here we view all the available coaches and their current levels. Look to get more in-depth and see what type of offensive and defensive schemes your potential coaches would be running. Coaches will already have certain packages unlocked along with certain influences, depending on how long they have been around. You can go for a newer coach who you can mold into your own, or go with a veteran who already knows all the tricks. You can always withdraw your offer later if you decide to go in another direction.

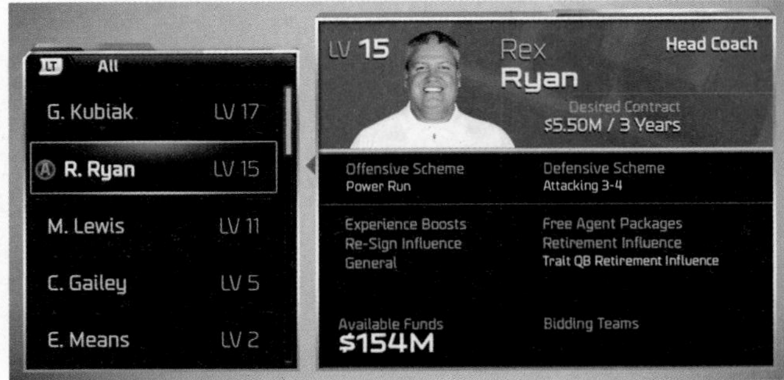

> **CHECK OUT THE BIDDING TEAMS LIST TO SEE IF YOUR TARGET COACH IS IN HIGH DEMAND AROUND THE LEAGUE!**

OFF SEASON

The first stage of the off-season is to resign your players. Think about their value to your franchise and scheme and how much money they would be worth on the open market. You can also delegate this task and allow your staff to handle it. Keep your salary cap room in mind if you have multiple players to resign.

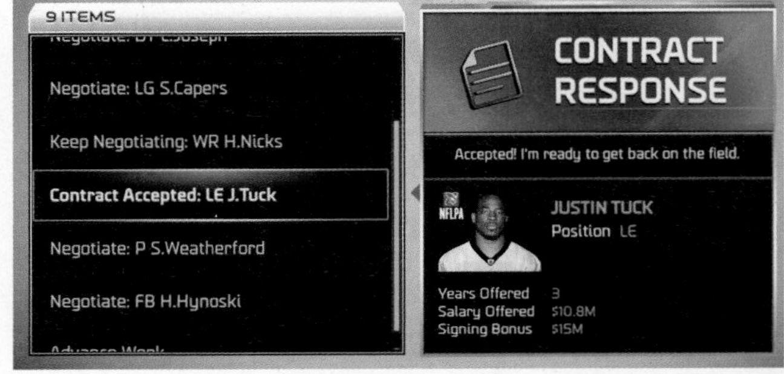

> **YOU CAN NEGOTIATE EXTENSIONS WITH PLAYERS DURING THE SEASON; THEY WILL SHOW UP AS AN ITEM IN YOUR WEEKLY ACTIONS.**

FREE AGENCY BIDDING

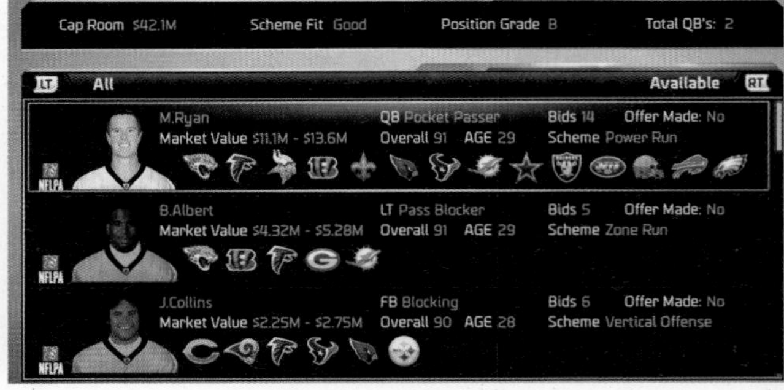

If a player rejects your negotiation offer, he will hit free agency! This is the place to go to see which players are available all around the league. If you need to add a star player to your team or find a good value replacement, this is the place. When you head into bidding, you can see all the available players along with their current scheme and player type. At the top of the screen, you will see your cap room, if the scheme is a fit, and your current grade at that position. On each player, there is a market value number that indicates where the bidding range is along with how many teams have made offers. Don't forget to check your team needs before getting into a bidding war for a player.

After you bid, you must wait a week for the player's agent to sort through offers and get back to you. Once you have offered all players that interest you, you can advance the week and get responses from your targets! You will get a few chances to advance weeks and sign free agents, so you may want to wait to hear back from your top choice before going after secondary options. If you have a backup plan, check and see how many bids they are getting and determine if you want to risk waiting. Once free agency ends, you will be able to view a recap and see who moved where!

> **DON'T FORGET TO CHECK FREE AGENCY BETWEEN PRE- AND REGULAR SEASON TO SEE WHO YOUR OPPONENTS CUT FROM THEIR TEAM!**

NFL DRAFT

TOP 5 NFL DRAFT TIPS

Once Free Agency wraps up, it is time for the NFL draft to get under way. This is where each team gets a chance to draft the biggest stars from college football. All the time you spent scouting will now pay off. Make time to complete this mode in one setting, especially for an online league with multiple users!

5 CHECK THE NEWS
4 FREE AGENTS
3 CONSIDER TRADING
2 SIGN YOUR ROOKIES
1 VIEW YOUR RATINGS

5 CHECK THE NEWS

During the draft, browse through your Twitter feed and news stories to hear the latest chatter around the league. This news can come in handy and help you keep track of who your opponents have selected. Remember that you only have two minutes to draft a player, and the game will automatically select someone for you when the clock runs out. You can always pause the draft clock if you need to step away for a moment.

> KEEP A NOTEPAD NEXT TO YOU AND CHECK OFF YOUR MOST WANTED PROSPECTS WHO GET DRAFTED!

4 FREE AGENTS

If you are unable to draft a player to fill every need on your roster, you can go into free agency after the draft and grab some players. There will always be a pool of leftover players from the earlier free agency period. These players will likely be available at a discounted rate since they were passed over the first time through!

> ALWAYS KEEP SOME MORE CONSISTENT VETERANS ON YOUR TEAMS WHILE YOU DEVELOP THE YOUNG TALENT.

3 CONSIDER TRADING

If you are waiting for the computer to pick but really want a player who might not be available later, you can try and trade up to the current selection. This will cost you a later pick or even a player, but if you want a special guy, it may be worth it. When it is your turn to select, you can always trade down your pick. This is a great strategy to get more assets, and it's always worth checking out the offers on the table.

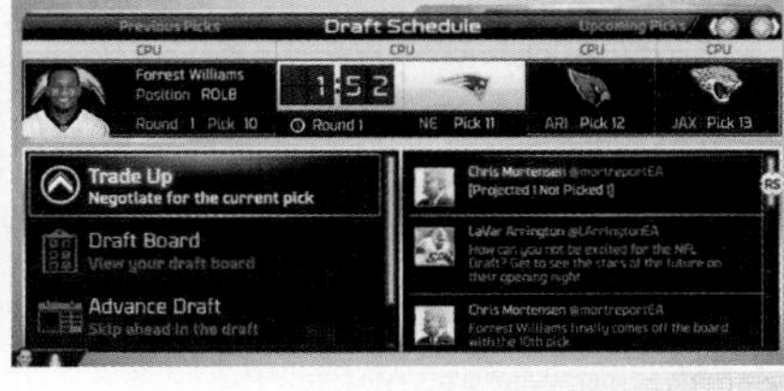

> IF YOU COMPLETE A SUCCESSFUL TRADE, THE CLOCK WILL RESET AND GIVE YOU A FULL SELECTION TIME.

2 SIGN YOUR ROOKIES

After the draft, you can check on the contracts that your rookies signed to see how valuable young talent is to your team. While these players are new, they have potential if you can manage their XP and hopefully turn them into stars. With the salary cap, it is important to get good value out of your young players.

> BRINGING IN A BIG CLASS OF ROOKIES IS A GREAT WAY TO KEEP THE VETERANS WORKING HARD.

1 VIEW YOUR RATINGS

If you took a chance and selected a player who wasn't on your draft board, you can now head to your depth chart and view their ratings. This is a great way to see if you might have struck gold in a specific rating. Picks that you scouted beforehand tend to be more safe, but you always have a chance to uncover a gem in the NFL draft!

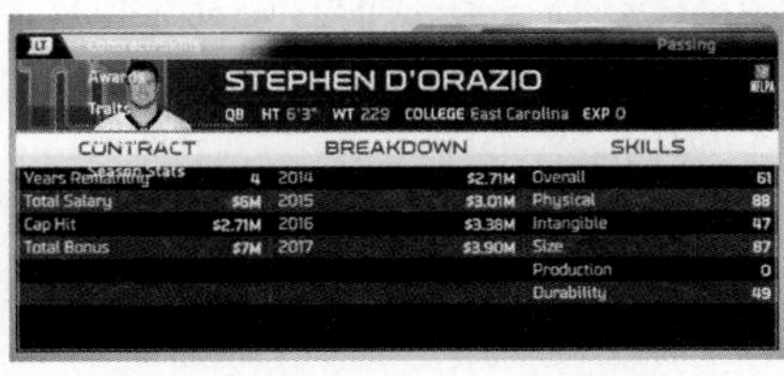

> GET ALL YOUR SCOUTING DONE BEFORE THE DRAFT, AS YOU WON'T BE ABLE TO GET ANY NEW INFORMATION ONCE IT STARTS.

START SEASON 2!

That completes an entire season of Connected Franchise Mode. Now you should have all the tools to turn your team into an NFL powerhouse. No matter if you play online or offline, CFM is a very deep mode that has something for everyone. By using the above tips, you can continue down the road toward Canton and the Football Hall of Fame!

Madden Ultimate Team

WHAT IS MADDEN ULTIMATE TEAM?

Madden Ultimate Team is a free-to-play game mode that combines player trading items with on-the-field *Madden NFL* action. Along the way, you can earn, buy, auction, and trade players to build your ultimate team of football legends past and present. In Ultimate Team mode you put together a team that fits any style or mold you want and then compete against other players!

Ultimate Team Checklist

- ❑ Start Your Team
- ❑ Set Your Lineup
- ❑ Play Solo Challenges
- ❑ Play Head-to-Head Seasons
- ❑ Earn Coins
- ❑ Complete Collections
- ❑ Use Trade Block
- ❑ Use Auction Block
- ❑ Adjust Chemistry
- ❑ Build Your Ultimate Lineup

GETTING STARTED

Head into the settings to redeem your special code for buying this strategy guide!

From the main menu, select the Ultimate Team panel to get started building your team. Since you picked up this strategy guide, you already have access to an 85 Overall Barry Sanders item, so you have a great back to build around. Open up the extra pack you received to see what type of team you can craft to start. The players in the extra pack should give you a few upgrades from your basic starter pack. Now, you will have to choose a player to build around from a list of current superstars. When choosing which player to start building around, focus on a defensive end or safety unless you already pulled a good one from your extra pack. There are already solid QB options available in the Skills Trainer, so building on defense is the smart move. If you are building a specific kind of squad to reflect your favorite team or player, you can also look to build there!

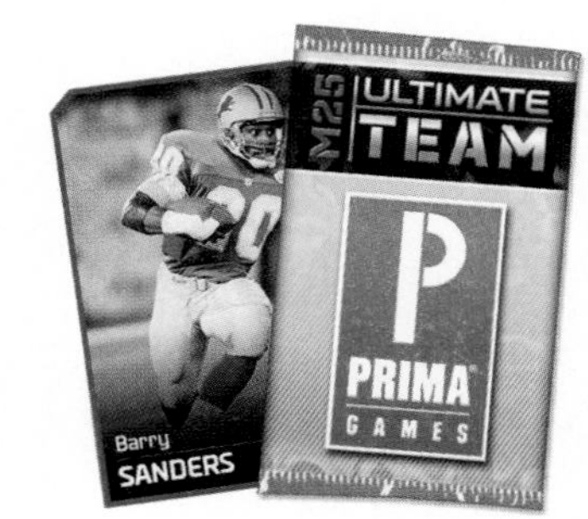

FREE Ultimate Team Pro Pack including Barry Sanders code can be found on the insert code page in this book. Follow the instructions on the insert page, then get off to a fast start in Ultimate Team by adding to your collection with the valuable offering. Have fun in Ultimate Team!

SOLO CHALLENGES

Play solo challenge games to test your team against many different teams played by the CPU. Solo challenges provide rewards such as coins or exclusive reward items. Many solo challenges have specific requirements to unlock them, such as completing a collection, having a certain team overall rating, or winning head-to-head games. Check often to find special seasonal or limited-time solo challenges!

THE ENTIRE ULTIMATE TEAM SYSTEM IS BUILT AROUND EARNING COINS, WITH WHICH YOU PICK UP MORE ITEMS.

HEAD-TO-HEAD SEASONS

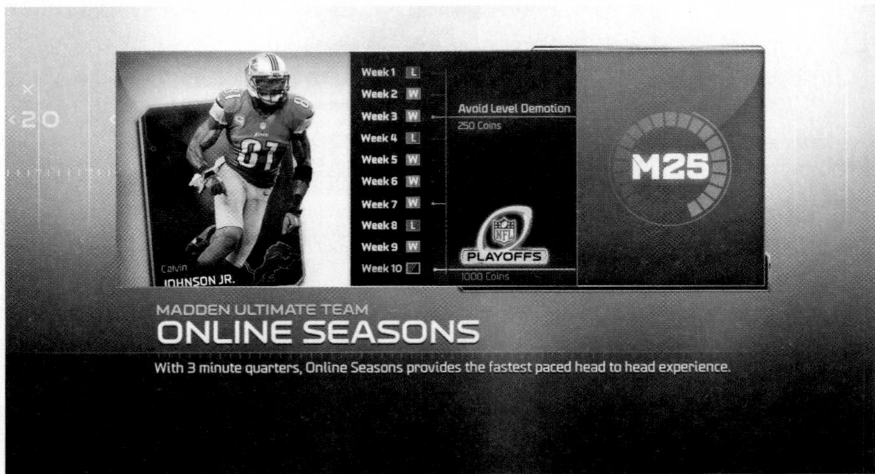

Select Head-to-Head Seasons to begin your championship career. Match up with another Madden Ultimate Team player at random. Each game you play during the season schedule has specific goals and rewards. There are eight levels of seasons. Keep winning to advance to a higher level, make the playoffs, and win the championship! As you progress, you can earn coins along the way. You can also View Season History, which includes your current record, post-season appearances, and championships won. The seasons are 10 games long in this mode and the playoffs feature eight teams.

IF YOU DON'T WIN THE REQUIRED NUMBER OF GAMES IN A SEASON, YOU MAY BE RELEGATED INTO A LOWER DIVISION.

MANAGING YOUR LINEUP

Each time you open up a new pack, you will see an assortment of items to manage. In the Team Management screen, you'll find three ways to view your items. Use Update Lineup to prepare for play by selecting your starters and updating your depth chart.

If you want to view your current roster, select it from the hub to examine your team and send items to the auction block or pending collections. These are items that are currently active in your collection.

YOU CAN COLLECT A HUGE NUMBER OF ITEMS IN ULTIMATE TEAM, BUT NOT ALL OF THEM CAN BE ACTIVE AT THE SAME TIME.

Last, you can view reserve items that you own but which are not part of your current roster. This is a great place to store lower-rated items until you need them. Some players like to keep their reserve pool small and trade or auction off their old items. This is up to you, but it's a good idea to keep a few items for backup.

YOU NEVER KNOW WHEN A NEW COLLECTION WILL BE ADDED, SO THINK TWICE BEFORE GETTING RID OF ITEMS!

COLLECTIONS

Make the most of your items by using them to complete "collections" to earn coins and exclusive item rewards. Each collection shows what to look for and tracks your progress. Be sure to scroll through all the available collections and check the hub often to see when new ones become available. Complete a collection to receive its reward.

When you're in Collections, view your Pending Collections to see what items you have ready to use. As you inspect the items required for a collection, the ones you can use will be highlighted. Fill in all the blanks to complete the collection and claim your reward.

> **MOVE ITEMS YOU WANT TO ADD TO COLLECTIONS TO YOUR CURRENT ROSTER. THEY HAVE TO COME FROM THERE TO BE PUT IN YOUR PENDING COLLECTIONS BIN.**

On the Collections panel, you'll see a notification of how many unopened packs you have. Select a pack to open it, and you'll see a panel of the items in that pack. Select one to view its possible actions, including Send to Current Roster, Send to Reserves, or Quick Sell/Discard for coins.

> **WHILE QUICK-SELLING YOUR ITEMS IS EASY, YOU CAN USUALLY GET MORE MONEY ON THE AUCTION BLOCK IF YOU SPEND THE EXTRA EFFORT.**

STORE

If you are looking to pick up packs without spending in-game coins, you can select the Store and buy items or packs. Opening new packs is a fun way to go hunting for new items that have been eluding you due to a lack of coins. You might even find a rare player that you don't need and put him up on the auction block.

> **ALWAYS STUDY THE MARKET BEFORE PUTTING AN ITEM UP FOR SALE, AS THE MARKET PRICES USUALLY CHANGE DAILY.**

TRADE BLOCK

In Madden Ultimate Team another great way to find items is to trade for them. This will allow you to swap an item from your collection with another player. Use the menu to locate the item you want to propose a trade for and then add the items you want to offer. The trade proposal will be sent and you will be notified of any activity. This is a great way to get new items without having to spend your hard-earned coins via the auction block.

AUCTIONS

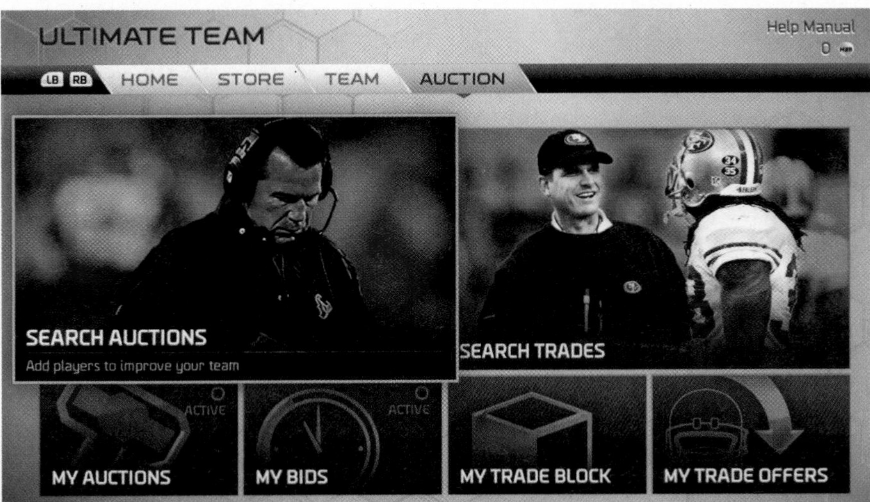

The Auctions screen allows players to search active auctions to find items to bid on or buy. You can also check your Current Bids and Posted Auctions. You set the price for an auction when you send an item from your Current Roster to the auction block. Auctions are a great way to earn extra coins or get new items to build your team. Be sure to check the current prices on the auction block so that you don't sell too cheaply!

> **IF YOU HAVE A GOOD ITEM THAT CAN'T CRACK YOUR CURRENT LINEUP, WHY NOT SELL IT TO PICK UP SOME COINS?**

CHEMISTRY

MAKE SURE TO CONSIDER CHEMISTRY WHEN BUILDING YOUR ULTIMATE TEAM TO MAXIMIZE YOUR RATINGS.

This season, chemistry is back in Madden Ultimate Team and a huge factor in the success and style of your team. There are four types of chemistry on offense and defense, and each of them will give your team a unique feel. The more chemistry you earn the more your team can unlock boosts. For example, a team that chooses "speed run" will receive boosts to elusiveness and run blocking.

HERE'S A DETAILED DESCRIPTION OF CHEMISTRY BENEFITS BROUGHT TO YOU BY EA SPORTS TIBURON GAME DESIGNER CHUCK KALLENBACH...

If you really want your Ultimate Team in Madden NFL 25 to be, well, Ultimate, you have to manage team chemistry. Chemistry is a system of boosts that offer certain attributes for all players on your team.

Players that provide chemistry have a special hex icon on the front of their player items to see how much of a boost your player provides. Team chemistry ranges from 0-99, and as you add more and more to your team, the attribute boosts get bigger and bigger. Tiers, position, and chemistry types determine how much chemistry a player provides. For example, every gold tier left end player with Pass Rush provides the same chemistry boost.

Only starters and players in their proper positions will give you a chemistry boost. If a Ground and Pound left tackle is playing out of position at right tackle, you won't receive anything from his chemistry. The chemistry icons of substitute players are highlighted when they match your team chemistry.

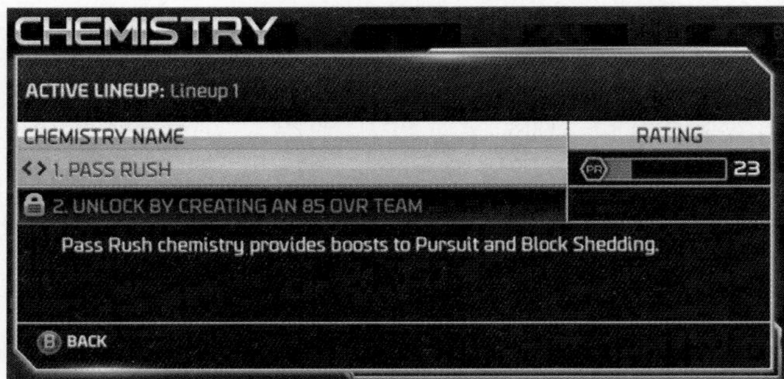

Upon unlocking your starter team, your captain provides some starting chemistry, which can be selected in the starting lineup. You can review your rating in team chemistry by selecting that tile on the lineup panel. Scroll left and right to see your totals in all the different chemistries.

JUST THE FACTS

There are four kinds of team chemistry for both offense and defense: Here's a list of the team chemistry choices, along with the attributes they boost.

OFFENSE

- Short Pass – PBLK Pass Blocking and CINT Catch in Traffic
- Long Pass – PBLK Pass Blocking and RRUN Route Running
- Ground and Pound – RBLK Run Blocking and TRCK Trucking
- Speed Run – RBLK Run Blocking and ELUS Elusiveness

DEFENSE

- Zone Defense – PREC Play Recognition and ZCOV Zone Coverage
- Man Defense – PREC Play Recognition and MCOV Man Coverage
- Pass Rush – BSHD Block Shedding and PUR Pursuit
- Run Stuff – BSHD Block Shedding and TCKL Tackling

DOUBLE YOUR FUN

Your team begins with one available chemistry slot, and you can choose any of the eight available types. When your OVR gets to 85, you'll receive a second slot, allowing you to experiment with different combinations of chemistry. You'll want to maximize the chemistries that complement your play style.

Looking to get a leg up on chemistry? Be sure to utilize the chemistry combinations like Long Pass and Short Pass, which result in a double boost to your pass blocking. Your three choices for chemistry combinations are as follows:

- Two offense or two defense that share an attribute, such as Pass Rush and Run Stuff
- Two offense or two defense that don't share an attribute, such as Long Pass and Speed Run
- One offense and one defense, such as Ground and Pound and Zone Defense

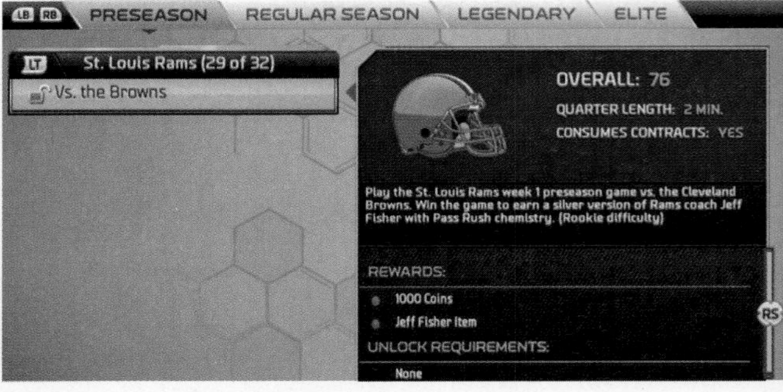

FIND A COACH WITH CHEMISTRY

The Preseason solo challenges are easier matchups that provide a coach item that has additional chemistry. Search through the list of games to find the chemistry you're looking for. For example, if you want Pass Rush chemistry, check out the St. Louis Rams' game against the Browns.

GET SOME LEGENDARY CHEMISTRY

The legendary solo challenges and collections provide a path to an elite player item that has chemistry. Win one of the legendary solo challenges to earn a collectible. Find the legendary player that matches that collectible in packs, and then proceed to the legendary collection to upgrade your player to a version with chemistry. The collection description tells you what kind of chemistry your elite legendary player will have.

EIGHT KINDS OF ELITE CHEMISTRY

In addition to providing important boosts for your players, chemistry is a requirement for the Elite series of solo challenges. For example, the first challenge in the sequence requires Run Stuff chemistry.

ONE TIP: MAKE SEVERAL LINEUPS TO HELP FULFILL THE VARIOUS CHEMISTRY REQUIREMENTS OF THESE CHALLENGES. THE REWARDS ARE WELL WORTH YOUR TROUBLE, AND YOU'LL LEARN A LOT ABOUT HOW TO MAXIMIZE YOUR TEAM CHEMISTRY.

TOP 5 BEST OVERALL PLAYERS

5 AARON RODGERS (QB), OVR 93
4 TOM BRADY (QB), OVR 93
3 CALVIN JOHNSON JR. (WR), OVR 94
2 J.J. WATT (LE), OVR 96
1 ADRIAN PETERSON (HB), OVR 98

When building your ultimate team, you want to work towards earning players with high ratings. This list features the best standard players in the game and items that will give your team an identity. Keep an eye out for these players, whether pulling packs or checking out the auction block. All of these players are currently NFL stars, and we know they will be stars for your team.

5 AARON RODGERS (QB), OVR 93

Aaron Rodgers is a great QB due to his blend of speed, accuracy, and throw power. Rodgers is an excellent talent who will give your team a reliable player under center with every snap. Rodgers has solid speed that can be used to move the chains on third down, too.

> IF YOU STALL ON THE GOAL LINE, MAKE SURE TO USE RODGERS'S SPEED TO GET YOU IN THE END ZONE!

4 TOM BRADY (QB), OVR 93

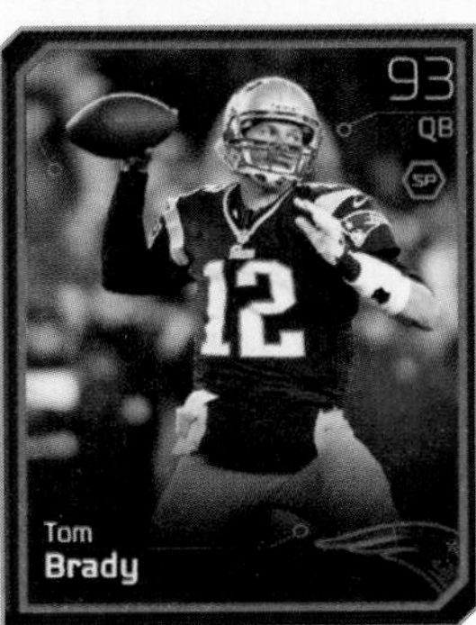

Tom Brady is the top QB in Madden Ultimate Team because of his ability to throw to every spot on the field. Brady has solid deep accuracy and can really use his accuracy to stress defenses in the seams. If you secure this item, you can start to build a passing offense that won't need the best WRs in the game to be effective.

> TOM BRADY IS A GREAT POCKET QB TO UTILIZE IF YOUR TEAM IS SERIOUS ABOUT THROWING THE BALL ON ALMOST EVERY DOWN.

3 CALVIN JOHNSON JR. (WR), OVR 94

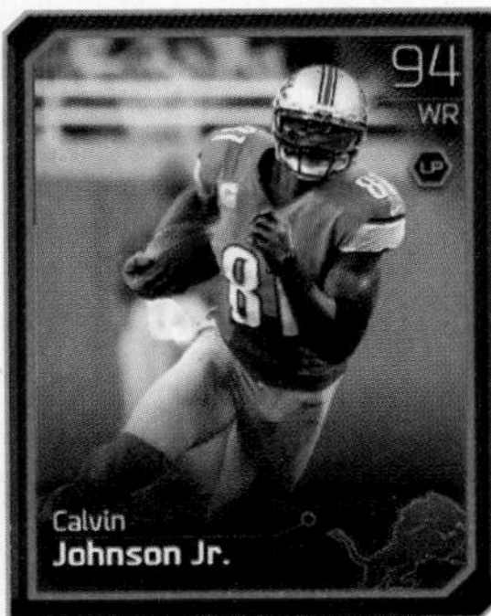

Calvin Johnson Jr. was on the cover of *Madden NFL 13* last season and was so talented that he didn't fall victim to the "Madden curse." Johnson set the single-season record for receiving yards, and now this item and your team will reap the rewards! Johnson has tremendous size and speed, which is a very rare combo, even in the NFL!

> CALVIN JOHNSON JR. CAN SUPPORT AN ENTIRE PASSING OFFENSE WITHOUT NEEDING MUCH HELP FROM ANOTHER RECEIVER OPPOSITE HIM!

2 J.J. WATT (LE), OVR 96

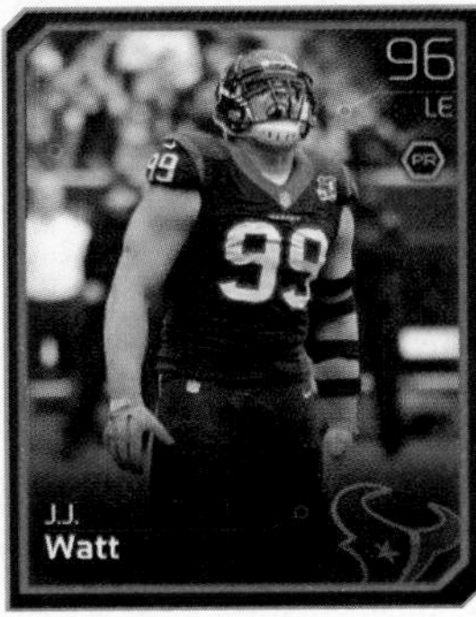

Watt is the perfect player for a defense that wants to stop the run consistently. Watt is a very strong player who can play at the defensive end position and will do a great job containing the edge. Watt also can get after the passer in rushing situations, showing why he is one of the best items in the game!

> WATT IS AN EVERY-DOWN TALENT WHO CAN STAY ON THE FIELD FOR PASSING DOWNS.

1 ADRIAN PETERSON (HB), OVR 98

Adrian Peterson was the MVP of the NFL last season and will be a great item in MUT this year. Peterson is the perfect type of back to build around because he is very well rounded. If you are the type of player who likes to run the ball and wants to try out the new Run Free moves, make sure to go for this item!

> WORK SCREEN PASSES INTO YOUR GAME PLAN WITH PETERSON, TOO; HE IS AN ALL-AROUND BACK!

TOP 5 OFFENSIVE STARTER CAPTAINS

When starting your ultimate team, you will be asked to choose from a list of current NFL stars. This can be a tough choice, as there are many ways to go about building the ultimate team. Here are some of the best options on the offensive side of the ball. Consider what type of team you want to become and what players or items you may already have for your team!

5 CALVIN JOHNSON JR. (WR), OVR 80
4 ROBERT GRIFFIN III (QB), OVR 80
3 TOM BRADY (QB), OVR 80
2 MARSHAWN LYNCH (HB), OVR 80
1 C.J. SPILLER (HB), OVR 80

5 CALVIN JOHNSON JR. (WR), OVR 80

Johnson will really help out your ultimate team if you are looking to pass the ball downfield! Your team will benefit from a +8 boost to Long Pass chemistry. Johnson has solid route running and can use his size to outwork defenders for the ball.

> JOHNSON IS ONE OF THE BEST PLAYERS IN THE RED ZONE, SO TARGET HIM ON FADE ROUTES DOWN THERE.

4 ROBERT GRIFFIN III (QB), OVR 80

RGIII burst onto the scene last year and forced defenses to worry about his legs! Once the defense over-committed to the run game, RGIII made them pay by going downfield. Your team will have a +10 boost to Long Pass chemistry if you choose him as your captain, and with his 86 Throw Power rating, it is a wise decision.

> GRIFFIN IS A SOLID CHOICE FOR GAMERS LOOKING TO RUN THE READ OPTION.

3 TOM BRADY (QB), OVR 80

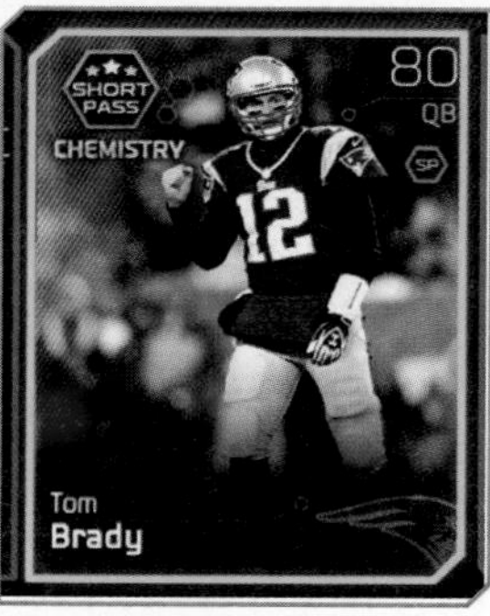

Tom Brady is a master of placing the ball where his receivers can catch it and pick up more yards. Some of his throws don't go much past the line of scrimmage, but they allow his teammates to make huge plays. Brady is the perfect QB for a short-pass offense, and your team will get a +10 boost to Short Pass chemistry.

> BRADY IS ONE OF THE MOST ACCURATE QBS THAT YOU CAN CHOOSE TO CAPTAIN YOUR TEAM.

2 MARSHAWN LYNCH (HB), OVR 80

Marshawn Lynch is known to be one of the toughest runners in the entire NFL. With an 88 Truck rating, he will also be one of the toughest starting backs in Madden Ultimate Team this season. If you want to ground and pound the ball, choose Lynch, as you will earn a +10 boost to your chemistry in that category. Lynch is perfect for the new Infinity Engine 2!

> LYNCH IS A GREAT ASSET TO HAVE IN SHORT-YARDAGE SITUATIONS, TOO.

1 C.J. SPILLER (HB), OVR 80

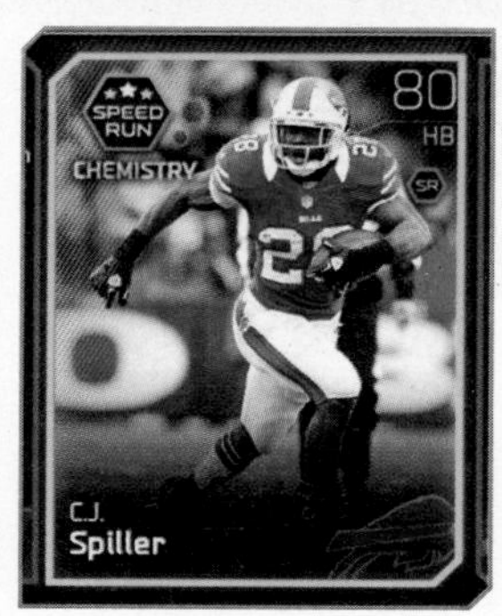

Spiller made huge plays last season nearly any time he got his hands on the ball. He was extremely elusive, which is reflected with his 92 rating! With the new Run Free system, going with a halfback may be a smart move. Your team will earn a +10 Speed Run boost.

> SPILLER ALSO HAS A SOLID CATCH RATING AND CAN BE UTILIZED ON SCREEN PASSES.

TOP 5 DEFENSIVE STARTER PLAYERS

5 ERIC WEDDLE (FS), OVR 80
4 LANCE BRIGGS (LOLB), OVR 80
3 ANTONIO CROMARTIE (CB), OVR 80
2 CLAY MATTHEWS (ROLB), OVR 80
1 LUKE KUECHLY (ROLB), OVR 80

Defense wins championships, and with the new head-to-head seasons in MUT, you can actually win one this season, so why not start with defense! When choosing your captain, consider what type of team you want to build and what style of defense you want to play. If you want to play heavy man-to-man defense, that requires different players than playing zone. No matter what team style you go after, there are plenty of great players to start out with; here are the five best!

5 ERIC WEDDLE (FS), OVR 80

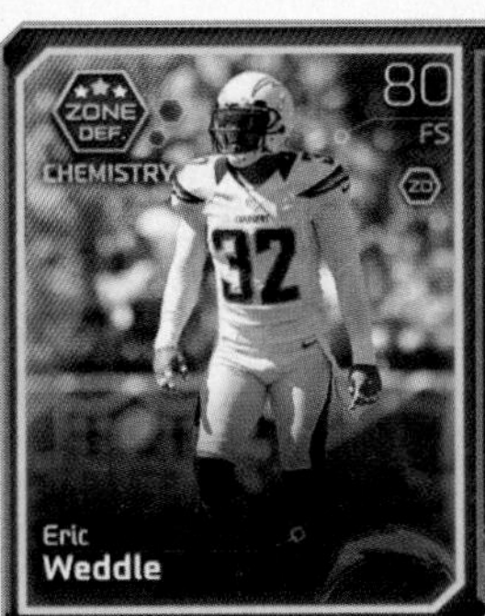

Eric Weddle has quickly become one of the top safeties in the NFL and now in Madden Ultimate Team. Gamers who want to utilize a zone coverage defense will earn a +6 boost in that chemistry category. Weddle won't excel in any specific category, but he brings a wide range of skills that can help slow down the opponent's passing game.

> WEDDLE IS A VERY SOLID ALL-AROUND PLAYER WHO IS PERFECT FOR A ZONE COVERAGE SCHEME

4 LANCE BRIGGS (LOLB), OVR 80

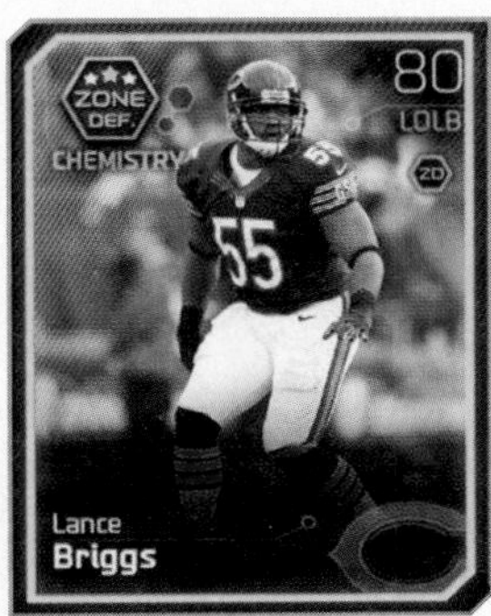

Lance Briggs has been an extremely solid player for many seasons and would be a great choice for your team. Starting with him gives your team a +7 boost to Zone Defense chemistry and a player to roam the middle of the field with. Briggs will be perfect for shutting down those pesky tight ends over the middle.

> LANCE BRIGGS CAN LAY SOME HIT STICKS THAT MIGHT JUST KNOCK THE BALL LOOSE.

3 ANTONIO CROMARTIE (CB), OVR 80

Cromartie has been one of our favorite defenders in *Madden NFL* for many years. He has always had great man coverage skills, and now your team will benefit with a +7 boost to Man Defense chemistry. Having a guy like him on your defense allows you to put him on the other team's best threat and hopefully forget about it!

> YOU CAN SHADE YOUR COVERAGE BEFORE THE SNAP IF YOU SENSE WHAT TYPE OF ROUTE YOUR OPPONENT IS RUNNING!

2 CLAY MATTHEWS (ROLB), OVR 80

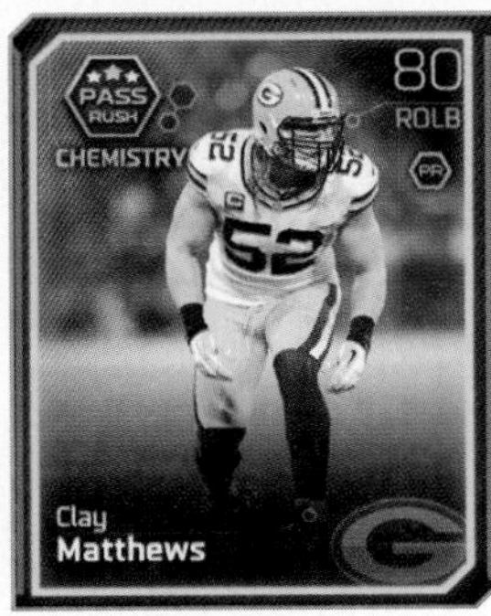

For teams that want to stop the passing game, rushing the passer is very important. Clay Matthews will give you a +7 boost to Pass Rush chemistry and allow your defense to get off the field on third downs with QB sacks. Matthews is an every down player and a great choice at LB.

> CLAY MATTHEWS IS VERSATILE AND CAN DROP BACK INTO ZONES ON PASSING DOWNS.

1 LUKE KUECHLY (ROLB), OVR 80

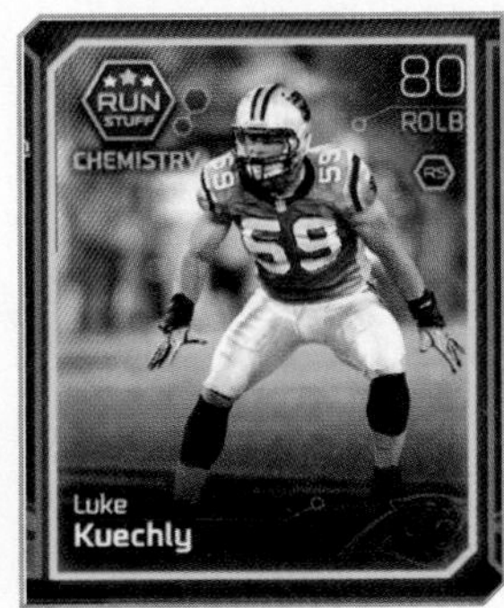

Stopping the run in *Madden NFL 25* will be difficult with all the new blocks added to the offensive line. For a +7 boost to Run Stuff, try a player like Kuechly and watch your defense improve. Kuechly has one of the highest Tackle ratings in the game, so you can be sure he will bring down the ball carrier very consistently!

> KUECHLY IS AN EVERY-DOWN LB, INCLUDING IN PASSING SITUATIONS WHERE YOU MIGHT SWITCH TO A DIME FORMATION.

TOP 5 COLLECTION TYPES

For many gamers, Ultimate Team is all about collecting! There are five different types of collections, but some are easier to complete than others. Here is everything you will see, from easiest to most difficult to collect. Remember—the bigger and tougher the collection, the better the rewards!

5 PROMO COLLECTIONS
4 LEGENDARY COLLECTIONS
3 PREMIUM COLLECTIONS
2 COACHES COLLECTIONS
1 TEAMS COLLECTIONS

5 PROMO COLLECTIONS

Promo collections require gamers to collect player items that include gold and elite items. These are some of the toughest challenges to complete, but the rewards can really improve your team. The gold and elite items are often some of the best at their position!

> CHECK THE COLLECTIONS PAGE AT LEAST ONCE EVERY WEEK TO SEE WHAT COLLECTIONS WERE ADDED.

4 LEGENDARY COLLECTIONS

To complete a legendary collection, gamers must locate legendary players from packs to earn a reward. This is another challenging collection category, but completing one will really give your team a unique player to use in Ultimate Team!

> DON'T ASSUME EVERY COLLECTION THAT HAS A SMALL NUMBER OF ITEMS IS EASY. THE ITEMS COULD BE VERY RARE.

3 PREMIUM COLLECTIONS

Premium collections are great because they allow you to choose your reward. This gives you more flexibility and allows you to choose whatever will help your team out. A premium collection requires a set of 10 collectibles from packs.

> SOME COLLECTIONS WILL CONSUME YOUR ITEMS, WHILE OTHERS WILL RETURN THEM TO YOU. MAKE SURE TO READ THE INFORMATION!

2 COACH COLLECTIONS

This is one of the easier collection types in the game, although it may take a while to earn all 32 of them. These require one gold coach from packs and a solo challenge reward.

> YOU CAN ADD ITEMS TO YOUR COLLECTIONS ONLY FROM YOUR ACTIVE ROSTER, NOT FROM YOUR RESERVES!

1 TEAM COLLECTIONS

This is a great collection to get started on as it is the easiest in the game. Look to see which teams you have a good start on—you must collect 10 bronze player items. There are 32 of these collections, and most of them will happen with the more packs you pull!

> YOU CAN ALWAYS USE THE AUCTION BLOCK IF YOU DON'T GET THE ITEMS YOU NEED FROM PACKS.

TOP 5 COIN-COLLECTING TIPS

5 COMPLETE COLLECTIONS
4 PLAY SOLO CHALLENGES
3 PLAY HEAD-TO-HEAD SEASONS
2 VISIT THE AUCTION BLOCK
1 QUICK-SELL

To buy items and improve your ultimate team you will need to open new packs or hit the auction block. This is where having coins will come in handy, as they are the in-game currency needed to make these buys. While there is no way to buy coins directly in Madden Ultimate Team, with these tips you can start building your fortune.

5 COMPLETE COLLECTIONS

One of the best things about collections is the reward that you receive after completing one! Depending on the size and difficulty of the collection, you can see some big coin rewards. Some collections also come with items that you can post to the auction block for extra coins.

> IF YOUR REWARD ITEM IS SELLING LOWER THAN EXPECTED, USE IT IN YOUR LINEUP AND SELL THE PLAYER IT MAKES EXPENDABLE.

4 PLAY SOLO CHALLENGES

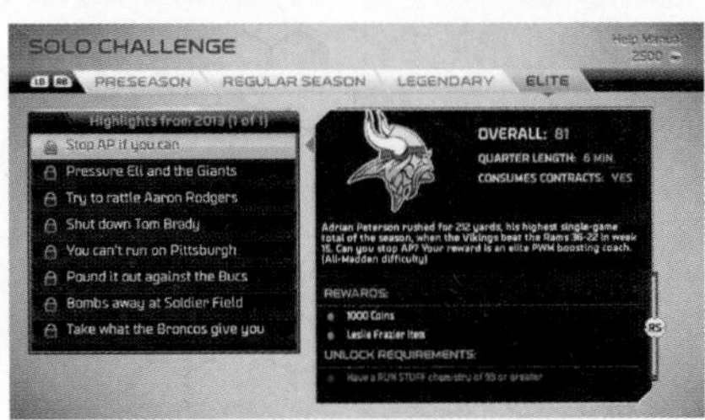

You earn coins as rewards for playing solo challenges. One of the first challenges is to get started playing your team's preseason schedule. These games will be on an easier difficulty and should allow you to get some easier wins even if your team isn't stacked yet!

> YOUR TEAM RATING WILL TAKE TIME TO BUILD, SO BE CAREFUL ABOUT PLAYING ON ALL-MADDEN DIFFICULTY TOO EARLY!

3 PLAY HEAD-TO-HEAD SEASONS

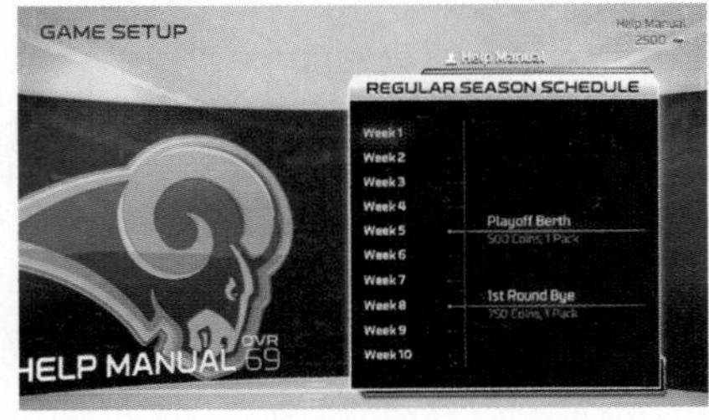

Playing online in head-to-head seasons is a great way to test your skill level as well as earn coins. The more games you play and win, the higher your rewards will be. The competition will get tougher, but you will start to see big rewards that will allow you to upgrade your team. The games are shorter than regular online ranked games and will keep track of all your statistics!

> ALWAYS KICK OFF THE BALL TO START A GAME ONLINE, ESPECIALLY WITH THE SHORTENED GAME TIME.

2 VISIT THE AUCTION BLOCK

The auction block is a live market that fluctuates constantly. Check similar items on the auction block before you price your item. Make sure you're not selling something hot for a base price. By making note of hot items and current prices, you can try to speculate on trends to be sure you are buying and selling at the right time! If you are a little light on coins, try the trade block instead, which allows you to trade your items!

If you see an item you need right away on the auction block, you can buy it immediately for a specific price rather than bid and wait.

1 QUICK-SELL

You can quick-sell most items for coins directly from New Items, Current Roster, or Reserves. This allows you to quickly make some coins any time you see a player or item that you don't have a need for at the moment. A set price is shown on the back of the item. Quick-selling can sometimes give you the coin boost you need to grab a new item!

The more coins you have on hand, the more flexibility you have when completing collections.

Top 5 Lists

CONTENTS

THE TOP 25 PLAYS IN *MADDEN NFL 25*! 48

TOP 5 NEW GAMEPLAY TIPS 50

NEW GAMEPLAY MECHANICS 50
NEW RUN GAME TIPS 51
NEW GAMEPLAY CONTROLS 52
NEW HOT ROUTES 53
PRECISION MODIFIER MOVES 54
TOP 5 MADDEN SHARE TIPS 55

TOP 5 BEGINNER TIPS 56

HOW TO PLAY OFFENSE 56
HOW TO PLAY DEFENSE 58
HOW TO PLAY SPECIAL TEAMS 60
CHOOSING A PLAYBOOK 62
SETTING YOUR LINEUP 63
HOW TO SET YOUR OFFENSIVE AUDIBLES 64
HOW TO SET YOUR DEFENSIVE AUDIBLES 65
HOW TO STOP THE RUN 66
TOP 5 GAME PLAN TIPS 67

TOP 5 EXPERT TIPS 68

COMMONLY ASKED QUESTIONS 68
TOP 5 OFFENSIVE FORMATIONS 70
DEFENSIVE FORMATIONS 71
OPTION REQUIREMENTS 72
WAYS TO DEFEND THE OPTION 73
WAYS TO USE PRACTICE MODE 74
WAYS TO READ DEFENSIVE COVERAGES 75
WAYS TO STOP SCRAMBLING QBS 76
WAYS TO DEFEND TIGHT ENDS 77
WAYS TO DEFEND SCREEN PASSES 78
WAYS TO STOP SLOT WRS 79
WAYS TO DEFEND THE RED ZONE 80
WAYS TO DEFEND A NO-HUDDLE ATTACK 81
WAYS TO SET UP BLITZES 82

TOP 5 DEVELOPER TIPS 83

NEW THINGS TO LOOK OUT FOR WITH REX DICKSON 83
NEW PLAYBOOKS WITH ANTHONY WHITE 84
BLOCKING TIPS WITH CLINT OLDENBURG 85
OFFENSIVE RATINGS WITH DONNY MOORE 86
DEFENSIVE RATINGS WITH DONNY MOORE 87
TOP 5 PLAYERS 88
QUARTERBACKS 89
HALFBACKS 90
WIDE RECEIVERS 91
TIGHT ENDS 92
DEFENSIVE ENDS 93
DEFENSIVE TACKLES 94
LINEBACKERS 95
CORNERBACKS 96
SAFETIES 97

TOP 5 TEAMS 98

ONLINE RANKED GAME TEAMS 98
RUSHING TEAMS 99
PASSING TEAMS 100
DEFENSIVE TEAMS 101
SLEEPER TEAMS 102

THE TOP 25 PLAYS IN *MADDEN NFL 25*!

Knowing where to find some of the best plays in *Madden NFL 25* can be an instant boost to your game. Here we share our Top 25 plays in the game this season and let you know what makes them great. We call out plays for both sides of the ball and many different situations, including both running and passing on offense. Once you test these plays out and pick your own favorites, consider making a custom playbook to pack them all into one book!

25 GUN FLIP TRIPS—HB WHEEL

Team Playbook: Cardinals

What Makes It Great: The HB is set out to the right of the formation, which makes it very tough for the defense to balance against.

How to Run It: Look quickly to the flat for the HB, or wait until he hits the sideline and test the defender's speed deep!

24 GUN BUNCH WK—VERTICALS

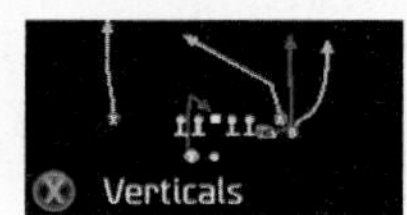

Team Playbook: Falcons

What Makes It Great: This play is great for beating Cover 2 and Cover 3 zone because of the tender areas of the field the WR routes reach.

How to Run It: Block the HB to give yourself time to look downfield, work the right side of the field first, and then scan back left.

23 SHOTGUN SPLIT PANTHER—689 HOOK

Team Playbook: Panthers

What Makes It Great: With two players in the backfield, gamers can feel confident they can pick up any blitz their opponent sends!

How to Run It: Look to use the backfield routes on short-yardage downs, or block them and look downfield on third and long.

22 5-2 NORMAL—FIRE ZONE 2

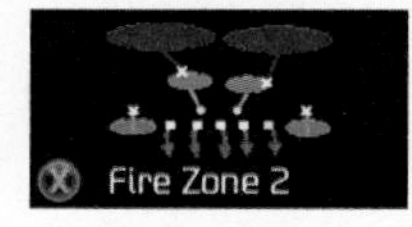

Team Playbook: Lions

What Makes It Great: For teams with great defensive linemen, the 5-2 gets them all on the field to really threaten offensive lines.

How to Run It: This play will work best near the goal line or against runs to the outside. Crash your linemen out to protect the edge.

21 GUN TIGHT DOUBLES ON—BROWNS CROSS

Team Playbook: Browns

What Makes It Great: This play has a TE on the line of scrimmage who can be used as an outlet or blocked for added protection.

How to Run It: Slant both inside receivers and streak the outside right WR. Your WR on the wheel should beat man coverage to the inside.

20 GUN DOUBLES FLEX WING—HB DIVE

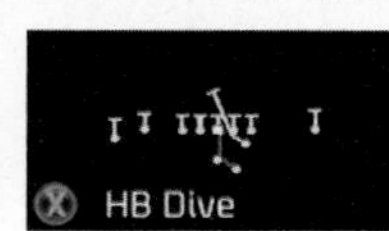

Team Playbook: Packers

What Makes It Great: The position of the TE gives this play a consistent lead blocker for the HB to get behind.

How to Run It: If your opponent is really packing the box, motion your outside WR over for an extra blocker. Keep it inside!

19 STRONG PRO—FB DIVE

Team Playbook: Jaguars

What Makes It Great: The quick handoff to the FB is a consistent way to pick up short yardage that moves the chains.

How to Run It: Make sure to sub a player with a good Truck rating into the game. Hand off the ball and look get behind your blockers.

18 GUN BUNCH QUADS—BUNCH TRAIL

Team Playbook: Chiefs

What Makes It Great: This play will easily defeat man-to-man coverage and will give your QB a safe, easy throw over the middle.

How to Run It: At the snap, look for the first receiver to clear out the middle and wait for the trail receiver to run through wide open!

17 SUB 4-1-6—SUGAR COVER 3 BLUFF

Team Playbook: Bears

What Makes It Great: The LBs will approach the line before the snap but drop back after and really confuse your opponent.

How to Run It: Call this when your opponent expects pressure; your defenders should drop right into the throwing lanes.

16 SINGLEBACK NORMAL PATRIOTS—PATS SLANTS

Team Playbook: Patriots

What Makes It Great: Quick passes from under center can be very tough for a defense to stop!

How to Run It: At the snap, look for any player who gets inside his defender. Against zone, wait for your target to clear his defender's zone.

15 GUN DOUBLESWK—HB SLIP SCREEN

Team Playbook: Saints

What Makes It Great: The screen pass is a great way to beat the blitz and can really gash your opponent for big yards.

How to Run It: Roll with the QB away from the screen and, at the last second, look to pop the ball over the defender for a big gain.

14 STRONG CLOSE—QUICK TOSS

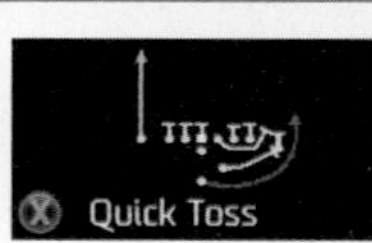

Team Playbook: Rams

What Makes It Great: Defenses that over-commit to the middle on short yardage can easily be burned by this play call.

How to Run It: Once your back gets the toss, let your blockers get set up before accelerating towards the edge!

13 I-FORM TIGHT PAIR—PA SPOT

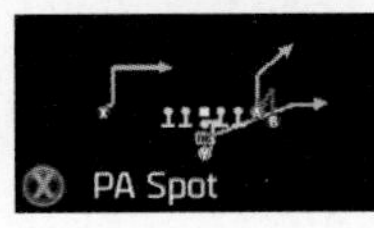

Team Playbook: Bills

What Makes It Great: Setting up your opponent with run plays leaves them vulnerable to play action, especially in the red zone.

How to Run It: Once you complete the handoff fake, look to the corner route or hit your safety valve on the hitch route underneath.

12 NICKEL 2-4-5 DT—OVER STORM BRAVE

Team Playbook: Packers

What Makes It Great: For teams with solid LBs, this blitz will unleash them towards the QB without any additional setup.

How to Run It: Wait until your opponent is in third and long, which will force them to get the ball out quickly but not far enough to move the chains.

11 PISTOL FULL PANTHER—TRIPLE OPTION

Team Playbook: Panthers

What Makes It Great: The Triple Option really forces a defense to be disciplined and doesn't allow them to overplay the edge.

How to Run It: Look to read the defensive end first and determine whether to keep it or hand it off. Next read the pitch man outside!

10 SINGLEBACK Y-TRIPS—WR SCREEN

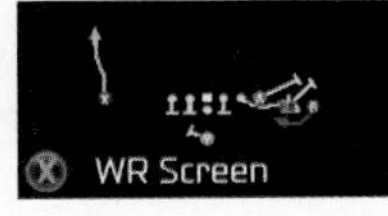

Team Playbook: Giants

What Makes It Great: With the new Run Free controls in Madden NFL 25, getting the ball quickly to your playmakers is a great move.

How to Run It: Any time you catch the opponent playing off coverage, quickly turn and get the ball out to your WR and let him make a play.

9 QUARTER 3 DEEP—MAN UP 3 DEEP

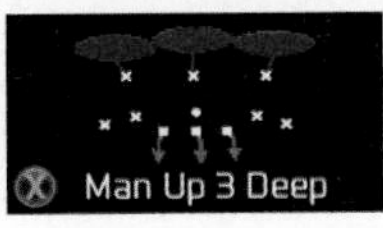

Team Playbook: Ravens

What Makes It Great: This will force your opponent to take all underneath throws due to three deep safeties.

How to Run It: Wait for heavy passing situations and call this coverage. It is one of the best plays because it rarely needs adjustments.

8 PISTOL TRIPS—READ OPTION

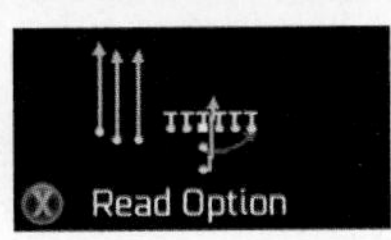

Team Playbook: Seahawks

What Makes It Great: The Read Option is an explosive play that forces the defense to pick their poison, especially against the trips set.

How to Run It: Use the read key to locate the DE: If he stands up, give it to the HB; if he crashes down keep it with the QB!

7 I-FORM TIGHT—POWER O

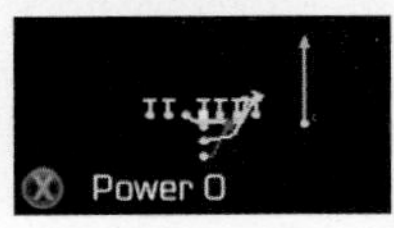

Team Playbook: 49ers

What Makes It Great: Gamers who have a solid power back can patiently wait for the hole to open up and get consistent gains

How to Run It: Start out by holding the precision modifier, and then unleash the acceleration burst once you see the hole.

6 GUN HEAVY—Z STREAK

Team Playbook: Run N Gun

What Makes It Great: The formation is very tight and will force defenses to move inside to defend it.

How to Run It: Block players in the backfield if you sense the blitz, but otherwise look to the TE on the corner route as your main read.

5 GUN NORMAL—SPEED OPTION

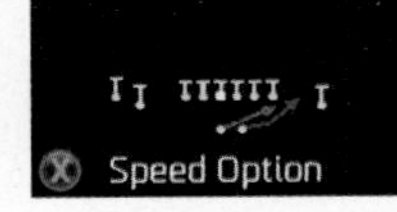

Team Playbook: Eagles

What Makes It Great: A quick QB who can cut the ball upfield really turns this play into a huge threat!

How to Run It: Read the DE, and if he commits to the QB, pitch the ball to the HB for a big gain. Don't force it!

4 NICKEL 3-3-5—2 MAN UNDER

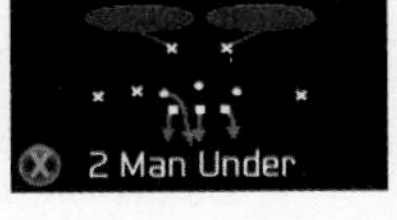

Team Playbook: Buccaneers, Saints, 49ers

What Makes It Great: This is a basic man-to-man coverage that will force your opponents to prove they know how to get players free

How to Run It: Move the blitzing LB out wide to maximize his rush angle, and user-control the LB guarding the HB.

3 PISTOL WEAK TWINS FLEX—SMASH Y-CORNER

Team Playbook: Redskins

What Makes It Great: Creating a full pistol scheme is finally possible in *Madden NFL 25*, and this formation is one of the best.

How to Run It: Look to hit the FB out of the backfield for a quick gain, or hold the ball and throw to either corner route as they break.

2 4-4 SPLIT—MONSTER GREEN

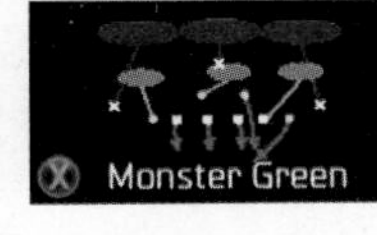

Team Playbook: 4-3 Defense

What Makes It Great: With the Read Option being a popular play, gamers will need a solid way to send defenders off the edge.

How to Run It: Flip this play depending on the formation and where you expect the run—the blitzing defenders will do the rest.

1 GUN TIGHT FLEX—WR CROSS

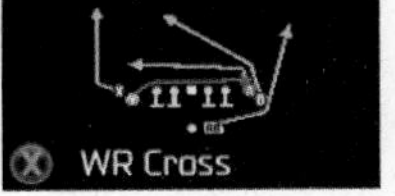

Team Playbook: Run N Gun

What Makes It Great: The wheel route by the HB is extremely tough to defend, and the crossing routes will beat man-to-man.

How to Run It: Streak both inside receivers if you sense zone coverage. Look to the WR on the left first, or air it out deep right if you get time.

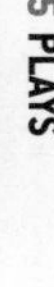

TOP 5 NEW GAMEPLAY TIPS

NEW GAMEPLAY MECHANICS

Every season, the team at EA SPORTS adds new features to *Madden NFL* to make the gameplay more authentic. Gamers who can quickly grasp the new gameplay mechanics will always have a competitive advantage. Here are the biggest additions to *Madden NFL 25* and tips on how you can master them.

- 5 READ AND PITCH KEYS
- 4 AUDIBLES BY PERSONNEL
- 3 SKILLS TRAINER
- 2 PRECISION MOVES
- 1 INFINITY ENGINE 2

5 READ AND PITCH KEYS

LEARNING HOW TO READ THE DEFENSIVE END WHILE RUNNING THE OPTION IS THE MOST IMPORTANT THING YOU CAN DO ON LAUNCH DAY.

When calling an option run, you will now see an "R" over the player you should key in on when determining whether to make the handoff or keep the ball for yourself. If you're running a play like the Triple Option, with an option to pitch the ball, you will also see a "P" to let you know this is the defender you need to pay attention to if you're going to pitch the ball. There is plenty more advice on playing a successful option game in this guide, but knowing that the "R" is for read and "P" is for pitch will make knowing where to look much easier in *Madden NFL 25*!

4 AUDIBLES BY PERSONNEL

THIS SEASON YOU CAN SET ALL YOUR QUICK AUDIBLES FOR EVERY FORMATION!

The new audible system in *Madden NFL 25* removes the old five formation audibles you could set and replaces it with a deeper, more authentic system. Now, gamers can set their four "quick audibles" for every formation in their playbook. When you come out in a personnel package like "21," which is two HBs and one TE, you can audible to any formation that matches! So, no longer can players come out in a formation with five WRs and audible down to a formation like Goal Line to get players to line up out of position. Since you can set and audible to any play with matching personnel, you now have more options at the line of scrimmage!

3 SKILLS TRAINER

TRAINING ON OFFENSE IS FUN, BUT THE TRAINER IS GREAT FOR LEARNING DEFENSE, TOO!

The Skills Trainer in *Madden NFL 25* is valuable for multiple reasons. First, it doesn't require you to have deep experience with the series, as it walks you through all the needed controls. Second, it allows you to practice the concepts you've just learned. This is an amazing way to get better quickly. How many times have you been told to try something but not understood it until you actually did it for yourself? The Skills Trainer will set you up with all the skills you need in the game and then allow you to test them out in real scenarios. The only difference between the trainer and a game is that you don't have to fear giving up points, so you can really have no fear in trying everything out!

2 PRECISION MOVES

WHILE HALFBACKS WITH GREAT AGILITY CAN CUT QUICKLY, HBS WITH GREAT ACCELERATION GET UP TO FULL SPEED FASTER AND LEAVE DEFENDERS IN THE DUST.

One of the most visible improvements in *Madden NFL 25* is the brand-new running style that really has players planting their feet into the ground and driving to make cuts. These cuts give gamers great control to fake out defenders and often don't require the use of a move. This is all part of the new Run Free system, and an exciting facet of the system is precision moves! Elite players with a 90-plus rating in a specific category can pull off signature, or precision, moves. These moves not only look great, they provide an improved fake-out chance against the defender. Try these out in the Skills Trainer to learn their power!

1 INFINITY ENGINE 2

LOOK FOR PLAYERS IN YOUR LINEUP WITH 90-PLUS HIT POWER TO REALLY MAXIMIZE THE TACKLE.

The Infinity Engine 2 has reinvented the way you play *Madden NFL 25*. Aside from just the visual upgrades, the brand-new Force Impact system will bring more power to the gridiron on tackles and runner moves. Stiff arms are now capable of packing a real punch to a defender, depending on the timing of the blow. Since everybody on the field has physics, you can no longer run into your lineman and expect success. Now, your runner will place his arm out and feel for bodies when he senses trouble near the hole. Learning the feel of the improved Infinity Engine 2 will take some time, but it is just one more thing to make *Madden NFL 25* feel more like football on Sunday.

5 DON'T FORCE IT OUTSIDE
4 USE YOUR MOVES
3 READ YOUR BLOCKERS
2 CUT BACK
1 FOLLOW YOUR BLOCKERS AND RUN PATH

NEW GAMEPLAY TIPS TOP 5

NEW RUN GAME TIPS

Let's go over some tips to help you be more successful in the run game. With so much focus going into the brand-new Run Free system and improvements in blocking, there are plenty of chances to win with a ground-and-pound style this season. Here are the most noticeable areas of improvement and tips for how you can quickly relearn how to pound the ball this season.

5 DON'T FORCE IT OUTSIDE

> TOO MANY GAMERS FORCE RUNS LIKE THE POWER O OUTSIDE—TRUST YOUR BLOCKERS TO OPEN HOLES!

Last season, gamers learned you can't just lazily run up the back of your lineman and expect success, so many gamers wanted to bounce the runs outside. In *Madden NFL 25,* if you're running a play that is designed between the tackles, do your best to keep it inside. There will be a hole that you can wait for and then time a nice acceleration burst right through. The easiest way to be consistent in the run game is to keep the majority of the runs inside, especially with the new contextual awareness, which will have backs more aware of their surroundings. Last season, runs were either huge gains or negative runs, but with this one change, the running game has become a more consistent chain mover!

4 USE YOUR MOVES

> SETTING UP YOUR MOVES CAN PAY OFF LATER IN THE GAME, AS A FEW EARLY JUKES CAN LEAD TO TRUCKS LATER!

Madden NFL 25 is set up to run with any position player who has the ball in his hands, but not every player has a full move arsenal like an HB. You must understand which player you have carrying the ball. You don't want to risk your QB taking a big hit because you decided to spin into traffic when you could have easily slid. If you have a power-style back on third and 1, look to use a truck move. With the combo moves and vast skill sets of all the players, using not just any move but the right move will be crucial this season.

3 READ YOUR BLOCKERS

> THE NUMBER ONE RULE OF THE ZONE RUNNING GAME IS: SLOW TO THE HOLE, FAST THROUGH IT!

Reach blocks are one new type of block in *Madden NFL 25.* These look different from anything you have seen before, and you need to learn how to read them! A reach block is when the offensive line works to steer or turn their defensive linemen one direction or the other. This works to create different openings for the HB to run through. If you are trying to get to the outside on a toss play but your lineman misses his block, you could possibly see an inside lane open up. Yes, the play you wanted to run wasn't a success, but you still may be able to pick up a few yards on the fly. There is also much better downfield blocking this year. If you see a defender slip off a block one way, look to help your lineman out and improvise off of it. Not only does it make the run game more fun, but it will absolutely increase your yards per carry.

2 CUT BACK

> WORK ON RUNNING THE HB STRETCH IN PRACTICE MODE TO LEARN THE TIMING OF DOUBLE-TEAM BLOCKS ON THE EDGE.

With a shifty HB, a well-timed hard cut can really gash the defense. On the HB Stretch run, the TE and tackle double-team the defensive end towards your run path. This should create a great edge seal before the TE slips upfield to pick up the LB. If anybody slips off the edge, be ready to use that left stick to really dig in and cut upfield. Learning the timing of these plays and running towards your strongest lineman is a great way to build around the run game. Read your blocks, make *one* cut, and then *go*!

1 FOLLOW YOUR BLOCKERS AND RUN PATH

> YOUR BLOCKERS WILL HEAD DOWNFIELD TO HELP YOU OUT, BUT THEY USUALLY PLAN FOR WHERE THE RUN IS SUPPOSED TO BE GOING!

With the updates to the run-block targeting system this year, your teammates will often help build you a convoy. They will create holes based on where the run should be headed, so trust them. Last season, the WRs on the edges didn't always hold up in the run game. As a result, many gamers kept their runs too far inside until the last minute, which meant their blockers were too far in front. Now, all the runs are blocked just as they are drawn up on Sunday, and the WRs will get involved. The more you stick to a run game that is authentic and follows the plays, the more success you will have in *Madden NFL 25*!

TOP 5 NEW GAMEPLAY TIPS

NEW GAMEPLAY CONTROLS

5 ACCELERATION BURST
4 STUMBLE RECOVERY
3 HEAT SEEKER
2 BALLHAWK
1 COMBO MOVES

While most of the controls remain the same, EA SPORTS has added some new elements that give you more control of the players on the screen than ever before. By understanding not only which new buttons to press, but when, you will be racking up more wins. There are some new ways not only to gain yardage but to take down the ball carrier.

> FOR A FULL LIST OF CONTROLS, CHECK OUT THE IN-GAME MANUAL.

5 ACCELERATION BURST

PLAYSTATION 3: R2
XBOX 360: RT

> WHEN CHANGING DIRECTION, USE THE ACCELERATION BURST TO QUICKLY GET BACK UP TO SPEED!

Gone are the days of speed burst or turbo! By using the Acceleration Burst button, gamers will simply get their player running to top speed sooner. If you are a running back who is looking to hit the hole, use this button to accelerate to 100 percent of your max speed. This is great for running plays like the toss, where the player needs to wait for his blocks to be set up before going to top gear. Although the game has featured "auto-sprint" the last few seasons, you are now in full control!

4 STUMBLE RECOVERY

Pull up on the right stick when your player is falling down and the icon flashes on his player ring.

> A SUCCESSFUL STUMBLE RECOVERY WILL MAKE THE RING FLASH GREEN; BAD TIMING WILL MAKE IT FLASH RED.

With the new Infinity Engine 2 in *Madden NFL 25*, gamers will experience their players starting to fall after taking a hit. Now that you are no longer stuck in an animation, you will sometimes be able to fight the fall and recover your balance! When this happens, a ring appears underneath your player and you have to react quickly! If you can get the timing down, your runner may recover his balance by placing a hand down on the ground. This is a great way to make highlight reel runs after the defense thinks they have already taken you down. Even if you don't fully recover, you can still stumble forward for extra yards!

3 HEAT SEEKER

PLAYSTATION 3: ■ **while using the left stick to steer**
XBOX 360: Ⓧ **while using the left stick to steer**

> IF YOU'RE ABOUT TO TAKE ON A BLOCKER, TAP THE TACKLE BUTTON TO TRY TO DIVE AROUND HIM AND BLOW UP THE PLAY!

Heat seeker is a great option for players who are looking to make the leap from beginner to average. When you're going for tackles in *Madden NFL 25*, heat seeker allows you to hold down the Tackle button and continue steering the player towards the ball carrier. This is huge for beginner players who used to control defensive linemen but now want to move towards controlling a linebacker. Controlling a linebacker gives the user more control of the defense and allows for big plays all over the field. Much like ballhawk last season, heat seeker makes it easier for players to control defenders and improve their game! It works by holding down the Hit Stick or the Tackle button. Learn which situation is the best time to go for the big hit or to make the safe tackle!

2 PRECISION MOVES

PLAYSTATION 3: L2
XBOX 360: LT

> USING A PRECISION HURDLE IS THE ONLY WAY TO LEAP OVER A TACKLER IN *MADDEN NFL 25*!

For the first time in *Madden NFL 25*, gamers have more than 30 running moves to utilize. By holding down the precision modifier, gamers can unleash special moves that will leave defenders scratching their heads. Research your players' ratings to find out what 90-plus ratings they have for certain moves. Remember that not just RBs can pull off these moves—WRs who make catches in the open field can use these moves to pick up yards after the catch!

1 COMBO MOVES

PLAYSTATION 3: **right stick** XBOX 360: **right stick**

> TRY ROLLING THE STICK IN MULTIPLE DIRECTIONS TO COMBINE MOVES LIKE A TRUCK AND A SPIN!

We talked about the new hard cuts in the run game, but we can't overlook combo moves. The ability to string together moves using the right stick opens up the running game in *Madden NFL 25*. A great combo move to use when a defender is approaching you at an angle is to start with a juke towards the middle and keep rolling the stick forward to lower your head for a truck. There are so many combos you can pull off in the game that it is wise to leave your thumb on the right stick when running free in *Madden NFL 25*! Don't forget to try to turn precision moves into combo moves to really make highlight runs!

5 SMOKE ROUTE
4 HITCH ROUTE
3 COMEBACK ROUTE
2 HB OPTION ROUTE
1 FLAT ROUTE

NEW GAMEPLAY TIPS TOP 5

NEW HOT ROUTES

The ability to make adjustments at the line of scrimmage is a key to becoming a better player. While controlling the offense, gamers can "hot route" and tell their receivers what routes to run on the fly. This is essential for gamers who plan to run a hurry-up offense, because they won't have the benefit of the huddle to give their receivers instructions. This season, the gameplay team has added some new hot routes to the game that are not only more realistic but give the gamer even more control before the snap!

5 SMOKE ROUTE

TARGET YOUR BEST WEAPONS IN SPACE; OFTEN THEY ONLY NEED TO MAKE ONE DEFENDER MISS!

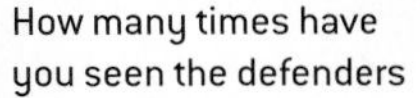

How many times have you seen the defenders backed way off your WR and just wanted to instantly get him the ball? The smoke route will let your WR know to turn and look towards the QB at the snap of the ball. If you have a numbers advantage, like two WRs against one CB, you can hopefully catch a block and bust it open. The smoke route can also be motioned from one side of the field to another to create imbalances against the defense. The smoke route is another great way to get the ball into the hands of your playmakers, especially against a conservative defense.

4 HITCH ROUTE

THIS ROUTE IS ESPECIALLY EFFECTIVE IN THE RED ZONE, SO DON'T FORGET TO SMART ROUTE IT!

One of our favorite ways to move the chains is by looking for safe and reliable targets over the middle. The hitch route can now be hot routed inside and is very effective against zones. If the defender doesn't try to get underneath the route, you should have a great window to throw the ball. Target players with strong Catch in Traffic ratings so they can hang onto the ball if they take a hit. Make sure to look out for defensive linemen who drop back into coverage, because they can often knock the pass down. These quick passes can also be used to set up the deep seam pass if the linebackers get too aggressive!

3 COMEBACK ROUTE

BLOCK AN EXTRA PLAYER, BECAUSE THIS ROUTE TAKES TIME TO DEVELOP.

The comeback route has always been one of our favorites when facing a third and long situation. If you see man coverage, your WR should get a free release at the line of scrimmage and make a sharp cut downfield. As long as no zone defender drops back to sit underneath (look out for buzz zones), you should be able to connect on this route. Time the throw as your WR starts to break out of his cut, rather than waiting on the throw, which can allow the defender to break on the ball. Having this route on the outside as a hot route will really force the defense to think about only playing over the top on long-yardage downs!

2 HB OPTION ROUTE

THIS IS A GREAT ROUTE THAT CAN BAIL OUT A QB WHO MISSES HIS PRIMARY READ.

The HB option is a perfectly named route. The back starts out of the backfield, and if he reads zone, he will turn around and sit underneath it. This is the perfect call in short-yardage situations and can also be used as a safety valve in the middle of the field for QBs who like to roll out. Against man coverage, the HB will cut towards the sideline and try to beat the defender. If you get a mismatch on the LB, you can often burn him for big yardage if you hit the HB in stride. Learn the timing of both routes and which defenses to unleash them against to maximize this great new addition.

1 FLAT ROUTE

IF YOU SENSE A BLITZ, HOT ROUTE THE SLOT WR TO A FLAT ROUTE AND USE HIM AS YOUR HOT READ.

The flat route has always been key to having a great offense in *Madden NFL*. Although it is one of the simplest routes in the game, it has never been available as a hot route. Last season, we were forced to use plays that had the stock route built in, but now you can simply add a flat route to the slot or TE on any given play! This means if you see the slot corner cheating inside, you can quickly throw a pass to the flat to make the defense pay. You can also now create a great passing concept like curl flats if you see Cover 3 zone from the defense. While many times you won't throw to the flat, just having it to keep the defense honest makes it one of the best weapons in the game.

TOP 5 NEW GAMEPLAY TIPS

5 PRECISION MODIFIER MOVES

Madden NFL 25 features precision moves that are the best way to run free in the game this year. These moves are available to any player who has a 90-plus move rating in a corresponding rating category. The gamer who can learn when to time the modifier will be rewarded with some special animations and an increased chance to break tackles. The Skills Trainer also has a great drill that can help you learn the timing for each move.

5 PRECISION HURDLE
4 PRECISION SPIN
3 PRECISION JUKE
2 PRECISION DIVE
1 PRECISION TRUCK

5 PRECISION HURDLE

> THIS MOVE HAS THE HIGHEST RISK/REWARD IN THE GAME; YOU COULD FUMBLE IF YOU DON'T CLEAR THE TACKLER!

Leaping over a defender will always make a highlight reel on Monday morning, and now it is possible in *Madden NFL 25*. This move is best in the open field, where you have fewer defenders to worry about. If you see a downed defender when running through a hole, just use the regular hurdle so you don't expose yourself to an increased fumble chance. For the precision hurdle, wait until you see a tackler start to break down and then go for it! If you time it properly, you can completely clear the defender! If you are facing a player with a great Hit Power rating, think twice before trying it out as you could fumble! Don't forget that you can use a precision dive near the goal line to go up and over the pile.

4 PRECISION SPIN

> A 90-PLUS SPIN MOVE RATING (SPM) IS NEEDED TO USE THIS PRECISION MOVE!

A well-timed spin can be one of the fanciest moves in the game, although it can lead to big hits if not timed properly. If you throw a swing pass out to the HB, look to use a well-timed precision spin to fake out the LB. This area of the field near the sideline has been an area of success, but careful not to spin into traffic if the defense is recovering to the middle of the field. A great thing about the spin is you can also break out of tackles with it!

3 PRECISION JUKE

> ANY PLAYER WITH A 90-PLUS JUKE RATING (JKM) CAN PULL OFF THIS MOVE, INCLUDING KICK RETURNERS!.

The precision juke is one of the most versatile precision moves in the game. You can juke in either direction depending on the situation and angle of the tackler. You can also back juke, which can really cause some missed tackles against human opponents. When going for the precision juke, you may completely make the defender miss, but you can also break tackles with it. If you are a fan of the back juke, try using the precision modifier in space, which will delay your steps and can throw off defenders! Think of using the precision modifier as a way to slow down your runner to get more control, and then use the move to get the fake-out!

2 PRECISION STIFF ARM

> LOOK FOR A PLAYER WITH A 90-PLUS STIFF ARM RATING (SFA) TO UNLEASH THIS MOVE.

Stiff arms give power backs another great move in *Madden NFL 25,* and the precision move only enhances it. If you're looking to be aggressive and use the force impact with a stiff arm simply tap the button. However, if you are running along the sideline and a defender comes in at an angle, hold down the button to put your arm out and string out the run. If you can time the precision stiff arm properly, you may see your HB go into beast mode like Marshawn Lynch and knock over the defender!

1 PRECISION TRUCK

> USE THIS MOVE WITH ANY PLAYER WHO HAS A 90-PLUS TRUCK RATING (TRK).

Using power backs is a great way to run the ball this year due to the trucking move. If you can time the right stick and get lower than the defender, you can knock him back and keep the chains moving. On short-yardage downs, it is key to get low and behind your blockers, but the real time to unleash this move is in the open field. If you turn the corner on an off tackle run and see the safety breaking down to make the tackle, look to flatten him and continue on your way to the end zone.

5 SLIDERS
4 ROSTERS
3 CUSTOM PLAYBOOKS
2 TOP DOWNLOADS
1 SHARE YOUR FILES

TOP 5 MADDEN SHARE TIPS

The Madden Share is a brand-new feature in *Madden NFL 25* that will heavily impact your gameplay experience. By heading to the Share tab on the home screen, gamers will be able to download rosters, sliders, and playbooks from the community! You could obtain a new playbook loaded with great plays or sliders that allow you to customize your on-the-field experience! Here are our favorite things about Madden Share!

5 SLIDERS

DEFAULT SLIDERS

PASSING	
QB Accuracy	58
Pass Blocking	34
This slider adjusts how effective pass blocking is.	
WR Catching	50
RUSHING	
Run Blocking	50
Fumbles	50
PASS DEFENSE	
Reaction Time	50
Interceptions	50

IF YOU WANT A REAL CHALLENGE, YOU CAN ALWAYS TURN UP THE COMPUTER'S SLIDERS OR TURN DOWN YOUR OWN!

Sliders allow for individual gamers to customize their experience. If you are struggling in a certain area, like dropped passes, you can adjust the sliders for catching to make it more to your liking. There are communities out there that will develop sliders to make the game more of a faster arcade-style experience—download a few different types and see what style you enjoy.

4 ROSTERS

MANAGE PLAYERS
Edit teams and trade players

IF YOU DOWNLOAD A ROSTER FILE THAT YOU ENJOY, YOU CAN BRING IT INTO CFM TO USE AS THE STARTING ROSTER!

Madden NFL 25 has an insane amount of equipment, ratings, and traits for every player that bring out an authentic experience. If you want to take a shot at being your own ratings czar, you can now edit every aspect and create your own ratings system. One of our favorite things to do is make sure the Giants (favorite team) are rated a 99 at every position! The key is being able to make the rosters and equipment fit your experience! You can also download a file from other players who have taken their shot at a roster!

3 CUSTOM PLAYBOOKS

CUSTOMIZE PLAYBOOKS
Update audibles and plays for all playbooks

YOU CAN DOWNLOAD SEPARATE FILES FOR BOTH OFFENSE AND DEFENSE.

Players who are big on gameplay are always trying out new playbooks to see which team has the best plays. In *Madden NFL 25*, not only can you make a custom playbook and add formations from different teams, but you can then share that playbook with the rest of the community. If you are looking for a new playbook to try out, check out the top downloads or sort by highest rated to see what players have been successful with. With all of the customization and creativity in the community, you will rarely see two identical playbooks this season!

2 TOP DOWNLOADS

TOP DOWNLOADS
Check out the most popular files...

IF YOU LIKE A SPECIFIC USER'S FILE, YOU CAN CHECK AND SEE WHAT OTHER FILES THEY HAVE UPLOADED.

When you bring together a community as passionate about gaming as the *Madden NFL* community, gamers will create some terrific content. Now that it is easy to share and download, expect to see awesome creations. To find out what is currently the talk of the community, head to the Top Downloads tab and sort to find something you enjoy. Once you try out the file, head into My Downloads and make sure to rate it to let others know if it is worth trying.

1 SHARE YOUR FILES

LOOK TO JOIN AN ONLINE COMMUNITY TO SEE WHAT FILES THE COMMUNITY WANTS THE MOST.

While downloading other files is a great way to use Madden Share, there wouldn't be anything available if people didn't upload. If you are a hard-core gamer, why not share your creations with the community? As the author of the guide, we will have a playbook available on the Madden Share that will be built for players who like to use a mobile QB—be sure to download and rate it!

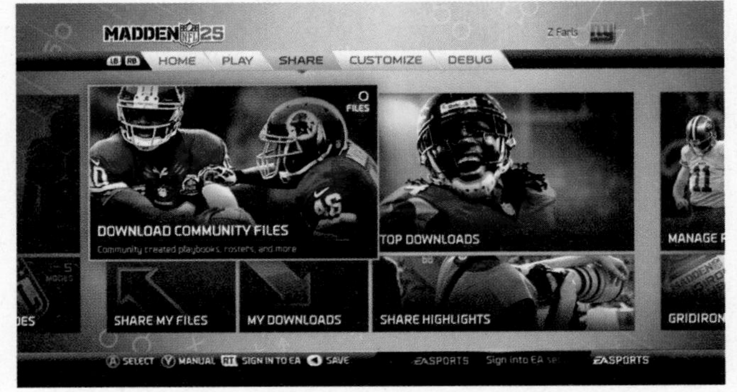

TOP 5 BEGINNER TIPS

5 CHOOSE YOUR PLAY
4 READ THE DEFENSE
3 MAKE YOUR READ
2 MAKE YOUR MOVE
1 HUDDLE UP

HOW TO PLAY OFFENSE

If you're new to either the sport of football or football video games, you need to first understand how the flow of the game works. Learning the controls will take a few days but can easily be accomplished with a combination of the Skills Trainer and practice mode. Once you have a feel for how to hold the controller, exit practice mode and start getting some real reps in a game, because playing live games is the only way to learn the timing. Set the difficulty level to Rookie to start—this is a good way to monitor your progress—and you can ramp up the difficulty when you start to improve. Here's how solid players get thinking about their offense in *Madden NFL 25*.

5 CHOOSE YOUR PLAY

> **CHOOSING A PLAY EARLY IN THE GAME TO SET UP THE DEFENSE FOR A LATER DRIVE IS A WAY TO BECOME MORE ADVANCED.**

Once you receive the kickoff, a great place to start is with the question, "What play should I call?" You will be in the Play Call screen and have many options from different formations. Formations are how your players line up, and each formation has different strengths and weaknesses. Every team tries to focus on its strengths, like its best players, and use those to attack their opponents' weaknesses. Beginners tend to play more conservatively with what plays they choose and usually start with a running play. If you think the defense isn't ready for the pass or can't defend your players, call a pass.

For basic play-calling, you can go with a run to the left, run to the right, run up the middle, or a passing play.

If you choose a pass, you want your passing play to do one of three things:

1. Beat the Blitz (Quick Pass)
2. Beat Man-to-Man Defense (Man Beater)
3. Beat Zone Defense (Zone Beater)

As you will see in the team breakdown chapter of the guide, every playbook has plays built into it to cover all these scenarios. The key is finding the plays you are comfortable running that maximize all of your talented players. Just because one play might work with one team doesn't mean it will be the best play for another team. When you are thinking about which play to choose, remember to consider factors like the score, how much time is left, and what has been working so far.

4 READ THE DEFENSE

> **BE SURE TO READ THE "WAYS TO READ DEFENSIVE COVERAGES" ARTICLE IN THE "TOP 5 EXPERT TIPS" SECTION.**

While reading the exact defense can be challenging for newer players, you can still learn valuable information by just paying attention. Although you may not know the exact play, think of everything you do know and ask yourself questions like:

- What types of players does my opponent have on the field? Are they set up to stop the run or the pass?
- Is the defense backed off my receivers, or are they up near the line?
- Are there any players who appear to be blitzing and drawing my attention?
- Where is the field position right now, and how could that affect the play call?
- Is my opponent controlling a certain player on defense? If so, how can I use that to my benefit?
- Do I think the play I called is going to work when I snap the ball?

All of these questions should be cycling through your head calmly after you call your play and *before* you snap the ball. If at any time you see something questionable and don't have a plan for it, make an adjustment or take a time-out. The number one mistake that beginners make is snapping the ball when they know a play isn't going to work. You have audibles that you can switch to based on what you see out there, so use them to your advantage. Hike!

3 MAKE YOUR READ

Mastering the timing of a few routes on one play gives you multiple windows to throw the ball.

Now that you have snapped the ball, you are getting ready to either hand off or throw the ball. Both the dropback of the QB and the handoff are automatic, so don't push the left stick too hard. For a run, make your read based on what you saw pre-snap. If you chose a read option, be looking at your read key from the pre-snap screen. If you're running the ball outside and see daylight, keep going, but if it looks sealed maybe cut it back towards the middle. Since you know where you're supposed to be going and what to expect, you shouldn't see any surprises.

On passing plays, you want to have a list of priorities on where to throw the ball based on what you saw before the play. Beginners should focus on just three players on any play.

Primary Read: This is your intended target based on what you saw before the snap. Make sure you were correct with what you saw and then deliver the football. A common mistake is to focus on this read too much and force the throw even when the receiver is not open.

Secondary Read: This route needs to break after your primary read. If your primary doesn't get open, this route won't help you if the receiver has already made a cut to try to get open. This is where timing windows and passing concepts start to be valuable.

Safety Valve: If both your reads are covered, move to your last read before throwing the ball away or taking off with the QB. The safety valve role is best served by a tight end (TE) or a halfback (HB) who blocks and then releases or is running a curl against zone defense or a drag across the field against man coverage. Since this will be your last read, it will be a few seconds before you dump it off, so make sure the timing is good.

If you can master just three easier reads on a few plays, you can prevent a good defensive player from user-controlling all your options on any given play. *Never* wait on an open primary read because you think the secondary read might get open; if you see an open player, throw him the ball. Otherwise, keep your progressions going quickly.

2 MAKE YOUR MOVE

If you are trailing late in the game, try to get out of bounds!

Once you get control of the ball carrier, start running! After you complete a pass or take the handoff, now is the time to have some fun. Between the directions you go with the left stick and the moves you pull off, you are now in true control. While running with your player, ask yourself these questions and scan the field:

- What skills does this player have? Is he a power runner or speed runner?
- From where is the defense running at me? Do I need to speed up or slow down?
- What angle is the nearest tackler taking, and what move will work in this situation?
- Do I need to cover up the ball to prevent a fumble?
- Is the player who is going to tackle me a big hitter, and does the quarterback (QB) I am running with need to slide for protection?
- Can I stretch out for extra yardage to try to get a first down or touchdown (TD)?

All of these things need to be quickly reevaluated with every step of the ball carrier, but most of them come naturally. You should have an idea of the game situation before you start to run, so you can quickly process this information. Every play in football is made of hundreds of small decisions by all 22 players on the field made quickly and updated every second. By having a plan, you can quickly make the right decisions and rack up more wins!

1 HUDDLE UP

To call a hurry-up offense after a successful play hold down Ⓨ on Xbox or ▲ on PS3 when the play ends!

After the play has ended and the runner has been tackled, has run out of bounds, has scored a TD, or has thrown an incomplete pass, you enter the final stage. Now is a good time to ask yourself a few more questions as you run back to the huddle:

- Did that play successfully achieve my goals?
- Do I want to call hurry up and skip the huddle to try to speed up this drive?
- How did my opponent react to that play? Would the play work later in the game?

As you ponder these questions, you will be back at the Play Call screen and ready to start the entire process all over again for the next play! If you can put together a long drive you can quickly see just how many decisions are needed to compete in a game of *Madden NFL 25!* Just remember to stay calm, ask questions, and be in control!

Offensive Checklist

- ❑ Choose a Run or Pass Play
- ❑ Look at the Defense
- ❑ Make Any Needed Audibles or Hot Routes
- ❑ Snap
- ❑ Make Your Reads
- ❑ Run with the Ball

TOP 5 BEGINNER TIPS

HOW TO PLAY DEFENSE

5 CHOOSE YOUR PLAY
4 READ THE OFFENSE
3 MAKE ADJUSTMENTS
2 MAKE YOUR MOVE
1 HUDDLE UP

Defense is often considered more challenging by beginner players than the offensive side of the ball. Let's see what we should be doing to start playing stout defense in *Madden NFL 25*. Most of this mirrors what we discussed on offense, as football is simply a chess match with the player getting the last adjustment in earning an advantage. Study up on the defensive buttons and adjustments with the Skills Trainer and practice mode! Knowing all your options is key to becoming a better player.

5 CHOOSE YOUR PLAY

> **PLAYING DEFENSE WITHOUT KNOWING THE PROPER CONTROLS IS VERY DETRIMENTAL TO LEARNING HOW TO PLAY. ON OFFENSE IT IS A MUCH SMALLER ISSUE!**

Most beginners have a conservative style of defense that allows them to give up some yardage but not the big play downfield. This allows the offense to take what is given to them. This is a great strategy at the start of the game to see what type of offense your opponent is running, especially if you don't know their play style. When it comes time to call a play, ask yourself a few questions:

- What is the down and distance?
- What do my opponents like to do on offense?
- What personnel are they putting on the field?

All of these questions should lead you towards calling one of the five types of plays in our "5 Sets for Success" system on defense.

1. Run Defense
2. Man Coverage Defense
3. Zone Coverage Defense
4. Man Blitz Defense
5. Zone Blitz Defense

If your opponent is likely to run the ball, you want to have more linemen and linebackers on the field. If you think they are going to pass, you want more cornerbacks and safeties in the game. While most beginner players don't like to send blitzes because it leaves them vulnerable, there are situations when a well-timed blitz can really throw off the offense! When looking to defend the pass, you must choose a man or zone defense. Man (or man-to-man) coverage means each defender is responsible for following an offensive player, while zone means that each defender plays an area of the field and only picks up a man if he runs through his area. Be sure to vary which you call so the offense doesn't get comfortable, but also cater to your team's strength. Check your defenders' ratings to see if they are better in man (MCV) or zone (ZCV) coverage. Calling a variety of plays out of the huddle will keep the offense guessing and give you a higher chance for success.

4 READ THE OFFENSE

> **IF THE OFFENSE IS HEAVILY WEIGHTED TO ONE SIDE, YOU CAN USE "BASE ALIGN" TO ADJUST YOUR DEFENSIVE BALANCE.**

Now that you have called your defensive play, you get to see where the offensive players line up, which is known as a formation. Each offensive formation has strengths and weaknesses, and it is the defense's job to match up against it. The game should do a good job readjusting to any weird alignments by the offense, but you should always be ready to make your own adjustments. This is a good time to ask questions like:

- Who are my opponent's biggest playmakers?
- Where are those players lining up?
- Where are my weaknesses if the ball is snapped right now?
- Who can I user-control on defense to give myself an advantage?
- Do I recognize this formation, and if so, what did I see from it last time?
- Do I need to audible?

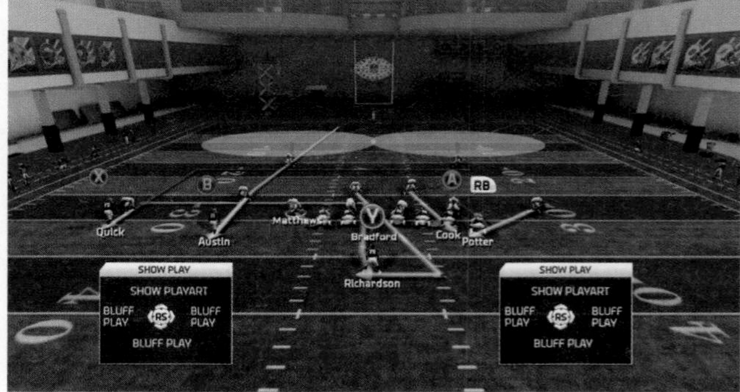

Now that you have made a few assumptions about what your opponent will run, get ready to make a few adjustments before the snap of the ball!

3 MAKE ADJUSTMENTS

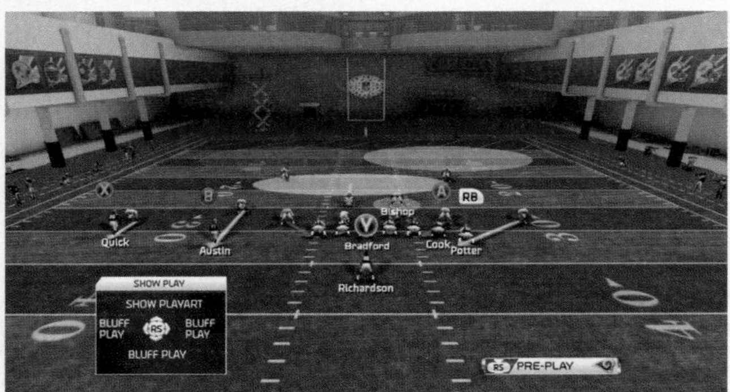

Dropping defensive linemen into zones can help stop short throws over the middle.

You will have a minimum of 7 seconds from the Play Call screen to the snap of the ball to get in any adjustments you need to feel confident! This doesn't seem like a long time, but with a little practice you can get in a lot of changes. You can adjust any individual player's assignment by clicking onto him, or you can control players by group, like linemen, linebackers, and secondary. To go from a beginner to an expert, you need to start realizing the tendencies of your opponent and reacting. If the QB keeps passing the ball to his TE over the middle of the field, you need to understand all the options you have to stop him. You can add a second man-to-man defender inside or drop a defensive lineman into a hook zone. Both of these will weaken another area of your coverage, but you must take away your opponent's first option. Always try to be ready for the snap of the ball and to see if the play you planned for was actually called!

2 MAKE YOUR MOVE

Never be afraid to "click on" to a defender and try to make a user play—this will lead to improvement in the long term!

One of the hardest things to learn on defense is just getting a feel for the defender you are controlling. Many players don't like to go for tackles because they fear they will miss them. Others don't like to try and defend in the passing game because they fear a mistake will cost them a TD. If you user-control a linebacker (LB) in a hook (yellow) zone, you can't hurt your team too badly, so that's what beginners should do. This will also start to improve your confidence, and you will be making plays in no time. Resist the urge to control a defensive lineman; it feels safe but won't make you better in the long term. Once you make your read and the play comes towards you, ask yourself these questions:

- Do I have an angle on the ball carrier?
- What move might the runner try to use here?
- Can I go for a hit stick, which is a higher risk but brings more reward?
- Can I hold down the Catch button for the interception, or should I use the safer Swat button?
- Is it safer for me to click off of my defender and let the CPU make a safe tackle?

There isn't a worse feeling than giving up a TD on a long throw that you let the CPU defend. As a player who has been in that situation, I know. You may be feeling a lack of confidence, but if the CPU ends up costing you the game when you chose not to "click on," you will regret it.

1 HUDDLE UP

You have a minimum of 7 seconds to get in your adjustments if the offense calls hurry up!

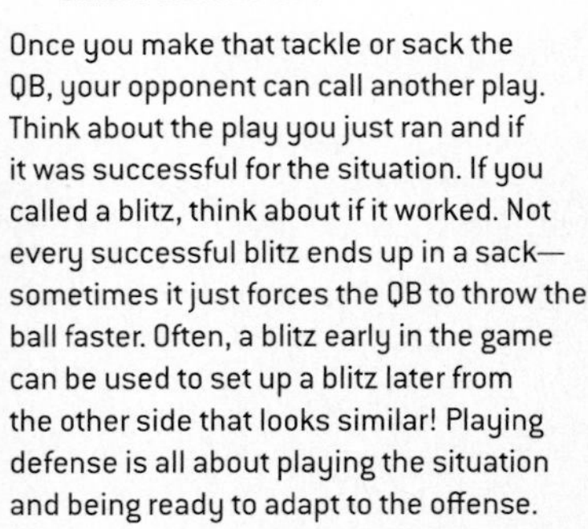

Once you make that tackle or sack the QB, your opponent can call another play. Think about the play you just ran and if it was successful for the situation. If you called a blitz, think about if it worked. Not every successful blitz ends up in a sack—sometimes it just forces the QB to throw the ball faster. Often, a blitz early in the game can be used to set up a blitz later from the other side that looks similar! Playing defense is all about playing the situation and being ready to adapt to the offense.

Now that you know everything you need to be scanning for over the course of a game on the defensive side of the ball, start working on the controls so you can quickly make those adjustments. Even the best players have a hard time getting stops early in the game if they haven't seen their opponent's best plays before. The key is learning what they like to do during the course of the game, so when the fourth quarter rolls around, you are ready to get a stop and win the game!

Defensive Checklist

- ❑ Choose a Run Defense or Man/Zone Pass Defense
- ❑ Look at the Offensive Formation and Personnel
- ❑ Make Any Needed Audibles or Adjustments
- ❑ Be Ready for the Snap
- ❑ Make Your Reads
- ❑ Make Your Move
- ❑ Make Plays

TOP 5 BEGINNER TIPS

HOW TO PLAY SPECIAL TEAMS

- 5 KICKOFF COVERAGE
- 4 PUNTING THE BALL
- 3 FIELD GOALS
- 2 PUNT RETURNS
- 1 KICK RETURNS

Most beginner players love to play on the offensive side of the ball, and while that is packed with excitement, there does come a time for the third phase of the game. Special teams are a crucial aspect of football but are often overlooked in video games. Gamers who take a few minutes to learn the basics, however, can often turn the tide of a game with a huge play. Think about your favorite team and how much a missed field goal or a returned kick changed the course of their season. Special teams are an area where a little bit of practice goes a long way. Here are some questions to think about and tips for improving.

5 KICKOFF COVERAGE

> **If you can't risk giving up a TD (for example, at the end of the half), use a Squib Kick from the Play Call menu.**

Kicking off the ball is simple: pull the right stick back and then push forward when the meter fills up. What happens afterward is more challenging; once the kick returner receives the kick, he will attempt to score. Here are some questions to consider:

- What is the game situation, including game time and score?
- Would a return for a TD really hurt my chance to win the game?
- Do I need to try to force a turnover with a big hit or strip?
- Does my opponent have a player with a high rating back there?
- Has my opponent had success with earlier kick returns?

All of these questions should help determine whether you take a tackler and run straight down the field or try to play back a little more. If you play back, you may give up more yards but prevent the big return for a TD. If you see an star player you don't want to kick towards, use the left stick to move the kicking arrow and aim for another player. With just a few minutes practicing power and direction, you can quickly learn all the places you can kick the ball. If you are losing late in a game, don't forget to try the onside kick to try to get the ball back.

4 PUNTING THE BALL

> **Check out the "Game Plan Tips" later in this section to learn more about when to punt vs. when to go for it on fourth down.**

The controls for punting the ball are the same as for kicking off and just as easy, but making the choice to punt can be challenging. Most gamers think they can get the first down even when punting is the safe choice. Resist the urge to make a risky choice and ask yourself these questions on the punt:

- Should I try to kick the ball out of bounds?
- Can I try to pin the ball inside the 10-yard line?
- Should I try for max distance on this punt?
- Does my opponent have a dangerous returner back there?
- Does my opponent appear to be sending pressure to try to block my punt?

Once you factor in all these questions, you can set the angle and direction of the kicking arrow with the left stick. The right stick back and forward controls the power. If you are near midfield, look to kick the ball out of bounds. If you are buried deep near your own end zone, kick it as far as possible. If you angle the kick low and away from the returner, you may pick up some yards on the roll. Punting may not be glamorous, but a great kick can leave your opponents starting their next drive at their own 1-yard line!

3 FIELD GOALS

Always have a favorite short yardage play call ready for a 2-point conversion try!

Taking the points with a field goal (FG) is a great way to salvage a drive that stops short of a TD! By selecting the Field Goal play from the special teams formation, you are likely going to earn 3 points. Here are questions to think about when kicking a field goal:

> How far can my kicker make an attempt from?

> How much time is left in the game—can I run one more play to get closer?

> What hash mark is the ball spotted on, and will that make the kick too difficult?

> Should I consider going for the TD instead?

To kick a FG with max distance, lower the kicking arrow all the way down. Aim it left and right with the left stick depending on the spot between the hash marks. Start the meter by pulling back on the right stick, and push it forward as the bar fills at the top. How far you can kick depends on your kicker's Kick Power rating (KPW), the angle of the arrow, the wind, and how much you fill up the meter. Test this in practice mode so you know exactly what yard line you need to be at to convert a successful chance. The player who is better prepared will increase the chance of success in a close game, and FGs can be the difference between a win and a loss! Remember to add 17 yards to your current yard line to account for the holder and end zone distance!

2 PUNT RETURNS

Since blocked punts are rare, look to set up your return game instead!

A great punt return can swing the tide of a football game, but so can a dropped or fumbled punt. When your opponent is getting ready to punt you the ball, start by grabbing your defender (backup LB) over the center and running him backwards. This will give you one more blocker in the return game. If you start to feel uncomfortable at any point when the ball is in the air, you can always press the Fair Catch button (Y on Xbox, ▲ on PS3) while controlling the returner. This lets your returner catch the ball without being hit by a defender but will prevent further return. The main goal of a punt return is to catch the ball and pick up as many yards as possible without risking a turnover. Every now and then you may spring a big return, but never force it. Last, remember a key returner rule, which is to never field a punt inside your own 10-yard line.

1 KICK RETURNS

Always be ready to audible to an onside kick return if your opponent tries to catch you off guard.

Starting off the game with a kick return for a TD can really put the momentum in your favor. With just a little bit of practice and a skilled player, you can become a great returner! Returning up the middle is the option that will give you the most consistent blocking. When you catch the ball automatically, start straight ahead, and at the last second before the defense breaks down, try to break the return outside. There is too much traffic in the middle of the field to weave through, so you want to get to the edge. The longer you can stay in the middle before busting outside containment, the greater the chance you have to make a big play for your team. There is no worse feeling for your opponent than to score a TD and then immediately give up a return TD, so work on your kick return game in practice mode!

TOP 5 BEGINNER TIPS

5 FIND A STYLE
4 TEST IT OUT
3 CREATE A MINI SCHEME
2 GO CUSTOM
1 SET YOUR AUDIBLES

CHOOSING A PLAYBOOK

No matter which team you choose to play with in *Madden NFL 25*, you can always choose any playbook that you like. This is one of the most overlooked strategies by new players. We always recommend picking a specific playbook before heading into a game, rather than waiting to see what plays your default team playbook contains. Once you start to develop some familiarity with one playbook, it will be a breeze to not only play with new teams, but also to explore new playbooks and carry over the concepts you have learned. By consistently using the same playbook, you can learn your reads and eliminate the calling of random plays.

5 FIND A STYLE

> **BE SURE TO EXPLORE ALL THE NEW OPTION-STYLE PLAYS IN *MADDEN NFL* THIS SEASON.**

Are you the type of player who likes to spread out your offense and pass every down? Or now that you have read all about the new run controls and tips, are you going to try a ground-and-pound approach? There are multiple ways to be successful in the game, but you have to commit to one and try it out. Depending on the strengths of your team, you must choose a playbook that fits your talents and the scheme you want to run. It doesn't make sense to take a pocket passer with no speed and run the Pistol playbook, which contains option runs with the QB!

3 CREATE A MINI SCHEME

> **WORK ON FINDING PLAYS THAT LOOK SIMILAR TO THE DEFENSE BUT ATTACK DIFFERENT AREAS OF THE FIELD.**

A mini scheme is a small group of plays out of one formation that you save for later in the game. If you need a quick drive at the end of the half, you can go to your mini scheme and give the defense a look they have never seen before. Some playbooks feature overlap of formations, so if you find a few formations from different books, look around and see if there is one that contains all of them! A good example is a formation like Singleback Bunch. You can have a Four Verticals play that attacks downfield with a Y Trail play that attacks underneath. Mix this in with a draw from the formation and you have three different plays from one formation that can be mixed up quickly and effectively. Having a solid mini scheme will give you confidence on drives at the end of the game and in the red zone!

4 TEST IT OUT

> **IF YOU EVER END UP IN A GAME WITHOUT YOUR FAVORITE PLAYBOOK, LOOK FOR SIMILAR FORMATIONS AND CONCEPTS TO WORK WITH!**

Once you have figured out the strength of your team and what style of offense you want to run, take your playbook into practice mode. Practice mode will help you start to learn the timing of certain plays and find out what routes are effective for beating certain coverages. You should run through your "5 Sets for Success" and learn how all the plays work together. Most mistakes happen during games when players simply call random plays they have never worked on before and expect them to work. Every team in the NFL practices their playbook all off-season to be ready for their first game, and you should too!

2 GO CUSTOM

> **DON'T ADD RANDOM PLAYS TO FILL UP A CUSTOM PLAYBOOK—LESS IS MORE!**

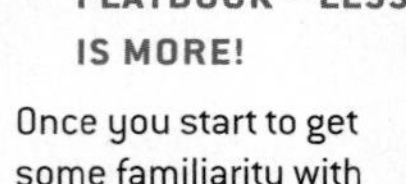

Once you start to get some familiarity with multiple playbooks, you can take the best of what you've found and make a custom playbook. This is a solid feature that the hard-core fans of *Madden NFL* utilize to really give their playbook a feel of its own. You can take out those formations that you never use to make it cleaner and add any new formations you find effective. This is something you can constantly tweak during the season and that can even fit multiple styles of play. Don't think custom playbooks aren't for newer players or you will be stunting your growth! Also make sure to check out Madden Share to find a playbook that is already finished!

1 SET YOUR AUDIBLES

> **TESTING OUT YOUR QUICK AUDIBLES (QUICK PASS, PLAY-ACTION PASS, DEEP PASS, RUN) IS A GOOD IDEA AND GIVES YOU MORE OPTIONS AT THE LINE!**

When you choose a playbook or build a custom book, make sure to set and save your audibles. With the brand-new deeper system in *Madden NFL 25*, setting up your audibles is very important. Learning how to get to multiple formations quickly through the use of personnel audibles will put stress on your opponent to make adjustments. Now, when you finally get into a game, you will have the perfect play call ready to beat the defense!

5 START AT QB
4 CHECK YOUR SPECIAL TEAMS
3 DEFENSIVE VERSATILITY
2 BUILD YOUR GAME PLAN
1 HIDDEN GEMS

BEGINNER TIPS **TOP 5**

SETTING YOUR LINEUP

The depth chart in *Madden NFL 25* is one of the most visited places in the game for expert players. Players who are using a new team for the first time want to see who their best players are and where they excel. If you are constantly using the same team, be sure to save your best lineup and have it automatically load into the game! If the team you chose has great WRs but you like to run the ball, you may need to adjust your lineup or game plan.

5 START AT QB

Only one player handles the ball every snap, so make sure you are using your best option!

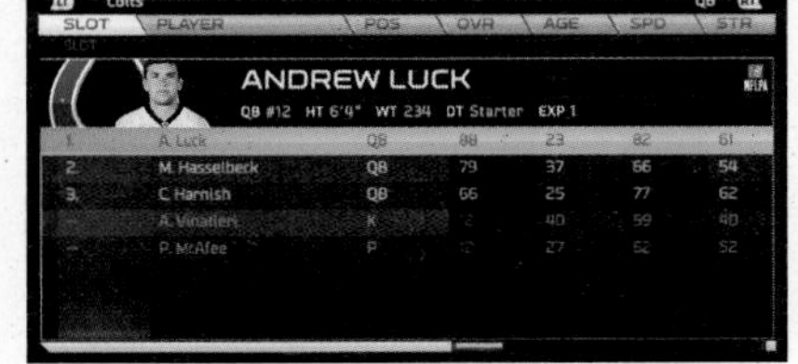

While searching for a new team to play with, you should always look to the QB position. If you head into the Roster menu, you can sort by any category and position to give yourself a look at how every play stacks up! Some teams have multiple QBs who can get the job done depending on how you want to play. If you have a veteran pocket passer but a scrambling rookie, you can work to get both some snaps. With all the different types of game plans, you need to have a QB who will set your team up for success, so make sure to focus on it!

4 CHECK YOUR SPECIAL TEAMS

Try lower-rated players when you get a big lead; they may be special!

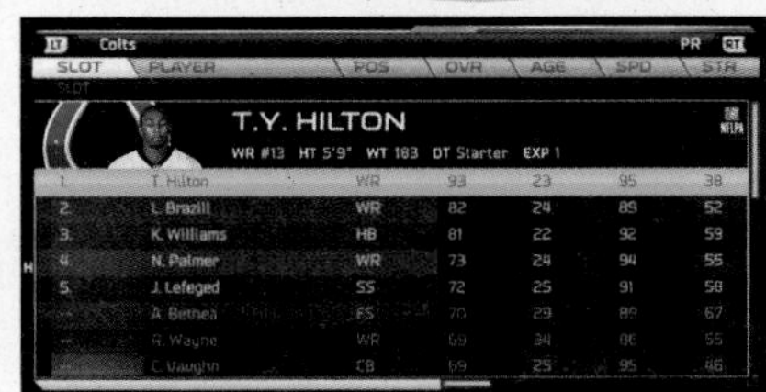

Setting your offense and defense but skipping over special teams is a common mistake that even veteran gamers make. Always be sure to check your kicker's Kick Power rating and just how fast your returner is. If you overlook a better player on the bench, you may be costing your team points later in the game. For a great returner, look at attributes like Speed (SPD), Agility (AGI), and Acceleration (ACC)!

3 DEFENSIVE VERSATILITY

Some outside linebackers (OLBs) may receive a ratings boost when going down to play defensive end!

Great coaches will find a way to line up their best 11 players on the field no matter what position they are. If you have three amazing safeties, try moving one down to cornerback (CB) to get him on the field. Take a look at what positions are utilized with your main defensive strategy, and then line up your best guys in those positions. When trying to stop a great running opponent, we often put our stronger backup defensive tackles (DTs) in at the defensive end (DE) position. This gives us some extra weight on the field to support our linebackers. Defensive players are capable of shifting around, so it's your job to get them into position to make plays!

2 BUILD YOUR GAME PLAN

If you have too many great backs, try moving one with a high Catch rating to wide receiver!

We talked about finding a great playbook already, but make sure that it fits with your team. The key is to make sure that your personnel matches up when you switch from one formation to another. It is okay for a TE to line up at wide receiver (WR), but he won't be able to move down to HB. If you're going to use a run-heavy game plan, make sure your fullback (FB) doesn't line up elsewhere if you audible to a pass. Where you set up each player in the depth chart determines where he lines up in every formation. You may want your fastest WR in the slot, rather than lining up at the number one position in the depth chart, depending on how you have set up your attack!

1 HIDDEN GEMS

A valuable rating for the WR/TE position is Catch in Traffic (CIT), which helps the receiver hang onto the ball in congested areas.

The Overall rating is a great snapshot of how good a player is, but a true coach will get the most out of his lower-rated players, too. If you have a lower-rated player who is only good at carrying the ball, put him in at the end of the game to protect the ball. If your QB has poor accuracy, look to help him out by running screen passes to the HB and WR. You only have so much talent on the roster, so take a minute to run through your lineup and really dig so you can maximize it. Finding a great sleeper player on your bench and turning him into a star is one of the best feelings in *Madden NFL 25*!

Chargers — SS

SEAN CATTOUSE — SS #40 HT 6'3" WT 218 DT 3rd String EXP 1

SLOT	PLAYER	POS	TAK	POW (HIT POWER)	PMV
1.	M. Gilchrist	SS	64	55	39
2.	B. Taylor	SS	72	73	60
3.	S. Cattouse	SS	64	86	49
--	E. Weddle	FS	94	77	39
--	D. Cox	CB	61	52	20
--	S. Wright	CB	63	62	35
--	D. Stuckey	FS	68	64	42
--	J. Patrick	CB	55	45	25

TOP 5 BEGINNER TIPS

HOW TO SET YOUR OFFENSIVE AUDIBLES

Setting your audibles using the new system is one of the fastest ways to improve in *Madden NFL 25*. Having plays that you know how to run available to switch to at the line of scrimmage is very important. By setting our four audibles for each formation from the Customize tab before we enter the game, we will have confidence to change the play if we sense our original play call won't work. By following the "5 Sets for Success" on both offense and defense, we know we will always have the right play ready to beat our opponent! To get into a comfort zone, we always come out in the same formation, which is our "base set." This will give us a good look at the defense, and then we can always audible to another play from our "5 Sets for Success"!

OFFENSIVE 5 SETS FOR SUCCESS

5 BASE FORMATION
4 RUN FORMATION
3 BLITZ BEATER FORMATION
2 MAN BEATER FORMATION
1 ZONE BEATER FORMATION

5 BASE FORMATION

EXAMPLE:
Gun Normal Y-Slot

> **FINDING A GOOD FORMATION FOR YOUR FIVE MOST TALENTED OFFENSIVE PLAYERS IS KEY TO GETTING THEM PLENTY OF SNAPS.**

Our base formation is very important in putting our best passing personnel on the field and finding a formation that is versatile. For our base formation to work, it must help us get a read on the defense and have the ability to beat both man and zone. Our audibles from this formation should contain a run if the defense is dropping back their players to play the pass! The importance of coming out in the same formation is that it gives us confidence due to the repetition. The more formations we can audible to from it, the better!

4 RUN FORMATION

EXAMPLE:
Strong Close

> **BE SURE TO KNOW WHICH SIDE YOUR BEST LINEMEN PLAY ON, AND RUN TOWARDS THEM IN BIG SITUATIONS!**

Being able to run the ball is an important part of a game plan even for players who like to pass in *Madden NFL 25*. Make sure that your playbook contains a formation that you feel comfortable with if your QB got injured and you had to change your style for a game. By choosing a formation and setting the audibles so we have a run left, run middle, and run right, we can make sure the defense can't key in on our plans! In the last audible slot, make sure to include a quick play-action pass that can beat players who are too aggressive against the run.

3 BLITZ BEATER FORMATION

EXAMPLE:
Gun Split Offset

> **TO BEAT THE BLITZ, YOU CAN EITHER GET THE BALL OUT FAST OR BLOCK EXTRA PLAYERS AND TRY TO PICK UP THE RUSHERS!**

Gun Split Offset puts two players lined up next to the QB, which makes it a great formation against players who like to bring pressure. The key is to switch up between blocking the two players in the backfield and sending them out on routes. If your opponent sends pressure, you can always block both and look to get the ball downfield. If your opponent gets frustrated and sends too many rushers, you can have those players go out on quick routes and really beat the defense. Make sure to have some quick screen passes saved in your audibles to always have a blitz-beating play ready.

2 MAN BEATER

EXAMPLE:
Gun Tight Flex

> **IF WE USE COMPRESSED SETS, THE DEFENDERS WILL HAVE TO CRAM INTO A SMALL AREA, WHICH MAKES IT TOUGH FOR THEM TO PLAY MAN-TO-MAN DEFENSE!**

We always start the game in our base set to find out what our opponent likes to do on defense, and then once we have an idea, we can switch to our man or zone beater formation. The man-beating formation is usually from a compressed-style set where everyone lines up tight, which makes it hard for defenders to line up. If you can set three man-beating concepts like Mesh, Slants, and Inside Cross to your audibles, you can switch up how you beat your opponent. For the fourth audible, always add a draw to the formation, because defenders have to turn their backs when playing man-to-man and can't react as fast!

1 ZONE BEATER

EXAMPLE: **Gun Bunch Wk**

> **BUNCH FORMATIONS CONTAIN MANY PLAYS YOU CAN USE TO DEFEAT ZONE COVERAGE.**

While our base play can already beat zone, having even more options to switch to is a great idea. When we sense our opponent calling their base zone defense, we love a play that can really stress a zone defense downfield, like Four Verticals. Make sure to set plays that can beat different types of zones, like Smash to beat Cover 2. If your opponent is playing Cover 3, have a Curl Flats play or use your hot routes to make one at the line of scrimmage. All zones have holes—it is just a matter of determining where they are and getting the ball out to your receiver there. By flooding one area of the field with receivers, you should feel confident you can hit an open target.

DEFENSIVE SETS FOR SUCCESS

5 RUN DEFENSE
4 BASE MAN
3 BASE ZONE
2 MAN BLITZ
1 ZONE BLITZ

HOW TO SET YOUR DEFENSIVE AUDIBLES

Setting your audibles is a huge part of having success in *Madden NFL 25* on the defensive side of the ball. When selecting a play, always wait to see what personnel your opponent is putting on the field. This can help you decide what type of formation to respond with. When you get to the line, look at your opponent's formation and either make adjustments or be ready to completely change your play. Depending on your team's strengths, play either 70 percent man, 30 percent zone or vice versa. Notice how four of our plays on the list come from the same formation; set these as audibles!

5 RUN DEFENSE

EXAMPLE:
4-3 Stack—Thunder Smoke

STARTING THE GAME IN YOUR RUN DEFENSE IS A GREAT WAY TO GET YOUR OPPONENT TO BECOME ONE-DIMENSIONAL.

Run defenses can be conservative or aggressive. Here we have selected a formation and play that will really ramp up the pressure. Although we will be vulnerable to the pass, the pressure should arrive before the offense can get the ball downfield. If we show blitz before the snap, we can get our players up to the line of scrimmage for the snap. Having a solid run defense to come out in on early downs is a great way to show the opponent you are ready to lock up.

4 BASE MAN

EXAMPLE:
Nickel Normal—2 Man Under

BY GOING WITH 2 MAN UNDER, YOU CAN BE PRETTY CONFIDENT YOUR COVERAGE WILL BE SOLID ACROSS THE BOARD.

If you think the opponent is getting ready to pass the ball, switching to your base man defense is a great idea. When you mix up man and zone, your opponent will always be guessing and be forced to make good reads. Man-to-man coverage means that each player on the field follows the receiver he is covering all across the field. You can see who is matched up against whom by following the line from your defender to a player on offense. If your defenders have good Man Coverage (MCV) ratings, play about 70 percent man coverage.

3 BASE ZONE

EXAMPLE:
Nickel Normal—Cover 3

COVER 4 IS A GREAT DEFENSE TO CALL WHEN YOUR OPPONENT IS ATTACKING YOU WITH THE PASS GAME AND YOU NEED TIME TO ADJUST.

A great base zone defense can force your opponent to drive slowly down the field. Zone defense works by having your players split up sections of the field. Any time an opponent runs through one of your defender's zones, your defender will play him man to man. Once your opponent leaves a zone, the defender lets him go and gets ready for another player to enter. If your team has solid Zone Coverage (ZCV) ratings, play about 70 percent zone vs. 30 percent man.

2 MAN BLITZ

EXAMPLE:
Nickel Normal—Over Storm Brave

BRINGING THE SAME BLITZER WHETHER THE PLAY IS ZONE OR MAN-TO-MAN IS A GREAT WAY TO FOOL YOUR OPPONENT!

A man-to-man blitz is a great way to force your opponent to get rid of the ball quickly or risk taking a sack. By sending lots of defenders towards the QB on situations like third and long, we can force the opponents to dump the ball off and not be able to pick up all the yards they need. While blitzing can be risky if your rushers get blocked by the offense, it is a great tactic to mix in! Sometimes the offense will keep extra blockers in if they fear you are blitzing, which means you will have extra defenders ready to stop the pass.

1 ZONE BLITZ

EXAMPLE: **Nickel Normal—Over Storm Brave 2**

ZONE BLITZES TEND TO BE SAFER THAN MAN-TO-MAN BLITZES; YOU MAY GIVE UP SHORT PASSES BUT RARELY WILL ALLOW DOWNFIELD THROWS.

Zone blitzes are the perfect combination to go along with man-to-man blitzes. One key to a great blitz is sending as few players as possible while still getting one rusher free. The longer you can wait to send your rusher towards the line of scrimmage, the better chance you have of not tipping off the offense that pressure is coming! By having a blitz ready as an audible, we can quickly adjust and bring pressure if we sense the offense is vulnerable!

TOP 5 BEGINNER TIPS

HOW TO STOP THE RUN

Stopping the run is one of the most important aspects of playing defense in *Madden NFL 25*. If you can't stop your opponent's run game, it will be hard to focus on anything else for the rest of the game. Nothing is more frustrating than an opponent who knows you can't stop the ground attack and sticks with it all game. Here are some tips to give you all the tools you need to stop the run this season!

5 BRING ON THE BEEF
4 INVERTED COVER 2
3 USER THE SAFETY
2 SET THE EDGE
1 TACKLE

5 BRING ON THE BEEF

> **FORMATIONS LIKE THE 5-2 AND 4-4 ARE GREAT TO HAVE IN YOUR PLAYBOOK AGAINST OPTION OPPONENTS.**

Making sure your best players are on the field to stop the run is crucial. Look for defensive linemen with good Strength (STR) and Block Shed (BSH) ratings. The 5-2 will add an extra defensive lineman up front, while the 4-4 will give you an extra linebacker. Look for linebackers with good Pursuit (PUR), Play Recognition (PRC), and Tackle (TAK) ratings. The quicker your computer players react to the run, the more containment you will see on the play. Have a consistent formation you feel comfortable with as your base run defense.

4 INVERTED COVER 2

> **ZONE DEFENSE IS A MORE CONSERVATIVE RUN DEFENSE. MAN-TO-MAN CAN BE RISKIER BUT MORE REWARDING.**

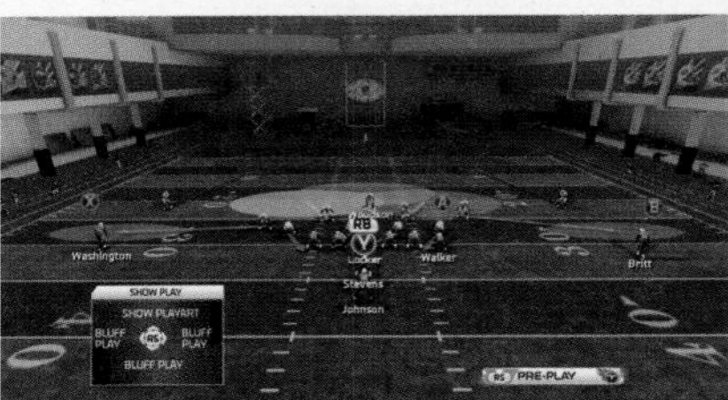

After choosing your formation, look for a Cover 3 play. Use the defensive controls to shade the safeties in. Now you are protecting the middle of the field with your safeties. Depending on where you see your opponent's strength, you can shift your line or linebackers in that direction. If your opponent is using a formation that has one TE on each side of the line, stay balanced and try spreading your linemen. The goal is to have every gap covered against the defense and not leave yourself with a weakness before the snap!

3 USER THE SAFETY

> **USER-CONTROL A LOW-RATED PLAYER WITH GOOD PHYSICAL SKILLS AND HE WILL PLAY ABOVE HIS RATING!**

You called a Cover 3 but just made it into an inverted Cover 2. You can now take control of the safety and move him down in the box. This puts eight defenders up in the box and should make your opponent think twice about running the ball. Your safety is free to roam anywhere—have him moving at the snap of the ball so he can quickly get to top speed.

2 SET THE EDGE

> **LOOK OUT FOR DOUBLE-TEAM BLOCKS BY THE OFFENSIVE LINE!**

With your safety now in motion, read the handoff. Your goal with your defender is to set the edge and not let the running back outside of your containment. The key is not to try and fight through the line with this player, but to eat a blocker, which will free up someone else to make the play. If the play is something to the outside like a toss, scrape down the line towards the sideline and try to beat the HB there. Don't be a hero—just be another player doing his job.

1 TACKLE

> **DON'T GO FOR A HIT STICK WITH A PLAYER LIKE A CB UNLESS HE HAS FULL MOMENTUM.**

If you do get to the ball, think about what type of tackle to attempt. If a blocker is between you and the ball carrier, tap the Tackle button to lunge and try to avoid the block. If it is just you and the ball carrier, hold the Tackle button and steer in cautiously while waiting for him to attempt a move. If you have teammates with you, consider going for a hit stick with the right stick. This move is risky if you miss, but since you have backup, it can be worth the chance. It can be frustrating to get in position but have your tackle get broken. Once you shut down your opponents on the first few runs, they should abandon the strategy and you can focus on the passing game. Defense is much easier when your opponent is one dimensional, and it all starts with stopping the run!

5 PUNT CAREFULLY
4 HURRY UP
3 SCRIPT YOUR FIRST 15 PLAYS
2 TAKE THE POINTS
1 MANAGE YOUR TIME-OUTS

TOP 5 GAME PLAN TIPS

Managing a game plan is very important in *Madden NFL 25*. You must develop a strategy for the upcoming game that takes into account not only your strengths and weaknesses but also your opponents'! Everything from the coin toss to team selection can mean the difference between a win and a loss. All of the small decisions that are made during a game add up and are huge factors in your success. Don't overlook any of these keys for planning to win!

5 PUNT CAREFULLY

> IF YOU DON'T GET THE LOOK YOU WANT ON FOURTH DOWN, SIMPLY CALL A TIME-OUT AND THEN PUNT. NEVER FORCE A PLAY IF YOU DON'T HAVE A GOOD FEELING.

Although punting is necessary when on your own half of the field and facing fourth and long, many gamers punt too much. Any time you get across midfield and face fewer than 7 yards to go, you should consider going for it. We also go for it in most fourth and 3 (or fewer) situations, if the results would help us put the game away. Always keep a few special quick passing plays for these situations to give the opponents a look they haven't seen. Rely on your best players in these spots and look to utilize their best ratings, such as Catch in Traffic. Some online gamers are stereotyped as "Goes on fourth and 20 from own 1-yard line and then quits," while the best players are likely to punt less often but always know when to kick. Don't let your emotions get the best of you.

4 HURRY UP

> WHEN SLOWING DOWN THE GAME WITH THE RUN, USE A BACK WITH A GOOD CARRY RATING (CAR), BECAUSE TURNOVERS ARE COSTLY.

Look to either speed up or slow down your offense to give yourself an advantage. While using hurry up (after the play, hold down Y on Xbox, ▲ on PS3), call the same play again. You can then audible when you get to the line of scrimmage.

Many gamers don't consider slowing down the pace of play and grinding down the defense with the run game. If you're playing aggressive opponents, forcing them to be patient can really frustrate them. If you feel you may be outmatched, slow the game down and look to shorten it while leveling the playing field. This will make your opponent become aggressive, and you can then try to use play action for a deep pass!

3 SCRIPT YOUR FIRST 15 PLAYS

> WHEN USING PLAY ACTION, MAKE SURE TO USE THE SAME RUN FAKE. DON'T CALL POWER O RUNS AND THEN TRY TO RUN A PLAY-ACTION FAKE WITH A STRETCH ROLLOUT. MAKE EVERYTHING LOOK THE SAME TO YOUR OPPONENT!

This is a common tactic used by real coaches every week. They plan out their first 15 plays of the game. By setting up and practicing exactly what plays you want to run, you will be ready for success. Keep a pool of around 25 possible plays and shift your game plan to take advantage of your opponent's weaknesses. If you're in an online franchise, check out the other team's statistics to see what their tendencies are before the game. Look for trends that show off their weaknesses, and then try to exploit those deficiencies.

2 TAKE THE POINTS

> THIS GOES FOR THE END OF THE HALF, TOO: DON'T FORCE AN EXTRA PLAY IF TIME IS TICKING DOWN—TAKE THE 3!

One of the toughest things to do in football is to take the emotion out of the game. Not only do we want to beat our opponents, we want to beat them convincingly. Gamers often bypass going for a field goal early in the game because they think they can easily score TDs. One of the biggest lessons learned from last season was to take the points when you get the chance. It stinks when your 12-play drive stalls out on the 3-yard line, but you are often better off getting 3 points than 0. There are multiple games from last season that would have been completely different had we kicked a simple FG. Managing the game, situation, and opponent are all factors to consider when making a big coaching call!

1 MANAGE YOUR TIME-OUTS

> IF YOU WIN THE COIN TOSS, ALWAYS *KICK*!

Some gamers feel it is great to save time-outs, but on the other hand you can't take them home with you. In the first half, we recommend using them whenever you want, but in the second half, save them to stop the clock. Early in the game, try using your time-outs any time you see something you are not ready for before the snap. Ideally, you want to have the time-outs to stop the clock, but too often they go to waste. What if your defense wasn't ready and you used a time-out to prevent a potential blown coverage! In the second half, it is extremely important to use them only in key situations. A time-out is so crucial in helping a trailing team that they become very valuable late in the game. If you can pick up first downs to stop the clock or get out of bounds while trailing, this adds to the time you have. Learning how to manage the game comes from experience and playing as many games as possible, but by staying calm and using common sense, you will be ready to win close games!

TOP 5 EXPERT TIPS

COMMONLY ASKED QUESTIONS

Over the years we have compiled feedback to help us better answer some of the most common questions that expert gamers have. By learning the answers and practicing on your game, you too can become an expert player quickly!

5 WHAT TEAM SHOULD I USE?
4 WHAT OFFENSIVE PLAYBOOK SHOULD I USE?
3 HOW DO YOU MAKE FAST OFFENSIVE AND DEFENSIVE ADJUSTMENTS?
2 HOW DO YOU MAKE DEPTH CHART DECISIONS?
1 IS OFFENSE OR DEFENSE MOST IMPORTANT?

5 WHAT TEAM SHOULD I USE?

> **SELECT THE TEAM THAT FITS YOUR PLAY STYLE. *DON'T USE LOWER-RATED TEAMS JUST TO BE DIFFERENT.***

There are two types of *Madden NFL* players: those who use their favorite team every game and those who are looking to gain a competitive edge against their opponent through team selection. If you are the latter, then we recommend you use the Seattle Seahawks or San Francisco 49ers. The 49ers have the ability to win games with their defense and run game, while Seattle has a great balance of talent all over the field. You don't gain style points by using lower-rated teams. If you feel the urge to be different, we recommend using the Green Bay Packers, as they have one of the most dangerous offenses in *Madden NFL 25*.

4 WHAT OFFENSIVE/DEFENSIVE PLAYBOOK SHOULD I USE?

> **CHECK OUT THE RUN N GUN OFFENSIVE AND 4-3 DEFENSIVE PLAYBOOKS. THEY HAVE THE MOST VARIETY OF FORMATIONS IN THE GAME.**

The Pistol playbook is new to *Madden NFL 25* and will be one of the most used playbooks this season. The overhaul to the option game will allow you to take full advantage of this playbook's strengths. Look to spread defenses out to isolate defenders into space where you can take advantage of Read Option plays in the open field. Don't forget to utilize screens in this offense. Some of the biggest plays in the game are the result of HB and WR screens.

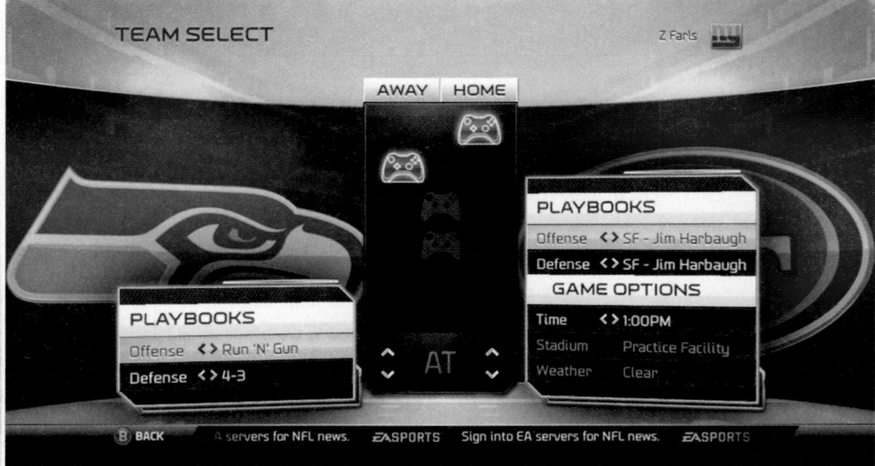

3 HOW DO I MAKE FAST OFFENSIVE AND DEFENSIVE ADJUSTMENTS?

CONTINUE PLAYING

Practice and more

FAIL 1,000 TIMES SO THAT ON ATTEMPT 1,001 YOU NAIL IT.

Practice and time will help you develop faster adjustments. When we give you adjustments to make to enhance your play-calling, it's something you should be practicing every time you load up the game. Head into practice mode and use two controllers so you can work on both offensive and defensive setups. In as little as five minutes you can feel confident with setups for one play. Don't make the mistake of reading the setups and then heading directly into a game.

2 HOW DO I MAKE DEPTH CHART DECISIONS?

SKILLS

Overall	93
Speed	69
Agility	69
Awareness	89
Throw Power	98
Short Acc	89
Mid Acc	87
Deep Acc	82

KEY IN ON SPECIFIC RATINGS. THIS WILL HELP YOU FORM AN IDENTITY ON BOTH SIDES OF THE BALL.

Making key depth chart decisions is all about what type of football you want your team to play. First decide if you are going to be a run first, pass first, or balanced offense. Next determine if your defense will be built to stop the run or the pass. Once you make these key decisions you can then fall back on what your team's identity is. When you are deciding between the 6'5" WR with a 70 Overall rating or the 6'4" TE at 74 Overall, it will be easier to choose based on what style of offense you selected. Pick the 6'5" WR for passing offenses and pick the 6'4" TE for rushing offenses. It's also important to look for key ratings when making depth chart moves. On offense look for things like Catch in Traffic for WRs and TEs. On defense focus on ratings like Hit Power and Block Shed. If you see someone with a high rating in these categories you should get them on the field.

1 IS OFFENSE OR DEFENSE MOST IMPORTANT?

DEFENSE WINS CHAMPIONSHIPS.

Without a doubt, defense is the most important side of the ball. Everyone can score points, but not everyone can lock up on defense. Spend the first few days of the season working on your offense and then the rest of the season focusing on defense. The best players each year have the best defense. This isn't a debatable topic. If you want to be an elite player you need to have lockdown defense.

TOP 5 EXPERT TIPS

TOP 5 OFFENSIVE FORMATIONS

Each year new formations are added to the series, and each year we spend countless hours testing out the most effective ones. Here are the best.

5 I-FORM HULK
4 PISTOL FULL HOUSE TE
3 GUN SPLIT PANTHER
2 GUN BUNCH HB STR
1 GUN WING TRIPS OFFSET

5 I-FORM HULK

I Form | Hulk | 2 RB 2 TE 0 WR

TE - LG - C - RG - RT - RT - LT - TE
QB
FB
HB

THIS FORMATION CAN BE FOUND IN THE COLTS PLAYBOOK.

The I-Form Hulk is new to *Madden NFL 25* and will be one of the most used run formations this season. This formation is all about pounding the rock and letting your opponent know it in advance. The formation is loaded to the right side of the field with two extra offensive tackles, which makes it extremely difficult for defenses to defend. If you are serious about running the ball then you want to use this formation. Mix in play action, which will be an effective tactic because defenses will anticipate run when they see the I-Form Hulk.

4 PISTOL FULL HOUSE TE

THIS FORMATION CAN BE FOUND IN THE 49ERS OFFENSIVE PLAYBOOK.

The Full House TE is a great formation for running an option-style offense. The compressed nature of the formation allows our offense to pick up key blocks in the run game. Defenders tend to not like tight spaces, as it can cause confusion and traffic when looking to chase after ball carriers. This is a great formation to use with custom playbooks because it's not entirely reliant on the QB's speed to be effective. We recommend trying some option plays out of this formation. This will make defenses guard the middle, leaving the edges wide open for our skill players.

3 GUN SPLIT PANTHER

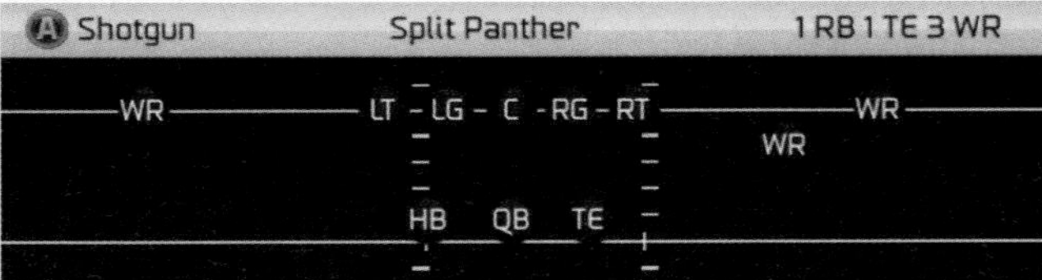

THIS FORMATION CAN BE FOUND IN CAROLINA'S OFFENSIVE PLAYBOOK.

Pass protection is important in *Madden NFL 25*. That is why we love this formation so much. We can pick up defensive blitzes from any point on the field. This formation also has one of the best QB runs in the entire game, the QB Wrap. Look to utilize the QB Wrap with mobile QBs to take full advantage of this formation.

2 GUN BUNCH HB STR

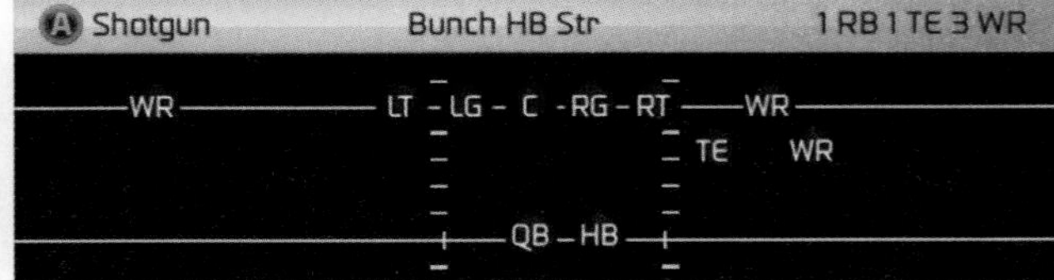

THIS FORMATION CAN BE FOUND IN THE 49ERS PLAYBOOK.

The Shotgun Bunch HB Str is a unique formation because it has four offensive players split to the right of the QB. This makes defenses extremely vulnerable to various offensive tactics. If we want to attack man-to-man the defense has to show their hand by over-aligning their defense to defend properly against the formation. If we want to attack zone the defense typically won't have enough zone defenders to cover all four offensive options as the play develops. That is why this is our second favorite formation in the game.

1 GUN WING TRIPS OFFSET

THIS FORMATION CAN BE FOUND IN THE EAGLES PLAYBOOK.

If you are looking to run the ball all over your opponent from the shotgun formation, then you'd better look to the Eagles playbook in *Madden NFL 25*. The Gun Wing Trips Offset is without a doubt the best formation in this year's game. By lining up our players offset, we have a huge advantage in the run game for a few reasons. First, the lead blockers pick up most blitzes and push to the linebacker level to create holes. Second, the shotgun run gives us more time as a user player to read running lanes. Expect to see a lot of this formation online this season!

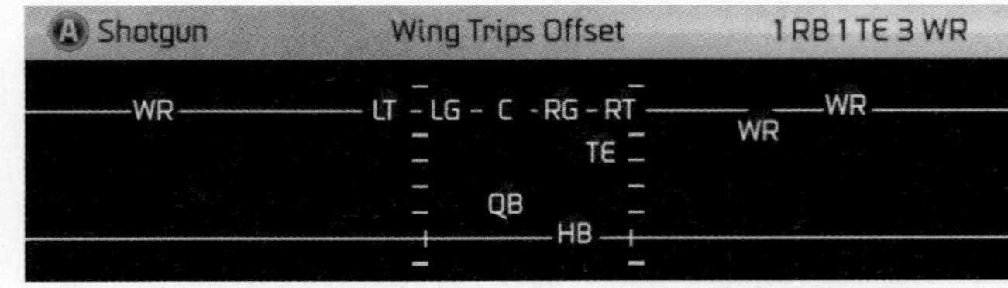

5 4-3 OVER PLUS
4 DOLLAR 3-2-6
3 4-4 SPLIT
2 4-3 STACK
1 NICKEL 3-3-5

HONORABLE MENTION:
NICKEL 1-5-5
PROWL, 5-2
NORMAL

EXPERT TIPS TOP 5

DEFENSIVE FORMATIONS

Defense wins championships, and in this Top 5 list we show you the formations that you need to use in *Madden NFL 25* to start winning more online. You must be able to stop the run, play lockdown coverage, and bring pressure that bursts pipes, and that's exactly what we show you.

5 4-3 OVER PLUS

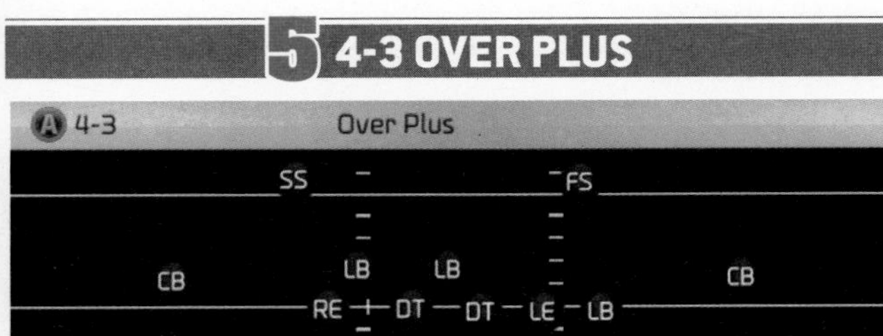

THIS FORMATION CAN BE FOUND IN THE 4-3 DEFENSIVE PLAYBOOK.

The 4-3 Over Plus can be an intimidating formation to run against. This is a great way to play an aggressive defense that will force your opponent to start throwing. If you are looking to play a more laid-back defense then we recommend using the 4-3 Under formation, as it will allow you to play a lot of soft zone coverages. This defensive mind-set is all about forcing your opponent to make the first mistake.

4 DOLLAR 3-2-6

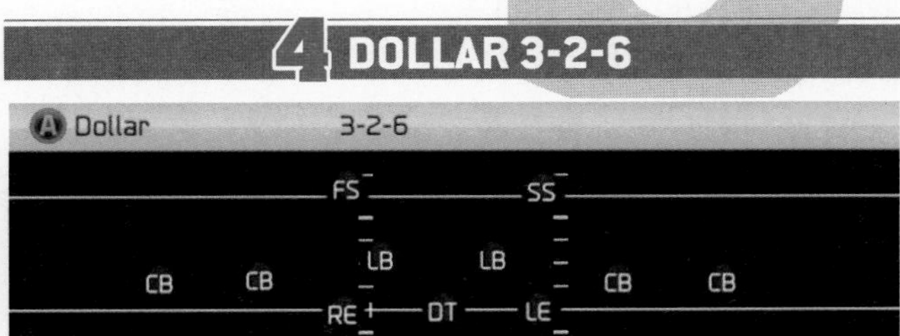

THIS FORMATION CAN BE FOUND IN THE 4-3 DEFENSIVE PLAYBOOK.

We love the personnel that the Dollar 3-2-6 brings to the field. It has three big defensive linemen, two agile linebackers, and five cover secondary players on the field. This formation is designed to be used all game and to stop whatever formation your opponent might use offensively. If you are facing a faster team consider subbing in linebackers at DE. If you are facing a running team consider putting DTs at DE.

3 4-4 SPLIT

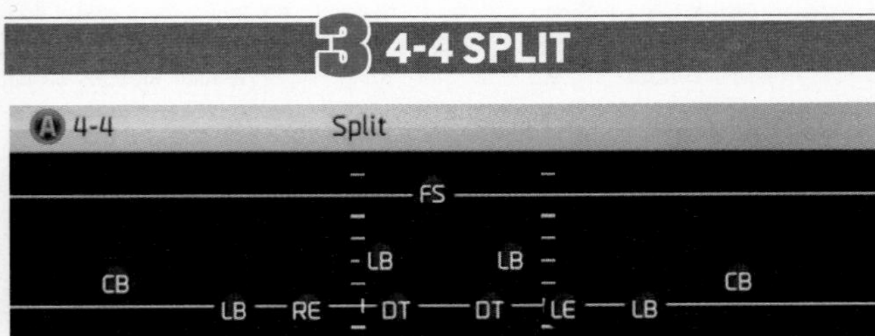

THIS FORMATION CAN BE FOUND IN THE 4-3 DEFENSIVE PLAYBOOK.

The 4-4 Split is the ultimate formation if your team has a lot of depth at linebacker. This formation makes a return to *Madden NFL 25* and should help to combat the read option game. We like this formation so much because it places so many defenders in the box, which makes it difficult for offenses to run the ball. However, if you don't have the correct personnel you will struggle to stop both the run and the pass. The 4-4 Split is an advanced defense that is used by the best players in the country.

2 4-3 STACK

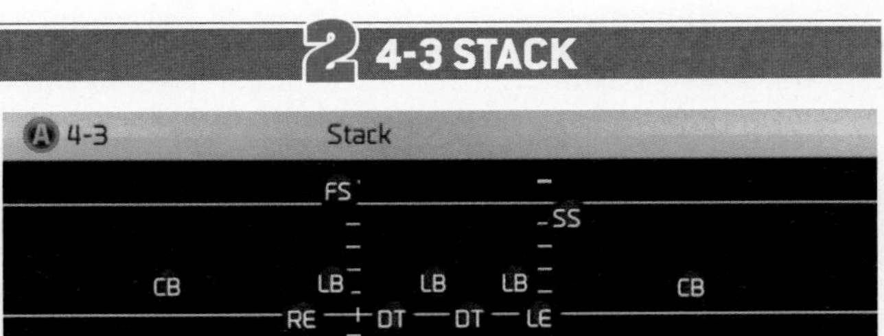

THIS FORMATION CAN BE FOUND IN THE 4-3 DEFENSIVE PLAYBOOK.

Our favorite formation to bring pressure from is the 4-3 Stack. We like this formation because we can bring pressure easily by using global linebacker commands. This is a huge reason why this is the most used formation by professional tournament players. You are also able to bring pressure from multiple looks, which is vital to the success of blitzing. If you are serious about improving your defense you will learn more about how to dominate defensively with the 4-3 Stack. For more information on how to use the 4-3 Stack, please visit www.MaddenTips.com.

1 NICKEL 3-3-5

THIS FORMATION CAN BE FOUND IN THE 4-3 DEFENSIVE PLAYBOOK.

Defensively, 2 Man Under is the best base coverage in the game. The best specific 2 Man Under play in the game is from the Nickel 3-3-5. The blitzing ROLB has a unique blitzing angle that gives him a boost at the snap of the ball. This one blitz angle allows us to put extra pressure on opposing QBs without altering the coverage on the field. Typically, we like to user-control the MLB who is covering the HB on this play to enhance coverage over the middle of the field. Change up between 2 Man Under and zone coverages so your opponent can't key in on coverage tendencies.

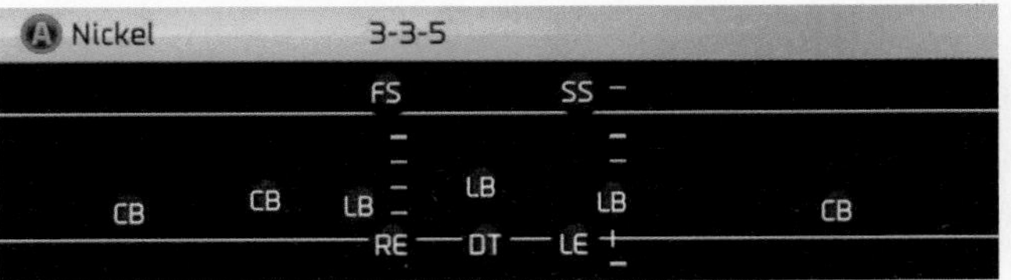

TOP 5 EXPERT TIPS

OPTION REQUIREMENTS

One of the best ways to move the ball offensively in *Madden NFL 25* is via the read option game. Here we showcase how to run a devastatingly effective option offense.

5 QB WITH 80 SPEED
4 BETTER BLOCKING WRS AND TES
3 VERTICAL THREAT WR
2 SPEED AND POWER IN THE BACKFIELD
1 PATIENCE

5 QB WITH 80 SPEED

> WE RECOMMEND AN 80 SPEED RATING FOR YOUR QB. YOU CAN GET BY WITH 75 SPEED BUT SHOULD GO NO LOWER THAN 70.

We have run the option in *Madden NFL 25* for hours and have determined that to run the option at its full potential your QB should have an 80 Speed rating. This is the threshold that allows your QB to break long runs down the sideline and create enough separation from defenders that you can expect to pick up big gains on the ground. This doesn't mean you can't run the option with slower QBs. It does mean that you should expect to gain minimal yards.

4 BETTER BLOCKING WRS AND TES

> THE IMPACT BLOCK RATING (IBL) IS WHAT DETERMINES THE BIG BLOCKS DOWNFIELD.

If you are pushing all in on running an option offense you need to sub in blocking WRs and TEs. This means that you will be sitting your better receiving options in favor of gaining an advantage in the run game. This isn't always the sexy move, because it will be hard to sit your star players, but it's a move that will benefit your option offense in the long run. We tend to focus more on the IBL rating than any other as it's the best indicator of whether or not we will see our blocker pancake the defender. Don't worry—number three on our list will satisfy your passing needs in this offense.

3 VERTICAL THREAT WR

> LOOK FOR SPEED AND HEIGHT WHEN TARGETING A VERTICAL THREAT WR.

While we recommend that you sub in WRs and TEs with better blocking skills, we also believe that *one* of your wide receivers should be a vertical threat to opposing defenses. We always want your opponents to worry about the deep ball so that they can't load up the box to try and stop the option. Speed WRs should have at least a 95 Speed rating, and when looking for height you should target 6'2" and taller. Any combination of the two should work for your offense. This means that a 97 Speed 5'8" WR will be effective and that an 88 Speed 6'4" WR will be effective. Make sure that you have an option you can target downfield on every play.

2 SPEED AND POWER IN THE BACKFIELD

> WANT TO TURN UP THE HEAT ON YOUR OPPONENT? USE TWO SPEEDY HBS IN YOUR BACKFIELD.

If you are running a read option-style offense then you want to use a speedy HB. A fast HB should have a 92 Speed rating, and a power HB should have a 90-plus Truck rating. This puts your HBs in the best position possible. When the DE crashes down on your HB, keep the ball with your QB. If the DE stands up to protect against the QB scramble be sure to give the ball to your power HB, so that he can fight through the line of scrimmage for tough yards.

1 PATIENCE

> NEVER FORCE THE OPTION. TAKE WHAT THE DEFENSE GIVES YOU.

The most important rule to understand when running the option is to always take what the defense gives you. If you do otherwise you will not be successful when running this offense. This might be frustrating if you are looking to scramble with your QB, but your opponent always takes that option away. You need to have the patience to be repetitive with your decisions so that you can have long-term success. When running the option it's often the first person to lose patience who is defeated. If the key DE stands up, always give the ball to your HB. If the key DE attacks the QB, then always keep the ball with the QB and look to pitch it to your HB. The option is simple and can be very effective as long as you have patience.

5 CALL ENGAGE EIGHT
4 USER-DEFEND AND COMMIT
3 SEND SIX DEFENDERS
2 COMMIT TO HB
1 COMMIT TO QB

EXPERT TIPS TOP 5

WAYS TO DEFEND THE OPTION

The option is quickly becoming one of the most popular ways to move the ball in *Madden NFL 25*. We've shown you how to run the option, and in this section we show you how to stop it.

5 ENGAGE EIGHT

ENGAGE EIGHT FROM ANY FORMATION WILL BE EFFECTIVE, BUT WE RECOMMEND IT FROM THE 4-4 OR 4-3.

This is an extremely high-risk, high-reward defense. If you are looking to stop your opponent completely, then calling Engage Eight will do the trick. Expect to get beaten by any type of pass if your opponent expects it's coming. We wanted to give you this option not as an every-down defense against the option, but as a last-ditch effort in stopping it. If you are in a pinch use this play.

4 USER-DEFEND AND COMMIT

DON'T JUST SIT BACK AND HOPE TO STOP THE OPTION. ATTACK IT.

User-defending and committing towards the option means to grab hold of the MLB or a deep safety and to attack the QB from the play side. This can be tricky because you have to dodge blockers to make a play on the QB. User-control ability is extremely important here, so make sure that you only attempt this if you are confident with yours. Remember that if your opponent throws a play action towards you that you must recover back into your coverage assignment.

3 SEND SIX DEFENDERS

SENDING SIX DEFENDERS IS MORE CONSERVATIVE THAN CALLING ENGAGE EIGHT BUT IS AGGRESSIVE ENOUGH TO DISRUPT THE OPTION.

This can be done from any formation and any play in the game. The only rule is to make sure you send six defenders, excluding your user defender. You will want to clean up with your user defender and try to make a play on the ball carrier. Sit back and let your opponent decide who to give the ball to and then attack. Don't commit too early, as you will take yourself out of the play by getting picked up by blockers.

2 COMMIT TO HB

THIS MEANS THAT YOU ARE FORCING THE QB TO KEEP THE BALL.

If you are facing a team with a QB you don't fear, then it's a good idea to use your pre-snap tools to select Commit to HB. This means that your defense will always give your opponent the option to run with the QB, but it will take away the option to hand off to the HB. Decide early in the game what your game plan is and consider changing it throughout the game so that your opponent doesn't get comfortable with the same read. The indicator for this will be your DE crashing in towards the snap of the ball.

1 COMMIT TO QB

THIS MEANS THAT YOU ARE FORCING THE HB TO TAKE THE BALL.

A general rule of thumb when facing the option in *Madden NFL 25* is that your opponent wants to run the ball with the QB. Don't allow it. Using your pre-snap adjustments, select Commit to QB, which will make your defense always contain the QB. Your indicator for this will be your DE standing up at the snap of the ball. If your opponent keeps the ball with the QB he will get crushed by the DE. This forces the handoff to the HB, and we can anticipate making a play on the ball carrier in the open field. Over the course of time this is without a doubt the best way to not only stop the option, but also to frustrate your opponents because they won't be able to do what they want to when running the option.

TOP 5 EXPERT TIPS

5 WAYS TO USE PRACTICE MODE

Practice is where champions are born. Spend 10 minutes in practice every time you turn *Madden NFL* on and your game will improve drastically. Here we go over the five most important things you should be doing with those 10 minutes.

5 RED ZONE EFFICIENCY
4 ROUTE TIMING
3 ADJUSTMENTS
2 DEPTH CHART
1 EXPERIMENTS

HONORABLE MENTION: **TEST TEAMS AND PLAYBOOKS**

5 RED ZONE EFFICIENCY

ON OFFENSE THE RED ZONE IS THE AREA BETWEEN YOUR OPPONENT'S GOAL LINE AND 20-YARD LINE. ON DEFENSE THE RED ZONE IS THE AREA BETWEEN YOUR GOAL LINE AND THE 20-YARD LINE.

Learning to score in the red zone will lead not only to more points on the scoreboard, but also to overall success in other areas of the field. As you approach the red zone the amount of field you have to operate in shrinks. So most of your favorite plays become ineffective. In the red zone it's important to attack the field horizontally, or from sideline to sideline, in order to move the ball. Windows become tighter and decisions need to be quicker. Spend most of your time in practice mode finding plays you have success with. You win games by scoring in the red zone.

4 ROUTE TIMING

TIMING IS ONE OF THE MOST OVERLOOKED FACTORS IN THE PASSING GAME.

When we use practice mode we tend to be repetitive with how we use our time. First, we start by calling any passing play and picking Cover 3 zone. We then make every available hot route to each receiver in succession. The goal here is to learn when to throw the ball against specific defenses. We repeat this against all defensive coverages so that over the course of time we will know when to throw specific routes against any defense we face. This is something that needs to be done for every route in the game. The absolute worst thing you can do is run a route in-game that you have never thrown before. If you do, you'd better be a wrap-up tackler.

3 ADJUSTMENTS

IF YOU ARE THINKING ABOUT MAKING ADJUSTMENTS THEN YOU ARE ALREADY BEATEN.

You should never have to think about making adjustments in *Madden NFL 25*; they should just happen. This means that you should be spending time in practice mode working on all the adjustments you have for every play that you typically call. This causes a chain reaction in your play-call system, which will become automated to the point where the only thing you are thinking about is how you can score more points. Make sure that you never question how to hot route a slant or any other available adjustment option.

2 DEPTH CHART

THE BEST PLACE TO LEARN YOUR TEAM'S DEPTH CHART IS IN PRACTICE MODE.

What we love about practice mode is that if you spend enough time there you will learn your team's roster up and down its depth chart. When you play games you rarely play the lower-rated players on your team, and this is a big-time mistake. Often you can find hidden gems on your bench. Scan your team's depth chart and look for players who are good at specific things. Maybe you have an HB on your bench who has a great Carry rating, or maybe you have an MLB who has an elite Hit Power rating. The more time you spend in practice mode the more you will know about your team's entire roster.

1 EXPERIMENTS

TEST. EVERYTHING.

Use practice mode as if it's your own personal laboratory. Anything and everything goes. Want to see how a kicker will do at QB? Test it. Maybe you want to know if your DT can effectively play lockdown coverage at CB in goal line situations. Whatever you can think up in your head you should try in practice mode. The more things you test the better prepared you will be for game situations. Practice mode is also great for experimenting against conventional wisdom. For example, people might say that speed is the only thing that matters for vertical passing plays. I beg to differ; acceleration is just as important as speed because it allows your receiver the burst he needs to get past the defender. The only way to find out is to test this in practice mode. Test anything and everything.

5 COVER 4 ZONE
4 COVER 3 ZONE
3 COVER 2 ZONE
2 2 MAN UNDER
1 BLITZING DEFENSE

WAYS TO READ DEFENSIVE COVERAGES

One of the hardest things to do in football is read what the defense is doing. In this section we show you exactly how to determine what type of coverage the defense is playing.

5 COVER 4 ZONE

Cover 4 zone's strength is defending the deep halves of the field. Cover 4's weakness is defending the flat and short middle.

When facing a Cover 4 zone you will see that the safeties are split deep across the top of the screen. You will also see both CBs playing off coverage. This is your indicator that the defense is in a Cover 4 zone. Look to attack the flats and the short middle of the field. Don't target downfield receivers because you will be throwing into the strength of the defense.

4 COVER 3 ZONE

Cover 3 zone's strength is being able to play the run and pass equally. Cover 3 zone's weakness is defending the seams and corner sideline routes.

A standard defense for most teams is the Cover 3 zone. It can defend the run and pass and has solid coverage at all parts of the field. The defense breaks down as plays develop and can be attacked in the seams of the field as well with corner routes to the sideline. Cover 3 zone is one of the most popular defenses in the game, so expect to see it a lot.

3 COVER 2 ZONE

Cover 2 zone's strength is defending the flat and short middle. Cover 2 zone's weakness is defending against vertical passing concepts.

When facing Cover 2 zone you will see both safeties split deep across the top of the screen. The CBs will be showing press coverage. This is your indicator that the defense could be in a Cover 2 zone. After the snap of the ball, read the outside CBs. If they press the WRs and let them release then you know the defense is in a Cover 2 zone. Anticipate Cover 2 zone in the red zone as well in short-yardage situations. The best players online use Cover 2 zone as a base to blitz from, so be ready to get the ball out quickly.

2 2 MAN UNDER

The strength of 2 Man Under is to be able to take away the offense's best player. Its weakness is against screens and mobile QBs.

The best defenses each season are directly related to being able to play effective man-to-man defense. When facing 2 Man Under you will see the safeties split deep across the top of the screen. The CBs show press coverage. This is your indicator that the defense could be in 2 Man Under coverage. This look is similar to Cover 2 zone, so be sharp with your post-snap reads.

1 BLITZING DEFENSES

The strength of a blitzing defense is that it puts pressure on offenses and forces mistakes. The weakness of a blitzing defense is that it has poor coverage and relies heavily on poor decisions by the QB.

We can't always tell when our opponent is blitzing, but the best available tell is to key in on the deep safeties. If they appear to be out of position from the typical Cover 4 zone, 2 Man Under, etc., then you should anticipate some type of blitz. Note if defenders appear to be out of position on each play, and if they are make sure to get the ball out quickly.

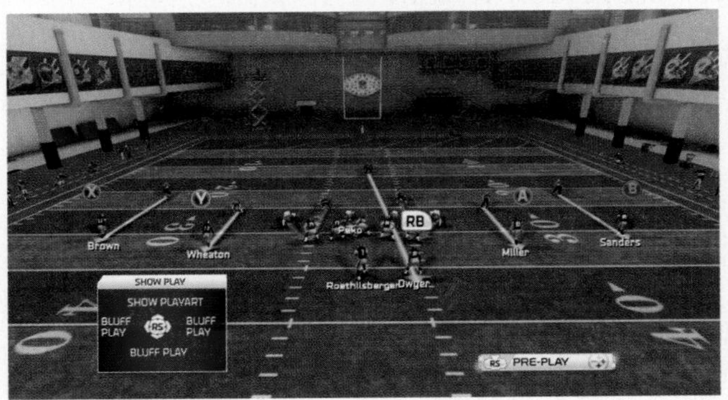

TOP 5 EXPERT TIPS

5 WAYS TO STOP SCRAMBLING QBS

Sooner or later you will come across an opponent who likes to run around with the QB. This can be the worst thing that has ever happened to you, but with this section we show you exactly how to prevent the QB scramble on passing plays.

5 ZONE COVERAGE
4 MAN QB SPY COVERAGE
3 PRESSURE OFF THE EDGE
2 CB BLITZES
1 CONTAIN DEFENSIVE ENDS

HONORABLE MENTION: **MAX COVERAGE DEFENSE WITH QB SPIES**

5 ZONE COVERAGE

> ZONE COVERAGE TYPICALLY KEEPS YOUR DEFENDERS SQUARED UP TO THE LINE OF SCRIMMAGE, WHICH ALLOWS YOUR DEFENDERS TO ATTACK THE QB IF HE SCRAMBLES.

Picking any zone play is a good idea if you don't want to get too advanced with your defensive setups to stop scrambling QBs. Man-to-man defenses force defenders to trail offensive players as they cover them all around the field. This results in defenders turning their backs to the line of scrimmage and losing sight of the scrambling QB. Playing zone coverage ensures that your defenders never lose their line of sight to the QB, which means faster reactions to the QB who likes to scramble.

4 MAN QB SPY COVERAGE

> THERE ARE A TON OF MAN QB SPY PLAYS IN *MADDEN NFL 25*, IN MULTIPLE FORMATIONS. NO ADJUSTMENTS ARE REQUIRED.

We like using Man QB Spy coverage as the quickest way to spy the QB. The play already has a QB spy built into the coverage, so no adjustments are required. Call the play and you are ready to go. If your opponent is skilled, the QB might be able to shake the QB spy defender, so be cautious with your user defender and be ready to chase down the QB if needed. Consider adding a second spy if the QB escapes a few times!

3 PRESSURE OFF THE EDGE

> DIME DB BLITZ AND DB BLITZ 2 ARE THE BEST PLAYS IN THE GAME TO PRESSURE SCRAMBLING QBS OFF THE EDGE.

Pressure off the edge will prevent scrambling QBs from getting outside of the pass rush and force them back into the interior of the offensive line. This is exactly what we want to happen, as it's extremely difficult to maneuver into space here. The only weakness to this style of defense is if your opponent recognizes the blitz and passes the ball quickly instead of scrambling with his QB. Mix up your play calling and you will have major success with this tip. Try to bring the pressure from the side of the QB's throwing arm, as he won't be able to throw as well if he is rolling to his weak side.

2 CB BLITZES

> SENDING A CB BLITZ IS NOT AN EVERY-DOWN DEFENSE TO STOP SCRAMBLING QBS, BUT IT IS A LOCKDOWN DEFENSE WHEN NEEDED.

What makes CB Blitzes difficult for scrambling QBs is that they can't always see the pressure because usually their vision is directed toward the line of scrimmage and middle of the field. Often, at the snap of the ball the QB will see open running lanes outside and will immediately be sacked by our blitzing corners. Deception is the CB Blitz's biggest strength. *Do not call this defense* for anything other than stopping opponents who scramble with their QBs.

1 CONTAIN YOUR DES

> WORK ON ADJUSTING THE CONTAINS FOR YOUR LINEMEN QUICKLY, FOR EXTRA COVERAGE, HOT ROUTE YOUR MLB TO A QB SPY.

This is our number one tip for stopping scrambling QBs, because it can be called upon from any play and any formation in the game and will absolutely prevent your opponent from scrambling with the QB. This defense will get beaten by HB draws and will also struggle to get pressure on pocket QBs, but you will track down the QB!

5 MAX COVERAGE DEFENSE
4 USER-CONTROL
3 HOT ROUTE DES INTO MAN-TO-MAN COVERAGE
2 MANUALLY PRESS
1 MAN ALIGN TWICE

HONORABLE MENTION: **USING TIPS 1–5 TOGETHER**

EXPERT TIPS TOP 5

WAYS TO DEFEND TIGHT ENDS

How many times have you been beaten by an opponent who snapped the ball and immediately threw to the TE for an easy completion? That won't be a problem for you anymore.

5 MAX COVERAGE DEFENSE

> MAX COVERAGE DEFENSE WILL GENERATE VERY LITTLE PASS RUSH AND ALLOW EASY YARDS VIA HB DRAWS AND QB SCRAMBLES.

Call any play in the game and hot route both DEs into hook zones. Also, hot route one DT to a QB spy. This defense will force any throw over the middle of the field into tight coverage. This is especially effective against opponents who enjoy throwing quickly to TEs directly over the middle of the field.

4 USER CONTROL

> USER-CONTROL IS ALWAYS THE BEST ANSWER FOR STOPPING ANYTHING IN *MADDEN NFL 25!*

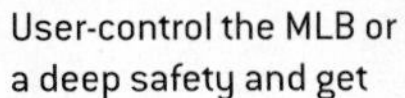

User-control the MLB or a deep safety and get him in position directly where your opponent is throwing. At the snap of the ball, stay in place and wait for the throw. With this tactic we are forcing your opponent to either throw the ball directly at your user defender or to wait and make another read. You won't always make the play, but the fact that you have a defender in the exact area where the QB wants to throw the ball should be enough to slow down TEs over the middle.

3 HOT ROUTE DES INTO MAN-TO-MAN COVERAGE

> THE SETUP FOR THIS WILL TAKE SOME PRACTICE. SPEND THE TIME LEARNING THE BUTTONS.

We love to hot route our DEs into man-to-man coverage against TEs, especially if we are already playing man-to-man coverage, because we will have inside-out coverage. At the snap of the ball your opponent will see the TE blanketed by two defenders. There will be absolutely no place to throw the ball. The biggest issue we see with this is the actual setup. You must get the button presses down before you attempt this in-game.

2 MANUALLY PRESS

> TES WON'T TYPICALLY GET PRESSED UNLESS WE DO IT MANUALLY. THIS IS A BIG-TIME TIP THAT MOST PLAYERS WON'T BE DOING.

Before the ball is snapped, user-control the MLB or deep safety and position him directly in front of the TE you want to manually press. At the snap of the ball hold down RB (Xbox) or R1 (PS3) to activate the press on the TE. This should shock your opponent as this is out of the ordinary. Be sure to manually cover the TE as he continues on his route.

1 MAN ALIGN TWICE

> THIS IS ONE OF THE MOST ADVANCED DEFENSIVE TIPS IN *MADDEN NFL 25*.

This tip is primarily used when calling zone defensive coverage. We like to call Cover 4 zone from the Dollar formation. We then hot route both DEs into hook zones and then man align the defense twice. This rebalances the hook zones on the field to defend the field equally. This type of coverage is an absolute nightmare for opponents who target TEs.

TOP 5 EXPERT TIPS

5 WAYS TO DEFEND SCREEN PASSES

5 COVER 2 ZONE
4 HOT ROUTE THE DE TO QB CONTAIN
3 USER-DEFEND
2 MAN AND ZONE COMBINATION DEFENSE
1 ALL OF THE ABOVE

HONORABLE MENTION: **BLITZ**

Screen passes are always a popular way to move the ball. The threat of a TD on nearly any play is the draw for screens. In this section we show you how we like to stop screen plays in *Madden NFL 25*. Remember, if you rush the QB and instantly get in, it is probably too good to be true—look out for the screen!

5 COVER 2 ZONE

Cover 2 zone places a flat defender in the area that most screens attack.

The most popular screens are the FL Screen and HB Slip Screen. Both of these plays target the flat, so we look to clog this space with one of our defenders. It's about a 50/50 split on whether the defender will get picked by a blocker or if our defender will shed the block and take down the ball carrier.

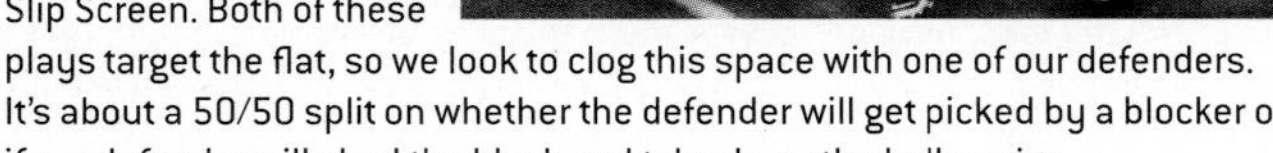

4 HOT ROUTE THE DE TO QB CONTAIN

If you don't want to play zone coverage then you can play man-to-man and drop a DE into a QB contain. The QB contain will slow things down.

We like QB contains over flat zones because the QB contain player will actually make a play on the ball. Many times this adjustment results in a batted down pass or an interception. Nothing is better than making this adjustment and having it result in 6.

3 USER-DEFEND

High risk, high reward.

User-defending screens can be extremely rewarding, but it can also result in big plays for your opponent. At the snap of the ball you need to read that the screen is happening. Take control of your user defender and scrape through the pulling blockers. If you are quick you can beat them to the point of attack and take down the ball carrier before he can move upfield. The issue with this is that it can be difficult to get by the blockers. If you get taken out of the play there is potential for a big play by your opponent.

2 MAN AND ZONE COMBINATION DEFENSE

Playing a man and zone combination can result in confusion and big plays for your defense.

This defense requires two rules. Rule #1 is to always have a defender playing man-to-man on the screen player. Rule #2 is to always have a defender playing a flat zone on the screen side. Come up with any combination of defenses, but stick to those two rules and you will have great success stopping any screen in the game.

1 ALL OF THE ABOVE

The perfect scenario for stopping screens would be to use Dollar 3-2-6—Cover 2 zone and make all the other adjustments.

Say your opponent is beating you with an HB Slip Screen. We would recommend the following: Call Dollar 3-2-6—Cover 2 zone. Hot route one of your LBs to man coverage on the HB. Hot route your DE to a QB contain. There is no way the HB Slip Screen will gain yards with this coverage. This is absolute lockdown defense.

5 DOUBLE-TEAM
4 PRESS COVERAGE
3 DOUBLE QB SPIES
2 BRACKET COVERAGE (VERTICAL)
1 BRACKET COVERAGE (HORIZONTAL)

HONORABLE MENTION: **MAX COVERAGE DEFENSE**

EXPERT TIPS TOP 5

5 WAYS TO STOP SLOT WRS

Slot WRs like Wes Welker and Randall Cobb are the movable chess pieces that are key to the success of most offenses. We show you what to expect and how to slow them down in *Madden NFL 25*!

5 DOUBLE-TEAM

> PLACE YOUR TWO BEST COVER CBS ON THE SLOT WR AND HE WON'T BE A FACTOR.

To slow down a slot WR we like to simply call any man-to-man play in the game and then hot route one of our safeties or DEs to double-cover the intended WR. This prevents any gain after the catch and will force your opponent to look elsewhere for big plays. If you have the skill, try user-controlling the extra defender instead of placing him in man-to-man coverage.

4 PRESS COVERAGE

> EVERY 2 MAN UNDER PLAY IN THE GAME WILL HAVE AUTOMATIC PRESS COVERAGE.

Pick any man-to-man play in the game and use your coverage audible to call press coverage. This will press the slot WR at the line of scrimmage and slow down his route. The timing will be off between him and the QB, which can result in mistakes and big plays for your defense. Make sure to check your slot CB's Press (PRS) rating against the slot WR's Release (RLS) rating to see who has the advantage.

3 DOUBLE QB SPIES

> THIS IS VERY UNCONVENTIONAL BUT VERY EFFECTIVE.

Slot WRs are usually most effective over the middle of the field. We have found that hot routing two defenders into QB spies will do an amazing job of stopping routes over the short middle of the field. When two QB spies are on the field they split the middle of the field and follow the eyes of the QB. The result is two players defending the exact spot on the field that is most effective for slot WRs.

2 BRACKET COVERAGE (VERTICAL)

> EXPECTING DOWNFIELD ROUTES? USE THIS TYPE OF COVERAGE.

Vertical bracket coverage is when your defense has two defenders splitting the slot WR, with one trailing him and one leading him. An example of this would be to have one defender play man-to-man press coverage and then to hot route another defender to play a deep zone over the top of the slot WR. This is a great way to prevent any big play downfield.

1 BRACKET COVERAGE (HORIZONTAL)

> EXPECTING SIDELINE-TO-SIDELINE ROUTES? USE THIS COVERAGE.

Horizontal bracket coverage is when your defense has two defenders splitting the slot WR, with one trailing him and one between him and the sideline. An example of this would be to have one defender play man-to-man press coverage and then to hot route another defender to play any combination of a hook zone, buzz zone, or flat zone. If you anticipate a corner pattern you would want to hot route the extra defender to a buzz zone. If you are looking for a route over the middle of the field then hot route him to a hook zone.

TOP 5 EXPERT TIPS

WAYS TO DEFEND THE RED ZONE

To win consistently in *Madden NFL 25* you must defend the red zone. In this section we show you high-pressure defense as well as blanket coverage.

5 COVER 2 WITH ADJUSTMENTS
4 5-2 MONSTER (RUN DEFENSE)
3 TAKE AWAY THE #1 OPTION
2 MAX COVERAGE DEFENSE
1 COVER 0

HONORABLE MENTION: **GOAL LINE FORMATION**

5 COVER 2 ZONE WITH ADJUSTMENTS

> THE FLAT IS TYPICALLY WHERE THE OFFENSE FIRST LOOKS IN THE RED ZONE.

Defending in the red zone should be easy because the offense has less space to work with, but often it's the hardest area to defend. We like to call any Cover 2 zone and then hot route both safeties to buzz zones. Next, we user-control the MLB and look to take away the middle of the field. At the snap of the ball our flat defenders press the outside WRs and look to take away any flat pattern. If the offense runs a curl-to-flat pattern our buzz zones will be in position to make a play on the ball. Last, we will patrol the middle of the field with our MLB to take away anything that comes our way.

4 5-2 MONSTER (RUN DEFENSE)

> THIS IS A VERY SPECIFIC DEFENSE FOR RUNNING SITUATIONS IN THE RED ZONE.

The 5-2 Monster defense was one of the most popular defensive schemes for multiple decades in professional football. The idea behind it is to give the illusion to the offense that they can attack the weak side of our defense. We set this up by calling 5-2 Normal Cover 3, shifting the LBs right, and then user-controlling the FS over the DE on the left of the screen. If the offense looks to run to the strong side of the formation there will be too many defenders and they will most likely lose yards. They will then look to run to the weak side, towards your user defender, where we will still have the advantage in run support but give the illusion that we don't. If you are looking to stop the run in the red zone, this is a must-have defense.

3 TAKE AWAY THE #1 OPTION

> AT ALL COSTS TAKE AWAY YOUR OPPONENT'S PRIMARY OPTION. NO EXCEPTIONS.

If taking away the number one option means putting three defenders on one offensive player, by all means put three defenders on him. Make your opponents feel uncomfortable in the red zone and force them to go where they don't want to go. Remember that space is tight in this area of the field, which means you can get away with paying extra attention to one offensive player. A good example of this would be to play man-to-man coverage and then have another zone defender play the anticipated area. You would user-defend him as well.

2 MAX COVERAGE DEFENSE

> MIX THIS IN WITH THE COVER 0 SETUP FOR MAXIMUM EFFICIENCY.

When setting up max coverage defense we are looking to frustrate our opponent into being patient. Call any 2 Man Under in the game and hot route both DEs into buzz zones. Next, hot route one of your safeties to a QB spy. Last, user-control the other safety. This defense isn't set up to generate pressure; its purpose is to frustrate your opponent into bad decisions.

1 COVER 0

> HEAVY PRESSURE EQUALS HIGH PROBABILITY OF MISTAKES.

Call 4-3 Under—Edge Sting. Use your coverage audibles to call press coverage. User-control the MLB covering the HB and be ready for anything over the middle of the field as well as the HB breaking to the flat. This defense will get all over your opponent's QB quickly, especially if he is under center. The pressure will come through the left A gap and will force a quick throw. Test your opponents early and see if they can handle this pressure in the red zone.

5 RUN DEFENSE
4 MAN-TO-MAN DEFENSE
3 ZONE DEFENSE
2 BLITZING DEFENSE
1 MAX COVERAGE DEFENSE

HONORABLE MENTION: **RED ZONE DEFENSE**

EXPERT TIPS TOP 5

WAYS TO DEFEND A NO-HUDDLE ATTACK

The real problem with the no-huddle offense is that as a defense we aren't set up to stop the onslaught that the offense throws at us. Unless of course we prepare for it. We give you five tools to add to your very own "no-huddle defense."

5 RUN DEFENSE

Always have a run defense to counter a run-heavy offense.

A few formations we recommend for stopping the run are the 5-2, 4-4, and 4-3 Stack. One of these three is in almost every defensive playbook in the game. Have your run defense in mind so that when your opponent starts no-huddling you can quickly audible to your run defense and not miss a beat. The problem isn't that the no-huddle is over-powered; the problem is that most times our defense isn't ready. Be ready.

4 MAN-TO-MAN DEFENSE

Our favorite man-to-man defense is the Dollar 3-2-6—2 Man Under.

No-huddle offenses aren't just getting to the line of scrimmage as fast as they can and snapping the ball. They are often changing their play in the process. This means that you need to change your defense. A lot will rely on your innate ability to anticipate what your opponent is going to do to you, but have your man-to-man defense ready so that you can shut down that third and 2 slant route.

3 ZONE DEFENSE

Our favorite zone defense is the Dollar 3-2-6—Cover 4.

Some players can't beat man-to-man, and some can't beat zone. Make sure you can get to your zone play as fast as possible during the no-huddle. Defending the no-huddle isn't so much about what play you are using but about having a plan for specific situations. If you face an opponent who uses a lot of trips formations then look to use man-to-man. If you are facing someone who likes to spread out the offense then consider using zone, but make sure you have a plan for what you want to do.

2 BLITZING DEFENSE

Our favorite blitzing defense is the 4-3 Stack—OLB Fire Man

You are probably starting to notice a trend. We need to have a defense for every situation. Adding a blitzing defense to the mix is the next step. Be ready to call upon this blitz when needed. One of our favorite things to do is to play a ton of coverage defense and then sneak in our heavy blitz on third down. It almost always gets our defense off the field.

1 MAX COVERAGE DEFENSE

Our favorite coverage defense is the Nickel 3-3-5—2 Man Under with adjustments.

Max coverage defense is a must when playing *Madden NFL 25*. Just as we like to blitz on third downs we also like to keep our opponents on their toes by dropping as many defenders into coverage as possible and rushing only a couple of defenders. The Nickel 3-3-5—2 Man Under is a unique defensive play because the blitzing LB has a rush angle that gives him a turbo rush after the QB. We like to hot route the weak-side DE into a buzz zone and to hot route the DT to a QB spy. This defense is great for third and long situations, especially when your opponent anticipates pressure and blocks six-plus players.

TOP 5 EXPERT TIPS

WAYS TO SET UP BLITZES

The key to defense in *Madden NFL 25* is being able to effectively blitz your opponent. This means to send more pass rushers than there are pass blockers. We show you the best ways to set up blitzes quickly!

5 COVER 0 BLITZES
4 SHOW BLITZ
3 MANUALLY MOVE DEFENDERS
2 DEFENSIVE LINE CRASHES AND SHIFTS
1 GLOBAL LINEBACKER COMMANDS

HONORABLE MENTION: **SHIFT LINEBACKERS**

5 COVER 0 BLITZES

> COVER 0 INDICATES THAT THERE IS NO SAFETY SUPPORT IN THE DEFENSIVE SECONDARY. TYPICALLY SIX OR MORE DEFENDERS ARE RUSHING THE QB.

Most Cover 0 blitzes don't require any defensive adjustment. A good example of this would be the 3-4 Over—Sting Pinch. In the play art you can see that every defender is matched up in man-to-man coverage. We aren't required to do anything for pressure to get in against our opponent. Sting Pinch Zone is the complementary blitz; it brings the same pressure but has zone coverage behind the blitz.

4 SHOW BLITZ

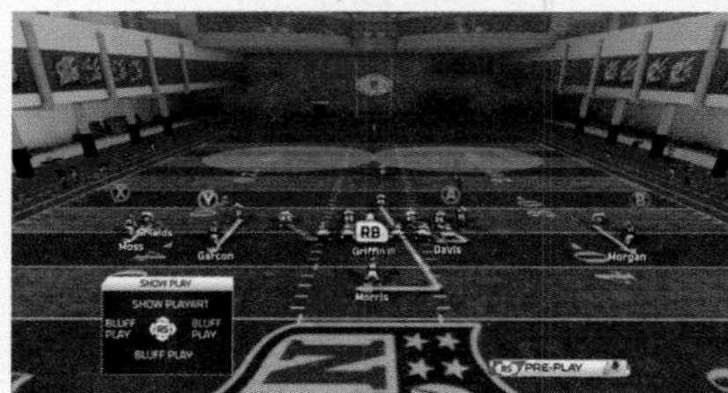

> ONE OF THE MOST UNDER-USED TOOLS IN THE GAME, THE SHOW BLITZ COMMAND IS SOMETHING WE HIGHLY RECOMMEND.

The Show Blitz command allows your defense to get into position extremely quickly. Most defenses in the game provide a Bear defensive front when Show Blitz is called. To show blitz simply call a coverage audible and then hit left on the D-pad. We use Show Blitz because it gets our defenders into the same position each time before the snap of the ball. This allows us to disguise coverage as well as blitzes.

3 MANUALLY MOVE DEFENDERS

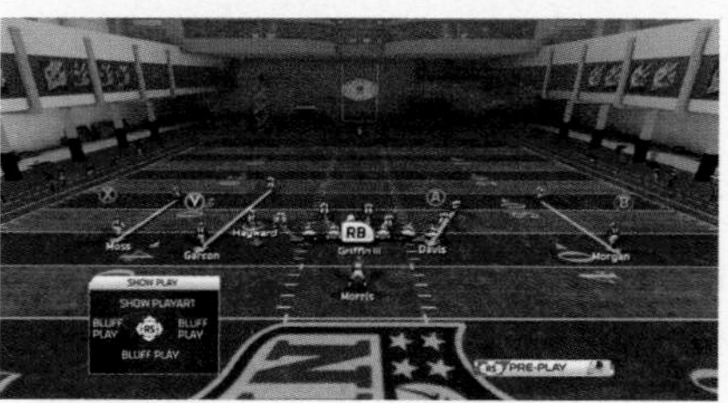

> DEFENDERS WILL RESET BACK TO THEIR ORIGINAL POSITIONS IF YOU PLACE THEM TOO CLOSE TO THE LINE OF SCRIMMAGE.

A great example of manually moving defenders is from Dime Normal—DB Blitz. We move the slot defenders closer to the line of scrimmage, which results in quicker pressure on the QB. The movement is slight, but it makes a huge difference between getting to the QB or not. We also like to do this with safeties, as they typically have unique blitzing angles, which can help them get to the QB faster.

2 DEFENSIVE LINE CRASHES AND SHIFTS

> DEFENSIVE LINE CRASHES AND SHIFTS ARE GREAT FOR CREATING OVERLOAD BLITZES.

There are four different line shifts and crashes 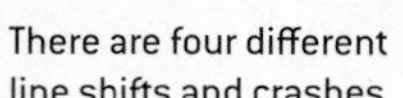 in *Madden NFL 25*. You can shift and crash your line in, out, left, or right. Each has its strengths and weaknesses. Line crashes and shifts are independent of each other, which means you could shift your defensive line in but crash them out. Typically we crash our defensive line towards where we want to bring pressure. An example of this would be to call Cover 3 zone from 4-3 Stack. Shift and crash your defensive line right. Next you would blitz the ROLB. With this setup we are looking to bring pressure off the right edge of the line of scrimmage.

1 GLOBAL LINEBACKER COMMANDS

> THE QUICKEST BLITZ IN THE GAME TO SET UP IS FROM THE NICKEL 1-5-5 FORMATION.

The fastest way to generate pressure in *Madden NFL 25* is by using the global linebacker commands. With these commands you have the ability to blitz all linebackers, blitz the ROLB, blitz the LOLB, and hook zone all linebackers. It's important to use global commands so that you don't have to individually click on each player to make an adjustment. You could be controlling a safety but still hot route your linebackers to blitz. One of our favorite formations in the game to do this from is the Nickel 1-5-5. Globally blitz all your linebackers and you will have instantly created an overload blitz that will get to the QB.

5 CPU RUSHING GAME
4 PERSONNEL AUDIBLES
3 STOP THE READ OPTION
2 HELP ME HELP YOU
1 RUNNING MOVES

DEVELOPER TIPS TOP 5

NEW THINGS TO LOOK OUT FOR WITH REX DICKSON

Rex Dickson is the creative director for *Madden NFL 25* gameplay. Under his direction, the game has continued a march towards true authenticity to deliver the experience you see on the gridiron on Sunday! As a former college football offensive lineman, Rex knows football, and his ability on the virtual gridiron has really taken a leap. Here is Rex's list of Top 5 New Things to Look Out for in *Madden NFL 25*.

5 CPU RUSHING GAME

THE COMPUTER IS ALSO MUCH DEADLIER WITH THE READ OPTION THIS SEASON.

The CPU this season is more dedicated to the rushing game, so make sure you have solid run defense before taking it on. Not only will the CPU stick with the game plan and really wear down your defense, but halfbacks are much improved with their moves and ability to identify running lanes. Learning to quickly identify runs and where the CPU will attack is the key to getting your defenders there and the gaps plugged. Look for keys like pulling linemen to help figure out where the action is advancing on the play.

4 PERSONNEL AUDIBLES

PLAYERS ONLINE WILL BE UNABLE TO AUDIBLE DOWN FROM SPREAD PASSING SETS TO RUN-HEAVY SETS WITH THE NO-HUDDLE AND GET PLAYERS OUT OF POSITION.

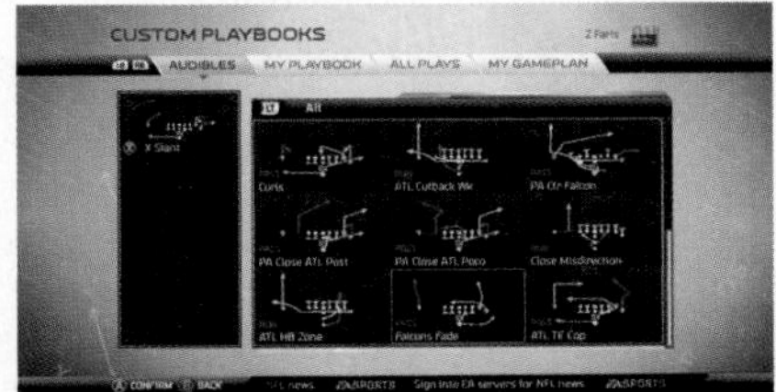

Learning how to calls plays with the new By Personnel option will be big for players this season. If you are a spread passing team that uses four WRs and one HB, don't expect to be able to audible to formations using TEs. When you call By Personnel, you will see a list of all the possible formations you can audible to. Working out of sets that have multiple options will keep the defense on their heels longer.

3 STOP THE READ OPTION

BY USING THE PRE-SNAP ADJUSTMENTS MENU, GAMERS CAN QUICKLY CHOOSE TO PLAY THE HB OR CONTAIN THE QB. MAKE IT A HABIT TO DO THIS BEFORE EVERY SNAP!

Players looking to stop the read option should check out plays that send LBs off the edge. One play we suggest is 3-4 Odd—OLB Stud Spy. On most downs, we look to contain the QB and allow the running back to pick up small chunks of yardage. On big downs, we choose to attack the HB and make sure our user defender watches the QB off the edge. By mixing up our play calls and bringing consistent edge pressure, we can force our opponents to abandon the read option early in the game and make them one-dimensional.

2 HELP ME HELP YOU

THE USER HAS MORE OPTIONS THAN EVER IN THE GAMEPLAY MENU TO CHANGE UP SETTINGS!

The gameplay in *Madden NFL 25* really empowers the user to "click on" to defenders and make plays. In years past, you might have tried to switch to a player on defense and started running the wrong way. However, now the game has a buffer that will make sure you are on the correct player by reading your direction. Gamers who are active and get into plays after the snap will be more successful this season.

1 RUNNING MOVES

THE CPU WILL ATTEMPT MORE DIVE TACKLES, SO BE READY TO HURDLE!

With all the improvements to run blocking this season, why not give pounding the rock a try. Offensive linemen love to run-block, especially for talented backs. With all the new hard cuts and combo and precision moves, you truly do have the ability to build a punishing ground game. Between the option, WR screens, and HB screens, gamers have plenty of power when they get the ball in space this season. Downfield blocking is also better this season, so give those linemen a few seconds to get set up downfield and be ready to reap the rewards!

TOP 5 DEVELOPER TIPS

NEW PLAYBOOKS WITH ANTHONY WHITE

5 WASHINGTON REDSKINS
4 NEW ENGLAND PATRIOTS
3 SAN FRANCISCO 49ERS
2 PHILADELPHIA EAGLES
1 PISTOL

HONORABLE MENTION: **RUN AND SHOOT, GREEN BAY PACKERS**

Each season, developer Anthony White watches football on Sunday and translates the X's and O's into plays inside the game. If a coach changes teams or schemes, White quickly reacts and fits the team with a new playbook. Making sure each team feels authentic and has its real scheme is important, so he keeps on top of all the moves. Here is a look at just a few of the updates you will see in *Madden NFL 25* with some of his favorite new playbooks!

5 REDSKINS

MUST-TRY FORMATION: **Pistol Wing Offset**

> CHECK OUT THE "TEAMS" CHAPTER TO SEE A MORE IN-DEPTH BREAKDOWN OF THE REDSKINS PLAYBOOK.

WAS - M. SHANAHAN

The Redskins proved they were a force on the ground last season. In *Madden NFL 25* their playbook will benefit from an improved run game. Even for gamers who don't want all the responsibility of the option game but still want to run the ball, Washington's playbook is still a great choice. While there are plenty of unique option plays from their multiple pistol formations, the playbook can still handle a pure power run attack. The best thing about this playbook is that many of the formations feature the same concepts . This way, you have less to master but many variations.

4 NEW ENGLAND PATRIOTS

> IF YOU HAVE A TRULY DOMINANT STYLE, SIMPLY GO ALL OUT UNTIL THE DEFENSE PROVES THEY CAN STOP YOU.

MUST-TRY FORMATION: **Gun Ace Trips Y-Iso**

NE - NE COACH

The New England Patriots playbook is perfect for gamers who like to use one type of personnel and stick with it all drive long. The Patriots have plenty of great formations for teams that have two strong TEs. This will stress the defense, which will have to figure out if they want to try to use LBs or safeties to match up against them. If the defense goes with a smaller lineup, look to use the Patriots' quick running plays to gash the defense! Finding a great playbook that gives you a lot of options to audible to at the line of scrimmage is a great move in *Madden NFL 25*!

3 SAN FRANCISCO 49ERS

> THE 49ERS REALLY SHOWED WHAT THEIR OFFENSE COULD DO WITH A DYNAMIC QB UNDER CENTER!

MUST-TRY FORMATION: **Pistol Full House Base**

SF - JIM HARBAUGH

Jim Harbaugh came to the NFL from college, and last year he unleashed a few tactics from his past on the league! By choosing to start QB Colin Kaepernick, he was able to use plays like the Read Option to pound the ball all the way to the Super Bowl. For gamers who are looking to play a power run game, the 49ers book is a great option. They have a great variety of plays from under center as well as pistol and shotgun formations to keep the defense from keying in on your tactics. Make sure your team has multiple halfbacks if you want to use this scheme, as stamina is very important in *Madden NFL 25*!

2 PHILADELPHIA EAGLES

> THE SIGNING OF NEW HEAD COACH CHIP KELLY BRINGS PLENTY OF EXCITEMENT TO THE EAGLES, ESPECIALLY BECAUSE OF HIS OFFENSIVE SCHEME.

MUST-TRY FORMATION: **Gun Trips Offset**

PHI - C. KELLY

The Eagles playbook in *Madden NFL 25* is going to be excellent for the gamer who wants to bring a fast-paced style to the gridiron. Look to use plays like 0 1 Trap, Cake Read Option, and Midline Read Option to give defenses looks they are not used to seeing. If you can run a disciplined scheme that limits turnovers and focuses on moving the chains, Philly may be the optimal playbook for your offense. You must commit to using screens and runs out of shotgun, however, to really maximize this book's potential.

1 PISTOL PLAYBOOK

> THE PISTOL PLAYBOOK WILL BE ONE OF THE MOST POPULAR ONLINE BECAUSE OF ITS RUN OF SUCCESS IN THE NFL LAST SEASON!

MUST-TRY FORMATION: **Pistol Twin TE Slot**

PISTOL

Gamers are always looking for the brand-new plays in *Madden NFL* to catch their opponents off guard. This season, the completely new Pistol playbook is the answer. Not only is the whole book new, but many of the plays and formations are brand-new to the series! To take full advantage of this book, keep an up-tempo pace and use similar looks to set your opponent up. If you can harness the full power of the multiple option types found in this book, you will rack up not only tons of yards but tons of wins! Make sure to use a QB who has enough mobility that defenses will fear him getting to the edge!

New Defensive Playbooks

Madden NFL 25 also added some great new plays and formations on the defensive side of the ball too. Check out new hybrid fronts from the Patriots and Falcons playbooks, which will have their 4-3 fronts looking more like a 3-4 with the DE in a two-point stance.

One other great thing on the defensive side of the ball is the addition of the 4-4 formation into the 4-3 playbook. This formation will pack the box with defenders and make it extremely difficult to run the ball. If you are having trouble stopping plays like the Read Option, try out the 4-4!.

Be sure to try these playbooks when selecting yours at the Team Selection screen!

5 GET THE BALL OUT
4 SLIDE PROTECT
3 RUN THE BALL
2 FORMATION, FORMATION, FORMATION
1 BUILD A POCKET

DEVELOPER TIPS TOP 5

BLOCKING TIPS WITH CLINT OLDENBURG

Clint Oldenburg has been working on the trenches in *Madden NFL 25* all off-season to deliver a gaming experience that reminds him of what he experienced on Sundays. Oldenburg knows a thing or two about blocking as he spent time on the line in the NFL, where his job was keeping his QB's jersey clean. As he continues to work on the line play, he takes a step back to reveal some tips on winning the line battle this season.

5 GET THE BALL OUT

Spread formations leave you vulnerable to the blitz, so make sure to hit your hot reads!

Too many online players try to counter sacks by the defense by spreading out their formation. Adding more WRs and neglecting to diagnose the real problem will only lead to more sacks. If you don't have your passing timing down yet, the spread will only lead to more problems. The more players you have on the line, the more protection and time in the pocket you will be afforded. Try a formation like Gun Ace, which moves the slot WRs to the line, and sub in a TE who will hold up better if asked to block.

4 SLIDE PROTECT

Making great pre-snap adjustments can stop pressure before it starts.

If a defense appears to be overloading one side of the line, bring up the Slide Protection option from the pre-snap menu. This allows you to choose a direction to have your linemen slide towards. They can easily pick up pressure from a defense that shows its pressure too early. Aside from left and right, you can slide protect in the up or down direction. "Down" pinches your offensive line if your opponent is trying to send pressure at the middle of your line. "Up" gives your linemen the go-ahead to be more aggressive and can also help stop pressure in the middle.

3 RUN THE BALL

Set up your blocks by drawing defenders to your blockers by pressing the line of scrimmage and then cutting through the running lane.

If you are facing an opponent who is unleashing on your passing game, run the ball to take the pressure off. Offensive linemen love to run-block because it gives them the chance to attack the defense. If you can slip outside the blitzing defenders' containment, you can spring a play for a huge gain and make the defense think twice about being aggressive. Quick passes with high conversion percentages, like HB and WR screens, are a great way to get the ball out of the dangerous areas.

2 FORMATION, FORMATION, FORMATION

Utilize the block-and-release hot route with players in your backfield. It will give great protection first and later act as a safety valve.

Certain formations have better blitz protection in *Madden NFL 25* because of where players line up. One of the best formations in the game to stop pressure is Gun Split Offset, which has multiple variations throughout the playbooks. The key to this formation is having both players in the backfield lined up next to the QB. If you sense the defense is up to something, quickly block one or both of the players. If the defense looks to be sending more players than you can block, hot route the player to a route and quickly pass him the ball. These two players should give you great confidence to pick up any type of pressure.

1 BUILD A POCKET

Offensive linemen expect their QBs to stay in the pocket, so trust your line!

Learning to stay calm in the pocket with your QB is crucial to becoming a better player. Many gamers hold the left stick at the snap and try to run away from the line. This actually makes it much easier for the rushers on the edge to break from their blocks and sack the QB. If you have completed the other steps we covered, you should have all the confidence to stand in the pocket and make your reads. By hanging tough in the pocket and waiting for routes to develop, you will begin to learn the timing in the trenches needed to become better. Learning to trust your offensive linemen will show your opponent you are ready to beat the blitz.

TOP 5 DEVELOPER TIPS

OFFENSIVE RATINGS WITH DONNY MOORE

5 CATCH IN TRAFFIC
4 DEEP THROW ACCURACY
3 SPEED
2 JUKE MOVE
1 OVERALL

Donny Moore is the man in charge of the ratings for *Madden NFL 25*. Over his long career working at EA SPORTS, he has spent years scouting young rookies and reviewing tape of old veterans to make sure you get an authentic experience. With over 132,000 ratings and traits to monitor, being the ratings czar isn't an easy job, like many gamers think. Moore must also stay up on more than 275,000 possible equipment combinations! Here are the areas on both offense and defense that are key this season.

5 CATCH IN TRAFFIC (CIT)

- PLAYER EXAMPLE: WES WELKER, BRONCOS
- ANY PRO CAN CATCH THE BALL WHEN OPEN—IT IS HANGING ONTO IT IN A CROWD THAT IS THE HARD PART!

When a player goes over the middle of the field and consistently hangs onto the ball, he earns a high rating in the ability to "catch in traffic." These players are extremely valuable to their QB due their ability to hang onto those big third down conversions. Any player that earns trust in big situations will also see more targets in the red zone! There is a fine line between regular catching, spectacular catches, and catching in traffic, but all must be separated to give gamers a true feel to each player.

4 DEEP THROW ACCURACY (DAC)

- PLAYER EXAMPLE: PEYTON MANNING, BRONCOS
- THANKS TO TUNED PASS LEAD THIS SEASON, A QB'S DAC RATING WILL BE MORE IMPORTANT THAN EVER!

Any player who uses a QB with a high deep accuracy rating is going to take more shots downfield during the course of a game. The higher the rating, the more consistent the accuracy of the pass will be, and this will stress defenses since they must respect the deep ball. A big part of *Madden NFL* is picking up those third and long situations, and having a QB with the confidence to unleash the ball is huge. If your QB is still developing his rating in this category, use route concepts that free up the receiver into open spaces and deliver the ball there.

3 SPEED (SPD)

- PLAYER EXAMPLE: DESEAN JACKSON, EAGLES
- SPEED IS STILL IMPORTANT, BUT HAVING GREAT AGILITY AND ACCELERATION TO GO ALONG WITH IT ARE HUGE.

The idea of "speed kills" has been a popular one in football, because it is fun to see those highlight reel runs where the back leaves the defense in the dust. With everything being equal it is always great to have fast players, since they can often make up for their mistakes with their speed. Just make sure to look into their other categories as well and remember that there is no "speed burst" or turbo this season. If you do find yourself with an elite speedster like WR Mike Wallace, make sure to test the defense and don't let the quickness go to waste!

2 JUKE MOVE (JKM)

- PLAYER EXAMPLE: LESEAN MCCOY, EAGLES
- REMEMBER THAT A PLAYER WITH A 90-PLUS RATING IN A MOVE CATEGORY CAN PULL OFF A PRECISION MOVE THIS SEASON.

With the new Run Free gameplay in *Madden NFL 25*, gamers should focus in on their back's best move. For some, it might be a Juke Move rating that can be used to combo into another move, or done with the precision modifier to really maximize it. For other runners, it might be a 90-plus Jump rating (JMP) that results in a great hurdle, or a 90-plus Stiff Arm rating (SFA) that results in the ability to ward off defenders. Whatever running move your back has the ability to unleash, make sure you work on the timing so you are ready to bust it out when the moment strikes. My personal favorite is the precision spin move!

1 OVERALL (OVR)

- PLAYER EXAMPLE: CALVIN JOHNSON, LIONS
- WHEN SETTING YOUR DEPTH CHART, ALWAYS REMEMBER THAT YOU CAN SORT BY ANY RATING CATEGORY!

Many gamers like to go through and analyze every rating, but the best way to really start testing players is to look at the Overall rating. Depending on the position and type of player, Overall will give you a solid snapshot of your player and what you should expect from him out on the field. Any player who is a 90-plus Overall or higher in *Madden NFL 25* is considered an elite talent and should be a focus of your offense. Follow along with the NFL season and look for roster and rating updates all season long!

5 PRESS
4 BLOCK SHED
3 SPEED
2 TACKLE
1 OVERALL

DEVELOPER TIPS **TOP 5**

DEFENSIVE RATINGS WITH DONNY MOORE

In this section, the ratings czar talks about key ratings on the defensive side of the ball! Remember, defense wins championships, and having players with the skills to make plays in the right position can be the difference between a win and a loss.

5 PRESS (PRS)

- **Player Example: Richard Sherman**
- **There are some very talented WRs in the league; try slowing them down by pressing them at the start of a play!**

For gamers who like to play an aggressive style in *Madden NFL 25*, pressing the WRs can be a great way to slow down the offense. Lining up right over the WR and bumping them as they start their route can really disrupt the timing of a pass play. This tactic isn't without risk though as a WR with a solid beat press rating can burn your defender and get open downfield for a huge gain. Make sure to study both of these key ratings and make sure your not leaving.

3 SPEED (SPD)

- **Player Example: Patrick Peterson**
- **If you have a lower rated player with great speed, look to user-control him to maximize his ratings.**

Speed on defense is important not just in the secondary, but in the front seven as well. Linebackers who have great speed can play sideline to sideline and should have no problem matching up against HBs and TEs in the passing game. If you find a pass rusher with great speed, you can send him off the edge and let him chase down even the fastest QBs in the game. When looking into speed, don't forget to check out agility and acceleration, as these two categories will enhance just how fast a player feels on defense. If you are trying to stop a QB with a QB spy, make sure your spy has ample speed to catch the QB once he takes off past the line!

4 BLOCK SHED (BSH)

- **Player Example: Vince Wilfork**
- **If you drop a player on the defensive line into a pass coverage assignment, he will still engage on standard run plays but not draws.**

With all the new running moves on offense, gamers will need to be ready to stop the run on defense, and it all starts up front! Having players on the defensive line with great Block Shed ratings means they will be likely to get off blocks and into the backfield. To really load up on these players, consider moving some of your DTs to DE in your main run-stuffing formation. Even if all your defenders get blocked at the snap of the ball, it just takes one guy to slip off his block to really disrupt a running play in the backfield.

2 TACKLE (TAK)

- **Player Example: Luke Kuechly**
- **Go for the more conservative tackle and not a hit stick if you are all alone with a ball carrier.**

With all of the weapons that an HB has in *Madden NFL 25* this season, gamers must be ready to wrap up the ball carrier. While Hit Power is an important stat that can force fumbles with the hit stick, wrapping up should be your top priority. Make sure to use the new Heat Seeker feature to steer in your tackle and bring down the ball carrier. Learning how to tackle and limiting broken and missed tackles is a quick way to get better, and it all starts with the Tackle rating!

1 OVERALL (OVR)

- **Player Example: J.J. Watt**
- **Every player is always working towards the rare 100 Overall rating!**

When looking at a team like the 49ers, it is clear that their defense is elite because of the number of 90-plus-rated players in their lineup. While going through your depth chart and checking in on the other stats can be fun, knowing that you have great players that have talent in every category across the board is best! The Overall rating gives gamers a great idea of just how strong a player is at specific stats that factor into his position. Pass rushers will have high Overall ratings if a skill like Finesse Move (FMV) or Power Move (PMV) is strong. Players like kickers and punters will benefit from having Kick Power (KPW) and Kick Accuracy (KAC). Every important rating is always a big factor in the overall!

TOP 5 PLAYERS

In this section we provide four Top 5 player lists for each position in *Madden NFL 25*. One is the official list by Overall rating from EA SPORTS, while the next gives our personal favorites. Then we highlight the top rookies, and finally we point out a few unknown sleepers you might want to check out.

EA SPORTS' TOP 5

These are the official ratings from EA SPORTS listing the top players at each position. All of these players are Pro Bowl caliber, and many are on their way to the Hall of Fame. Every season, gamers quickly load up the rosters for *Madden NFL* to see which players have the highest ratings in the game. Every Overall rating is analyzed by each team's fans and of course its rivals. The players on this list have consistently out-performed their peers and are considered the best players in the league. These players have the statistics to be ranked above their peers and are expected to repeat these performances, especially if they want to stay on this list.

PRIMA'S TOP 5

While EA SPORTS does a tremendous job rating players, all fans love to dig through the ratings and argue for their favorite players and teams. By testing out every team, player, and rating in the game, ZFarls and SGibs have developed some of their own favorite players they think can win you more games in *Madden NFL 25*. Many of these players can be found on the EA SPORTS list, but all of them are worthy of checking out and taking out for a test run this season. Each player has a unique style and blend of ratings that gives him a distinctive feel, and by testing them out you can learn which players are most effective for how you want to play the game.

TOP 5 ROOKIES

Every season, thousands of hours of scouting and work go into the NFL Draft, which determines where college talent ends up in the NFL. All of the rookies discussed here have a special style and blend of ratings that can make them huge factors during the course of a *Madden NFL* season. Many factors determine which rookies are at the top of their position, including draft order, which team selected them, style, and position. Never overlook a rookie just because you haven't seen him play on Sunday yet. Last season, three rookie QBs made huge impacts early in their careers, and there will surely be more at every position this season. Here are our favorite rookies at each position in *Madden NFL 25*!

TOP 5 SLEEPERS

Not every player in *Madden NFL 25* is a superstar yet—many players are still working their way up the depth chart, and some are even fighting to make the team. It would be a mistake to overlook players who aren't household names yet. Many of these players, despite not having great Overall ratings, are still very capable of helping your team win games in *Madden NFL 25*. We have put together this list to help determine which players are sleepers in *Madden NFL 25*. It takes 53 players to win on Sunday, and with this list, you should see some future stars who will really help fill out your roster at each position.

QUARTERBACKS

Last season, there was a shift in the mind-set of NFL fans about what makes a truly great QB. Many fans had formed an opinion that you need a pocket passing QB who can throw the ball downfield to win a championship. However, after watching three young QBs lead their teams to the playoffs with an exciting dual-threat style, many fans have reshaped their opinions. Ultimately, a more prototypical QB—Joe Flacco of the Ravens—stood with the Lombardi trophy, allowing those favoring the old school to retain bragging rights for another season. This year, defenses won't be caught off guard by the new school of QBs, who must maintain their high level of play to remain atop these lists. Here are some of our favorite QBs in what is still the most important position in football!

EA SPORTS' TOP 5 QBS

	POSITION	NAME	TEAM	OVR	SPD	THP	THA	DAC
5	QB	Matt Ryan	Falcons	94	65	89	91	86
4	QB	Drew Brees	Saints	96	65	89	96	87
3	QB	Peyton Manning	Broncos	97	60	89	95	89
2	QB	Aaron Rodgers	Packers	97	80	95	89	87
1	QB	Tom Brady	Patriots	98	57	95	93	82

TOP 5 ROOKIE QBS

	POSITION	NAME	TEAM	OVR	SPD	THP	THA	DAC
5	QB	Matt Barkley	Eagles	73	65	84	84	68
4	QB	B.J. Daniels	49ers	63	84	84	68	69
3	QB	Mike Glennon	Buccaneers	6	54	95	76	81
2	QB	E.J. Manuel	Bills	74	83	94	77	77
1	QB	Geno Smith	Jets	73	85	92	82	84

PRIMA'S TOP 5 QBS

	POSITION	NAME	TEAM	OVR	SPD	THP	THA	DAC
5	QB	Cam Newton	Panthers	90	85	97	84	84
4	QB	Russell Wilson	Seahawks	89	86	93	86	85
3	QB	Aaron Rodgers	Packers	97	80	95	89	87
2	QB	Robert Griffin III	Redskins	89	92	95	87	85
1	QB	Colin Kaepernick	49ers	89	88	96	84	88

TOP 5 SLEEPER QBS

	POSITION	NAME	TEAM	OVR	SPD	THP	THA	DAC
5	QB	Tim Tebow	Patriots	73	81	86	71	73
4	QB	Dennis Dixon	Eagles	68	84	84	70	69
3	QB	Tyrod Taylor	Ravens	73	87	92	72	75
2	QB	Brock Osweiler	Broncos	73	69	96	79	80
1	QB	Terrelle Pryor	Raiders	70	90	94	72	66

ANDREW LUCK LIVED UP TO THE HYPE LAST YEAR AND SHOULD BE A POPULAR PLAYER ONLINE THIS SEASON.

QB BROCK OSWEILER IS A GREAT OPTION IF YOU WANT TO DEVELOP A POCKET PASSER IN YOUR FRANCHISE.

HALFBACKS

With all of the new Run Free moves in *Madden NFL 25*, having a great HB will be more important than ever. Gamers who commit to running the ball will have more success if they are handing it off to a superstar in the backfield. There are a few styles you should consider when looking at players from this list. Some backs are more elusive and use their speed and agility to avoid and break tackles. Other backs tend to be more powerful and can use their strength to truck defenders and break tackles. The best have a combination of both and are even capable of catching passes out of the backfield, too. If you can get a star HB on your team, it will ease up pressure on your QB and force the defense to prove they can stop the run.

EA SPORTS' TOP 5 HBS

	POSITION	NAME	TEAM	OVR	SPD	AGI	ACC	TRK/ELU
5	HB	Jamaal Charles	Chiefs	95	93	99	97	67/97
4	HB	Ray Rice	Ravens	95	91	96	97	79/84
3	HB	Arian Foster	Texans	96	92	94	96	95/77
2	HB	Marshawn Lynch	Seahawks	97	94	96	95	99/78
1	HB	Adrian Peterson	Vikings	97	96	97	97	98/97

TOP 5 ROOKIE HBS

	POSITION	NAME	TEAM	OVR	SPD	AGI	ACC	TRK/ELU
5	HB	Johnathan Franklin	Packers	73	90	91	88	83/65
4	HB	Denard Robinson	Jaguars	67	92	95	96	51/91
3	HB	Montee Ball	Broncos	75	86	86	90	87/68
2	HB	Chris Thompson	Redskins	66	93	86	97	34/78
1	HB	Eddie Lacy	Packers	76	87	88	86	91/71

PRIMA'S TOP 5 HBS

	POSITION	NAME	TEAM	OVR	SPD	AGI	ACC	TRK/ELU
5	HB	LeSean McCoy	Eagles	93	91	98	98	32/49
4	HB	Chris Johnson	Titans	87	99	95	98	55/81
3	HB	C.J. Spiller	Bills	92	96	98	96	62/99
2	HB	Jamaal Charles	Chiefs	94	98	97	97	67/97
1	HB	Adrian Peterson	Vikings	97	96	97	97	98/97

TOP 5 SLEEPER HBS

	POSITION	NAME	TEAM	OVR	SPD	AGI	ACC	TRK/ELU
5	HB	Michael Smith	Buccaneers	66	95	91	94	77/73
4	HB	Jeff Demps	Buccaneers	63	98	95	98	55/84
3	HB	Lamar Miller	Dolphins	73	95	93	96	55/82
2	HB	Taiwan Jones	Raiders	68	97	92	95	54/84
1	HB	LaMichael James	49ers	74	93	96	97	49/93

ADRIAN PETERSON IS THE BEST OVERALL HB IN THE GAME, NO MATTER WHAT STYLE YOU UTILIZE!

HB LAMICHAEL JAMES GIVES THE 49ERS A GREAT SPEED OPTION TO COMPLEMENT THE POWERFUL FRANK GORE.

WIDE RECEIVERS

Finding great WRs in *Madden NFL 25* is easy, as there are plenty of great players out there. Not only will HBs benefit from the new Run Free controls, but so will WRs, who will now have more weapons after the catch. No matter the style of passing offense, having players who can hang onto the ball and run after the catch is very important. Some WRs in the game can do it all on their own, while others have a great target on the other side of the field that makes them even better. Once you develop confidence in the relationship with your QB and WR, you will move the chains more consistently. Think about the specific type of WR you want to throw to. Some players are outside WRs while some work better in the slot. Some slot WRs like to work quickly over the middle and need to catch the ball in traffic, while others have great straight-line speed and can burn any defender in the game. Here are some favorite WRs in *Madden NFL 25*!

EA SPORTS' TOP 5 WRS

	POSITION	NAME	TEAM	OVR	SPD	CTH	RLS	RTE
5	WR	Roddy White	Falcons	93	89	96	86	97
4	WR	A.J. Green	Bengals	94	90	96	97	90
3	WR	Brandon Marshall	Bears	95	88	94	99	98
2	WR	Andre Johnson	Texans	97	91	97	97	97
1	WR	Calvin Johnson Jr	Lions	99	95	97	99	96

TOP 5 ROOKIE WRS

	POSITION	NAME	TEAM	OVR	SPD	CTH	RLS	RTE
5	WR	Marquise Goodwin	Bills	64	98	74	53	64
4	WR	DeAndre Hopkins	Texans	73	89	87	71	72
3	WR	Cordarrelle Patterson	Vikings	73	93	81	75	53
2	WR	Justin Hunter	Titans	69	92	84	76	65
1	WR	Tavon Austin	Rams	76	95	82	63	73

PRIMA'S TOP 5 WRS

	POSITION	NAME	TEAM	OVR	SPD	CTH	RLS	RTE
5	WR	Randall Cobb	Packers	87	92	93	79	82
4	WR	Mike Wallace	Dolphins	87	98	86	81	84
3	WR	Percy Harvin	Seahawks	92	96	91	77	88
2	WR	Julio Jones	Falcons	92	95	90	98	88
1	WR	Calvin Johnson Jr	Lions	99	95	97	99	96

TOP 5 SLEEPER WRS

	POSITION	NAME	TEAM	OVR	SPD	CTH	RLS	RTE
5	WR	T.Y. Hilton	Colts	79	95	85	40	64
4	WR	Trindon Holliday	Broncos	67	98	70	40	64
3	WR	Jason Avant	Eagles	79	82	86	87	82
2	WR	Andrew Hawkins	Bengals	72	94	79	49	73
1	WR	Danario Alexander	Chargers	82	89	69	91	79

CALVIN JOHNSON SHOULD BE THE NUMBER ONE WR CHOSEN IN ANY FANTASY DRAFT!

ANDREW HAWKINS IS A GREAT PLAYER TO TARGET ON SCREEN PASSES, BECAUSE HE CAN BREAK BIG RUNS AFTER THE CATCH.

TIGHT ENDS

Tight ends are some of the most versatile players on the field. They must have the size to block against defensive ends but be quick enough to run past safeties and LBs in the passing game. On this list, you will find many great TEs who can not only beat their man-to-man defenders deep but are capable of finding soft spots in zone coverage. Consider your offensive style: If you like to run, you want a player who is solid in run blocking and can hang onto tough passes when you do decide to pass it. If you are more passing based, consider a player who can shift out to the WR position and can create mismatches with his speed against an LB, or with his size against a defender in the secondary. These lists are filled with all types of players who can really add another dimension to your passing game in *Madden NFL 25*!

EA SPORTS' TOP 5 TES

	POSITION	NAME	TEAM	OVR	SPD	CTH	CIT	IBL
5	TE	Vernon Davis	49ers	94	90	78	75	78
4	TE	Tony Gonzalez	Falcons	95	78	96	95	66
3	TE	Jimmy Graham	Saints	96	85	90	95	71
2	TE	Jason Witten	Cowboys	96	75	96	96	70
1	TE	Rob Gronkowski	Patriots	98	83	90	97	68

TOP 5 ROOKIE TES

	POSITION	NAME	TEAM	OVR	SPD	CTH	CIT	IBL
5	TE	Gavin Escobar	Cowboys	72	75	85	87	55
4	TE	Vance McDonald	49ers	71	84	79	68	72
3	TE	Zach Ertz	Eagles	75	77	88	74	73
2	TE	Luke Willson	Seahawks	63	88	74	69	65
1	TE	Tyler Eifert	Bengals	80	82	88	84	67

PRIMA'S TOP 5 TES

	POSITION	NAME	TEAM	OVR	SPD	CTH	CIT	IBL
5	TE	Jermichael Finley	Packers	85	85	82	74	67
4	TE	Vernon Davis	49ers	94	90	78	75	78
3	TE	Jason Witten	Cowboys	96	75	96	96	70
2	TE	Rob Gronkowski	Patriots	98	83	90	97	68
1	TE	Jimmy Graham	Saints	96	85	90	95	71

TOP 5 SLEEPER TES

	POSITION	NAME	TEAM	OVR	SPD	CTH	CIT	IBL
5	TE	Jordan Cameron	Browns	77	84	77	78	64
4	TE	Jordan Reed	Redskins	69	79	80	84	55
3	TE	Michael Egnew	Dolphins	70	84	81	82	55
2	TE	James Hanna	Cowboys	71	88	73	77	57
1	TE	Chase Coffman	Falcons	68	71	49	49	60

JASON WITTEN IS A CONSISTENT PLAYER WHO CAN USE HIS SIZE TO HIS ADVANTAGE.

TE JAMES HANNA HAS ALL THE RAW PHYSICAL SKILLS TO DEVELOP INTO A GREAT PASS CATCHER.

DEFENSIVE ENDS

Defensive ends make the highlight reel for getting after the QB and bringing him down for a sack. However, a truly dominant defensive end is one who causes the offense nightmares all week leading up to the game. The opposing coach knows he must keep extra players in to block and can't run at their side, which gives the DE's team a huge advantage. There are a few different types of moves that defensive ends use to try to beat the offensive linemen. Faster, lighter players might go with a finesse move to try to run right past the offensive linemen, while other ends will go with a power move and try and push the linemen back. All great players change up their style of moves to keep the offensive linemen on their heels! Here are some players who can help you get to the QB and force those big third down stops!

EA SPORTS' TOP 5 DES

	POSITION	NAME	TEAM	OVR	SPD	STR	PMV/FMV	BSH
5	RE	DeMarcus Ware	Cowboys	94	84	86	93/83	72
4	RE	Haloti Ngata	Ravens	94	68	98	88/55	97
3	RE	Jason Pierre-Paul	Giants	94	86	82	75/94	84
2	LE	Cameron Wake	Dolphins	97	84	79	69/97	75
1	LE	J.J. Watt	Texans	99	77	97	99/67	98

TOP 5 ROOKIE DES

	POSITION	NAME	TEAM	OVR	SPD	STR	PMV/FMV	BSH
5	DE	Olivier Vernon	Dolphins	69	83	82	85/67	78
4	DE	Quanterus Smith	Broncos	68	78	66	88/72	67
3	DE	Margus Hunt	Bengals	70	85	88	66/79	80
2	DE	Cornelius Washington	Bears	69	85	91	86/52	77
1	DE	Ezekiel Ansah	Lions	78	83	84	88/82	76

PRIMA'S TOP 5 DES

	POSITION	NAME	TEAM	OVR	SPD	STR	PMV/FMV	BSH
5	DE	Julius Peppers	Bears	92	84	85	79/93	67
4	DE	J.J. Watt	Texans	99	77	97	99/67	98
3	DE	Carlos Dunlap	Bengals	89	84	81	71/94	75
2	DE	Cameron Wake	Dolphins	97	84	79	69/97	75
1	DE	Jason Pierre-Paul	Giants	94	86	82	75/94	84

TOP 5 SLEEPER DES

	POSITION	NAME	TEAM	OVR	SPD	STR	PMV/FMV	BSH
5	DE	Kroy Biermann	Falcons	74	75	80	54/78	75
4	DE	Robert Quinn	Rams	78	83	78	89/90	73
3	DE	Thaddeus Gibson	Titans	69	82	71	72/83	64
2	DE	Dontay Moch	Bengals	65	90	65	78/52	64
1	DE	Bruce Irvin	Seahawks	79	90	70	95/67	69

JASON PIERRE-PAUL IS AN ALL-AROUND TALENT WHO HAS GREAT PASS-RUSHING MOVES.

BRUCE IRVIN IS A TRUE SPEED RUSHER WHOM YOU WANT TO SAVE FOR THOSE ALL-OUT PASSING DOWNS!

DEFENSIVE TACKLES

Defensive tackle is an often overlooked position by many gamers, but the penalty for this mistake can be painful. A great DT is going to help stop the run without committing extra resources from your defense that can leave you vulnerable. Many of these players take on two blocks at the same time, which leaves LBs free to come in and make tackles. The best DTs can also help push the pocket on passing downs and cause the QB discomfort. Most DTs have tremendous size and strength and are very tough to move out of the way. The best players also mix in some pass-rushing moves, which allows them to stay on the field for every down. While they may not rack up huge numbers, don't forget to pay attention to the players doing battle in the trenches on every snap!

EA SPORTS' TOP 5 DTS

	POSITION	NAME	TEAM	OVR	SPD	STR	PMV/FMV	BSH
5	DT	Henry Melton	Bears	90	74	85	97/75	82
4	DT	Gerald McCoy	Buccaneers	91	72	90	96/70	83
3	DT	Ndamukong Suh	Lions	93	72	96	97/72	85
2	DT	Vince Wilfork	Patriots	93	56	96	88/47	98
1	DT	Geno Atkins	Bengals	97	73	91	99/72	93

TOP 5 ROOKIE DTS

	POSITION	NAME	TEAM	OVR	SPD	STR	PMV/FMV	BSH
5	DT	Akeem Spence	Buccaneers	71	64	94	64/76	88
4	DT	Johnathan Hankins	Giants	70	60	92	76/43	91
3	DT	Sharrif Floyd	Vikings	78	74	84	84/67	89
2	DT	Kwame Geathers	Chargers	61	48	89	74/40	83
1	DT	Star Lotulelei	Panthers	81	61	96	85/55	93

PRIMA'S TOP 5 DTS

	POSITION	NAME	TEAM	OVR	SPD	STR	PMV/FMV	BSH
5	DT	Henry Melton	Bears	90	74	85	97/75	82
4	DT	Vince Wilfork	Patriots	93	56	96	88/47	98
3	DT	Nick Fairley	Lions	90	73	88	95/72	91
2	DT	Gerald McCoy	Buccaneers	91	72	90	96/70	83
1	DT	Geno Atkins	Bengals	97	73	91	99/72	93

TOP 5 SLEEPER DTS

	POSITION	NAME	TEAM	OVR	SPD	STR	PMV/FMV	BSH
5	DT	John Jenkins	Saints	70	63	92	75/40	92
4	DT	Terrence Cody	Ravens	74	45	97	81/34	92
3	DT	Phil Taylor	Browns	83	62	93	85/54	95
2	DT	Torell Troup	Bills	68	50	93	82/30	92
1	DT	Stephen Paea	Bears	76	63	98	84/45	88

GENO ATKINS IS ONE OF THE BEST PASS-RUSHING OPTIONS AT DT.

PUTTING A PLAYER LIKE TERRENCE CODY IN THE RIGHT SITUATION WILL FORCE A TOUGH MATCHUP FOR YOUR OPPONENT!

LINEBACKERS

Linebackers have many jobs on the football field, and the more a certain player can do the more valuable he will be to his team! Certain teams like to use four LBs on the field at once, while others like to go with three. In a three linemen/four linebacker scheme, a player who lines up on the outside must be able to rush the passer off the edge. The players in the middle of this scheme must be quick and able to shed any linemen who try to block them. With a four linemen/three linebacker scheme, the LBs must be solid in coverage against TEs and HBs out of the backfield, while the MLB must work the whole field and make tackles. A truly great LB will also be able to stay in the game in nickel and dime packages when the opponent is throwing the ball, even though most of his position mates will be taken out of the game. With all the different styles and positions of LB, make sure you are maximizing your players' ratings and putting them in a position for success!

EA SPORTS' TOP 5 LBS

	POSITION	NAME	TEAM	OVR	SPD	POW	TAK	PUR
5	LB	Jerod Mayo	Patriots	94	85	91	96	98
4	LB	Aldon Smith	49ers	95	84	90	90	97
3	LB	Clay Matthews	Packers	95	86	95	90	97
2	LB	Von Miller	Broncos	97	88	89	95	99
1	LB	Patrick Willis	49ers	97	90	98	96	93

TOP 5 ROOKIE LBS

	POSITION	NAME	TEAM	OVR	SPD	POW	TAK	PUR
5	LB	Vontaze Burfict	Bengals	77	74	95	89	85
4	LB	Zaviar Gooden	Titans	65	90	87	69	74
3	LB	Alec Ogletree	Rams	77	83	89	79	93
2	LB	Corey Lemonier	49ers	68	85	90	74	87
1	LB	Barkevious Mingo	Browns	76	87	78	80	91

PRIMA'S TOP 5 LBS

	POSITION	NAME	TEAM	OVR	SPD	POW	TAK	PUR
5	LB	Navorro Bowman	49ers	93	83	91	99	97
4	LB	Lamarr Woodley	Steelers	89	82	90	90	93
3	LB	Von Miller	Broncos	97	88	89	95	99
2	LB	Clay Matthews	Packers	95	86	95	90	97
1	LB	Patrick Willis	49ers	97	90	98	96	93

TOP 5 SLEEPER LBS

	POSITION	NAME	TEAM	OVR	SPD	POW	TAK	PUR
5	LB	Bruce Carter	Cowboys	81	88	90	86	89
4	LB	Thomas Davis	Panthers	79	84	91	77	88
3	LB	Thomas Howard	Free Agent	82	87	77	79	91
2	LB	Joe Mays	Broncos	79	78	98	97	87
1	LB	Manny Lawson	Bills	82	88	73	77	94

VON MILLER IS A FORCE WHILE RUSHING THE PASSER.

JOE MAYS IS A SOLID LB WHO CAN REALLY LAY SOME BIG HITS THIS SEASON.

CORNERBACKS

Some of the best athletes in the world play CB in the NFL. Not only are they faced with the task of guarding incredibly talented WRs, but they must do everything in reverse! A truly great CB can shut down half of the field and take away a QB's favorite passing option. There has been a boom of big CBs lately who like to play physical press-style coverage to attempt to slow WRs down. Other CBs play off coverage and have raw ability that allows them to run and cut with any WR. Look beyond the Overall rating to check size and speed to know which type of CB is out there and how he can be best utilized! Some players might be best when playing man-to-man, while others may be more effective in zone coverage.

EA SPORTS' TOP 5 CBS

	POSITION	NAME	TEAM	OVR	SPD	PRS	MCV	ZCV
5	CB	Champ Bailey	Broncos	93	55	75	92	89
4	CB	Brandon Flowers	Chiefs	94	60	85	96	92
3	CB	Charles Tillman	Bears	95	73	95	92	90
2	CB	Richard Sherman	Seahawks	96	61	97	98	92
1	CB	Darrelle Revis	Buccaneers	97	64	90	99	93

TOP 5 ROOKIE CBS

	POSITION	NAME	TEAM	OVR	SPD	PRS	MCV	ZCV
5	CB	Logan Ryan	Patriots	70	87	80	79	87
4	CB	Brandon McGee	Rams	67	92	81	75	82
3	CB	Steve Williams	Chargers	69	91	48	83	73
2	CB	Desmond Trufant	Falcons	77	93	53	87	84
1	CB	Dee Milliner	Jets	81	94	82	88	86

PRIMA'S TOP 5 CBS

	POSITION	NAME	TEAM	OVR	SPD	PRS	MCV	ZCV
5	CB	Patrick Peterson	Cardinals	89	98	92	91	85
4	CB	Richard Sherman	Seahawks	96	61	97	98	92
3	CB	Darrelle Revis	Buccaneers	97	64	90	99	93
2	CB	Dominique Rodgers-Cromartie	Broncos	79	98	51	88	74
1	CB	Antonio Cromartie	Jets	92	96	86	98	88

TOP 5 SLEEPER CBS

	POSITION	NAME	TEAM	OVR	SPD	PRS	MCV	ZCV
5	CB	Teddy Williams	Cowboys	59	97	40	69	67
4	CB	Bradley Fletcher	Eagles	82	87	75	94	84
3	CB	Josh Wilson	Redskins	83	95	69	69	77
2	CB	Josh Robinson	Vikings	73	97	53	79	81
1	CB	DeMarcus Van Dyke	Steelers	69	98	76	74	69

THE LONGER YOUR CB IS FORCED TO COVER, THE BETTER THE CHANCE A WR CAN GET OPEN!

GIVE YOUR CB HELP WITH A SAFETY OR A LB IF HE IS GETTING BEATEN.

SAFETIES

The importance of the safety position in the NFL has continued to grow due to the explosion of the passing game. Safeties must be able to shift all over the field and change up their role on any given play. Safeties are split into two positions, free safety and strong safety. While free safeties usually are more known to play in the passing game while strong safeties get up in the box to stop the run, these lines have been blurred. With the greater prevalence of mobile QBs, the free safety sometimes needs to get involved in the running game. With HBs and TEs being split out wide with different shifts, a strong safety must be ready to go with them and cover them. Consider all of these skills and ratings when looking at this position. One factor for a safety can also be his ability to knock the ball loose with his hit power.

EA SPORTS' TOP 5 SAFETIES

	POSITION	NAME	TEAM	OVR	SPD	PRC	POW	TAK
5	FS	Devin McCourty	Patriots	92	93	81	64	68
4	SS	Reshad Jones	Dolphins	92	86	75	88	84
3	FS	Jairus Byrd	Bills	95	87	88	60	81
2	SS	Troy Polamalu	Steelers	95	89	92	85	80
1	FS	Eric Weddle	Chargers	96	84	91	77	94

PRIMA'S TOP 5 SAFETIES

	POSITION	NAME	TEAM	OVR	SPD	PRC	POW	TAK
5	SS	Troy Polamalu	Steelers	95	89	92	66	64
4	FS	Devin McCourty	Patriots	92	93	81	64	68
3	FS	Earl Thomas	Seahawks	90	93	77	74	81
2	SS	LaRon Landry	Colts	86	91	65	86	63
1	SS	Kam Chancellor	Seahawks	90	84	79	93	83

SAFETIES WHO CAN HELP IN THE RUN GAME WILL BE A HUGE ASSET THIS SEASON.

TOP 5 ROOKIE SAFETIES

	POSITION	NAME	TEAM	OVR	SPD	PRC	POW	TAK
5	SS	Duke Williams	Bills	70	91	61	82	66
4	SS	Kenny Vaccaro	Saints	80	83	74	86	74
3	SS	Shamarko Thomas	Steelers	72	91	72	90	70
2	FS	Tyrann Mathieu	Cardinals	72	90	74	83	67
1	FS	Eric Reid	49ers	76	88	65	93	79

TOP 5 SLEEPER SAFETIES

	POSITION	NAME	TEAM	OVR	SPD	PRC	POW	TAK
5	FS	Jerron McMillian	Packers	71	93	56	83	69
4	SS	Nate Ebner	Patriots	63	87	39	91	74
3	SS	Mike Mitchell	Panthers	75	87	55	91	76
2	SS	Christian Thompson	Ravens	67	90	45	82	71
1	SS	Taylor Mays	Bengals	74	94	54	86	66

WITH THE ALL-NEW FORCE IMPACT SYSTEM, SAFETIES CAN REALLY LAY SOME BIG HITS.

TOP 5 TEAMS

ONLINE RANKED GAME TEAMS

5 PHILADELPHIA EAGLES
4 WASHINGTON REDSKINS
3 GREEN BAY PACKERS
2 SEATTLE SEAHAWKS
1 SAN FRANCISCO 49ERS

HONORABLE MENTION: **FALCONS, TEXANS, BRONCOS**

Each season, gamers sign online and try to climb atop the online leaderboards. While some gamers pick their favorite team, many others take the best team available. Knowing what areas of the roster to look for can be crucial in determining what team to use. If you are best with a scrambling QB, you need to find a player with the ratings to fit your scheme. If you can find a style that meshes with your playbook, you will be well ahead of the competition. Here are our picks to use online in *Madden NFL 25*

5 PHILADELPHIA EAGLES

The Eagles have a unique playbook with their new head coach, Chip Kelly!

The Eagles have one of the best *Madden NFL* QBs of all-time in Michael Vick, who can stress defenses with his arm or his legs. With all of the new option-style plays in their playbook, Vick should once again dominate defenses. HB LeSean McCoy is another speedy player who has a great ability to cut back and find running lanes. On the outside, make sure to target speedy WR DeSean Jackson downfield at least once per half, as not many defenders can run stride for stride with him. On defense, the Eagles still have a solid pass rusher in Trent Cole, who will be the anchor for your defensive line. With all of the buzz surrounding their offense, Philly should be seen plenty online!

4 WASHINGTON REDSKINS

Make sure to try out all of the new pistol plays in the Redskins playbook.

Last season rookie QB Robert Griffin III came into the league and led an offense that got fans very excited. He led the Redskins to a playoff berth with an efficient passing attack and solid ground game. In *Madden NFL 25*, you can utilize the Redskins' pistol attack to test your opponents' run defense. Try handing the ball to HB Alfred Morris, who is a big, bruising back that can pick up first downs. If the defense over-commits, keep the ball with RGIII and burn them downfield. The Redskins also have a solid corps of rushers off the edge and will be a very popular team online this season. If they continue their winning ways from the end of last season, their ratings will only improve.

3 GREEN BAY PACKERS

Green Bay is has the best overall QB in the game with Aaron Rodgers, and there is nothing he can't do for your team.

There is no doubt that using the best QB in the game makes everything easier for your team. Aaron Rodgers has elite accuracy and plenty of weapons to throw the ball to on offense. Despite the loss of Greg Jennings, Green Bay still has three great WRs with Jordy Nelson, James Jones, and Randall Cobb. Use Cobb on screen passes and in the slot, where he can get separation from defenders. Jones and Nelson are targets that can play outside and hang onto the ball in the red zone. On defense, Green Bay is a popular team due to LB Clay Matthews's ability to get after the passer. With their solid defensive line, you won't need to work too hard to stop the run, and DT B.J. Raji is fast enough to keep QBs contained in the pocket. Don't sleep on the Packers if you are looking to pass the ball as your primary offensive attack.

2 SEATTLE SEAHAWKS

With all the new focus on the read option this year, Seattle will be a popular team!

Between all the brand-new combo moves and run blocking this year, aren't you ready to hop online and start pounding the ball? If so, Seattle is an ideal team. Not only can their QB help out in the run game, but they likely have the most powerful HB in the league. HB Marshawn Lynch is a weapon who can move the chains consistently. Use him not just between the tackles but on options and screen passes, too. On defense, the line has some speedy players who can rush the QB and close out games. The secondary also has the talent to match up with nearly any team in the game. A significant factor for Seattle is their size in the secondary!

1 SAN FRANCISCO 49ERS

The 49ers' decision to go with QB Colin Kaepernick turned out to be a good one!

Last season in the biggest *Madden NFL* tournaments, every game featured the San Francisco 49ers, thanks to their amazing defense and balanced offensive attack. With their great corps of LBs, the 49ers forced more turnovers and got crucial stops. On offense, the 49ers benefitted from mid-season roster upgrades due to their success on the field with rookie QB Colin Kaepernick. Although they lost a few of their offensive players, they maintained all of their best ones and even added some firepower with WR Anquan Boldin. Boldin will be a great weapon to team with Michael Crabtree due to their ability to hang onto passes in traffic. Use TE Vernon Davis to stretch defenses down the seam with his great speed. With the ability to run any style of offense and defense, SF should be popular once again this year.

5 KANSAS CITY CHIEFS
4 BUFFALO BILLS
3 SEATTLE SEAHAWKS
2 SAN FRANCISCO 49ERS
1 MINNESOTA VIKINGS

HONORABLE MENTION:
RAIDERS, TEXANS, REDSKINS

TEAMS TOP 5

RUSHING TEAMS

Running the ball in *Madden NFL 25* is a great way to win more games. Not only will you cut down on turnovers, but you will control the clock and keep your defense rested. If you can consistently keep the chains moving, defenses will get frustrated, which will open up the passing game! With all-new blocking this year, there has never been a better time to get committed to the run game. Here are our favorite rushing teams. They have a multitude of styles. Some running teams are built for power, while others are built for speed. No matter which team you choose from this list, you will be built to win on the ground!

5 KANSAS CITY CHIEFS

By giving the ball to Jamaal Charles at least 25 times a game, you can improve your chances of winning!

Although the Chiefs will be getting a new coach with Andy Reid, the safe bet is that Jamaal Charles will be a big part of his scheme. If your opponents don't commit to stopping the run, punish them. Your back is one of the most talented speed backs in the game, and he has a great burst that lets him shoot through the line. Stick with formations that load up one side of the line, like Singleback Ace Pair Chief, and let the defense know where you are going. They will have to prove they can stop it. Allow your back to carry the load, but feel free to let your new QB, Alex Smith, get to the edge every now and then, as he has decent speed the defense will need to worry about.

4 BUFFALO BILLS

Buffalo has three options at the QB position, so find out which one complements your style best.

C.J. Spiller is one of the best backs in *Madden NFL* and right on the brink of stardom. By using a two-back system in Buffalo, gamers can be assured they will be able to pull off every style of run. Use rookie QB E.J. Manuel and involve him in the run game as well. If the defense gets too aggressive against the run, work the play action and screen-pass game to get the ball to your backs in space. Buffalo also has some big TEs who should do well in the run-block game.

3 SEATTLE SEAHAWKS

Seattle has a playbook that is committed to the power run game!

While everyone loves a star HB, most gamers overlook the players who do the real work. The offensive line is a crucial part of having success in the run game. They can make a back's job extremely easy. Marshawn Lynch is a true power-run back who will benefit from the new force impact moves in the game this year. Don't forget about QB Russell Wilson, who put together some highlight runs last season too. The combo of these two guys going inside and outside should cause nightmares for the defense. Make sure to try out the stiff arm and truck moves with Lynch!

2 SAN FRANCISCO 49ERS

The only question for the 49ers is which HB to use.

While the 49ers are a great defensive team, their ground game can not be overlooked. They have four HBs who can carry the load, depending on which style you want to use. Frank Gore is a tremendous power back who should be your number one option. One way to stress the defense is to get as many of your backs as you can on the field at once. This way, the defense can't key in on who will be carrying the ball on any given play. Another way to rack up ground yards is to take off with QB Colin Kaepernick on passing plays. This can be devastating to a defense that thinks they have a stop on third down, only to see the QB scramble and move the chains. No matter what style of run offense you want to use, San Francisco has the pieces to fit.

1 MINNESOTA VIKINGS

Learn how to use the read option, as it can be very effective when run properly!

The Vikings have the highest-rated back in the game in Adrian Peterson, and he is perfect for trying out the new running moves in *Madden NFL 25*. All the moves work the same in the open field, so don't worry about how you get him the ball! Your QB is also a great threat in the read option game, so work those runs in to keep that defensive end occupied. By learning all the options available to you in the run game with Minnesota, you can easily transfer your skills to other teams and dominate on the ground!

TOP 5 TEAMS

PASSING TEAMS

5 ATLANTA FALCONS
4 NEW ENGLAND PATRIOTS
3 DENVER BRONCOS
2 DETROIT LIONS
1 GREEN BAY PACKERS

HONORABLE MENTION: **NEW ORLEANS SAINTS, NEW YORK GIANTS, DALLAS COWBOYS**

For many gamers, passing the ball is their preferred way to light up the scoreboard. While some players favor a pocket passer, others like QBs who have more mobility. Great passing teams have great receivers not only at the WR position, but also in the middle of the field with the TE. Finding the right combination of these lineups can result in an offense that is nearly impossible to stop. Once you find your team, find the right playbook for it and learn your reads to limit mistakes!

5 ATLANTA FALCONS

> **The Falcons have two tremendous WRs on the outside!**

For players who like to throw outside the numbers, the Falcons are a great option. QB Matt Ryan has found two of the better WRs in the NFL with Julio Jones and Roddy White. These two players can go up and make nearly any catch in traffic and are great options in the red zone. By bringing in HB Steven Jackson, the Falcons should have a solid veteran in the lineup who is versatile. If you need to convert on a big third down in the air, look for TE Tony Gonzalez over the middle, as he has made clutch catches his entire career.

4 NEW ENGLAND PATRIOTS

> **Keep extra blockers in to help in pass protection against opponents with great defenses.**

The Patriots have one of the best pocket passers in the game with QB Tom Brady. Brady can make all the big throws, and he is extremely accurate in the short passing game. Having such an elite QB comes with responsibility, however, as you must protect him at all costs. If you are under duress, look to get the ball downfield to some of your larger TE threats. While making throws under pressure can result in turnovers, these players have the skills needed to go up and make catches in traffic. The quicker you can make your reads in the passing game, the more success you will enjoy with the New England. Don't forget to work a fast tempo to keep defenses off-balance.

3 DENVER BRONCOS

> **Attempt one down-the-field pass every quarter with Peyton Manning to keep the defense back.**

The Broncos added WR Wes Welker to their lineup last season, and this should give QB Peyton Manning another great target in his second season in Denver. WR Eric Decker already benefitted from having Manning under center, as his ability to make quick decisions paid off for their offense. The Broncos have a few options at HB but none really jump out from the depth chart. Instead, work on ways to get speedy WR Trindon Holliday the ball in space, and see if he can take it the distance.

2 DETROIT LIONS

> **Work on using bullet passes by holding down the target's icon to really fit the ball into tight windows.**

While having a QB with one of the most powerful arms in *Madden NFL 25* can be a gift, it can also be a curse. Don't rely on QB Matt Stafford's cannon of an arm so much that you to make sloppy reads. Aside from star WR Calvin Johnson, the Lions have some other weapons. Look for their two talented HBs on streaks up the middle. If you can find a more reliable target to go along with Johnson, the Lions could be one of the best offensive teams in the game. Work both of your TEs to find out which one fits your style best.

1 GREEN BAY PACKERS

> **To be truly successful with the Packers, you need to get your HBs involved in the passing game!**

Green Bay is one of the best offensive teams all-around, and it all starts with QB Aaron Rodgers. Rodgers is mostly known for his arm, but he does have enough speed to pick up third downs with his legs. The Packers also drafted two rookie HBs who should be able to get involved in the passing game. Randall Cobb is a versatile WR who can line up anywhere. Allow James Jones and Jordy Nelson to fill in for the loss of Greg Jennings.

5 GREEN BAY PACKERS
4 HOUSTON TEXANS
3 CINCINNATI BENGALS
2 SEATTLE SEAHAWKS
1 SAN FRANCISCO 49ERS

HONORABLE MENTION:
BILLS, COWBOYS, GIANTS

TEAMS TOP 5

DEFENSIVE TEAMS

"Defense wins championships" is a motto that is uttered by all the top online players every season. Any player can find a team that will let them score 50 points a game, but the real key is being able to get a stop when the game is on the line. Some defenses are balanced, while others can bring pressure that will upset the offense's rhythm and force turnovers. No matter what style you favor, finding a team with the talent to match is a key part of *Madden NFL 25!*

5 GREEN BAY PACKERS

HAVING ONE DOMINANT DEFENSIVE PLAYER TO UNLEASH IN CRUNCH TIME IS VERY IMPORTANT!

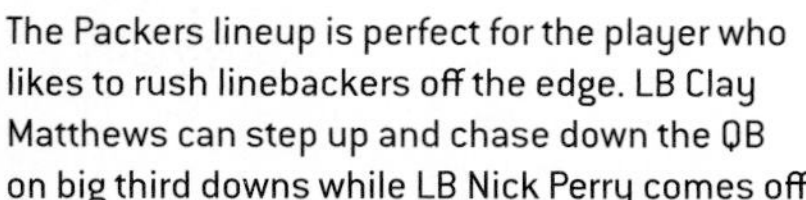

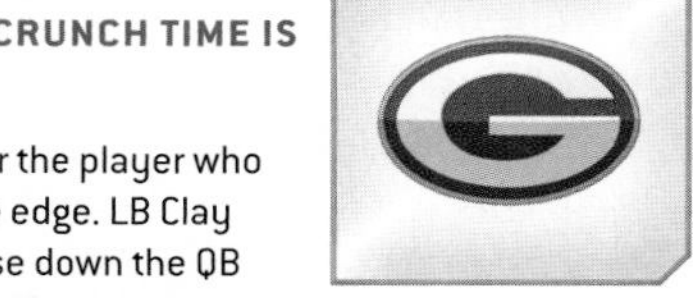

The Packers lineup is perfect for the player who likes to rush linebackers off the edge. LB Clay Matthews can step up and chase down the QB on big third downs while LB Nick Perry comes off the other side. The Packers still have plenty of talent in their secondary despite losing Charles Woodson to the Raiders. Find a way to get all their LBs on the field, as their defensive ends are good against the run but can be too slow to chase down QBs who escape the pocket!

4 HOUSTON TEXANS

FEEL FREE TO CHANGE UP YOUR DEFENSIVE PLAYBOOK IF YOU THINK IT WILL MAXIMIZE YOUR TALENT OR CONFUSE YOUR OPPONENT.

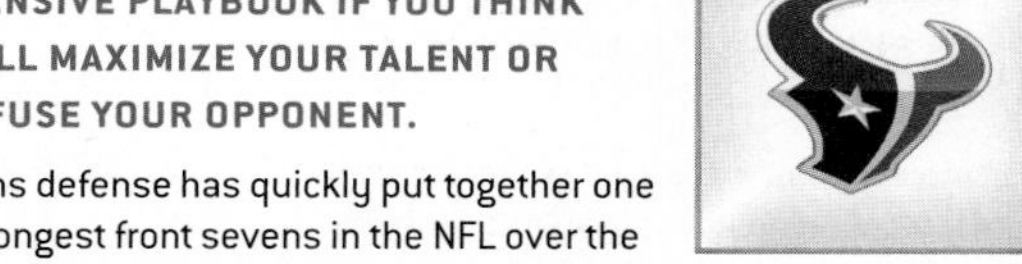

The Texans defense has quickly put together one of the strongest front sevens in the NFL over the last few seasons. Although they have had some players move on via free agency, they still have star players like J.J. Watt, who will make any offensive linemen nervous. Backing up Watt is LB Brian Cushing, who will be free to roam and put big hits on players coming over the middle. By adding future Hall of Fame safety Ed Reed to the lineup, the Texans did a good job solidifying their secondary with playmakers.

3 CINCINNATI BENGALS

SET YOUR DEPTH CHART TO MAXIMIZE THE TALENT ON YOUR ROSTER.

The Bengals have great athletic ability on defense to match their talent on the offensive side of the ball. Your speedy linebackers have the skill to drop back and match up with slot WRs or get out on the edge and play the run. The Bengals also have enough talent with the ends that you shouldn't have to blitz often, which is great for conservative players. This team is also capable of forcing a solid number of turnovers, which can set up their offense for success. Make sure to dig through your full lineup to find some of their gems on the bench!

2 SEATTLE SEAHAWKS

THE MARK OF A GREAT DEFENSE IS CAPITALIZING ON BAD THROWS BY THE OFFENSE WITH CATCHES INSTEAD OF DROPS.

The Seattle secondary has not only solid speed but great size that can defend against big TEs and WRs. Use fast pass rushers like Bruce Irvin to chase down the QB. The key to the Seattle defense is in the middle with LB Bobby Wagner, a big hitter who can force fumbles at any time. Look to play a nickel defense for most of the game, as new CB Antoine Winfield is solid against the run.

1 SAN FRANCISCO 49ERS

THE MORE HIT POWER POSSESSED BY YOUR DEFENSE, THE MORE FUMBLES YOU WILL FORCE!

There is only one team in *Madden NFL 25* with a truly dominant core of linebackers, and that is the 49ers. Their offensive style lines up perfectly with their ability to limit opponents. Teams will find it very hard to crack their defense. The most impressive thing about the lineup is its depth. At nearly any position, you can find a backup who would be a starter on other teams. You can play an aggressive style with them because you have plenty of fresh players to rotate. There is no limit to the defensive coverages you can play, and that means your opponent must be ready for anything, which will give you a huge advantage.

TOP 5 TEAMS

SLEEPER TEAMS

5 CAROLINA PANTHERS
4 DETROIT LIONS
3 TENNESSEE TITANS
2 BUFFALO BILLS
1 KANSAS CITY CHIEFS

HONORABLE MENTION: **RAIDERS, BUCCANEERS**

For gamers who are looking to truly test their skill level, playing with a less skilled team can be a great challenge. Choosing a lower-rated team can be a good way to even the playing field against a friend who isn't as talented. Although the teams on the list might not be playoff teams, they all bring something to the field that is unique. If your opponents aren't ready to play their best game, they will have their hands full. Here are five sleeper teams you can use to shock your opponent in *Madden NFL 25*!

5 CAROLINA PANTHERS

A UNIQUE PLAY STYLE LIKE THE OPTION CAN REALLY THROW YOUR OPPONENTS FOR A LOOP!

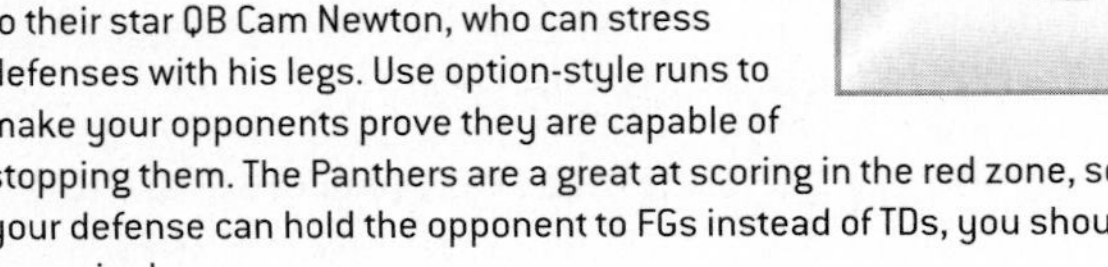

The Carolina Panthers are a distinctive team due to their star QB Cam Newton, who can stress defenses with his legs. Use option-style runs to make your opponents prove they are capable of stopping them. The Panthers are a great at scoring in the red zone, so if your defense can hold the opponent to FGs instead of TDs, you should earn wins!

4 DETROIT LIONS

A TRUE STAR PLAYER CAN REALLY MAKE A LOWER-RATED TEAM STAND OUT!

The Lions have one of the best passing combos in *Madden NFL 25* with QB Matt Stafford and WR Calvin Johnson. Johnson is the best WR in the entire game and can still be targeted even when facing double coverage. Force your opponent to commit tons of resources to stop him, which will open up the run game for free agent signee Reggie Bush out of the backfield. On defense, the Lions have a strong defensive line and some solid hit power in the back seven.

3 TENNESSEE TITANS

USE PLAY ACTION AND ROLL-OUTS TO MAKE THROWS EASIER FOR QB JAKE LOCKER.

The Titans have one of the fastest HBs in the game with Chris Johnson, and his ability to take any play the distance will keep you in every game. QB Jake Locker has a strong arm to get the ball downfield, but don't force it into tight windows because his accuracy is still improving. On defense, the Titans won't win you any games, but by running the ball you should be able to hang in and surprise some people.

2 BUFFALO BILLS

IF YOU ARE OFF TO A SLOW START WITH YOUR STARTING QB, TRY PLAYING ONE OF YOUR BACKUPS FOR A SPARK.

Buffalo has put together a great group of running backs that will dominate against any player who doesn't have their run defense down. Rookie QB E.J. Manuel is a great threat who can break containment if defenses don't key in on him. With a fast secondary, the Bills can hang with any WR corps. Unleash star pass rusher Mario Williams after the QB to get your defense off the field.

1 KANSAS CITY CHIEFS

HAVING A BACK LIKE CHARLES MEANS THAT KC IS A REAL CONTENDER WITH THE ALL NEW RUN FREE CONTROLS!

The Chiefs have missed the playoffs the last few seasons, but they have quietly put together a solid defense. They solidified their team by trading for efficient QB Alex Smith to go with star HB Jamaal Charles. The Chiefs can control the game with their defense thanks to talent in each of their corps. Your opponent can't attack a certain area and must commit to a balanced game plan to beat you. Offensively, there is some great speed at the HB position that can be used to grind out games. For the balanced player who can use a good short passer, the Chiefs can shock some people!

Teams

CONTENTS

OVERVIEW 104

HOW TO USE THE TEAMS CHAPTER: OFFENSIVE PLAYS 104

HOW TO USE THE TEAMS CHAPTER: DEFENSIVE PLAYS 105

CHICAGO BEARS 106

CINCINNATI BENGALS 112

BUFFALO BILLS 118

DENVER BRONCOS 124

CLEVELAND BROWNS 130

TAMPA BAY BUCCANEERS 136

ARIZONA CARDINALS 142

SAN DIEGO CHARGERS 148

KANSAS CITY CHIEFS 154

INDIANAPOLIS COLTS 160

DALLAS COWBOYS 166

MIAMI DOLPHINS 172

PHILADELPHIA EAGLES 178

ATLANTA FALCONS 184

SAN FRANCISCO 49ERS 190

NEW YORK GIANTS 196

JACKSONVILLE JAGUARS 202

NEW YORK JETS 208

DETROIT LIONS 214

GREEN BAY PACKERS 220

CAROLINA PANTHERS 226

NEW ENGLAND PATRIOTS 232

OAKLAND RAIDERS 238

ST. LOUIS RAMS 244

BALTIMORE RAVENS 250

WASHINGTON REDSKINS 256

NEW ORLEANS SAINTS 262

SEATTLE SEAHAWKS 268

PITTSBURGH STEELERS 274

HOUSTON TEXANS 280

TENNESSEE TITANS 286

MINNESOTA VIKINGS 292

OVERVIEW

HOW TO USE THE TEAMS CHAPTER: OFFENSIVE PLAYS

In this year's guide we have redesigned how we deliver each team's best offensive plays. We did this by listening to fan feedback and have once again simplified the information you're about to read. The offensive play section is set up so that you can take the running and passing tips we provide and put them to use right when you start playing *Madden NFL 25*. Here are the five most important pieces of information broken down in each team's offensive play section.

5 BEST PERSONNEL
4 PRO TIPS
3 PLAY CALL SHEET
2 RUNNING FORMATION
1 PASSING FORMATION

5 BEST PERSONNEL

OFFENSE

RECOMMENDED OFFENSIVE PASS FORMATION:
GUN SNUGS FLIPPED (1 HB, 1 TE, 3 WR)

> **THERE ARE MANY OTHER FORMATIONS WITHIN EACH TEAM'S PLAYBOOK THAT HAVE THE SAME PERSONNEL AS THE ONE WE GIVE YOU. USE THEM ALL.**

In this section we give you the best personnel grouping for your team. We also give you the best formation to use with that personnel. It's extremely important that you are consistently playing to your team's strengths and that you are getting enough repetitions for each of your team's superstars. Over the course of a game it can be hard to manage which formations and players should see the field. We take that question and throw it out the window by telling you what formation and plays you should be using in *Madden NFL 25*.

4 PRO TIPS

PRO TIPS

> WR MARQUISE GOODWIN'S 98 SPD WILL BE THE FASTEST ON THE FIELD.
> WR T.J. GRAHAM IS ANOTHER SPEEDSTER, WITH 96 SPD.
> ROOKIE WR DA'RICK ROGERS'S 81 CIT RATING IS THE SECOND HIGHEST AMONG RECEIVERS.

> **MAKE SURE TO USE THE PRO TIP PLAYERS IN MULTIPLE SITUATIONS.**

Maximizing your team's depth chart takes hours of studying your team's rosters and ratings. We are giving you the cheat sheet to unlock your team's hidden stars so that you can make the right substitutions at the right time. Each Pro Tip offers valuable information that you can use to increase your team's in-game ability. These depth chart moves are crucial to your team's overall success, and you will want to make them each and every game.

3 PLAY CALL SHEET

CHICAGO BEARS RUNNING PLAY CALL SHEET

LEGEND: Inside Run | Outside Run | Shotgun Run | QB Run

1ST DOWN RUNS	2ND AND SHORT	3RD AND SHORT	GOAL LINE RUNS	2ND AND LONG	3RD AND LONG
I-Form Pro—HB Toss	Singleback Doubles—Inside Zone	I-Form Twins Flex—FB Dive Strong	I-Form Tight—HB Blast	Gun Split Offset—Power O	Gun 5WR Trio—QB Draw
I-Form Pro—Iso	Weak Twin Flex—HB Lead	I-Form Twins Flex—HB Toss	I-Form Tight—Iso	I-Form Pro—Lead Draw	Gun Trey Open—QB Draw
Weak Twins Flex—Power O	Strong Tight Pair—HB Blast	Singleback Ace—HB Stretch	Weak Twins Flex—Toss Weak	Gun Spread Flex Wk—HB Mid Draw	Gun Trey Open—HB Mid Draw

CHICAGO BEARS PASSING PLAY CALL SHEET

LEGEND: Base Play | Man Beater | Zone Beater | Blitz Beater

1ST DOWN PLAY	2ND AND SHORT	3RD AND SHORT	GOAL LINE PASSING	2ND AND LONG	3RD AND LONG
Gun 5 WR Trio—Hitch Corner	Gun Trey Open—Y Short Cross	Gun Spread Flex Wk—HB Slip Screen	Gun Empty Trey—Quick Slants	Singleback Ace—Close PA HB Wheel	Gun Trey Open—Trail Shake
Gun Bunch—Z Spot Dig	Singleback Tight Flex—Mesh	Strong Pro—Go's Y Post	I-Form Pro—PA End Around	Gun Y Trips Wk—Comebacks Dig	Singleback Ace Pair Twins—Smash
Singleback Ace—Y Shallow Cross	Gun Trio—Curl Flat	I-Form Twins Flex—Bears Fk Toss Scrn	I-Form Tight—Goal Line Fade	Gun Empty Trey—Bears Smash	Gun Split Offset—Shakes

> **WE PROVIDE EACH TEAM WITH 12 FULLY BROKEN DOWN PLAYS.**

Each team has a play call sheet that will provide situational play calls. These 48 plays give you a play to use in almost any situation you face. Make sure you hit practice mode and spend time running the plays suggested in the play call sheet. Perfect practice makes perfect, so spend ample time working on these plays.

2 RUNNING FORMATION

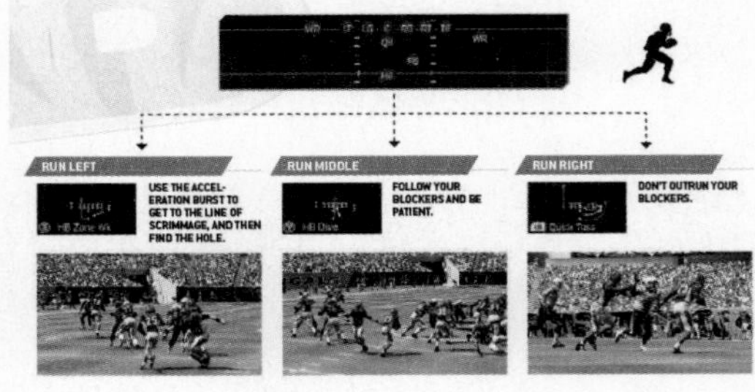

> **USE PLAY ACTION OFF OF YOUR FAVORITE RUNS TO CONFUSE YOUR OPPONENT.**

Each team has a recommended offensive running formation that is best used to run the ball with. We have gone through every playbook for every team and hand picked the best running formations and plays for your team. Make sure to use this formation when you want to run the ball. The formation provided is the best option within your team's playbook.

1 PASSING FORMATION

> **MIX IN RUNNING PLAYS FROM THIS FORMATION TO KEEP YOUR OPPONENTS ON THEIR TOES!**

Each team has a recommended offensive passing formation that is best used to pass the ball with. We have gone through every playbook for every team and hand-picked the best passing formations and plays for your team. Make sure to use this formation when you want to pass the ball. The formation provided is the best option within your team's playbook.

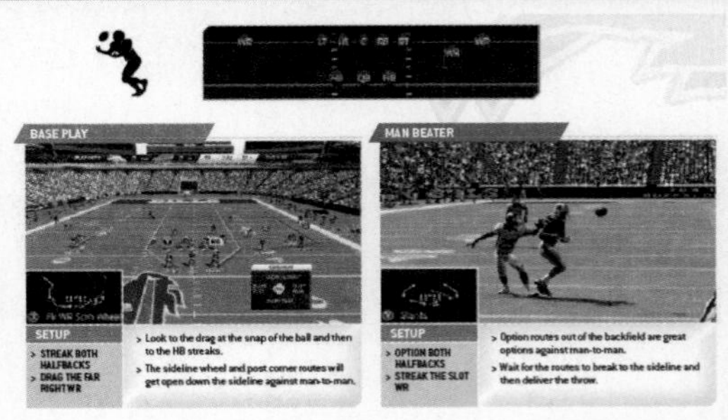

5 GOAL LINE DEFENSE
4 PRO TIPS
3 PLAY CALL SHEET
2 RUNNING FORMATION
1 PASSING FORMATION

HOW TO USE THE TEAMS CHAPTER: DEFENSIVE PLAYS

In this year's guide we have redesigned how we deliver each teams best defensive plays. We did this by listening to fan feedback and have once again simplified the information you're about to read. The defensive play section is set up so that you can instantly take the tips we provide and put them to use right when you start playing *Madden NFL 25*. Here are the five most important pieces of information broken down in each team's defensive play section.

5 GOAL LINE DEFENSE

DEFENSE

RECOMMENDED DEFENSIVE PASS FORMATION:
NICKEL NORMAL

GO WITH SIZE AND STRENGTH IN THE GOAL LINE RATHER THAN SPEED AND QUICKNESS.

One of the most important areas on the field is the goal line. This is where games are won and lost. Within each team's play call sheet we provide you with the best plays within your team's playbook for goal line situations. Use these plays to improve your defense in this crucial area of the field. If you want to use other plays in the goal line we recommend using any type of Cover 2 zone.

4 PRO TIPS

PRO TIPS

- PLACE CB STEPHON GILMORE ON YOUR OPPONENT'S BEST WR.
- USE CB RON BROOKS TO COVER YOUR OPPONENT'S FASTEST WR.
- CB LEODIS MCKELVIN SHOULD BE USED AS THE NICKEL DB.

THE PRO TIP SUBSTITUTIONS ARE VITAL TO YOUR TEAM'S SUCCESS.

Within each defensive play section we provide you with the key depth chart moves that will help you win more games. Each team has bench players who prove to be valuable when you break down their ratings. Rather than study the rosters and ratings yourself we have done the work for you. Simply look at each team's Pro Tips to learn the secrets of the roster!

3 PLAY CALL SHEET

CHICAGO BEARS DEFENSIVE RUN PLAY CALL SHEET

1ST DOWN RUN DEFENSE	2ND AND SHORT	3RD AND SHORT	GOAL LINE RUN DEFENSE	2ND AND LONG	3RD AND LONG
4-3 Over—Cover 1	4-3 Over Plus—Fire Man	4-6 Normal—Weak Blitz	Goal Line 5-3-3—Jam Cover 1	Nickel Wide 9—2 Man Under	4-6 Normal—2 Man Under
4-3 Over—Smoke Mid Zone 2	4-3 Over Plus—Fire Zone 2	4-6 Normal—Fire Zone 3	Goal Line 5-3-3—Flat Buzz	Nickel Wide 9—Cover 4	4-6 Normal—Cover 4

CHICAGO BEARS DEFENSIVE PASS PLAY CALL SHEET

1ST DOWN PLAY	2ND AND SHORT	3RD AND SHORT	GOAL LINE PASSING	2ND AND LONG	3RD AND LONG
Man Coverage	Sub 4-1-6—2 Man Under	Nickel Normal—Cover 1 Robber	Goal Line 6-3-2—GL Man	Nickel Normal—Over Storm Brave	Dime Normal—MLB Blitz
Zone Coverage	Sub 4-1-6—Cover 2 Sink	Nickel Normal—Sugar 3 Seam	Goal Line 6-3-2—GL Zone	Nickel Normal—FS Slant 3	Dime Normal—Fox Fire Zone

LEGEND: Man Coverage | Zone Coverage | Man Blitz | Zone Blitz

WE PROVIDE EACH TEAM WITH 12 FULLY BROKEN DOWN PLAYS.

Each team has a play call sheet that will provide situational play calls. These 48 plays will give you a play to use in almost any situation you face. Make sure you hit practice mode and spend time running the plays suggested in the play call sheet. Perfect practice makes perfect, so spend ample time working on these plays.

2 RUNNING FORMATION

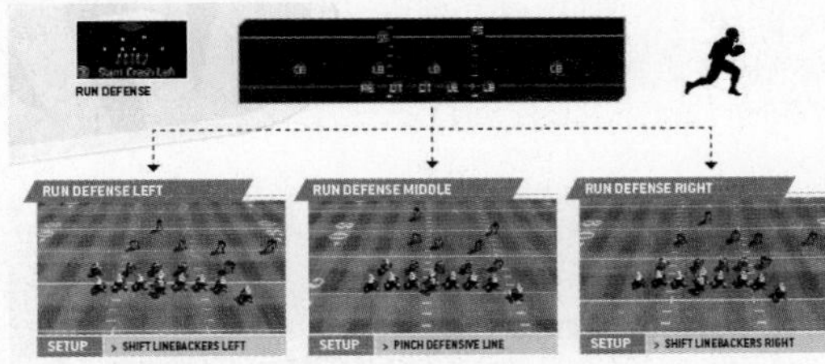

WE TEACH YOU HOW TO STOP THE RUN ALL OVER THE FIELD.

Each team has a recommended defensive running formation that is best used to stop the run. We have gone through every playbook for every team and hand-picked the best run-stuffing formations and plays for your team. Make sure to use this formation when you want to stop the run. The formation provided is the best option within your team's playbook.

1 PASSING FORMATION

DEFENSE IS ALL ABOUT CONFUSING THE OFFENSE, SO MAKE SURE TO MIX UP YOUR PLAY CALLS!

Each team has a recommended defensive passing formation that is best used to stop the pass. We have gone through every playbook for every team and hand-picked the best defensive passing formations and plays for your team. Make sure to use this formation when you want to stop the pass. The formation provided is the best option within your team's playbook.

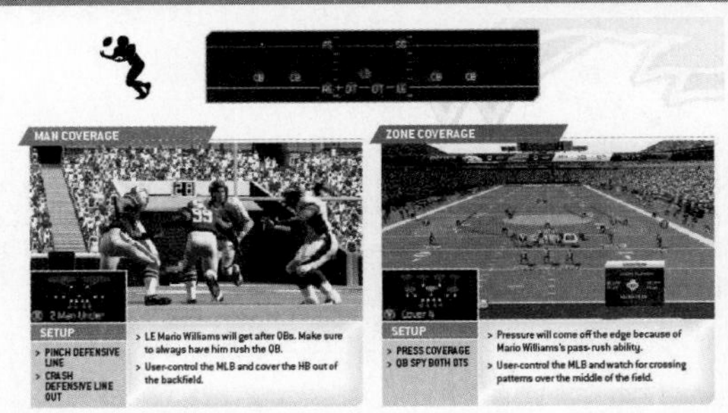

OVERVIEW

Chicago Bears

2012 TEAM RANKINGS

3rd NFC North (10-6-0)

PASSING OFFENSE: **29th**
RUSHING OFFENSE: **10th**
PASSING DEFENSE: **8th**
RUSHING DEFENSE: **8th**

2012 TEAM LEADERS

PASSING: **Jay Cutler: 3,033**
RUSHING: **Matt Forte: 1,094**
RECEIVING: **Brandon Marshall: 1,508**
TACKLES: **Lance Briggs: 103**
SACKS: **Julius Peppers: 11.5**
INTS: **Tim Jennings: 9**

KEY ADDITIONS

TE Martellus Bennett
LOLB James Anderson
MLB D.J. Williams

KEY ROOKIES

MLB Jon Bostic
RT Jordan Mills
WR Marquess Wilson

CONNECTED FRANCHISE MODE STRATEGY

CFM TEAM RATING: **74**
OFFENSIVE SCHEME: **West Coast**
DEFENSIVE SCHEME: **Base 4-3**
STRENGTHS: **QB, HB, LT, RE, LOLB, ROLB**
WEAKNESSES: **WR, TE, LE, FS, SS**

SCHEDULE

1	Sep 8	1:00 PM ET		BENGALS
2	Sep 15	1:00 PM ET		VIKINGS
3	Sep 22	8:30 PM ET	AT	STEELERS
4	Sep 29	1:00 PM ET	AT	LIONS
5	Oct 6	1:00 PM ET		SAINTS
6	Oct 10	8:25 PM ET		GIANTS
7	Oct 20	1:00 PM ET	AT	REDSKINS
8	BYE			
9	Nov 4	8:40 PM ET	AT	PACKERS
10	Nov 10	1:00 PM ET		LIONS
11	Nov 17	1:00 PM ET		RAVENS
12	Nov 24	1:00 PM ET	AT	RAMS
13	Dec 1	1:00 PM ET	AT	VIKINGS
14	Dec 9	8:40 PM ET		COWBOYS
15	Dec 15	1:00 PM ET	AT	BROWNS
16	Dec 22	1:00 PM ET	AT	EAGLES
17	Dec 29	1:00 PM ET		PACKERS

FRANCHISE OVERVIEW

BEARS GAMEPLAY RATING

85

> SEE THE INSIDE BACK COVER FOR A QUICK REFERENCE TO THE GAME ABBREVIATIONS USED THROUGHOUT THIS GUIDE.

> IMPROVE WITH YOUR TEAM BY VISITING PRIMAGAMES.COM/MADDENNFL25 FOR MORE INFORMATION AND HOW-TO VIDEOS.

OFFENSIVE SCOUTING REPORT

> QB Jay Cutler has a 90 OVR rating, but he is also 30 years old and in the final year of his contract. Use him as trade bait or use him for one last playoff push before you start rebuilding the franchise around a younger QB.

> The Bears desperately need help at the WR position. Outside of WR Brandon Marshall they don't have a receiver they can rely on. Consider packaging Cutler and Marshall together to trade for future draft picks.

> HB Matt Forte will carry the load offensively for the Bears, but he doesn't have a suitable backup. Look for speed in the draft.

DEFENSIVE SCOUTING REPORT

> RE Shea McClellin and LE Cornelius Washington are the future of this defensive squad. Build around them with strong interior DTs.

> The acquisition of LOLB James Anderson and MLB D.J. Williams will help fill a linebacker need for the Bears, but neither is a long-term solution. Not to mention that ROLB Lance Briggs will need to be replaced soon. The linebacking corps in Chicago needs a face-lift in the coming years.

> The Bears CBs lack speed, but they do have good size with Charles Tillman. This is another position that will need attention in the draft. Speed kills at CB, so look for that in the later rounds.

OWNER & COACH PROFILES

TED PHILLIPS
LEGACY SCORE: 300 | OFF. SCHEME: West Coast
DEF. SCHEME: Base 4-3

MARC TRESTMAN
LEVEL: 1 | LEGACY SCORE: 0
OFF. SCHEME: West Coast | DEF. SCHEME: Base 4-3

TEAM OVERVIEW

KEY PLAYERS

WR #15

BRANDON MARSHALL

KEY RATINGS

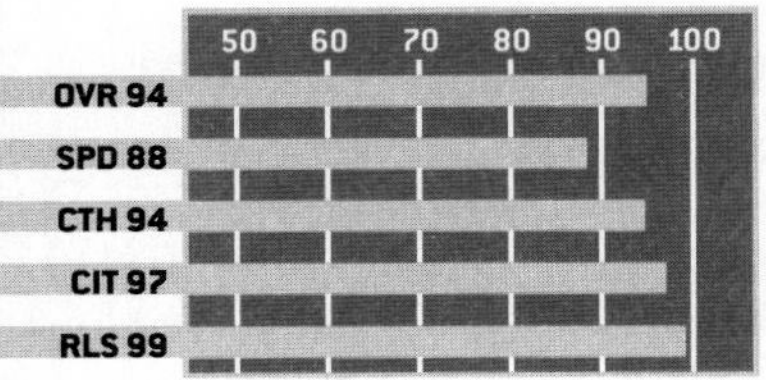

- End zone fades are a great way to utilize Marshall's height in the red zone.
- Look to get the ball to Marshall on third down. He has a 97 CIT rating, which means he won't drop many passes.
- Marshall can catch any ball thrown his way. Make sure to target him in the red zone as he is great catching end zone fades.
- Marshall has two years remaining on his contract. Consider extending his contract—he will be a solid player for years to come.

RE #90

JULIUS PEPPERS

KEY RATINGS

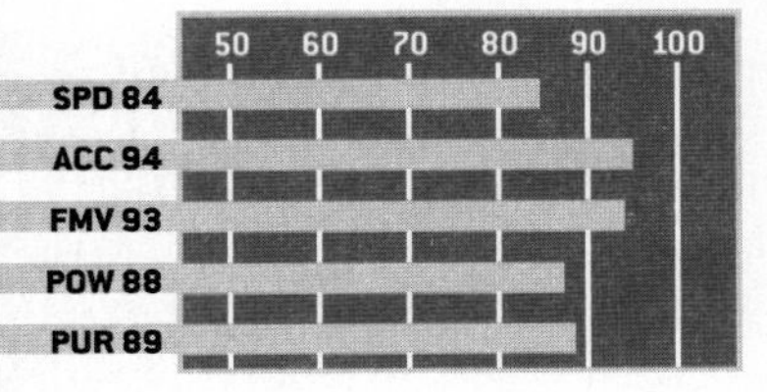

- Peppers has a nice Overall rating, but he doesn't have the elite ratings to really dominate games.
- He will be good in spurts and will be a contributor if you use the Bears in online ranked matches.
- Peppers will appeal to a lot of teams around the league. Consider trading him to drop his heavy contract and let your young DEs flourish.
- At 33 years of age and with three years left on his contract, Peppers could quickly become a concern on this roster.

PRE-GAME SETUP

KEY RUNNING SUBSTITUTION

Who: HB Michael Bush

Where: Backup HB

Why: Use Bush in late-game situations. His 95 CAR rating will ensure you don't turn the ball over.

Key Stats: 95 CAR, 74 CTH

KEY PASSING SUBSTITUTION

Who: WR Earl Bennett

Where: #2 WR

Why: Bennett doesn't have blazing speed like Devin Hester, but he does have 89 CIT. He needs to see the field every down for the Bears.

Key Stats: 89 CIT

KEY RUN DEFENSE SUBSTITUTION

Who: DT Stephen Paea

Where: Starting DT

Why: Paea has 88 BSH, which is the best of the DTs on this team. He will help clog the middle of the field and allow linebackers to make plays.

Key Stats: BSH 88, TAK 86, 87 POW

KEY PASS DEFENSE SUBSTITUTION

Who: CB Zack Brown

Where: Nickel CB

Why: Brown has great hands for a CB and will provide a defensive boost against pass-heavy teams.

Key Stats: 72 CTH, 89 JMP

OFFENSIVE DEPTH CHART

POS	FIRST NAME	LAST NAME	OVR
QB	Jay	Cutler	86
QB	Josh	McCown	71
QB	Matt	Blanchard	64
HB	Matt	Forte	91
HB	Michael	Bush	81
HB	Armando	Allen	67
FB	Harvey	Unga	74
FB	Tony	Fiammetta	69
WR	Brandon	Marshall	95
WR	Earl	Bennett	77
WR	Alshon	Jeffery	75
WR	Devin	Hester	73
WR	Eric	Weems	73
WR	Marquess	Wilson	66
WR	Terrence	Toliver	61
WR	Joe	Anderson	61
TE	Martellus	Bennett	88
TE	Steve	Maneri	69
TE	Kyle	Adams	66
TE	Brody	Eldridge	65
TE	Fendi	Onobun	62
LT	Jermon	Bushrod	86
LT	Eben	Britton	70
LT	Cory	Brandon	59
LG	Matt	Slauson	79
LG	Edwin	Williams	73
LG	James	Brown	65
C	Roberto	Garza	76
C	Patrick	Mannelly	66
C	Taylor	Boggs	61
RG	Kyle	Long	75
RG	Derek	Dennis	60
RT	J'Marcus	Webb	77
RT	Jonathan	Scott	72
RT	Jordan	Mills	70

DEFENSIVE DEPTH CHART

POS	FIRST NAME	LAST NAME	OVR
LE	Corey	Wootton	78
LE	Turk	McBride	72
LE	Cornelius	Washington	69
LE	Cheta	Ozougwu	64
RE	Julius	Peppers	92
RE	Shea	McClellin	73
RE	Kyle	Moore	72
DT	Henry	Melton	90
DT	Sedrick	Ellis	77
DT	Stephen	Paea	76
DT	Nate	Collins	67
DT	Corvey	Irvin	67
LOLB	James	Anderson	82
LOLB	J.T.	Thomas	64
LOLB	Patrick	Trahan	62
MLB	D.J.	Williams	80
MLB	Blake	Costanzo	69
MLB	Jon	Bostic	67
ROLB	Lance	Briggs	94
ROLB	Khaseem	Greene	71
ROLB	Lawrence	Wilson	66
ROLB	Jerry	Franklin	60
CB	Charles	Tillman	95
CB	Tim	Jennings	90
CB	Kelvin	Hayden	75
CB	Zack	Bowman	74
CB	Sherrick	McManis	66
CB	Isaiah	Frey	60
FS	Chris	Conte	74
FS	Brandon	Hardin	70
FS	Anthony	Walters	68
FS	Tom	Nelson	63
SS	Major	Wright	81
SS	Tom	Zbikowski	79
SS	Craig	Steltz	72
SS	Cyhl	Quarles	57

SPECIAL TEAMS DEPTH CHART

POS	FIRST NAME	LAST NAME	OVR
K	Robbie	Gould	93
P	Adam	Podlesh	73

Chicago Bears

RECOMMENDED OFFENSIVE RUN FORMATION: I-FORM PRO (2 RB, 1 TE, 2 WR)

PRO TIPS

- > HB MICHAEL BUSH WILL BE GREAT IN LATE-GAME SITUATIONS WITH HIS 95 CAR RATING.
- > USE THE RIGHT STICK TO PLAYMAKER ANY RUN THE OPPOSITE DIRECTION.
- > FB EVAN RODRIGUEZ HAS 83 SPD AND WILL BE AN EFFECTIVE WEAPON IN THE PASSING GAME.
- > USE PLAY ACTION TO TRY TO FREE UP WR DEVIN HESTER DOWNFIELD.

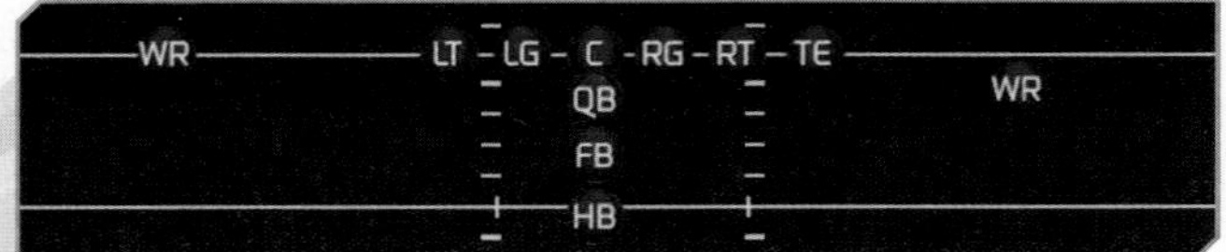

RUN LEFT

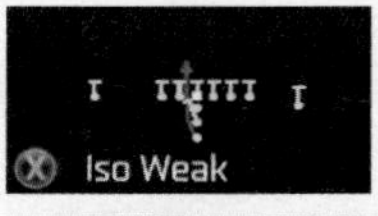

FOLLOW YOUR BLOCKS OFF THE LEFT EDGE.

RUN MIDDLE

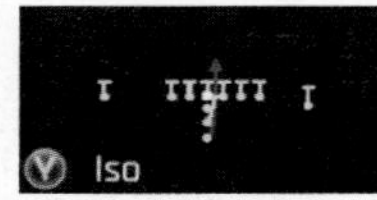

KEEP THIS RUN BETWEEN THE TACKLES.

RUN RIGHT

USE THE ACCELERATION BURST TO GET TO THE OUTSIDE EDGE.

CHICAGO BEARS RUNNING PLAY CALL SHEET

LEGEND: Inside Run | Outside Run | Shotgun Run | QB Run

1ST DOWN RUNS	2ND AND SHORT	3RD AND SHORT	GOAL LINE RUNS	2ND AND LONG	3RD AND LONG
I-Form Pro—HB Toss	Singleback Doubles—Inside Zone	I-Form Twins Flex—FB Dive Strong	I-Form Tight—HB Blast	Gun Split Offset—Power O	Gun 5WR Trio—QB Draw
I-Form Pro—Iso	Weak Twin Flex—HB Lead	I-Form Twins Flex—HB Toss	I-Form Tight—Iso	I-Form Pro—Lead Draw	Gun Trey Open—QB Draw
Weak Twins Flex—Power O	Strong Tight Pair—HB Blast	Singleback Ace—HB Stretch	Weak Twins Flex—Toss Weak	Gun Spread Flex Wk—HB Mid Draw	Gun Trey Open—HB Mid Draw

CHICAGO BEARS PASSING PLAY CALL SHEET

LEGEND: Base Play | Man Beater | Zone Beater | Blitz Beater

1ST DOWN PLAY	2ND AND SHORT	3RD AND SHORT	GOAL LINE PASSING	2ND AND LONG	3RD AND LONG
Gun 5 WR Trio—Hitch Corner	Gun Trey Open—Y Short Cross	Gun Spread Flex Wk—HB Slip Screen	Gun Empty Trey—Quick Slants	Singleback Ace—Close PA HB Wheel	Gun Trey Open—Trail Shake
Gun Bunch—Z Spot Dig	Singleback Tight Flex—Mesh	Strong Pro—Go's Y Post	I-Form Pro—PA End Around	Gun Y Trips Wk—Comebacks Dig	Singleback Ace Pair Twins—Smash
Singleback Ace—Y Shallow Cross	Gun Trio—Curl Flat	I-Form Twins Flex—Bears Fk Toss Scrn	I-Form Tight—Goal Line Fade	Gun Empty Trey—Bears Smash	Gun Split Offset—Shakes

In these play call sheets we picked the best plays for specific situations so that you will have a play for every down and distance.

OFFENSE

RECOMMENDED OFFENSIVE PASS FORMATION: GUN SNUGS FLIPPED (1 HB, 1 TE, 3 WR)

PRO TIPS

> WR ALSHON JEFFERY ADDS A TON OF SIZE TO THE FIELD. USE HIS 6'3" HEIGHT FOR JUMP BALL SITUATIONS.

> WR DEVIN HESTER IS BEST USED FOR SCREENS, DRAGS, AND ZIG ROUTES.

> TE MARTELLUS BENNETT IS A MISMATCH FOR MOST DEFENSES BECAUSE OF HIS HEIGHT AND JUMPING ABILITY.

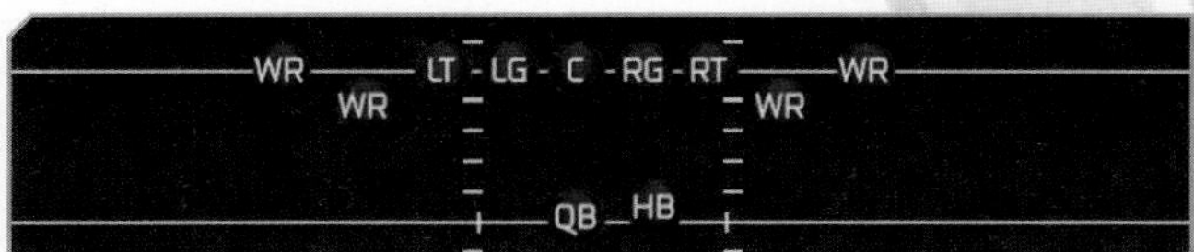

BASE PLAY

SETUP

> STREAK THE FAR LEFT WR
> DRAG THE FAR RIGHT WR

> The wheel routes on the sideline crush most coverages.

> Hit the drag underneath to open up the sideline wheels.

MAN BEATER

SETUP

> WHEEL THE HB
> STREAK THE FAR LEFT WR

> The corner route will be open for big plays down the sideline.

> One of the underneath drags will get open. Deliver the ball with a high lead pass.

ZONE BEATER

SETUP

> STREAK BOTH OUTSIDE RECEIVERS
> WHEEL THE HB

> The route combination on the right side of the field will beat any zone. Find the open receiver.

> The HB running the wheel is usually open quickly at the snap.

BLITZ BEATER

SETUP

> HITCH BOTH OUTSIDE RECEIVERS

> If you face a zone blitz look to the flats.

> If you face a man-to-man blitz look to the hitches.

Chicago Bears

RECOMMENDED DEFENSIVE RUN FORMATION: 46 NORMAL

PRO TIPS

- > GET ROOKIE LE CORNELIUS WASHINGTON ON THE FIELD. HIS STRENGTH ALONE MAKES HIM PLAY WORTHY.
- > DT STEPHEN PAEA'S 98 STR RATING MAKES HIM ONE OF THE BEST RUN-STOPPING DEFENSIVE TACKLES IN THE GAME.
- > DT NATE COLLINS CAN HELP YOUR DEFENSIVE LINE IN RUNNING SITUATIONS.
- > ROOKIE MLB JON BOSTIC HAS THE SPEED TO STOP RUNS OUTSIDE.

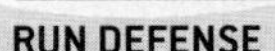

RUN DEFENSE

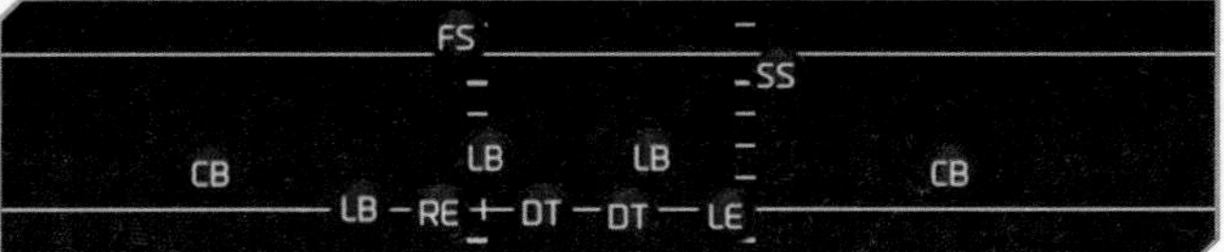

RUN DEFENSE LEFT

SETUP > SHIFT LINEBACKERS LEFT

RUN DEFENSE MIDDLE

SETUP > PINCH DEFENSIVE LINE

RUN DEFENSE RIGHT

SETUP > SHIFT LINEBACKERS RIGHT

CHICAGO BEARS DEFENSIVE RUN PLAY CALL SHEET

1ST DOWN RUN DEFENSE	2ND AND SHORT	3RD AND SHORT	GOAL LINE RUN DEFENSE	2ND AND LONG	3RD AND LONG
4-3 Over—Cover 1	4-3 Over Plus—Fire Man	4-6 Normal—Weak Blitz	Goal Line 5-3-3—Jam Cover 1	Nickel Wide 9—2 Man Under	4-6 Normal—2 Man Under
4-3 Over—Smoke Mid Zone 2	4-3 Over Plus—Fire Zone 2	4-6 Normal—Fire Zone 3	Goal Line 5-3-3—Flat Buzz	Nickel Wide 9—Cover 4	4-6 Normal—Cover 4

CHICAGO BEARS DEFENSIVE PASS PLAY CALL SHEET

1ST DOWN PLAY	2ND AND SHORT	3RD AND SHORT	GOAL LINE PASSING	2ND AND LONG	3RD AND LONG
Man Coverage	Sub 4-1-6—2 Man Under	Nickel Normal—Cover 1 Robber	Goal Line 6-3-2—GL Man	Nickel Normal—Over Storm Brave	Dime Normal—MLB Blitz
Zone Coverage	Sub 4-1-6—Cover 2 Sink	Nickel Normal—Sugar 3 Seam	Goal Line 6-3-2—GL Zone	Nickel Normal—FS Slant 3	Dime Normal—Fox Fire Zone

LEGEND: Man Coverage | Zone Coverage | Man Blitz | Zone Blitz

In these play call sheets we picked the best plays for specific situations so that you will have a play for every down and distance.

DEFENSE

RECOMMENDED DEFENSIVE PASS FORMATION: NICKEL NORMAL

PRO TIPS

- MATCH UP CB TIM JENNINGS ON YOUR OPPONENT'S FASTEST WR.
- CB CHARLES TILLMAN SHOULD COVER YOUR OPPONENT'S BEST OVERALL WR.
- USER-CONTROL CB ZACK BOWMAN FOR HIS ELITE CTH RATING.
- FS TOM NELSON'S 92 SPD RATING GIVES THE BEARS DEFENSE MORE SPEED IN THE SECONDARY.

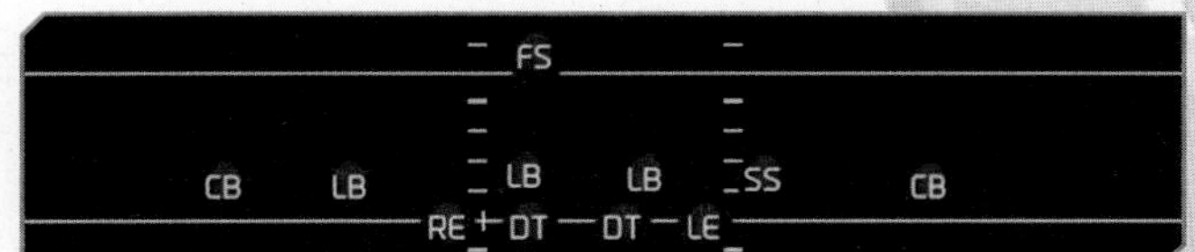

MAN COVERAGE

SETUP

- CRASH DEFENSIVE LINE OUT
- QB SPY BOTH DEFENSIVE TACKLES

- We are looking to generate an outside pass rush here with solid coverage.
- Peppers should be able to get after the QB while we maintain max coverage on the field.

ZONE COVERAGE

SETUP

- BUZZ ZONE BOTH FLAT DEFENDERS
- PRESS COVERAGE

- If your opponent attacks the flat we will have it covered.
- User-control the deep FS and help cover the middle of the field.

MAN BLITZ

SETUP

- PRESS COVERAGE
- USER-CONTROL THE MLB

- Pressure will be quick, so be ready for a throw to the flats.
- If your corners get beaten off the line of scrimmage it will result in a big play.

ZONE BLITZ

SETUP

- PRESS COVERAGE
- REBLITZ THE LEFT DT

- User-control the ROLB covering the HB.
- If the HB stays in to block, drop into coverage. If the HB runs a route, cover him.

Cincinnati Bengals

FRANCHISE OVERVIEW

BENGALS GAMEPLAY RATING

81

> SEE THE INSIDE BACK COVER FOR A QUICK REFERENCE TO THE GAME ABBREVIATIONS USED THROUGHOUT THIS GUIDE.

> IMPROVE WITH YOUR TEAM BY VISITING PRIMAGAMES.COM/MADDENNFL25 FOR MORE INFORMATION AND HOW-TO VIDEOS.

2012 TEAM RANKINGS

2nd AFC North (10-6-0)

PASSING OFFENSE: **17th**
RUSHING OFFENSE: **18th**
PASSING DEFENSE: **7th**
RUSHING DEFENSE: **12th**

2012 TEAM LEADERS

PASSING: **Andy Dalton: 3,669**
RUSHING: **BenJarvus Green-Ellis: 1,094**
RECEIVING: **A.J. Green: 1,350**
TACKLES: **Vontaze Burfict: 127**
SACKS: **Geno Atkins: 12.5**
INTS: **Reggie Nelson: 3**

KEY ADDITIONS

LB James Harrison
TE Alex Smith

KEY ROOKIES

RB Giovani Bernard
DE Margus Hunt
SS Shawn Williams

CONNECTED FRANCHISE MODE STRATEGY

CFM TEAM RATING: **73**
OFFENSIVE SCHEME: **Balanced**
DEFENSIVE SCHEME: **Base 4-3**
STRENGTHS: **QB, TE, RE, DT, FS**
WEAKNESSES: **HB, FB, WR**

SCHEDULE

	Date	Time		Opponent
1	Sep 8	1:00	AT	BEARS
2	Sep 16	8:40		STEELERS
3	Sep 22	1:00		PACKERS
4	Sep 29	1:00	AT	BROWNS
5	Oct 6	1:00		PATRIOTS
6	Oct 13	1:00	AT	BILLS
7	Oct 20	1:00	AT	LIONS
8	Oct 27	4:05		JETS
9	Oct 31	8:25	AT	DOLPHINS
10	Nov 10	1:00	AT	RAVENS
11	Nov 17	1:00		BROWNS
12	BYE			
13	Dec 1	4:25	AT	CHARGERS
14	Dec 8	1:00		COLTS
15	Dec 15	8:30	AT	STEELERS
16	Dec 22	1:00		VIKINGS
17	Dec 29	1:00		RAVENS

OFFENSIVE SCOUTING REPORT

> The offensive corps of the Bengals looks to be solid for many years to come. With QB Andy Dalton and WR A.J. Green leading the way expect to have many years of success.

> Rookie HB Giovani Bernard needs to be your starting HB from day one. He is the most explosive HB and has the most upside. Give him the reps he needs to become an elite player and spell him with the aging BenJarvus Green-Ellis.

> Outside of A.J. Green the Bengals don't have another threat at WR. Focus on WRs in your team's first draft.

DEFENSIVE SCOUTING REPORT

> The defensive line is stacked with athleticism and playmakers. There is a ton of versatility in terms of scheme, so make sure to plug and play each player at different positions.

> The Bengals linebackers are solid and have a lot of hit power, but they do lack top end speed. Look for speedy linebackers in free agency or in the draft. This pickup will help with your team's overall coverage ability.

> You have tons of speed in the secondary but no real standout player to build a defensive powerhouse around. Try to shop around some of the extra speed and see if you can strike a good deal with owners who covet this rating.

OWNER & COACH PROFILES

MIKE BROWN

LEGACY SCORE: 150
OFF. SCHEME: Balanced Offense
DEF. SCHEME: Base 4-3

MARVIN LEWIS

LEVEL: 12
LEGACY SCORE: 1250
OFF. SCHEME: Balanced Offense
DEF. SCHEME: Base 4-3

TEAM OVERVIEW

KEY PLAYERS

WR #18

A.J. GREEN

KEY RATINGS

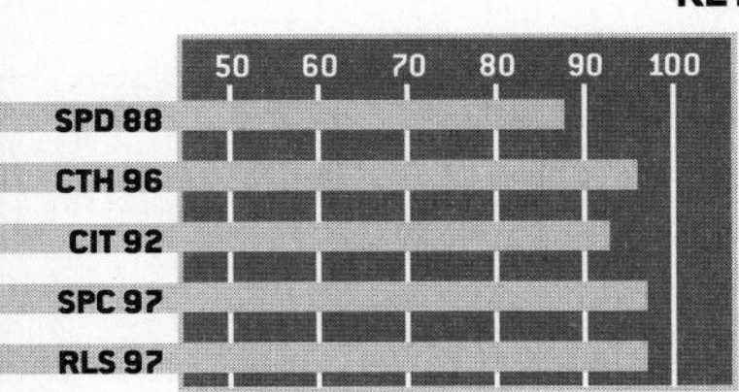

> Green will dominate in the red zone, so look to get him the ball on end-zone fades.

> Make sure to target Green at least 10 times a game. Make this your goal each game to ensure he gets enough touches.

DT #97

GENO ATKINS

KEY RATINGS

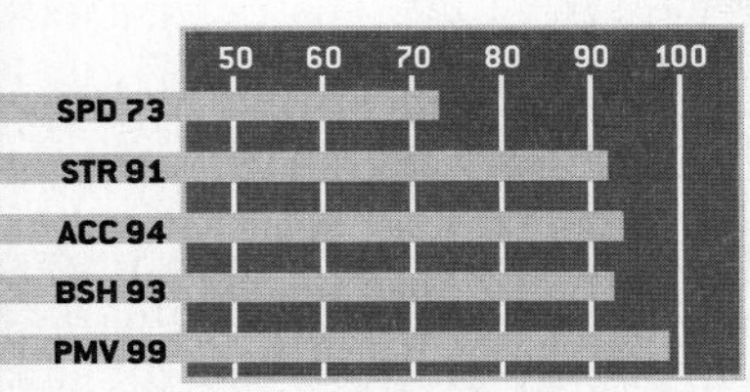

> Atkins will be crucial for blitzes that require elite acceleration. He provides your defense great flexibility with a 94 ACC rating at DT.

> Mix in max coverage defense because Atkins is a one-man rushing crew. He gets to the QB quickly with his 99 PMV.

PRE-GAME SETUP

KEY RUNNING SUBSTITUTION

Who: HB Giovani Bernard

Where: Starting HB

Why: Bernard might be a rookie, but he will have to lead the Bengals' rushing attack this season.

Key Stats: 94 AGI, 94 ACC

KEY PASSING SUBSTITUTION

Who: TE Tyler Eifert

Where: #2 WR

Why: Eifert is a TE, but this rookie will be a huge target split wide for QB Andy Dalton. Utilize his height for big plays down the sideline.

Key Stats: 6'5", 88 CTH, 84 CIT, 90 JMP

KEY RUN DEFENSE SUBSTITUTION

Who: LE Margus Hunt

Where: #2 DT

Why: Rookie LE Margus Hunt is huge. At 6'8" he will be a force on the field. He also has great athleticism, which will help for coverage purposes.

Key Stats: 6'8", 85 SPD, 89 ACC, 83 POW

KEY PASS DEFENSE SUBSTITUTION

Who: CB Onterio McCalebb

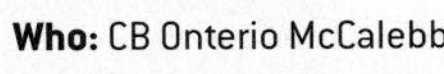

Where: Nickel/Dime CB

Why: McCalebb has speed for days. Get him on the field at all costs. He will be great for blitzing situations as well as for covering the league's fastest WRs.

Key Stats: 97 SPD, 91 ACC, 94 ACC

OFFENSIVE DEPTH CHART

POS	FIRST NAME	LAST NAME	OVR
QB	Andy	Dalton	84
QB	Josh	Johnson	70
QB	John	Skelton	67
QB	Zac	Robinson	64
HB	BenJarvus	Green-Ellis	82
HB	Giovani	Bernard	75
HB	Bernard	Scott	74
HB	Cedric	Peerman	70
HB	Rex	Burkhead	68
HB	Daniel	Herron	68
FB	Chris	Pressley	79
FB	John	Conner	74
WR	A.J.	Green	94
WR	Mohamed	Sanu	74
WR	Andrew	Hawkins	72
WR	Brandon	Tate	70
WR	Marvin	Jones	70
WR	Ryan	Whalen	68
WR	Cobi	Hamilton	67
WR	Dane	Sanzenbacher	65
TE	Tyler	Eifert	80
TE	Jermaine	Gresham	80
TE	Alex	Smith	77
TE	Orson	Charles	71
TE	Richard	Quinn	70
TE	Clark	Harris	63
LT	Andrew	Whitworth	90
LT	Dennis	Roland	69
LT	Tanner	Hawkinson	66
LG	Travelle	Wharton	82
LG	Clint	Boling	78
C	Trevor	Robinson	76
C	Kyle	Cook	75
RG	Kevin	Zeitler	87
RG	Mike	Pollak	77
RT	Andre	Smith	92
RT	Anthony	Collins	78
RT	Reid	Fragel	69

DEFENSIVE DEPTH CHART

POS	FIRST NAME	LAST NAME	OVR
LE	Carlos	Dunlap	89
LE	Margus	Hunt	70
LE	Wallace	Gilberry	70
RE	Michael	Johnson	89
RE	Robert	Geathers	76
RE	Dontay	Moch	65
RE	DeQuin	Evans	60
DT	Geno	Atkins	97
DT	Domata	Peko	81
DT	Devon	Still	74
DT	Brandon	Thompson	66
LOLB	James	Harrison	86
LOLB	Aaron	Maybin	74
MLB	Rey	Maualuga	76
MLB	J.K.	Schaffer	58
ROLB	Vontaze	Burfict	77
ROLB	Sean	Porter	70
ROLB	Vincent	Rey	66
ROLB	Emmanuel	Lamur	64
CB	Leon	Hall	90
CB	Terence	Newman	85
CB	Adam	Jones	79
CB	Dre	Kirkpatrick	76
CB	Brandon	Ghee	68
CB	Shaun	Prater	67
CB	Onterio	McCalebb	58
FS	Reggie	Nelson	88
FS	George	Iloka	65
SS	Taylor	Mays	74
SS	Shawn	Williams	72
SS	Jeromy	Miles	71

SPECIAL TEAMS DEPTH CHART

POS	FIRST NAME	LAST NAME	OVR
K	Mike	Nugent	83
P	Kevin	Huber	84

Cincinnati Bengals

RECOMMENDED OFFENSIVE RUN FORMATION: STRONG CLOSE (2 RB, 1 TE, 2 WR)

PRO TIPS

- ROOKIE HB GIOVANI BERNARD SHOULD BE YOUR STARTING HB.
- USE HB BENJARVUS GREEN-ELLIS FOR LATE-GAME SITUATIONS BECAUSE OF HIS 96 CAR RATING.
- GREEN-ELLIS ALSO HAS A 92 TRK RATING, WHICH IS IDEAL FOR SHORT-YARD SITUATIONS.
- TIGHT ENDS RICHARD QUINN AND ALEX SMITH ARE YOUR BEST RUN-BLOCKING TIGHT ENDS.

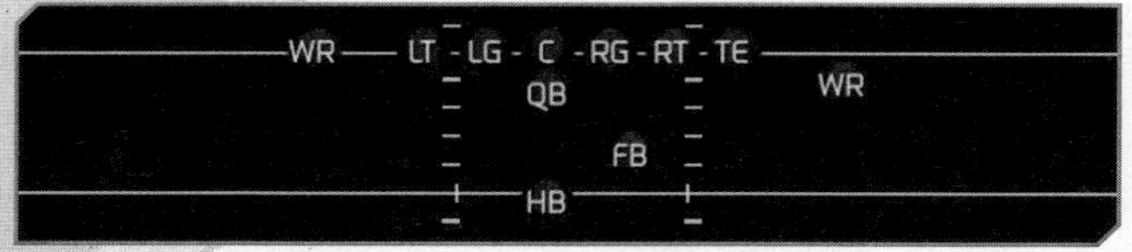

RUN LEFT

HB Zone Wk

USE THE ACCELERATION BURST TO GET TO THE LINE OF SCRIMMAGE, AND THEN FIND THE HOLE.

RUN MIDDLE

FOLLOW YOUR BLOCKERS AND BE PATIENT.

RUN RIGHT

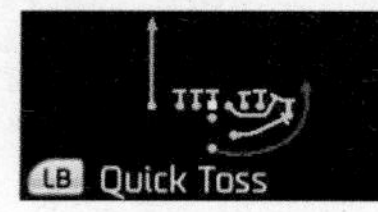

DON'T OUTRUN YOUR BLOCKERS.

CINCINNATI BENGALS RUNNING PLAY CALL SHEET

LEGEND: Inside Run | Outside Run | Shotgun Run | QB Run

1ST DOWN RUNS	2ND AND SHORT	3RD AND SHORT	GOAL LINE RUNS	2ND AND LONG	3RD AND LONG
Strong Close—Quick Toss	Strong Pro—Power O	I-Form Tight Pair—FB Dive	Goal Line Normal—QB Sneak	Gun Y-Trips Bengal—HB Base	Gun Trips Y-Flex—HB Draw
Strong Pro—HB Blast	Singleback Ace Pair—Close Zone Strg	I-Form Tight Pair—Strong Stretch	Goal Line Normal—HB Dive	Singleback Wing Trips—Power O	Gun Split Slot—Power O
Singleback Ace Pair—HB Toss Crack	Singleback Y-Trips—HB Plunge	I-Form Tight Pair—HB Toss	Goal Line Normal—Power O	Gun Trio Open—HB Draw	Gun Y-Trips Bengal HB Draw

CINCINNATI BENGALS PASSING PLAY CALL SHEET

LEGEND: Base Play | Man Beater | Zone Beater | Blitz Beater

1ST DOWN PLAY	2ND AND SHORT	3RD AND SHORT	GOAL LINE PASSING	2ND AND LONG	3RD AND LONG
Gun Y-Trips Bengal—Y Trail	Gun Y-Trips Bengal—Sluggo Seam	I-Form Pro—Mesh	Goal Line—PA Waggle	I-Form Pro—Z Spot	Gun Trio—Stick
Gun Spread Y-Slot—Inside Cross	Gun Y-Trips Bengals—Stick N Nod	Singleback Doubles—Curl Flats	Goal Line—PA Spot	Strong Pro—494 F Flat	Gun Trio—X Spot
Gun Split Slot—689 Hook	Gun Spread Y-Slot—Weak Flood	Singleback Snugs Flip—Bench	Goal Line—PA Power O	Full House Normal Wide—Close Z Corner	Singleback Ace—Double Sluggo

In these play call sheets we picked the best plays for specific situations so that you will have a play for every down and distance.

OFFENSE

RECOMMENDED OFFENSIVE PASS FORMATION:
GUN TRIPS Y ISO (1 HB, 1 TE, 3 WR)

PRO TIPS

- WR MARVIN JONES WILL MAKE SPECTACULAR CATCHES WITH HIS 90 SPC RATING.
- WR RYAN WHALEN'S 85 CIT IS SECOND HIGHEST ON THE TEAM.
- TIGHT ENDS TYLER EIFERT AND JERMAINE GRESHAM WILL BE VITAL TO YOUR TEAM'S PASSING SUCCESS.

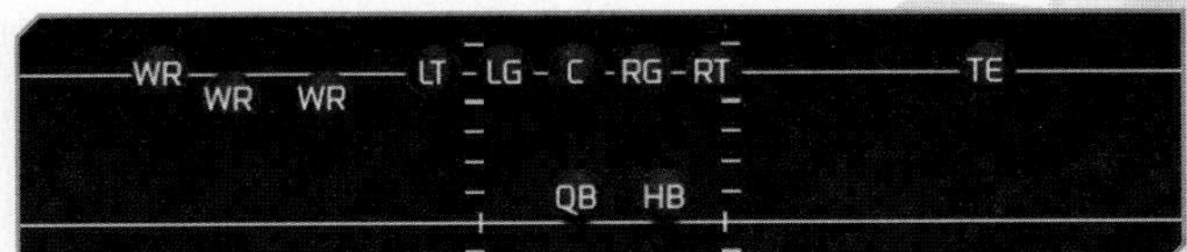

BASE PLAY

Deep Attack

SETUP

- ZIG THE INSIDE SLOT WR
- DRAG THE OUTSIDE SLOT WR

- A.J. Green will be a nice option outside. Throw a high lead pass so he can go up and get it.
- If Green isn't open down the sideline look to the drag and zig combination underneath.

MAN BEATER

Slants Flat

SETUP

- ZIG THE INSIDE SLOT WR
- DRAG THE OUTSIDE SLOT WR

- Against man-to-man defenses we look to both outside slants as our first options.
- These slants get separation after the cut inside. Lead pass inside and high to lead the WR upfield.

ZONE BEATER

Four Verticals

SETUP

- OPTION THE HB
- HITCH THE OUTSIDE SLOT WR

- Against Cover 2 zones look to the sideline streaks.
- Against Cover 3 and Cover 4 zones look to the HB option and the slot WR's hitch and angled streak.

BLITZ BEATER

HB Slip Screen

SETUP

- STREAK BOTH OUTSIDE RECEIVERS
- SLANT THE INSIDE SLOT WR

- Your first option is the HB on the screen.
- If the HB is covered look to the inside slot WR running the slant.

Cincinnati Bengals

RECOMMENDED DEFENSIVE RUN FORMATION: 4-3 OVER

PRO TIPS

> LE MARGUS HUNT HAS THE SIZE TO PLAY DT AND BE A FORCE IN STOPPING THE RUN.

> TO STOP THE RUN YOUR DEFENSIVE LINE SHOULD CONSIST OF LE MARGUS HUNT, DT GENO ATKINS, AND DT DOMATA PEKO.

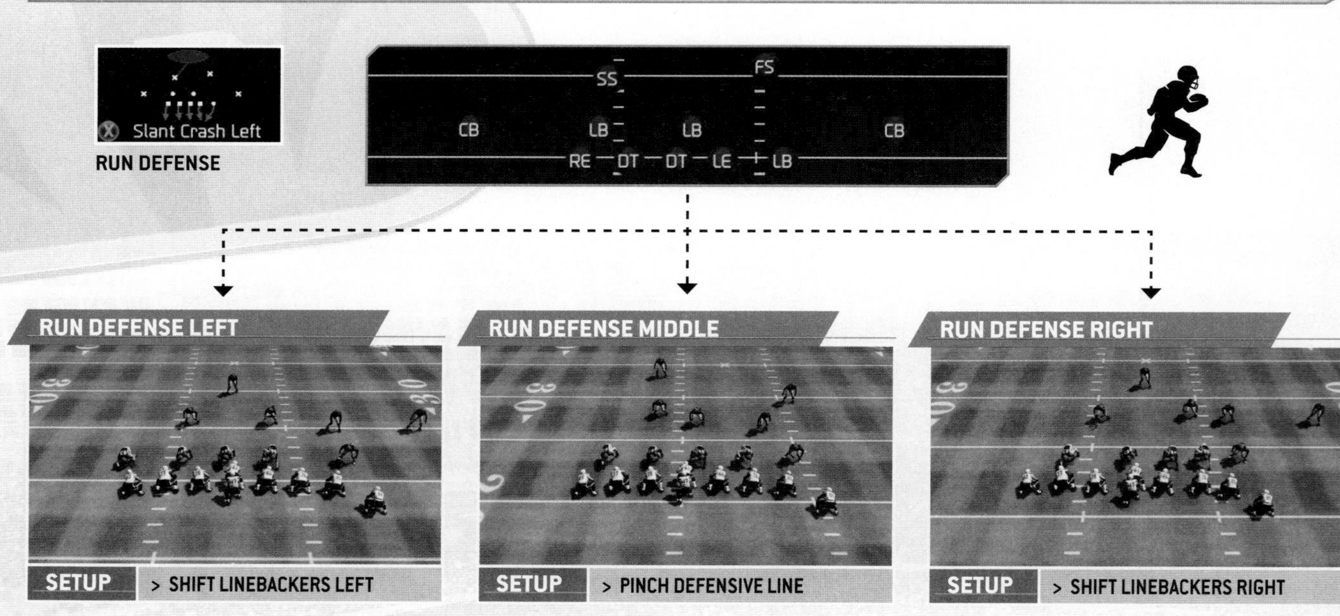

CINCINNATI BENGALS DEFENSIVE RUN PLAY CALL SHEET

1ST DOWN RUN DEFENSE	2ND AND SHORT	3RD AND SHORT	GOAL LINE RUN DEFENSE	2ND AND LONG	3RD AND LONG
Nickel Normal—Cover 1 Press	4-3 Under—Free Fire	46 Normal—Weak Blitz	Goal Line 5-3-3—Jam Cover 1	Nickel 3-3-5—Cover 1	Dime Normal—2 Man Under
Nickel Normal—Cover 3	4-3 Under—Will Punch 3 Seam	46 Normal—Fire Zone 3	Goal Line 5-3-3—Flat Buzz	Nickel 3-3-5—Cover 4	Dime Normal—Cover 2 Sink

CINCINNATI BENGALS DEFENSIVE PASS PLAY CALL SHEET

1ST DOWN PLAY	2ND AND SHORT	3RD AND SHORT	GOAL LINE PASSING	2ND AND LONG	3RD AND LONG
4-3 Over—2 Man Under	4-3 Over Plus—Cover 1	4-3 Stack—OLB Fire	Goal Line 6-3-2—GL Man	Dime Normal—2 Man Under	4-3 Under—Edge Sting
4-3 Over—Cover 3	4-3 Over Plus—Cover 2	4-3 Stack—Will 2 Fire	Goal Line 6-3-2—GL Zone	Dime Normal—3 Double Buzz	4-3 Under—Under Same Shark 3

LEGEND: Man Coverage | Zone Coverage | Man Blitz | Zone Blitz

In these play call sheets we picked the best plays for specific situations so that you will have a play for every down and distance.

DEFENSE

RECOMMENDED DEFENSIVE PASS FORMATION: NICKEL NORMAL

PRO TIPS

- MATCH UP CB TERENCE NEWMAN AGAINST THE OPPOSING TEAM'S FASTEST WR.
- MATCH UP CB DRE KIRKPATRICK AGAINST THE OPPOSING TEAM'S TALLEST WR.
- KIRKPATRICK AND CB LEON HALL HAVE THE TEAM'S BEST PRESS RATINGS.
- USE CB ONTERIO MCCALEBB'S 97 SPD FOR BLITZING SITUATIONS.

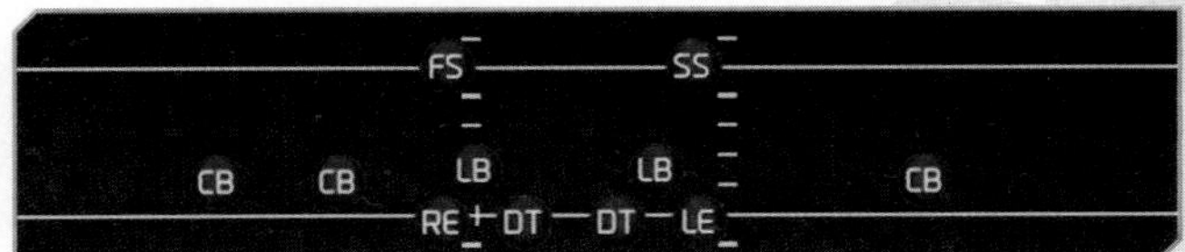

MAN COVERAGE

SETUP

- SPREAD DEFENSIVE LINE
- REBLITZ BOTH DEFENSIVE ENDS

- Reblitzing the defensive ends will create a better pass rush.
- User-control the MLB to take away anything over the middle of the field.

ZONE COVERAGE

SETUP

- SHIFT DEFENSIVE LINE LEFT
- QB SPY THE RE

- User-control the MLB and take away TEs over the middle of the field.
- Watch out for HB draws.

MAN BLITZ

SETUP

- GLOBAL BLITZ LINEBACKERS
- USER-CONTROL THE FS COVERING THE HB AND COVER OVER THE MIDDLE OF THE FIELD

- Press coverage will slow down WRs off the line of scrimmage. Consider calling press if you are starting Hall and Kirkpatrick.
- If you are using your speed CBs (Newman and McCalebb), make sure not to press.

ZONE BLITZ

SETUP

- GLOBAL BLITZ LINEBACKERS
- SHADE SECONDARY COVERAGE IN

- User-control the FS.
- The middle of the field will be open, but the sidelines will be blanketed.

Buffalo Bills

2012 TEAM RANKINGS

4th AFC East (6-10-0)

PASSING OFFENSE: **25th**
RUSHING OFFENSE: **6th**
PASSING DEFENSE: **10th**
RUSHING DEFENSE: **31st**

2012 TEAM LEADERS

PASSING: **Ryan Fitzpatrick: 3,400**
RUSHING: **C.J. Spiller: 1,244**
RECEIVING: **Steve Johnson: 1,046**
TACKLES: **Nick Barnett: 112**
SACKS: **Mario Williams: 10.5**
INTS: **Jairus Byrd: 5**

KEY ADDITIONS

LB Jerry Hughes
QB Kevin Kolb
DT Alan Branch

KEY ROOKIES

QB E.J. Manuel
WR Robert Woods
LB Kiko Alonso

CONNECTED FRANCHISE MODE STRATEGY

CFM TEAM RATING: **68**
OFFENSIVE SCHEME: **West Coast**
DEFENSIVE SCHEME: **Base 4-3**
STRENGTHS: **HB, LE, ROLB, FS, CB**
WEAKNESSES: **QB, FB, WR, TE**

SCHEDULE

1	Sep 8	1:00 PM ET		PATRIOTS
2	Sep 15	1:00 PM ET		PANTHERS
3	Sep 22	4:25 PM ET	AT	JETS
4	Sep 29	1:00 PM ET		RAVENS
5	Oct 3	8:25 PM ET	AT	BROWNS
6	Oct 13	1:00 PM ET		BENGALS
7	Oct 20	1:00 PM ET	AT	DOLPHINS
8	Oct 27	1:00 PM ET	AT	SAINTS
9	Nov 3	1:00 PM ET		CHIEFS
10	Nov 10	1:00 PM ET	AT	STEELERS
11	Nov 17	1:00 PM ET		JETS
12	BYE			
13	Dec 1	4:05 PM ET		FALCONS
14	Dec 8	1:00 PM ET	AT	BUCCANEERS
15	Dec 15	1:00 PM ET	AT	JAGUARS
16	Dec 22	1:00 PM ET		DOLPHINS
17	Dec 29	1:00 PM ET	AT	PATRIOTS

FRANCHISE OVERVIEW

> SEE THE INSIDE BACK COVER FOR A QUICK REFERENCE TO THE GAME ABBREVIATIONS USED THROUGHOUT THIS GUIDE.

> IMPROVE WITH YOUR TEAM BY VISITING PRIMAGAMES.COM/MADDENNFL25 FOR MORE INFORMATION AND HOW-TO VIDEOS.

OFFENSIVE SCOUTING REPORT

- Depending on how rookie QB E.J. Manuel pans out you might consider drafting a QB in the near future. Manuel has great throwing power, but you will need to work on his accuracy ratings and give him major upgrades.
- HB Fred Jackson is all but done in Buffalo, so let him go as soon as his contract ends at the end of next season.
- Build your offense around QB E.J. Manuel and HB C.J. Spiller. Focus on an option-style offensive attack and look to score as many points as possible.

DEFENSIVE SCOUTING REPORT

- FS Jairus Byrd is untouchable in the Bills' front office, so focus your defense around his strengths. He is great in coverage, and a hard-hitting SS would complement him well.
- LE Mario Williams takes a big chunk out of your team's salary cap. If he doesn't produce right away, try to trade him to dump cap. If you can get a blockbuster deal and future draft picks take it.
- LB Manny Lawson is a valuable chess piece for the Bills defense. He has great size and speed, which will allow you to play multiple formations with the same personnel. If you can upgrade Lawson in the tackle department he has potential to flourish late in his career.

OWNER & COACH PROFILES

RALPH WILSON

LEGACY SCORE: 4025 OFF. SCHEME: Balanced Offense
DEF. SCHEME: Base 4-3

DOUG MARRONE

LEVEL: 1 LEGACY SCORE: 0
OFF. SCHEME: Balanced Offense DEF. SCHEME: Base 4-3

TEAM OVERVIEW

KEY PLAYERS

HB #28

C.J. SPILLER

KEY RATINGS

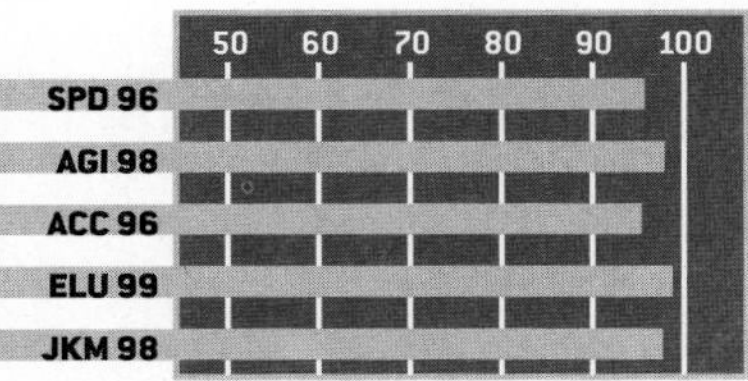

> Get Spiller the ball in open spaces with screens and wheel patterns out of the backfield.

> Use motion to get him out of the backfield and to create mismatches against linebackers. Not many defenders can cover Spiller in one-on-one situations.

FS #31

JAIRUS BYRD

KEY RATINGS

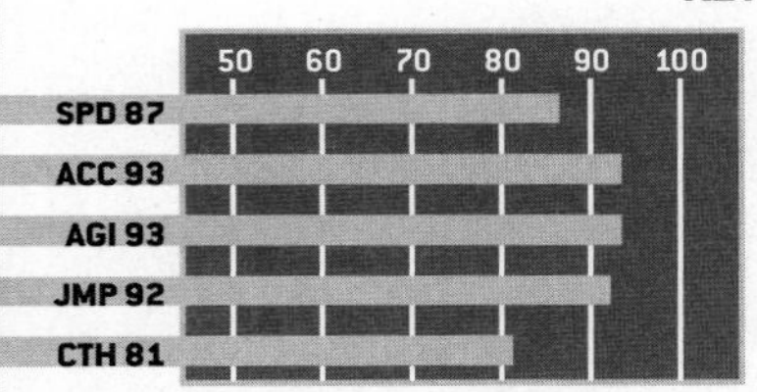

> An 81 CTH rating is amazing for a FS. User-control Byrd in the secondary and be super aggressive when going for ballhawk interceptions.

> Byrd has a great blend of size and speed, and you can user-control him in the box as an extra defender to help in run support.

PRE-GAME SETUP

KEY RUNNING SUBSTITUTION

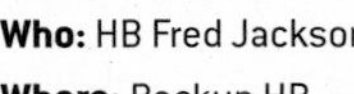

Who: HB Fred Jackson

Where: Backup HB

Why: Jackson does a lot of things very well and will be a solid backup option to HB C.J. Spiller.

Key Stats: 87 SPD, 87 AGI, 88 ACC

KEY PASSING SUBSTITUTION

Who: WR Marquise Goodwin

Where: #2 WR

Why: Rookie WR Marquise Goodwin has lightning speed. His 98 SPD rating is tops in the league, and he will beat just about any defender downfield.

Key Stats: 98 SPD, 92 AGI, 96 ACC

KEY RUN DEFENSE SUBSTITUTION

Who: DT Alan Branch

Where: #2 DT

Why: Branch is a beast on the field and is a huge body for offensive lines to move. His 92 BSH rating in combination with starting DT Kyle Williams will make it difficult for teams to run the ball up the middle.

Key Stats: 92 BSH, 85 TAK

KEY PASS DEFENSE SUBSTITUTION

Who: CB Ron Brooks

Where: Nickel/Dime CB

Why: Use Brooks for blitzing situations and match him up against your opponent's fastest WR.

Key Stats: 95 SPD, 90 ACC, 93 AGI

OFFENSIVE DEPTH CHART

POS	FIRST NAME	LAST NAME	OVR
QB	Kevin	Kolb	76
QB	E.J.	Manuel	74
QB	Jeff	Tuel	64
HB	C.J.	Spiller	92
HB	Fred	Jackson	83
HB	Tashard	Choice	73
HB	Zach	Brown	66
FB	Dorin	Dickerson	72
FB	Frank	Summers	67
WR	Stevie	Johnson	89
WR	Brad	Smith	73
WR	Robert	Woods	70
WR	T.J.	Graham	70
WR	Marcus	Easley	66
WR	Da'Rick	Rogers	66
WR	Marquise	Goodwin	64
WR	Chris	Hogan	63
WR	DeMarco	Sampson	62
WR	Kevin	Elliott	60
TE	Scott	Chandler	83
TE	Lee	Smith	73
TE	Chris	Gragg	69
TE	Mike	Caussin	66
TE	Mickey	Shuler	62
LT	Cordy	Glenn	77
LT	Chris	Hairston	74
LT	Thomas	Welch	60
LG	Sam	Young	72
LG	Chris	Scott	68
LG	Colin	Brown	62
C	Eric	Wood	82
C	Doug	Legursky	73
C	David	Snow	69
C	Garrison	Sanborn	57
RG	Kraig	Urbik	81
RG	Zack	Chibane	63
RG	Keith	Williams	61
RT	Erik	Pears	78
RT	Zebrie	Sanders	66

DEFENSIVE DEPTH CHART

POS	FIRST NAME	LAST NAME	OVR
LE	Mario	Williams	92
LE	Jarron	Gilbert	69
RE	Kyle	Williams	91
RE	Alan	Branch	75
RE	Alex	Carrington	71
RE	Jay	Ross	57
DT	Marcell	Dareus	88
DT	Torell	Troup	68
DT	Corbin	Bryant	66
LOLB	Mark	Anderson	73
LOLB	Jerry	Hughes	72
LOLB	Kourtnei	Brown	56
MLB	Nigel	Bradham	73
MLB	Arthur	Moats	70
MLB	Kiko	Alonso	70
MLB	Brian	Smith	61
MLB	Marcus	Dowtin	52
ROLB	Manny	Lawson	82
ROLB	Bryan	Scott	73
ROLB	Chris	White	61
CB	Stephon	Gilmore	82
CB	Leodis	McKelvin	77
CB	Ron	Brooks	68
CB	Justin	Rogers	67
CB	Crezdon	Butler	67
CB	T.J.	Heath	60
FS	Jairus	Byrd	95
FS	Aaron	Williams	75
SS	Da'Norris	Searcy	75
SS	Duke	Williams	70
SS	Mana	Silva	65
SS	Jonathan	Meeks	64

SPECIAL TEAMS DEPTH CHART

POS	FIRST NAME	LAST NAME	OVR
K	Rian	Lindell	84
K	Dustin	Hopkins	71
P	Shawn	Powell	65

Buffalo Bills

RECOMMENDED OFFENSIVE RUN FORMATION: PISTOL STRONG SLOT BILLS (2 HB, 0 TE, 3 WR)

PRO TIPS

- > ROOKIE QB E.J. MANUEL WILL BE EFFECTIVE RUNNING AN OPTION-STYLE OFFENSE.
- > HB FRED JACKSON IS ONE OF THE BEST BACKUP HALFBACKS IN THE GAME.
- > HB C.J. SPILLER SHOULD GET THE MAJORITY OF SNAPS IN THIS OFFENSE.
- > LEE SMITH AND MICKEY SHULER JR. ARE THE BILLS' BEST BLOCKING TIGHT ENDS.

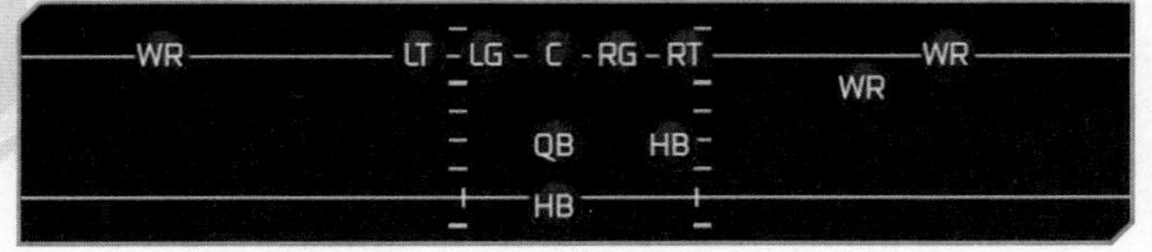

RUN LEFT

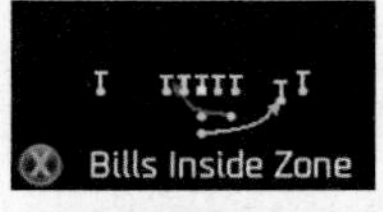

SPILLER CAN BREAK THIS RUN FOR A TD AT ANY TIME.

RUN MIDDLE

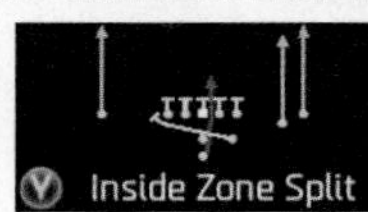

USE THE PRECISION MODIFIER TO CUT THROUGH THE LINE.

RUN RIGHT

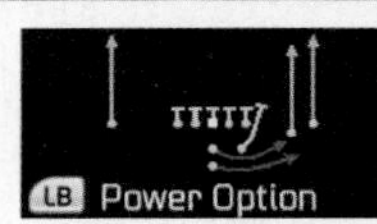

GET TO THE SIDELINE AND CUT UPFIELD.

BUFFALO BILLS RUNNING PLAY CALL SHEET

LEGEND: Inside Run | Outside Run | Shotgun Run | QB Run

1ST DOWN RUNS	2ND AND SHORT	3RD AND SHORT	GOAL LINE RUNS	2ND AND LONG	3RD AND LONG
Singleback Wing Trips—Bills Zone	I-Form Pro—FB Dive	Pistol Strong Slot Bills—HB Draw	Goal Line Normal—QB Sneak	Gun Trips Open—Read Option	Gun Split Slot—HB Inside
Singleback Tight Doubles—HB Dive	I-Form Twins Flex—HB Lead Draw	Singleback Wing Trips—Bills Zone Wk	Goal Line Normal—HB Dive	Pistol Wing Trips—HB Dive	Gun Doubles Wing—HB Off Tackle
Singleback Tight Doubles—HB Cutback	Strong Close—HB Dive	Pistol Strong Slot Bills—HB Counter	Goal Line Normal—Power O	Gun Trips Open—Cntr Read Option	Gun Doubles Wing—HB Mid Draw

BUFFALO BILLS PASSING PLAY CALL SHEET

LEGEND: Base Play | Man Beater | Zone Beater | Blitz Beater

1ST DOWN PLAY	2ND AND SHORT	3RD AND SHORT	GOAL LINE PASSING	2ND AND LONG	3RD AND LONG
Gun Split Slot—Slants	Singleback Wing Trips—China Under	Singleback Wing Trips—HB Slip Screen	Goal Line—PA Waggle	Gun Bunch Wk—Bunch Trail	Gun Normal Y-Flex—Slot Flats
Gun Doubles Wing—HB Angle	Pistol Strong Slot Bills—Mesh Dig	Gun Trio Open—HB Slip Sceen	Goal Line—PA Spot	Gun Trio Open—Inside Cross	Gun Normal Y-Flex—Deep Curl
Gun Trio Open—Flood Post	Gun Bunch Wk—Z Spot	I-Form Tight Pair—PA Power O	Goal Line—PA Power O	Gun Trips Open—Stick	Gun Trips Y-Flex—Slot Drive

In these play call sheets we picked the best plays for specific situations so that you will have a play for every down and distance.

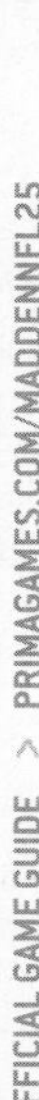

OFFENSE

RECOMMENDED OFFENSIVE PASS FORMATION: GUN SPLIT SLOT (2 HB, 0 TE, 3 WR)

PRO TIPS

> WR MARQUISE GOODWIN'S 98 SPD WILL BE THE FASTEST ON THE FIELD.
> WR T.J. GRAHAM IS ANOTHER SPEEDSTER, WITH 96 SPD.
> ROOKIE WR DA'RICK ROGERS'S 81 CIT RATING IS THE SECOND HIGHEST AMONG RECEIVERS.

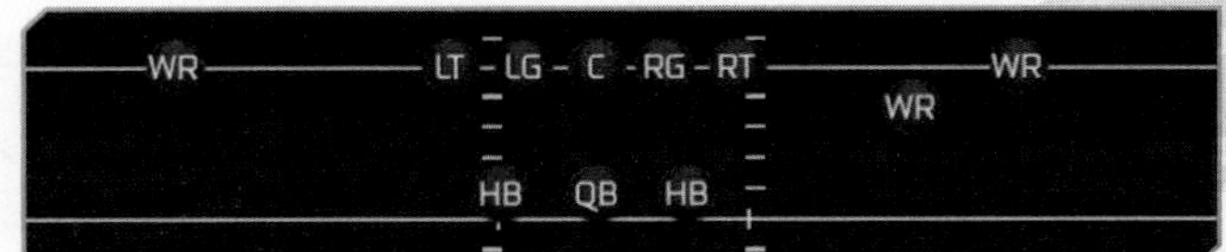

BASE PLAY

SETUP

> STREAK BOTH HALFBACKS
> DRAG THE FAR RIGHT WR

> Look to the drag at the snap of the ball and then to the HB streaks.
> The sideline wheel and post corner routes will get open down the sideline against man-to-man.

MAN BEATER

SETUP

> OPTION BOTH HALFBACKS
> STREAK THE SLOT WR

> Option routes out of the backfield are great options against man-to-man.
> Wait for the routes to break to the sideline and then deliver the throw.

ZONE BEATER

SETUP

> BLOCK THE LEFT HB
> STREAK THE FAR LEFT WR

> Against Cover 2 and Cover 3 zones look to the corner route and sideline streaks.
> Against Cover 4 zones look to the flat route.

BLITZ BEATER

SETUP

> SWING RIGHT THE LEFT HB
> DRAG THE FAR RIGHT WR

> The HB will get open quickly and will have a ton of lead blockers.
> If you can't get the ball to the HB look to the drag underneath.

Buffalo Bills

RECOMMENDED DEFENSIVE RUN FORMATION: 3-4 EVEN

PRO TIPS

- > TORELL TROUP IS QUIETLY ONE OF THE BEST RUN-STOPPING DEFENSIVE TACKLES IN *MADDEN NFL 25*.
- > USE DT ALAN BRANCH ON RUNNING DOWNS TO STUFF THE RUN.
- > MIDDLE LINEBACKERS NIGEL BRADHAM AND ARTHUR MOATS HAVE ELITE HIT POWER AND WILL CAUSE HALFBACKS TO FUMBLE.

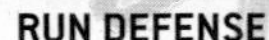

RUN DEFENSE

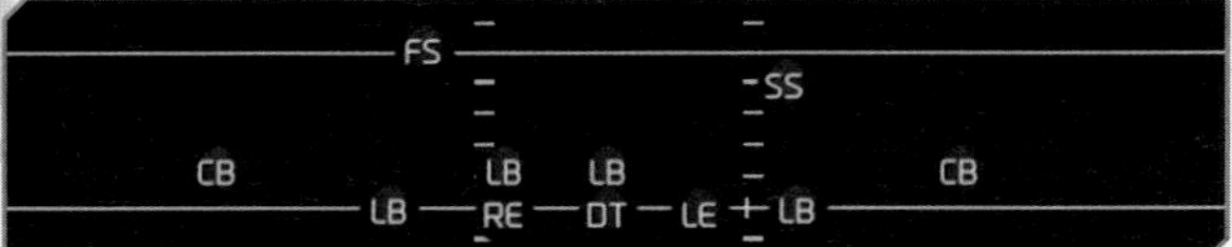

RUN DEFENSE LEFT

SETUP > SHIFT LINEBACKERS LEFT

RUN DEFENSE MIDDLE

SETUP > PINCH DEFENSIVE LINE

RUN DEFENSE RIGHT

SETUP > SHIFT LINEBACKERS RIGHT

BUFFALO BILLS DEFENSIVE RUN PLAY CALL SHEET

1ST DOWN RUN DEFENSE	2ND AND SHORT	3RD AND SHORT	GOAL LINE RUN DEFENSE	2ND AND LONG	3RD AND LONG
3-4 Odd—MLB Storm Blitz	3-4 Predator—2 Man Under	4-3 Over Odd—LB Dogs	Goal Line 5-3-3—Jam Cover 1	Nickel 3-3-5—Cover 1 Robber	Nickel 3-3-5 Will—Cover 1 Spy
3-4 Odd—Cover 3	3-4 Predator—Cover 2 Sink	4-3 Over Odd—Cover 2	Goal Line 5-3-3—Flat Buzz	Nickel 3-3-5—Cover 3	Nickel 3-3-5 Will—Cover 6

BUFFALO BILLS DEFENSIVE PASS PLAY CALL SHEET

1ST DOWN PLAY	2ND AND SHORT	3RD AND SHORT	GOAL LINE PASSING	2ND AND LONG	3RD AND LONG
3-4 Even—MLB Cross Fire	4-3 Over Plus—Cover 1	4-3 Over Plus—Dbl Safety Blitz	Goal Line 6-3-2—GL Man	Dime Normal—2 Man Under	Dime Normal—MLB Loop
3-4 Even—MLB Cross Fire 3	4-3 Over Plus—Cover 2	4-3 Over Plus—SS Fire 3 Seam	Goal Line 6-3-2—GL Zone	Dime Normal—3 Double Buzz	Dime Normal—SS Overload 3

LEGEND: Man Coverage | Zone Coverage | Man Blitz | Zone Blitz

In these play call sheets we picked the best plays for specific situations so that you will have a play for every down and distance.

DEFENSE

RECOMMENDED DEFENSIVE PASS FORMATION: DIME NORMAL

PRO TIPS

- PLACE CB STEPHON GILMORE ON YOUR OPPONENT'S BEST WR.
- USE CB RON BROOKS TO COVER YOUR OPPONENT'S FASTEST WR.
- CB LEODIS MCKELVIN SHOULD BE USED AS THE NICKEL DB.
- START CB CREZDON BUTLER AT SS. HE WILL PROVIDE EXTRA SPEED AND COVERAGE FOR YOUR DEFENSE.

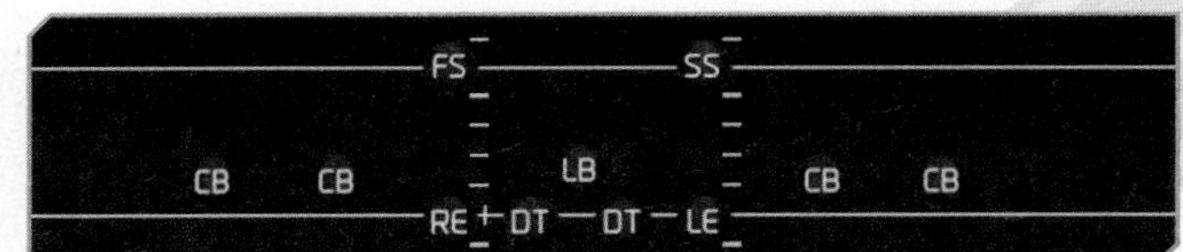

MAN COVERAGE

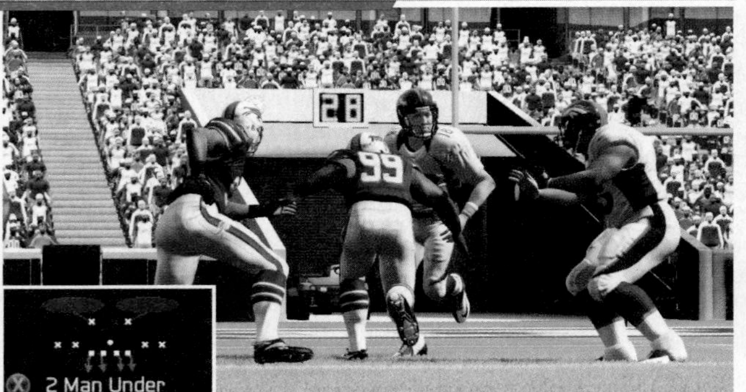

SETUP

- PINCH DEFENSIVE LINE
- CRASH DEFENSIVE LINE OUT

- LE Mario Williams will get after QBs. Make sure to always have him rush the QB.
- User-control the MLB and cover the HB out of the backfield.

ZONE COVERAGE

SETUP

- PRESS COVERAGE
- QB SPY BOTH DTS

- Pressure will come off the edge because of Mario Williams's pass-rush ability.
- User-control the MLB and watch for crossing patterns over the middle of the field.

MAN BLITZ

SETUP

- SPREAD THE DEFENSIVE LINE AND CRASH IN
- PRESS COVERAGE

- Pressure will come off the right edge, so anticipate a quick throw there as well.
- Many times this blitz gets two rushers after the QB free.

ZONE BLITZ

SETUP

- SPREAD THE DEFENSIVE LINE AND CRASH IN
- HOT ROUTE BOTH BUZZ ZONE DEFENDERS TO FLAT ZONES

- User-control the FS.
- The right flat will look open at the snap of the ball because the SS starts deep.
- The SS in the flat zone will get to the flat in time, but your opponent will think it's open. Interception City.

Denver Broncos

2012 TEAM RANKINGS

1st AFC West (13-3-0)

PASSING OFFENSE: **5th**
RUSHING OFFENSE: **16th**
PASSING DEFENSE: **3rd**
RUSHING DEFENSE: **3rd**

2012 TEAM LEADERS

PASSING: **Peyton Manning: 4,659**
RUSHING: **Willis McGahee: 731**
RECEIVING: **Demaryius Thomas: 1,434**
TACKLES: **Wesley Woodyard: 117**
SACKS: **Von Miller: 18.5**
INTS: **Wesley Woodyard: 3**

KEY ADDITIONS

WR Wes Welker
LOLB Stewart Bradley
CB Dominique Rodgers-Cromartie

KEY ROOKIES

HB Montee Ball
DT Sylvester Williams
CB Kayvon Webster

CONNECTED FRANCHISE MODE STRATEGY

CFM TEAM RATING: **76**
OFFENSIVE SCHEME: **Balanced**
DEFENSIVE SCHEME: **Attacking 4-3**
STRENGTHS: **QB, WR, LT, LOLB, CB**
WEAKNESSES: **HB, C, LE, DT, SS**

SCHEDULE

Week	Date	Time		Opponent
1	Sep 5	8:30		RAVENS
2	Sep 15	4:25	at	GIANTS
3	Sep 23	8:40		RAIDERS
4	Sep 29	4:25		EAGLES
5	Oct 6	4:25	at	COWBOYS
6	Oct 13	4:05		JAGUARS
7	Oct 20	8:30	at	COLTS
8	Oct 27	4:25		REDSKINS
9	BYE			
10	Nov 10	4:25	at	CHARGERS
11	Nov 17	4:05		CHIEFS
12	Nov 24	8:30	at	PATRIOTS
13	Dec 1	1:00	at	CHIEFS
14	Dec 8	4:05		TITANS
15	Dec 12	8:25		CHARGERS
16	Dec 22	1:00	at	TEXANS
17	Dec 29	4:25	at	RAIDERS

FRANCHISE OVERVIEW

BRONCOS GAMEPLAY RATING

89

> SEE THE INSIDE BACK COVER FOR A QUICK REFERENCE TO THE GAME ABBREVIATIONS USED THROUGHOUT THIS GUIDE.

> IMPROVE WITH YOUR TEAM BY VISITING PRIMAGAMES.COM/MADDENNFL25 FOR MORE INFORMATION AND HOW-TO VIDEOS.

OFFENSIVE SCOUTING REPORT

> QB Peyton Manning is a 15-year NFL pro. That's good and bad for your front office. It means your team is ready to win right *now*. It also means that you will need to rebuild the franchise when he retires. Keep your eye out for under-the-radar rookies in the coming years.

> The Broncos are in desperate need of an elite HB. Your first order of business with the Broncos is to find a halfback in the draft or free agency. Look for two while you're at it—an every-down player and a shifty third-down back.

> Free agent splash pickup WR Wes Welker will help the Broncos immediately. Whatever you do, don't keep him for a second contract. You have two stud WRs who need more long-term attention in Demaryius Thomas and Eric Decker. Keep them around as long as you have Peyton.

DEFENSIVE SCOUTING REPORT

> In the secondary you have three lockdown cover corners: 35-year-old Champ Bailey, 24-year-old Chris Harris, and 27-year-old Dominique Rodgers-Cromartie. Bailey is costing you $10 million a year. Get rid of him, sign Rodgers-Cromartie long-term, and call it a day.

> LOLB Von Miller is 24 years old and is already one of the league's best pass-rushing linebackers. His contract is up in two years. With the money you save by dumping Champ Bailey you can sign Miller to a long-term deal now. Miller is the future; Bailey isn't.

> In the draft you will need to look for defensive linemen. Look for DEs who rush the passer and DTs who have enough strength to anchor the middle of the field.

OWNER & COACH PROFILES

PAT BOWLEN

LEGACY SCORE: 7650
DEF. SCHEME: Attacking 4-3
OFF. SCHEME: Balanced Offense

JOHN FOX

LEVEL: 20
OFF. SCHEME: Balanced Offense
LEGACY SCORE: 1050
DEF. SCHEME: Attacking 4-3

TEAM OVERVIEW

KEY PLAYERS

QB #18

PEYTON MANNING

KEY RATINGS

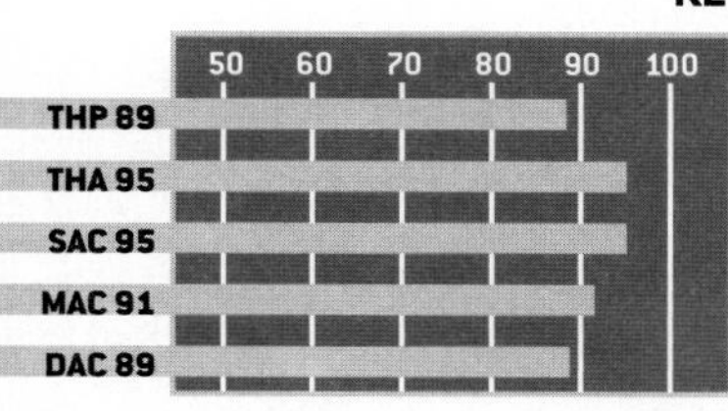

> Manning has lost some zip on his fastball, but he can still make every throw you need. An elite DAC rating is tough to come by in *Madden NFL 25,* and Manning has it.

> Don't even think about running any type of option offense with Manning. If he gets hurt your team will be in trouble.

LOLB #52

VON MILLER

KEY RATINGS

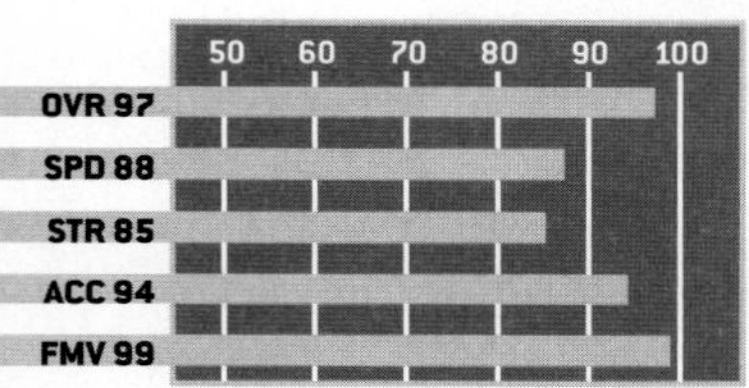

> Miller can create pressure for your defense without blitzing. Play a lot of 2 Man Under coverage and send Miller after the QB.

> Not only can Miller rush the QB, he can also deliver big-time hits. His 89 POW rating goes great with his 95 TAK rating.

PRE-GAME SETUP

KEY RUNNING SUBSTITUTION

Who: HB Ronnie Hillman

Where: Starting HB

Why: He might only have a 72 OVR rating, but he is the best overall HB on this team. He has just enough speed and quickness to be a threat to opposing defenses.

Key Stats: 91 SPD, 94 AGI, 93 ACC, 92 ELU

KEY PASSING SUBSTITUTION

Who: WR Trindon Holliday

Where: Deep ball and screen plays

Why: Holliday has blazing speed. Get him the ball in space and it can result in instant points for your offense.

Key Stats: 98 SPD, 95 AGI, 97 ACC

KEY RUN DEFENSE SUBSTITUTION

Who: DT Sealver Siliga

Where: #2 DT

Why: Siliga might only have a 65 OVR rating, but he has an 87 BSH rating, which is the second best on the line. If you need to stop the run get him in the game.

Key Stats: 87 BSH, 89 STR

KEY PASS DEFENSE SUBSTITUTION

Who: FS Quinton Carter

Where: Starting FS

Why: Carter has a little pop in his bat. A 92 POW rating means you see the field, no matter what.

Key Stats: 92 POW, 70 PUR

OFFENSIVE DEPTH CHART

POS	FIRST NAME	LAST NAME	OVR
QB	Peyton	Manning	97
QB	Brock	Osweiler	73
QB	Zac	Dysert	68
HB	Knowshon	Moreno	76
HB	Montee	Ball	75
HB	Ronnie	Hillman	72
HB	Lance	Ball	70
HB	Jeremiah	Johnson	65
FB	Jacob	Hester	79
WR	Wes	Welker	93
WR	Demaryius	Thomas	90
WR	Eric	Decker	87
WR	Andre	Caldwell	74
WR	Trindon	Holliday	67
WR	Tavarres	King	65
WR	Gerell	Robinson	62
WR	Greg	Orton	61
TE	Joel	Dreessen	83
TE	Jacob	Tamme	80
TE	Virgil	Green	71
TE	Julius	Thomas	65
TE	Aaron	Brewer	39
LT	Ryan	Clady	94
LT	Chris	Clark	64
LG	Zane	Beadles	81
LG	Manny	Ramirez	76
C	J.D.	Walton	79
C	Philip	Blake	68
C	C.J.	Davis	65
C	Quentin	Saulsberry	64
C	Justin	Boren	61
RG	Louis	Vasquez	89
RG	Chris	Kuper	81
RT	Orlando	Franklin	86
RT	Vinston	Painter	64

DEFENSIVE DEPTH CHART

POS	FIRST NAME	LAST NAME	OVR
LE	Derek	Wolfe	74
LE	Jeremy	Beal	66
LE	Malik	Jackson	65
RE	Robert	Ayers	81
RE	Shaun	Phillips	79
RE	Quanterus	Smith	68
DT	Terrance	Knighton	80
DT	Kevin	Vickerson	78
DT	Sylvester	Williams	76
DT	Mitch	Unrein	66
DT	Sealver	Siliga	65
LOLB	Von	Miller	97
LOLB	Stewart	Bradley	72
MLB	Joe	Mays	79
MLB	Nate	Irving	66
MLB	Steven	Johnson	60
ROLB	Wesley	Woodyard	80
ROLB	Danny	Trevathan	68
CB	Champ	Bailey	93
CB	Chris	Harris	82
CB	Dominique	Rodgers-Cromartie	79
CB	Tony	Carter	74
CB	Omar	Bolden	71
CB	Kayvon	Webster	69
CB	Mario	Butler	66
FS	Rahim	Moore	82
FS	Quentin	Jammer	79
FS	Quinton	Carter	72
SS	Mike	Adams	78
SS	David	Bruton	71
SS	Duke	Ihenacho	61

SPECIAL TEAMS DEPTH CHART

POS	FIRST NAME	LAST NAME	OVR
K	Matt	Prater	84
P	Britton	Colquitt	81

Denver Broncos

RECOMMENDED OFFENSIVE RUN FORMATION: SINGLEBACK DEUCE (1 HB, 2 TE, 2 WR)

PRO TIPS

- > START HB RONNIE HILLMAN AS HE IS THE TEAM'S BEST OVERALL OPTION.
- > USE HB MONTEE BALL FOR LATE-GAME SITUATIONS BECAUSE OF HIS 96 CAR RATING.
- > HB KNOWSHON MORENO WILL BE YOUR BEST OPTION TO BACK UP MONTEE BALL.
- > TE JOEL DREESSEN AND FB JACOB HESTER ARE YOUR BEST RUN-BLOCKING OPTIONS.

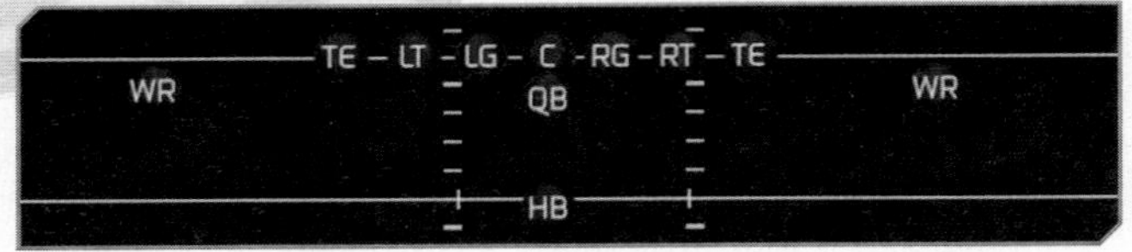

RUN LEFT

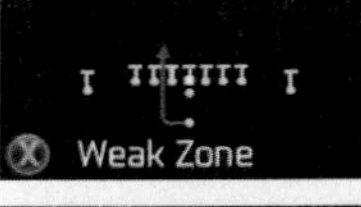

HILLMAN HAS GREAT ACCELERATION, SO MAKE SURE TO USE IT.

RUN MIDDLE

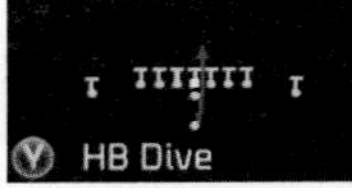

COVER UP WHEN RUNNING BETWEEN THE TACKLES.

RUN RIGHT

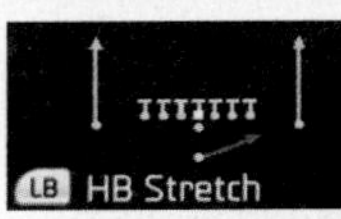

HILLMAN HAS JUST ENOUGH SPEED TO GET TO THE EDGE.

DENVER BRONCOS RUNNING PLAY CALL SHEET

LEGEND: Inside Run | Outside Run | Shotgun Run | QB Run

1ST DOWN RUNS	2ND AND SHORT	3RD AND SHORT	GOAL LINE RUNS	2ND AND LONG	3RD AND LONG
Strong Pro—Toss Crack	Singleback Deuce—HB Dive	Strong Pro—HB Zone Wk	Goal Line Normal—QB Sneak	Gun Dice Y-Flex—45 Quick Base	Gun Deuce Trips—HB Base
Strong Pro—HB Blast	Singleback Deuce—HB Stretch	Singleback Dice Slot—HB Cutback	Goal Line Normal—HB Dive	Singleback Deuce—Weak Zone	Gun Dice Slot—HB Mid Draw
I-Form Tight Pair—DEN Cutback Wk	Singleback Bunch—HB Dive	Singleback Deuce Twins—HB Slant 18	Goal Line Normal—Power O	Gun Y-Trips Wk—HB Mid Draw	Gun Dice Slot—HB Off Tackle

DENVER BRONCOS PASSING PLAY CALL SHEET

LEGEND: Base Play | Man Beater | Zone Beater | Blitz Beater

1ST DOWN PLAY	2ND AND SHORT	3RD AND SHORT	GOAL LINE PASSING	2ND AND LONG	3RD AND LONG
Gun Dice Slot—Curls Slot Shake	Singleback Deuce—Slants	Gun Trey 4WR Str—Comebacks	Goal Line—PA Waggle	Gun Split Slot—Y Shallow Cross	Gun Trey 4WR—Mesh
Gun Dice Slot—HB Angle	Singleback Deuce—Double Sluggo	Gun Trey 4WR Str—Quick Slants	Goal Line—PA Spot	Gun Dice—Corner Strike	Gun Bunch Wk—Close Bronco Cross
Gun Dice Wk—Slants Middle	Gun Dice Y-Flex—Deep Curl	Gun Trips Over—Stick Bubble	Goal Line—PA Power O	Gun Split Slot—46 Z Cross	Gun Bunch Wk—Close Mesh

In these play call sheets we picked the best plays for specific situations so that you will have a play for every down and distance.

OFFENSE

RECOMMENDED OFFENSIVE PASS FORMATION: SHOTGUN DOUBLES ON (1 HB, 1 TE, 3 WR)

PRO TIPS

- WR TRINDON HOLLIDAY SHOULD SEE SOME PLAYING TIME. GET HIM THE BALL ON WR SCREENS AND PLAY ACTION DEEP.
- WR WES WELKER HAS SOME OF THE BEST HANDS IN THE LEAGUE. USE HIS 98 CIT RATING FOR BIG THIRD DOWN PLAYS.
- THE BRONCOS HAVE FOUR TIGHT ENDS WHO SHOULD ALL SEE PLAYING TIME. GOAL LINE WOULD BE A NICE FORMATION TO SHOW RUN BUT DELIVER PASS.

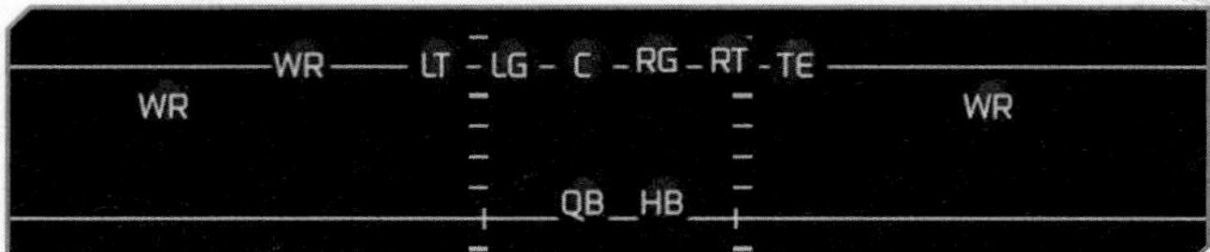

BASE PLAY

SETUP

- STREAK THE TE
- DRAG THE FAR RIGHT WR

- The HB releases if your opponent doesn't send pressure, and he will be open against both man and zone coverage.
- Look to the TE streak and the slot streak against zone.

MAN BEATER

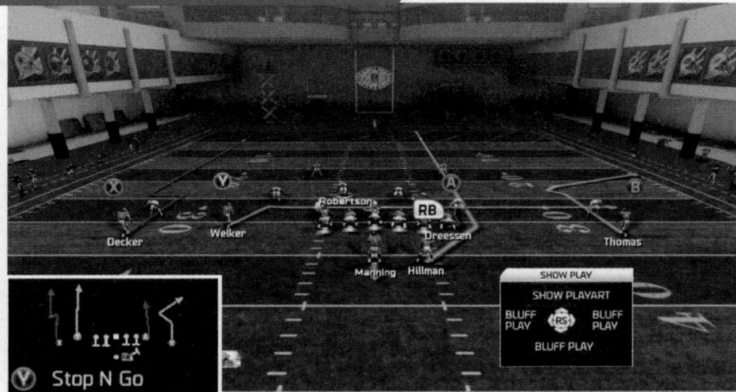

SETUP

- STREAK THE HB
- DRAG THE SLOT WR

- The post corner route crushes man-to-man coverage, as does the out-n-up route.
- The underneath drag will be open with a high lead pass, and look to the HB against slower LBs.

ZONE BEATER

SETUP

- SMOKE SCREEN THE FAR RIGHT WR
- STREAK THE FAR LEFT WR

- Against Cover 2 and Cover 3 zones look to the receivers running the corner routes.
- Against Cover 4 zones look to the smoke screen for an easy 5-yard gain.

BLITZ BEATER

SETUP

- WHEEL THE HB
- DRAG THE FAR RIGHT WR

- Wait for the HB to cut upfield and then throw a sideline lead pass.
- The underneath drag is a nice option for over-committed user defenders.

Denver Broncos

RECOMMENDED DEFENSIVE RUN FORMATION: 4-3 STACK

PRO TIPS

- > USER-CONTROL FS QUINTON CARTER AND HIS 92 POW RATING TO HELP IN RUN SUPPORT.
- > MLB JOE MAYS HAS A 95 POW RATING, WHICH WILL BE GREAT FOR RUN SITUATIONS.
- > START DT SEALVER SILIGA DURING RUNNING SITUATIONS.

RUN DEFENSE

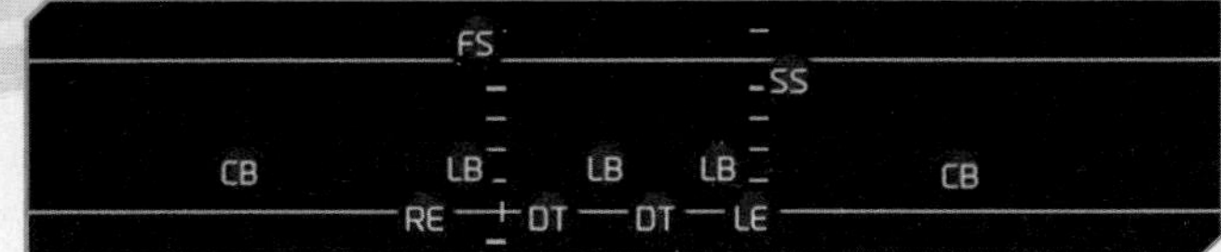

RUN DEFENSE LEFT

SETUP > SHIFT LINEBACKERS LEFT

RUN DEFENSE MIDDLE

SETUP > PINCH DEFENSIVE LINE

RUN DEFENSE RIGHT

SETUP > SHIFT LINEBACKERS RIGHT

DENVER BRONCOS DEFENSIVE RUN PLAY CALL SHEET

1ST DOWN RUN DEFENSE	2ND AND SHORT	3RD AND SHORT	GOAL LINE RUN DEFENSE	2ND AND LONG	3RD AND LONG
4-3 Over Plus—Cover 1	4-3 Under—2 Man Under	4-3 Odd—Safety Blitz	Goal Line 5-3-3—Jam Cover 1	Nickel 3-3-5 Sam—Overload 1 Roll	Nickel 3-3-5—Cover 1
4-3 Over Plus—Cover 2	4-3 Under—Sam Blitz 2	4-3 Odd—Will Go Fire 3	Goal Line 5-3-3—Flat Buzz	Nickel 3-3-5 Sam—Cover 6	Nickel 3-3-5—Cover 4

DENVER BRONCOS DEFENSIVE PASS PLAY CALL SHEET

1ST DOWN PLAY	2ND AND SHORT	3RD AND SHORT	GOAL LINE PASSING	2ND AND LONG	3RD AND LONG
3-4 Even—MLB Cross Fire	4-3 Over Plus—Cover 1	4-3 Over Plus—Dbl Safety Blitz	Goal Line 6-3-2—GL Man	Dime Normal—2 Man Under	Dime Normal—MLB Loop
3-4 Even—MLB Cross Fire 3	4-3 Over Plus—Cover 2	4-3 Over Plus—SS Fire 3 Seam	Goal Line 6-3-2—GL Zone	Dime Normal—3 Double Buzz	Dime Normal—SS Overload 3

LEGEND: Man Coverage | Zone Coverage | Man Blitz | Zone Blitz

In these play call sheets we picked the best plays for specific situations so that you will have a play for every down and distance.

DEFENSE

RECOMMENDED DEFENSIVE PASS FORMATION: NICKEL WIDE 9

PRO TIPS

- PLACE CB CHAMP BAILEY ON YOUR OPPONENT'S BEST WR.
- USE CB DOMINIQUE RODGERS-CROMARTIE TO COVER YOUR OPPONENT'S FASTEST WR.
- CB CHRIS HARRIS SHOULD BE USED AS THE NICKEL DB.
- FS QUINTON CARTER HAS A 92 POW RATING. START HIM AT FS.

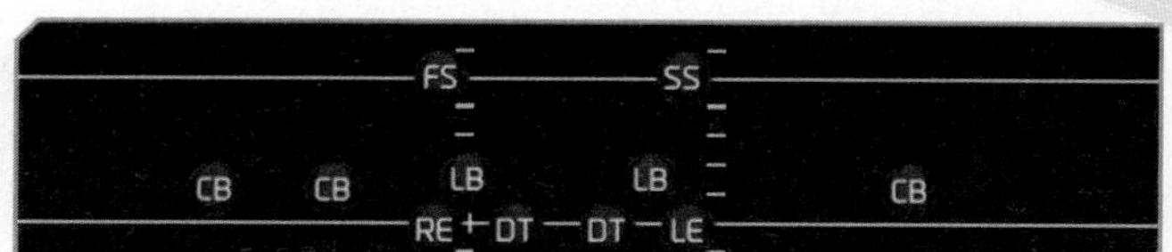

MAN COVERAGE

SETUP

- PINCH DEFENSIVE LINE
- REBLITZ BOTH DES

- When you reblitz a defensive end in the Nickel Wide 9 it creates a unique rush angle.
- This pass rush allows our defenders to get after the QB quicker.

ZONE COVERAGE

SETUP

- HOOK ZONE BOTH BUZZ ZONE DEFENDERS
- MAN ALIGN TWICE

- Man aligning twice will rebalance the hook zones across the field evenly.
- This will leave the flat open but blanket the middle of the field as well as anything deep.

MAN BLITZ

SETUP

- SHOW BLITZ
- USER-CONTROL THE FS COVERING THE HB

- Pressure will come off the left edge.
- Use press coverage to slow down your opponent's read at the snap of the ball.

ZONE BLITZ

SETUP

- SHOW BLITZ
- SHADE SAFETY COVERAGE IN

- User-control the FS over the middle of the field. If your opponent blocks an extra player the blitz won't get in.
- Place both hook zone defenders in flats to fool your opponent into thinking the flat is open.

Cleveland Browns

2012 TEAM RANKINGS

4th AFC North (5-11-0)

PASSING OFFENSE: **5th**
RUSHING OFFENSE: **16th**
PASSING DEFENSE: **3rd**
RUSHING DEFENSE: **3rd**

2012 TEAM LEADERS

PASSING: **Brandon Weeden: 3,385**
RUSHING: **Trent Richardson: 950**
RECEIVING: **Josh Gordon: 805**
TACKLES: **D'Qwell Jackson: 118**
SACKS: **Jabaal Sheard: 7**
INTS: **Sheldon Brown: 3**

KEY ADDITIONS

QB Brian Hoyer
TE Kellen Davis
TE Gary Barnidge

KEY ROOKIES

DE Barkevious Mingo
SS Jamoris Slaughter

CONNECTED FRANCHISE MODE STRATEGY

CFM TEAM RATING: **69**
OFFENSIVE SCHEME: **West Coast**
DEFENSIVE SCHEME: **Base 4-3**
STRENGTHS: **TE, LT, RE, CB**
WEAKNESSES: **QB, WR, FS, DT**

SCHEDULE

1	Sep 8	1:00 PM ET		DOLPHINS
2	Sep 15	1:00 PM ET	AT	RAVENS
3	Sep 22	1:00 PM ET	AT	VIKINGS
4	Sep 29	1:00 PM ET		BENGALS
5	Oct 3	8:25 PM ET		BILLS
6	Oct 13	1:00 PM ET		LIONS
7	Oct 20	4:25 PM ET	AT	PACKERS
8	Oct 27	1:00 PM ET	AT	CHIEFS
9	Nov 3	4:25 PM ET		RAVENS
10	BYE			
11	Nov 17	1:00 PM ET	AT	BENGALS
12	Nov 24	1:00 PM ET		STEELERS
13	Dec 1	1:00 PM ET		JAGUARS
14	Dec 8	1:00 PM ET	AT	PATRIOTS
15	Dec 15	1:00 PM ET		BEARS
16	Dec 22	1:00 PM ET	AT	JETS
17	Dec 29	1:00 PM ET	AT	STEELERS

FRANCHISE OVERVIEW

BROWNS GAMEPLAY RATING

> SEE THE INSIDE BACK COVER FOR A QUICK REFERENCE TO THE GAME ABBREVIATIONS USED THROUGHOUT THIS GUIDE.

> IMPROVE WITH YOUR TEAM BY VISITING PRIMAGAMES.COM/MADDENNFL25 FOR MORE INFORMATION AND HOW-TO VIDEOS.

OFFENSIVE SCOUTING REPORT

> QB Brandon Weeden is a second-year pro, but he's already 29 years old. Plan on replacing him if you can't upgrade him enough over the course of the first season and into the off season. QB should be your number one priority with the Browns.

> HB Trent Richardson is the franchise. As he goes so does your team's success. Upgrade his stats throughout the season and try to improve his Catching rating to make him a three-down HB.

> WR Josh Gordon has three years left on his contract, and he is a future star in the making. Look to improve his Catching rating, as it's only an 84 and has room for improvement.

DEFENSIVE SCOUTING REPORT

> The interior of the Browns' defensive line is young and talented. DT Phil Taylor and LE Ahtyba Rubin both have two years remaining on their contracts and can anchor your defensive line for years to come.

> Rookie ROLB Barkevious Mingo is talented but needs playing time to progress into an elite player. Make sure he starts and plays as many snaps as possible. Mingo is the future of this defense.

> SS T.J. Ward is a free agent at the end of the first season. Make him your number one priority once free agency begins.

OWNER & COACH PROFILES

JIMMY HASLAM

LEGACY SCORE: 0
OFF. SCHEME: Power Run
DEF. SCHEME: Base 4-3

ROB CHUDZINSKI

LEVEL: 1
LEGACY SCORE: 0
OFF. SCHEME: Power Run
DEF. SCHEME: Base 4-3

TEAM OVERVIEW

KEY PLAYERS

HB #33

TRENT RICHARDSON

KEY RATINGS

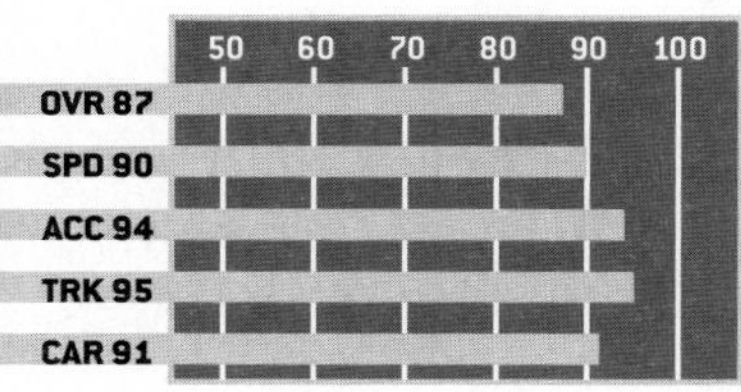

Richardson doesn't have breakaway speed, but he does have the ability to run over defenders. Focus on straight-ahead downhill runs to be most effective with him.

Keep Richardson in on third down situations—he has solid pass blocking ratings: 66 PBK, 60 IBL, and 60 RBS.

CB #23

JOE HADEN

KEY RATINGS

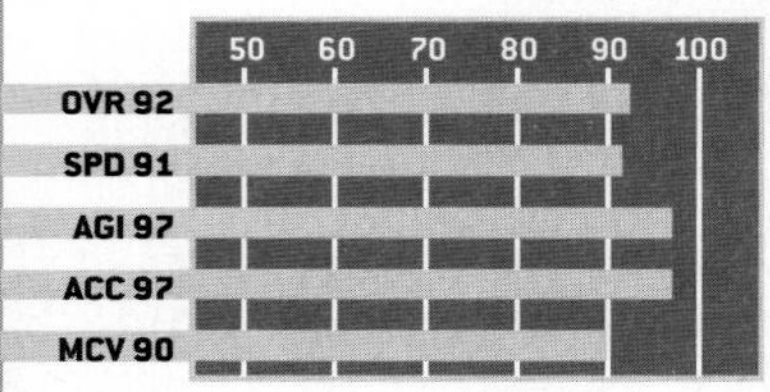

Haden is one of the quickest CBs in the game. Use him to lock down opposing team's #1 wide receivers. His 75 CTH rating is impressive for a defensive player.

Press coverage will be an effective way to use Haden. His 84 PRS rating allows you to call press coverage on an every down basis.

PRE-GAME SETUP

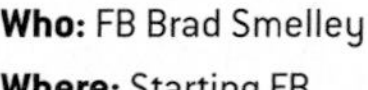

KEY RUNNING SUBSTITUTION

Who: FB Brad Smelley

Where: Starting FB

Why: Smelley is one of the best blocking FBs in the game. Use him in short-yard situations to get the needed push at the line of scrimmage.

Key Stats: 76 RBK, 83 IBL

KEY PASSING SUBSTITUTION

Who: WR Travis Benjamin

Where: #2 WR

Why: Benjamin is the Browns' only speed threat. Get him on the field for screens and deep balls.

Key Stats: 96 SPD, 95 AGI, 95 ACC

KEY RUN DEFENSE SUBSTITUTION

Who: DT Ishmaa'ily Kitchen

Where: Starting DE in run situations

Why: Kitchen has a 92 STR rating, which will allow him to hold his ground on running plays. He will help prevent weaker offensive linemen from getting a push upfield.

Key Stats: 92 STR

KEY PASS DEFENSE SUBSTITUTION

Who: CB Buster Skrine

Where: #2 CB

Why: Skrine has the speed to cover opposing teams' fastest WRs.

Key Stats: 96 SPD, 92 AGI, 94 ACC

OFFENSIVE DEPTH CHART

POS	FIRST NAME	LAST NAME	OVR
QB	Brandon	Weeden	76
QB	Jason	Campbell	75
QB	Brian	Hoyer	71
HB	Trent	Richardson	87
HB	Montario	Hardesty	72
HB	Brandon	Jackson	71
HB	Dion	Lewis	71
HB	Chris	Ogbonnaya	70
HB	Miguel	Maysonet	64
FB	Owen	Marecic	75
FB	Brad	Smelley	73
FB	Dan	Gronkowski	64
WR	Josh	Gordon	81
WR	Davone	Bess	76
WR	Greg	Little	76
WR	David	Nelson	74
WR	Travis	Benjamin	68
WR	Jordan	Norwood	66
WR	Josh	Cooper	64
WR	Tori	Gurley	63
TE	Jordan	Cameron	77
TE	Kellen	Davis	77
TE	Gary	Barnidge	74
LT	Joe	Thomas	97
LT	Oniel	Cousins	66
LT	Chris	Faulk	60
LG	John	Greco	77
LG	Jason	Pinkston	74
C	Alex	Mack	91
C	Braxston	Cave	64
C	Christian	Yount	57
RG	Shawn	Lauvao	75
RG	Jarrod	Shaw	64
RG	Dominic	Alford	60
RT	Mitchell	Schwartz	83
RT	Rashad	Butler	74
RT	Ryan	Miller	65

DEFENSIVE DEPTH CHART

POS	FIRST NAME	LAST NAME	OVR
LE	Ahtyba	Rubin	84
LE	Billy	Winn	75
LE	Hall	Davis	64
LE	Brian	Sanford	64
RE	Desmond	Bryant	88
RE	John	Hughes	68
RE	Armonty	Bryant	64
DT	Phil	Taylor	83
DT	Ishmaa'ily	Kitchen	67
DT	Nicolas	Jean-Baptiste	58
LOLB	Paul	Kruger	87
LOLB	Quentin	Groves	76
LOLB	James-Michael	Johnson	67
MLB	D'Qwell	Jackson	87
MLB	Craig	Robertson	73
MLB	Tank	Carder	66
MLB	L.J.	Fort	66
MLB	Adrian	Moten	55
ROLB	Jabaal	Sheard	82
ROLB	Barkevious	Mingo	76
CB	Joe	Haden	91
CB	Buster	Skrine	74
CB	Christopher	Owens	73
CB	Leon	McFadden	71
CB	Trevin	Wade	65
FS	Tashaun	Gipson	71
FS	Johnson	Bademosi	67
SS	T.J.	Ward	90
SS	Jamoris	Slaughter	70

SPECIAL TEAMS DEPTH CHART

POS	FIRST NAME	LAST NAME	OVR
K	Shayne	Graham	83
P	Spencer	Lanning	69
P	T.J.	Conley	67

Cleveland Browns

RECOMMENDED OFFENSIVE RUN FORMATION: I-FORM TIGHT PAIR (1 HB, 2 TE, 2 WR)

PRO TIPS

> FB BRAD SMELLEY WILL HELP YOUR RUN GAME BECAUSE OF HIS IBL RATING.
> HB DION LEWIS SHOULD BACK UP HB TRENT RICHARDSON.
> HB BRANDON JACKSON IS THE BROWN'S BEST RECEIVING HB.
> TE KELLEN DAVIS IS 6'7" AND HAS 76 IBL.

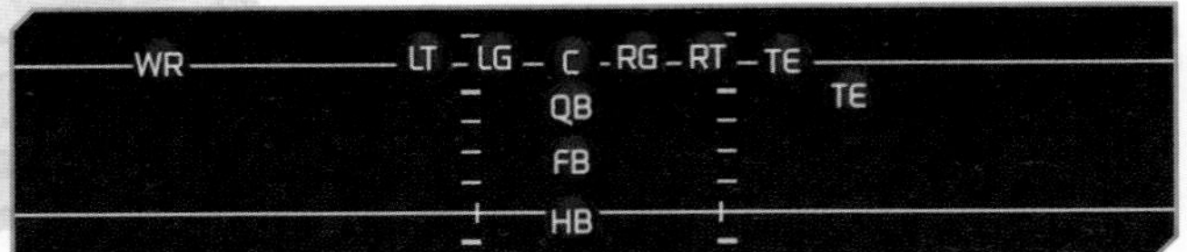

RUN LEFT

FOLLOW YOUR BLOCKS AND PUNISH DEFENDERS WITH RICHARDSON.

RUN MIDDLE

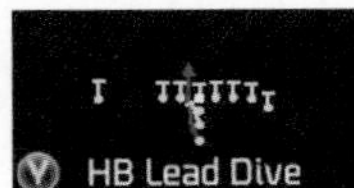

RICHARDSON IS BEST WHEN RUNNING UP THE MIDDLE.

RUN RIGHT

OFF TACKLES AND POWER O PLAYS ARE THE BEST OUTSIDE RUN OPTIONS FOR RICHARDSON.

CLEVELAND BROWNS RUNNING PLAY CALL SHEET

LEGEND: Inside Run | Outside Run | Shotgun Run | QB Run

1ST DOWN RUNS	2ND AND SHORT	3RD AND SHORT	GOAL LINE RUNS	2ND AND LONG	3RD AND LONG
Split Pro—Off Tackle	I-Form—HB Misdirection	Strong Pro—FB Dive	Goal Line Normal—QB Sneak	Gun Snugs Flip—HB Mid Draw	Gun Normal Y-Flex Tight—HB Draw
I-Form Pro—Iso	I-Form—Browns Zone Wk	Singleback Dice Slot—HB Cutback	Goal Line Normal—HB Dive	Strong Pro—HB Toss Crack	Gun Normal Y-Flex Tight—HB Quick Base
I-Form Pro—HB Toss	Singleback Y-Trips—Pump HB Draw	Singleback Deuce Twins—HB Slant 18	Goal Line Normal—Power O	Gun Splut Y-Flex—HB Off Tackle	Gun Trips TE—HB Mid Draw

CLEVELAND BROWNS PASSING PLAY CALL SHEET

LEGEND: Base Play | Man Beater | Zone Beater | Blitz Beater

1ST DOWN PLAY	2ND AND SHORT	3RD AND SHORT	GOAL LINE PASSING	2ND AND LONG	3RD AND LONG
Gun Split Y-Flex—Mesh	Singleback Browns Doubles—Slants	Strong Twins—PA FB Flat	Goal Line—PA Waggle	Gun Spread—Curl Flats	Gun Tight Doubles On—DBL Stick
Gun Y-Trips Open—Stick N Nod	Gun Spread—Slot Outs	Gun Trey Open—WR Screen	Goal Line—PA Spot	Gun Split Y-Flex—Y Shallow Cross	Gun Tight Doubles On—Z Spot
Singleback Browns Doubles—Slot Shake	Gun Spread—Four Verticals	Gun Trey Open—Fk WR Screen	Goal Line—PA Power O	Gun Split Slot—46 Z Cross	Gun Y-Trips Open—Inside Attack

In these play call sheets we picked the best plays for specific situations so that you will have a play for every down and distance.

OFFENSE

RECOMMENDED OFFENSIVE PASS FORMATION: GUN TREY OPEN (1 HB, 0 TE, 4 WR)

PRO TIPS

- WR DAVID NELSON IS 6'5" AND HAS 83 CIT. HE WILL BE A NICE TARGET ON THE OUTSIDE AND IN THE RED ZONE.
- WR TRAVIS BENJAMIN, WITH 96 SPD, IS A GAME CHANGER. GET HIM THE BALL IN OPEN SPACES SO HE CAN MAKE BIG PLAYS.
- WR DAVONE BESS HAS A 90 CTH RATING, WHICH MAKES HIM A GREAT SLOT OPTION. USE HIM FOR SHORT ROUTES OVER THE MIDDLE OF THE FIELD.
- THE BROWNS HAVE THREE TIGHT ENDS WHO CAN ALL CATCH PASSES. WORK THEM INTO YOUR SCHEME.

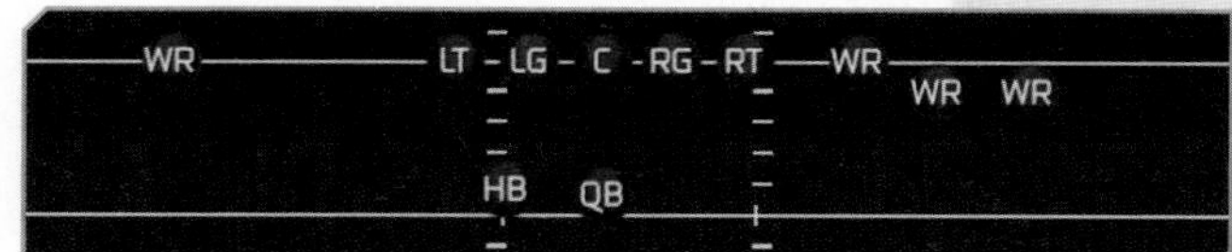

BASE PLAY

SETUP

- STREAK THE INSIDE SLOT WR
- DRAG THE FAR RIGHT WR

- The far left WR's stock fade route is great for user catching. Throw a high inside pass lead.
- The right sideline wheel will get inside position, and the drag will be open with a high pass lead.

MAN BEATER

SETUP

- BLOCK THE HB
- DRAG THE MIDDLE SLOT WR

- The far left corner torches man-to-man coverage with a sideline lead pass. Wait for him to break to the sideline.
- The inside slot streak gets great separation deep if there is no safety coverage. User-catch the far right fade.

ZONE BEATER

SETUP

- OPTION ROUTE THE HB
- STREAK BOTH OUTSIDE RECEIVERS

- Against Cover 2 and Cover 3 zones the sidelines will be open.
- Against Cover 4 zones look to the HB option and the angle post over the middle.

BLITZ BEATER

SETUP

- SWING THE HB RIGHT
- DRAG THE FAR RIGHT WR

- You can also motion the HB right to get a burst at the snap of the ball.
- Follow your blockers and get upfield quickly. This screen can result in TDs.

Cleveland Browns

RECOMMENDED DEFENSIVE RUN FORMATION: 3-4 OVER

PRO TIPS

- > DT ISHMAA'ILY KITCHEN WILL ADD STRENGTH TO YOUR RUN SUPPORT.
- > LOLB JAMES-MICHAEL JOHNSON IS ON THE BENCH WITH 85 POW. GET HIM IN THE GAME DURING RUNNING SITUATIONS.
- > SS T.J. WARD IS THE MOST IMPORTANT PLAYER FOR STOPPING THE RUN.

RUN DEFENSE

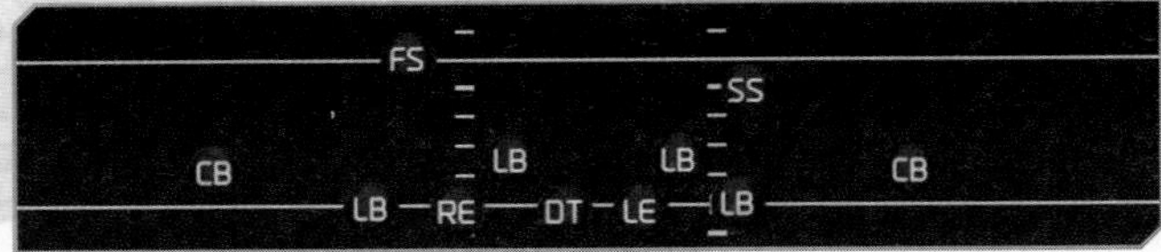

RUN DEFENSE LEFT

SETUP > SHIFT LINEBACKERS LEFT

RUN DEFENSE MIDDLE

SETUP > PINCH DEFENSIVE LINE

RUN DEFENSE RIGHT

SETUP > SHIFT LINEBACKERS RIGHT

CLEVELAND BROWNS DEFENSIVE RUN PLAY CALL SHEET

1ST DOWN RUN DEFENSE	2ND AND SHORT	3RD AND SHORT	GOAL LINE RUN DEFENSE	2ND AND LONG	3RD AND LONG
3-4 Odd—Cover 1 Lurk	3-4 Under—Pinch	3-4 Over—Cross Fire 3	Goal Line 5-3-3—Jam Cover 1	Nickel 1-5-5 Prowl—OLB Fire	Quarter 1-3-7—Inside Blitz
3-4 Odd—Cover 6	3-4 Under—Cover 3	3-4 Over—Sting Pinch Zone	Goal Line 5-3-3—Flat Buzz	Nickel 1-5-5 Prowl—Dbl Loop 3	Quarter 1-3-7—Under Smoke 3

CLEVELAND BROWNS DEFENSIVE PASS PLAY CALL SHEET

1ST DOWN PLAY	2ND AND SHORT	3RD AND SHORT	GOAL LINE PASSING	2ND AND LONG	3RD AND LONG
3-4 Even—2 Man Under	3-4 Solid—Gap Press	3-4 Odd—Pinch Cover 0	Goal Line 6-3-2—GL Man	Nickel 2-4-5 DT—Cross Fire	Nickel 1-5-5 Prowl—Overload Blitz
3-4 Even—Cover 2 Sink	3-4 Solid—Trio Sky Zone	3-4 Odd—Sam Mike 3 Seam	Goal Line 6-3-2—GL Zone	Nickel 2-4-5 DT—Cross Fire 3 Seam	Nickel 1-5-5 Prowl—Strg Corner 2 Fire

LEGEND: Man Coverage | Zone Coverage | Man Blitz | Zone Blitz

In these play call sheets we picked the best plays for specific situations so that you will have a play for every down and distance.

DEFENSE

RECOMMENDED DEFENSIVE PASS FORMATION: NICKEL 1-5-5 PROWL

PRO TIPS

- > PLACE CB JOE HADEN ON YOUR OPPONENT'S BEST WR.
- > USE CB BUSTER SKRINE TO COVER YOUR OPPONENT'S FASTEST WR.
- > CB LEON MCFADDEN SHOULD BE USED AS THE NICKEL DB.
- > START CB CHRISTOPHER OWENS AT FS.

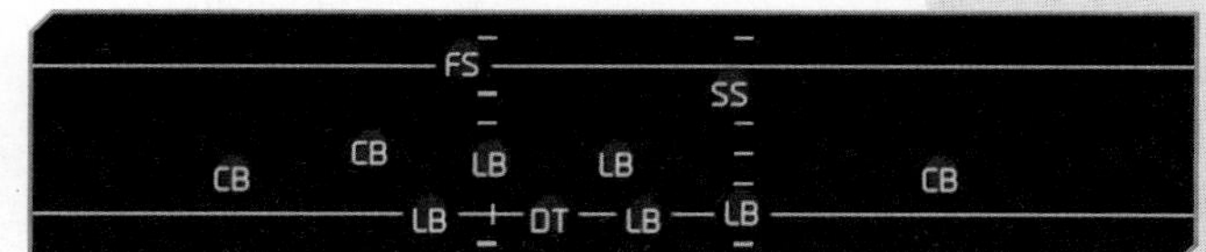

MAN COVERAGE

SETUP

- > SHOW BLITZ
- > QB SPY THE DT

> Showing blitz gives the illusion of pressure, which can force your opponent's QB to leave the pocket early.

> The QB spy will track him down if he does leave the pocket.

ZONE COVERAGE

SETUP

- > SHOW BLITZ
- > FLAT ZONE BOTH BLITZING OUTSIDE LINEBACKERS

> The seams and sidelines will be covered.

> User-control the hook zone MLB and watch for any route over the middle of the field.

MAN BLITZ

SETUP

- > SHOW BLITZ
- > GLOBAL BLITZ LINEBACKERS

> Manually cover the HB with the FS.

> Pressure will be quick, so watch for a throw to the flat or over the short middle.

ZONE BLITZ

SETUP

- > SHOW BLITZ
- > GLOBAL BLITZ LINEBACKERS

> User-control the FS.

> Defend the deep middle and make sure to protect any route downfield.

> Place both hook zone defenders in flats to fool your opponent into thinking the flat is open.

Tampa Bay Buccaneers

2012 TEAM RANKINGS

4th NFC South (7-9-0)

PASSING OFFENSE: **10th**
RUSHING OFFENSE: **15th**
PASSING DEFENSE: **32nd**
RUSHING DEFENSE: **1st**

2012 TEAM LEADERS

PASSING: **Josh Freeman: 4,065**
RUSHING: **Doug Martin: 1,454**
RECEIVING: **Vincent Jackson: 1,384**
TACKLES: **Lavonte David: 139**
SACKS: **Michael Bennett: 9.0**
INTS: **Ronde Barber: 4**

KEY ADDITIONS

CB Darrelle Revis
HB Jeff Demps
WR Kevin Ogletree

KEY ROOKIES

Banks, Johnthan CB
Glennon, Mike QB
Spence, Akeem DT

CONNECTED FRANCHISE MODE STRATEGY

CFM TEAM RATING: **71**
OFFENSIVE SCHEME: **Power Run**
DEFENSIVE SCHEME: **Base 4-3**
STRENGTHS: **QB, HB, WR, DT, CB, FS**
WEAKNESSES: **TE, LOLB, MLB, DT**

SCHEDULE

Week	Date	Time		Opponent
1	Sep 8	1:00	AT	JETS
2	Sep 15	4:05		SAINTS
3	Sep 22	1:00	AT	PATRIOTS
4	Sep 29	1:00		CARDINALS
5	BYE			
6	Oct 13	1:00		EAGLES
7	Oct 20	1:00	AT	FALCONS
8	Oct 24	8:25		PANTHERS
9	Nov 3	4:05	AT	SEAHAWKS
10	Nov 11	8:40		DOLPHINS
11	Nov 17	1:00		FALCONS
12	Nov 24	1:00	AT	LIONS
13	Dec 1	1:00	AT	PANTHERS
14	Dec 8	1:00		BILLS
15	Dec 15	1:00		49ERS
16	Dec 22	1:00	AT	RAMS
17	Dec 29	1:00	AT	SAINTS

FRANCHISE OVERVIEW

BUCCANEERS GAMEPLAY RATING

81

> SEE THE INSIDE BACK COVER FOR A QUICK REFERENCE TO THE GAME ABBREVIATIONS USED THROUGHOUT THIS GUIDE.

> IMPROVE WITH YOUR TEAM BY VISITING PRIMAGAMES.COM/MADDENNFL25 FOR MORE INFORMATION AND HOW-TO VIDEOS.

OFFENSIVE SCOUTING REPORT

> QB Josh Freeman leads the Buccaneers' pirate ship. As he goes so does this offense. He has great throw power and mobility but needs upgrades to his throw accuracy ratings to become one of the league's best.

> Save as many upgrade points as possible to give to HB Doug Martin's Speed rating. Currently he has 91 SPD, and if you can upgrade that to the 95 range he will be an absolute monster on the virtual gridiron.

> Look for TEs during free agency as well as in the draft. The Buccaneers have no real standout at this position.

DEFENSIVE SCOUTING REPORT

> The Buccaneers are weak at the linebacking position. Outside of ROLB Lavonte David they have no linebacker rated higher than a 75 OVR.

> CB Darrelle Revis was brought in to fix the Buccaneers' league-worst passing defense. If he can't recover from his knee injury you will need to focus on finding young talent in the NFL draft or free agency.

> FS Dashon Goldson and SS Mark Barron are big-time hitting safeties. Look to complement their power with speed cornerbacks who can cover.

OWNER & COACH PROFILES

MALCOLM GLAZER

LEGACY SCORE: 1325
OFF. SCHEME: Power Run
DEF. SCHEME: Base 4-3

GREG SCHIANO

LEVEL: 1
LEGACY SCORE: 0
OFF. SCHEME: Power Run
DEF. SCHEME: Base 4-3

TEAM OVERVIEW

KEY PLAYERS

WR #83

VINCENT JACKSON

KEY RATINGS

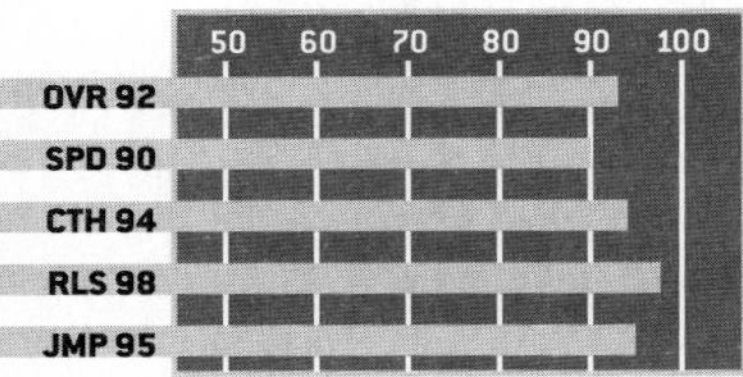

> Target Jackson on the most important plays of the game. His 96 CIT rating means he will hold onto the ball when getting hit by opposing defenders.

> Defenders will find it extremely difficult to press Jackson at the line of scrimmage. His 98 RLS rating is tops in the game.

CB #24

DARRELLE REVIS

KEY RATINGS

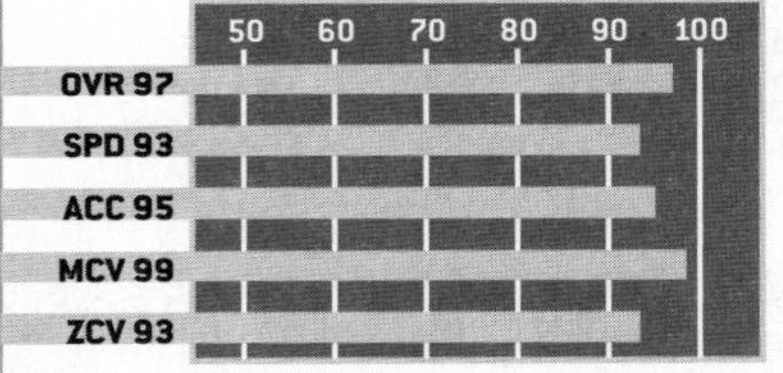

Revis can do it all, but what he does best is to completely take away your opponent's number one receiving option.

Revis can play lockdown man and zone coverage. He can also press most receivers at the line of scrimmage with his 90 PRS rating.

PRE-GAME SETUP

KEY RUNNING SUBSTITUTION

Who: HB Jeff Demps

Where: Backup HB

Why: Demps is the fastest HB in the game. Give him at least five carries a game and expect one of them to go the distance.

Key Stats: 98 SPD, 95 AGI, 98 ACC

KEY PASSING SUBSTITUTION

Who: WR Kevin Ogletree

Where: #3 WR

Why: Ogletree brings speed to the Buccaneers receiving corps. Use him for screens and short passes over the middle.

Key Stats: 96 SPD, 95 AGI, 95 ACC

KEY RUN DEFENSE SUBSTITUTION

Who: DT Akeem Spence

Where: Starting DE in run situations

Why: Spence is a rookie DT who has the defensive line's best Block Shedding rating. Get him in the game to stop the run.

Key Stats: 88 BSH

KEY PASS DEFENSE SUBSTITUTION

Who: CB Johnthan Banks

Where: #2 CB

Why: Banks doesn't have top-end speed, but he has the size to lock down any big receiver in the game. At 6'2" and with 78 CTH and 87 PRS ratings he will be a playmaker on this defense.

Key Stats: 6'2", 78 CTH, 87 PRS

OFFENSIVE DEPTH CHART

POS	FIRST NAME	LAST NAME	OVR
QB	Josh	Freeman	82
QB	Dan	Orlovsky	70
QB	Adam	Weber	66
QB	Mike	Glennon	66
HB	Doug	Martin	90
HB	Brian	Leonard	73
HB	Mike	James	68
HB	Michael	Smith	66
HB	Jeff	Demps	63
FB	Erik	Lorig	76
WR	Vincent	Jackson	92
WR	Mike	Williams	85
WR	Kevin	Ogletree	74
WR	Derek	Hagan	72
WR	Tiquan	Underwood	69
WR	Carlton	Mitchell	67
WR	Eric	Page	63
WR	David	Douglas	62
WR	Chris	Owusu	62
TE	Luke	Stocker	77
TE	Tom	Crabtree	74
TE	Zach	Miller	70
TE	Nate	Byham	68
TE	Danny	Noble	63
LT	Donald	Penn	87
LT	Mike	Remmers	64
LG	Carl	Nicks	95
C	Jeremy	Zuttah	77
C	Ted	Larsen	73
C	Cody	Wallace	69
C	Andrew	Economos	62
RG	Davin	Joseph	88
RG	Jamon	Meredith	71
RT	Demar	Dotson	79
RT	Gabe	Carimi	75
RT	Jason	Weaver	61

DEFENSIVE DEPTH CHART

POS	FIRST NAME	LAST NAME	OVR
LE	Da'Quan	Bowers	77
LE	Aaron	Morgan	67
LE	William	Gholston	67
RE	Adrian	Clayborn	80
RE	Daniel	Te'o-Nesheim	68
RE	Steven	Means	67
RE	Markus	White	64
DT	Gerald	McCoy	91
DT	Derek	Landri	74
DT	Gary	Gibson	74
DT	Akeem	Spence	71
DT	Andre	Neblett	65
DT	Lazarius	Levingston	64
DT	Matthew	Masifilo	60
LOLB	Adam	Hayward	72
LOLB	Dekoda	Watson	70
LOLB	Jacob	Cutrera	66
MLB	Mason	Foster	75
MLB	Najee	Goode	59
MLB	Joe	Holland	55
ROLB	Lavonte	David	89
ROLB	Jonathan	Casillas	73
CB	Darrelle	Revis	97
CB	Johnthan	Banks	72
CB	Anthony	Gaitor	70
CB	Leonard	Johnson	70
CB	Myron	Lewis	67
CB	Danny	Gorrer	64
FS	Dashon	Goldson	90
FS	Ahmad	Black	75
FS	Keith	Tandy	69
SS	Mark	Barron	80
SS	Cody	Grimm	71

SPECIAL TEAMS DEPTH CHART

POS	FIRST NAME	LAST NAME	OVR
K	Connor	Barth	85
P	Michael	Koenen	82
P	Chas	Henry	68

Tampa Bay Buccaneers

RECOMMENDED OFFENSIVE RUN FORMATION: STRONG CLOSE (2 HB, 1 TE, 2 WR)

PRO TIPS

- HB BRIAN LEONARD HAS THE BEST HANDS OF ANY BUCCANEERS HB, WITH AN 80 CTH RATING.
- HB JEFF DEMPS'S 98 SPD WILL MAKE BIG PLAYS IF YOU GET HIM TOUCHES.
- FB ERIK LORIG HAS AN AMAZING 90 IBL RATING. HE WILL PANCAKE PEOPLE IN THE RUN GAME.

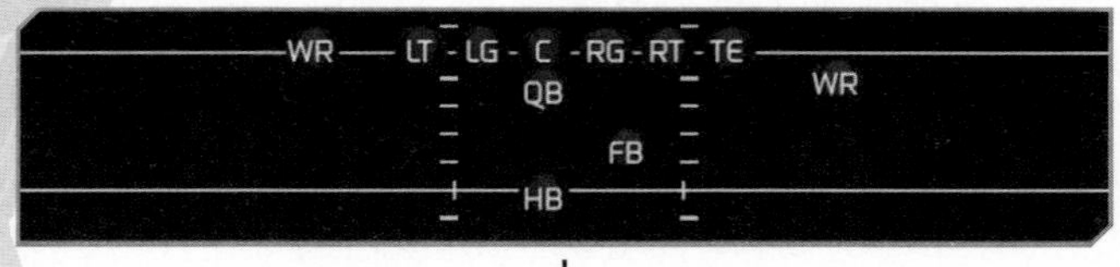

RUN LEFT

MARTIN HAS ENOUGH SPEED TO GET OUTSIDE ON THE COUNTER.

RUN MIDDLE

FOLLOW YOUR BLOCKERS UP THROUGH THE HOLE.

RUN RIGHT

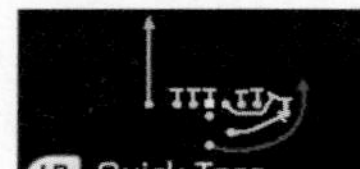

KEEP TIGHT TO THE OFFENSIVE LINE AND THEN USE ACCELERATION BURST TOWARDS THE SIDELINE.

TAMPA BAY BUCCANEERS RUNNING PLAY CALL SHEET

LEGEND: Inside Run | Outside Run | Shotgun Run | QB Run

1ST DOWN RUNS	2ND AND SHORT	3RD AND SHORT	GOAL LINE RUNS	2ND AND LONG	3RD AND LONG
Strong H Pro—Counter Weak	I-Form Pro—FB Dive	Goal Line—HB Dive	Goal Line—QB Sneak	Gun Split Slot—Power O	Gun Buc Trips—Read Option
Singleback Ace—Close HB Draw	Singleback Ace—HB Dive	Strong Tight Pair—HB Toss	I-Form Pro—Iso	I-Form Slot Flex—HB Zone Wk	Gun Buc Trips—HB Draw
Strong H Pro—Power O	Singleback Ace—HB Blast	I-Form Pro—End Around	Goal Line—Strong Toss	Gun Buc Trips—HB Base	Gun Spread—HB Sweep

TAMPA BAY BUCCANEERS PASSING PLAY CALL SHEET

LEGEND: Base Play | Man Beater | Zone Beater | Blitz Beater

1ST DOWN PLAY	2ND AND SHORT	3RD AND SHORT	GOAL LINE PASSING	2ND AND LONG	3RD AND LONG
Singleback Bunch—Z Spot	Gun Empty Trey—TE Slot Cross	Singleback Y-Trips—HB Slip Screen	Goal Line—PA Power O	I-Form Tight Pair—X Slant	Gun Bunch Wk—Bunch Trail
Gun Wing Trips Wk—Fork Dig	I-Form Pro—Mesh	Singleback Doubles—PA TE Screen	Strong Close—Bucs Y-Trail	Gun Spread—Deep Attack	Gun Empty Buc—Curl Flats
Gun Empty Buc—Deep In	Gun Snugs Flip—Bench Switch	Gun Doubles—Angle Smash	Weak Pro Twins—PA Bucs Read	Gun Bunch Wk—Z Spot	Gun Empty Buc—Slot Stick Nod

In these play call sheets we picked the best plays for specific situations so that you will have a play for every down and distance.

OFFENSE

RECOMMENDED OFFENSIVE PASS FORMATION: GUN DOUBLES (1 HB, 1 TE, 3 WR)

PRO TIPS

- RECEIVERS KEVIN OGLETREE AND TIQUAN UNDERWOOD BOTH PROVIDE SPEED TO THIS OFFENSE. LOOK TO TARGET THEM DEEP OFF PLAY ACTION.
- WR DAVONE BESS HAS 90 CTH, WHICH MAKES HIM A GREAT SLOT OPTION. USE HIM FOR SHORT ROUTES OVER THE MIDDLE OF THE FIELD.
- THE BUCCANEERS HAVE THREE TIGHT ENDS WHO CAN ALL CATCH PASSES. WORK THEM INTO YOUR SCHEME.

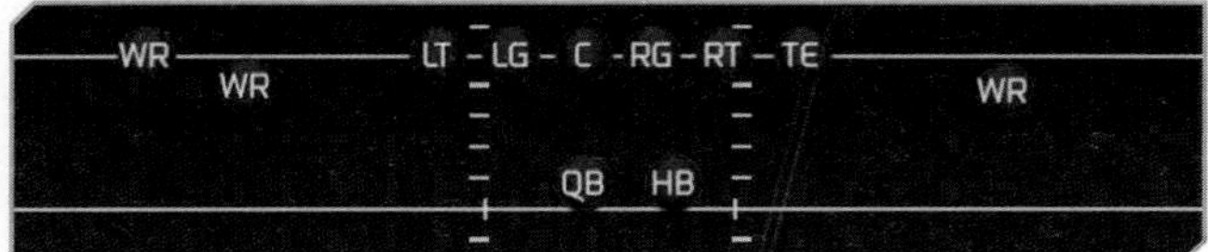

BASE PLAY

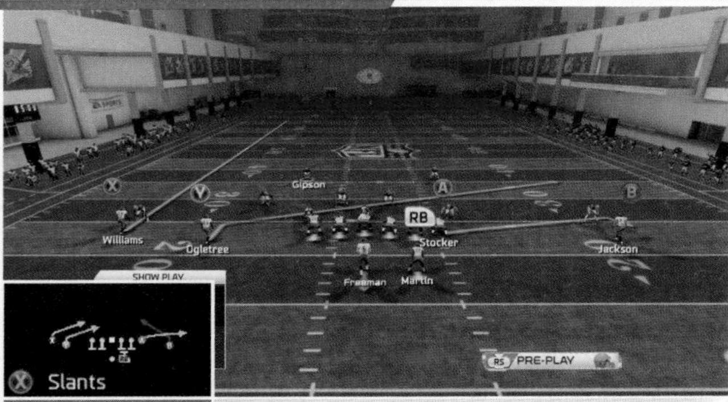

SETUP

- DRAG THE FAR RIGHT WR
- STREAK THE FAR LEFT WR

- Look to the drag against zone, the TE flat against the blitz, and the slant against man-to-man.
- The streak is for a sideline user catch.

MAN BEATER

SETUP

- DRAG THE SLOT WR
- DRAG THE TE

- The two drags will create a mesh over the middle of the field. Find the open one and throw a high lead pass.
- The outside double move routes get open after they make their initial cut. Throw a high inside lead pass.

ZONE BEATER

SETUP

- BLOCK OR OPTION THE HB
- ZIG THE SLOT WR

- Against Cover 2 and Cover 3 zones look to the sidelines or TE over the middle.
- Against Cover 4 zones look to the HB option or the slot zig.

BLITZ BEATER

SETUP

- DRAG THE FAR RIGHT WR
- BLOCK THE TE

- Blocking the TE will give you extra time in the pocket to throw to the HB
- If the HB is covered look to the drag underneath.

Tampa Bay Buccaneers

RECOMMENDED DEFENSIVE RUN FORMATION: 5-2 NORMAL

PRO TIPS

- > DT AKEEM SPENCE IS YOUR BEST BLOCK SHEDDING DEFENSIVE LINEMAN.
- > ROOKIE RE STEVEN MEANS HAS THE SECOND BEST BSH RATING (83) ON THE TEAM.
- > INVOLVE FS DASHON GOLDSON AND SS MARK BARRON IN RUN SUPPORT. THEY ARE BIG-TIME HITTERS IN THE SECONDARY.

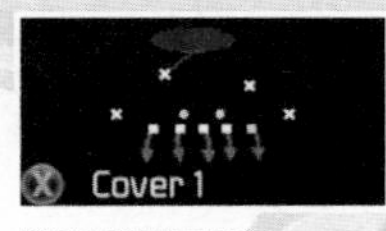

RUN DEFENSE

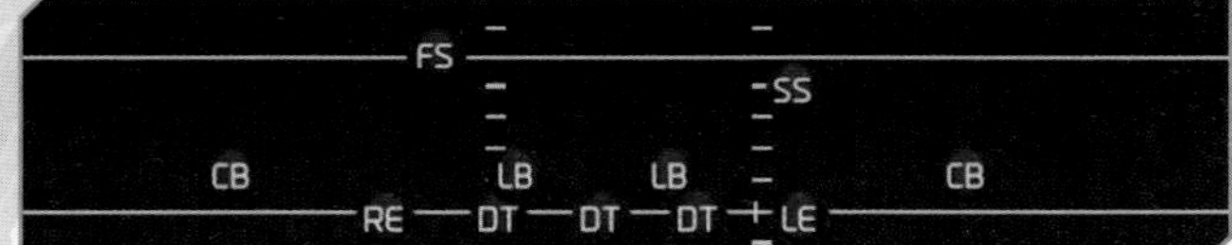

RUN DEFENSE LEFT

SETUP > SHIFT LINEBACKERS LEFT

RUN DEFENSE MIDDLE

SETUP > PINCH DEFENSIVE LINE

RUN DEFENSE RIGHT

SETUP > SHIFT LINEBACKERS RIGHT

TAMPA BAY BUCCANEERS DEFENSIVE RUN PLAY CALL SHEET

1ST DOWN RUN DEFENSE	2ND AND SHORT	3RD AND SHORT	GOAL LINE RUN DEFENSE	2ND AND LONG	3RD AND LONG
5-2 Normal—Cover 1	4-3 Stack—2 Man Under	4-3 Under—Free Fire	Goal Line 5-3-3—Jam Cover 1	Nickel 3-3-5—2 Man Under	Nickel 3-3-5—Cover 1
5-2 Normal—Cover 3	4-3 Stack—Cover 2 Buc	4-3 Under—Sam Blitz 2	Goal Line 5-3-3—Flat Buzz	Nickel 3-3-5—Cover 4	Nickel 3-3-5—Cover 2 Buc

TAMPA BAY BUCCANEERS DEFENSIVE PASS PLAY CALL SHEET

1ST DOWN PLAY	2ND AND SHORT	3RD AND SHORT	GOAL LINE PASSING	2ND AND LONG	3RD AND LONG
Dime Normal—2 Man Under	Dime Normal—Cover 1 Press	Dollar 3-2-6—Mike Edge 1 Dog	Goal Line 6-3-2—GL Man	Nickel Normal—Over Storm Brave	Nickel 3-3-5—LB Cross Blitz
Dime Normal—Cover 4	Dime Normal—Cover 6	Dollar 3-2-6—Cross 3 Fire	Goal Line 6-3-2—GL Zone	Nickel Normal—Overload Blitz	Nickel 3-3-5—LB Cross 3

LEGEND: Man Coverage | Zone Coverage | Man Blitz | Zone Blitz

In these play call sheets we picked the best plays for specific situations so that you will have a play for every down and distance.

DEFENSE

RECOMMENDED DEFENSIVE PASS FORMATION: DOLLAR 3-2-6

PRO TIPS

> PLACE CB DARRELLE REVIS ON YOUR OPPONENT'S BEST WR.
> USE CB JOHNTHAN BANKS TO COVER YOUR OPPONENT'S TALLEST WR.
> PLAY MORE ZONE COVERAGE WITH THIS DEFENSE.

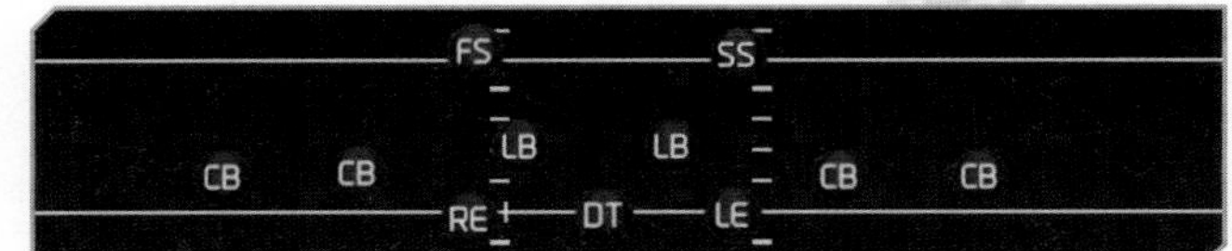

MAN COVERAGE

SETUP

> PINCH DEFENSIVE LINE
> QB SPY THE DT

> User-control the blitzing MLB in coverage.
> Revis will lock down one side of the field so you can user-defend other options.

ZONE COVERAGE

SETUP

> PINCH DEFENSIVE LINE
> QB SPY THE DT

> User-control either MLB and cover routes over the short middle.
> The flats will be weak with this coverage, but you will not be beaten deep.

MAN BLITZ

SETUP

> PRESS COVERAGE
> USER-CONTROL EITHER MLB

> Cover over the short middle with the MLB.
> If you see any CB get beaten at the line of scrimmage, drop deep and defend with the MLB.

ZONE BLITZ

SETUP

> PRESS COVERAGE
> FLAT ZONE BOTH HOOK ZONE DEFENDERS

> User-control the MLB and defend the short middle.
> It's better to protect deep with the MLB and get beaten underneath than to protect short and get beaten deep.
> Place both hook zone defenders in flats to fool your opponent into thinking the flat is open.

Arizona Cardinals

2012 TEAM RANKINGS

4th NFC West (5-11-0)

PASSING OFFENSE: **28th**
RUSHING OFFENSE: **32nd**
PASSING DEFENSE: **5th**
RUSHING DEFENSE: **28th**

2012 TEAM LEADERS

PASSING: **John Skelton: 1,132**
RUSHING: **LaRod Stephens-Howling: 356**
RECEIVING: **Larry Fitzgerald: 798**
TACKLES: **Daryl Washington: 134**
SACKS: **Daryl Washington: 9.0**
INTS: **Patrick Peterson: 7**

KEY ADDITIONS

QB Carson Palmer
HB Rashard Mendenhall
CB Antoine Cason

KEY ROOKIES

OG Jonathan Cooper
ILB Kevin Minter
CB Tyrann Mathieu

CONNECTED FRANCHISE MODE STRATEGY

CFM TEAM RATING: **68**
OFFENSIVE SCHEME: **West Coast**
DEFENSIVE SCHEME: **Base 4-3**
STRENGTHS: **WR, LE, MLB, CB**
WEAKNESSES: **RG, LOLB, ROLB, FS, SS**

SCHEDULE

1	Sep 8	4:25 ET	AT	RAMS
2	Sep 15	4:05 ET		LIONS
3	Sep 22	1:00 ET	AT	SAINTS
4	Sep 29	1:00 ET	AT	BUCCANEERS
5	Oct 6	4:05 ET		PANTHERS
6	Oct 13	4:25 ET	AT	49ERS
7	Oct 17	8:25 ET		SEAHAWKS
8	Oct 27	4:25 ET		FALCONS
9	BYE			
10	Nov 10	4:25 ET		TEXANS
11	Nov 17	1:00 ET	AT	JAGUARS
12	Nov 24	4:05 ET		COLTS
13	Dec 1	1:00 ET	AT	EAGLES
14	Dec 8	4:25 ET		RAMS
15	Dec 15	1:00 ET	AT	TITANS
16	Dec 22	4:05 ET	AT	SEAHAWKS
17	Dec 29	4:25 ET		49ERS

FRANCHISE OVERVIEW

CARDINALS GAMEPLAY RATING

74

> See the inside back cover for a quick reference to the game abbreviations used throughout this guide.

> Improve with your team by visiting PrimaGames.com/MaddenNFL25 for more information and how-to videos.

OFFENSIVE SCOUTING REPORT

- QB Carson Palmer was brought in to ease the process of finding a franchise QB. This is your number one priority with the Cardinals. Find a QB that can help this team get back to the Super Bowl.
- HB Rashard Mendenhall has shown flashes of brilliance in his young NFL career. Injuries have also come to light, and that is a major concern for your organization.
- HB Ryan Williams is another young talent who with potential to become one of the league's best, but injuries have kept him from seeing significant playing time in his two-year NFL career. If you can keep Mendenhall and Williams healthy you could have a dominant backfield for years to come.

DEFENSIVE SCOUTING REPORT

- LE Calais Campbell is one of the biggest defensive linemen in the game. He is also one of the best. He is locked into a contract for the next four years, until he's 30.
- Opposite Campbell is RE Darnell Dockett, who is entering the back nine of his career. Dockett has three years left on his deal, all of which are costing you $9 million a year. For a 79 OVR rating this is far too much money to be spending. You need to dump him—and do it sooner rather than later.
- CB Patrick Peterson is the best defensive player the Cardinals have. He is also one of the most coveted players in the game. If you can strike a deal that brings in different needs it might be a nice option for a Cardinals squad with a ton of team needs.

OWNER & COACH PROFILES

BILL BIDWILL
LEGACY SCORE: 650
OFF. SCHEME: Power Run
DEF. SCHEME: Attacking 3-4

BRUCE ARIANS
LEVEL: 10
LEGACY SCORE: 0
OFF. SCHEME: Power Run
DEF. SCHEME: Attacking 3-4

TEAM OVERVIEW

KEY PLAYERS

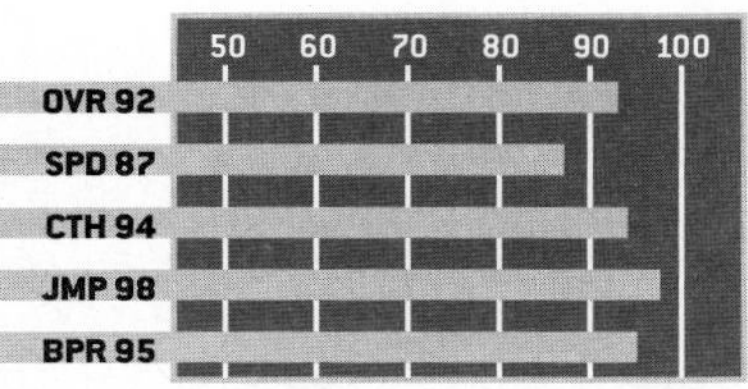

WR #11
LARRY FITZGERALD

KEY RATINGS

OVR	92
SPD	87
CTH	94
JMP	98
BPR	95

> Fitzgerald is one of the league's best WRs. Get him the ball early and often. He is best in third down situations because of his tremendous catching ability.

> In red zone situations hot route Fitzgerald to a fade. Snap the ball and lob it to him. This is a great way to get him the ball in tight spaces.

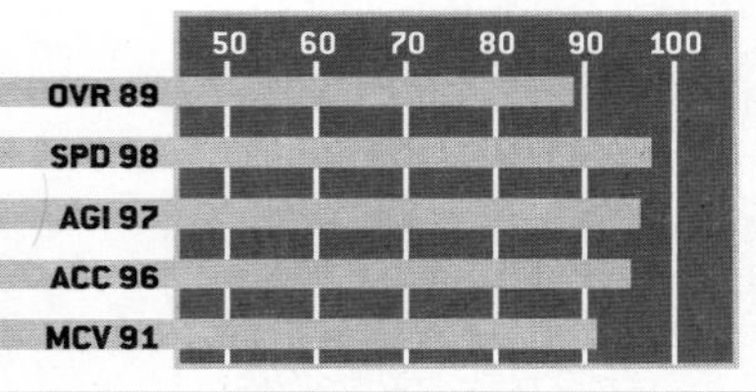

CB #21
PATRICK PETERSON

KEY RATINGS

OVR	89
SPD	98
AGI	97
ACC	96
MCV	91

> Peterson is the best CB in *Madden NFL 25*—not because of his Overall rating but because of his rare athletic ability. He can cover speed WRs and he can cover tall WRs.

> Put Peterson on an island and never worry about him getting beaten. Build your defense around this rare player.

PRE-GAME SETUP

KEY RUNNING SUBSTITUTION

Who: HB Alfonso Smith

Where: Backup HB

Why: Smith has the highest speed on the Cardinals' HB depth chart. Get him in the game to give your run game a boost.

Key Stats: 93 SPD

KEY PASSING SUBSTITUTION

Who: WR Ryan Swope

Where: #3 WR

Why: Swope has great speed to take advantage of over the middle of the field.

Key Stats: 94 SPD, 95 ACC, 85 CIT

KEY RUN DEFENSE SUBSTITUTION

Who: MLB Kevin Minter

Where: Backup MLB

Why: Minter can help the defensive battle in stopping the run game because of his 87 TAK rating.

Key Stats: 87 TAK

KEY PASS DEFENSE SUBSTITUTION

Who: CB Bryan McCann

Where: #2 CB

Why: McCann has the speed to cover the opposing team's fastest WR.

Key Stats: 96 SPD, 92 AGI, 98 ACC

OFFENSIVE DEPTH CHART

POS	FIRST NAME	LAST NAME	OVR
QB	Carson	Palmer	84
QB	Drew	Stanton	73
QB	Ryan	Lindley	65
HB	Rashard	Mendenhall	80
HB	Ryan	Williams	74
HB	William	Powell	69
HB	Stepfan	Taylor	68
HB	Alfonso	Smith	67
HB	Andre	Ellington	67
FB	Jim	Dray	71
WR	Larry	Fitzgerald	92
WR	Andre	Roberts	78
WR	Michael	Floyd	75
WR	Ryan	Swope	65
WR	Jarett	Dillard	65
WR	LaRon	Byrd	63
WR	Kerry	Taylor	58
TE	Jeff	King	75
TE	Rob	Housler	74
TE	Mike	Leach	71
TE	D.C.	Jefferson	71
TE	Kory	Sperry	67
LT	Levi	Brown	74
LT	Nate	Potter	67
LG	Jonathan	Cooper	83
LG	Daryn	Colledge	80
LG	Chilo	Rachal	71
C	Lyle	Sendlein	77
C	Scott	Wedige	61
RG	Earl	Watford	70
RG	Mike	Gibson	70
RG	Senio	Kelemete	64
RT	Bobby	Massie	76
RT	Paul	Fanaika	70

DEFENSIVE DEPTH CHART

POS	FIRST NAME	LAST NAME	OVR
LE	Calais	Campbell	93
LE	Matt	Shaughnessy	77
LE	Ronald	Talley	63
RE	Darnell	Dockett	79
RE	Frostee	Rucker	77
DT	Dan	Williams	81
DT	David	Carter	72
DT	Ricky	Lumpkin	60
LOLB	Lorenzo	Alexander	78
LOLB	O'Brien	Schofield	76
LOLB	Alex	Okafor	68
MLB	Daryl	Washington	90
MLB	Karlos	Dansby	83
MLB	Jasper	Brinkley	75
MLB	Kevin	Minter	71
MLB	Reggie	Walker	70
MLB	Zack	Nash	52
ROLB	Sam	Acho	74
ROLB	Tim	Fugger	62
CB	Patrick	Peterson	89
CB	Antoine	Cason	81
CB	Jerraud	Powers	78
CB	Javier	Arenas	76
CB	Jamell	Fleming	67
CB	Bryan	McCann	66
FS	Yeremiah	Bell	74
FS	Tyrann	Mathieu	72
FS	Justin	Bethel	71
SS	Rashad	Johnson	76
SS	Jonathon	Amaya	68
SS	Curtis	Taylor	63

SPECIAL TEAMS DEPTH CHART

POS	FIRST NAME	LAST NAME	OVR
K	Jay	Feely	85
P	Dave	Zastudil	91

Arizona Cardinals

RECOMMENDED OFFENSIVE RUN FORMATION: SINGLEBACK DOUBLES (1 HB, 1 TE, 3 WR)

PRO TIPS

- FB JIM DRAY SHOULD BE USED WHEN YOU PLAN ON RUNNING THE BALL.
- HB RASHARD MENDENHALL SHOULD BE YOUR EVERY-DOWN HB.
- ROOKIE HB STEPFAN TAYLOR IS THE TEAM'S BEST PASS-CATCHING HB.

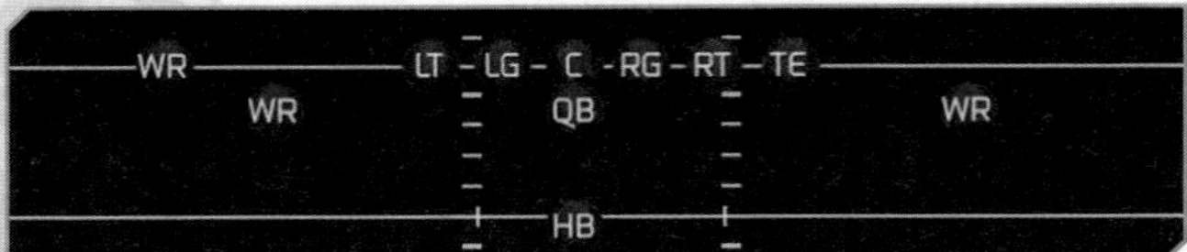

RUN LEFT

MENDENHALL STILL HAS THE QUICKNESS TO GET TO THE EDGE.

RUN MIDDLE

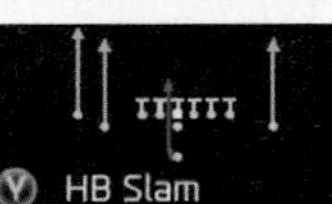

POWER THROUGH THE MIDDLE OF THE FIELD WITH MENDENHALL.

RUN RIGHT

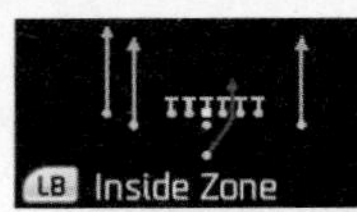

KEEP TIGHT TO THE OFFENSIVE LINE AND THEN EXPLODE TO THE SIDELINE.

ARIZONA CARDINALS RUNNING PLAY CALL SHEET

LEGEND: Inside Run | Outside Run | Shotgun Run | QB Run

1ST DOWN RUNS	2ND AND SHORT	3RD AND SHORT	GOAL LINE RUNS	2ND AND LONG	3RD AND LONG
Singleback Ace—Stretch	Pistol Strong—Inside Zone Split	Goal Line—HB Dive	I-Form Tight Pair—Iso	Singleback Zona Y-Trips—HB Draw	Gun Split Close—FB Inside
Singleback Doubles—Inside Zone	Singleback Ace Close—Tight Slots Wham	I-Form Tight—HB Toss	I-Form Tight Pair—FB Dive	I-Form Pro—FB Dive	Gun Y-Trips Wk—HB Mid Draw
I-Form Pro—HB Toss	Singleback Flex—HB Slam	I-Form Tight—Power O	Strong Pro—HB Toss Crack	Gun Snugs—HB Draw	Gun Spread—HB Draw

ARIZONA CARDINALS PASSING PLAY CALL SHEET

LEGEND: Base Play | Man Beater | Zone Beater | Blitz Beater

1ST DOWN PLAY	2ND AND SHORT	3RD AND SHORT	GOAL LINE PASSING	2ND AND LONG	3RD AND LONG
Singleback Zona Y-Trips—Slot Drive	Gun Empty Trey—TE Slot Cross	Gun Spread—HB Slip Screen	Goal Line—PA Power O	Singleback Ace Twins—Cards Flood	Gun Split Close—WR Corner
Gun Trio—Verticals	Gun Spread—Zona Corner	Singleback Ace Twins—HB Slip Screen	Singleback Ace Twins—HB Slip Screen	Singleback Zona Y-Trips—Slants	Gun Y-Trips Wk—Four Verticals
Gun Empty Trey—Inside Cross	Singleback Ace Twins—Smash	Gun Trio—HB Slip Screen	Singleback Ace Pair—Close PA Cross	Weak Flex Twins—Zona Corner	Gun 5WR Trips—Smash

In these play call sheets we picked the best plays for specific situations so that you will have a play for every down and distance.

OFFENSE

RECOMMENDED OFFENSIVE PASS FORMATION: GUN SNUGS (1 HB, 0 TE, 4 WR)

PRO TIPS

- WR MICHAEL FLOYD IS A BIG TARGET IN THE RED ZONE.
- ROOKIE WR RYAN SWOPE WILL PROVIDE SPEED TO THIS OFFENSE.
- LOOK TO WR LARRY FITZGERALD ON ALL CRUCIAL THIRD DOWNS.

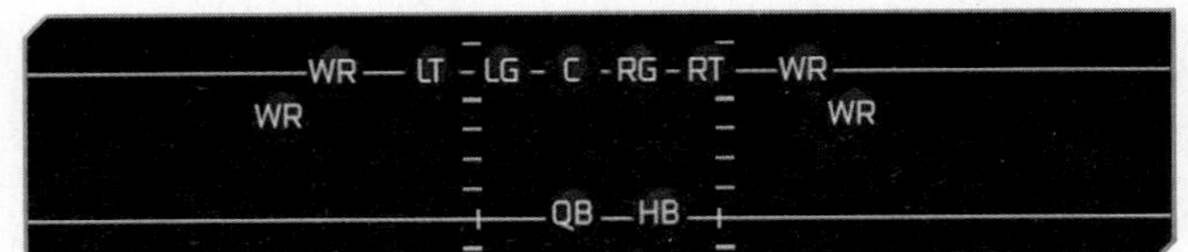

BASE PLAY

SETUP

- STREAK THE RIGHT SLOT
- MOTION THE FAR LEFT WR OUTSIDE

- Against a zone blitz the motioned WR will be open in the flat.
- Against man-to-man coverage the corner route and underneath drag are your best options.

MAN BEATER

SETUP

- DRAG THE FAR LEFT WR
- MOTION THE FAR LEFT WR OUTSIDE

The motioned WR will destroy man-to-man coverage.

The deep corner route is your home-run hitter, while the HB's route is great against the blitz.

ZONE BEATER

SETUP

- OPTION ROUTE THE HB
- MOTION THE FAR LEFT WR OUTSIDE

- Against Cover 2 and Cover 3 zones look to the deep corner.
- Against Cover 4 zones look to the HB option and the far right angled streak.

BLITZ BEATER

SETUP

- HITCH THE LEFT SLOT WR
- HITCH THE RIGHT SLOT WR

- If you face a zone blitz look to either flat route.
- If you face a man-to-man blitz look to either slot hitch route.

Arizona Cardinals

RECOMMENDED DEFENSIVE RUN FORMATION: 3-4 SOLID

PRO TIPS

- RE FROSTEE RUCKER BRINGS EXPERIENCE TO THE DEFENSIVE LINE AND WILL HELP OUT IN RUNNING SITUATIONS.
- DT RICKY LUMPKIN HAS 88 STR AND IS ONE OF THE CARDINALS' STRONGER DEFENDERS.
- MLB KARLOS DANSBY IS A VETERAN WHO NEEDS TO SEE THE FIELD ON RUNNING SITUATIONS. HE ALSO HAS AN 83 STR RATING.

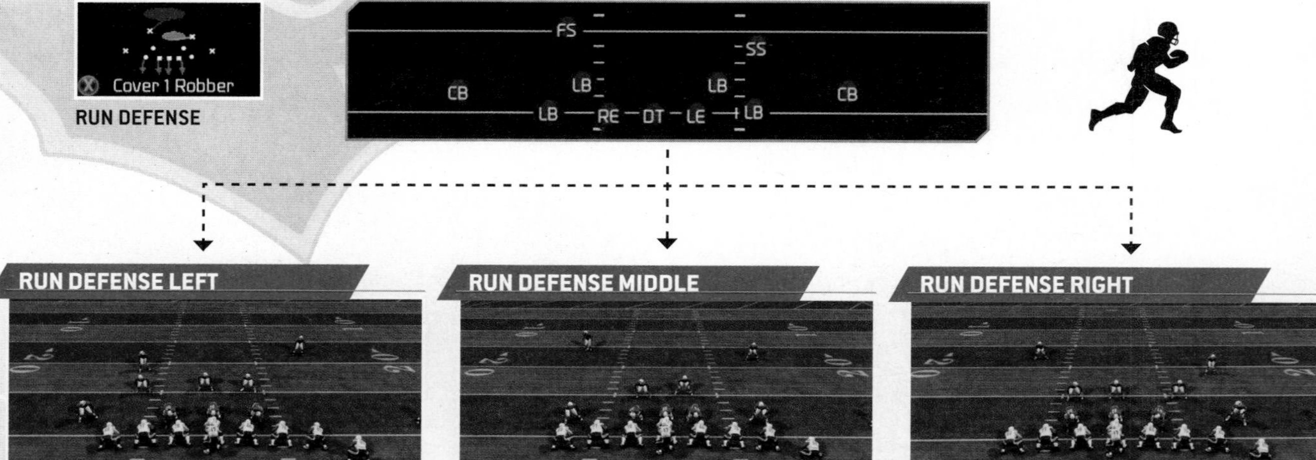

RUN DEFENSE LEFT

SETUP > SHIFT LINEBACKERS LEFT

RUN DEFENSE MIDDLE

SETUP > PINCH DEFENSIVE LINE

RUN DEFENSE RIGHT

SETUP > SHIFT LINEBACKERS RIGHT

ARIZONA CARDINALS DEFENSIVE RUN PLAY CALL SHEET

1ST DOWN RUN DEFENSE	2ND AND SHORT	3RD AND SHORT	GOAL LINE RUN DEFENSE	2ND AND LONG	3RD AND LONG
3-4 Even—2 Man Under	3-4 Solid—Gap Press	Nickel 1-5-5 Prowl—Dbl Loop	Goal Line 5-3-3—Jam Cover 1	3-4 Odd—2 Man Under	3-4 Over—Cross Fire
3-4 Even—Cover 3	3-4 Solid—Cover 6	Nickel 1-5-5 Prowl—Dbl Loop 3	Goal Line 5-3-3—Flat Buzz	3-4 Odd—Cover 2 Spy	3-4 Over—Cross 3 Fire

ARIZONA CARDINALS DEFENSIVE PASS PLAY CALL SHEET

1ST DOWN PLAY	2ND AND SHORT	3RD AND SHORT	GOAL LINE PASSING	2ND AND LONG	3RD AND LONG
Nickel 2-4-5 DT—2 Man Under	Quarter 1-3-7—Inside Blitz	Sub 1-4-6—Mike SS Dog 1	Goal Line 6-3-2—GL Man	Nickel 2-4-5 DT—Overload 1 Roll	Sub 2-3-6 Will—Spinner
Nickel 2-4-5 DT—Cover 4	Quarter 1-3-7—Cover 3 Buzz	Sub 1-4-6—Cross 3 Fire	Goal Line 6-3-2—GL Zone	Nickel 2-4-5 DT—Cover 3	Sub 2-3-6 Will—DB Fire 2

LEGEND: Man Coverage | Zone Coverage | Man Blitz | Zone Blitz

In these play call sheets we picked the best plays for specific situations so that you will have a play for every down and distance.

DEFENSE

RECOMMENDED DEFENSIVE PASS FORMATION: NICKEL 1-5-5 PROWL

PRO TIPS

- PLACE CB PATRICK PETERSON ON YOUR OPPONENT'S BEST WR.
- USE CB BRYAN MCCANN TO COVER YOUR OPPONENT'S FASTEST WR.
- USE CB JAVIER ARENAS AS YOUR #2 CB.

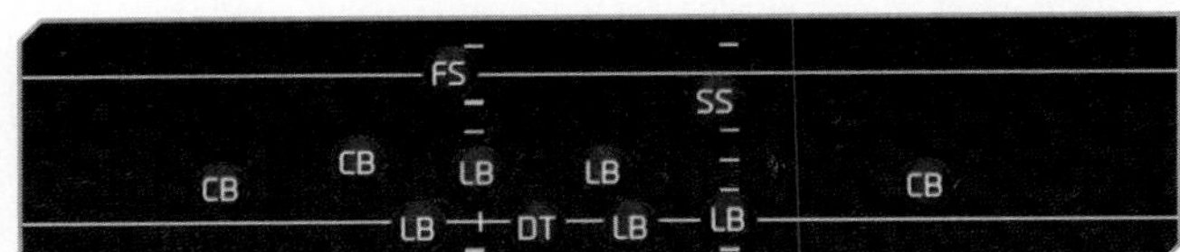

MAN COVERAGE

SETUP

- GLOBAL BLITZ BOTH OUTSIDE LINEBACKERS
- USER-CONTROL ONE OF THE BLITZING MIDDLE LINEBACKERS

- We are looking to force pressure off the outside edge with our pass rushers.
- This will force QBs to step up into the pocket and make throws in tight spaces.

ZONE COVERAGE

SETUP

- PRESS COVERAGE
- FLAT ZONE BOTH BLITZING OUTSIDE LINEBACKERS

- When you put nine defenders into coverage you make your opponent be patient with the ball.
- Opposing QBs will also be forced into making throws in tight coverage, which results in big hits for our defense.

MAN BLITZ

SETUP

- PRESS COVERAGE
- GLOBAL BLITZ LINEBACKERS

- User-control the FS.
- Stay deep with the FS and look to help out if you see a beat press animation at the line of scrimmage.

ZONE BLITZ

SETUP

- PRESS COVERAGE
- GLOBAL BLITZ LINEBACKERS

- User-control the FS.
- Feel free to place the hook zone defenders in different coverage assignments as you see fit.
- The flats will be wide open, but that is something we are willing to give up with this blitz.

San Diego Chargers

2012 TEAM RANKINGS

2nd AFC West (7-9-0)

PASSING OFFENSE: **24th**
RUSHING OFFENSE: **27th**
PASSING DEFENSE: **18th**
RUSHING DEFENSE: **16th**

2012 TEAM LEADERS

PASSING: **Philip Rivers: 3,606**
RUSHING: **Ryan Mathews: 707**
RECEIVING: **Malcom Floyd: 814**
TACKLES: **Eric Weddle: 97**
SACKS: **Shaun Phillips: 9.5**
INTS: **Quentin Jammer: 3**

KEY ADDITIONS

ROLB Dwight Freeney
HB Danny Woodhead
CB Derek Cox

KEY ROOKIES

RT D.J. Fluker
MLB Manti Te'o
WR Keenan Allen

CONNECTED FRANCHISE MODE STRATEGY

CFM TEAM RATING: **72**
OFFENSIVE SCHEME: **Balanced**
DEFENSIVE SCHEME: **Attacking 3-4**
STRENGTHS: **QB, HB, TE, ROLB, FS**
WEAKNESSES: **RG, RE, DT, CB, SS**

SCHEDULE

Week	Date	Time		Opponent
1	Sep 9	10:20 PM ET		TEXANS
2	Sep 15	1:00 PM ET	AT	EAGLES
3	Sep 22	1:00 PM ET	AT	TITANS
4	Sep 29	4:25 PM ET		COWBOYS
5	Oct 6	4:25 PM ET	AT	RAIDERS
6	Oct 14	8:40 PM ET		COLTS
7	Oct 20	1:00 PM ET	AT	JAGUARS
8	BYE			
9	Nov 3	1:00 PM ET	AT	REDSKINS
10	Nov 10	4:25 PM ET		BRONCOS
11	Nov 17	1:00 PM ET	AT	DOLPHINS
12	Nov 24	1:00 PM ET	AT	CHIEFS
13	Dec 1	4:25 PM ET		BENGALS
14	Dec 8	4:25 PM ET		GIANTS
15	Dec 12	8:25 PM ET	AT	BRONCOS
16	Dec 22	4:25 PM ET		RAIDERS
17	Dec 29	4:25 PM ET		CHIEFS

FRANCHISE OVERVIEW

CHARGERS GAMEPLAY RATING

73

> SEE THE INSIDE BACK COVER FOR A QUICK REFERENCE TO THE GAME ABBREVIATIONS USED THROUGHOUT THIS GUIDE.

> IMPROVE WITH YOUR TEAM BY VISITING PRIMAGAMES.COM/MADDENNFL25 FOR MORE INFORMATION AND HOW-TO VIDEOS.

OFFENSIVE SCOUTING REPORT

QB Philip Rivers has been in the NFL for nine seasons. He has been the starting QB for seven of those years. Rivers was once thought of as a premiere QB in the league. His current contract has three years remaining and a ton of cash loaded on the back end. Consider dumping him for a younger, more promising QB.

TE Antonio Gates is in a similar situation. At age 33 and with three years remaining on his contract, what is the best move? He still has production left in him, but how much? We think it will be best for your team to dump Rivers and Gates in a package deal and take draft picks or younger, lower-rated players in return.

HB Ryan Mathews is also in a similar situation. What do you do with a guy that has a 71 INJ rating? If he plays he's amazing, but that's a big *if*. Mathews has two years remaining on his contract, and we think that you can get a ton of value by packaging Rivers, Gates, and Mathews together and seeing what you get in return. Don't focus so much on HB needs because you have Danny Woodhead, who is 28 and will be a stud for a year or two.

DEFENSIVE SCOUTING REPORT

The defensive line is in shambles for the Chargers. You need to hope you can package Rivers, Gates, and Mathews for workable offensive pieces and then rebuild your entire defensive line through the draft and free agency. Use your high picks for pass-rushing DEs and use your researching skills to find strong DTs.

The linebacking group for the Chargers has value if you play the right guys. Start LOLB Melvin Ingram, MLB Donald Butler, and ROLB Dwight Freeney. Back all of them up with rookie MLB Manti Te'o.

CB Derek Cox will need to see the bulk of your upgrades during the season. Also pay attention to rookie CB Steve Williams, who needs to start right away. Luckily, FS Eric Weddle can patrol the deep secondary and keep this entire defense in line. Weddle can do it all, and with a 96 OVR rating he is going to have to.

OWNER & COACH PROFILES

ALEX SPANOS
LEGACY SCORE: 900
OFF. SCHEME: Balanced Offense
DEF. SCHEME: Attacking 4-3

MIKE MCCOY
LEVEL: 1
LEGACY SCORE: 0
OFF. SCHEME: Balanced Offense
DEF. SCHEME: Attacking 4-3

TEAM OVERVIEW

KEY PLAYERS

WR #84

DANARIO ALEXANDER

KEY RATINGS

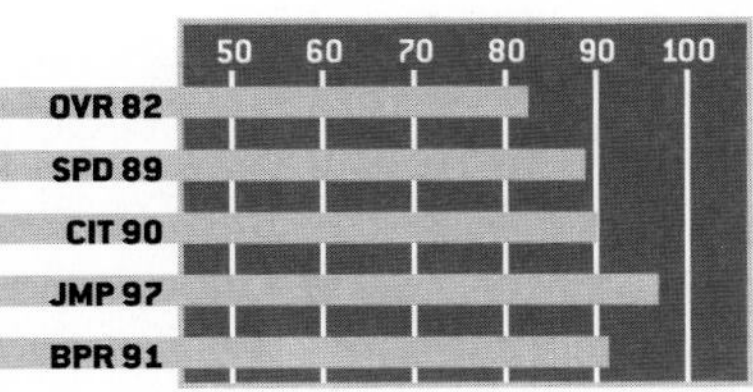

Alexander only caught 37 balls last season, but those catches totaled 658 yards and 7 TDs.

He is a play-making WR who is an amazing deep threat. Throw the ball up to him and let him make a play!

FS #32

ERIC WEDDLE

KEY RATINGS

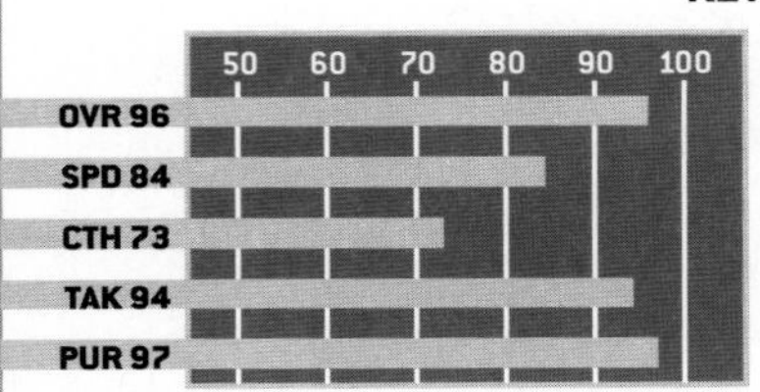

What Weddle lacks in natural ability he makes up for with his ability to read plays and always be in the right place at the right time.

Weddle is a tackling machine with a 97 TAK rating; you can expect him to make every tackle he attempts.

PRE-GAME SETUP

KEY RUNNING SUBSTITUTION

Who: HB Danny Woodhead

Where: Starting HB

Why: Mathews is the guy in San Diego, but we think Woodhead is a better player in *Madden NFL 25*. Make him your every-down HB.

Key Stats: 91 SPD, 95 AGI, 95 ACC, 88 CAR, 83 CTH

KEY PASSING SUBSTITUTION

Who: WR Eddie Royal

Where: #3 WR

Why: Royal has enough speed to make defenses respect him deep. Get him in the ballgame in your three-wide-receiver formations.

Key Stats: 94 SPD, 94 AGI, 95 ACC

KEY RUN DEFENSE SUBSTITUTION

Who: MLB Manti Te'o

Where: Backup MLB

Why: Te'o will make a ton of plays in the run game. He will also cause fumbles because of his POW rating.

Key Stats: 88 TAK, 85 POW

KEY PASS DEFENSE SUBSTITUTION

Who: CB Steve Williams

Where: #2 CB

Why: Williams is the second-best corner on this team. He is only a 69 OVR, but he has the ability to be a solid player.

Key Stats: 91 SPD, 93 AGI, 95 ACC

OFFENSIVE DEPTH CHART

POS	FIRST NAME	LAST NAME	OVR
QB	Philip	Rivers	84
QB	Charlie	Whitehurst	73
QB	Brad	Sorensen	64
HB	Ryan	Mathews	82
HB	Danny	Woodhead	82
HB	Ronnie	Brown	78
HB	Edwin	Baker	62
FB	Le'Ron	McClain	81
FB	Chris	Gronkowski	65
WR	Danario	Alexander	82
WR	Malcom	Floyd	81
WR	Vincent	Brown	74
WR	Keenan	Allen	74
WR	Eddie	Royal	74
WR	Robert	Meachem	73
WR	Deon	Butler	70
WR	Richard	Goodman	66
WR	Mike	Willie	56
TE	Antonio	Gates	87
TE	John	Phillips	76
TE	Ladarius	Green	68
TE	Mike	Windt	49
LT	King	Dunlap	78
LT	Max	Starks	75
LT	Mike	Harris	57
LG	Chad	Rinehart	76
LG	Rich	Ohrnberger	70
C	Nick	Hardwick	78
C	David	Molk	68
C	Colin	Baxter	68
RG	Jeromey	Clary	73
RG	Stephen	Schilling	70
RG	Johnnie	Troutman	64
RT	D.J.	Fluker	78
RT	Brandyn	Dombrowski	72

DEFENSIVE DEPTH CHART

POS	FIRST NAME	LAST NAME	OVR
LE	Corey	Liuget	84
LE	Jarius	Wynn	73
RE	Kendall	Reyes	80
RE	Damik	Scafe	64
DT	Cam	Thomas	76
DT	Kwame	Geathers	61
LOLB	Jarret	Johnson	82
LOLB	Melvin	Ingram	77
LOLB	Thomas	Keiser	66
MLB	Donald	Butler	85
MLB	Manti	Te'o	74
MLB	D.J.	Smith	73
MLB	Jonas	Mouton	69
MLB	Andrew	Gachkar	64
MLB	Phillip	Dillard	64
MLB	Bront	Bird	62
ROLB	Dwight	Freeney	88
ROLB	Larry	English	77
ROLB	Tourek	Williams	63
CB	Derek	Cox	84
CB	Shareece	Wright	75
CB	Johnny	Patrick	70
CB	Steve	Williams	69
CB	Gregory	Gatson	62
CB	Cornelius	Brown	60
FS	Eric	Weddle	96
FS	Darrell	Stuckey	74
SS	Marcus	Gilchrist	72
SS	Brandon	Taylor	70
SS	Sean	Cattouse	62

SPECIAL TEAMS DEPTH CHART

POS	FIRST NAME	LAST NAME	OVR
K	Nick	Novak	79
P	Mike	Scifres	89

San Diego Chargers

RECOMMENDED OFFENSIVE RUN FORMATION: I-FORM PRO TWINS (2 HB, 1 TE, 2 WR)

PRO TIPS

> HALFBACKS RYAN MATHEWS AND DANNY WOODHEAD SHOULD SPLIT CARRIES IN THE BACKFIELD.

> USE HB RONNIE BROWN IN LATE-GAME SITUATIONS BECAUSE OF HIS 93 CAR RATING.

> FB LE'RON MCCLAIN HAS AN 87 TRK RATING AND CAN BE USED IN SHORT-YARD SITUATIONS.

> TE JOHN PHILLIPS HAS A 72 IBL RATING AND WILL BE A GREAT LEAD BLOCKER IF USED AT FB.

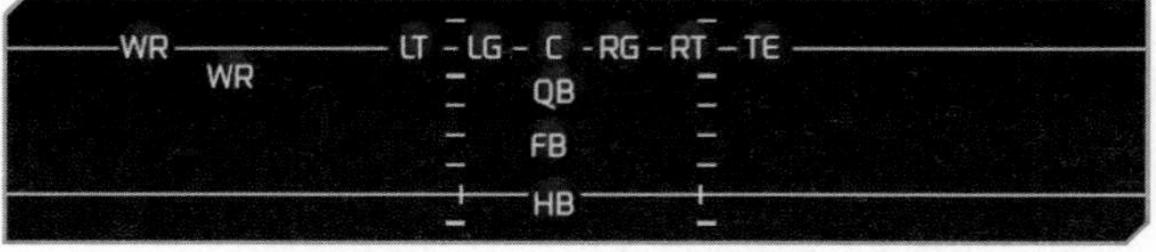

RUN LEFT

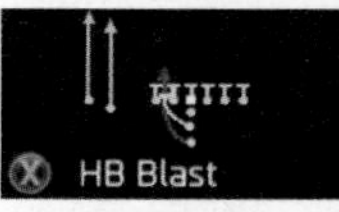

ONCE YOU BREAK THE RUN OFF THE LEFT EDGE GET UPFIELD.

RUN MIDDLE

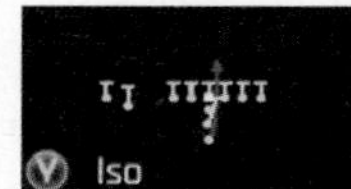

BE PATIENT WHEN RUNNING IN BETWEEN THE TACKLES.

RUN RIGHT

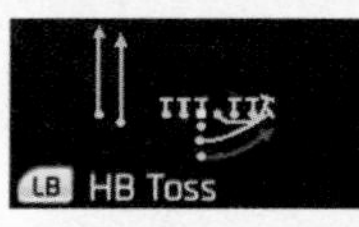

WOODHEAD HAS THE QUICKNESS TO BREAK ANY RUN FOR A TOUCHDOWN!

SAN DIEGO CHARGERS RUNNING PLAY CALL SHEET

LEGEND: Inside Run | Outside Run | Shotgun Run | QB Run

1ST DOWN RUNS	2ND AND SHORT	3RD AND SHORT	GOAL LINE RUNS	2ND AND LONG	3RD AND LONG
Singleback Tight Doubles—HB Cutback	Singleback Ace Pair—HB Dive	Singleback Jumbo—HB Dive	Goal Line Normal—QB Sneak	Gun Doubles Wk—HB Delay	Gun Trips TE—HB Off Tackle
Singleback Tight Doubles—HB Dive	I-Form Tight—Iso	Singleback Jumbo—HB Toss	Goal Line Normal—HB Dive	Strong Pro—HB Iso	Gun Trips TE—HB Mid Draw
Strong Pro—HB Dive	I-Form Tight—HB Zone Wk	Singleback Jumbo—HB Ace Power	Goal Line Normal—Power O	Gun Bunch Wk—HB Mid Draw	Gun Normal Y-Flex Tight—HB Quick Base

SAN DIEGO CHARGERS PASSING PLAY CALL SHEET

LEGEND: Base Play | Man Beater | Zone Beater | Blitz Beater

1ST DOWN PLAY	2ND AND SHORT	3RD AND SHORT	GOAL LINE PASSING	2ND AND LONG	3RD AND LONG
Gun Split Y-Flex—FL Drive	Gun Doubles Wk—Ins Y-Corner	Singleback Doubles—Sluggo Seam	Goal Line—PA Waggle	Gun Bunch Wk—SD Bunch	Gun Trips TE—Slot Quick Flat
Gun Normal Y-Flex Tight—Y-Sail	Gun Doubles Wk—Slot Post	I-Form Pro—HB Slip Screen	Goal Line—PA Spot	Gun Trips TE—Curl Flat	Gun Bunch Wk—Spacing
Gun Bunch Wk—Z Spot Dig	Gun Doubles Wk—Double Smash	I-Form—PA Charger Wheel	Goal Line—PA Power O	Gun Split Y-Flex—Close FB Trail	Gun Normal Y-Flex—Flood

In these play call sheets we picked the best plays for specific situations so that you will have a play for every down and distance.

OFFENSE

RECOMMENDED OFFENSIVE PASS FORMATION: GUN DOUBLES WK (1 HB, 1 TE, 3 WR)

PRO TIPS

- WR EDDIE ROYAL HAS 94 SPD—USE HIM FOR SCREENS AND ROUTES OVER THE MIDDLE.
- WR ROBERT MEACHEM IS 6'2" AND HAS 92 SPD. HE IS THE MOST WELL-ROUNDED RECEIVER ON THIS TEAM.
- MAKE SURE TO SUB IN TE ANTONIO GATES AS A WR IN FOUR-WIDE-RECEIVER FORMATIONS.

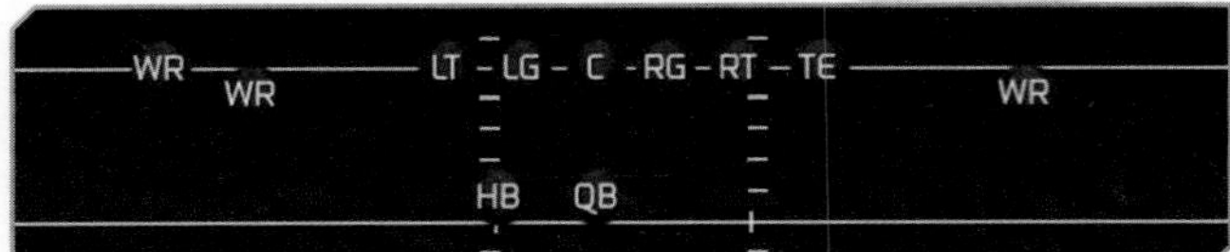

BASE PLAY

SETUP

- BLOCK THE HB
- ZIG THE TE

- Early in games we like to take shots downfield to Malcom Floyd and Danario Alexander on the outside.
- They both have the ability to win jump balls in the end zone!

MAN BEATER

SETUP

- BLOCK THE HB
- DRAG THE SLOT WR

- Look to Antonio Gates on the corner route. As he breaks to the sideline he will separate from his defender.
- The slot drag will be your next option. You can playmaker this route upfield as well.

ZONE BEATER

SETUP

- STREAK THE HB
- SMART ROUTE BOTH CORNER ROUTES

- Against Cover 2 and Cover 3 zones look to the corner routes.
- Against Cover 4 zones look to the outside hitches.

BLITZ BEATER

SETUP

- SWING THE HB RIGHT
- DRAG THE FAR RIGHT WR

- Throw the ball to the HB sooner rather than later.
- The longer you wait to throw the ball to the HB the better chance defenders have to block shed.

San Diego Chargers

RECOMMENDED DEFENSIVE RUN FORMATION: 3-4 ODD

PRO TIPS

- > MOVE ROLB LARRY ENGLISH TO DE, WHERE HIS OVR RATING BECOMES 81.
- > JARIUS WYNN IS THE BEST AVAILABLE DT TO USE DURING RUNNING SITUATIONS, BEHIND CAM THOMAS.
- > MANTI TE'O NEEDS TO BE ON THE FIELD DURING RUNNING SITUATIONS.

RUN DEFENSE

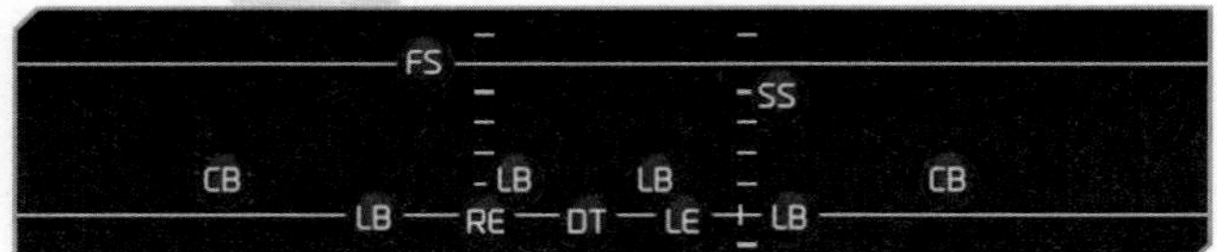

RUN DEFENSE LEFT

SETUP > SHIFT LINEBACKERS LEFT

RUN DEFENSE MIDDLE

SETUP > PINCH DEFENSIVE LINE

RUN DEFENSE RIGHT

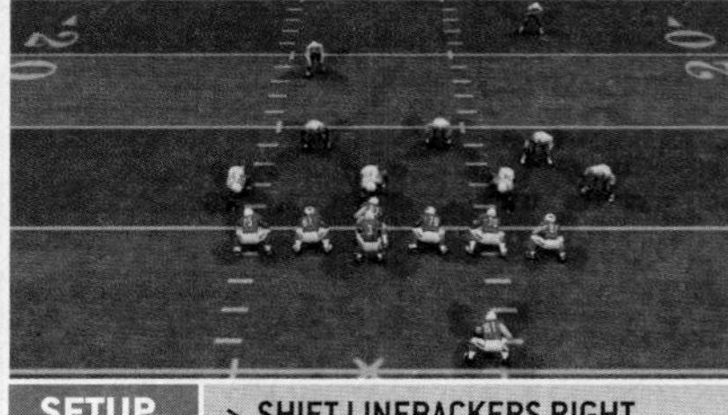

SETUP > SHIFT LINEBACKERS RIGHT

SAN DIEGO CHARGERS DEFENSIVE RUN PLAY CALL SHEET

1ST DOWN RUN DEFENSE	2ND AND SHORT	3RD AND SHORT	GOAL LINE RUN DEFENSE	2ND AND LONG	3RD AND LONG
3-4 Over—2 Man Under	3-4 Even—MLB Cross Fire	3-4 Solid—OLB Blitz	Goal Line 5-3-3—Jam Cover 1	Nickel 3-3-5—Cover 1	Quarter Normal—2 Man Under Spy
3-4 Over—Cover 3	3-4 Even—Cover 2	3-4 Solid—Weak Blitz 3	Goal Line 5-3-3—Flat Buzz	Nickel 3-3-5—Cover 4	Quarter Normal—Cover 3

SAN DIEGO CHARGERS DEFENSIVE PASS PLAY CALL SHEET

1ST DOWN PLAY	2ND AND SHORT	3RD AND SHORT	GOAL LINE PASSING	2ND AND LONG	3RD AND LONG
Sub 2-3-6 Will—2 Man Under	Nickel 2-4-5—Over Storm Brave	3-4 Over—Cross Fire Chuck	Goal Line 6-3-2—GL Man	Nickel 2-4-5—Overload 1 Roll	Nickel 3-3-5—Dogs All Go
Sub 2-3-6 Will—Cover 2	Nickel 2-4-5—Cover 6	3-4 Over—OLB Fire 2	Goal Line 6-3-2—GL Zone	Nickel 2-4-5—Overload 3 Seam	Nickel 3-3-5—LB Cross 3

LEGEND: Man Coverage | Zone Coverage | Man Blitz | Zone Blitz

In these play call sheets we picked the best plays for specific situations so that you will have a play for every down and distance.

DEFENSE

RECOMMENDED DEFENSIVE PASS FORMATION: 3-4 OVER

PRO TIPS

> PLACE CB DEREK COX ON YOUR OPPONENT'S BEST WR.
> USE CB STEVE WILLIAMS TO COVER YOUR OPPONENT'S FASTEST WR.
> CB SHAREECE WRIGHT SHOULD BE THE NICKEL CORNER.

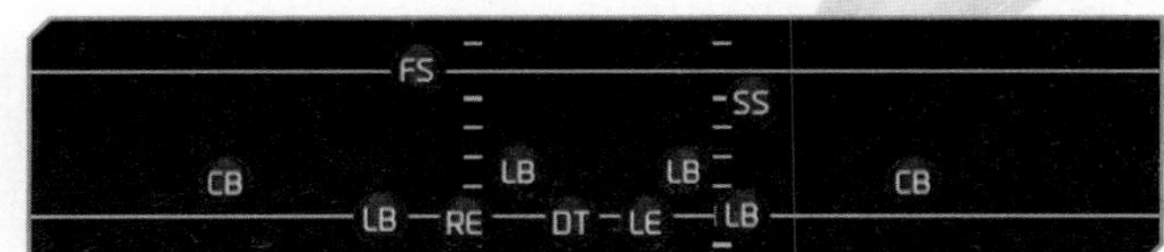

MAN COVERAGE

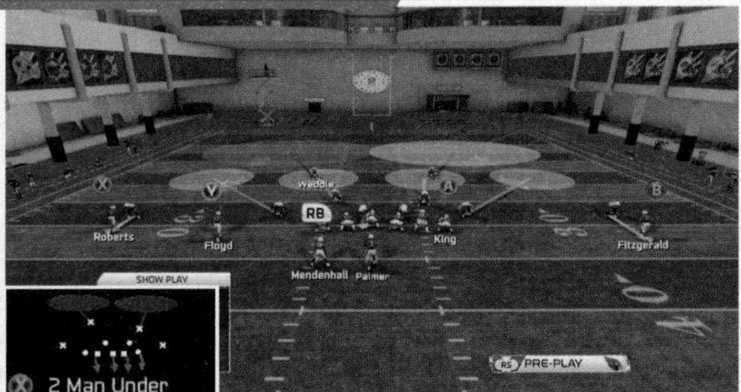

SETUP

> GLOBAL ZONE LINEBACKERS
> BASE ALIGN TWICE

> This setup allows better coverage on the field. The Chargers don't have the best cover CBs in the game.
> User-control one of the MLBs and look to jump any route over the short middle.

ZONE COVERAGE

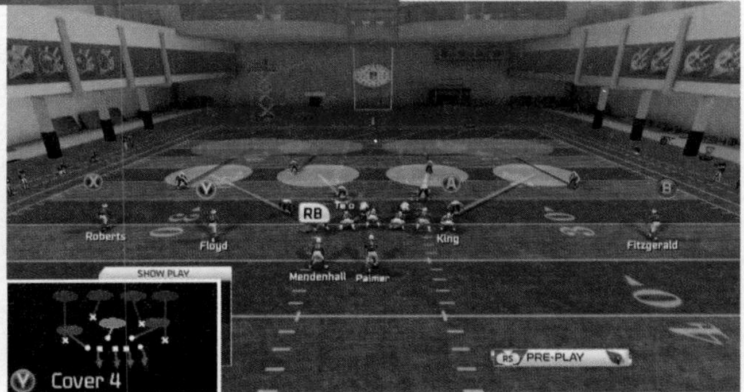

SETUP

> GLOBAL ZONE LINEBACKERS
> BASE ALIGN TWICE

> Base aligning twice will rebalance your defensive zones, resulting in better coverage on the field.
> This is one of our favorite zone setups in the game. The field is absolutely blanketed with defenders.

MAN BLITZ

SETUP

> PINCH DEFENSIVE LINE
> GLOBAL BLITZ BOTH OUTSIDE LINEBACKERS

> This setup will generate A gap pressure.
> Pressure will be extremely quick, so be ready for wild throws from your opponent.

ZONE BLITZ

SETUP

> PINCH DEFENSIVE LINE
> GLOBAL BLITZ BOTH LINEBACKERS

> User-control the FS.
> This blitz mimics our man-to-man setup, but we play zone coverage behind it.
> We like to mix this setup in to confuse our opponents and throw off their timing.

Kansas City Chiefs

2012 TEAM RANKINGS

4th AFC West (2-14-0)

PASSING OFFENSE: **32nd**
RUSHING OFFENSE: **5th**
PASSING DEFENSE: **12th**
RUSHING DEFENSE: **27th**

2012 TEAM LEADERS

PASSING: **Matt Cassel: 1,796**
RUSHING: **Jamaal Charles: 1,509**
RECEIVING: **Dwayne Bowe: 801**
TACKLES: **Derrick Johnson: 125**
SACKS: **Justin Houston: 10**
INTS: **Brandon Flowers: 3**

KEY ADDITIONS

QB Alex Smith
CB Sean Smith
ROLB Frank Zombo

KEY ROOKIES

OT Eric Fisher
TE Travis Kelce
RB Knile Davis

CONNECTED FRANCHISE MODE STRATEGY

CFM TEAM RATING: **78**
OFFENSIVE SCHEME: WEST **Coast**
DEFENSIVE SCHEME: **Base 4-3**
STRENGTHS: **QB, HB, WR, LOLB, MLB, CB, SS**
WEAKNESSES: **LG, LE, DT, FS**

SCHEDULE

Week	Date	Time		Opponent
1	Sep 8	1:00	AT	JAGUARS
2	Sep 15	1:00		COWBOYS
3	Sep 19	8:25	AT	EAGLES
4	Sep 29	1:00		GIANTS
5	Oct 6	1:00	AT	TITANS
6	Oct 13	1:00		RAIDERS
7	Oct 20	1:00		TEXANS
8	Oct 27	1:00		BROWNS
9	Nov 3	1:00	AT	BILLS
10	BYE			
11	Nov 17	4:05	AT	BRONCOS
12	Nov 24	1:00		CHARGERS
13	Dec 1	1:00		BRONCOS
14	Dec 8	1:00	AT	REDSKINS
15	Dec 15	4:05	AT	RAIDERS
16	Dec 22	1:00		COLTS
17	Dec 29	4:25	AT	CHARGERS

FRANCHISE OVERVIEW

CHIEFS GAMEPLAY RATING

77

> See the inside back cover for a quick reference to the game abbreviations used throughout this guide.

> Improve with your team by visiting PrimaGames.com/MaddenNFL25 for more information and how-to videos.

OFFENSIVE SCOUTING REPORT

> The signing of QB Alex Smith is exactly what the Chiefs needed. Smith brings a reliable option at the QB position. He is locked in for two years, which is exactly what we would want with a 29-year-old QB. If Smith performs and upgrades his skills, give him a long-term deal to end his career with the Chiefs.

> HB Jamaal Charles is 26 years old and is already the best HB in *Madden NFL 25*. He has no weak spots in his game, and the only place you could say is an issue is his 85 CAR rating. Charles will always be the fastest player on the field, and he can also be split wide and catch passes as well. Lock him up long-term at the end of his current deal and keep him around for another three years.

> Rookie HB Knile Davis has potential to be a solid contributor to the Chiefs offense. Spend time upgrading his stats, as Charles needs no updates. Focus on his Agility rating; it's currently 83 and needs to be closer to 90.

DEFENSIVE SCOUTING REPORT

> DT Dontari Poe can be the anchor that holds this defense together. His 96 STR rating is an elite rating, and if you can upgrade his BSH rating then he will take over games.

> LOLB Justin Houston, MLB Derrick Johnson, and ROLB Tamba Hali are one of the top linebacking groups in the league. Houston currently has two years left on his contract; consider signing him long-term now to save yourself money later. Both Johnson and Hali have three years left on their contracts.

> Rookie CB Sanders Commings needs to see the field if you want him to develop. This will require sitting CB Dunta Robinson, who currently has an 82 OVR rating.

OWNER & COACH PROFILES

CLARK HUNT
LEGACY SCORE: 50
DEF. SCHEME: Base 4-3
OFF. SCHEME: West Coast

ANDY REID
LEVEL: 24
OFF. SCHEME: West Coast
LEGACY SCORE: 2300
DEF. SCHEME: Base 4-3

TEAM OVERVIEW

KEY PLAYERS

HB #25

JAMAAL CHARLES

KEY RATINGS

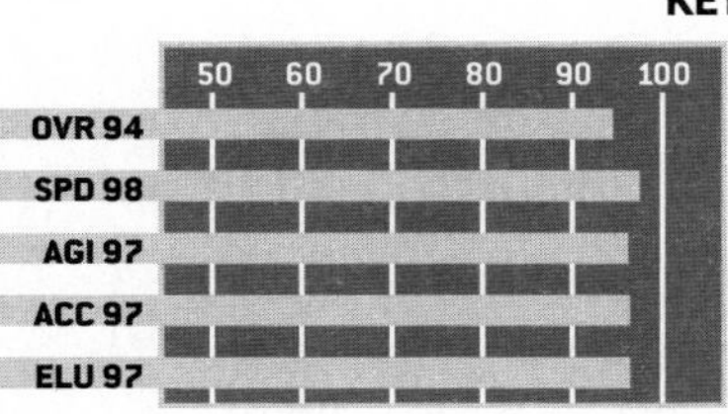

> Charles is the best HB in the game. Give him 20-plus touches every game rushing and at least five targets receiving.

> We like to split Charles wide and take advantage of his speed deep against slower defenders.

CB #24

BRANDON FLOWERS

KEY RATINGS

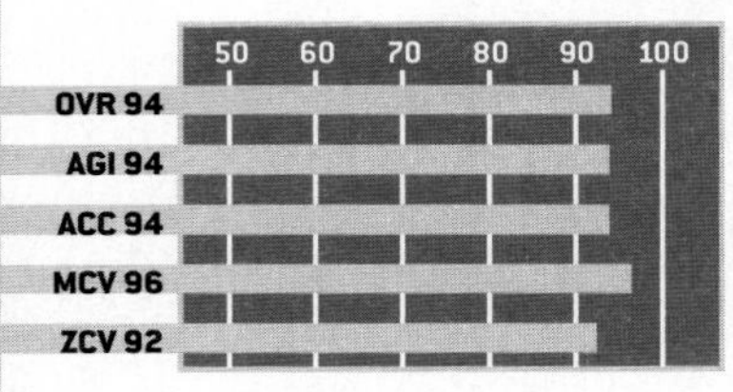

> Flowers can play man-to-man as well as zone coverage. This versatility is invaluable to the Chiefs' defensive success.

> Avoid matching Flowers up with WRs any faster than 93 SPD, as he will struggle defending them because of his 90 SPD.

PRE-GAME SETUP

KEY RUNNING SUBSTITUTION

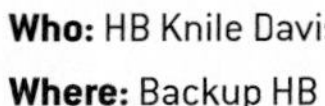

Who: HB Knile Davis

Where: Backup HB

Why: Davis is a rookie, but he will be a valuable backup to Charles.

Key Stats: 94 SPD, 73 CTH

KEY PASSING SUBSTITUTION

Who: WR Dexter McCluster

Where: #3 WR

Why: McCluster is an X factor for this offense. Move him around the field and use him in different packages to take advantage of his quickness.

Key Stats: 92 SPD, 94 AGI, 95 ACC, 80 CTH

KEY RUN DEFENSE SUBSTITUTION

Who: RE Allen Bailey

Where: Starting LE

Why: Bailey will provide run support because of his 91 STR. He also has 75 SPD, which will allow him to start full time.

Key Stats: 91 STR

KEY PASS DEFENSE SUBSTITUTION

Who: CB Sanders Commings

Where: #3 CB

Why: Sanders has the best Press rating on the team and will be a lockdown defender against the opposing team's third WR.

Key Stats: 6'0", 90 SPD, 90 PRS

OFFENSIVE DEPTH CHART

POS	FIRST NAME	LAST NAME	OVR
QB	Alex	Smith	87
QB	Chase	Daniel	75
QB	Ricky	Stanzi	65
QB	Tyler	Bray	64
HB	Jamaal	Charles	94
HB	Shaun	Draughn	69
HB	Knile	Davis	66
HB	Cyrus	Gray	66
FB	Anthony	Sherman	73
FB	Braden	Wilson	71
WR	Dwayne	Bowe	88
WR	Donnie	Avery	76
WR	Dexter	McCluster	74
WR	Jonathan	Baldwin	73
WR	Terrance	Copper	65
WR	Devon	Wylie	64
WR	Mardy	Gilyard	63
WR	Junior	Hemingway	62
WR	Jamar	Newsome	60
TE	Tony	Moeaki	80
TE	Anthony	Fasano	80
TE	Travis	Kelce	73
TE	Thomas	Gafford	69
TE	Kevin	Brock	65
LT	Branden	Albert	89
LT	Steven	Baker	56
LG	Geoff	Schwartz	77
LG	Jeff	Allen	69
C	Rodney	Hudson	76
C	Eric	Kush	62
RG	Jon	Asamoah	88
RG	Ryan	Durand	69
RT	Eric	Fisher	84
RT	Donald	Stephenson	72
RT	Matt	Reynolds	59

DEFENSIVE DEPTH CHART

POS	FIRST NAME	LAST NAME	OVR
LE	Tyson	Jackson	75
LE	Marcus	Dixon	73
LE	Austen	Lane	72
RE	Mike	Devito	80
RE	Allen	Bailey	70
DT	Dontari	Poe	78
DT	Anthony	Toribio	71
DT	Jerrell	Powe	70
LOLB	Justin	Houston	91
LOLB	Edgar	Jones	65
MLB	Derrick	Johnson	93
MLB	Akeem	Jordan	71
MLB	Zac	Diles	68
MLB	Nico	Johnson	65
MLB	Orie	Lemon	57
ROLB	Tamba	Hali	89
ROLB	Frank	Zombo	70
CB	Brandon	Flowers	94
CB	Dunta	Robinson	82
CB	Sean	Smith	82
CB	Sanders	Commings	70
CB	Jalil	Brown	66
CB	Neiko	Thorpe	57
FS	Kendrick	Lewis	79
FS	Tysyn	Hartman	65
SS	Eric	Berry	88
SS	Husain	Abdullah	78

SPECIAL TEAMS DEPTH CHART

POS	FIRST NAME	LAST NAME	OVR
K	Ryan	Succop	78
P	Dustin	Colquitt	88

Kansas City Chiefs

RECOMMENDED OFFENSIVE RUN FORMATION: STRONG TIGHT PAIR (2 HB, 2 TE, 1 WR)

PRO TIPS

- GET ROOKIE HB KNILE DAVIS A FEW TOUCHES EACH GAME WHEN CHARLES FATIGUES.
- QB ALEX SMITH HAS 77 SPD, SO MAKE DEFENSES ACCOUNT FOR HIM EVERY PLAY.
- FB ANTHONY SHERMAN HAS GOOD HANDS OUT OF THE BACKFIELD, BUT ALSO HAS 82 IBL.
- TE ANTHONY FASANO IS YOUR BEST BLOCKING TE.

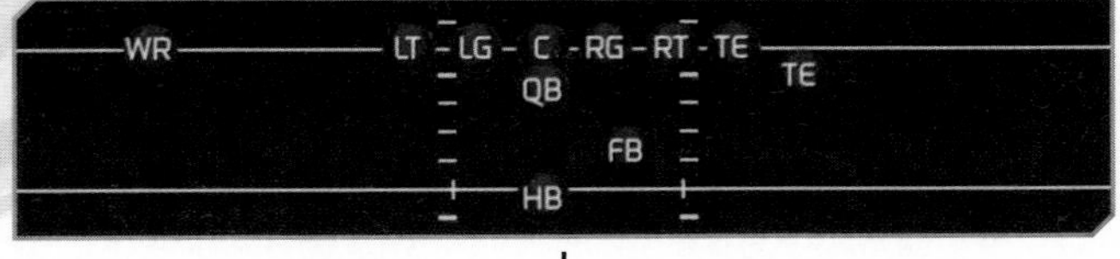

RUN LEFT

CHARLES ATTEMPTS TO JUMP OVER THE DEFENDER!

RUN MIDDLE

SPIN MOVE!

RUN RIGHT

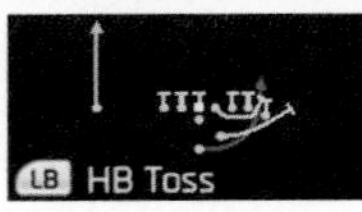

PATIENCE IS KEY WITH A HALFBACK LIKE CHARLES.

KANSAS CITY CHIEFS RUNNING PLAY CALL SHEET

LEGEND: Inside Run | Outside Run | Shotgun Run | QB Run

1ST DOWN RUNS	2ND AND SHORT	3RD AND SHORT	GOAL LINE RUNS	2ND AND LONG	3RD AND LONG
Singleback Y-Trips—HB Draw	I-Form Slot Flex—HB Iso	Singleback Chief Doubles—HB Inside Zone	Goal Line Normal—QB Sneak	Gun Doubles Wk—Read Option	Gun Split Offset—Power O
Singleback Y-Trips—HB Toss Strong	I-Form Slot Flex—HB Blast	Singleback Chief Doubles—Toss Crack	Goal Line Normal—HB Dive	I-Form Pro—Iso	Gun Trey Open—HB Mid Draw
Strong Tight Pair—Power O	I-Form Tight Pair—Power O	Singleback Ace—HB Off Tackle	Goal Line Normal—Power O	Gun Doubles Wk—QB Power	Gun Empty Trey—QB Draw

KANSAS CITY CHIEFS PASSING PLAY CALL SHEET

LEGEND: Base Play | Man Beater | Zone Beater | Blitz Beater

1ST DOWN PLAY	2ND AND SHORT	3RD AND SHORT	GOAL LINE PASSING	2ND AND LONG	3RD AND LONG
Gun Trey Open—KC Corner	I-Form Slot Flex—WR Drag	Singleback Doubles—Sluggo Seam	Goal Line—PA Waggle	Gun Y-Trips Wk—KC Dig	Pistol Trips—Stick
Gun Empty Trey—Spacing	I-Form Slot Flex—Verticals HB Out	I-Form Pro—HB Slip Screen	Goal Line—PA Spot	Gun Doubles—TE Stick	Pistol Trips—Flood
Gun Empty Chief—KC Stick N Nod	Gun Empty Chief—KC Fork	I-Form—PA Charger Wheel	Goal Line—PA Power O	Gun Y-Trips Wk—Strong Flood	Pistol Trips—PA Boot Lt

In these play call sheets we picked the best plays for specific situations so that you will have a play for every down and distance.

OFFENSE

RECOMMENDED OFFENSIVE PASS FORMATION: SINGLEBACK ACE PAIR CHIEF (1 RB, 2 TE, 2 WR)

PRO TIPS

- START WR DEXTER MCCLUSTER IF YOUR OFFENSE IS MORE SPEED BASED.
- START WR JONATHAN BALDWIN IF YOUR OFFENSE IS MORE USER-CATCH BASED.
- ROOKIE TE TRAVIS KELCE IS 6'4" AND HAS 91 JMP, WHICH MAKES HIM A GREAT RED ZONE TARGET.

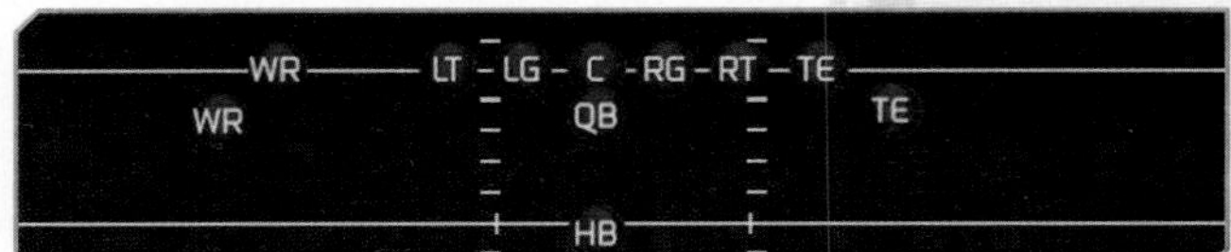

BASE PLAY

SETUP

- ZIG THE INSIDE TE
- ZIG THE OUTSIDE WR

- At the snap of the ball throw the ball to the HB.
- This play is very difficult to stop and is one of the best quick passes in the game.

MAN BEATER

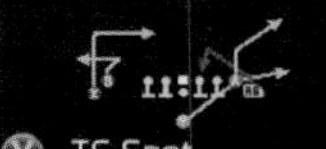

SETUP

- STREAK THE OUTSIDE WR
- STREAK THE OUTSIDE TE

- This is another snap-throw play to the HB.
- The combination of this play and our base play will make it impossible for defenses to defend both options at the same time.

ZONE BEATER

SETUP

- OPTION THE HB
- STREAK THE INSIDE TE

- Against Cover 2 and Cover 3 zones look to the sidelines.
- Against Cover 4 zones look to the HB hitch.

BLITZ BEATER

SETUP

- BLOCK BOTH TIGHT ENDS
- DRAG THE FAR LEFT WR

- Let the HB get into position and then throw a high bullet pass.
- The pass lead is important because it will lead him upfield.

Kansas City Chiefs

RECOMMENDED DEFENSIVE RUN FORMATION: 3-4 OVER ED

PRO TIPS

- DT JERRELL POWE WILL PROVIDE ADDED STRENGTH TO THE DEFENSIVE LINE WITH HIS 92 STR RATING.
- ROOKIE MLB NICO JOHNSON IS A WRAP-UP TACKLER (88 TAK RATING) WHO NEEDS TO PLAY DURING RUNNING SITUATIONS.
- SS ERIC BERRY CAN PROVIDE RUN SUPPORT FROM THE SS POSITION.

RUN DEFENSE

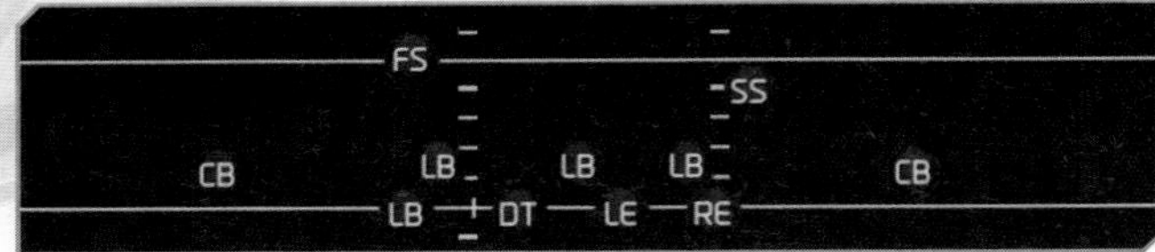

RUN DEFENSE LEFT

SETUP > SHIFT LINEBACKERS LEFT

RUN DEFENSE MIDDLE

SETUP > PINCH DEFENSIVE LINE

RUN DEFENSE RIGHT

SETUP > SHIFT LINEBACKERS RIGHT

KANSAS CITY CHIEFS DEFENSIVE RUN PLAY CALL SHEET

1ST DOWN RUN DEFENSE	2ND AND SHORT	3RD AND SHORT	GOAL LINE RUN DEFENSE	2ND AND LONG	3RD AND LONG
3-4 Solid—1 Man Under	3-4 Odd—Cross Fire	3-4 Even—Strong Blitz	Goal Line 5-3-3—Jam Cover 1	Sub 2-3-6—2 Man Under	Sub 1-4-6—Buck Dog 1
3-4 Solid—Cover 2	3-4 Odd—FS Zone Blitz	3-4 Even—Trio Sky Zone	Goal Line 5-3-3—Flat Buzz	Sub 2-3-6—Cover 4	Sub 1-4-6—DB Sting 2 Buzz

KANSAS CITY CHIEFS DEFENSIVE PASS PLAY CALL SHEET

1ST DOWN PLAY	2ND AND SHORT	3RD AND SHORT	GOAL LINE PASSING	2ND AND LONG	3RD AND LONG
3-4 Over Ed—Cover 1	Nickel 2-4-5 Even—Cover 1 Spy	3-4 Odd—Pinch Cover 0	Goal Line 6-3-2—GL Man	Nickel 3-3-5—Dogs All Go	Sub 2-3-6—Silver Shoot Pinch
3-4 Over Ed—Cover 3	Nickel 2-4-5 Even—Bucks 3 Slant	3-4 Odd—Zorro Will Jack 3	Goal Line 6-3-2—GL Zone	Nickel 3-3-5—LB Cross 3	Sub 2-3-6—Mid Zone Blitz

LEGEND: Man Coverage | Zone Coverage | Man Blitz | Zone Blitz

In these play call sheets we picked the best plays for specific situations so that you will have a play for every down and distance.

DEFENSE

RECOMMENDED DEFENSIVE PASS FORMATION: NICKEL 2-4-5 EVEN

PRO TIPS

- PLACE CB BRANDON FLOWERS ON YOUR OPPONENT'S BEST WR.
- USE CB SANDERS COMMINGS TO COVER YOUR OPPONENT'S FASTEST WR.
- CB SEAN SMITH SHOULD BE USED AS THE NICKEL CORNER.

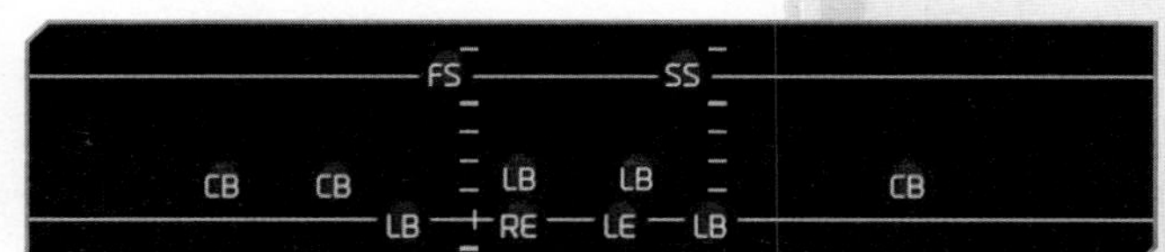

MAN COVERAGE

SETUP

- GLOBAL ZONE LINEBACKERS
- BASE ALIGN TWICE

- Aligning twice balances the zones on the field, creating better coverage.
- User-control one of the MLBs over the short middle.

ZONE COVERAGE

SETUP

- GLOBAL ZONE LINEBACKERS
- BASE ALIGN TWICE

- As with our man coverage setup we are looking to protect short with four hook zones.
- User-control the FS and drop deep at the snap of the ball.

MAN BLITZ

SETUP

- PRESS COVERAGE
- GLOBAL BLITZ LINEBACKERS

- Make sure Flowers and Commings are in the game for this setup.
- User-control the FS and watch for any beat press animations; cover deep if you see one.

ZONE BLITZ

SETUP

- SHADE SAFETY COVERAGE IN
- GLOBAL BLITZ LINEBACKERS

- User-control the FS.
- If your opponent starts attacking the flat, drop two of the hook zones into flats.
- We like to mix this setup in to confuse our opponents and throw off their timing.

Indianapolis Colts

2012 TEAM RANKINGS

2nd AFC South (11-5-0)

PASSING OFFENSE: **7th**
RUSHING OFFENSE: **22nd**
PASSING DEFENSE: **21st**
RUSHING DEFENSE: **29th**

2012 TEAM LEADERS

PASSING: **Andrew Luck: 4,374**
RUSHING: **Vick Ballard: 814**
RECEIVING: **Reggie Wayne: 1,355**
TACKLES: **Jerrell Freeman: 145**
SACKS: **Robert Mathis: 8**
INTS: **Darius Butler: 4**

KEY ADDITIONS

WR Darrius Heyward-Bey
LOLB Erik Walden
SS LaRon Landry

KEY ROOKIES

DE Bjoern Werner
OG Hugh Thornton
C Khaled Holmes

CONNECTED FRANCHISE MODE STRATEGY

CFM TEAM RATING: **68**
OFFENSIVE SCHEME: **Power Run**
DEFENSIVE SCHEME: **Hybrid Multiple Front**
STRENGTHS: **QB, TE, WR, RT, ROLB, FS, SS**
WEAKNESSES: **HB, LE, RE, DT, LOLB, MLB**

SCHEDULE

Week	Date	Time		Opponent
1	Sep 8	1:00		RAIDERS
2	Sep 15	1:00		DOLPHINS
3	Sep 22	4:25	AT	49ERS
4	Sep 29	1:00	AT	JAGUARS
5	Oct 6	1:00		SEAHAWKS
6	Oct 14	8:40	AT	CHARGERS
7	Oct 20	8:30		BRONCOS
8	BYE			
9	Nov 3	8:30	AT	TEXANS
10	Nov 10	1:00		RAMS
11	Nov 14	8:25	AT	TITANS
12	Nov 24	4:05	AT	CARDINALS
13	Dec 1	1:00		TITANS
14	Dec 8	1:00	AT	BENGALS
15	Dec 15	1:00		TEXANS
16	Dec 22	1:00	AT	CHIEFS
17	Dec 29	1:00		JAGUARS

FRANCHISE OVERVIEW

COLTS GAMEPLAY RATING

83

> SEE THE INSIDE BACK COVER FOR A QUICK REFERENCE TO THE GAME ABBREVIATIONS USED THROUGHOUT THIS GUIDE.

> IMPROVE WITH YOUR TEAM BY VISITING PRIMAGAMES.COM/MADDENNFL25 FOR MORE INFORMATION AND HOW-TO VIDEOS.

OFFENSIVE SCOUTING REPORT

- QB Andrew Luck is the best young QB in the league, and he is untouchable on this roster. You can run any type of offense with him and have success doing it.
- You need to start surrounding Luck with talent at the HB and WR positions. The current HBs on the roster will not be long-term answers. This will be your number one priority heading into the off season and the draft.
- WR Reggie Wayne is 34 years old and has two years remaining on his contract. Let him go once this contract ends and look to get younger at this position.

DEFENSIVE SCOUTING REPORT

- The Colts defensive line over the past decade had been one of the most feared pass-rushing lines in the league. That is a thing of the past, and you must focus on the defensive line moving forward. Start with pass-rushing DEs because you have a few DTs that can clog the middle of the field.
- ROLB Robert Mathis is still an effective pass-rushing linebacker, but he is aging and you will need to replace him. The rest of the Colts linebackers also need some attention, as there is no standout player on this roster.
- The bright spot of the Colts defense is their secondary. They have speed at CB and have big-time hitters at safety. The addition of SS LaRon Landry will give this defense a swagger that they will need to be competitive.

OWNER & COACH PROFILES

JIM IRSAY
LEGACY SCORE: 2350 OFF. SCHEME: Power Run
DEF. SCHEME: Hybrid Multiple Front

CHUCK PAGANO
LEVEL: 1 LEGACY SCORE: 500
OFF. SCHEME: Power Run DEF. SCHEME: Hybrid Multiple Fro

TEAM OVERVIEW

KEY PLAYERS

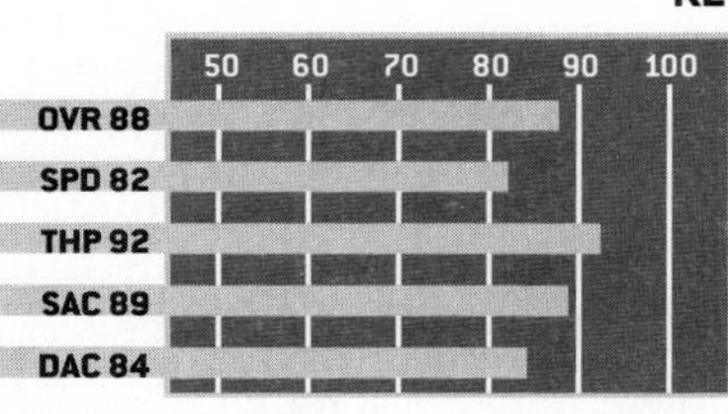

QB #12
ANDREW LUCK

KEY RATINGS

OVR	88
SPD	82
THP	92
SAC	89
DAC	84

- Luck is one of the best QBs in *Madden NFL 25*. His mobility is an added bonus to his already stellar arm.
- Make sure to use option plays with Luck. Don't be afraid to make big plays with him.

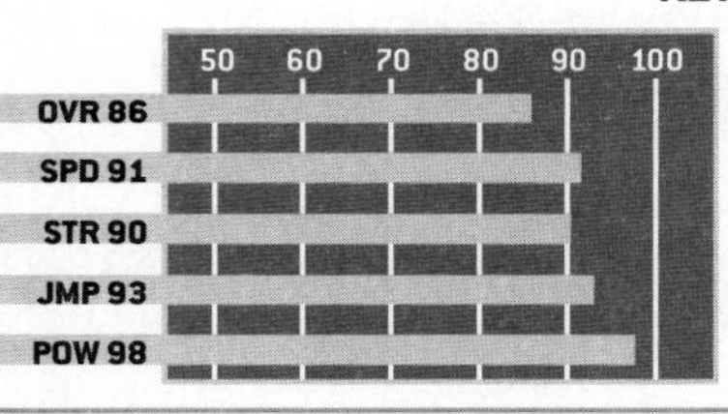

SS #30
LARON LANDRY

KEY RATINGS

OVR	86
SPD	91
STR	90
JMP	93
POW	98

- Landry is the hardest-hitting safety in the league. He also has elite speed, which is hard to come by at SS.
- User-control Landry to benefit from his hit power. He is one of the best defensive players in *Madden NFL 25*.

PRE-GAME SETUP

KEY RUNNING SUBSTITUTION

Who: HB Kerwynn Williams

Where: Starting HB

Why: Williams is the quickest HB on this roster and is the best receiving option.

Key Stats: 92 SPD, 75 CTH

KEY PASSING SUBSTITUTION

Who: TE Coby Fleener

Where: #3 WR

Why: Fleener is rare talent at the TE position. He can line up at TE as well as split wide as a receiver.

Key Stats: 6'6", 87 SPD, 82 CIT, 89 JMP

KEY RUN DEFENSE SUBSTITUTION

Who: DT Kellen Heard

Where: #2 DT

Why: Heard has a 65 OVR rating but 91 STR, and he is the second strongest defensive lineman on the Colts' roster.

Key Stats: 91 STR

KEY PASS DEFENSE SUBSTITUTION

Who: CB Darius Butler

Where: #2 CB

Why: Butler has great hands for a CB and has outstanding jumping ability.

Key Stats: 91 SPD, 70 CTH, 94 JMP

OFFENSIVE DEPTH CHART

POS	FIRST NAME	LAST NAME	OVR
QB	Andrew	Luck	88
QB	Matt	Hasselbeck	79
QB	Chandler	Harnish	66
HB	Ahmad	Bradshaw	83
HB	Vick	Ballard	77
HB	Donald	Brown	74
HB	Delone	Carter	72
HB	Kerwynn	Williams	64
FB	Stanley	Havili	73
WR	Reggie	Wayne	91
WR	T.Y.	Hilton	79
WR	Darrius	Heyward-Bey	79
WR	LaVon	Brazill	67
WR	Griff	Whalen	67
WR	Nathan	Palmer	63
TE	Dwayne	Allen	84
TE	Coby	Fleener	77
TE	Weslye	Saunders	73
TE	Justice	Cunningham	69
TE	Matt	Overton	50
LT	Anthony	Castonzo	79
LT	Bradley	Sowell	62
LT	Justin	Anderson	59
LG	Donald	Thomas	81
LG	Jeff	Linkenbach	70
LG	Joe	Reitz	69
C	Samson	Satele	78
C	Khaled	Holmes	69
RG	Mike	McGlynn	72
RG	Hugh	Thornton	69
RG	Robert	Griffin	61
RT	Gosder	Cherilus	90
RT	Ben	Ijalana	72
RT	Lee	Ziemba	64

DEFENSIVE DEPTH CHART

POS	FIRST NAME	LAST NAME	OVR
LE	Cory	Redding	83
LE	Ricardo	Mathews	73
LE	Lawrence	Guy	63
LE	Kellen	Heard	59
RE	Ricky	Jean Francois	75
RE	Drake	Nevis	73
RE	Fili	Moala	73
DT	Aubrayo	Franklin	82
DT	Brandon	McKinney	71
DT	Josh	Chapman	67
DT	Martin	Tevaseu	66
DT	Montori	Hughes	63
LOLB	Erik	Walden	74
LOLB	Justin	Hickman	66
LOLB	Quinton	Spears	60
MLB	Pat	Angerer	77
MLB	Kelvin	Sheppard	76
MLB	Jerrell	Freeman	74
MLB	Kavell	Conner	73
MLB	Mario	Harvey	63
MLB	Scott	Lutrus	59
ROLB	Robert	Mathis	86
ROLB	Bjoern	Werner	74
ROLB	Lawrence	Sidbury	66
CB	Vontae	Davis	87
CB	Greg	Toler	77
CB	Darius	Butler	74
CB	Cassius	Vaughn	72
CB	Josh	Gordy	69
CB	Marshay	Green	61
CB	Teddy	Williams	59
FS	Antoine	Bethea	87
FS	John	Boyett	70
FS	Larry	Asante	68
FS	Delano	Howell	66
SS	LaRon	Landry	86
SS	Joe	Lefeged	74
SS	Sergio	Brown	70

SPECIAL TEAMS DEPTH CHART

POS	FIRST NAME	LAST NAME	OVR
K	Adam	Vinatieri	87
P	Pat	McAfee	94

Indianapolis Colts

RECOMMENDED OFFENSIVE RUN FORMATION: I-FORM HULK (2 HB, 2 TE, 0 WR)

PRO TIPS

> QB ANDREW LUCK HAS ENOUGH SPEED TO RUN AN OPTION-STYLE OFFENSE.

> HB KERWYNN WILLIAMS IS THE BEST AVAILABLE HB ON THE COLTS' ROSTER

> USE HB VICK BALLARD IN LATE-GAME SITUATIONS BECAUSE OF HIS 91 CAR RATING.

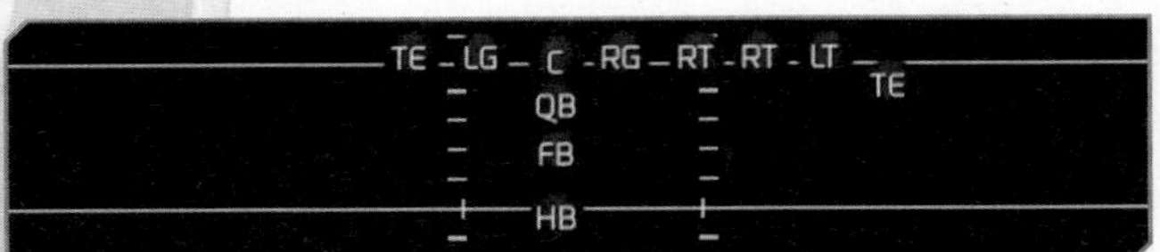

RUN LEFT

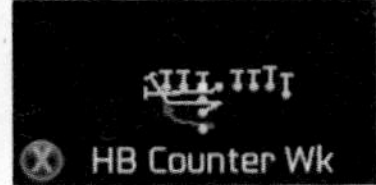

WILLIAMS HAS SPEED TO GET TO THE EDGE.

RUN MIDDLE

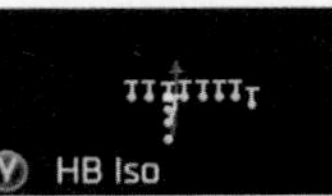

DON'T USE ACCELERATION BURST RUNNING UP THE MIDDLE.

RUN RIGHT

GET TO THE EDGE AS FAST AS YOU CAN.

INDIANAPOLIS COLTS RUNNING PLAY CALL SHEET

LEGEND: Inside Run | Outside Run | Shotgun Run | QB Run

1ST DOWN RUNS	2ND AND SHORT	3RD AND SHORT	GOAL LINE RUNS	2ND AND LONG	3RD AND LONG
I-Form Tight—HB Counter	I-Form Pro—FB Dive	Singleback Indy Y-Trips—HB Slam	Goal Line Normal—QB Sneak	Gun Y-Trips Wk—HB Mid Draw	Gun Trey Open—HB Counter
I-Form Tight—Iso	Singleback Jumbo—HB Dive	Weak Flex Twins—Toss Weak	Goal Line Normal—HB Dive	I-Form Pro—Iso	Gun Trey Open—HB Draw
I-Form Pro—Outside Zone	Singleback Jumbo—Inside Zone	Weak Flex Twins—Counter Wk	Goal Line Normal—Power O	Gun Bunch TE—HB Off Tackle	Gun Bunch TE—HB Draw

INDIANAPOLIS COLTS PASSING PLAY CALL SHEET

LEGEND: Base Play | Man Beater | Zone Beater | Blitz Beater

1ST DOWN PLAY	2ND AND SHORT	3RD AND SHORT	GOAL LINE PASSING	2ND AND LONG	3RD AND LONG
Gun Bunch TE—Mesh	Singleback Doubles—Flanker Drive	Weak Pro—HB Slip Screen	Goal Line—PA Waggle	Gun Spread Y-Slot—Hitch Seam	Pistol Y-Trips—Double China
Singleback Bunch—Colts Verticals	Weak Flex Twins—Drive	Singleback Indy Y-Trips—Stick N Slide	Goal Line—PA Spot	Gun Snugs—WR Crosses	Pistol Y-Trips—Smash
Gun Y-Trips Wk—Colts Slot Seam	Gun Empty Trey—Strong Flood	Gun Split Close—Scat	Goal Line—PA Power O	Gun Snugs—Bench	Gun Bunch TE—Curl Flat Corner

In these play call sheets we picked the best plays for specific situations so that you will have a play for every down and distance.

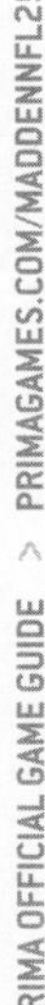

OFFENSE

RECOMMENDED OFFENSIVE PASS FORMATION: PISTOL Y-TRIPS (1 RB, 1 TE, 3 WR)

PRO TIPS

- SEND WR DARRIUS HEYWARD-BEY ON DEEP PATTERNS TO TAKE ADVANTAGE OF HIS SPEED.
- T.Y. HILTON SHOULD BE USED AS THE FOURTH WR.
- TE COBY FLEENER SHOULD BE USED AS THE THIRD WR.

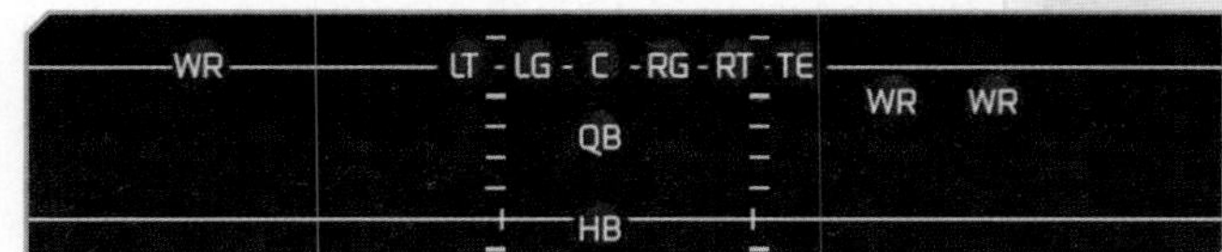

BASE PLAY

SETUP

- BLOCK THE HB
- STREAK THE TE

- The sideline wheel is a great option against man-to-man coverage.
- The TE streak will be effective against zone coverages.

MAN BEATER

SETUP

- STREAK THE HB
- DRAG THE SLOT WR

- The far left WR running the slant will get inside position against man-to-man press coverage.
- Throw a high lead pass once he gets inside position.

ZONE BEATER

SETUP

- OPTION THE HB

- Against Cover 2 and Cover 3 zones look to the sidelines.
- Against Cover 4 zones look to the HB option and the slot WR's angled streak.

BLITZ BEATER

SETUP

- SWING RIGHT THE HB
- DRAG THE FAR RIGHT WR

The drag will be an underneath option if the defense is able to defend the HB.

Look to the HB at the snap of the ball and get him the ball quickly.

Indianapolis Colts

RECOMMENDED DEFENSIVE RUN FORMATION: 3-4 STACK OVER ED

PRO TIPS

> SUB IN DEFENSIVE TACKLES MARTIN TEVASEU AND KELLEN HEARD FOR RUNNING SITUATIONS.

> MIDDLE LINEBACKERS KELVIN SHEPPARD AND KAVELL CONNER ARE WRAP-UP TACKLERS.

> SS LARON LANDRY'S 98 POW RATING WILL CAUSE FUMBLES WHEN USED TO STOP THE RUN.

RUN DEFENSE

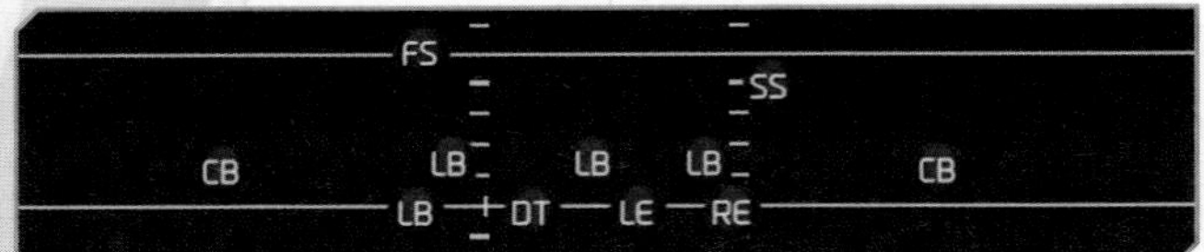

RUN DEFENSE LEFT

SETUP > SHIFT LINEBACKERS LEFT

RUN DEFENSE MIDDLE

SETUP > PINCH DEFENSIVE LINE

RUN DEFENSE RIGHT

SETUP > SHIFT LINEBACKERS RIGHT

INDIANAPOLIS COLTS DEFENSIVE RUN PLAY CALL SHEET

1ST DOWN RUN DEFENSE	2ND AND SHORT	3RD AND SHORT	GOAL LINE RUN DEFENSE	2ND AND LONG	3RD AND LONG
3-4 Over Ed—2 Man Under	3-4 Even—MLB Cross Fire	3-4 Odd—Pinch Cover 0	Goal Line 5-3-3—Jam Cover 1	Nickel 2-4-5 Even—Overload 1 Roll	Nickel 1-5-5 Prowl—2 Man Under
3-4 Over Ed—Cover 2 Sink	3-4 Even—MLB Cross Fire 3	3-4 Odd—Sam Mike 2 Sting	Goal Line 5-3-3—Flat Buzz	Nickel 2-4-5 Even—Overload 3 Seam	Nickel 1-5-5 Prowl—Cover 4

INDIANAPOLIS COLTS DEFENSIVE PASS PLAY CALL SHEET

1ST DOWN PLAY	2ND AND SHORT	3RD AND SHORT	GOAL LINE PASSING	2ND AND LONG	3RD AND LONG
3-4 Predator—Weak Blitz	3-4 Predator—Cover 1 Lurk	3-4 Even—Strong Blitz	Goal Line 6-3-2—GL Man	Sub 2-3-6 Flex—Spinner Buck Dog 1	Nickel 2-4-5 Even—Over Storm Brave
3-4 Predator—Roll Eagle 2 Invert	3-4 Predator—MLB Cross Fire 3	3-4 Even—Trio Sky Zone	Goal Line 6-3-2—GL Zone	Sub 2-3-6 Flex—DB Fire 2	Nickel 2-4-5 Even—Sugar 3 Seam

LEGEND: Man Coverage | Zone Coverage | Man Blitz | Zone Blitz

In these play call sheets we picked the best plays for specific situations so that you will have a play for every down and distance.

DEFENSE

RECOMMENDED DEFENSIVE PASS FORMATION: NICKEL 1-5-5 PROWL

PRO TIPS

- > PLACE CB VONTAE DAVIS ON YOUR OPPONENT'S BEST WR.
- > USE CB CASSIUS VAUGHN TO COVER YOUR OPPONENT'S FASTEST WR.
- > CB DARIUS BUTLER SHOULD BE USED AS YOUR SECOND CB.

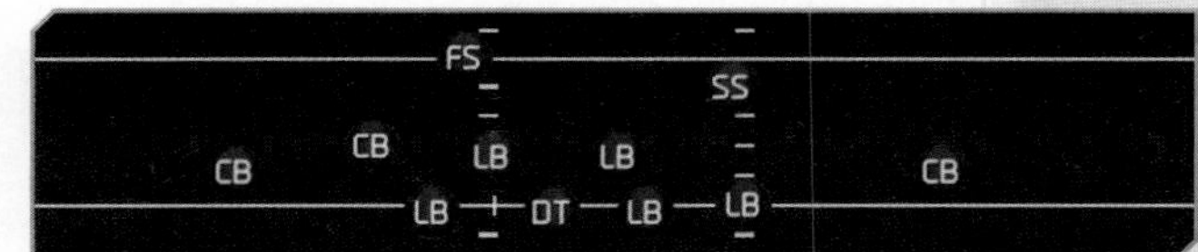

MAN COVERAGE

SETUP

- > HOOK ZONE THE SS
- > GLOBAL BLITZ BOTH OUTSIDE LINEBACKERS

- > We set this play up specifically to take advantage of SS LaRon Landry.
- > Cover over the short field with Landry and look for hit stick opportunities.

ZONE COVERAGE

SETUP

- > HOOK ZONE THE SS
- > DEEP ZONE THE LOLB

- > We are again setting our defense up around the strengths of SS LaRon Landry.
- > User-control Landry over the short middle and always be ready to deliver the big hit.

MAN BLITZ

SETUP

- > PRESS COVERAGE
- > GLOBAL BLITZ LINEBACKERS

- > Using press coverage puts your secondary at risk of getting beaten deep.
- > User-control the FS and take away your opponent's first option.

ZONE BLITZ

SETUP

- > PRESS COVERAGE
- > GLOBAL BLITZ LINEBACKERS

- > To change things up with this blitz you can place either hook zone defender into a flat zone.
- > In third and long situations put the hook zone defenders into deep zones.
- > We like to mix this setup in to confuse our opponents and throw off their timing.

Dallas Cowboys

2012 TEAM RANKINGS

3rd NFC East (8-8-0)

PASSING OFFENSE: **3rd**
RUSHING OFFENSE: **31st**
PASSING DEFENSE: **19th**
RUSHING DEFENSE: **22nd**

2012 TEAM LEADERS

PASSING: **Tony Romo: 4,903**
RUSHING: **DeMarco Murray: 663**
RECEIVING: **Dez Bryant: 1,382**
TACKLES: **Anthony Spencer: 95**
SACKS: **DeMarcus Ware: 11.5**
INTS: **Brandon Carr: 3**

KEY ADDITIONS

LOLB Justin Durant
WR Anthony Armstrong

KEY ROOKIES

C Travis Frederick
TE Gavin Escobar
WR Terrance Williams

CONNECTED FRANCHISE MODE STRATEGY

CFM TEAM RATING: **72**
OFFENSIVE SCHEME: **Balanced**
DEFENSIVE SCHEME: **Attacking 3-4**
STRENGTHS: **QB, WR, TE, LE, RE, MLB, CB**
WEAKNESSES: **LG, C, RG, DT, FS, SS**

SCHEDULE

Week	Date	Time		Opponent
1	Sep 8	8:30		GIANTS
2	Sep 15	1:00	AT	CHIEFS
3	Sep 22	1:00		RAMS
4	Sep 29	4:25	AT	CHARGERS
5	Oct 6	4:25		BRONCOS
6	Oct 13	8:30		REDSKINS
7	Oct 20	1:00	AT	EAGLES
8	Oct 27	1:00	AT	LIONS
9	Nov 3	1:00		VIKINGS
10	Nov 10	8:30	AT	SAINTS
11	BYE			
12	Nov 24	4:25	AT	GIANTS
13	Nov 28	4:30		RAIDERS
14	Dec 9	8:40	AT	BEARS
15	Dec 15	4:25		PACKERS
16	Dec 22	1:00	AT	REDSKINS
17	Dec 29	1:00		EAGLES

FRANCHISE OVERVIEW

COWBOYS GAMEPLAY RATING

79

> See the inside back cover for a quick reference to the game abbreviations used throughout this guide.

> Improve with your team by visiting PrimaGames.com/MaddenNFL25 for more information and how-to videos.

OFFENSIVE SCOUTING REPORT

> QB Tony Romo has always put up amazing numbers as the Cowboys' QB, but he has yet to get them to the promised land. Romo has seven years remaining on his contract, which means he's going to be playing for you until he's 40. This isn't a good contract for you, to be paying a 40-year-old $28 million in the final year of his contract. Keep Romo around for a year or two and then cut ties.

> HB DeMarco Murray has the potential to be a special player in this league. Give him upgrades in agility and acceleration and you could see him quickly become the best HB in the game.

> WR Miles Austin and TE Jason Witten have been the foundation of the Cowboys offense over the past few years. In a year or two you will need to think about replacing both of them with younger, more talented players.

DEFENSIVE SCOUTING REPORT

LE Anthony Spencer's contract is up at the end of the first season. RE DeMarcus Ware is signed on with the team for the next three. Match Ware's contract for Spencer and keep this tandem together for the next three seasons.

Keep the core of your secondary together over the next five seasons. CBs Brandon Carr, Morris Claiborne, and Orlando Scandrick are all young and can cover.

Your first priority during free agency and the draft is to find a starting FS and SS.

OWNER & COACH PROFILES

JERRY JONES
LEGACY SCORE: 9625 OFF. SCHEME: Balanced Offense
DEF. SCHEME: Attacking 3-4

JASON GARRETT
LEVEL: 6 LEGACY SCORE: 75
OFF. SCHEME: Balanced Offense DEF. SCHEME: Attacking 3-4

TEAM OVERVIEW

KEY PLAYERS

WR #88

DEZ BRYANT

KEY RATINGS

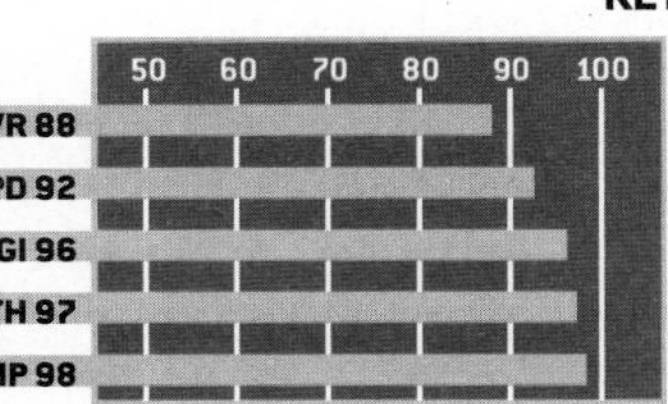

> Bryant is a matchup nightmare. Use him to stretch the field vertically.

> Bryant is great at running underneath patterns and has great hands to hold onto the ball.

RE #94

DEMARCUS WARE

KEY RATINGS

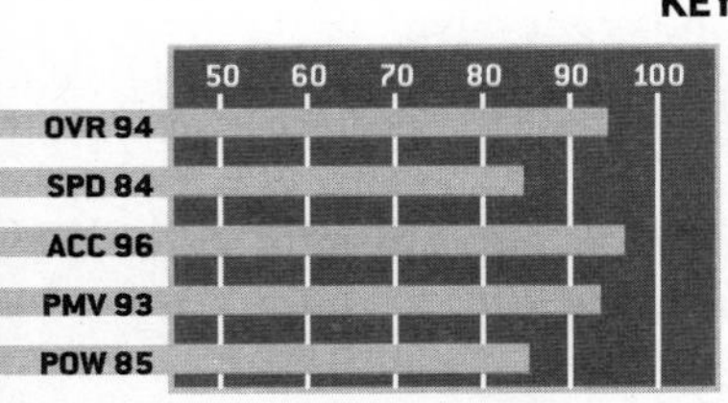

> Ware can't be blocked in most situations. Send him after the QB on every down.

> Ware can be used as an interior DT as well. Put him inside to create matchup problems for the offense.

PRE-GAME SETUP

KEY RUNNING SUBSTITUTION

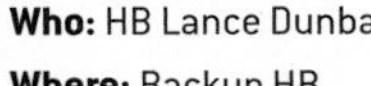

Who: HB Lance Dunbar

Where: Backup HB

Why: Dunbar is the best backup option for the Cowboys.

Key Stats: 87 SPD, 92 AGI, 92 ACC

KEY PASSING SUBSTITUTION

Who: TE James Hanna

Where: Backup TE

Why: Hanna is one of the fastest TEs in the game and is a matchup problem for most defenses.

Key Stats: 6'4", 89 SPD

KEY RUN DEFENSE SUBSTITUTION

Who: DT Sean Lissemore

Where: #2 DT for run situations

Why: Lissemore has the second highest BSH rating for DTs. Sub out Ratliff for Lissemore in run situations.

Key Stats: 84 BSH

KEY PASS DEFENSE SUBSTITUTION

Who: SS Danny McCray

Where: Starting FS

Why: McCray is only rated 66 OVR, but he has solid ratings for a user-controlled FS.

Key Stats: 6'1", 87 SPD

OFFENSIVE DEPTH CHART

POS	FIRST NAME	LAST NAME	OVR
QB	Tony	Romo	88
QB	Kyle	Orton	77
HB	DeMarco	Murray	84
HB	Joseph	Randle	69
HB	Phillip	Tanner	69
HB	Lance	Dunbar	65
WR	Dez	Bryant	92
WR	Miles	Austin	84
WR	Dwayne	Harris	71
WR	Terrance	Williams	67
WR	Anthony	Armstrong	67
WR	Cole	Beasley	65
WR	Danny	Coale	63
WR	Tim	Benford	60
TE	Jason	Witten	96
TE	James	Hanna	72
TE	Gavin	Escobar	72
TE	Colin	Cochart	69
TE	Andre	Smith	68
TE	L.P.	Ladouceur	52
LT	Tyron	Smith	87
LT	Darrion	Weems	60
LG	Nate	Livings	78
LG	Ronald	Leary	62
C	Phil	Costa	74
C	Travis	Frederick	73
C	Ryan	Cook	72
C	Kevin	Kowalski	63
RG	Mackenzy	Bernadeau	76
RG	David	Arkin	69
RG	Ray	Dominguez	64
RT	Doug	Free	77
RT	Jermey	Parnell	76

DEFENSIVE DEPTH CHART

POS	FIRST NAME	LAST NAME	OVR
LE	Anthony	Spencer	89
LE	Tyrone	Crawford	72
RE	DeMarcus	Ware	94
RE	Kyle	Wilber	71
RE	DeVonte	Holloman	64
DT	Jason	Hatcher	87
DT	Jay	Ratliff	84
DT	Sean	Lissemore	76
DT	Nick	Hayden	67
DT	Jeris	Pendleton	64
DT	Ben	Bass	61
LOLB	Justin	Durant	81
LOLB	Alex	Albright	63
LOLB	Caleb	McSurdy	58
MLB	Sean	Lee	90
MLB	Cameron	Sheffield	63
ROLB	Bruce	Carter	81
ROLB	Ernie	Sims	71
CB	Brandon	Carr	88
CB	Morris	Claiborne	82
CB	Orlando	Scandrick	76
CB	Sterling	Moore	68
CB	B.W.	Webb	68
FS	Matt	Johnson	71
FS	J.J.	Wilcox	68
FS	Brandon	Underwood	67
SS	Barry	Church	75
SS	Will	Allen	69
SS	Eric	Frampton	67
SS	Danny	McCray	66
SS	Micah	Pellerin	51

SPECIAL TEAMS DEPTH CHART

POS	FIRST NAME	LAST NAME	OVR
K	Dan	Bailey	83
P	Chris	Jones	67

Dallas Cowboys

RECOMMENDED OFFENSIVE RUN FORMATION: STRONG CLOSE (2 HB, 1 TE, 2 WR)

PRO TIPS

- HB DEMARCO MURRAY SHOULD SEE THE MAJORITY OF CARRIES FOR THE COWBOYS.
- QB TONY ROMO HAS 73 SPD, WHICH IS ENOUGH SPEED TO RUN AN OPTION OFFENSE.
- FB LAWRENCE VICKERS'S 82 IBL RATING MAKES HIM AN IMPORTANT PIECE OF THE RUN OFFENSE.

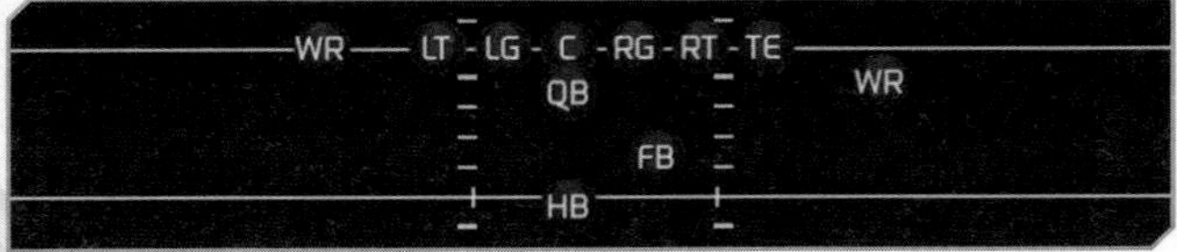

RUN LEFT

MURRAY HAS THE SIZE AND SPEED FOR ANY RUN.

RUN MIDDLE

MURRAY IS GREAT BETWEEN THE TACKLES.

RUN RIGHT

MURRAY'S SPEED ALLOWS HIM TO GET TO THE EDGE.

DALLAS COWBOYS RUNNING PLAY CALL SHEET

LEGEND: Inside Run | Outside Run | Shotgun Run | QB Run

1ST DOWN RUNS	2ND AND SHORT	3RD AND SHORT	GOAL LINE RUNS	2ND AND LONG	3RD AND LONG
Singleback Jumbo—HB Toss	Strong Y-Flex—HB Dive	Strong Close—HB Dive	Goal Line—HB Dive	Gun Y-Trips Cowboy—HB Draw	Gun Doubles—HB Base
Singleback Jumbo—HB Plunge	Weak Twins Flex—HB Lead	Singleback Ace—Close HB Stretch	Goal Line—FB Dive	Strong Y-Flex—HB Draw	Gun Norm Y-Flex Tight—HB Quick Base
Weak Twins Flex—Toss Weak	Singleback Doubles—HB Dive	Strong Close—Counter Weak	Goal Line—Power O	Gun Y-Flex Tight—HB Draw	Gun Flip Trips—HB Mid Draw

DALLAS COWBOYS PASSING PLAY CALL SHEET

LEGEND: Base Play | Man Beater | Zone Beater | Blitz Beater

1ST DOWN PLAY	2ND AND SHORT	3RD AND SHORT	GOAL LINE PASSING	2ND AND LONG	3RD AND LONG
Gun Doubles—Cowboys Shake	Singleback Bunch—Flanker Drive	Singleback Jumbo—Cowboy Verts Drag	I-Form Pro—PA Scissors	I-Form Slot Flex—Go's HB Out	Gun Flip Trips—Slot Trail
Gun Split Cowboy—Cowboy Y-Out	Singleback Bunch—Y Trail	Gun Doubles—Slants	Goal Line—PA Spot	Singleback Ace Pair—Flanker Dig	Gun Flip Trips—Fades
Gun Y-Trips Cowboy—Cowboys Y-Sail	Singleback Y-Trips—Y Option	Gun Norm Y-Flex Tight—Under Y-Option	I-Form Slot Flex—Slants	Gun Doubles—Flex DAL Semi	Gun Snugs Flip—Bench

In these play call sheets we picked the best plays for specific situations so that you will have a play for every down and distance.

OFFENSE

RECOMMENDED OFFENSIVE PASS FORMATION: GUN FLIP TRIPS (1 RB, 0 TE, 4 WR)

PRO TIPS

> TE JAMES HANNA CAN BE USED IN FOUR-WIDE-RECEIVER PACKAGES TO GET EXTRA SIZE ON THE FIELD.

> HB DEMARCO MURRAY IS AN EXCELLENT RECEIVER OUT OF THE BACKFIELD.

> LOOK TO TE JASON WITTEN FOR ALL CRUCIAL THIRD DOWN SITUATIONS BECAUSE OF HIS 96 CIT RATING.

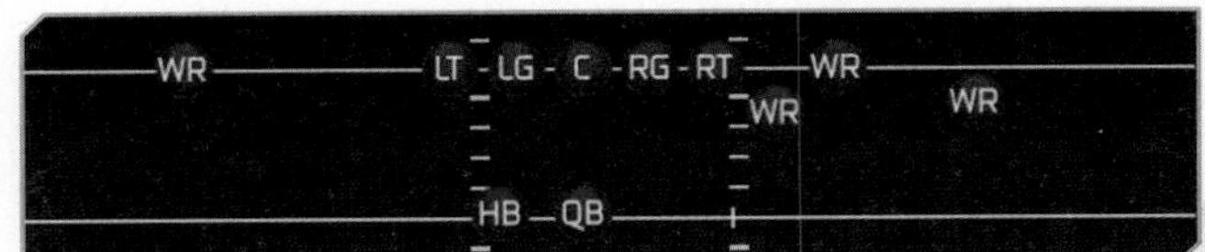

BASE PLAY

SETUP

> STREAK THE HB

> STREAK THE FAR LEFT WR

> Against zone coverages look to the curl flat route combination on the right.

> If you see HB DeMarco Murray in a one-on-one man-to-man situation look to air it out deep to him.

MAN BEATER

SETUP

> STREAK THE HB

> STREAK THE FAR LEFT WR

The auto-motion receiver is an unbumpable route that gets great separation over the middle.

The trail route is our primary route on this play. Look to throw the ball to that receiver as he cuts upfield.

ZONE BEATER

SETUP

> OUT THE FAR RIGHT WR

> DRAG THE FAR LEFT WR

> Against Cover 2 and Cover 3 zones look to the deep post and corner.

> Against Cover 4 zones look to the HB out of the backfield and the drag route.

BLITZ BEATER

SETUP

> DRAG THE FAR RIGHT WR

> STREAK THE FAR LEFT WR

> The WR running the wheel route on the right is a great option if the screen is covered at the snap of the ball.

> In this example the screen is covered and we throw a high lead pass to the wheel receiver.

Dallas Cowboys

RECOMMENDED DEFENSIVE RUN FORMATION: 4-3 OVER PLUS

PRO TIPS

- > SUB IN DT SEAN LISSEMORE FOR DT JAY RATLIFF IN RUN SITUATIONS.
- > MLB SEAN LEE IS ONE OF THE GAME'S BEST TACKLERS; HE HAS A 97 TAK RATING.
- > ROLB BRUCE CARTER HAS A 90 POW RATING, SO HE WILL CAUSE FUMBLES.

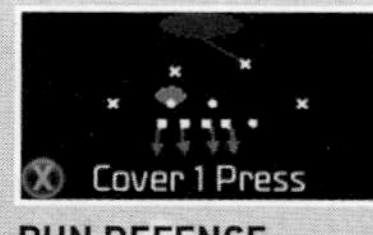

RUN DEFENSE

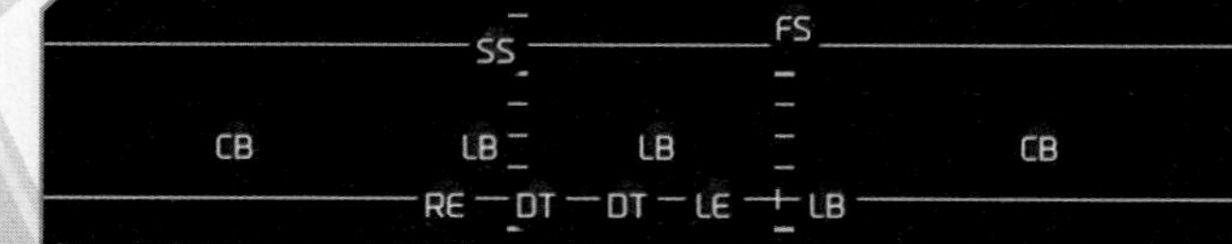

RUN DEFENSE LEFT

SETUP > SHIFT LINEBACKERS LEFT

RUN DEFENSE MIDDLE

SETUP > PINCH DEFENSIVE LINE

RUN DEFENSE RIGHT

SETUP > SHIFT LINEBACKERS RIGHT

DALLAS COWBOYS DEFENSIVE RUN PLAY CALL SHEET

1ST DOWN RUN DEFENSE	2ND AND SHORT	3RD AND SHORT	GOAL LINE RUN DEFENSE	2ND AND LONG	3RD AND LONG
4-3 Over Plus—Cover 2 Man	4-3 Stack—Free Fire	4-3 Under—Safety Blitz	Goal Line 5-3-3—Jam Cover 1	4-6 Normal—Man QB Spy	Nickel Wide 9—Cover 1 Robber
4-3 Over Plus—Cover 2 Sink	4-3 Stack—Sam 3 Fire	4-3 Under—Under Sam 3 Shark	Goal Line 5-3-3—Flat Buzz	4-6 Normal—Cover 4	Nickel Wide 9—Sugar Cover 3 Bluff

DALLAS COWBOYS DEFENSIVE PASS PLAY CALL SHEET

1ST DOWN PLAY	2ND AND SHORT	3RD AND SHORT	GOAL LINE PASSING	2ND AND LONG	3RD AND LONG
Nickel Normal—Cover 1 Press	Nickel Normal—Cover 1 Robber	Dime Normal—All Out Blitz	Goal Line 6-3-2—GL Man	Dime Normal—2 Man Under	Quarter Normal—Inside Blitz
Nickel Normal—Cover 4	Nickel Normal—9 Velcro	Dime Normal—MLB Loop 2	Goal Line 6-3-2—GL Zone	Dime Normal—Cover 3	Quarter Normal—Zone Blitz

LEGEND: Man Coverage | Zone Coverage | Man Blitz | Zone Blitz

In these play call sheets we picked the best plays for specific situations so that you will have a play for every down and distance.

DEFENSE

RECOMMENDED DEFENSIVE PASS FORMATION: 46 NORMAL

PRO TIPS

> PLACE CB BRANDON CARR ON YOUR OPPONENT'S BEST WR.

> USE CB ORLANDO SCANDRICK TO COVER YOUR OPPONENT'S FASTEST WR.

> CB MORRIS CLAIBORNE SHOULD BE USED AS YOUR SECOND CB.

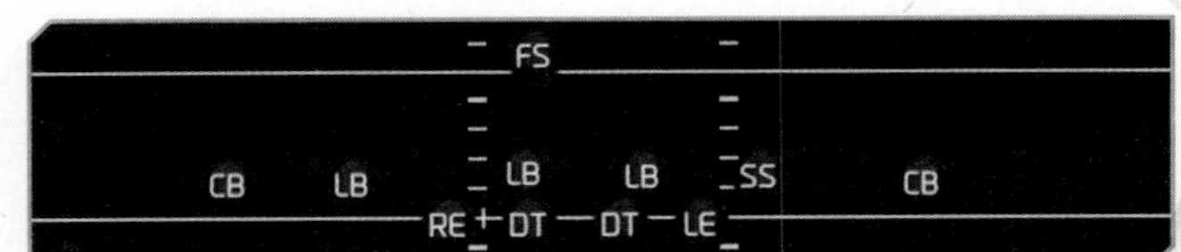

MAN COVERAGE

SETUP

> SHIFT DEFENSIVE LINE RIGHT

> BLITZ SS

> User-control the FS deep and look to play over the middle of the field.

> The Cowboys' CBs are great in man coverage, so protect the middle of the field and let the pressure from this play get after the QB.

ZONE COVERAGE

SETUP

> SHIFT DEFENSIVE LINE RIGHT

> BLITZ THE SS

> User-control the MLB and protect the middle of the field.

> If your opponent starts attacking the flats, hot route both DEs into flat zones and don't blitz the SS.

MAN BLITZ

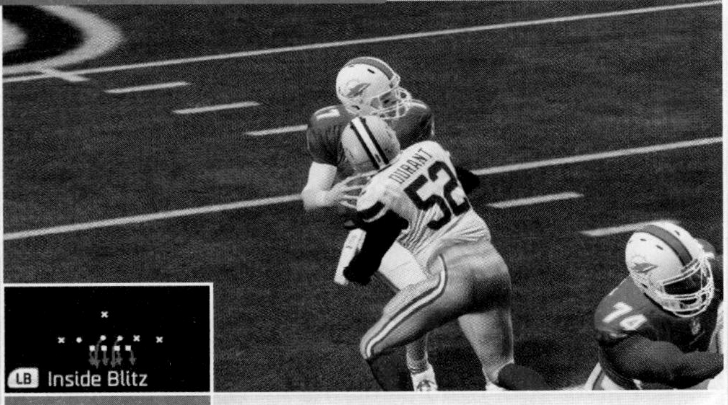

SETUP

> NONE

> Don't make any adjustments to this play or you will change the alignment of the blitz.

> This is one of the fastest A gap blitzes in the game.

ZONE BLITZ

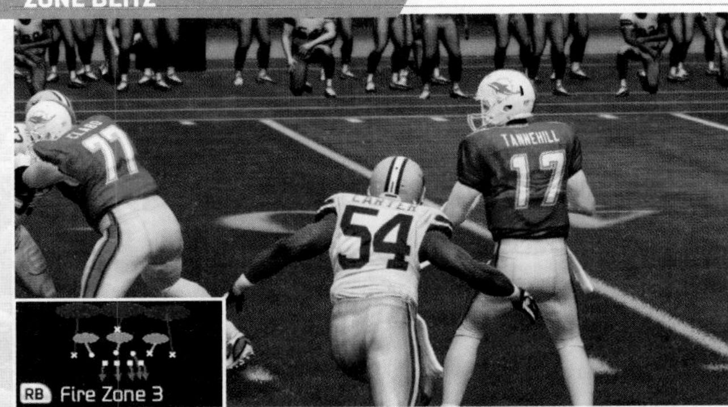

SETUP

> PRESS COVERAGE

> GLOBAL BLITZ THE ROLB

> Depending on your opponent's blocking scheme, pressure will come off the left edge of the A gap.

> User-control the MLB and protect anything over the middle of the field.

> We like to mix this setup in to confuse our opponents and throw off their timing.

Miami Dolphins

2012 TEAM RANKINGS

2nd AFC East (7-9-0)

PASSING OFFENSE: **26th**
RUSHING OFFENSE: **17th**
PASSING DEFENSE: **27th**
RUSHING DEFENSE: **13th**

2012 TEAM LEADERS

PASSING: **Ryan Tannehill: 3,294**
RUSHING: **Reggie Bush: 986**
RECEIVING: **Brian Hartline: 1,083**
TACKLES: **Karlos Dansby: 134**
SACKS: **Cameron Wake: 15**
INTS: **Reshad Jones: 4**

KEY ADDITIONS

WR Mike Wallace
WR Brandon Gibson
TE Dustin Keller

KEY ROOKIES

RE Dion Jordan
CB Jamar Taylor
LG Dallas Thomas

CONNECTED FRANCHISE MODE STRATEGY

CFM TEAM RATING: **68**
OFFENSIVE SCHEME: **West Coast**
DEFENSIVE SCHEME: **Base 4-3**
STRENGTHS: **WR, C, RT, LE, RE, SS**
WEAKNESSES: **HB, LT, RG, CB, FS**

SCHEDULE

Week	Date	Time		Opponent
1	Sep 8	1:00 PM ET	AT	BROWNS
2	Sep 15	1:00 PM ET	AT	COLTS
3	Sep 22	4:05 PM ET		FALCONS
4	Sep 30	8:40 PM ET	AT	SAINTS
5	Oct 6	1:00 PM ET		RAVENS
6	BYE			
7	Oct 20	1:00 PM ET		BILLS
8	Oct 27	1:00 PM ET	AT	PATRIOTS
9	Oct 31	8:25 PM ET		BENGALS
10	Nov 11	8:40 PM ET	AT	BUCCANEERS
11	Nov 17	1:00 PM ET		CHARGERS
12	Nov 24	1:00 PM ET		PANTHERS
13	Dec 1	1:00 PM ET	AT	JETS
14	Dec 8	1:00 PM ET	AT	STEELERS
15	Dec 15	1:00 PM ET		PATRIOTS
16	Dec 22	1:00 PM ET	AT	BILLS
17	Dec 29	1:00 PM ET		JETS

FRANCHISE OVERVIEW

DOLPHINS GAMEPLAY RATING

78

> SEE THE INSIDE BACK COVER FOR A QUICK REFERENCE TO THE GAME ABBREVIATIONS USED THROUGHOUT THIS GUIDE.

> IMPROVE WITH YOUR TEAM BY VISITING PRIMAGAMES.COM/MADDENNFL25 FOR MORE INFORMATION AND HOW-TO VIDEOS.

OFFENSIVE SCOUTING REPORT

- QB Ryan Tannehill is one of the best young QBs in the league. Surround him with talent and you will have a star in the making.
- During free agency and the draft look to find HBs that can play right away.
- WR Mike Wallace was signed during the off season and will help Tannehill develop as quarterback. Wallace is one of the fastest players in the game, and you should complement his speed with another speed receiver.

DEFENSIVE SCOUTING REPORT

LE Cameron Wake is a premiere pass rusher in the NFL. Heading into this season he will have rookie RE Dion Jordan to accompany him after the QB.

Not only do the Dolphins have great DEs, but also they have great DTs. Do everything you can in the off season to keep both Randy Starks and Paul Soliai in town.

The contract of SS Reshad Jones is up at the end of the first season. While he's only been in the league for three seasons he is already 27. Don't sign him for longer than three seasons.

OWNER & COACH PROFILES

STEPHEN ROSS

LEGACY SCORE: 0
OFF. SCHEME: West Coast
DEF. SCHEME: Base 4-3

JOE PHILBIN

LEVEL: 1
LEGACY SCORE: 0
OFF. SCHEME: West Coast
DEF. SCHEME: Base 4-3

TEAM OVERVIEW

KEY PLAYERS

WR #15
MIKE WALLACE

KEY RATINGS

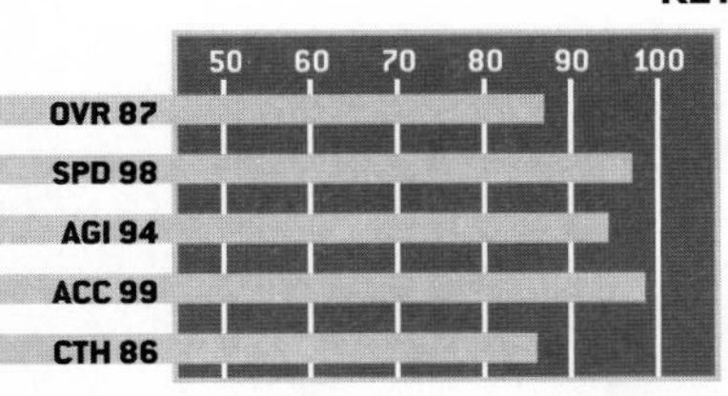

> Wallace should be used on streaks, screens, and underneath drags.

> Very few defenders in the league can defend him one on one.

LE #91
CAMERON WAKE

KEY RATINGS

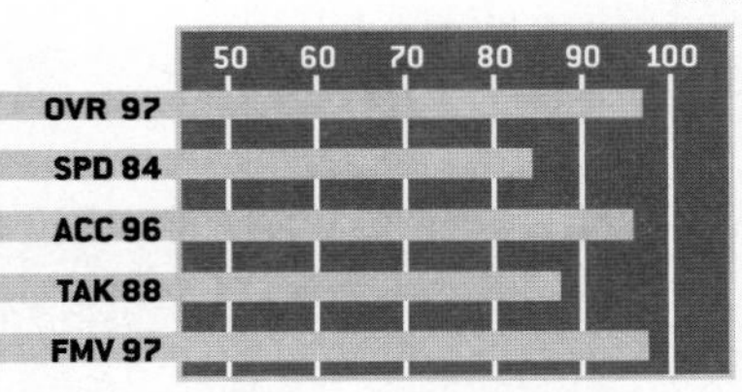

> Wake is nearly unblockable. His speed and strength make him one of the best pass rushers in the game.

> Wake also has enough speed to be dropped into zone coverage.

PRE-GAME SETUP

KEY RUNNING SUBSTITUTION

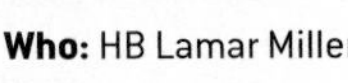

Who: HB Lamar Miller

Where: Starting HB

Why: Miller is the best available HB for the Dolphins. He has great speed and will hold onto the ball.

Key Stats: 95 SPD, 93 AGI, 96 ACC, 86 CAR

KEY PASSING SUBSTITUTION

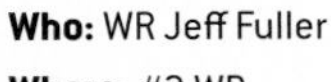

Who: WR Jeff Fuller

Where: #3 WR

Why: Fuller is the Dolphins' best red zone target, and with 82 CIT he will be crucial on third downs.

Key Stats: 6'4", 82 CIT

KEY RUN DEFENSE SUBSTITUTION

Who: DT Vaughn Martin

Where: #3 DT for run situations

Why: Martin has the strength to push back the offensive line in run situations.

Key Stats: 91 STR, 81 BSH

KEY PASS DEFENSE SUBSTITUTION

Who: CB Nolan Carroll

Where: Nickel CB

Why: Carroll has great size and speed for a CB.

Key Stats: 6'1", 93 SPD

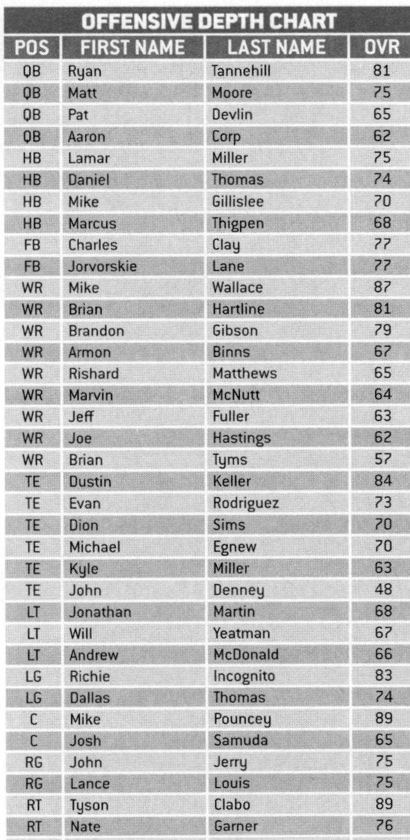

OFFENSIVE DEPTH CHART

POS	FIRST NAME	LAST NAME	OVR
QB	Ryan	Tannehill	81
QB	Matt	Moore	75
QB	Pat	Devlin	65
QB	Aaron	Corp	62
HB	Lamar	Miller	75
HB	Daniel	Thomas	74
HB	Mike	Gillislee	70
HB	Marcus	Thigpen	68
FB	Charles	Clay	77
FB	Jorvorskie	Lane	77
WR	Mike	Wallace	87
WR	Brian	Hartline	81
WR	Brandon	Gibson	79
WR	Armon	Binns	67
WR	Rishard	Matthews	65
WR	Marvin	McNutt	64
WR	Jeff	Fuller	63
WR	Joe	Hastings	62
WR	Brian	Tyms	57
TE	Dustin	Keller	84
TE	Evan	Rodriguez	73
TE	Dion	Sims	70
TE	Michael	Egnew	70
TE	Kyle	Miller	63
TE	John	Denney	48
LT	Jonathan	Martin	68
LT	Will	Yeatman	67
LT	Andrew	McDonald	66
LG	Richie	Incognito	83
LG	Dallas	Thomas	74
C	Mike	Pouncey	89
C	Josh	Samuda	65
RG	John	Jerry	75
RG	Lance	Louis	75
RT	Tyson	Clabo	89
RT	Nate	Garner	76
RT	Jeff	Adams	64

DEFENSIVE DEPTH CHART

POS	FIRST NAME	LAST NAME	OVR
LE	Cameron	Wake	97
LE	Jared	Odrick	79
LE	Derrick	Shelby	66
RE	Dion	Jordan	83
RE	Olivier	Vernon	69
DT	Randy	Starks	88
DT	Paul	Soliai	85
DT	Vaughn	Martin	79
DT	Kheeston	Randall	64
DT	Chas	Alecxih	60
LOLB	Koa	Misi	82
LOLB	Jason	Trusnik	73
MLB	Dannell	Ellerbe	84
MLB	Jelani	Jenkins	66
MLB	Austin	Spitler	66
ROLB	Philip	Wheeler	87
ROLB	Jonathan	Freeny	62
ROLB	Josh	Kaddu	61
CB	Brent	Grimes	89
CB	Richard	Marshall	79
CB	Jamar	Taylor	76
CB	Nolan	Carroll	72
CB	Dimitri	Patterson	70
CB	Will	Davis	68
CB	R.J.	Stanford	64
CB	Julian	Posey	62
CB	De'Andre	Presley	57
FS	Chris	Clemons	79
FS	Jimmy	Wilson	68
FS	Kelcie	McCray	62
SS	Reshad	Jones	92
SS	Don	Jones	63

SPECIAL TEAMS DEPTH CHART

POS	FIRST NAME	LAST NAME	OVR
K	Dan	Carpenter	78
K	Caleb	Sturgis	71
P	Brandon	Fields	92

Miami Dolphins

RECOMMENDED OFFENSIVE RUN FORMATION: FULL HOUSE WIDE (2 HB, 1 TE, 2 WR)

PRO TIPS

> HB LAMAR MILLER SHOULD BE YOUR STARTING HB.

> FB CHARLES CLAY WILL BE A NICE OPTION IN THE BACKFIELD WITHIN THE FULL HOUSE FORMATION.

> HB DANIEL THOMAS SHOULD BACK UP LAMAR MILLER.

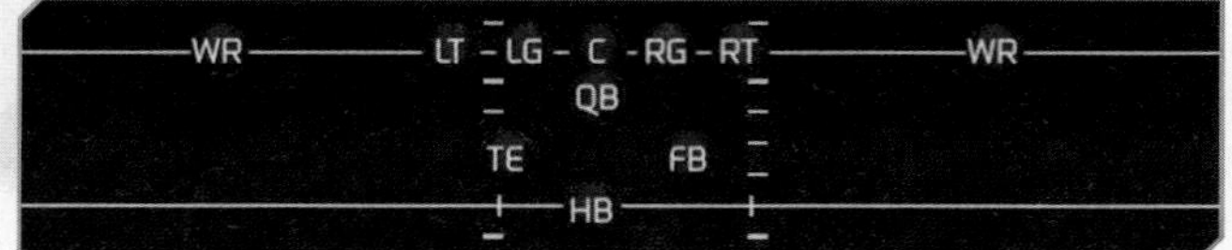

RUN LEFT

Weak Zone

MILLER IS SHIFTY, BUT DON'T LET HIM TAKE TOO MANY BIG HITS.

RUN MIDDLE

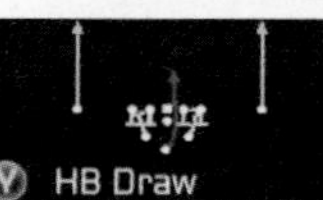

USE MILLER'S SPEED TO GET UPFIELD AS QUICKLY AS POSSIBLE.

RUN RIGHT

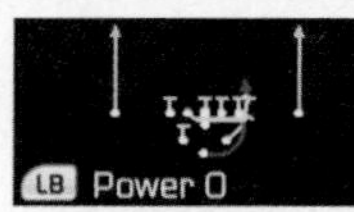

MILLER IS A TOUCHDOWN THREAT ON EVERY RUN.

MIAMI DOLPHINS RUNNING PLAY CALL SHEET

LEGEND: Inside Run | Outside Run | Shotgun Run | QB Run

1ST DOWN RUNS	2ND AND SHORT	3RD AND SHORT	GOAL LINE RUNS	2ND AND LONG	3RD AND LONG
I-Form Pro—HB Toss	Singleback Ace Pair—Inside Zone	Strong Pro—HB Blast	Goal Line Normal—QB Sneak	Gun Trips TE—HB Mid Draw	Gun Snugs Flip—HB Mid Draw
I-Form Pro—Iso	Singleback Ace Pair—HB Toss Strong	Strong Pro—Toss Crack	Goal Line Normal—HB Dive	Singleback Jumbo—Power O	Gun Split Dolphin—Power O
Singleback Ace—Counter Wk	Strong Pro—HB Dive	Singleback Jumbo—HB Off Tackle	Goal Line Normal—Power O	Gun Snugs Flip—HB Sweep	Gun Doubles Wk—HB Draw

MIAMI DOLPHINS PASSING PLAY CALL SHEET

LEGEND: Base Play | Man Beater | Zone Beater | Blitz Beater

1ST DOWN PLAY	2ND AND SHORT	3RD AND SHORT	GOAL LINE PASSING	2ND AND LONG	3RD AND LONG
Gun Doubles Wk—Slants	Singleback Jumbo—Y Shallow Cross	Singleback Wing Trio—Inside Cross	Goal Line—PA Waggle	Gun Dolphins Trips—Slot Out	Gun Doubles Wing TE—Dolphins X Spot
Gun Split Dolphin—Mesh	Singleback Bunch—Y Trail	Gun Split Dolphin—HB Wheel	Goal Line—PA Spot	Gun Doubles Flex Wing—Slants	Singleback Flex—Curl Flats
Gun Tight Doubles On—PA WR Cross	Singleback Ace—Levels Divide	Full House Wide—Comebacks	Goal Line—PA Power O	Gun Wing Trio Wk—Corner Strike	Gun Empty Base—Spacing

In these play call sheets we picked the best plays for specific situations so that you will have a play for every down and distance.

OFFENSE

RECOMMENDED OFFENSIVE PASS FORMATION: GUN DOUBLES FLEX WING (1 RB, 1 TE, 3 WR)

PRO TIPS

- USE WR JEFF FULLER IN THE END ZONE FOR JUMP BALL SITUATIONS.
- TE MICHAEL EGNEW HAS GREAT SPEED FOR HIS POSITION.
- FB CHARLES CLAY IS 6'3" AND HAS THE HANDS OF A RECEIVER.

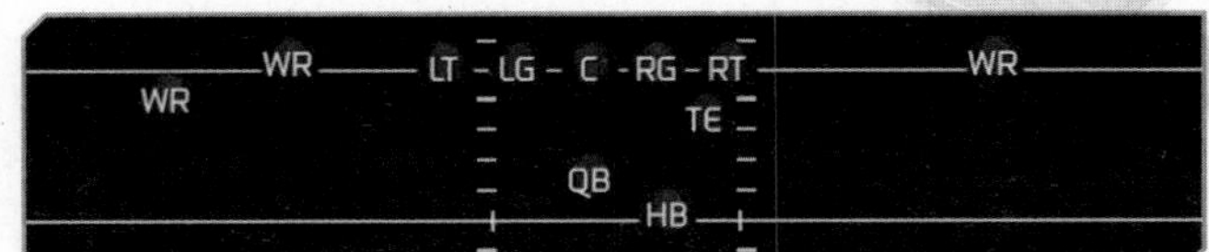

BASE PLAY

SETUP
- STREAK THE TE
- OPTION THE HB

- Against zone coverages look to the curl-flat route combination on the left.
- Lamar Miller will get great separation against man-to-man underneath.

MAN BEATER

SETUP
- BLOCK THE TE
- BLOCK THE HB

- The slot WR gets inside position once his route breaks over the middle of the field.
- Throw a high lead pass to the right and lead the defender upfield for big yards.

ZONE BEATER

SETUP
- STREAK THE TE
- OPTION THE HB

- Against Cover 2 and Cover 3 zones look to the TE streak and the slot post.
- Against Cover 4 zones look to the HB out of the backfield.

BLITZ BEATER

SETUP
- BLOCK AND RELEASE THE TE
- SWING RIGHT THE HB

- The TE will stay in to block at the snap of the ball. If he has no one to block he will release to the flat.
- With lead blockers in front of him Miller can spring this play for a touchdown.

Miami Dolphins

RECOMMENDED DEFENSIVE RUN FORMATION: 4-3 OVER

PRO TIPS

- > DT VAUGHN MARTIN IS A GREAT SUBSTITUTION FOR RUNNING SITUATIONS.
- > ROOKIE MLB JELANI JENKINS HAS 83 TAK AND 88 POW; GET HIM ON THE FIELD FOR RUNNING SITUATIONS.
- > SS RESHAD JONES CAN HELP WITH RUN SUPPORT. GET HIM IN THE BOX WHEN YOU EXPECT THE RUN.

RUN DEFENSE

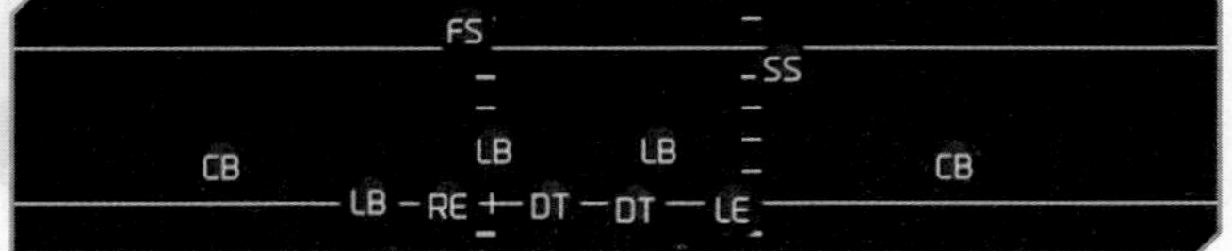

RUN DEFENSE LEFT

SETUP > SHIFT LINEBACKERS LEFT

RUN DEFENSE MIDDLE

SETUP > PINCH DEFENSIVE LINE

RUN DEFENSE RIGHT

SETUP > SHIFT LINEBACKERS RIGHT

MIAMI DOLPHINS DEFENSIVE RUN PLAY CALL SHEET

1ST DOWN RUN DEFENSE	2ND AND SHORT	3RD AND SHORT	GOAL LINE RUN DEFENSE	2ND AND LONG	3RD AND LONG
4-3 Over—2 Man Under	4-3 Over Plus—Cover 1	4-3 Stack—Thunder Smoke	Goal Line 5-3-3—Jam Cover 1	Dollar 3-2-6—Spinner Buck Dog 1	Nickel Wide 9—Odd Overload Blitz
4-3 Over—Cover 2 Sink	4-3 Over Plus—Cover 2	4-3-Stack—Thunder Smoke 2	Goal Line 5-3-3—Flat Buzz	Dollar 3-2-6—Fire Zone 3	Nickel Wide 9—Odd Overload 4

MIAMI DOLPHINS DEFENSIVE PASS PLAY CALL SHEET

1ST DOWN PLAY	2ND AND SHORT	3RD AND SHORT	GOAL LINE PASSING	2ND AND LONG	3RD AND LONG
4-3 Under—2 Man Under	46 Bear Under—LB Dogs	4-3 Stack—Free Fire	Goal Line 6-3-2—GL Man	Nickel Normal—Under Smoke	Dollar 3-2-6—Fire Dog 1
4-3 Under—Snake 3 Deep	46 Bear Under—LB Dogs 3	4-3 Stack—Sam 3 Fire	Goal Line 6-3-2—GL Zone	Nickel Normal—Mid Zone Blitz	Dollar 3-2-6—DB Fire 2

LEGEND: Man Coverage | Zone Coverage | Man Blitz | Zone Blitz

In these play call sheets we picked the best plays for specific situations so that you will have a play for every down and distance.

DEFENSE

RECOMMENDED DEFENSIVE PASS FORMATION: 46 BEAR UNDER

PRO TIPS

- PLACE CB BRENT GRIMES ON YOUR OPPONENT'S BEST WR.
- USE CB JAMAR TAYLOR TO COVER YOUR OPPONENT'S FASTEST WR.
- CB RICHARD MARSHALL SHOULD BE USED AS YOUR SECOND CB.

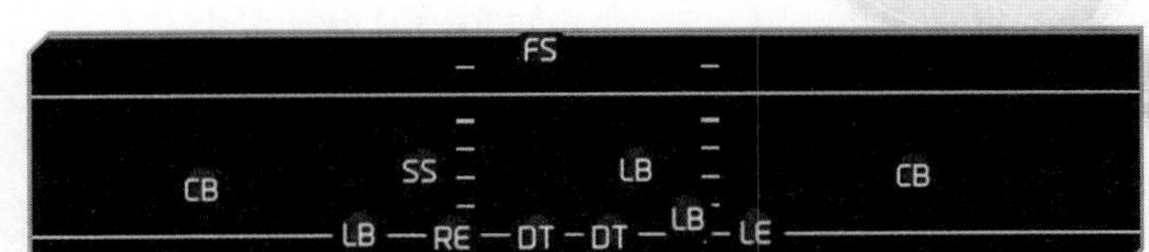

MAN COVERAGE

SETUP

- QB SPY THE DT
- BUZZ ZONE BOTH DEFENSIVE ENDS

This setup creates a unique pass rush angle for LE Cameron Wake to get after the QB.

Coverage will be lockdown and the pressure will eventually get to the QB because of Wake.

ZONE COVERAGE

SETUP

- DEEP ZONE THE SS
- QB SPY THE DT
- BLITZ THE SS

- User-control the MLB and protect the middle of the field.
- If your opponent starts attacking the flats, hot route both DEs into flat zones.

MAN BLITZ

SETUP

- MAN ALIGN
- PRESS COVERAGE

- Pressure will come from different areas of the offensive line depending on your opponent's blocking scheme.
- If the HB stays in to block, drop back into coverage with the MLB. If he runs a route, make sure to cover him.

ZONE BLITZ

SETUP

- PRESS COVERAGE
- BLITZ THE LE

If your opponent starts attacking the flats, drop both hook zone defenders into flat zones.

- User-control the MLB and protect the short and deep middle.
- We like to mix this setup in to confuse our opponents and throw off their timing.

Philadelphia Eagles

2012 TEAM RANKINGS

4th NFC East (4-12-0)

PASSING OFFENSE: **13th**
RUSHING OFFENSE: **13th**
PASSING DEFENSE: **9th**
RUSHING DEFENSE: **23rd**

2012 TEAM LEADERS

PASSING: **Michael Vick: 2,362**
RUSHING: **LeSean McCoy: 840**
RECEIVING: **Jeremy Maclin: 857**
TACKLES: **DeMeco Ryans: 113**
SACKS: **Fletcher Cox: 5.5**
INTS: **Dominique Rodgers-Cromartie: 3**

KEY ADDITIONS

WR Arrelious Benn
HB Felix Jones
QB Dennis Dixon

KEY ROOKIES

QB Matt Barkley
TE Zach Ertz
SS Earl Wolff

CONNECTED FRANCHISE MODE STRATEGY

CFM TEAM RATING: **72**
OFFENSIVE SCHEME: **Spread**
DEFENSIVE SCHEME: **Base 4-3**
STRENGTHS: **HB, WR, TE, LG, MLB, P**
WEAKNESSES: **LE, C, RE, DT, K**

SCHEDULE

Week	Date	Time		Opponent
1	Sep 9	7:10 PM ET	AT	REDSKINS
2	Sep 15	1:00 PM ET		CHARGERS
3	Sep 19	8:25 PM ET		CHIEFS
4	Sep 29	4:25 PM ET	AT	BRONCOS
5	Oct 6	1:00 PM ET	AT	GIANTS
6	Oct 13	1:00 PM ET	AT	BUCCANEERS
7	Oct 20	1:00 PM ET		COWBOYS
8	Oct 27	1:00 PM ET		GIANTS
9	Nov 3	4:05 PM ET	AT	RAIDERS
10	Nov 10	1:00 PM ET	AT	PACKERS
11	Nov 17	1:00 PM ET		REDSKINS
12	BYE			
13	Dec 1	1:00 PM ET		CARDINALS
14	Dec 8	1:00 PM ET		LIONS
15	Dec 15	1:00 PM ET	AT	VIKINGS
16	Dec 22	1:00 PM ET		BEARS
17	Dec 29	1:00 PM ET	AT	COWBOYS

FRANCHISE OVERVIEW

EAGLES GAMEPLAY RATING

76

> SEE THE INSIDE BACK COVER FOR A QUICK REFERENCE TO THE GAME ABBREVIATIONS USED THROUGHOUT THIS GUIDE.

> IMPROVE WITH YOUR TEAM BY VISITING PRIMAGAMES.COM/MADDENNFL25 FOR MORE INFORMATION AND HOW-TO VIDEOS.

OFFENSIVE SCOUTING REPORT

- QB Michael Vick is a special talent that doesn't come around very often. With that said, his age is starting to creep up on him. If he doesn't have a lights out season don't re-sign him this off season.
- HB LeSean McCoy is one of the league's best young HBs, but you will want to focus more of your attention on upgrading HB Bryce Brown's stats. McCoy is already an elite player and Brown needs more attention in areas like CAR and CTH.
- WR Jeremy Maclin's contract is up at the end of the first season. This is a tough decision to make as he is a solid player, but he will ask for a big time contract. We recommend keeping him around unless you can find a respectable replacement for him.

DEFENSIVE SCOUTING REPORT

- RE Fletcher Cox is entering his second NFL season and is a solid player with no real standout rating. Using upgrades you could go a few different ways with him. Upgrade his PMV rating to make him a better pass rusher or upgrade his BSH rating to make him a better run stopper. You could even upgrade his speed and move him to outside linebacker.
- MLB Mychal Kendricks is the feature of this defense. He is a rare player at the MLB position with his 90 SPD. Focus on upgrading his AGI and TAK ratings. Kendricks has potential to be the best MLB in the game.
- During free agency and the draft your number one priority should be focused on the secondary. Specifically, improving your CBs will improve this defense tenfold.

OWNER & COACH PROFILES

JEFFREY LURIE

LEGACY SCORE: 1075
OFF. SCHEME: Vertical Offense
DEF. SCHEME: Attacking 3-4

CHIP KELLY

LEVEL: 15
LEGACY SCORE: 0
OFF. SCHEME: Vertical Offense
DEF. SCHEME: Attacking 3-4

TEAM OVERVIEW

KEY PLAYERS

HB #25
LESEAN MCCOY

KEY RATINGS

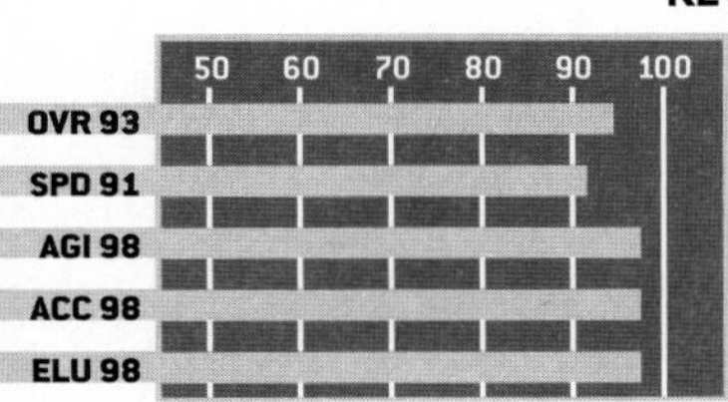

> McCoy is an every-down HB and can be split wide as a receiver.

> McCoy's best runs are counters, tosses, and off tackles.

FS #21
KENNY PHILLIPS

KEY RATINGS

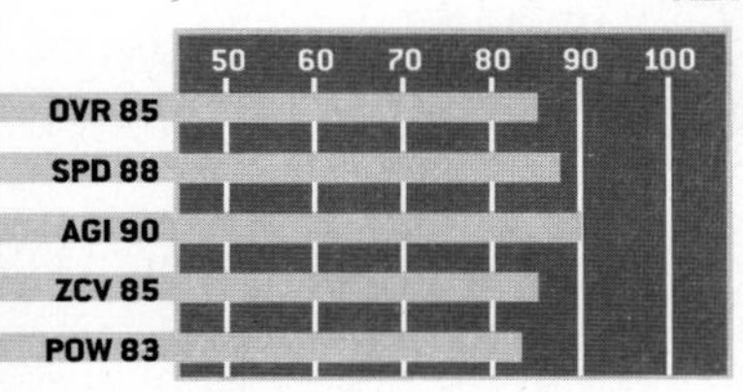

> Phillips stands at 6'2" and has enough speed to cover sideline to sideline.

> User-control Phillips on every down. He is a playmaker.

PRE-GAME SETUP

KEY RUNNING SUBSTITUTION

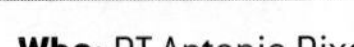

Who: HB Bryce Brown

Where: Backup HB

Why: Brown showed last season that he has what it takes to be a productive NFL HB.

Key Stats: 93 SPD, 92 AGI, 93 ACC

KEY PASSING SUBSTITUTION

Who: WR Jason Avant

Where: #2 WR

Why: Avant has some of the best clutch hands in the game. Throw to him on third down.

Key Stats: 95 CIT

KEY RUN DEFENSE SUBSTITUTION

Who: DT Antonio Dixon

Where: #2 DT

Why: Dixon is the Eagles' second-best run-stopping DT. Get him on the field in running situations.

Key Stats: 90 STR

KEY PASS DEFENSE SUBSTITUTION

Who: CB Brandon Boykin

Where: Nickel CB

Why: Boykin is the fastest CB the Eagles have. His 90 SPD is going to have to go a long way for this defense.

Key Stats: 90 SPD

OFFENSIVE DEPTH CHART

POS	FIRST NAME	LAST NAME	OVR
QB	Michael	Vick	81
QB	Nick	Foles	75
QB	Matt	Barkley	73
QB	Dennis	Dixon	68
QB	G.J.	Kinne	63
HB	LeSean	McCoy	93
HB	Bryce	Brown	77
HB	Felix	Jones	76
HB	Chris	Polk	67
FB	James	Casey	82
FB	Emil	Igwenagu	62
WR	DeSean	Jackson	85
WR	Jeremy	Maclin	83
WR	Jason	Avant	79
WR	Arrelious	Benn	73
WR	Riley	Cooper	70
WR	Damaris	Johnson	67
WR	Greg	Salas	65
WR	B.J.	Cunningham	64
WR	Nick	Miller	56
TE	Brent	Celek	85
TE	Zach	Ertz	75
TE	Clay	Harbor	74
TE	Derek	Carrier	62
TE	Jon	Dorenbos	45
LT	Jason	Peters	88
LT	Ed	Wang	67
LT	Matt	Kopa	58
LG	Evan	Mathis	98
LG	Danny	Watkins	73
LG	Allen	Barbre	69
C	Jason	Kelce	79
C	Dallas	Reynolds	68
C	Matt	Tennant	65
RG	Todd	Herremans	87
RG	Julian	Vandervelde	64
RT	Lane	Johnson	79
RT	Dennis	Kelly	70
RT	Nate	Menkin	65

DEFENSIVE DEPTH CHART

POS	FIRST NAME	LAST NAME	OVR
LE	Cedric	Thornton	71
LE	Clifton	Geathers	66
RE	Fletcher	Cox	79
RE	Vinny	Curry	70
DT	Isaac	Sopoaga	80
DT	Antonio	Dixon	70
DT	Bennie	Logan	69
LOLB	Connor	Barwin	83
LOLB	Brandon	Graham	76
LOLB	Joe	Kruger	66
MLB	DeMeco	Ryans	85
MLB	Mychal	Kendricks	72
MLB	Jason	Phillips	70
MLB	Jamar	Chaney	70
MLB	Emmanuel	Acho	65
MLB	Casey	Matthews	62
ROLB	Trent	Cole	84
ROLB	Phillip	Hunt	65
CB	Cary	Williams	83
CB	Bradley	Fletcher	82
CB	Brandon	Boykin	72
CB	Brandon	Hughes	69
CB	Jordan	Poyer	68
CB	Curtis	Marsh	67
CB	Trevard	Lindley	63
FS	Kenny	Phillips	85
FS	Kurt	Coleman	70
FS	David	Sims	63
SS	Patrick	Chung	82
SS	Earl	Wolff	71
SS	Colt	Anderson	70
SS	Nate	Allen	69

SPECIAL TEAMS DEPTH CHART

POS	FIRST NAME	LAST NAME	OVR
K	Alex	Henery	80
P	Donnie	Jones	91

Philadelphia Eagles

RECOMMENDED OFFENSIVE RUN FORMATION: GUN WING TRIPS OFFSET (1 HB, 1 TE, 3 WR)

PRO TIPS

> ROOKIE TE ZACH ERTZ PROVIDES THE BEST BLOCKING AT THE TE POSITION.

> USE HB BRYCE BROWN TO BACK UP HB LESEAN MCCOY.

> PLAY ACTION DEEP TO WR DESEAN JACKSON WILL OPEN UP THE RUN GAME.

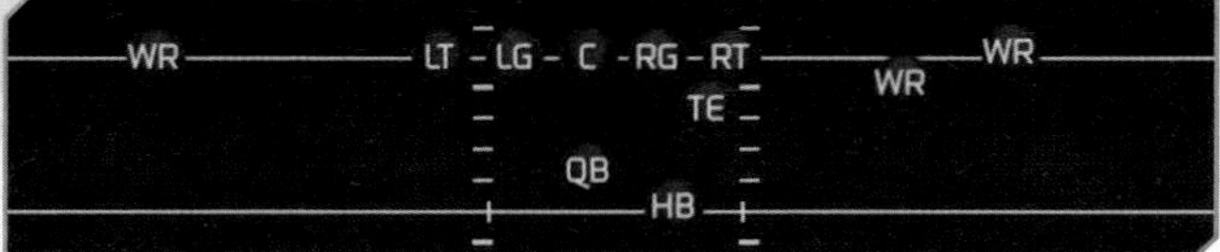

RUN LEFT

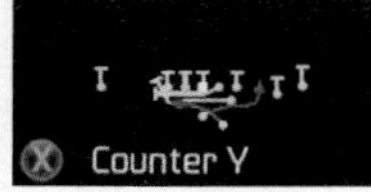

MCCOY'S QUICKNESS MAKES HIM A THREAT ON EVERY PLAY.

RUN MIDDLE

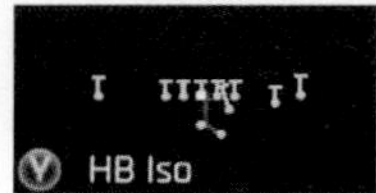

USE MCCOY'S AGILITY AND ACCELERATION TO FIND HOLES THROUGH THE MIDDLE.

RUN RIGHT

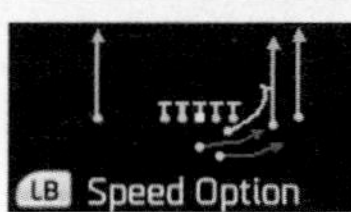

WE KEEP THE BALL WITH QB MIKE VICK.

PHILADELPHIA EAGLES RUNNING PLAY CALL SHEET

LEGEND: Inside Run | Outside Run | Shotgun Run | QB Run

1ST DOWN RUNS	2ND AND SHORT	3RD AND SHORT	GOAL LINE RUNS	2ND AND LONG	3RD AND LONG
Singleback Ace—Off Tackle	I-Form Tight Pair—Weak Iso	I-Form Pro—Inside Zone	Goal Line—HB Dive	Gun Normal—Buck Sweep	Gun Normal—Read Option
Singleback Ace—HB Blast	Singleback Tight Slots—HB Dive	I-Form Pro—Iso	Goal Line—HB Sting	Gun Trio Offset—0 1 Trap	Gun Normal—Speed Option
I-Form Tight Pair—Stretch	Strong Close—HB Dive	Strong Close—HB Off Tackle	Goal Line—Power 0	Gun Spread Offset—Read Option	Gun Ace Pair Twins—Speed Option

PHILADELPHIA EAGLES PASSING PLAY CALL SHEET

LEGEND: Base Play | Man Beater | Zone Beater | Blitz Beater

1ST DOWN PLAY	2ND AND SHORT	3RD AND SHORT	GOAL LINE PASSING	2ND AND LONG	3RD AND LONG
Gun Split Eagle—Slot Cross	Gun Spread Offset—Fake Screen Wheel	Gun Trio Offset—HB Slip Screen	Gun Empty Spread—Stick	Gun Ace Pair Twins—Smash	Gun Normal—HB Angle
Gun Normal—X-tra HB Wheel	Gun Spread Offset—SE Screen	Gun Wing Trips Offset—WR Screen	Goal Line—PA Spot	Gun Ace Pair Twins—Posts	Gun Trips Offset—Smash
Gun Y-Trips Offset—Slot Drive	Gun Spread HB Wk—Quick Slants	Gun Trio 4WR—HB Slip Screen	Goal Line—PA Power 0	Gun 5WR Trio—Flood Switch	Gun Trips Offset—Verticals

In these play call sheets we picked the best plays for specific situations so that you will have a play for every down and distance.

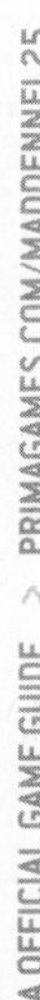

OFFENSE

RECOMMENDED OFFENSIVE PASS FORMATION: GUN WING TRIPS OFFSET (1 HB, 1 TE, 3 WR)

PRO TIPS

- WR JASON AVANT HAS 95 CIT.
- QB DENNIS DIXON CAN FILL IN NICELY FOR QB MIKE VICK IF NEEDED.
- HB FELIX JONES CAN BE USED AS A WR TO ADD EVEN MORE SPEED TO THIS OFFENSE.

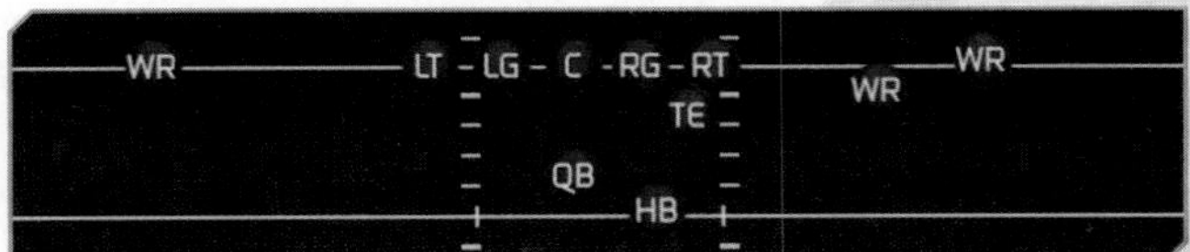

BASE PLAY

SETUP

- DRAG THE FAR RIGHT WR
- OPTION THE HB

- Against zone look to the underneath drag route.
- Against man-to-man look to the sideline wheel and the HB out of the backfield.

MAN BEATER

SETUP

- STREAK THE TE
- BLOCK THE HB

- Against man-to-man defenses the slants on the outside will get inside position after the press coverage.
- Throw a high-and-inside lead pass to get the most yards after the catch.

ZONE BEATER

SETUP

- STREAK THE TE AND MOTION HIM LEFT
- OPTION THE HB

- Against Cover 2 and Cover 3 zones look to the slot WR, Avant, who will hang on to the ball during big hits.
- Against Cover 4 zones look to the HB out of the backfield.

BLITZ BEATER

SETUP

- BLOCK THE HB
- DRAG THE SLOT WR

- If the HB is open, throw a sideline lead pass to keep him moving upfield.
- McCoy has the speed to make this a touchdown against the blitz.

Philadelphia Eagles

RECOMMENDED DEFENSIVE RUN FORMATION: 3-4 PREDATOR

PRO TIPS

> DT ANTONIO DIXON SHOULD BE USED ON RUNNING DOWNS.

> LOLB BRANDON GRAHAM HAS 88 POW, WHICH WILL FORCE FUMBLES.

> MLB DEMECO RYANS IS YOUR BEST TACKLER. USER-CONTROL HIM TO TAKE DOWN THE BALL CARRIER.

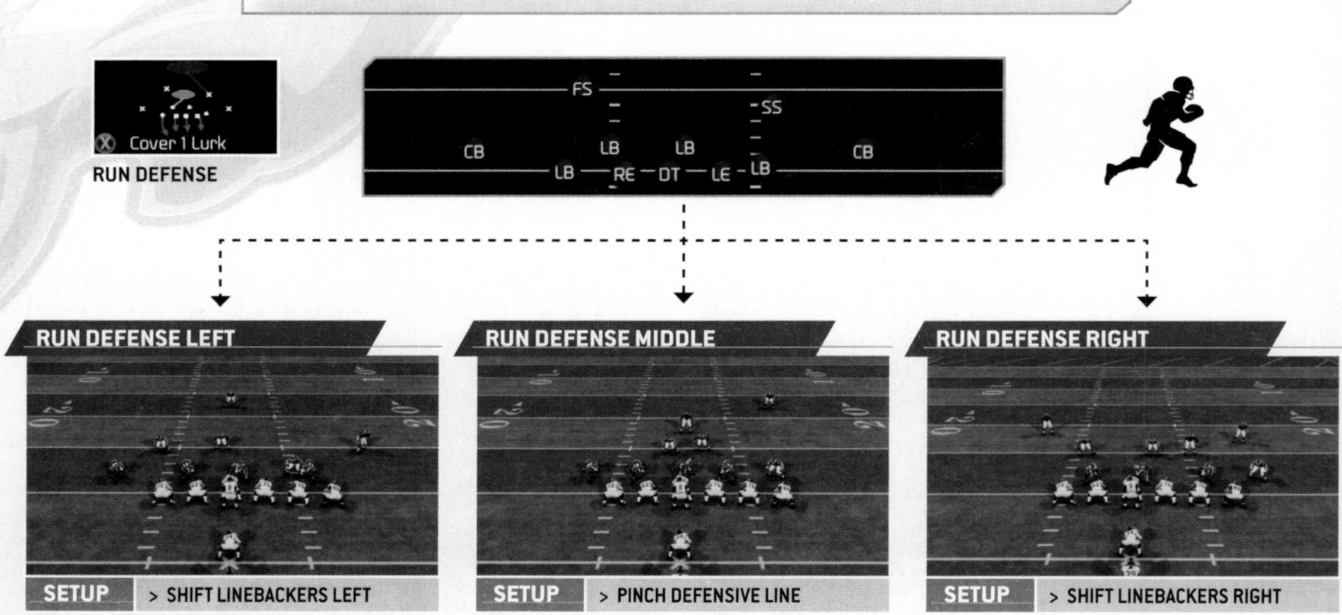

PHILADELPHIA EAGLES DEFENSIVE RUN PLAY CALL SHEET

1ST DOWN RUN DEFENSE	2ND AND SHORT	3RD AND SHORT	GOAL LINE RUN DEFENSE	2ND AND LONG	3RD AND LONG
3-4 Predator—2 Man Under	3-4 Solid—Sting Pinch	Nickel 1-5-5 Prowl—Dbl Loop	Goal Line 5-3-3—Jam Cover 1	3-4 Over Stack—2 Man Under	Sub 2-3-6 Even—Cover 1 Robber
3-4 Predator—Cover 2 Sink	3-4 Solid—Cover 3 Buzz	Nickel 1-5-5 Prowl—Dbl Loop 3	Goal Line 5-3-3—3 Deep Under	3-4 Over Stack—Cover 4	Sub 2-3-6 Even—Cover 4

PHILADELPHIA EAGLES DEFENSIVE PASS PLAY CALL SHEET

1ST DOWN PLAY	2ND AND SHORT	3RD AND SHORT	GOAL LINE PASSING	2ND AND LONG	3RD AND LONG
3-4 Odd—Cover 1 Robber	Sub 2-3-6 Even—Overload 1 Roll	Nickel 1-5-5 Prowl—Overload Blitz	Goal Line 6-3-2—GL Man	Nickel 2-4-5—Over Storm Brave	Sub 2-3-6 Will—Zero Blitz
3-4 Odd—Cover 2 Sink	Sub 2-3-6 Even—Cover 2	Nickel 1-5-5 Prowl—Prowl Bear 2	Goal Line 6-3-2—GL Zone	Nickel 2-4-5—Overload 3 Seam	Sub 2-3-6 Will—Spinner Dog 3

LEGEND: Man Coverage | Zone Coverage | Man Blitz | Zone Blitz

In these play call sheets we picked the best plays for specific situations so that you will have a play for every down and distance.

DEFENSE

RECOMMENDED DEFENSIVE PASS FORMATION: SUB 2-3-6 WILL

PRO TIPS

- PLACE CB CARY WILLIAMS ON YOUR OPPONENT'S BEST WR.
- USE CB BRANDON BOYKIN TO COVER YOUR OPPONENT'S FASTEST WR.
- CB BRADLEY FLETCHER SHOULD BE USED AS YOUR SECOND CB.

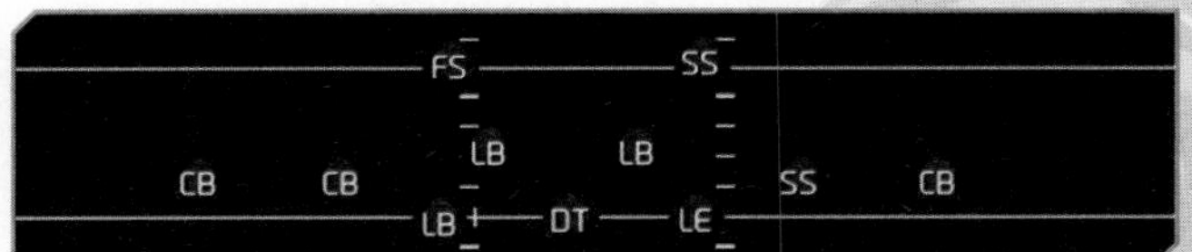

MAN COVERAGE

SETUP

- GLOBAL ZONE THE LINEBACKERS
- USER-CONTROL THE MLB

- Every receiver but one will be covered, and we will have three extra defenders over the middle of the field.
- This is one of our favorite ways to slow down opponents who attack the middle of the field.

ZONE COVERAGE

SETUP

- GLOBAL ZONE THE LINEBACKERS
- USER-CONTROL THE MLB
- BLITZ THE SS

- The only real weakness this defense has is the short flat.
- If your opponent throws deep, anticipate interceptions by the secondary.

MAN BLITZ

SETUP

- MAN ALIGN
- PRESS COVERAGE
- USER-CONTROL THE FS

- Your opponent has to block seven players in order to pick this pressure up.
- We like using this blitz against opponents who always block at least six players.

ZONE BLITZ

SETUP

- BLITZ THE LOLB
- USER-CONTROL THE MLB

- The flat will be covered even if they get rid of the ball before pressure gets to the QB.
- Be ready for any pass over the short middle of the field.
- We like to mix this setup in to confuse our opponents and throw off their timing.

Atlanta Falcons

2012 TEAM RANKINGS

1st NFC South (13-3-0)

PASSING OFFENSE: **8th**
RUSHING OFFENSE: **29th**
PASSING DEFENSE: **23rd**
RUSHING DEFENSE: **21st**

2012 TEAM LEADERS

PASSING: **Matt Ryan: 4,719**
RUSHING: **Michael Turner: 800**
RECEIVING: **Roddy White: 1,351**
TACKLES: **Stephen Nicholas: 95**
SACKS: **John Abraham: 10**
INTS: **Thomas DeCoud: 6**

KEY ADDITIONS

HB Steven Jackson
RE Osi Umenyiora

KEY ROOKIES

CB Desmond Trufant
CB Robert Alford
DE Malliciah Goodman

CONNECTED FRANCHISE MODE STRATEGY

CFM TEAM RATING: **76**
OFFENSIVE SCHEME: **Power Run**
DEFENSIVE SCHEME: **Attacking 4-3**
STRENGTHS: **QB, HB, WR, TE, CB**
WEAKNESSES: **C, RG, RT, LE, MLB**

SCHEDULE

1	Sep 8	1:00 PM ET	AT	SAINTS
2	Sep 15	1:00 PM ET		RAMS
3	Sep 22	4:05 PM ET	AT	DOLPHINS
4	Sep 29	8:30 PM ET		PATRIOTS
5	Oct 7	8:40 PM ET		JETS
6	BYE			
7	Oct 20	1:00 PM ET		BUCCANEERS
8	Oct 27	4:25 PM ET	AT	CARDINALS
9	Nov 3	1:00 PM ET	AT	PANTHERS
10	Nov 10	1:00 PM ET		SEAHAWKS
11	Nov 17	1:00 PM ET	AT	BUCCANEERS
12	Nov 21	8:25 PM ET		SAINTS
13	Dec 1	4:05 PM ET	AT	BILLS
14	Dec 8	8:30 PM ET	AT	PACKERS
15	Dec 15	1:00 PM ET		REDSKINS
16	Dec 23	8:40 PM ET	AT	49ERS
17	Dec 29	1:00 PM ET		PANTHERS

FRANCHISE OVERVIEW

FALCONS GAMEPLAY RATING

86

> See the inside back cover for a quick reference to the game abbreviations used throughout this guide.

> Improve with your team by visiting PrimaGames.com/MaddenNFL25 for more information and how-to videos.

OFFENSIVE SCOUTING REPORT

- The contract of the most important piece of the Falcons franchise is up at the end of the season. QB Matt Ryan needs to be signed to a long-term deal.
- HB Steven Jackson is a short-term solution to a long-term problem. Backing him up is HB Jacquizz Rodgers, who lacks the top-end speed to be a feature HB in this league. You have two options: try to upgrade Rodgers's speed or look to the draft for a starting HB.
- WRs Roddy White, Julio Jones, and TE Tony Gonzalez all have two years remaining on their contracts. Let both White and Gonzalez go and sign Jones long-term.

DEFENSIVE SCOUTING REPORT

- Focus on the defensive line in the upcoming draft as well as in free agency. You need to rebuild it from top to bottom.
- You are also going to need to do something about your current linebackers. TE Tony Gonzalez is expendable—try to bring in a two-for-one deal via trade.
- CB Desmond Trufant is a rookie who has lockdown coverage skills, but he needs upgrades to his PRS and CTH ratings.

OWNER & COACH PROFILES

ARTHUR BLANK
LEGACY SCORE: 300 | OFF. SCHEME: Power Run
DEF. SCHEME: Attacking 4-3

MIKE SMITH
LEVEL: 21 | LEGACY SCORE: 150
OFF. SCHEME: Power Run | DEF. SCHEME: Attacking 4-3

TEAM OVERVIEW

KEY PLAYERS

QB #2
MATT RYAN

KEY RATINGS

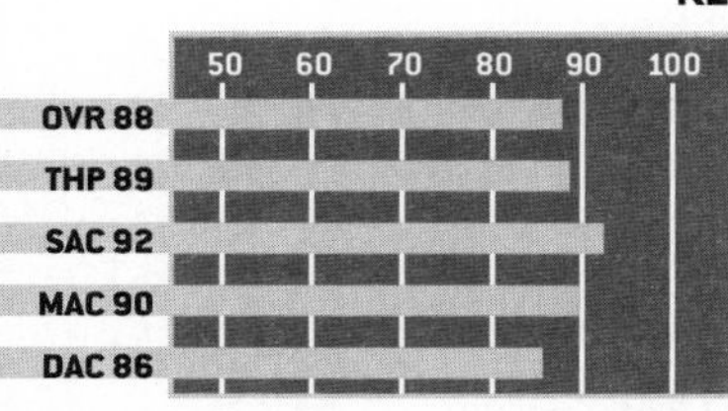

- Ryan can make every throw on the field. The Falcons have the best receiving threats in the game.
- Focus on hitting Julio Jones downfield, and look for Roddy White and Tony Gonzalez over the middle.

CB #22
ASANTE SAMUEL

KEY RATINGS

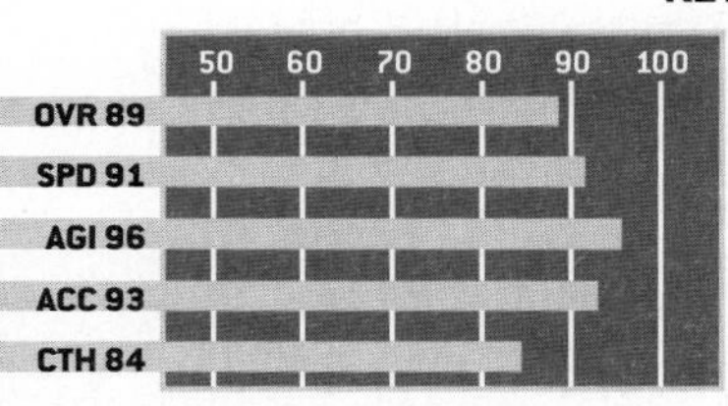

- Samuel takes a lot of risks as a lockdown corner. He also makes a lot of plays for the Falcons.
- With an 84 CTH rating Samuel has some of the best hands among CBs in the game.

PRE-GAME SETUP

KEY RUNNING SUBSTITUTION

Who: HB Jacquizz Rodgers

Where: Backup HB

Why: Rodgers doesn't have top-end speed, but he is one of the quickest HBs in the game.

Key Stats: 94 AGI, 96 ACC

KEY PASSING SUBSTITUTION

Who: TE Chase Coffman

Where: Backup TE

Why: Coffman is 6'6" and has great hands. He gives the Falcons offense the flexibility to use two-tight-end formations.

Key Stats: 90 CIT

KEY RUN DEFENSE SUBSTITUTION

Who: DT Travian Robertson

Where: #3 DT for running situations

Why: Use Robertson for running situations and in your goal line formations.

Key Stats: 90 STR

KEY PASS DEFENSE SUBSTITUTION

Who: CB Robert Alford

Where: #2 CB

Why: Alford is a rookie, but he should see time playing nickel CB. His speed alone is reason for him to see playing time.

Key Stats: 93 SPD, 96 AGI, 95 ACC

OFFENSIVE DEPTH CHART

POS	FIRST NAME	LAST NAME	OVR
QB	Matt	Ryan	94
QB	Sean	Renfree	70
QB	Dominique	Davis	68
HB	Steven	Jackson	89
HB	Jacquizz	Rodgers	81
HB	Jason	Snelling	74
HB	Antone	Smith	65
HB	Josh	Vaughan	64
FB	Patrick	DiMarco	76
FB	Bradie	Ewing	65
WR	Roddy	White	93
WR	Julio	Jones	92
WR	Harry	Douglas	76
WR	Drew	Davis	66
WR	Kevin	Cone	63
WR	James	Rodgers	61
WR	Tim	Toone	59
TE	Tony	Gonzalez	95
TE	Chase	Coffman	68
TE	Levine	Toilolo	65
TE	Tommy	Gallarda	64
TE	Josh	Harris	57
LT	Sam	Baker	80
LT	Alec	Savoie	59
LG	Justin	Blalock	82
LG	Jacques	McClendon	71
C	Peter	Konz	72
C	Joe	Hawley	70
RG	Garrett	Reynolds	74
RG	Phillipkeith	Manley	64
RG	Harland	Gunn	62
RT	Lamar	Holmes	72
RT	Mike	Johnson	68

DEFENSIVE DEPTH CHART

POS	FIRST NAME	LAST NAME	OVR
LE	Kroy	Biermann	74
LE	Cliff	Matthews	68
LE	Malliciah	Goodman	67
RE	Osi	Umenyiora	84
RE	Jonathan	Massaquoi	65
RE	Stansly	Maponga	64
DT	Jonathan	Babineaux	85
DT	Peria	Jerry	77
DT	Corey	Peters	74
DT	Travian	Robertson	66
DT	Micanor	Regis	63
LOLB	Stephen	Nicholas	78
LOLB	Nick	Clancy	61
MLB	Akeem	Dent	77
MLB	Pat	Schiller	60
MLB	Brian	Banks	57
ROLB	Sean	Weatherspoon	83
ROLB	Robert	James	67
CB	Asante	Samuel	89
CB	Desmond	Trufant	77
CB	Robert	McClain	73
CB	Dominique	Franks	72
CB	Robert	Alford	72
CB	Terrence	Johnson	63
CB	Peyton	Thompson	63
FS	Thomas	DeCoud	84
FS	Charles	Mitchell	69
FS	Kemal	Ishmael	68
SS	William	Moore	87
SS	Zeke	Motta	71
SS	Shann	Schillinger	67

SPECIAL TEAMS DEPTH CHART

POS	FIRST NAME	LAST NAME	OVR
K	Matt	Bryant	87
P	Matt	Bosher	81

Atlanta Falcons

RECOMMENDED OFFENSIVE RUN FORMATION: STRONG CLOSE (2 HB, 1 TE, 2 WR)

PRO TIPS

> CHASE COFFMAN HAS 90 CIT, WHICH IS ELITE FOR TIGHT ENDS.
> QB DOMINIQUE DAVIS HAS 83 SPD AND CAN BE USED TO SCRAMBLE FOR YARDS.
> HB JASON SNELLING HAS 92 TRK AND IS THE TEAM'S BEST TRUCKING HB.

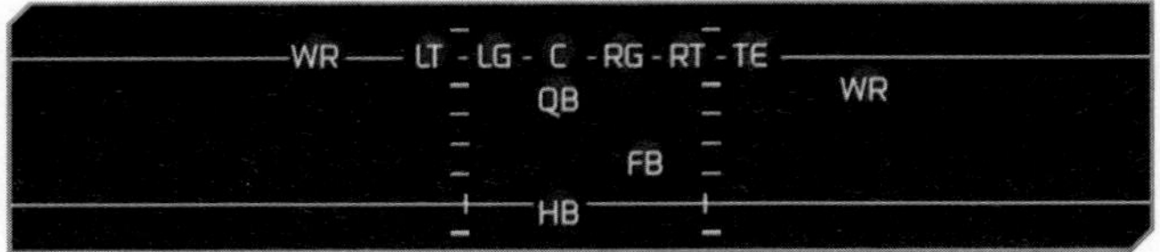

RUN LEFT

STEVEN JACKSON CAN RUN OVER ANY DEFENDER.

RUN MIDDLE

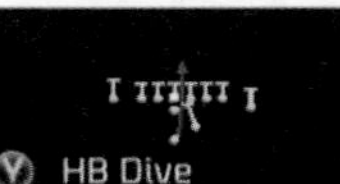

JACKSON IS BEST USED RUNNING UP THE MIDDLE.

RUN RIGHT

KEEP THE RUN INSIDE EVEN ON OUTSIDE RUNS WITH JACKSON.

ATLANTA FALCONS RUNNING PLAY CALL SHEET

LEGEND: Inside Run | Outside Run | Shotgun Run | QB Run

1ST DOWN RUNS	2ND AND SHORT	3RD AND SHORT	GOAL LINE RUNS	2ND AND LONG	3RD AND LONG
Singleback Ace—HB Toss Strg	I-Form Tight Pair—Iso	Singleback Ace—HB Dive	Full House Normal Wide—HB Slam	Gun Split Offset—Power O	Gun Bunch Wk—HB Base
I-Form Pro—HB Blast	Singleback Ace—ATL Zone Wk	Weak Pro Twins—Strong Stretch	Goal Line—HB Dive	I-Form Pro—HB Draw	Gun Trio Falcon—HB Draw
Strong Pro—Power O	Strong Pro—HB Blast	Full House Normal Wide—HB Sweep	Goal Line—Power O	Gun Bunch Wk—HB Mid Draw	Gun Tight Flex—HB Draw

ATLANTA FALCONS PASSING PLAY CALL SHEET

LEGEND: Base Play | Man Beater | Zone Beater | Blitz Beater

1ST DOWN PLAY	2ND AND SHORT	3RD AND SHORT	GOAL LINE PASSING	2ND AND LONG	3RD AND LONG
Gun Trey Open—Y-Drag	Gun Trio Falcon—ATL Stick	Singleback Bunch—Falcon HB Angle	Goal Line—PA Spot	Singleback Tight Doubles—Bench Switch	Gun Wing Trips—Y-Trail
Gun Tight Flex—HB Option	Gun Split Offset—Close Mesh	Singleback Ace Pair—HB Slip Screen	Goal Line—PA Power O	Singleback Y-Trips—Y Trail	Gun Wing Trips—Slot Drive
Gun Trio Falcon—Mesh Corner	Gun Doubles On—Smash Corner	Gun Spread Y-Flex—HB Slip Screen	Gun Empty Base—Spacing	Singleback Y-Trips—Four Verticals	Gun Bunch Wk—Bunch Trail

In these play call sheets we picked the best plays for specific situations so that you will have a play for every down and distance.

OFFENSE

RECOMMENDED OFFENSIVE PASS FORMATION: GUN TIGHT FLEX (1 HB, 0 TE, 4 WR)

PRO TIPS

- SUB IN TE TONY GONZALEZ AS THE THIRD WR.
- SUB IN TE CHASE COFFMAN AS THE FOURTH WR.
- HB JACQUIZZ RODGERS IS A GREAT CHANGE-OF-PACE HB FOR THIRD DOWN SITUATIONS.

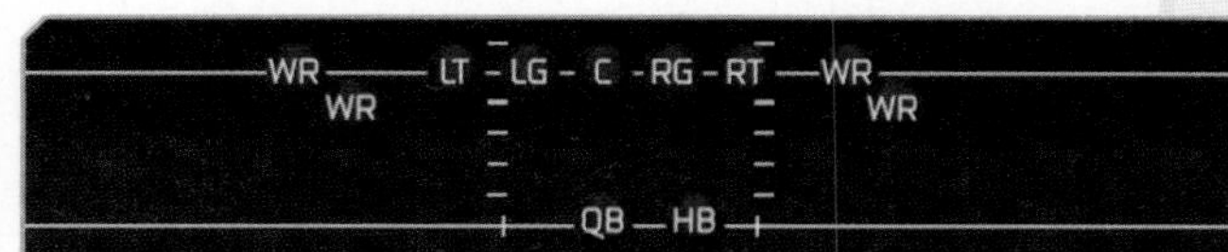

BASE PLAY

SETUP

- NONE

- Against zone look to the crossing mesh routes as well as the deep post.
- Against man-to-man look to the sideline wheel and the HB wheel routes.

MAN BEATER

SETUP

- OPTION THE HB
- MOTION THE LEFT SLOT WR TO THE LEFT

- User-catch the motioned WR down the sideline. This is extremely difficult to defend.
- The underneath curl routes and HB option are your secondary options.

ZONE BEATER

SETUP

- STREAK BOTH OUTSIDE WRS
- OPTION THE HB

- Against Cover 2 and Cover 3 zones look to the corner routes.
- Against Cover 4 zones look to the HB out of the backfield.

BLITZ BEATER

SETUP

- BLOCK THE HB

- Against zone blitzes look to the flat routes
- Against man blitzes look to the short curls.

Atlanta Falcons

RECOMMENDED DEFENSIVE RUN FORMATION: 4-3 ODD

PRO TIPS

> DT TRAVIAN ROBERTSON HAS AN 88 STR RATING AND WILL HELP WITH RUN SUPPORT ON THE DEFENSIVE LINE.

> SS WILLIAM MOORE HAS THE TEAM'S BEST POW RATING WITH A 90.

> MLB AKEEM DENT IS THE TEAM'S BEST TACKLER, WITH A 89 TAK RATING.

RUN DEFENSE

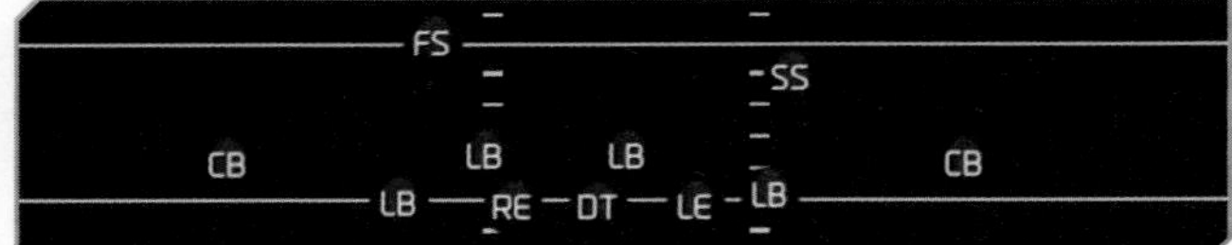

RUN DEFENSE LEFT

SETUP > SHIFT LINEBACKERS LEFT

RUN DEFENSE MIDDLE

SETUP > PINCH DEFENSIVE LINE

RUN DEFENSE RIGHT

SETUP > SHIFT LINEBACKERS RIGHT

ATLANTA FALCONS DEFENSIVE RUN PLAY CALL SHEET

1ST DOWN RUN DEFENSE	2ND AND SHORT	3RD AND SHORT	GOAL LINE RUN DEFENSE	2ND AND LONG	3RD AND LONG
4-3 Stack—Cover 1 Robber	4-3 Over Plus—Cover 1	4-3 Under—Engage Eight	Goal Line 5-3-3—Jam Cover 1	4-3 Under—2 Man Under	Dime Normal—2 Man Under
4-3 Stack—Cover 3 Cloud	4-3 Over Plus—Cover 2	4-3 Under—Sam Blitz 2	Goal Line 5-3-3—Flat Buzz	4-3 Under—Snake 3 Deep	Dime Normal—Cover 2 Sink

ATLANTA FALCONS DEFENSIVE PASS PLAY CALL SHEET

1ST DOWN PLAY	2ND AND SHORT	3RD AND SHORT	GOAL LINE PASSING	2ND AND LONG	3RD AND LONG
Nickel Strong—Robber	Nickel Strong—2 Man Under	Nickel Normal—Sugar Blitz	Goal Line 6-3-2—GL Man	Nickel Normal—Under Smoke	Dime Normal—MLB Blitz
Nickel Strong—Cover 2 Sink	Nickel Strong—Cover 3	Nickel Normal—Sugar 2 Buzz	Goal Line 6-3-2—GL Zone	Nickel Normal—Buck Slant 3	Dime Normal—Fox Fire Zone

LEGEND: Man Coverage | Zone Coverage | Man Blitz | Zone Blitz

In these play call sheets we picked the best plays for specific situations so that you will have a play for every down and distance.

DEFENSE

RECOMMENDED DEFENSIVE PASS FORMATION: NICKEL 3-3-5

PRO TIPS

> PLACE CB ASANTE SAMUEL ON YOUR OPPONENT'S BEST WR.

> USE CB ROBERT ALFORD TO COVER YOUR OPPONENT'S FASTEST WR.

> CB DESMOND TRUFANT SHOULD BE USED AS YOUR 2ND CB.

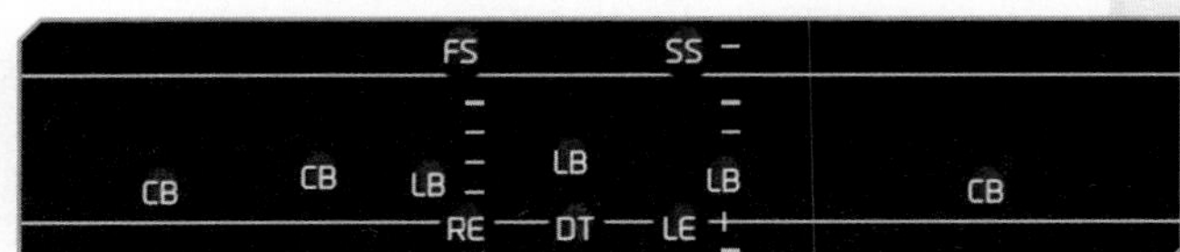

MAN COVERAGE

SETUP

> SHIFT DEFENSIVE LINE LEFT AND CRASH OUT

> SHIFT LINEBACKERS LEFT

> The defensive line shifts and crash will create a stunt that will confuse the offensive line.

> The confusion will result in one of our pass rushers getting free after the QB.

ZONE COVERAGE

SETUP

> SHIFT DEFENSIVE LINE LEFT AND CRASH OUT

> SHIFT LINEBACKERS LEFT

> BLITZ THE SS

> This is the same setup as the man-to-man setup, but we have changed the coverage behind the pressure.

> This is a great play call for third and long situations.

MAN BLITZ

SETUP

> MAN ALIGN

> PRESS COVERAGE

> GLOBAL BLITZ ALL LINEBACKERS

> User-control the nickel corner over the middle of the field.

> The safeties have a good chance of getting beaten off the press.

ZONE BLITZ

SETUP

> PRESS COVERAGE

> GLOBAL BLITZ ALL LINEBACKERS

> If you are getting beaten to the flat, place both hook zone defenders into flats.

> When you want to blitz on third and long, place both hook zone defenders in deep zones.

> We like to mix this setup in to confuse our opponents and throw off their timing.

San Francisco 49ers

2012 TEAM RANKINGS

1st NFC West (11-4-1)

PASSING OFFENSE: **23rd**
RUSHING OFFENSE: **4th**
PASSING DEFENSE: **4th**
RUSHING DEFENSE: **4th**

2012 TEAM LEADERS

PASSING: **Colin Kaepernick: 1,814**
RUSHING: **Frank Gore: 1,214**
RECEIVING: **Michael Crabtree: 1,105**
TACKLES: **NaVorro Bowman: 148**
SACKS: **Aldon Smith: 19.5**
INTS: **Dashon Goldson: 3**

KEY ADDITIONS

QB Colt McCoy
WR Anquan Boldin
K Phil Dawson

KEY ROOKIES

HB Marcus Lattimore
TE Vance McDonald
FS Eric Reid
ROLB Corey Lemonier

CONNECTED FRANCHISE MODE STRATEGY

CFM TEAM RATING: **84**
OFFENSIVE SCHEME: **Power Run**
DEFENSIVE SCHEME: **Base 3-4**
STRENGTHS: **QB, HB, WR, LB, RE, LT**
WEAKNESSES: **LE, DT, FS**

SCHEDULE

1	Sep 8	4:25 PM ET		PACKERS
2	Sep 15	8:30 PM ET	AT	SEAHAWKS
3	Sep 22	4:25 PM ET		COLTS
4	Sep 26	8:25 PM ET	AT	RAMS
5	Oct 6	8:30 PM ET		TEXANS
6	Oct 13	4:25 PM ET		CARDINALS
7	Oct 20	4:05 PM ET	AT	TITANS
8	Oct 27	1:00 PM ET	AT	JAGUARS
9	BYE			
10	Nov 10	4:05 PM ET		PANTHERS
11	Nov 17	4:25 PM ET	AT	SAINTS
12	Nov 25	8:40 PM ET	AT	REDSKINS
13	Dec 1	4:05 PM ET		RAMS
14	Dec 8	4:25 PM ET		SEAHAWKS
15	Dec 15	1:00 PM ET	AT	BUCCANEERS
16	Dec 23	8:40 PM ET		FALCONS
17	Dec 29	4:25 PM ET	AT	CARDINALS

FRANCHISE OVERVIEW

49ERS GAMEPLAY RATING

91

> SEE THE INSIDE BACK COVER FOR A QUICK REFERENCE TO THE GAME ABBREVIATIONS USED THROUGHOUT THIS GUIDE.

> IMPROVE WITH YOUR TEAM BY VISITING PRIMAGAMES.COM/MADDENNFL25 FOR MORE INFORMATION AND HOW-TO VIDEOS.

OFFENSIVE SCOUTING REPORT

> Invest in a quality backup QB. If Kaepernick goes down you will struggle with Colt McCoy. Use your first-round draft pick on a stud rookie QB.

> Kicker Phil Dawson is accurate with 90 KAC, but he won't be kicking any 60-yarders with 87 KPW. Scan the free agent market for a kicker with a big leg or wait for the draft.

> Ricardo Lockette is the 49ers' only true speed receiver. Look for speed late in your first draft.

DEFENSIVE SCOUTING REPORT

> Starting SS Donte Whitner turns 29 at the end of your first season and will hit the free agent market expecting to get paid top dollar for being one of the league's best. Consider using him as trade bait early in your first season or look to acquire a rookie in the draft.

> RE Justin Smith becomes a free agent at the end of the first season. He is the anchor of the defense, so pay attention to beast defensive linemen in free agency and the draft.

> Rookie DE Corey Lemonier makes LOLB Ahmad Brooks or LOLB Parys Haralson expendable. If you can get good value for either player pull the trigger and start the rookie. He has a ton of upside.

OWNER & COACH PROFILES

JED YORK

LEGACY SCORE: 625
OFF. SCHEME: Power Run
DEF. SCHEME: Base 3-4

JIM HARBAUGH

LEVEL: 21
LEGACY SCORE: 1300
OFF. SCHEME: Power Run
DEF. SCHEME: Base 3-4

TEAM OVERVIEW

KEY PLAYERS

QB #7

COLIN KAEPERNICK

KEY RATINGS

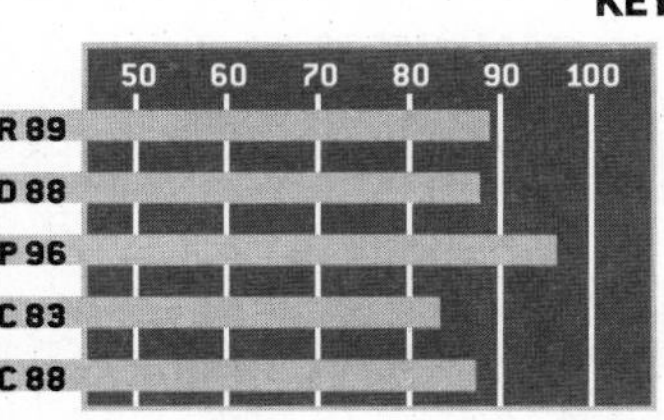

> Use a playbook that has option runs to take advantage of Kaepernick's speed.

> Air the ball out downfield to speedy WR Ricardo Lockette (96 SPD).

> Kaepernick has great athleticism but will need upgrades to his throw accuracy ratings.

MLB #52

PATRICK WILLIS

KEY RATINGS

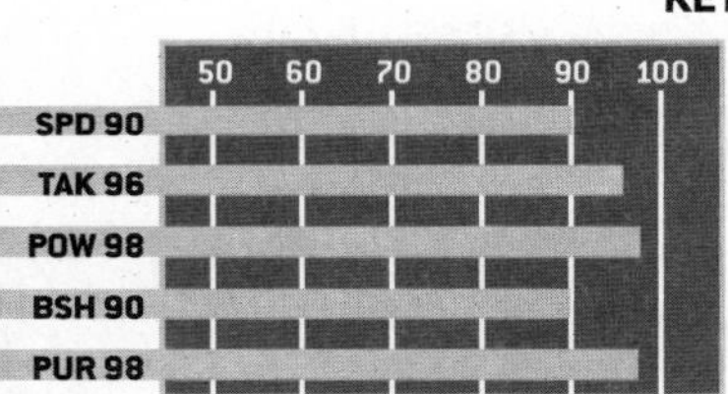

> User-control Willis and take advantage of his 98 POW.

> Willis is the single-most dominant defender in *Madden NFL 25*.

> Willis has no real weakness.

> Look to upgrade his 88 AGI.

PRE-GAME SETUP

KEY RUNNING SUBSTITUTION

Who: HB LaMichael James

Where: Backup HB

Why: James is one of the league's best backup HBs. He has great speed and lateral movement. Spell Gore with James.

Key Stats: 93 SPD, 96 AGI, 97 ACC, 93 ELU

KEY PASSING SUBSTITUTION

Who: WR Ricardo Lockette

Where: Slot WR

Why: Lockette is the 49ers' only true speed threat. Get him in the game to stretch defenses vertically.

Key Stats: 6'2", 96 SPD, 93 ACC, 94 JMP

KEY RUN DEFENSE SUBSTITUTION

Who: ROLB Corey Lemonier

Where: Starting DE

Why: Lemonier has 90 POW and 85 SPD. He is a must-start for this defense. You will be the beneficiary of hit stick fumbles courtesy of one Corey Lemonier.

Key Stats: 6'3", 85 SPD, 90 ACC, 90 POW

KEY PASS DEFENSE SUBSTITUTION

Who: CB Chris Culliver

Where: Nickel CB

Why: Culliver is a great nickel CB who can cover the faster slot WRs in the game.

Key Stats: 95 SPD, 92 JMP, 70 CTH

OFFENSIVE DEPTH CHART

POS	FIRST NAME	LAST NAME	OVR
QB	Colin	Kaepernick	89
QB	Colt	McCoy	73
QB	Scott	Tolzien	65
QB	B.J.	Daniels	63
HB	Frank	Gore	93
HB	Kendall	Hunter	79
HB	LaMichael	James	74
HB	Marcus	Lattimore	70
HB	Anthony	Dixon	68
HB	Jewel	Hampton	65
HB	D.J.	Harper	64
FB	Bruce	Miller	88
FB	Will	Tukuafu	65
WR	Michael	Crabtree	90
WR	Anquan	Boldin	88
WR	Mario	Manningham	81
WR	Kyle	Williams	72
WR	A.J.	Jenkins	71
WR	Quinton	Patton	69
WR	Kassim	Osgood	67
WR	Marlon	Moore	66
WR	Ricardo	Lockette	65
WR	Chad	Hall	65
TE	Vernon	Davis	94
TE	Vance	McDonald	71
TE	Garrett	Celek	67
TE	Brian	Jennings	64
TE	Demarcus	Dobbs	61
LT	Joe	Staley	96
LT	Kenny	Wiggins	56
LG	Mike	Iupati	95
LG	Joe	Looney	63
C	Jonathan	Goodwin	85
C	Daniel	Kilgore	64
RG	Alex	Boone	89
RG	Adam	Snyder	73
RT	Anthony	Davis	90
RT	Al	Netter	71

DEFENSIVE DEPTH CHART

POS	FIRST NAME	LAST NAME	OVR
LE	Ray	McDonald	89
LE	Tank	Carradine	75
LE	Tony	Jerod-Eddie	63
RE	Justin	Smith	94
RE	Glenn	Dorsey	82
DT	Ian	Williams	73
DT	Lamar	Divens	67
DT	Quinton	Dial	64
LOLB	Ahmad	Brooks	89
LOLB	Parys	Haralson	82
LOLB	Darius	Fleming	66
MLB	Patrick	Willis	97
MLB	NaVorro	Bowman	93
MLB	Dan	Skuta	68
MLB	Michael	Wilhoite	62
MLB	Nathan	Stupar	60
ROLB	Aldon	Smith	95
ROLB	Corey	Lemonier	68
ROLB	Nick	Moody	65
ROLB	Cam	Johnson	65
CB	Carlos	Rogers	90
CB	Tarell	Brown	88
CB	Nnamdi	Asomugha	83
CB	Chris	Culliver	78
CB	Tramaine	Brock	75
CB	Perrish	Cox	71
FS	Eric	Reid	76
FS	Craig	Dahl	74
FS	C.J.	Spillman	69
SS	Donte	Whitner	86
SS	Darcel	McBath	72
SS	Trenton	Robinson	69

SPECIAL TEAMS DEPTH CHART

POS	FIRST NAME	LAST NAME	OVR
K	Phil	Dawson	89
P	Andy	Lee	95

San Francisco 49ers

RECOMMENDED OFFENSIVE RUN FORMATION: I-FORM TIGHT (2 HB, 2 TE, 1 WR)

PRO TIPS

- USE FB BRUCE MILLER AND HIS 79 RBS AND 75 RBF TO LEAD THE WAY ON THE GROUND.
- MILLER ALSO HAS 74 CIT, WHICH MAKES HIM A RECEIVING THREAT OUT OF THE BACKFIELD.
- USE PLAY ACTION TO TARGET TE VERNON DAVIS DOWNFIELD.
- SUB IN ROOKIE TE VANCE MCDONALD AT WR TO LOAD THE FIELD UP WITH BLOCKERS.

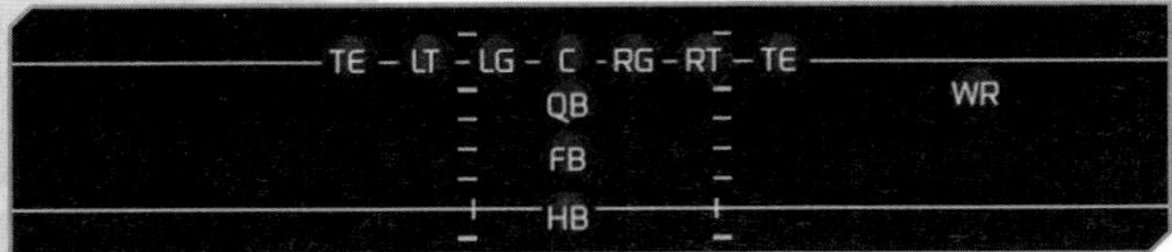

RUN LEFT

WAIT FOR THE PULLING BLOCKERS TO CLEAR THE WAY.

RUN MIDDLE

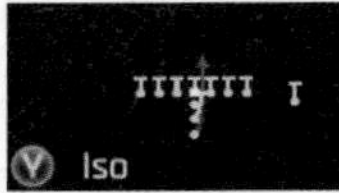

PATIENCE IS KEY WHEN RUNNING UP THE MIDDLE.

RUN RIGHT

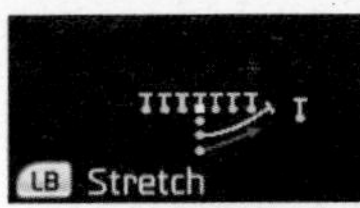

HIT THE EDGE AS FAST AS YOU CAN.

SAN FRANCISCO 49ERS RUNNING PLAYCALL SHEET

LEGEND: Inside Run | Outside Run | Shotgun Run | QB Run

1ST DOWN RUNS	2ND AND SHORT	3RD AND SHORT	GOAL LINE RUNS	2ND AND LONG	3RD AND LONG
Singleback Twin TE Flex—Counter Weak	Pistol Strong—Inside Zone Split	Goal Line—HB Dive	Weak Tight Pair—FB Dive	Gun Bunch HB Str—HB Draw	Pistol Full House TE—Niners Read Option
I-Form Tight—HB Blast	Singleback Ace Close—Tight Slots Wham	I-Form Tight—Stretch	I-Form Pro—FB Dive	I-Form Pro—HB Lead Draw	Pistol Ace Twins—Read Option
Pistol Full House TE—Counter Lead	Singleback Flex—HB Slam	Strong Tight Pair—HB Toss	I-Form Niners Heavy—Off Tackle	Gun Y-Trips—Inverted Veer	Empty Trey Flex—QB Draw

SAN FRANCISCO 49ERS PASSING PLAYCALL SHEET

LEGEND: Base Play | Man Beater | Zone Beater | Blitz Beater

1ST DOWN PLAY	2ND AND SHORT	3RD AND SHORT	GOAL LINE PASSING	2ND AND LONG	3RD AND LONG
Gun Bunch HB Str—Y-Trail	Gun Empty Trey Flex—Y Stick	Singleback Ace Pair—Drive	Goal Line—PA Power O	I-Form Pro—X Post	Gun Trey Open—Trail Shake
Gun Doubles On—HB Circle	Gun Trey Open—Stick N Nod	Singleback Bunch—Flanker Drive	Singleback Ace Close—Niners Pivot Seam	Singleback Jumbo Pair—Y Stick	Gun Trey Open—Four Verticals
Gun Y-Trips Wk—Y-Sail	Pistol Ace Twins—Niner Post Wheel	Gun Bunch Str—HB Slip Screen	I-Form Tight Pair—Niner Spacing	Pistol Strong PA Flood	Pistol Full House—PA X Post

In these play call sheets we picked the best plays for specific situations so that you will have a play for every down and distance.

OFFENSE

RECOMMENDED OFFENSIVE PASS FORMATION: GUN BUNCH HB STR (1 HB, 1 TE, 3 WR)

PRO TIPS

- HB LAMICHAEL JAMES AND HB KENDALL HUNTER ARE BETTER PASSING OPTIONS THAN HB FRANK GORE. GET THEM IN THE GAME FOR MORE SPEED.
- CONSIDER PLACING WR RICARDO LOCKETTE AS THE SOLO WR IN THIS FORMATION. ISOLATING HIM WILL GIVE HIS 96 SPD HOME-RUN CHANCES.
- KEEP WR ANQUAN BOLDIN AND WR MICHAEL CRABTREE ON THE FIELD TOGETHER. THEY BOTH HAVE ELITE CIT RATINGS.

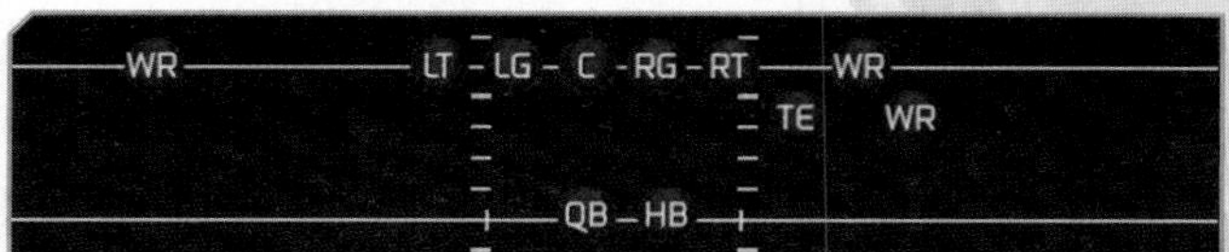

BASE PLAY

SETUP

- STREAK THE FAR LEFT WR
- STREAK THE RIGHT SLOT WR

- The HB is your number one option. Target him right away.
- Against zone coverage look to drag WR.

MAN BEATER

SETUP

- WHEEL THE HB
- STREAK THE FAR LEFT WR

- The TE running the angle route torches man coverage.
- The formation alignment allows the HB to beat his defender.

ZONE BEATER

SETUP

- BLOCK THE HB
- DRAG THE RIGHT SLOT WR

- Against blitzing zone defenses the sideline wheel will be open.
- This play can beat any zone defense. Let the routes develop downfield.

BLITZ BEATER

SETUP

- BLOCK THE TE

- If the defense isn't blitzing you will see DEs recognize the play.
- Save this play for big moments in games.

San Francisco 49ers

RECOMMENDED DEFENSIVE RUN FORMATION: 3-4 SOLID

PRO TIPS

> THE 3-4 SOLID FORMATION CALLS FOR OUR THREE BIGGEST DEFENDERS TO LINE UP DIRECTLY OVER THE CENTER AND TWO GUARDS.

> LOOK TO USE RE JUSTIN SMITH, LE RAY MCDONALD, AND RE GLENN DORSEY TO CLOG THE MIDDLE OF THE FIELD.

> START ALDON SMITH AND AHMAD BROOKS AT OLB AND USE PATRICK WILLIS AND NAVORRO BOWMAN AT MLB

> IN THE SECONDARY USE CARLOS ROGERS AND NNAMDI ASOMUGHA AT CB AND ERIC REID AND DONTE WHITNER AS SAFETIES.

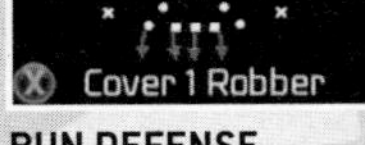

RUN DEFENSE

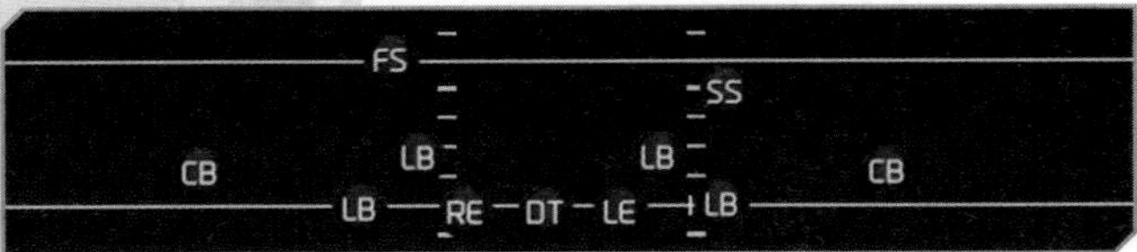

RUN DEFENSE LEFT

SETUP > SHIFT LINEBACKERS LEFT

RUN DEFENSE MIDDLE

SETUP > PINCH DEFENSIVE LINE

RUN DEFENSE RIGHT

SETUP > SHIFT LINEBACKERS RIGHT

SAN FRANCISCO 49ERS DEFENSIVE RUN PLAYCALL SHEET

1ST DOWN RUN DEFENSE	2ND AND SHORT	3RD AND SHORT	GOAL LINE RUN DEFENSE	2ND AND LONG	3RD AND LONG
3-4 Solid—Cover 1 Robber	3-4 Solid—2 Man Under	3-4 Over—Cat Blitz	Goal Line 5-3-3—Jam Cover 1	Nickel 2-4-5 Even—2 Man Under	Nickel 3-3-5—2 Man Under
3-4 Solid—Cover 3	3-4 Solid—Cover 4	3-4 Over—FS Zone Blitz	Goal Line 5-3-3—Flat Buzz	Nickel 2-4-5 Even—Cover 4	Nickel 3-3-5—Cover 4

SAN FRANCISCO 49ERS DEFENSIVE PASS PLAYCALL SHEET

1ST DOWN PLAY	2ND AND SHORT	3RD AND SHORT	GOAL LINE PASSING	2ND AND LONG	3RD AND LONG
Sub 2-3-6 Sam—2 Man LB Blitz	Sub 2-3-6 Sam—Cover 1 LB Spy	Sub 2-3-6—Cover 1 Spy	Goal Line 6-3-2—GL Man	Nickel 3-3-5 LB Dogs	Sub 2-3-6—Over Storm Brave
Sub 2-3-6 Sam—Cover 3	Sub 2-3-6 Sam—Cover 6	Sub 2-3-6—Slant Zone 2	Goal Line 6-3-2—GL Zone	Nickel 3-3-5 Loop Crash 3	Sub 2-3-6—Under Smoke 2

LEGEND: Man Coverage | Zone Coverage | Man Blitz | Zone Blitz

In these play call sheets we picked the best plays for specific situations so that you will have a play for every down and distance.

DEFENSE

RECOMMENDED DEFENSIVE PASS FORMATION: NICKEL 2-4-5 EVEN

PRO TIPS

> THIS FORMATION ALLOWS YOU TO SUB IN LINEBACKERS AT DE, SO YOU COULD POTENTIALLY HAVE SIX LINEBACKERS ON THE FIELD.

> THE 49ERS HAVE SIX STUD LINEBACKERS, SO BE SURE TO SUB THEM IN AT DE.

> FOR EXTRA RUN SUPPORT USE RE JUSTIN SMITH AND LE RAY MCDONALD AT DE.

> USE CB CHRIS CULLIVER AS THE EXTRA CB IN THIS FORMATION.

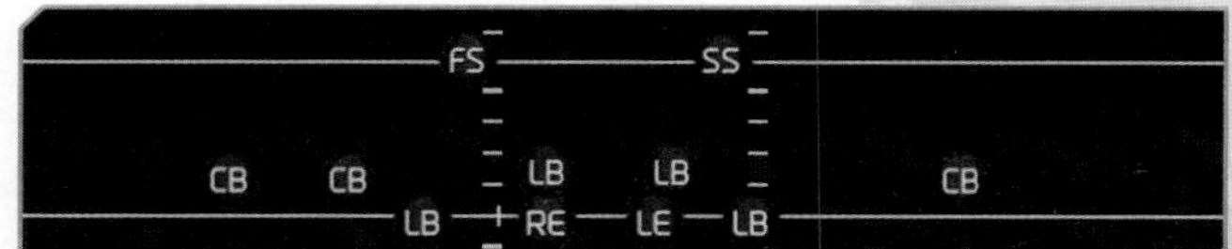

MAN COVERAGE

SETUP

> USER-CONTROL THE MLB
> QB SPY THE LEFT DT

> The 2 Man Under defenses have the best press in the game.

> This allows your pass rushers extra time to get after the QB.

ZONE COVERAGE

SETUP

> USER-CONTROL THE MLB
> HOOK ZONE THE LEFT DT

> Use Cover 4 to mix up your play calling with the 2 Man Under.

> This is a great defense for third and long situations.

MAN BLITZ

SETUP

> PRESS COVERAGE
> USER-CONTROL THE MLB

> Pressure will be quick, so be ready for a throw to the flats.

> If your corners get beaten off the line of scrimmage it will result in a big play.

ZONE BLITZ

SETUP

> PRESS COVERAGE
> GLOBAL BLITZ ALL LINEBACKERS

> User-control the deep FS over the middle of the field and jump any routes over the middle.

> The flats and deep seams will be very tender with this play.

New York Giants

2012 TEAM RANKINGS

2nd NFC East (9-7-0)

PASSING OFFENSE: **12th**
RUSHING OFFENSE: **14th**
PASSING DEFENSE: **28th**
RUSHING DEFENSE: **25th**

2012 TEAM LEADERS

PASSING: **Eli Manning: 3,948**
RUSHING: **Ahmad Bradshaw: 1,015**
RECEIVING: **Victor Cruz: 1,092**
TACKLES: **Antrel Rolle, 96**
SACKS: **Jason Pierre-Paul: 6.5**
INTS: **Stevie Brown: 8**

KEY ADDITIONS

WR Louis Murphy
TE Brandon Myers
DT Cullen Jenkins

KEY ROOKIES

RT Justin Pugh
DT Johnathan Hankins
RE Damontre Moore

CONNECTED FRANCHISE MODE STRATEGY

CFM TEAM RATING: **80**
OFFENSIVE SCHEME: **Balanced Offense**
DEFENSIVE SCHEME: **Attacking 4-3**
STRENGTHS: **QB, WR, LT, RG, LE, RE**
WEAKNESSES: **HB, LOLB, MLB, ROLB, CB**

SCHEDULE

1	Sep 8	8:30 PM ET	AT	COWBOYS
2	Sep 15	4:25 PM ET		BRONCOS
3	Sep 22	1:00 PM ET	AT	PANTHERS
4	Sep 29	1:00 PM ET	AT	CHIEFS
5	Oct 6	1:00 PM ET		EAGLES
6	Oct 10	8:25 PM ET	AT	BEARS
7	Oct 21	8:40 PM ET		VIKINGS
8	Oct 27	1:00 PM ET	AT	EAGLES
9	BYE			
10	Nov 10	1:00 PM ET		RAIDERS
11	Nov 17	8:30 PM ET		PACKERS
12	Nov 24	4:25 PM ET		COWBOYS
13	Dec 1	8:30 PM ET	AT	REDSKINS
14	Dec 8	4:25 PM ET	AT	CHARGERS
15	Dec 15	1:00 PM ET		SEAHAWKS
16	Dec 22	4:05 PM ET	AT	LIONS
17	Dec 29	1:00 PM ET		REDSKINS

FRANCHISE OVERVIEW

GIANTS GAMEPLAY RATING

84

> SEE THE INSIDE BACK COVER FOR A QUICK REFERENCE TO THE GAME ABBREVIATIONS USED THROUGHOUT THIS GUIDE.

> IMPROVE WITH YOUR TEAM BY VISITING PRIMAGAMES.COM/MADDENNFL25 FOR MORE INFORMATION AND HOW-TO VIDEOS.

OFFENSIVE SCOUTING REPORT

QB Eli Manning can make every throw on the field. Focus on adding in a mobile QB to this offense. Look for one during free agency and in the later rounds of the draft.

The Giants have two HBs that have potential to turn into stars. If you want a more explosive HB then upgrade David Wilson. If you want an HB who will run over people upgrade Andre Brown.

Victor Cruz recently signed an extension, whereas Hakeem Nicks has a contract ending at the end of the season. Do whatever it takes to keep them on your team. Also focus on WR Rueben Randle, as he has the ability to become a dominant receiver in this league. Upgrade Randle's AGI and ACC.

DEFENSIVE SCOUTING REPORT

Since the Giants' magical Super Bowl run during the 2007–2008 season they have been known for having DEs who get after the QB. This still holds true, but the Giants defense is aging, and they lost RE Osi Umenyiora to the Falcons. It's almost rebuilding time.

The most important thing you can do to improve this Giants defense is to focus on your linebackers. LOLBs Keith Rivers and Aaron Curry are both former first-round top 10 picks. We recommend signing them both to five-year deals and working on upgrading them to see if you can turn their careers around.

The Giants have five CBs who have potential to be number one corners. The problem with this secondary is that there isn't enough playing time for everyone. We recommend focusing on Prince Amukamara and Jayron Hosley.

OWNER & COACH PROFILES

STEVE TISCH

LEGACY SCORE: 4225
OFF. SCHEME: Balanced Offense
DEF. SCHEME: Attacking 4-3

TOM COUGHLIN

LEVEL: 29
LEGACY SCORE: 7800
OFF. SCHEME: Balanced Offense
DEF. SCHEME: Attacking 4-3

TEAM OVERVIEW

KEY PLAYERS

QB #10

ELI MANNING

KEY RATINGS

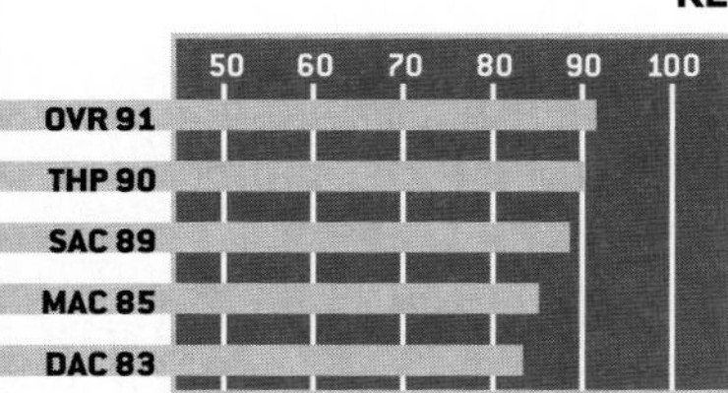

- Manning leads his team with gutsy play and big-time throws.
- Air the ball out to Victor Cruz and Hakeem Nicks. Don't forget about Rueben Randle.

RE #90

JASON PIERRE-PAUL

KEY RATINGS

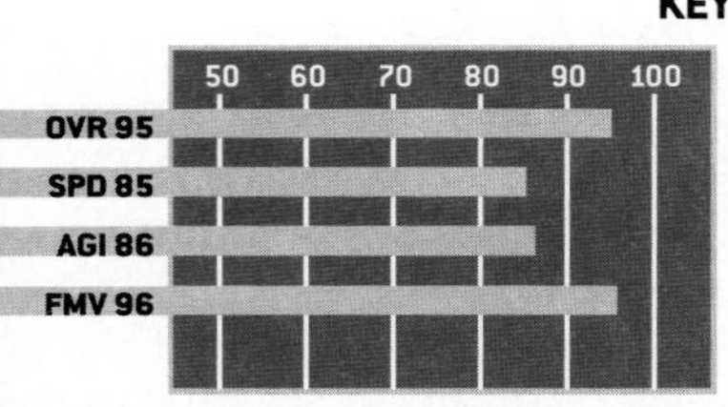

- Jason Pierre-Paul is an up-and-coming pass rusher who has taken the league by storm.
- JPP can't be stopped off the edge. Get him in one-on-one situations and he will get to the QB.

PRE-GAME SETUP

KEY RUNNING SUBSTITUTION

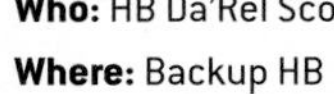

Who: HB Da'Rel Scott

Where: Backup HB

Why: Scott is a great backup whose speed is similar to that of starter David Wilson.

Key Stats: 96 SPD, 94 ACC

KEY PASSING SUBSTITUTION

Who: WR Jerrel Jernigan

Where: Backup to WR Victor Cruz

Why: Jernigan might not be the superstar that Cruz is, but he has the ratings to fill in nicely if needed.

Key Stats: 95 AGI, 94 ACC

KEY RUN DEFENSE SUBSTITUTION

Who: DT Shaun Rogers

Where: #2 DT

Why: Rogers was once one of the best DTs in the league. He still can be a playmaker.

Key Stats: 94 STR

KEY PASS DEFENSE SUBSTITUTION

Who: CB Jayron Hosley

Where: #3 CB

Why: Hosley is one of the Giants' fastest defenders. Use him to blitz off the edge and cover opposing teams' fastest WRs.

Key Stats: 92 SPD

OFFENSIVE DEPTH CHART

POS	FIRST NAME	LAST NAME	OVR
QB	Eli	Manning	91
QB	David	Carr	74
QB	Ryan	Nassib	72
HB	David	Wilson	78
HB	Andre	Brown	76
HB	Ryan	Torain	71
HB	Da'Rel	Scott	69
HB	Michael	Cox	64
FB	Henry	Hynoski	85
WR	Victor	Cruz	90
WR	Hakeem	Nicks	89
WR	Rueben	Randle	76
WR	Louis	Murphy	73
WR	Ramses	Barden	72
WR	Jerrel	Jernigan	66
WR	Kris	Adams	64
WR	Jeremy	Horne	64
TE	Brandon	Myers	81
TE	Bear	Pascoe	73
TE	Adrien	Robinson	69
TE	Zak	DeOssie	50
LT	Will	Beatty	90
LT	David	Diehl	75
LT	Matthew	McCants	62
LG	Kevin	Boothe	82
LG	Selvish	Capers	71
LG	Chris	DeGeare	70
C	David	Baas	78
C	Jim	Cordle	66
RG	Chris	Snee	90
RG	Brandon	Mosley	67
RG	Bryant	Browning	63
RG	Michael	Jasper	62
RT	Justin	Pugh	77
RT	James	Brewer	76

DEFENSIVE DEPTH CHART

POS	FIRST NAME	LAST NAME	OVR
LE	Justin	Tuck	87
LE	Mathias	Kiwanuka	83
LE	Adrian	Tracy	68
RE	Jason	Pierre-Paul	94
RE	Damontre	Moore	69
RE	Justin	Trattou	64
RE	Adewale	Ojomo	63
DT	Linval	Joseph	84
DT	Cullen	Jenkins	83
DT	Shaun	Rogers	75
DT	Mike	Patterson	75
DT	Marvin	Austin	71
DT	Johnathan	Hankins	70
DT	Frank	Okam	66
DT	Markus	Kuhn	64
LOLB	Keith	Rivers	77
LOLB	Aaron	Curry	76
MLB	Dan	Connor	76
MLB	Mark	Herzlich	66
ROLB	Jacquian	Williams	76
ROLB	Spencer	Paysinger	66
CB	Corey	Webster	81
CB	Prince	Amukamara	80
CB	Terrell	Thomas	77
CB	Aaron	Ross	76
CB	Jayron	Hosley	72
CB	Trumaine	McBride	70
CB	Terrence	Frederick	63
CB	Laron	Scott	60
FS	Antrel	Rolle	83
FS	Will	Hill	67
SS	Stevie	Brown	83
SS	Ryan	Mundy	74
SS	David	Caldwell	71
SS	Cooper	Taylor	68
SS	Tyler	Sash	63

SPECIAL TEAMS DEPTH CHART

POS	FIRST NAME	LAST NAME	OVR
K	Josh	Brown	82
K	David	Buehler	67
P	Steve	Weatherford	81

New York Giants

RECOMMENDED OFFENSIVE RUN FORMATION: I-FORM PRO (2 HB, 1 TE, 2 WR)

PRO TIPS

- HB DA'REL SCOTT IS ONE OF THE LEAGUE'S FASTEST BACKUP HALFBACKS,WITH A 96 SPD RATING.
- HB ANDRE BROWN IS THE TEAM'S BEST TRUCKING HB (88 TRK).
- TE BEAR PASCOE IS THE GIANT'S BEST BLOCKING TE (85 IBL).

WR — LT – LG – C – RG – RT – TE — WR
QB
FB
HB

RUN LEFT

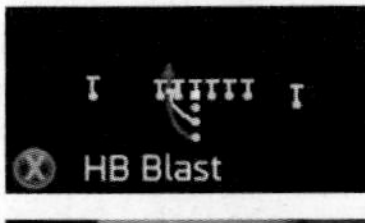

DAVID WILSON KICKS THE RUN OUT TO THE LEFT.

RUN MIDDLE

WILSON IS A TOUGH IN-BETWEEN-THE-TACKLES RUNNER.

RUN RIGHT

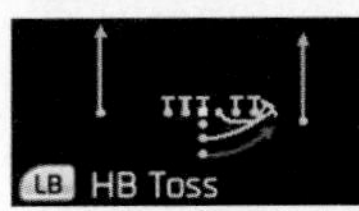

SPEED FOR DAYS!

NEW YORK GIANTS RUNNING PLAY CALL SHEET

LEGEND: Inside Run | Outside Run | Shotgun Run | QB Run

1ST DOWN RUNS	2ND AND SHORT	3RD AND SHORT	GOAL LINE RUNS	2ND AND LONG	3RD AND LONG
I-Form Pro—Power O	Strong H Pro—HB Blast	Singleback Y-Trips—Zone Weak	Goal Line—HB Sting	Gun Ace Twins—HB Mid Draw	Gun Trips TE—HB Mid Draw
Singleback Ace—HB Zone Wk	I-Form Pro—Iso	Singleback Ace—HB Toss	Goal Line—FB Dive	Singleback Y-Trips—HB Draw	Gun Wing Trips Wk NY—HB Power
Singleback Jumbo—Strech	Weak H Pro—HB Gut	Weak H Pro—Toss Weak	Singleback Ace—HB Stretch	Gun Doubles Wk—HB Mid Draw	Gun Snugs—HB Draw

NEW YORK GIANTS PASSING PLAY CALL SHEET

LEGEND: Base Play | Man Beater | Zone Beater | Blitz Beater

1ST DOWN PLAY	2ND AND SHORT	3RD AND SHORT	GOAL LINE PASSING	2ND AND LONG	3RD AND LONG
Gun Spread—Slot Outs	Gun Normal Wing NY—Giants Slot Trail	Gun Trips TE—HB Slip Screen	Goal Line—PA Spot	Gun Trips TE—Flood	Singleback Bunch—Y Trail
Gun Empty Giant—Slot Stick Nod	Gun Y-Trips Wk—Y Trail	Gun Spread—HB Slip Screen	Singleback Jumbo—Inside Cross	Gun Split Giant—Mesh	Gun Spread—Four Verticals
Gun Trips TE—Inside Cross	Gun Snugs—Giants Seams	Gun Doubles Wk—FL Screen	Gun Empty Spread—Spacing	Gun Ace Twins—Curl Flat Corner	Gun Ace Twins—Slot Under

In these play call sheets we picked the best plays for specific situations so that you will have a play for every down and distance.

OFFENSE

RECOMMENDED OFFENSIVE PASS FORMATION: GUN NORMAL WING NY (1 HB, 1 TE, 3 WR)

PRO TIPS

> SUB IN WR JERREL JERNIGAN AS THE THIRD WR.

> SUB IN WR RUEBEN RANDLE AS THE FOURTH WR.

> WR LOUIS MURPHY IS A GREAT SPEED THREAT OFF THE BENCH.

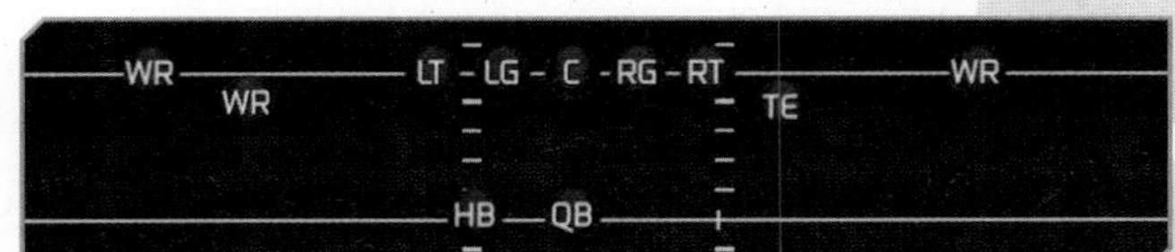

BASE PLAY

SETUP

> NONE

> Against zone look to the crossing mesh routes as well as the deep post.

> Against man-to-man look to the sideline wheel and the HB wheel routes.

MAN BEATER

SETUP

> OPTION THE HB

> MOTION THE LEFT SLOT WR TO THE LEFT

> Look to user-catch the motioned WR down the sideline. This is extremely difficult to defend.

> The underneath curl routes and HB option are your secondary options.

ZONE BEATER

SETUP

> STREAK BOTH OUTSIDE WRS

> OPTION THE HB

> Against Cover 2 and Cover 3 zones look to the corner routes.

> Against Cover 4 zones look to the HB out of the backfield.

BLITZ BEATER

SETUP

> BLOCK THE HB

> Against zone blitzes look to the flat routes.

> Against man blitzes look to the short curls.

New York Giants

RECOMMENDED DEFENSIVE RUN FORMATION: 5-2 NORMAL

PRO TIPS

> DT SHAUN ROGERS HAS A 94 STR RATING AND WILL HELP WITH RUN SUPPORT ON THE DEFENSIVE LINE.

> LOLB KEITH RIVERS HAS AN 88 POW RATING, WHICH IS BEST AMONG THE GIANTS' LINEBACKERS.

> MLB DAN CONNOR HAS THE TEAM'S BEST TACKLE RATING FOR LINEBACKERS.

RUN DEFENSE

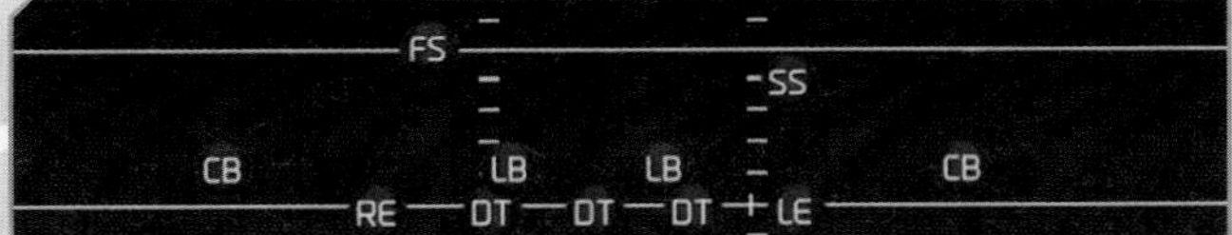

RUN DEFENSE LEFT

SETUP > SHIFT LINEBACKERS LEFT

RUN DEFENSE MIDDLE

SETUP > PINCH DEFENSIVE LINE

RUN DEFENSE RIGHT

SETUP > SHIFT LINEBACKERS RIGHT

NEW YORK GIANTS DEFENSIVE RUN PLAY CALL SHEET

1ST DOWN RUN DEFENSE	2ND AND SHORT	3RD AND SHORT	GOAL LINE RUN DEFENSE	2ND AND LONG	3RD AND LONG
5-2 Normal—Cover 1	4-3 Stack—Man QB Spy	5-2 Normal—Pinch	Goal Line 5-3-3—Jam Cover 1	Nickel Normal—Cover 1	Nickel Normal—2 Man Under
5-2 Normal—Cover 3	4-3 Stack—Cover 2 Sink	5-2 Normal—Fire Zone 2	Goal Line 5-3-3—Flat Buzz	Nickel Normal—Cover 6	Nickel Normal—9 Velcro

NEW YORK GIANTS DEFENSIVE PASS PLAY CALL SHEET

1ST DOWN PLAY	2ND AND SHORT	3RD AND SHORT	GOAL LINE PASSING	2ND AND LONG	3RD AND LONG
Sub 2-3-6 Flex—2 Man MLB Blitz	Quarter Normal—Inside Blitz	Sub 2-3-6 Flex—Spinner Buck Dog 1	Goal Line 6-3-2—GL Man	NASCAR Normal—Under Smoke	NASCAR Normal—Sugar Blitz
Sub 2-3-6 Flex—3 Double Buzz	Quarter Normal—Zone Blitz	Sub 2-3-6 Flex—Spinner Dog 3	Goal Line 6-3-2—GL Zone	NASCAR Normal—Odd Overload 3	NASCAR Normal—Sugar 2 Disguise

LEGEND: Man Coverage | Zone Coverage | Man Blitz | Zone Blitz

In these play call sheets we picked the best plays for specific situations so that you will have a play for every down and distance.

DEFENSE

RECOMMENDED DEFENSIVE PASS FORMATION: NICKEL NASCAR

PRO TIPS

> PLACE CB PRINCE AMUKAMARA ON YOUR OPPONENT'S BEST WR.

> USE CB JAYRON HOSLEY TO COVER YOUR OPPONENT'S FASTEST WR.

> CB COREY WEBSTER SHOULD BE YOUR SECONDCB.

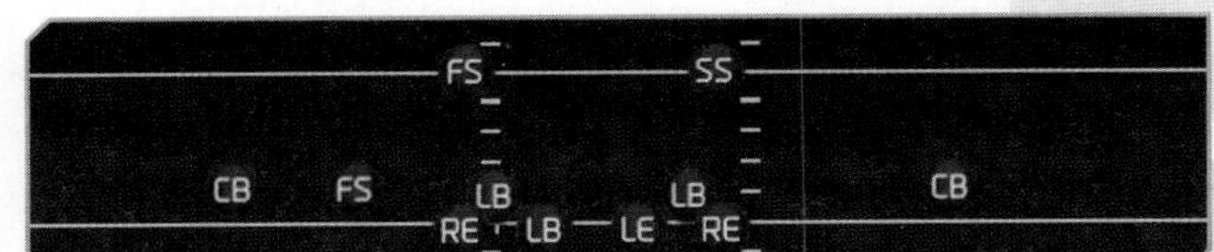

MAN COVERAGE

SETUP

> SHIFT DEFENSIVE LINE LEFT AND CRASH OUT

> SHIFT LINEBACKERS LEFT

> The defensive line shifts and crash will create a stunt that will confuse the offensive line.

> The confusion will result in one of our pass rushers getting free after the QB.

ZONE COVERAGE

SETUP

> SHIFT DEFENSIVE LINE LEFT AND CRASH OUT

> SHIFT LINEBACKERS LEFT

> BLITZ THE SS

> This is the same setup as the man-to-man setup, but we have changed the coverage behind the pressure.

> This is a great play call for third and long situations.

MAN BLITZ

SETUP

> MAN ALIGN

> PRESS COVERAGE

> GLOBAL BLITZ ALL LINEBACKERS

> User-control the nickel corner over the middle of the field.

> The safeties have a good chance of getting beaten off the press.

ZONE BLITZ

SETUP

> PRESS COVERAGE

> GLOBAL BLITZ ALL LINEBACKERS

> If you are getting beaten to the flat, place both hook zone defenders into flats.

> When you want to blitz on third and long, place both hook zone defenders in deep zones.

> We like to mix this setup in to confuse our opponents and throw off their timing.

Jacksonville Jaguars

2012 TEAM RANKINGS

4th AFC South (2-14-0)

PASSING OFFENSE: **21st**
RUSHING OFFENSE: **30th**
PASSING DEFENSE: **22nd**
RUSHING DEFENSE: **30th**

2012 TEAM LEADERS

PASSING: **Chad Henne: 2,084**
RUSHING: **Maurice Jones-Drew: 414**
RECEIVING: **Cecil Shorts: 979**
TACKLES: **Paul Posluszny: 139**
SACKS: **Tyson Alualu: 3.5**
INTS: **Derek Cox: 4**

KEY ADDITIONS

HB Justin Forsett
WR Mohamed Massaquoi
DT Kyle Love

KEY ROOKIES

RT Luke Joeckel
SS John Cyprien
CB Dwayne Gratz

CONNECTED FRANCHISE MODE STRATEGY

CFM TEAM RATING: **66**
OFFENSIVE SCHEME: **West Coast**
DEFENSIVE SCHEME: **Base 4-3**
STRENGTHS: **HB, TE, LT, CB, FS**
WEAKNESSES: **QB, LG, DT, LOLB, ROLB**

SCHEDULE

Wk	Date	Time		Opponent
1	Sep 8	1:00		CHIEFS
2	Sep 15	4:25	at	RAIDERS
3	Sep 22	4:25	at	SEAHAWKS
4	Sep 29	1:00		COLTS
5	Oct 6	1:00	at	RAMS
6	Oct 13	4:05	at	BRONCOS
7	Oct 20	1:00		CHARGERS
8	Oct 27	1:00		49ERS
9	BYE			
10	Nov 10	1:00	at	TITANS
11	Nov 17	1:00		CARDINALS
12	Nov 24	1:00	at	TEXANS
13	Dec 1	1:00	at	BROWNS
14	Dec 5	8:25		TEXANS
15	Dec 15	1:00		BILLS
16	Dec 22	1:00		TITANS
17	Dec 29	1:00	at	COLTS

FRANCHISE OVERVIEW

JAGUARS GAMEPLAY RATING

72

> SEE THE INSIDE BACK COVER FOR A QUICK REFERENCE TO THE GAME ABBREVIATIONS USED THROUGHOUT THIS GUIDE.

> IMPROVE WITH YOUR TEAM BY VISITING PRIMAGAMES.COM/MADDENNFL25 FOR MORE INFORMATION AND HOW-TO VIDEOS.

OFFENSIVE SCOUTING REPORT

- QB Blaine Gabbert is not the future in Jacksonville. Find a replacement quickly. Until this team gets a viable starting QB it will struggle to get wins consistently.
- We love the idea of trading away HB Maurice Jones-Drew in return for a QB or future draft picks. Rookie HB Denard Robinson and free agent signee Justin Forsett will be more than effective in the backfield.
- WRs Cecil Shorts III and Justin Blackmon are both young up-and-coming receivers in this league. With the addition of a solid starting QB the Jaguars offense looks promising in the near future.

DEFENSIVE SCOUTING REPORT

The Jaguars' entire defense needs to be rebuilt. Keep RE Jason Babin and RE Andre Branch and replace everyone on the defensive line.

MLB Paul Posluszny is the only player worth keeping long-term among the linebackers. ROLB Geno Hayes has enough speed to keep around, but look to rebuild this entire unit.

Veteran CB Marcus Trufant was brought in to keep this defensive unit afloat during the rebuilding phase. Trufant is a savvy player with good coverage skills.

OWNER & COACH PROFILES

SHAD KHAN
LEGACY SCORE: 0
OFF. SCHEME: Power Run
DEF. SCHEME: Attacking 4-3

GUS BRADLEY
LEVEL: 14
LEGACY SCORE: 0
OFF. SCHEME: Power Run
DEF. SCHEME: Attacking 4-3

TEAM OVERVIEW

KEY PLAYERS

HB #32
MAURICE JONES-DREW

KEY RATINGS

50 60 70 80 90 100
OVR 91
SPD 92
AGI 95
ACC 93
CAR 91

- Jones-Drew looks to rebound after the 2012 season.
- Jones-Drew has elite SPM and JKM ratings.

MLB #51
PAUL POSLUSZNY

KEY RATINGS

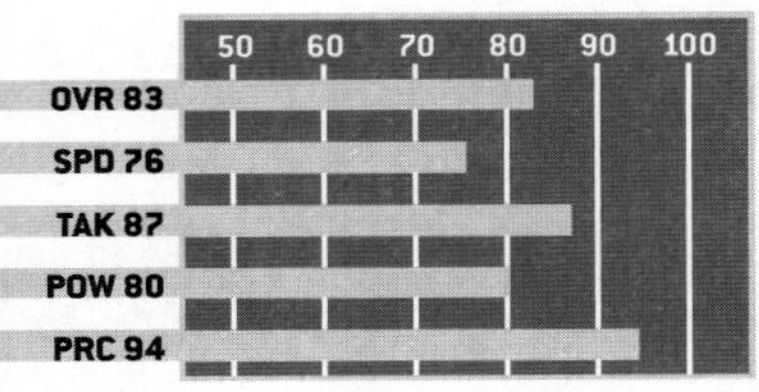

- The leader of the defense is also the team's leading tackler.
- Posluszny will not be fooled on play-action plays.

PRE-GAME SETUP

KEY RUNNING SUBSTITUTION

Who: HB Denard Robinson

Where: Backup HB

Why: Robinson played QB in college, but he is now an NFL HB. He has the speed to be an NFL running back.

Key Stats: 92 SPD, 95 AGI, 96 ACC

KEY PASSING SUBSTITUTION

Who: WR Taylor Price

Where: Deep-threat WR

Why: Price is the team's fastest offensive player. Get him the ball deep.

Key Stats: 95 SPD

KEY RUN DEFENSE SUBSTITUTION

Who: DT Roy Miller

Where: #1 DT

Why: Miller is the team's best DT. He has 85 BSH and 88 STR for stopping the run.

Key Stats: 85 BSH, 88 STR

KEY PASS DEFENSE SUBSTITUTION

Who: FS Antwon Blake

Where: #2 CB

Why: With the speed that Blake has he has to see the field. Start him as the second CB.

Key Stats: 95 SPD

OFFENSIVE DEPTH CHART

POS	FIRST NAME	LAST NAME	OVR
QB	Blaine	Gabbert	74
QB	Chad	Henne	74
QB	Mike	Kafka	71
QB	Matt	Scott	64
HB	Maurice	Jones-Drew	91
HB	Justin	Forsett	77
HB	Denard	Robinson	67
HB	Jonathan	Grimes	66
HB	Jordan	Todman	66
FB	Will	Ta'ufo'ou	70
FB	Lonnie	Pryor	67
WR	Cecil	Shorts III	83
WR	Justin	Blackmon	81
WR	Mohamed	Massaquoi	74
WR	Jordan	Shipley	73
WR	Taylor	Price	64
WR	Ace	Sanders	63
WR	Toney	Clemons	61
WR	Tobais	Palmer	56
TE	Marcedes	Lewis	88
TE	Allen	Reisner	70
TE	Isaiah	Stanback	67
TE	Ryan	Otten	66
TE	Brett	Brackett	60
TE	Jeremy	Cain	45
LT	Eugene	Monroe	89
LT	Mark	Asper	59
LG	Will	Rackley	72
LG	Austin	Pasztor	63
C	Brad	Meester	78
C	Mike	Brewster	66
C	Dan	Gerberry	62
RG	Uche	Nwaneri	80
RG	Jason	Spitz	76
RT	Luke	Joeckel	83
RT	Cameron	Bradfield	75

DEFENSIVE DEPTH CHART

POS	FIRST NAME	LAST NAME	OVR
LE	Tyson	Alualu	78
LE	Jeremy	Mincey	76
LE	Pannel	Egboh	70
RE	Jason	Babin	79
RE	Andre	Branch	71
RE	Ryan	Davis	64
DT	Sen'Derrick	Marks	77
DT	Roy	Miller	75
DT	Kyle	Love	75
DT	Brandon	Deaderick	73
DT	D'Anthony	Smith	65
LOLB	Russell	Allen	81
LOLB	Julian	Stanford	65
MLB	Paul	Posluszny	83
MLB	Michael	Zimmer	58
ROLB	Geno	Hayes	74
ROLB	Brandon	Marshall	65
CB	Marcus	Trufant	81
CB	Alan	Ball	71
CB	Dwayne	Gratz	71
CB	Demetrius	McCray	69
CB	Mike	Harris	68
CB	Kevin	Rutland	67
CB	Jeremy	Harris	63
FS	Dwight	Lowery	81
FS	Josh	Evans	67
FS	Antwon	Blake	65
SS	Johnathan	Cyprien	76
SS	Chris	Prosinski	66

SPECIAL TEAMS DEPTH CHART

POS	FIRST NAME	LAST NAME	OVR
K	Josh	Scobee	85
P	Bryan	Anger	78

Jacksonville Jaguars

RECOMMENDED OFFENSIVE RUN FORMATION: I-FORM TIGHT (2 HB, 2 TE, 1 WR)

PRO TIPS

- WITH 94 SPD, HB JORDAN TODMAN IS THE TEAM'S FASTEST HB.
- ROOKIE FB LONNIE PRYOR IS THE TEAM'S BEST TRUCKING RUNNER (84 TRK).
- TE MARCEDES LEWIS IS THE TEAM'S BEST BLOCKING TE (78 IBL).

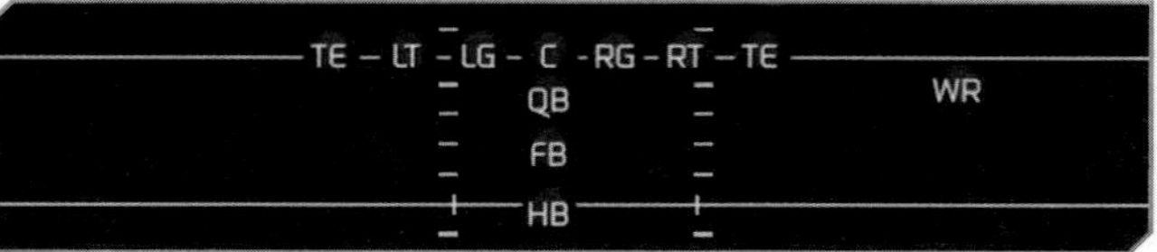

RUN LEFT

HB Blast

JONES-DREW KEEPS LOW TO THE GROUND.

RUN MIDDLE

JONES-DREW WILL RUN OVER ANY DEFENDER IN THE LEAGUE.

RUN RIGHT

JONES-DREW HAS THE SPEED TO GET OUTSIDE.

JACKSONVILLE JAGUARS RUNNING PLAY CALL SHEET

LEGEND: Inside Run | Outside Run | Shotgun Run | QB Run

1ST DOWN RUNS	2ND AND SHORT	3RD AND SHORT	GOAL LINE RUNS	2ND AND LONG	3RD AND LONG
Singleback Ace—Counter Wk	Singleback Ace Twins—HB Dive	I-Form Pro—Iso	Goal Line Normal—QB Sneak	Gun Trips TE—HB Mid Draw	Gun Bunch Wk—HB Mid Draw
I-Form Tight—HB Iso	Strong Pro—HB Blast	I-Form Pro—HB Toss	Goal Line Normal—HB Dive	Singleback Jumbo—Power O	Gun Y-Trips HB Wk—HB Off Tackle
I-Form Tight—HB Toss	Strong Pro—Power O	Singleback Bunch—HB Counter	Goal Line Normal—Power O	Gun Snugs Flip—HB Sweep	Gun Trips TE—45 Quick Base

JACKSONVILLE JAGUARS PASSING PLAY CALL SHEET

LEGEND: Base Play | Man Beater | Zone Beater | Blitz Beater

1ST DOWN PLAY	2ND AND SHORT	3RD AND SHORT	GOAL LINE PASSING	2ND AND LONG	3RD AND LONG
Gun Split Jaguar—Jags Under	Singleback Doubles—Sluggo Seam	Strong Twins—Double Slant	Goal Line—PA Waggle	Gun Spread Y-Flex—Four Verticals	Gun Ace Wing TE—Slants
Gun Trips TE—Slot Quick Flat	I-Form Tight—FL Drive	Gun Y-Trips HB Wk—HB Slip Screen	Goal Line—PA Spot	Gun Spread Y-Flex—Corner Stike	Gun Tight Flex—WR Corners
Gun Ace Wing TE—Whip Unders	Gun Trips TE—X Spot	Gun Empty Base—WR Screen	Goal Line—PA Power O	Gun Spread Y-Flex—Deep Attack	Gun Tight Flex—WR Cross

In these play call sheets we picked the best plays for specific situations so that you will have a play for every down and distance.

OFFENSE

RECOMMENDED OFFENSIVE PASS FORMATION: GUN TIGHT FLEX (1 HB, 0 TE, 4 WR)

PRO TIPS

- USE WR MOHAMED MASSAQUOI AS THE THIRD WR.
- USE WR TAYLOR PRICE AS THE FOURTHWR.
- WR JUSTIN BLACKMON HAS THE TEAM'S BEST CIT RATING.

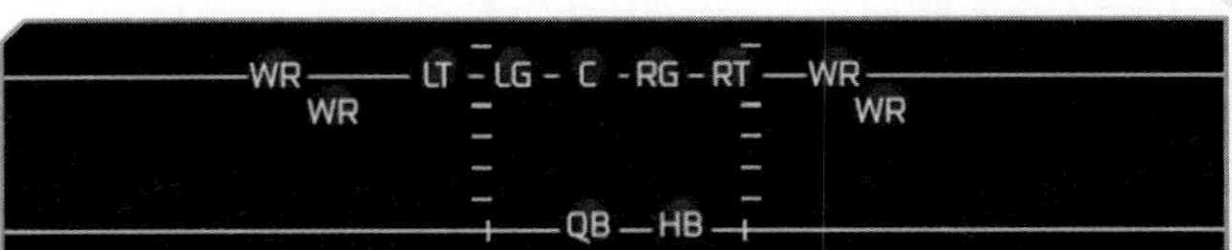

BASE PLAY

SETUP

- NONE

- Against zone look to the crossing mesh routes as well as the deep post.
- Against man-to-man look to the sideline wheel and the HB wheel routes.

MAN BEATER

SETUP

- OPTION THE HB
- MOTION THE LEFT SLOT WR TO THE LEFT

- Look to user-catch the motioned WR down the sideline. This is extremely difficult to defend.
- The underneath curl routes and HB option are your secondary options.

ZONE BEATER

SETUP

- STREAK BOTH OUTSIDE WRS
- OPTION THE HB

- Against Cover 2 and Cover 3 zones look to the corner routes.
- Against Cover 4 zones look to the HB out of the backfield.

BLITZ BEATER

SETUP

- BLOCK THE HB

- Against zone blitzes look to the flat routes.
- Against man blitzes look to the short curls.

Jacksonville Jaguars

RECOMMENDED DEFENSIVE RUN FORMATION: 4-3 OVER PLUS

PRO TIPS

- DT ROY MILLER IS THE TEAM'S STRONGEST DEFENSIVE LINEMAN.
- LOLB RUSSELL ALLEN HAS THE TEAM'S HIGHEST POW RATING.
- MLB PAUL POSLUSZNY HAS THE TEAM'S HIGHEST TAK RATING.

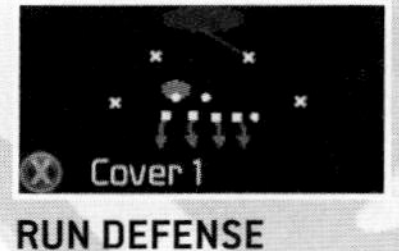

RUN DEFENSE

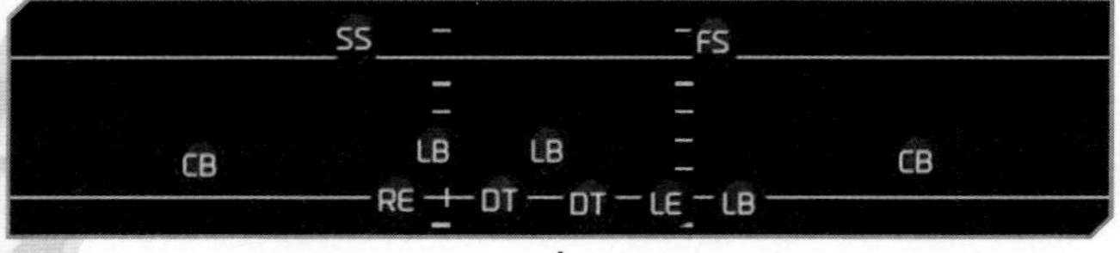

RUN DEFENSE LEFT

SETUP > SHIFT LINEBACKERS LEFT

RUN DEFENSE MIDDLE

SETUP > PINCH DEFENSIVE LINE

RUN DEFENSE RIGHT

SETUP > SHIFT LINEBACKERS RIGHT

JACKSONVILLE JAGUARS DEFENSIVE RUN PLAY CALL SHEET

1ST DOWN RUN DEFENSE	2ND AND SHORT	3RD AND SHORT	GOAL LINE RUN DEFENSE	2ND AND LONG	3RD AND LONG
4-3 Under—2 Man Under	4-3 Over—LB Dogs	4-3 Stack—Thunder Moke	Goal Line 5-3-3—Jam Cover 1	Dime Normal—2 Man Under	Nickel Normal—Cover 1 Press
4-3 Under—Cover 2 Buc	4-3 Over—Cover 6	4-3 Stack—Zip Shoot Gut	Goal Line 5-3-3—Flat Buzz	Dime Normal—Cover 3	Nickel Normal—3 Strong Cloud

JACKSONVILLE JAGUARS DEFENSIVE PASS PLAY CALL SHEET

1ST DOWN PLAY	2ND AND SHORT	3RD AND SHORT	GOAL LINE PASSING	2ND AND LONG	3RD AND LONG
46 Bear Under—2 Man Under	Nickel Wide 9—Sugar Blitz	4-3 Under—Safety Blitz	Goal Line 6-3-2—GL Man	Dime Normal—Cover 1 Press	Quarter Normal—Over Storm Brave
46 Bear Under—Cover 3	Nickel Wide 9—Sugar SS 2 Fire	4-3 Under—Smoke Mid Zone 2	Goal Line 6-3-2—GL Zone	Dime Normal—Cover 6	Quarter Normal—DB Strike Zone

LEGEND: Man Coverage | Zone Coverage | Man Blitz | Zone Blitz

In these play call sheets we picked the best plays for specific situations so that you will have a play for every down and distance.

DEFENSE

RECOMMENDED DEFENSIVE PASS FORMATION: DIME FLAT

PRO TIPS

- PLACE CB MARCUS TRUFANT ON YOUR OPPONENT'S BEST WR.
- USE FS ANTWON BLAKE TO COVER YOUR OPPONENT'S FASTEST WR.
- CB DWAYNE GRATZ SHOULD BE USED AS YOUR SECOND CB.

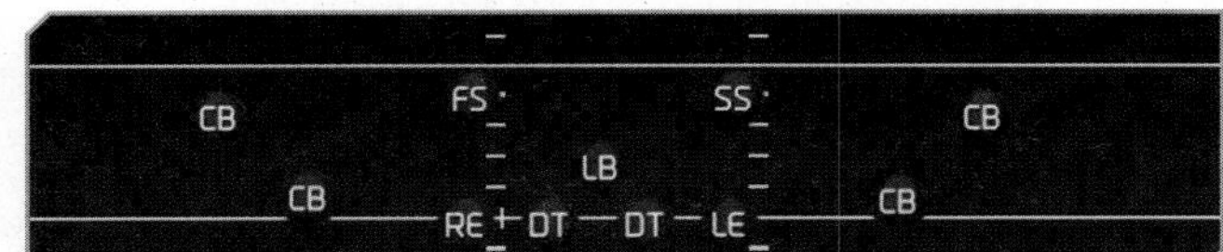

MAN COVERAGE

SETUP

- SHIFT DEFENSIVE LINE LEFT AND CRASH OUT
- SHIFT LINEBACKERS LEFT

- The defensive line shifts and crash will create a stunt that will confuse the offensive line.
- The confusion will result in one of our pass rushers getting free after the QB.

ZONE COVERAGE

SETUP

- SHIFT DEFENSIVE LINE LEFT AND CRASH OUT
- SHIFT LINEBACKERS LEFT
- BLITZ THE SS

- This is the same setup as the man-to-man setup, but we have changed the coverage behind the pressure.
- This is a great play call for thirdand long situations.

MAN BLITZ

SETUP

- MAN ALIGN
- PRESS COVERAGE
- GLOBAL BLITZ ALL LINEBACKERS

- User-control the nickel corner over the middle of the field.
- The safeties have a good chance of getting beat off the press.

ZONE BLITZ

SETUP

- PRESS COVERAGE
- GLOBAL BLITZ ALL LINEBACKERS

- If you are getting beaten to the flat, place both hook zone defenders into flats.
- When you want to blitz on third and long place both hook zone defenders in deep zones.
- We like to mix this setup in to confuse our opponents and throw off their timing.

New York Jets

2012 TEAM RANKINGS

3rd AFC East (6-10-0)

PASSING OFFENSE: **30th**
RUSHING OFFENSE: **12th**
PASSING DEFENSE: **2nd**
RUSHING DEFENSE: **26th**

2012 TEAM LEADERS

PASSING: **Mark Sanchez: 2,883**
RUSHING: **Shonn Greene: 1,063**
RECEIVING: **Jeremy Kerley: 827**
TACKLES: **David Harris: 123**
SACKS: **Quinton Coples: 5.5**
INTS: **Antonio Cromartie: 3**

KEY ADDITIONS

SS Dawan Landry
ROLB Antwan Barnes
HB Chris Ivory

KEY ROOKIES

QB Geno Smith
CB Dee Milliner
RE Sheldon Richardson

CONNECTED FRANCHISE MODE STRATEGY

CFM TEAM RATING: **74**
OFFENSIVE SCHEME: **Power Run**
DEFENSIVE SCHEME: **Attacking 3-4**
STRENGTHS: **LT, C, TE, LE, CB**
WEAKNESSES: **QB, TE, DT, LOLB, ROLB, FS**

SCHEDULE

1	Sep 8	1:00 PM ET		BUCCANEERS
2	Sep 12	8:25 PM ET	AT	PATRIOTS
3	Sep 22	4:25 PM ET		BILLS
4	Sep 29	4:05 PM ET	AT	TITANS
5	Oct 7	8:40 PM ET	AT	FALCONS
6	Oct 13	1:00 PM ET		STEELERS
7	Oct 20	1:00 PM ET		PATRIOTS
8	Oct 27	4:05 PM ET	AT	BENGALS
9	Nov 3	1:00 PM ET		SAINTS
10	BYE			
11	Nov 17	1:00 PM ET	AT	BILLS
12	Nov 24	1:00 PM ET	AT	RAVENS
13	Dec 1	1:00 PM ET		DOLPHINS
14	Dec 8	1:00 PM ET		RAIDERS
15	Dec 15	4:05 PM ET	AT	PANTHERS
16	Dec 22	1:00 PM ET		BROWNS
17	Dec 29	1:00 PM ET	AT	DOLPHINS

FRANCHISE OVERVIEW

JETS GAMEPLAY RATING

73

> SEE THE INSIDE BACK COVER FOR A QUICK REFERENCE TO THE GAME ABBREVIATIONS USED THROUGHOUT THIS GUIDE.

> IMPROVE WITH YOUR TEAM BY VISITING PRIMAGAMES.COM/MADDENNFL25 FOR MORE INFORMATION AND HOW-TO VIDEOS.

OFFENSIVE SCOUTING REPORT

- Start rookie QB Geno Smith right away. We love that Smith has an 85 SPD rating, which will allow you to run an option-style offense if needed.
- The Jets don't have any star HBs, but they do have three different HBs that are solid options. We don't think any are young enough to develop or sign long-term, but you have options with this backfield. Chris Ivory, with his 96 TRK rating, has the best chance to become a feature HB.
- The best-kept secret on this roster is WR Stephen Hill. He has special skills that could put him in the same category as WR Calvin Johnson Jr. He has a long way to go but has the potential.

DEFENSIVE SCOUTING REPORT

- LE Muhammad Wilkerson dominates games with his ability to tackle and interrupt running plays. He is only 23 years old and is already one of the league's best defensive linemen.
- The Jets linebackers aren't elite, but what they do have is speed. Consider playing a lot of man-to-man coverage with this unit, and blitz a ton with this secondary's ability to cover.
- The combination of CB Antonio Cromartie and rookie Dee Milliner is one that opposing QBs should fear. Neither has holes in his game, and they have the speed to turn any interception into a touchdown.

OWNER & COACH PROFILES

WOODY JOHNSON

LEGACY SCORE: 200 | OFF. SCHEME: Power Run
DEF. SCHEME: Attacking 3-4

REX RYAN

LEVEL: 11 | LEGACY SCORE: 200
OFF. SCHEME: Power Run | DEF. SCHEME: Attacking 3-4

TEAM OVERVIEW

KEY PLAYERS

WR #10

SANTONIO HOLMES

KEY RATINGS

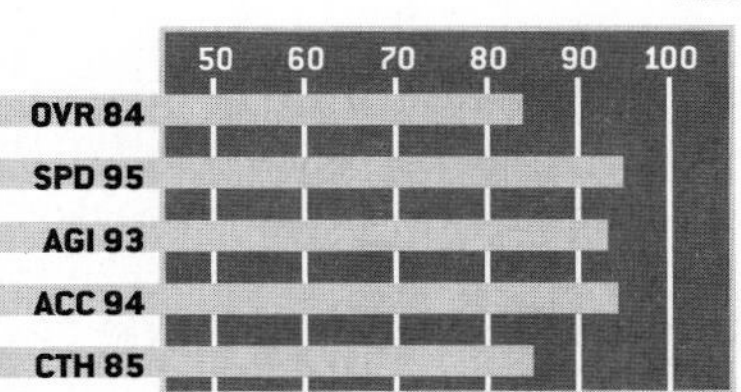

- Holmes will help rookie QB Geno Smith mature into an NFL starting QB.
- Holmes is best used as a deep-threat receiver and on screen patterns.

CB #31

ANTONIO CROMARTIE

KEY RATINGS

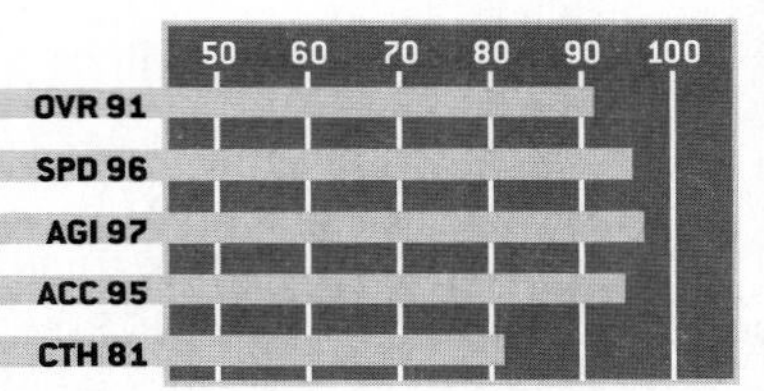

- Cromartie is the league's most physically gifted CB.
- Put Cromartie on any receiver in the game and he will be covered.

PRE-GAME SETUP

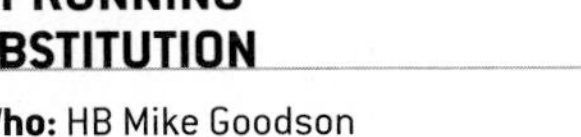

KEY RUNNING SUBSTITUTION

Who: HB Mike Goodson

Where: Starting HB

Why: Goodson has great speed and should be your starting HB

Key Stats: 94 SPD, 93 AGI, 95 ACC

KEY PASSING SUBSTITUTION

Who: WR Clyde Gates

Where: #3 WR

Why: Gates is the team's fastest receiver. Get him in the game for deep balls and screens.

Key Stats: 96 SPD, 97 ACC

KEY RUN DEFENSE SUBSTITUTION

Who: DT Antonio Garay

Where: #2 DT

Why: Garay provides added strength to the defensive line in run situations.

Key Stats: 89 STR

KEY PASS DEFENSE SUBSTITUTION

Who: CB Dee Milliner

Where: #2 CB

Why: Milliner has the skills to create his own island this season for the Jets.

Key Stats: 94 SPD

OFFENSIVE DEPTH CHART

POS	FIRST NAME	LAST NAME	OVR
QB	Geno	Smith	73
QB	Mark	Sanchez	73
QB	Greg	McElroy	72
QB	Matt	Simms	61
HB	Chris	Ivory	80
HB	Mike	Goodson	77
HB	Bilal	Powell	74
HB	Joe	McKnight	69
FB	Lex	Hilliard	75
FB	Tommy	Bohanon	72
WR	Santonio	Holmes	84
WR	Stephen	Hill	74
WR	Ben	Obomanu	73
WR	Jeremy	Kerley	73
WR	Clyde	Gates	68
WR	Jordan	White	63
WR	Thomas	Mayo	60
WR	Vidal	Hazelton	57
WR	Titus	Ryan	54
TE	Kellen	Winslow	79
TE	Jeff	Cumberland	76
TE	Konrad	Reuland	69
TE	Hayden	Smith	67
TE	Tanner	Purdum	54
LT	D'Brickashaw	Ferguson	91
LT	Oday	Aboushi	63
LG	Willie	Colon	80
LG	Brian	Winters	72
LG	Dennis	Landolt	64
C	Nick	Mangold	94
C	Caleb	Schlauderaff	66
RG	Stephen	Peterman	79
RG	Vladimir	Ducasse	71
RG	William	Campbell	64
RT	Austin	Howard	80
RT	Mark	Popek	65

DEFENSIVE DEPTH CHART

POS	FIRST NAME	LAST NAME	OVR
LE	Muhammad	Wilkerson	94
LE	Tevita	Finau	66
RE	Sheldon	Richardson	79
RE	Antonio	Garay	76
DT	Kenrick	Ellis	73
DT	Damon	Harrison	66
DT	Lanier	Coleman	60
LOLB	Calvin	Pace	75
LOLB	Quinton	Coples	75
LOLB	Garrett	McIntyre	67
MLB	David	Harris	81
MLB	Demario	Davis	71
MLB	Josh	Mauga	67
MLB	Nick	Bellore	65
ROLB	Antwan	Barnes	77
ROLB	Ricky	Sapp	65
ROLB	Jacquies	Smith	56
CB	Antonio	Cromartie	92
CB	Dee	Milliner	81
CB	Kyle	Wilson	78
CB	Ellis	Lankster	71
CB	Aaron	Berry	70
CB	Isaiah	Trufant	69
CB	Darrin	Walls	64
CB	Donnie	Fletcher	59
FS	Josh	Bush	72
FS	Antonio	Allen	67
FS	Bret	Lockett	66
SS	Dawan	Landry	79
SS	Jaiquawn	Jarrett	71

SPECIAL TEAMS DEPTH CHART

POS	FIRST NAME	LAST NAME	OVR
K	Nick	Folk	76
P	Robert	Malone	71

New York Jets

RECOMMENDED OFFENSIVE RUN FORMATION: SINGLEBACK ACE PAIR TWINS (1 HB, 2 TE, 2 WR)

PRO TIPS

- START QB GENO SMITH. HIS 85 SPD WILL OPEN UP YOUR OFFENSE.
- HB CHRIS IVORY SHOULD BE USED IN SHORT-YARDAGE SITUATIONS BECAUSE OF HIS 96 TRK RATING
- TE HAYDEN SMITH IS THE TEAM'S BEST BLOCKING TE WITH A 72 IBL RATING.

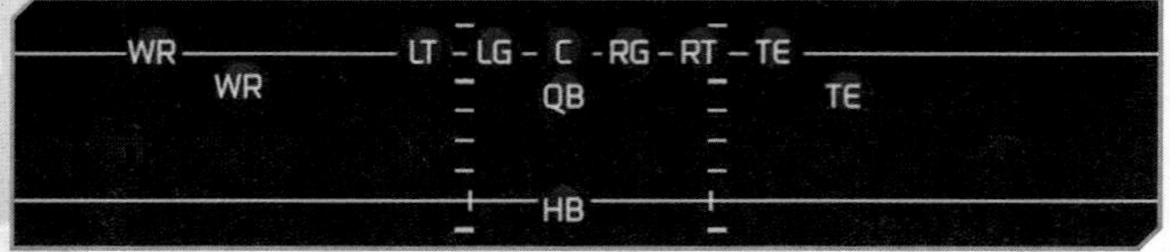

RUN LEFT

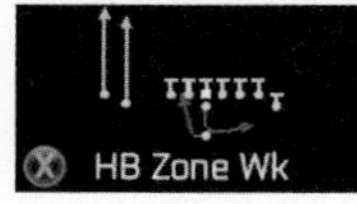

MIKE GOODSON CUTS THE RUN TO THE LEFT.

RUN MIDDLE

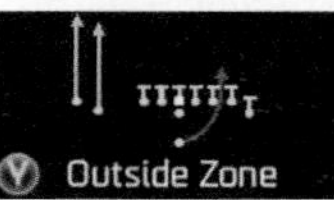

WAIT FOR RUNNING LANES TO OPEN UP.

RUN RIGHT

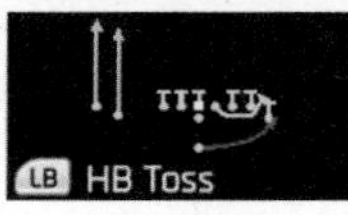

ATTACK THE OUTSIDE EDGE WITH GOODSON'S SPEED.

NEW YORK JETS RUNNING PLAY CALL SHEET

LEGEND: Inside Run | Outside Run | Shotgun Run | QB Run

1ST DOWN RUNS	2ND AND SHORT	3RD AND SHORT	GOAL LINE RUNS	2ND AND LONG	3RD AND LONG
Strong Close—Counter Weak	I-Form Pro—Power O	Singleback Doubles—Zone Weak	Goal Line Normal—QB Sneak	Gun Trey Open—HB Sweep	Gun Snugs—HB Draw
Singleback Doubles—HB Cutback	Weak Pro—Power O	Singleback Jumbo—HB Ace Power	Goal Line Normal—HB Dive	Singleback Bunch—HB Slash	Gun Y-Trips HB Wk—HB Off Tackle
Weak Pro—Power O	Singleback Y-Trips—Inside Zone	Singleback Jumbo—HB Toss	Goal Line Normal—Power O	Gun Snugs—HB Sweep	Gun Spread Y-Slot—45 Quick Base

NEW YORK JETS PASSING PLAY CALL SHEET

LEGEND: Base Play | Man Beater | Zone Beater | Blitz Beater

1ST DOWN PLAY	2ND AND SHORT	3RD AND SHORT	GOAL LINE PASSING	2ND AND LONG	3RD AND LONG
Gun Spread Y-Slot—Slot Outs	Singleback Doubles—TE Post	Singleback Bunch—Z Spot	Goal Line—PA Waggle	Gun Trey Open—Jets Deep Post	Gun Snugs—Jets Slot Post
Gun Bunch Wk—Deep Attack	Singleback Doubles—Corner Strike	Gun Snugs—Jets Drag	Goal Line—PA Spot	Gun Trey Open—Stick N Nod	Gun Empty Trey—Curl Flats
Gun Bunch Wk—Verticals	Singleback Y-Trips—Jets Flood	Strong Tight Pair—PA Spot	Goal Line—PA Power O	Gun Split Jet—Jets Slot Cross	Gun Empty Trey—Stick

In these play call sheets we picked the best plays for specific situations so that you will have a play for every down and distance.

OFFENSE

RECOMMENDED OFFENSIVE PASS FORMATION: GUN SNUGS (1 HB, 0 TE, 4 WR)

PRO TIPS

- WR STEPHEN HILL IS A BIG-TIME SLEEPER. HIS HEIGHT AND SPEED MAKE HIM A MISMATCH AGAINST MOST DEFENDERS.
- TE JEFF CUMBERLAND IS A BIG TARGET AT TE. USE HIM IN THE PASSING GAME.
- HB JOE MCKNIGHT HAS THE SKILLS TO BE SPLIT WIDE AS A RECEIVER. USE HIM IN EMPTY SETS.

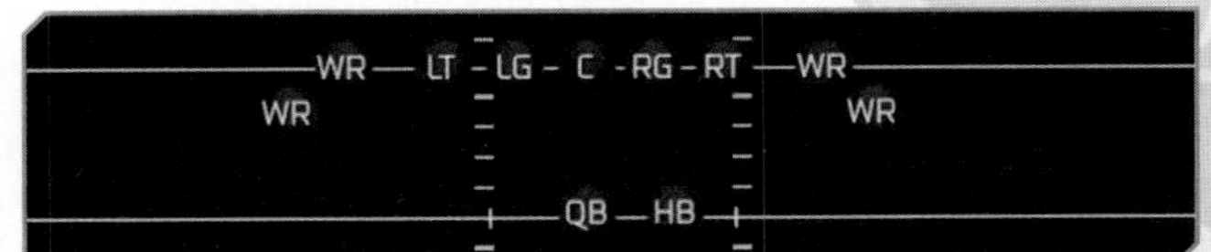

BASE PLAY

SETUP

- DRAG THE LEFT SLOT WR
- DRAG THE RIGHT SLOT WR

- Against man-to-man coverage the WR running the left wheel route will get crazy separation when he makes his first cut.
- Throw a sideline lead pass for a huge gain.

MAN BEATER

SETUP

- BLOCK THE HB
- STREAK THE RIGHT SLOT

- Either outside WR will destroy his man defender on the cut to the outside.
- Look to the underneath crossing pattern and the slot streak as a last resort.

ZONE BEATER

SETUP

- STREAK BOTH OUTSIDE WRS
- CURL THE HB

- Against Cover 2 and Cover 3 zones look to the sideline corner routes.
- Against Cover 4 zones look to the HB curl.

BLITZ BEATER

SETUP

- BLOCK THE HB

- If you are facing a zone blitz, either flat route is a good option.
- If you are facing a man-to-man blitz look to the slot curls.

New York Jets

RECOMMENDED DEFENSIVE RUN FORMATION: 3-4 PREDATOR

PRO TIPS

- LE MUHAMMAD WILKERSON WILL CONTROL THE LINE OF SCRIMMAGE FOR YOUR DEFENSE.
- MLB NICK BELLORE HAS THE TEAM'S BEST TACKLE RATING (84).
- MLB DAVID HARRIS HAS AN 88 POW RATING, WHICH WILL CAUSE FUMBLES.

RUN DEFENSE

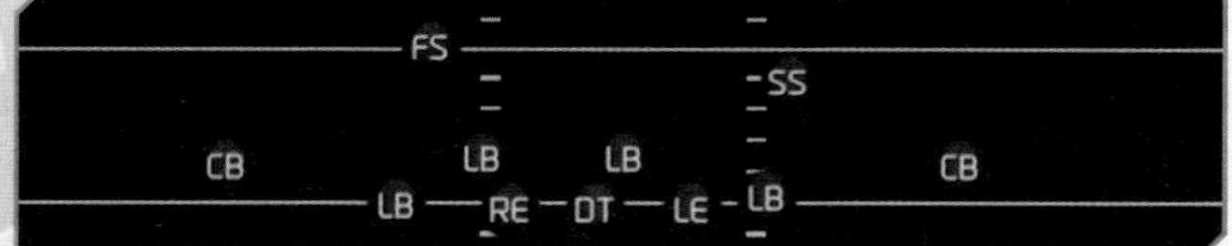

RUN DEFENSE LEFT

SETUP > SHIFT LINEBACKERS LEFT

RUN DEFENSE MIDDLE

SETUP > PINCH DEFENSIVE LINE

RUN DEFENSE RIGHT

SETUP > SHIFT LINEBACKERS RIGHT

NEW YORK JETS DEFENSIVE RUN PLAY CALL SHEET

1ST DOWN RUN DEFENSE	2ND AND SHORT	3RD AND SHORT	GOAL LINE RUN DEFENSE	2ND AND LONG	3RD AND LONG
3-4 Solid—2 Man Under	3-4 Over Ed—Cover 1	3-4 Odd—Cross Fire	Goal Line 5-3-3—Jam Cover 1	Nickel 2-4-5 Even—2 Man Under	Nickel 3-3-5—LB Cross Blitz
3-4 Solid—Cover 2	3-4 Over Ed—Cover 2	3-4 Odd—Cross 3 Fire	Goal Line 5-3-3—Flat Buzz	Nickel 2-4-5 Even—Cover 3	Nickel 3-3-5—LB Cross 3

NEW YORK JETS DEFENSIVE PASS PLAY CALL SHEET

1ST DOWN PLAY	2ND AND SHORT	3RD AND SHORT	GOAL LINE PASSING	2ND AND LONG	3RD AND LONG
3-4 Predator—2 Man Under	3-4 Odd—Cover 1 Robber	Sub 2-3-6—Silver Shoot Pinch	Goal Line 6-3-2—GL Man	Nickel 3-3-5—Cover 1	Nickel 3-3-5—LB Dogs
3-4 Predator—Cover 2	3-4 Odd—2 Deep MLB Spy	Sub 2-3-6—Buck Slant 3	Goal Line 6-3-2—GL Zone	Nickel 3-3-5—Cover 4	Nickel 3-3-5—3 Crash Switch

LEGEND: Man Coverage | Zone Coverage | Man Blitz | Zone Blitz

In these play call sheets we picked the best plays for specific situations so that you will have a play for every down and distance.

DEFENSE

RECOMMENDED DEFENSIVE PASS FORMATION: NICKEL 2-4-5 EVEN

PRO TIPS

- > PLACE CB ANTONIO CROMARTIE ON THE OPPOSING TEAM'S BEST WR.
- > USE CB DEE MILLINER ON THE OPPOSING TEAM'S FASTEST WR.
- > USE CB KYLE WILSON AS YOUR #2 CB.

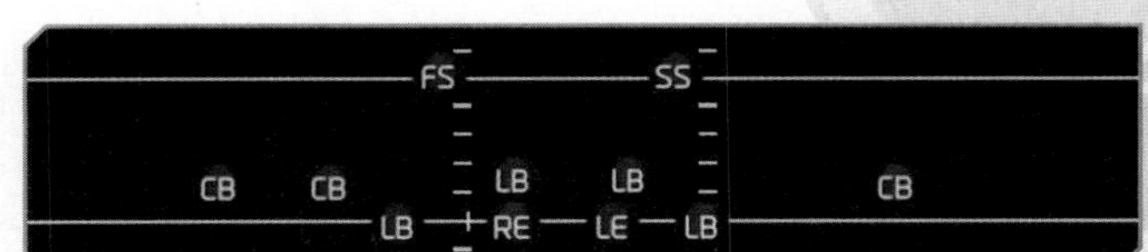

MAN COVERAGE

SETUP

- > GLOBAL HOOK ZONE THE LINEBACKERS
- > BASE ALIGN TWICE

- > This setup is amazing at stopping opponents who like passing over the middle of the field.
- > In this example you can see the opposing QB is trying to force a throw over the middle with three defenders covering the WR!

ZONE COVERAGE

SETUP

- > FLAT ZONE THE ROLB
- > FLAT ZONE THE LOLB

- > User-control the MLB over the middle of the field.
- > Watch for crossing patterns over the middle of the field as well as TE streaks.

MAN BLITZ

SETUP

- > PRESS COVERAGE
- > GLOBAL BLITZ LINEBACKERS

- > Press coverage will slow down our opponent's reads.
- > The goal is for the pressure to get to the QB before the WR releases off the press coverage.

ZONE BLITZ

SETUP

- > PRESS COVERAGE
- > GLOBAL BLITZ LINEBACKERS

- > User-control the FS over the deep middle.
- > Look to cover the short middle if there are no deep threats in the slots.

Detroit Lions

2012 TEAM RANKINGS

4th NFC North (4-12-0)

PASSING OFFENSE: **2nd**
RUSHING OFFENSE: **23rd**
PASSING DEFENSE: **14th**
RUSHING DEFENSE: **16th**

2012 TEAM LEADERS

PASSING: **Matthew Stafford: 4,967**
RUSHING: **Mikel Leshoure: 798**
RECEIVING: **Calvin Johnson Jr.: 1,964**
TACKLES: **Stephen Tulloch: 112**
SACKS: **Cliff Avril: 9.5**
INTS: **Don Carey: 2**

KEY ADDITIONS

HB Reggie Bush
LE Jason Jones
CB Ron Bartell

KEY ROOKIES

RE Ezekiel Ansah
CB Darius Slay
RG Larry Warford

CONNECTED FRANCHISE MODE STRATEGY

CFM TEAM RATING: **71**
OFFENSIVE SCHEME: **Vertical Offense**
DEFENSIVE SCHEME: **Attacking 3-4**
STRENGTHS: **QB, WR, LG, DT, MLB, SS**
WEAKNESSES: **LT, RG, LOLB, ROLB, CB**

SCHEDULE

Week	Date	Time		Opponent
1	Sep 8	1:00		VIKINGS
2	Sep 15	4:05	AT	CARDINALS
3	Sep 22	1:00	AT	REDSKINS
4	Sep 29	1:00		BEARS
5	Oct 6	1:00	AT	PACKERS
6	Oct 13	1:00	AT	BROWNS
7	Oct 20	1:00		BENGALS
8	Oct 27	1:00		COWBOYS
9	BYE			
10	Nov 10	1:00	AT	BEARS
11	Nov 17	1:00	AT	STEELERS
12	Nov 24	1:00		BUCCANEERS
13	Nov 28	12:30		PACKERS
14	Dec 8	1:00	AT	EAGLES
15	Dec 16	8:40		RAVENS
16	Dec 22	4:05		GIANTS
17	Dec 29	1:00	AT	VIKINGS

FRANCHISE OVERVIEW

LIONS GAMEPLAY RATING

76

> SEE THE INSIDE BACK COVER FOR A QUICK REFERENCE TO THE GAME ABBREVIATIONS USED THROUGHOUT THIS GUIDE.

> IMPROVE WITH YOUR TEAM BY VISITING PRIMAGAMES.COM/MADDENNFL25 FOR MORE INFORMATION AND HOW-TO VIDEOS.

OFFENSIVE SCOUTING REPORT

- QB Matt Stafford has put up amazing numbers as the Lions starter. At age 25 we think it's best to sign him to a long-term deal now to make sure he's still throwing passes to WR Calvin Johnson Jr.
- HB Reggie Bush is only 28 years old and can do a lot of different things for this offense. We think you should turn him into a WR and let HB Mikel Leshoure grow into a star HB.
- WR Calvin Johnson Jr. is the best player at his position and is the player most important to the future success of this team.

DEFENSIVE SCOUTING REPORT

- DTs Ndamukong Suh and Nick Fairley are two of the best at stopping the run and putting pressure on opposing QBs. Both their contracts end in two years, so make sure to sign them both to long-term extensions.
- MLB Stephen Tulloch is a few upgrades away from being one of the better MLBs in the game. He isn't a flashy player, but we love his 89 TAK and 91 POW ratings.
- CB Chris Greenwood has potential to be a future lockdown corner. He needs upgrades to his MCV and ZCV ratings.

OWNER & COACH PROFILES

WILLIAM FORD

LEGACY SCORE: 275
OFF. SCHEME: Vertical Offense
DEF. SCHEME: Attacking 4-3

JIM SCHWARTZ

LEVEL: 4
LEGACY SCORE: 0
OFF. SCHEME: Vertical Offense
DEF. SCHEME: Attacking 4-3

TEAM OVERVIEW

KEY PLAYERS

WR #81

CALVIN JOHNSON JR.

KEY RATINGS

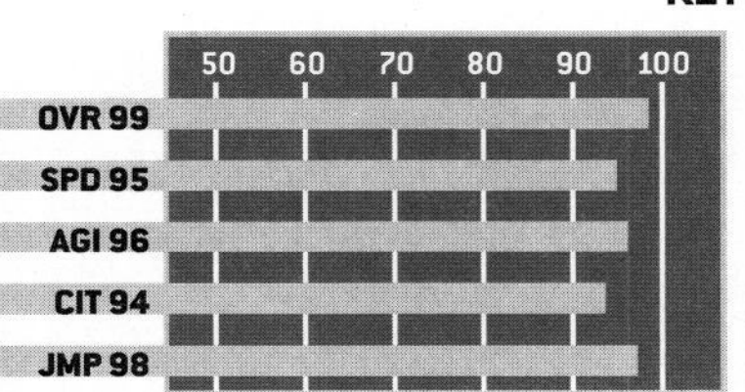

- Johnson is arguably one of the greatest WRs of all time. Get him the ball as often as possible.
- Johnson will win the majority of jump balls. Throw the ball up to him in the red zone.
- LionsDefStar

DT #90

NDAMUKONG SUH

KEY RATINGS

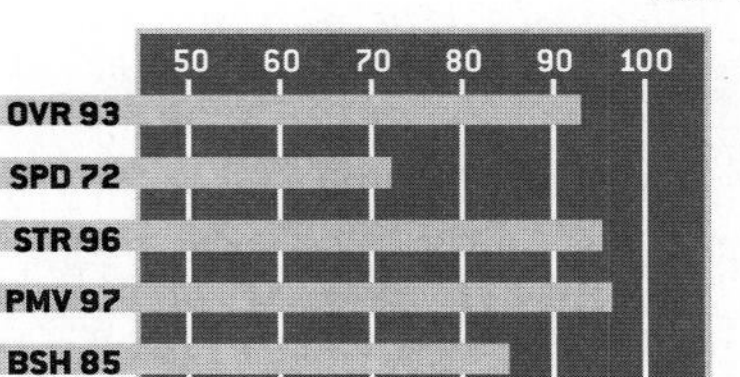

- Suh has the rare size and speed combination to make him one of the league's best DTs.
- You can place Suh at DE and have him rush the QB because of his 71 SPD.

PRE-GAME SETUP

KEY RUNNING SUBSTITUTION

Who: HB Mikel Leshoure

Where: Backup HB

Why: Leshoure is a great late-game HB because of his 95 CAR rating.

Key Stats: 95 CAR

KEY PASSING SUBSTITUTION

Who: TE Tony Scheffler

Where: #3 WR

Why: Scheffler has the skills of a WR but the body of a TE. Get him on the field and let him post defenders up!

Key Stats: 6'5", 87 CTH

KEY RUN DEFENSE SUBSTITUTION

Who: RE Ronnell Lewis

Where: #3 DE

Why: Lewis will cause fumbles with his ability to lay big hits on ball carriers.

Key Stats: 94 POW

KEY PASS DEFENSE SUBSTITUTION

Who: CB Chris Greenwood

Where: Nickel CB

Why: Greenwood's height and speed make him one of the better CBs on the Lions roster.

Key Stats: 6'1", 96 SPD

OFFENSIVE DEPTH CHART

POS	FIRST NAME	LAST NAME	OVR
QB	Matthew	Stafford	85
QB	Shaun	Hill	76
QB	Kellen	Moore	68
HB	Reggie	Bush	83
HB	Mikel	Leshoure	79
HB	Joique	Bell	76
HB	Montell	Owens	74
HB	Jahvid	Best	71
HB	Theo	Riddick	66
FB	Shaun	Chapas	71
WR	Calvin	Johnson Jr.	99
WR	Nate	Burleson	76
WR	Ryan	Broyles	73
WR	Mike	Thomas	73
WR	Chastin	West	67
WR	Devin	Thomas	66
WR	Kris	Durham	65
WR	Corey	Fuller	63
WR	Terrence	Austin	60
WR	Patrick	Edwards	56
TE	Brandon	Pettigrew	79
TE	Tony	Scheffler	78
TE	Michael	Williams	70
TE	Joseph	Fauria	65
TE	Nathan	Overbay	65
TE	Matt	Veldman	63
TE	Don	Muhlbach	58
LT	Riley	Reiff	77
LG	Rob	Sims	89
LG	Rodney	Austin	69
LG	Derek	Hardman	68
C	Dominic	Raiola	83
C	Dylan	Gandy	71
RG	Larry	Warford	72
RG	Bill	Nagy	71
RT	Corey	Hilliard	75
RT	Jason	Fox	69

DEFENSIVE DEPTH CHART

POS	FIRST NAME	LAST NAME	OVR
LE	Israel	Idonije	81
LE	Jason	Jones	81
LE	Willie	Young	74
RE	Ezekiel	Ansah	78
RE	Ronnell	Lewis	69
RE	Devin	Taylor	66
DT	Ndamukong	Suh	93
DT	Nick	Fairley	90
DT	C.J.	Mosley	75
DT	Ogemdi	Nwagbuo	70
DT	Jimmy	Saddler-McQueen	62
LOLB	Ashlee	Palmer	74
LOLB	Cory	Greenwood	69
LOLB	Tahir	Whitehead	66
MLB	Stephen	Tulloch	88
MLB	Travis	Lewis	66
ROLB	DeAndre	Levy	79
ROLB	Carmen	Messina	70
CB	Chris	Houston	85
CB	Ron	Bartell	75
CB	Bill	Bentley	72
CB	Darius	Slay	71
CB	Jonte	Green	70
CB	Chris	Greenwood	66
CB	DeQuan	Menzie	64
CB	Domonique	Johnson	64
CB	Ross	Weaver	61
FS	Glover	Quin	83
FS	Amari	Spievey	76
FS	Tyrell	Johnson	71
SS	Louis	Delmas	84
SS	Don	Carey	76
SS	John	Wendling	70
SS	Ricardo	Silva	66

SPECIAL TEAMS DEPTH CHART

POS	FIRST NAME	LAST NAME	OVR
K	David	Akers	81
P	Sam	Martin	63

Detroit Lions

RECOMMENDED OFFENSIVE RUN FORMATION: PISTOL ACE (1 HB, 2 TE, 2 WR)

PRO TIPS

- USE TE DON MUHLBACH AT FB, AS HE HAS A 78 IBL RATING, WHICH WILL BE GREAT FOR RUN SITUATIONS.
- HB JAHVID BEST IS A GREAT OPTION AT HB IF HE CAN STAY HEALTHY.
- HB MIKEL LESHOURE SHOULD BE USED LATE IN GAMES TO PROTECT THE BALL.

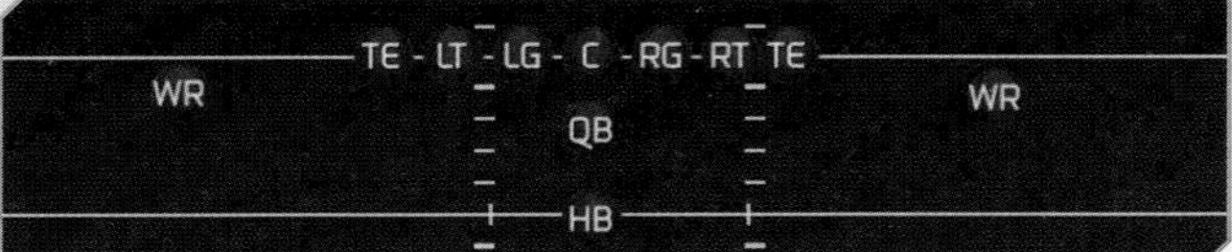

RUN LEFT

GET OUTSIDE AS QUICKLY AS POSSIBLE WITH REGGIE BUSH.

RUN MIDDLE

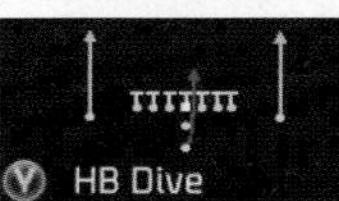

DON'T TAKE TOO MANY BIG HITS WITH BUSH UP THE MIDDLE.

RUN RIGHT

BUSH IS A TOUCHDOWN THREAT ON EVERY RUN.

DETROIT LIONS RUNNING PLAY CALL SHEET

LEGEND: Inside Run | Outside Run | Shotgun Run | QB Run

1ST DOWN RUNS	2ND AND SHORT	3RD AND SHORT	GOAL LINE RUNS	2ND AND LONG	3RD AND LONG
I-Form Pro—Power O	Weak Pro—HB Gut	I-Form Pro—FB Dive	Goal Line—HB Dive	Gun Split Lion—Power O	Pistol Strong—Read Option
Singleback Ace—HB Dive	I-Form Pro—Iso	Singleback Y-Trips Lion—HB Stretch	Goal Line—FB Dive	Singleback Ace Pair—HB Draw	Pistol Twin TE Flex—Read Option
Singleback Ace Pair—HB Sweep	Singleback Jumbo—HB Dive	Singleback Ace Pair Flex—Counter Weak	Goal Line—Strong Toss	Gun Doubles—HB Mid Draw	Gun Ace Twins—HB Mid Draw

DETROIT LIONS PASSING PLAY CALL SHEET

LEGEND: Base Play | Man Beater | Zone Beater | Blitz Beater

1ST DOWN PLAY	2ND AND SHORT	3RD AND SHORT	GOAL LINE PASSING	2ND AND LONG	3RD AND LONG
Pistol Twin TE Flex—X Curl	Gun Ace TE Slot—TE Option	Gun Spread Y-Flex—FL Screen	Goal Line—PA Spot	Singleback Bunch—Verticals	Gun Split Lion—Slot Cross
Gun Ace—Y Shallow Cross	Gun Doubles—Lions HB Angle	Gun Trey Open—HB Slip Screen	Pistol Ace—Quick Slants	Gun Ace Twins—Posts	Singleback Bunch—Lions Smash
Gun Ace Twins—Slot Under	Gun Snugs Flip—WR Corners	Gun Empty Trey—TE Screen	I-Form Pro—Lions Fade	Gun Spread Y-Flex—Smash HB Check	Pistol Twin TE Flex—U Drive

In these play call sheets we picked the best plays for specific situations so that you will have a play for every down and distance.

OFFENSE

RECOMMENDED OFFENSIVE PASS FORMATION: GUN ACE (1 HB, 2 TE, 2 WR)

PRO TIPS

- HB REGGIE BUSH CAN BE USED AT WR; THEN USE HB JAHVID BEST AS THE FEATURE HB.
- TE TONY SCHEFFLER CAN BE SPLIT WIDE TO TAKE ADVANTAGE OF SMALLER CORNERBACKS.
- USE WR NATE WASHINGTON FOR WR SCREENS AND DRAGS OVER THE MIDDLE.

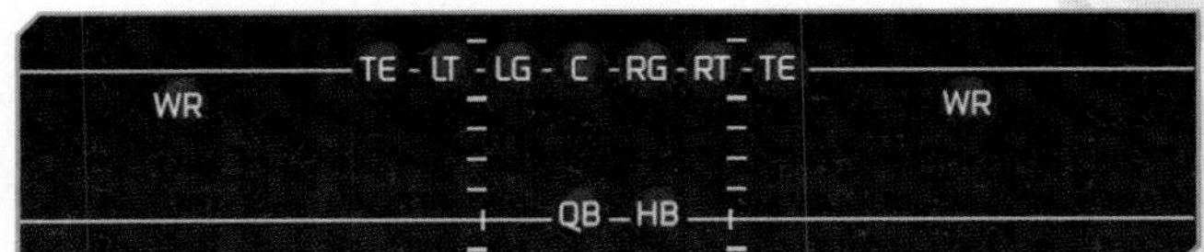

BASE PLAY

SETUP

- ZIG THE LEFT TE
- STREAK THE FAR LEFT WR

- Against man-to-man coverage look to the TE running the zig and the WR running the streak.
- Against zone coverage look to the curl-flat route combination on the right.

MAN BEATER

SETUP

- STREAK THE FAR LEFT WR
- STREAK THE HB

- The TE running the drag will get open underneath the TE running the short curl.
- We like throwing a high bullet pass to the TE running the short curl.

ZONE BEATER

SETUP

- SMOKE SCREEN THE FAR RIGHT WR
- STREAK THE FAR LEFT WR

- Against Cover 2 and Cover 3 zones look to the TEs running the corner routes.
- Against Cover 4 zones look to the WR running the smoke screen.

BLITZ BEATER

SETUP

- BLOCK BOTH TIGHT ENDS

- Blocking the TEs will allow better protection against aggressive defenses.
- Bush and Best are great options on this HB Slip Screen.

Detroit Lions

RECOMMENDED DEFENSIVE RUN FORMATION: 5-2 NORMAL

PRO TIPS

- > DEFENSIVE TACKLES FAIRLEY AND SUH ARE TWO OF THE LEAGUE'S BEST. YOU SHOULD HAVE NO ISSUE STOPPING THE RUN.
- > FIND A PLACE FOR RE RONNELL LEWIS TO PLAY. HIS 94 POW NEEDS TO SEE THE FIELD.
- > SS LOUIS DELMAS CAN HELP WITH RUN SUPPORT.

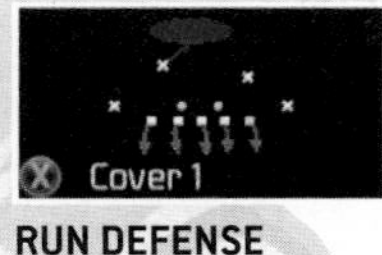

RUN DEFENSE

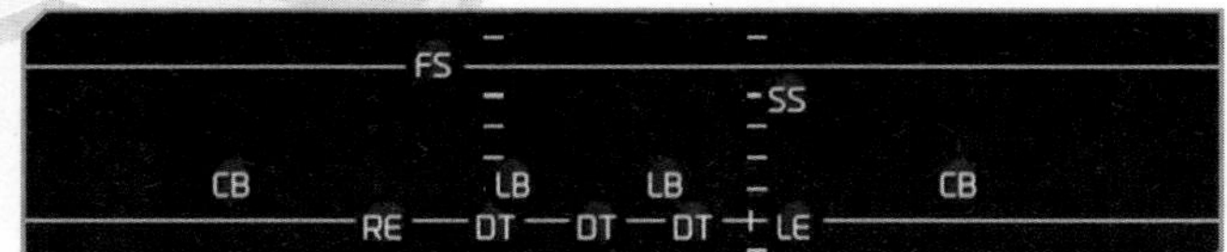

RUN DEFENSE LEFT

SETUP > SHIFT LINEBACKERS LEFT

RUN DEFENSE MIDDLE

SETUP > PINCH DEFENSIVE LINE

RUN DEFENSE RIGHT

SETUP > SHIFT LINEBACKERS RIGHT

DETROIT LIONS DEFENSIVE RUN PLAY CALL SHEET

1ST DOWN RUN DEFENSE	2ND AND SHORT	3RD AND SHORT	GOAL LINE RUN DEFENSE	2ND AND LONG	3RD AND LONG
5-2 Normal—Pinch	4-3 Stack—2 Man Under	Nickel Strong—Under Smoke	Goal Line 5-3-3—Jam Cover 1	Nickel Normal—Cover 1	Nickel Wide 9—2 Man Under
5-2 Normal—Cover 2	4-3 Stack—Cover 2 Buc	Nickel Strong—Zone Blitz	Goal Line 5-3-3—Flat Buzz	Nickel Wide 9—Cover 2 Sink	Nickel Wide 9—Cover 4

DETROIT LIONS DEFENSIVE PASS PLAY CALL SHEET

1ST DOWN PLAY	2ND AND SHORT	3RD AND SHORT	GOAL LINE PASSING	2ND AND LONG	3RD AND LONG
Nickel Strong—Robber	Dime Normal—2 Man Under	Quarter Normal—DB Strike 1	Goal Line 6-3-2—GL Man	Nickel Wide 9—Dbl Safety Blitz	Dime Normal—MLB Blitz
Nickel Strong—Cover 3	Dimen Normal—3 Double Buzz	Quarter Normal—Zone Blitz	Goal Line 6-3-2—GL Zone	Nickel Wide 9—Sugar 3 DB Fire	Dime Normal—Fox Fire Zone

LEGEND: Man Coverage | Zone Coverage | Man Blitz | Zone Blitz

In these play call sheets we picked the best plays for specific situations so that you will have a play for every down and distance.

DEFENSE

RECOMMENDED DEFENSIVE PASS FORMATION: NICKEL STRONG

PRO TIPS

> PLACE CB CHRIS HOUSTON ON YOUR OPPONENT'S BEST WR.
> USE CB CHRIS GREENWOOD ON YOUR OPPONENT'S FASTEST WR.
> CB DARIUS SLAY SHOULD BE YOUR SECOND CB.

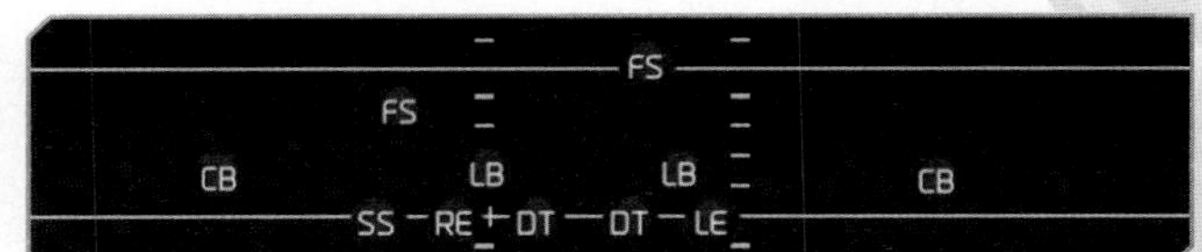

MAN COVERAGE

SETUP

> BLITZ THE FS AND MOVE HIM OFF THE LEFT EDGE OF THE DEFENSIVE LINE
> CRASH THE DEFENSIVE LINE DOWN

> Pressure will come off the right edge.
> Suh and Fairley will provide pressure up the middle, forcing QBs to take sacks from blitzing defenses.

ZONE COVERAGE

SETUP

> BLITZ THE FS AND MOVE HIM OFF THE LEFT EDGE OF THE DEFENSIVE LINE
> DEEP ZONE THE NICKEL CB

> User-control the MLB and defend the left flat.
> This defense will provide solid pressure but also protect the deep part of the field.

MAN BLITZ

SETUP

> PRESS COVERAGE
> USER-CONTROL THE MLB

> Cover the HB out of the backfield if he runs a route.
> If the HB stays in to block, drop into coverage with the MLB.

ZONE BLITZ

SETUP

> PRESS COVERAGE
> CRASH DEFENSIVE LINE DOWN

> User-control the MLB and protect the short middle of the field.
> Watch for TEs and slot WRs running crossing patterns.

DETROIT LIONS

Green Bay Packers

2012 TEAM RANKINGS

1st NFC North (11-5-0)

PASSING OFFENSE: **9th**
RUSHING OFFENSE: **20th**
PASSING DEFENSE: **11th**
RUSHING DEFENSE: **17th**

2012 TEAM LEADERS

PASSING: **Aaron Rodgers: 4,295**
RUSHING: **Alex Green: 464**
RECEIVING: **Randall Cobb: 954**
TACKLES: **Morgan Burnett: 123**
SACKS: **Clay Matthews: 13**
INTS: **Casey Hayward: 6**

KEY ADDITIONS

None

KEY ROOKIES

RE Datone Jones
HB Eddie Lacy
HB Johnathan Franklin

CONNECTED FRANCHISE MODE STRATEGY

CFM TEAM RATING: **82**
OFFENSIVE SCHEME: **West Coast**
DEFENSIVE SCHEME: **Attacking 3-4**
STRENGTHS: **QB, WR, TE, LG, ROLB, CB**
WEAKNESSES: **HB, C, RT, SS**

SCHEDULE

1	Sep 8	4:25	AT	49ERS
2	Sep 15	1:00		REDSKINS
3	Sep 22	1:00	AT	BENGALS
4	BYE			
5	Oct 6	1:00		LIONS
6	Oct 13	1:00	AT	RAVENS
7	Oct 20	4:25		BROWNS
8	Oct 27	8:30	AT	VIKINGS
9	Nov 4	8:40		BEARS
10	Nov 10	1:00		EAGLES
11	Nov 17	8:30	AT	GIANTS
12	Nov 24	1:00		VIKINGS
13	Nov 28	12:30	AT	LIONS
14	Dec 8	8:30		FALCONS
15	Dec 15	4:25	AT	COWBOYS
16	Dec 22	4:25		STEELERS
17	Dec 29	1:00	AT	BEARS

FRANCHISE OVERVIEW

PACKERS GAMEPLAY RATING

88

> SEE THE INSIDE BACK COVER FOR A QUICK REFERENCE TO THE GAME ABBREVIATIONS USED THROUGHOUT THIS GUIDE.

> IMPROVE WITH YOUR TEAM BY VISITING PRIMAGAMES.COM/MADDENNFL25 FOR MORE INFORMATION AND HOW-TO VIDEOS.

OFFENSIVE SCOUTING REPORT

> QB Aaron Rodgers is a dual-threat player. He can beat you with his arm and he can beat you with his legs. The only concern we have with Rodgers is injury. For that reason we believe you need to bring in a viable backup in preparation.

> The Packers don't have a star HB, but they have three HBs that all have value. Rookies Eddie Lacy and Johnathan Franklin are the future, but we think that DuJuan Harris is the best HB to win now.

> There may not be a better three-WR combination in the league than Jordy Nelson, Randall Cobb, and James Jones.

DEFENSIVE SCOUTING REPORT

> The Packers defensive line is built for pure strength, and they have that with LE B.J. Raji and DT Ryan Pickett. In the future we would like to see the transition to a more athletic line.

> The future is bright for LOLB Nick Perry. He has all the ratings needed to be a game changer in the league. He will need upgrades to his AGI and TAK ratings.

> Start FS Jerron McMillian at SS for the time being, but focus on finding a long-term solution for this position.

OWNER & COACH PROFILES

MARK MURPHY
LEGACY SCORE: 1250 | OFF. SCHEME: West Coast
DEF. SCHEME: Attacking 3-4

MIKE MCCARTHY
LEVEL: 28 | LEGACY SCORE: 1050
OFF. SCHEME: West Coast | DEF. SCHEME: Attacking 3-4

TEAM OVERVIEW

KEY PLAYERS

QB #12

AARON RODGERS

KEY RATINGS

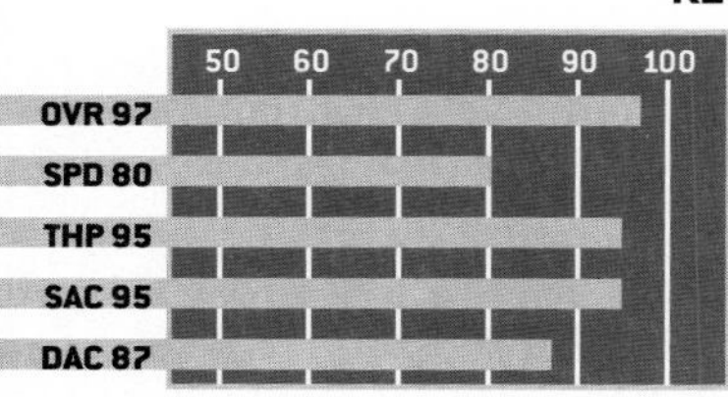

> Rodgers is close to the perfect QB. He can make every throw on the field and has the speed to disrupt defenses.

> Use Rodgers's speed to run read options in short-yardage situations as well as in the red zone.

ROLB #52

CLAY MATTHEWS

KEY RATINGS

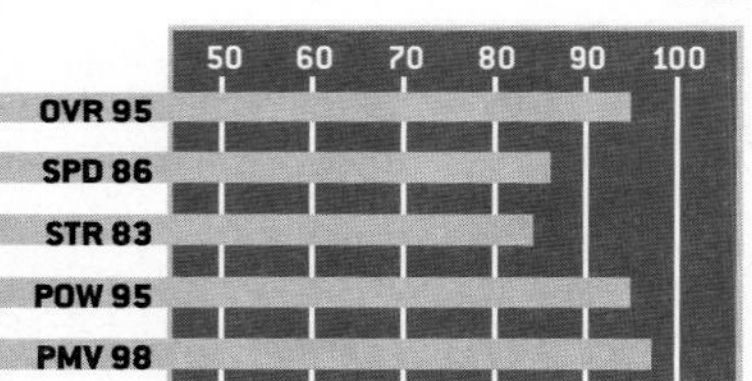

> Send Matthews after the QB every down.

> Look to generate one-on-one rushes for Matthews, as he will almost always get to the QB.

PRE-GAME SETUP

KEY RUNNING SUBSTITUTION

Who: HB DuJuan Harris

Where: Starting HB

Why: Harris is the most well-rounded HB the Packers have, even with their two rookie HBs.

Key Stats: 94 SPD, 93 AGI, 96 ACC

KEY PASSING SUBSTITUTION

Who: WR James Jones

Where: #2 WR

Why: Jones has 97 CIT and should be your primary target on third downs. Get him the ball on curls and outs.

Key Stats: 97 CIT

KEY RUN DEFENSE SUBSTITUTION

Who: RE C.J. Wilson

Where: #2 DT

Why: Wilson has elite strength for a DE. Get him on the field to stop the run.

Key Stats: 90 STR

KEY PASS DEFENSE SUBSTITUTION

Who: FS Jerron McMillian

Where: Starting SS

Why: McMillian is one of the fastest FSs in the game. Get him in the game for his coverage skills.

Key Stats: 93 SPD

OFFENSIVE DEPTH CHART

POS	FIRST NAME	LAST NAME	OVR
QB	Aaron	Rodgers	98
QB	Graham	Harrell	66
QB	B.J.	Coleman	63
HB	Eddie	Lacy	76
HB	Johnathan	Franklin	73
HB	James	Starks	72
HB	DuJuan	Harris	72
HB	Alex	Green	71
FB	John	Kuhn	88
WR	Jordy	Nelson	89
WR	Randall	Cobb	88
WR	James	Jones	87
WR	Jarrett	Boykin	67
WR	Charles	Johnson	65
WR	Jeremy	Ross	64
WR	Kevin	Dorsey	63
TE	Jermichael	Finley	85
TE	Andrew	Quarless	75
TE	D.J.	Williams	74
TE	Matthew	Mulligan	72
TE	Ryan	Taylor	67
LT	Bryan	Bulaga	82
LT	David	Bakhtiari	66
LT	Andrew	Datko	62
LG	Josh	Sitton	96
LG	Greg	Van Roten	64
C	Evan	Dietrich-Smith	75
C	Garth	Gerhart	66
C	Brett	Goode	63
RG	T.J.	Lang	85
RG	J.C.	Tretter	69
RG	Kevin	Hughes	65
RT	Derek	Sherrod	75
RT	Marshall	Newhouse	75
RT	Don	Barclay	72

GREEN BAY PACKERS

DEFENSIVE DEPTH CHART

POS	FIRST NAME	LAST NAME	OVR
LE	B.J.	Raji	83
LE	Mike	Neal	74
LE	Mike	Daniels	71
RE	Datone	Jones	74
RE	C.J.	Wilson	72
RE	Jerel	Worthy	70
RE	Josh	Boyd	63
DT	Ryan	Pickett	86
DT	Johnny	Jolly	74
DT	Jordan	Miller	68
LOLB	Nick	Perry	76
LOLB	Nate	Palmer	63
MLB	A.J.	Hawk	84
MLB	Brad	Jones	78
MLB	Robert	Francois	65
MLB	Terrell	Manning	64
MLB	Sam	Barrington	61
MLB	Jamari	Lattimore	56
ROLB	Clay	Matthews	95
ROLB	Dezman	Moses	65
CB	Tramon	Williams	86
CB	Casey	Hayward	86
CB	Sam	Shields	84
CB	Davon	House	74
CB	Jarrett	Bush	73
CB	Micah	Hyde	67
FS	Morgan	Burnett	85
FS	Jerron	McMillian	71
SS	M.D.	Jennings	76
SS	Sean	Richardson	65

SPECIAL TEAMS DEPTH CHART

POS	FIRST NAME	LAST NAME	OVR
K	Mason	Crosby	73
P	Tim	Masthay	78

Green Bay Packers

RECOMMENDED OFFENSIVE RUN FORMATION: GUN BUNCH WK (1 HB, 1 TE, 3 WR)

PRO TIPS

> USE HB DUJUAN HARRIS AS YOUR STARTING HB.

> TE MATTHEW MULLIGAN IS THE TEAM'S BEST RUN-BLOCKING TE WITH 84 IBL.

> USE HB EDDIE LACY FOR SHORT-YARDAGE SITUATIONS BECAUSE OF HIS 91 TRK RATING.

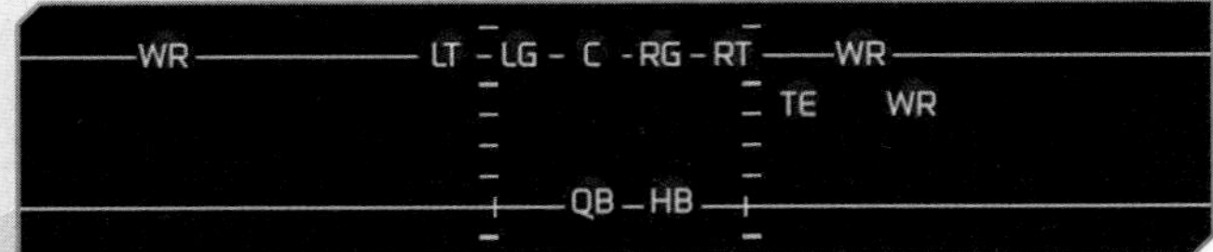

RUN LEFT

DUJUAN HARRIS STAYS LOW TO THE GROUND.

RUN MIDDLE

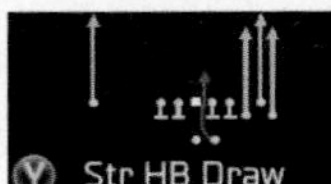

CONSIDER USING HB EDDIE LACY FOR RUNS UP THE MIDDLE.

RUN RIGHT

ONCE HARRIS GETS INTO OPEN SPACE HE IS DANGEROUS WITH THE BALL.

GREEN BAY PACKERS RUNNING PLAY CALL SHEET

LEGEND: Inside Run | Outside Run | Shotgun Run | QB Run

1ST DOWN RUNS	2ND AND SHORT	3RD AND SHORT	GOAL LINE RUNS	2ND AND LONG	3RD AND LONG
Singleback Ace—HB Stretch	Singleback Flex—HB Slam	I-Form Pro—FB Dive Fake HB	Goal Line—HB Dive	Gun Wing Offset Wk—Inside Zone Split	Gun Doubles Flex Wing—Read Option
I-Form Pro—HB Blast	Gun Doubles Flex Wing—HB Dive	I-Form Pro—FB Dive HB Flip	Full House Wide—HB Slam	Singleback Ace—HB Draw	Gun Wing Offset Wk—Read Option
Strong Close—Quick Toss	Singleback Ace—HB Dive	Singleback Bunch—Toss Crack	Full House Wide—Power O	Gun Wing Offset Wk—Counter Y	Normal Y-Flex Tight—HB Draw

GREEN BAY PACKERS PASSING PLAY CALL SHEET

LEGEND: Base Play | Man Beater | Zone Beater | Blitz Beater

1ST DOWN PLAY	2ND AND SHORT	3RD AND SHORT	GOAL LINE PASSING	2ND AND LONG	3RD AND LONG
Gun Doubles Flex Wing—Curl Flats	Strong Close—Y Trail	Full House Wide—Slants	I-Form Pro—PA Scissors	Gun Doubles On—HB Circle	Gun Flex Trey—Shallow Cross
Gun Normal Y-Flex Tight—Packer Y-Curl	Gun Doubles On—Inside Cross	Strong Close—HB Slip Screen	Weak Pro—Quick Slants	Gun Bunch Wk—Str Y Trail	Gun Pack Trips—Deep Corner
Singleback Tight Flex—Bench	Singleback Flex—Z Spot	Full House Wide—Angle Swing	Goal Line—PA Spot	Gun Empty Wing Trio—Smash	Gun Bunch Wk—Verticals

In these play call sheets we picked the best plays for specific situations so that you will have a play for every down and distance.

OFFENSE

RECOMMENDED OFFENSIVE PASS FORMATION: GUN BUNCH WK (1 HB, 1 TE, 3 WR)

PRO TIPS

> WR JAMES JONES HAS THE TEAM'S BEST CIT RATING.
> TE JERMICHAEL FINLEY IS A GREAT TARGET IN THE RED ZONE.
> USE WR RANDALL COBB ON SCREEN ROUTES, DRAGS, AND SLANTS.

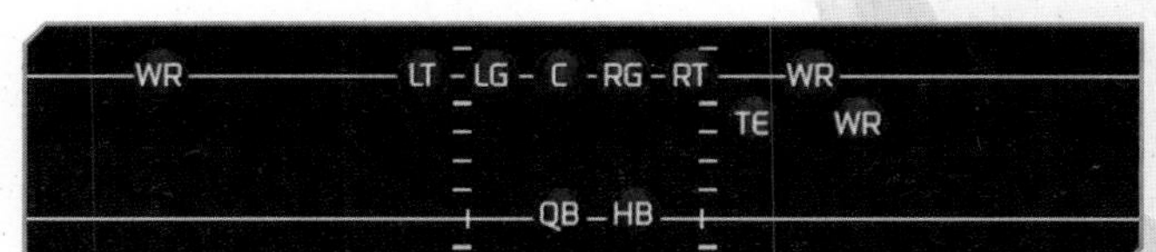

BASE PLAY

SETUP

> STREAK THE SLOT WR ON THE RIGHT
> PUT THE FAR LEFT WR ON A COMEBACK

> The HB out of the backfield is your first option. He releases out of the backfield for big gains.
> Next look to the wheel on the right and the far left comeback against man-to-man coverage.

MAN BEATER

SETUP

> WHEEL THE HB
> PUT THE FAR LEFT WR ON A COMEBACK

> The bunch alignment makes it difficult for man defenses to defend this play.
> Look to the HB at the snap of the ball and then look over the middle to the TE.

ZONE BEATER

SETUP

> STREAK THE HB
> STREAK THE FAR LEFT WR

> Against Cover 2 and Cover 3 look to the sideline streak and the deep post.
> Against Cover 4 zones look to the underneath drag.

BLITZ BEATER

SETUP

> PUT THE FAR LEFT WR ON A COMEBACK
> STREAK THE RIGHT SLOT WR

> For better pass blocking block the TE.
> If you block the TE, put the HB on a block-and-release, which will result in a delayed HB screen!

Green Bay Packers

RECOMMENDED DEFENSIVE RUN FORMATION: 3-4 EVEN

PRO TIPS

- MOVE LE B.J. RAJI TO #2 DT AND USE RE C.J. WILSON AS THE #3 DT FOR RUNNING SITUATIONS.
- ROLB CLAY MATTHEWS WILL FORCE FUMBLES WITH HIS 95 POW RATING.
- FS MORGAN BURNETT HAS A SOLID 88 POW RATING.

RUN DEFENSE

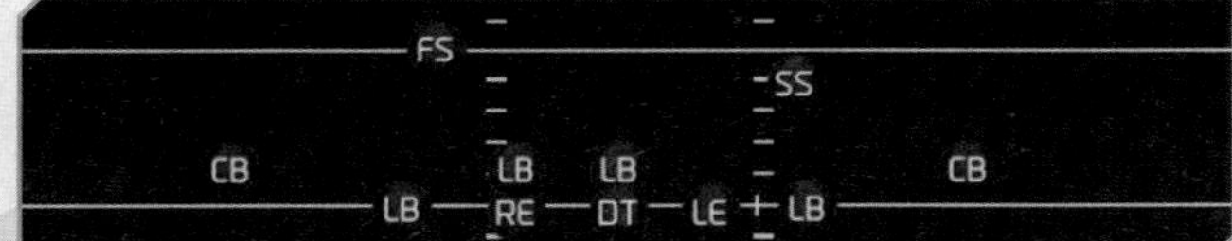

RUN DEFENSE LEFT

SETUP > SHIFT LINEBACKERS LEFT

RUN DEFENSE MIDDLE

SETUP > PINCH DEFENSIVE LINE

RUN DEFENSE RIGHT

SETUP > SHIFT LINEBACKERS RIGHT

GREEN BAY PACKERS DEFENSIVE RUN PLAY CALL SHEET

1ST DOWN RUN DEFENSE	2ND AND SHORT	3RD AND SHORT	GOAL LINE RUN DEFENSE	2ND AND LONG	3RD AND LONG
3-4 Odd—2 Man Under	3-4 Under—Cover 1 Lurk	Nickel Psycho—OLB Fire	Goal Line 5-3-3—Jam Cover 1	Nickel 2-4-5 DT—Cover 1 Spy	Nickel Psycho—2 Man Under
3-4 Odd—Cover 6	3-4 Under—Cover 3	Nickel Psycho—Invert 2 Fire	Goal Line 5-3-3—Flat Buzz	Nickel 2-4-5 DT—Cover 2 Sink	Nickel Psycho—Cover 4

GREEN BAY PACKERS DEFENSIVE PASS PLAY CALL SHEET

1ST DOWN PLAY	2ND AND SHORT	3RD AND SHORT	GOAL LINE PASSING	2ND AND LONG	3RD AND LONG
Sub 2-3-6 Sam—2 Man LB Blitz	Nickel 2-4-5 DT—Cover 1 Spy	Sub 2-3-6—Sugar Blitz	Goal Line 6-3-2—GL Man	Sub 2-3-6—Silver Shoot Pinch	Nickel Psycho—MLB Cross Fire
Sub 2-3-6 Sam—Cover 3	Nickel 2-4-5 DT—Cover 2 Sink	Sub 2-3-6—Cover 3 Bluff	Goal Line 6-3-2—GL Zone	Sub 2-3-6—Buck Slant 3	Nickel Psycho—Strg Corner 2 Fire

LEGEND: Man Coverage | Zone Coverage | Man Blitz | Zone Blitz

In these play call sheets we picked the best plays for specific situations so that you will have a play for every down and distance.

DEFENSE

RECOMMENDED DEFENSIVE PASS FORMATION: NICKEL PSYCHO

PRO TIPS

- PLACE CB TRAMON WILLIAMS ON YOUR OPPONENT'S BEST WR.
- USE CB SAM SHIELDS ON YOUR OPPONENT'S FASTEST WR.
- CB CASEY HAYWARD SHOULD BE YOUR #2 CB.

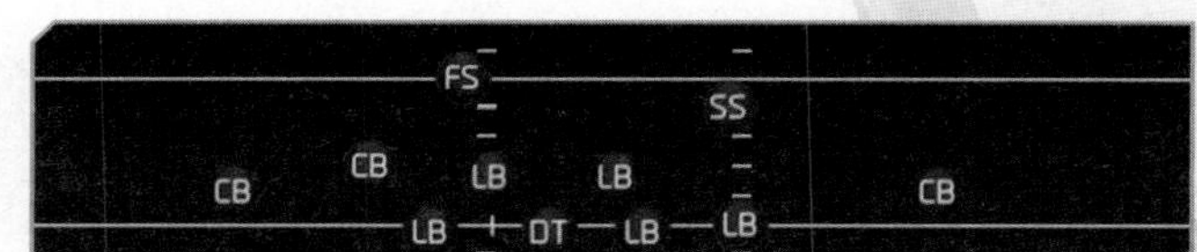

MAN COVERAGE

SETUP

- GLOBAL BLITZ BOTH OUTSIDE LINEBACKERS
- QB SPY THE DT

- Pressure will start wide and will collapse the pocket on the QB.
- The only place to go for the QB is to try and scramble up through the line of scrimmage.

ZONE COVERAGE

SETUP

- GLOBAL BLITZ BOTH OUTSIDE LINEBACKERS
- QB SPY THE DT

- In this example the QB tries to scramble up through the line of scrimmage.
- Clay Matthews chases him down from behind while the QB spy tackles the QB for a short gain.

MAN BLITZ

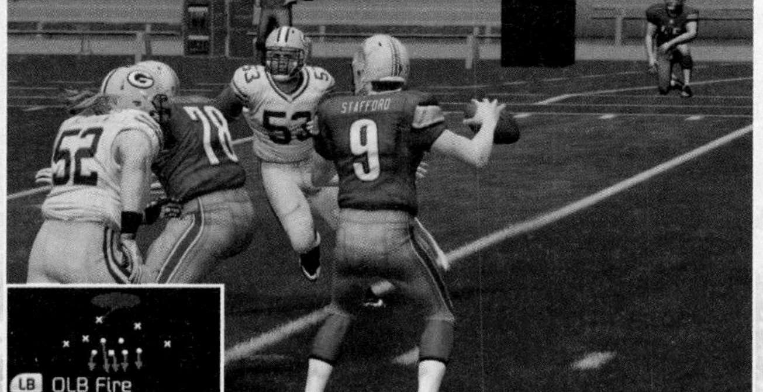

SETUP

- PRESS COVERAGE
- GLOBAL BLITZ LINEBACKERS

- User-control the corner blitzing corner.
- Drop into coverage with the blitzing corner. Make sure to leave him on his blitz assignment. This will cause confusion on the offensive line.

ZONE BLITZ

SETUP

- GLOBAL BLITZ LINEBACKERS
- FLAT ZONE BOTH HOOK ZONE DEFENDERS

- Pressure will come off either edge.
- The QB has to get rid of the ball quickly, but the flats will be covered!

Carolina Panthers

2012 TEAM RANKINGS

2nd NFC South (7-9-0)

PASSING OFFENSE: **16th**
RUSHING OFFENSE: **9th**
PASSING DEFENSE: **13th**
RUSHING DEFENSE: **14th**

2012 TEAM LEADERS

PASSING: **Cam Newton: 3,869**
RUSHING: **Cam Newton: 741**
RECEIVING: **Steve Smith: 1,174**
TACKLES: **Luke Kuechly: 164**
SACKS: **Charles Johnson: 12.5**
INTS: **Captain Munnerlyn: 2**

KEY ADDITIONS

WR Ted Ginn
WR Domenik Hixon
MLB Chase Blackburn

KEY ROOKIES

DT Star Lotulelei
DT Kawann Short
HB Kenjon Barner

CONNECTED FRANCHISE MODE STRATEGY

CFM TEAM RATING: **72**
OFFENSIVE SCHEME: **Balanced Offense**
DEFENSIVE SCHEME: **Base 4-3**
STRENGTHS: **QB, FB, LT, LE, RE, MLB, ROLB**
WEAKNESSES: **LG, RT, CB, FS, SS**

SCHEDULE

Week	Date	Time		Opponent
1	Sep 8	1:00 PM ET		SEAHAWKS
2	Sep 15	1:00 PM ET	AT	BILLS
3	Sep 22	1:00 PM ET		GIANTS
4	BYE			
5	Oct 6	4:05 PM ET	AT	CARDINALS
6	Oct 13	1:00 PM ET	AT	VIKINGS
7	Oct 20	1:00 PM ET		RAMS
8	Oct 24	8:25 PM ET	AT	BUCCANEERS
9	Nov 3	1:00 PM ET		FALCONS
10	Nov 10	4:05 PM ET	AT	49ERS
11	Nov 18	8:40 PM ET		PATRIOTS
12	Nov 24	1:00 PM ET	AT	DOLPHINS
13	Dec 1	1:00 PM ET		BUCCANEERS
14	Dec 8	1:00 PM ET	AT	SAINTS
15	Dec 15	4:05 PM ET		JETS
16	Dec 22	1:00 PM ET		SAINTS
17	Dec 29	1:00 PM ET	AT	FALCONS

FRANCHISE OVERVIEW

PANTHERS GAMEPLAY RATING

76

> SEE THE INSIDE BACK COVER FOR A QUICK REFERENCE TO THE GAME ABBREVIATIONS USED THROUGHOUT THIS GUIDE.

> IMPROVE WITH YOUR TEAM BY VISITING PRIMAGAMES.COM/MADDENNFL25 FOR MORE INFORMATION AND HOW-TO VIDEOS.

OFFENSIVE SCOUTING REPORT

- If you were starting a franchise tomorrow, QB Cam Newton would be the guy you wanted starting at QB for your team. He has only two years left on his contract, so make sure to sign him long-term.
- The Panthers have four different players who can carry the ball effectively. We think that rookie Kenjon Barner is the best long-term answer, and besides his CAR rating he is the best of the bunch.
- Trade WR Steve Smith as soon as possible. This offense is built to run the ball, and with the free-agent signing of WR Ted Ginn, Smith is no longer needed as a deep threat in the passing game. Try to get draft picks in return.

DEFENSIVE SCOUTING REPORT

- LE Greg Hardy and RE Charles Johnson are two of the best young pass rushers in the game. Hardy's contract is up at the end of the season. Bring him back for another few seasons.
- MLB Luke Kuechly is one of the best tacklers in the league. Currently he has three years remaining on his contract, and we think you should extend that to a max contract. He is only 22 and has a lot of football left ahead of him.
- The secondary needs major work in Carolina. During the draft make finding a lockdown CB your number one priority.

OWNER & COACH PROFILES

JERRY RICHARDSON

LEGACY SCORE: 750
OFF. SCHEME: Balanced Offense
DEF. SCHEME: Base 4-3

RON RIVERA

LEVEL: 6
LEGACY SCORE: 0
OFF. SCHEME: Balanced Offense
DEF. SCHEME: Base 4-3

TEAM OVERVIEW

KEY PLAYERS

QB #1

CAM NEWTON

KEY RATINGS

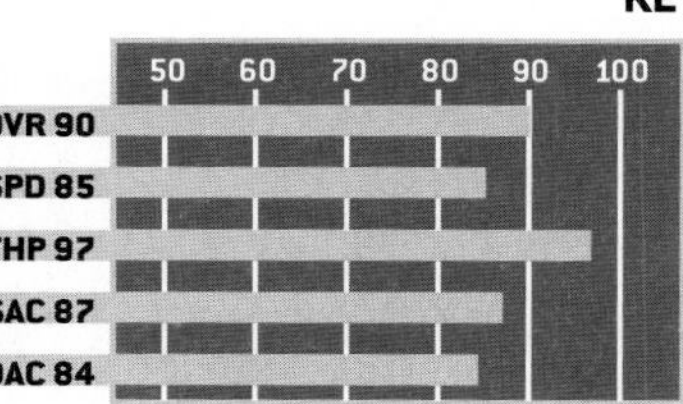

> Newton is a premiere young QB in the NFL. He has one of the best deep balls in the game.

> You should be running the read option at least 10 times a game with Newton.

MLB #59

LUKE KUECHLY

KEY RATINGS

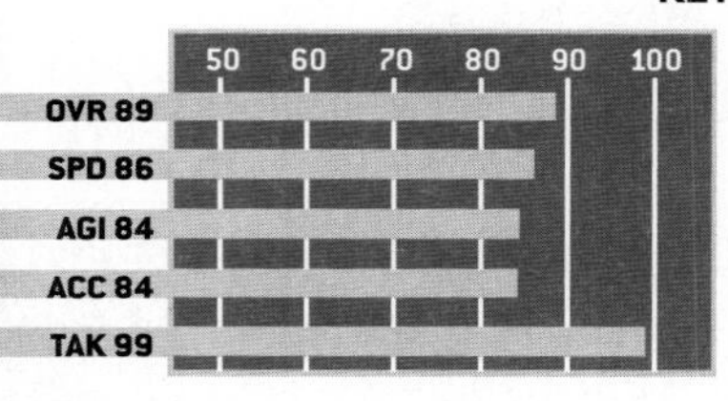

> Kuechly is arguably the game's best tackler. With a 99 TAK rating he will make every tackle on the field.

> User-control Kuechly when facing the run for an almost guaranteed tackle.

PRE-GAME SETUP

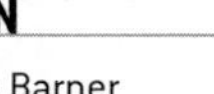

KEY RUNNING SUBSTITUTION

Who: HB Kenjon Barner

Where: Starting HB

Why: There's a lot of star power in the Panthers backfield. Don't be fooled; Barner is the best of the bunch.

Key Stats: 93 SPD, 92 AGI

KEY PASSING SUBSTITUTION

Who: WR Ted Ginn

Where: #3 WR

Why: Ginn will be great as a kick and punt returner as well as a deep ball threat.

Key Stats: 97 SPD

KEY RUN DEFENSE SUBSTITUTION

Who: DT Sione Fua

Where: #2 DT

Why: Fua has the strength to be a starting DT for running situations.

Key Stats: 90 STR

KEY PASS DEFENSE SUBSTITUTION

Who: FS Colin Jones

Where: #4 CB

Why: We like Jones for his speed. Use him as your dime CB and when you plan on blitzing.

Key Stats: 93 SPD

OFFENSIVE DEPTH CHART

POS	FIRST NAME	LAST NAME	OVR
QB	Cam	Newton	89
QB	Derek	Anderson	73
QB	Jimmy	Clausen	68
HB	DeAngelo	Williams	82
HB	Jonathan	Stewart	82
HB	Kenjon	Barner	69
HB	Tauren	Poole	68
HB	Armond	Smith	63
FB	Mike	Tolbert	92
FB	Richie	Brockel	69
WR	Steve	Smith	90
WR	Brandon	LaFell	77
WR	Domenik	Hixon	76
WR	Ted	Ginn	74
WR	David	Gettis	70
WR	Kealoha	Pilares	68
WR	Armanti	Edwards	66
WR	Joe	Adams	64
TE	Greg	Olsen	88
TE	Ben	Hartsock	75
TE	Nelson	Rosario	65
TE	J.J.	Jansen	49
LT	Jordan	Gross	88
LT	Bruce	Campbell	69
LT	Patrick	Brown	65
LG	Amini	Silatolu	74
LG	Edmund	Kugbila	66
LG	Hayworth	Hicks	62
C	Ryan	Kalil	85
C	Jeff	Byers	67
RG	Geoff	Hangartner	77
RG	Garry	Williams	74
RT	Byron	Bell	73
RT	Thomas	Austin	66

DEFENSIVE DEPTH CHART

POS	FIRST NAME	LAST NAME	OVR
LE	Greg	Hardy	90
LE	Frank	Alexander	67
RE	Charles	Johnson	93
RE	Mario	Addison	72
DT	Star	Lotulelei	81
DT	Dwan	Edwards	79
DT	Colin	Cole	75
DT	Sione	Fua	73
DT	Frank	Kearse	73
DT	Kawann	Short	73
DT	Nate	Chandler	63
LOLB	Thomas	Davis	80
LOLB	Jason	Williams	68
LOLB	A.J.	Klein	67
MLB	Luke	Kuechly	89
MLB	Chase	Blackburn	77
MLB	Ben	Jacobs	60
ROLB	Jon	Beason	88
ROLB	Jordan	Senn	72
ROLB	Doug	Hogue	66
CB	Captain	Munnerlyn	76
CB	Josh	Norman	74
CB	D.J.	Moore	72
CB	Drayton	Florence	70
CB	James	Dockery	69
CB	Josh	Thomas	69
FS	Haruki	Nakamura	74
FS	Colin	Jones	69
SS	Charles	Godfrey	80
SS	Mike	Mitchell	75
SS	Anderson	Russell	67
SS	D.J.	Campbell	66

SPECIAL TEAMS DEPTH CHART

POS	FIRST NAME	LAST NAME	OVR
K	Graham	Gano	76
P	Brad	Nortman	69

Carolina Panthers

RECOMMENDED OFFENSIVE RUN FORMATION: PISTOL FULL PANTHER (2 HB, 1 TE, 2 WR)

PRO TIPS

- > USE FB MIKE TOLBERT TO GET SHORT YARDAGE.
- > HB KENJON BARNER SHOULD BE YOUR STARTING HB.
- > MAKE SURE TO RUN THE BALL WITH CAM NEWTON.

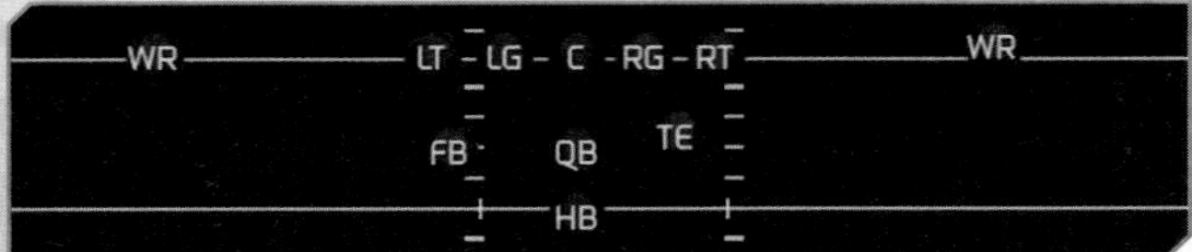

RUN LEFT

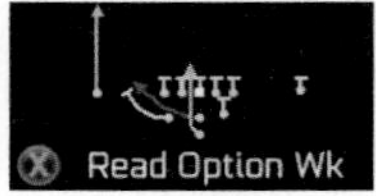

CAM NEWTON KEEPS THE BALL AND RUNS OFF THE LEFT EDGE.

RUN MIDDLE

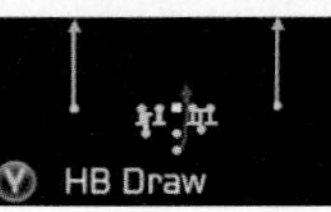

KENJON BARNER GETS THE RUN UPFIELD AS QUICKLY AS POSSIBLE.

RUN RIGHT

NEWTON KEEPS THE BALL AGAIN AND IS OFF TO THE END ZONE.

CAROLINA PANTHERS RUNNING PLAY CALL SHEET

LEGEND: Inside Run | Outside Run | Shotgun Run | QB Run

1ST DOWN RUNS	2ND AND SHORT	3RD AND SHORT	GOAL LINE RUNS	2ND AND LONG	3RD AND LONG
Strong Close—HB Off Tackle	Singleback Tight Slots—HB Dive	Weak Twins—HB Gut	Pistol Full Panther—HB Dive Wk	Gun Split Panther—Inside Zone Split	Gun Trips TE—Inverted Veer
Singleback Ace—HB Dive	I-Form Pro—Inside Zone	I-Form Tight Pair—HB Toss	Gun Heavy Panther—QB Power	Gun Doubles—HB Mid Draw	Gun Spread Y-Slot—QB Draw
Pistol Strong—Power Option	Pistol Weak—HB Zone Wk	Singleback Bunch Ace—Toss Crack	Pistol Full Panther—Read Option	Gun Doubles—Inside Zone	Gun Spread—HB Draw

CAROLINA PANTHERS PASSING PLAY CALL SHEET

LEGEND: Base Play | Man Beater | Zone Beater | Blitz Beater

1ST DOWN PLAY	2ND AND SHORT	3RD AND SHORT	GOAL LINE PASSING	2ND AND LONG	3RD AND LONG
Gun Ace—Inside Cross	Singleback Ace—Curl Flats	Gun Empty Base—Spacing	Gun Spread—Panther Curls	Singleback Panther Doubles—Panther Verts	Gun Doubles—Shark HB Wheel
Gun Spread Y-Slot—Deep Attack	Singleback Tight Slots—Drag Cross Ups	Singleback Ace Pair Flex—Quick Slant	Pistol Full Panther—Slants	Pistol Weak—Curls	Gun Spread Y-Slot—Four Verticals
Singleback Bunch Ace—Panther Go's	Pistol Strong—PA Flood	Singleback Panther Doubles—HB Slip Screen	Pistol Full Panther—Curl Deep Out	Gun Y-Trips TE Slot—Panther Y-Sail	Gun Empty Base—Verticals Shake

In these play call sheets we picked the best plays for specific situations so that you will have a play for every down and distance.

OFFENSE

RECOMMENDED OFFENSIVE PASS FORMATION: GUN DOUBLES (1 HB, 1 TE, 3 WR)

PRO TIPS

- TE GREG OLSEN IS ONE OF THE HARDEST TIGHT ENDS IN THE GAME TO DEFEND.
- USE WR TED GINN TO ATTACK OPPOSING DEFENSES DEEP.
- WR DAVID GETTIS IS A SLEEPER ON THE BENCH.

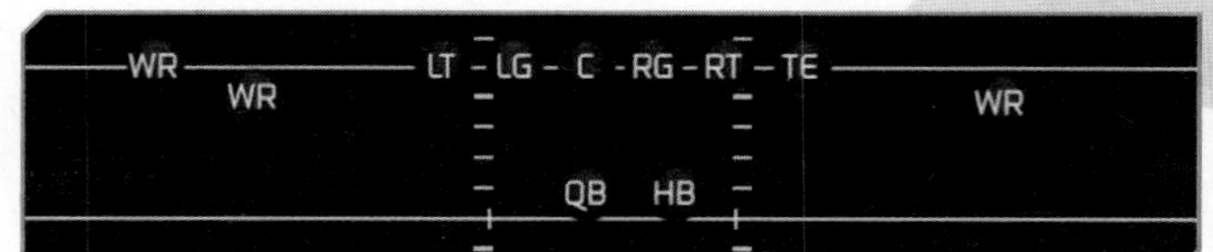

BASE PLAY

SETUP

- ZIG THE TE
- DRAG THE FAR RIGHT WR

- Look to the sideline wheel route as your first option on this play.
- If the wheel is covered look to the TE zig and the WR drag.

MAN BEATER

SETUP

- STREAK THE TE
- DRAG THE FAR RIGHT WR

- If a slower linebacker is covering TE Greg Olsen, look to hit him deep downfield.
- Otherwise target Kenjon Barner out of the backfield.

ZONE BEATER

SETUP

- STREAK THE TE
- OPTION THE HB

- Against Cover 2 and Cover 3 look to the sideline streaks.
- Against Cover 4 zones look to the HB option.

BLITZ BEATER

SETUP

- SWING RIGHT THE HB
- DRAG THE FAR RIGHT WR

- At the snap of the ball look to the drag; if he gets open throw him the ball.
- Otherwise get the HB the ball in the flat, where he has blockers to lead him upfield.

Carolina Panthers

RECOMMENDED DEFENSIVE RUN FORMATION: 5-2 NORMAL

PRO TIPS

- MLB CHASE BLACKBURN HAS 87 TAK AND WILL HELP STOP THE RUN.
- MLB LUKE KUECHLY IS A TACKLING MACHINE WITH A 99 TAK RATING.
- DEFENSIVE ENDS CHARLES JOHNSON AND GREG HARDY SHOULD REMAIN IN THE GAME ON RUNNING DOWNS.

RUN DEFENSE

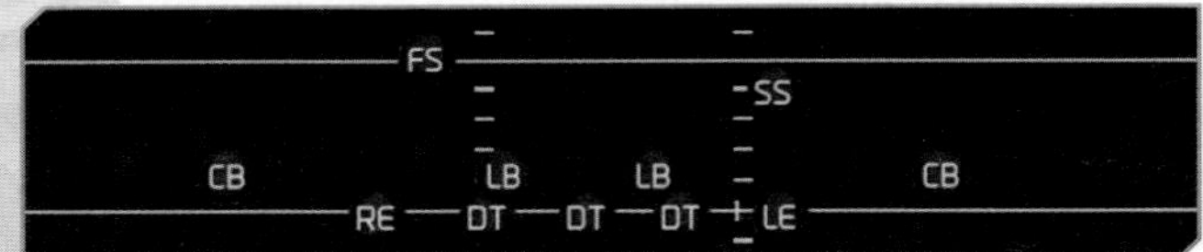

RUN DEFENSE LEFT

SETUP > SHIFT LINEBACKERS LEFT

RUN DEFENSE MIDDLE

SETUP > PINCH DEFENSIVE LINE

RUN DEFENSE RIGHT

SETUP > SHIFT LINEBACKERS RIGHT

CAROLINA PANTHERS DEFENSIVE RUN PLAY CALL SHEET

1ST DOWN RUN DEFENSE	2ND AND SHORT	3RD AND SHORT	GOAL LINE RUN DEFENSE	2ND AND LONG	3RD AND LONG
4-3 Stack—2 Man Under	5-2 Normal—Cover 1	5-2 Normal—Engage Eight	Goal Line 5-3-3—Jam Cover 1	Nickel 4 D Ends—Cover 1 Robber	Nickel Normal—2 Man Under
4-3 Stack—Cover 2 Buc	5-2 Normal—Cover 3	5-2 Normal—Trio Sky Zone	Goal Line 5-3-3—Flat Buzz	Nickel 4 D Ends—Cover 4	Nickel Normal—Cover 6

CAROLINA PANTHERS DEFENSIVE PASS PLAY CALL SHEET

1ST DOWN PLAY	2ND AND SHORT	3RD AND SHORT	GOAL LINE PASSING	2ND AND LONG	3RD AND LONG
Sub 4-1-6—2 Man Under	Dime Normal—Cover 1 Press	Sub 4-1-6—Silver Shoot Pinch	Goal Line 6-3-2—GL Man	Nickel Normal—Over Storm Brave	Sub 4-1-6—Overload 1 Roll
Sub 4-1-6—Cover 2 Sink	Dime Normal—Cover 6	Sub 4-1-6—Sugar 2 Buzz	Goal Line 6-3-2—GL Zone	Nickel Normal—Under Smoke 2	Sub 4-1-6—Overload 3 Seam

LEGEND: Man Coverage | Zone Coverage | Man Blitz | Zone Blitz

In these play call sheets we picked the best plays for specific situations so that you will have a play for every down and distance.

DEFENSE

RECOMMENDED DEFENSIVE PASS FORMATION: DIME NORMAL

PRO TIPS

- PLACE CB CAPTAIN MUNNERLYN ON YOUR OPPONENT'S BEST WR.
- USE CB DRAYTON FLORENCE ON YOUR OPPONENT'S FASTEST WR.
- CB JOSH NORMAN SHOULD BE YOUR #2 CB.

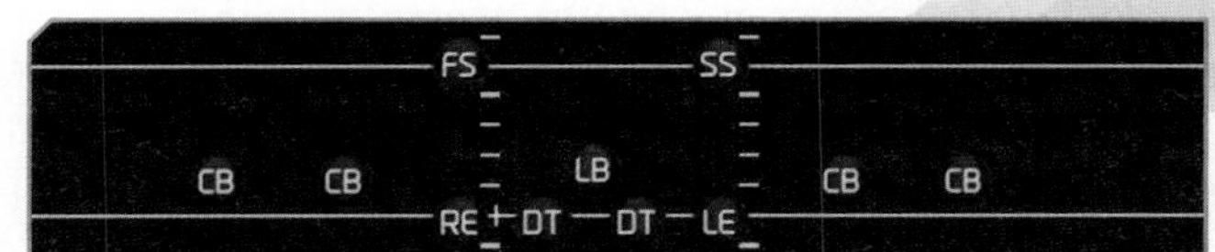

MAN COVERAGE

SETUP

- PINCH THE DEFENSIVE LINE
- CRASH THE DEFENSIVE LINE OUT

- By pinching the defensive line and crashing out, DEs Charles Johnson and Greg Hardy will get better pass rush angles.
- User-control the MLB covering the HB and watch for any routes over the middle of the field.

ZONE COVERAGE

SETUP

- PINCH THE DEFENSIVE LINE
- CRASH THE DEFENSIVE LINE OUT

- The 3 Double Buzz is unique because both safeties are playing hook zones.
- On most plays only one safety will play in a hook zone. This can result in confusion and interceptions for the defense.

MAN BLITZ

SETUP

- PRESS COVERAGE
- SHIFT LINEBACKERS RIGHT AND SLIDE THE BLITZING CB OFF THE EDGE OF THE LE

- We are trying to generate two free pass rushers after the QB.
- This blitz will force our opponent to block two extra offensive players to pick up this pressure.

ZONE BLITZ

SETUP

- SHIFT LINEBACKERS LEFT AND SLIDE THE BLITZING CB OFF THE EDGE OF THE RE
- CRASH THE DEFENSIVE LINE DOWN

- We are once again trying to generate two free pass rushers after the QB.
- If both defenders get in free, the QB will have to get rid of the ball quickly.

New England Patriots

2012 TEAM RANKINGS

1st AFC East (12-4-0)

PASSING OFFENSE: **4th**
RUSHING OFFENSE: **7th**
PASSING DEFENSE: **29th**
RUSHING DEFENSE: **9th**

2012 TEAM LEADERS

PASSING: **Tom Brady: 4,827**
RUSHING: **Stevan Ridley: 1,263**
RECEIVING: **Wes Welker: 1,354**
TACKLES: **Jerod Mayo: 147**
SACKS: **Rob Ninkovich: 8**
INTS: **Devin McCourty: 5**

KEY ADDITIONS

HB Leon Washington
HB LeGarrette Blount

KEY ROOKIES

ROLB Jamie Collins
WR Aaron Dobson
WR Josh Boyce

CONNECTED FRANCHISE MODE STRATEGY

CFM TEAM RATING: **82**
OFFENSIVE SCHEME: **Spread**
DEFENSIVE SCHEME: **Hybrid Multiple Front**
STRENGTHS: **QB, TE, LG, RT, DT, ROLB, FS, SS**
WEAKNESSES: **WR, CB**

SCHEDULE

1	Sep 8	1:00 PM ET	AT	BILLS
2	Sep 12	8:25 PM ET		JETS
3	Sep 22	1:00 PM ET		BUCCANEERS
4	Sep 29	8:30 PM ET	AT	FALCONS
5	Oct 6	1:00 PM ET	AT	BENGALS
6	Oct 13	4:25 PM ET		SAINTS
7	Oct 20	1:00 PM ET	AT	JETS
8	Oct 27	1:00 PM ET		DOLPHINS
9	Nov 3	4:25 PM ET		STEELERS
10	BYE			
11	Nov 18	8:40 PM ET	AT	PANTHERS
12	Nov 24	8:30 PM ET		BRONCOS
13	Dec 1	4:25 PM ET	AT	TEXANS
14	Dec 8	1:00 PM ET		BROWNS
15	Dec 15	1:00 PM ET	AT	DOLPHINS
16	Dec 22	8:30 PM ET	AT	RAVENS
17	Dec 29	1:00 PM ET		BILLS

FRANCHISE OVERVIEW

PATRIOTS GAMEPLAY RATING

88

> See the inside back cover for a quick reference to the game abbreviations used throughout this guide.

> Improve with your team by visiting PrimaGames.com/MaddenNFL25 for more information and how-to videos.

OFFENSIVE SCOUTING REPORT

> QB Tom Brady has a contract that will last until he's 40 years of age. That's five more years the Patriots have with this future hall of famer. The window is closing on the Brady era, so do everything you can to surround him with winning talent.

> The Patriots backfield has the most depth in the entire NFL. There are five HBs who could start for this team. The question is, who is the best long-term player? We think the future is brightest for HBs Stevan Ridley and Shane Vereen. Upgrade both these players during the off-season.

> TE Rob Gronkowski is arguably the best TE in the game today. His kryptonite right now is the injury bug. His 77 INJ rating is a cause for concern. Monitor his injuries closely and be prepared to make a drastic move if necessary.

DEFENSIVE SCOUTING REPORT

> RE Chandler Jones started his rookie season hot out of the gates. Injuries kept him from seeing the field for the majority of the second half of the season. If he can stay on the field he will be a force in this league.

> The future is bright for LOLB Dont'a Hightower. He has the speed of smaller linebackers but the size and strength of the biggest in the league. He is the definition of a hybrid player.

> Our favorite player in the Patriots secondary is SS Nate Ebner. With his 87 SPD and a 91 POW ratings, we see potential for him to become a quality player in this league.

OWNER & COACH PROFILES

ROBERT KRAFT
LEGACY SCORE: 11632
OFF. SCHEME: Spread
DEF. SCHEME: Hybrid Multiple Front

CHAD MASTERS
LEVEL: 30
LEGACY SCORE: 18325
OFF. SCHEME: Spread
DEF. SCHEME: Hybrid Multiple Fro

TEAM OVERVIEW

KEY PLAYERS

QB #12

TOM BRADY

KEY RATINGS

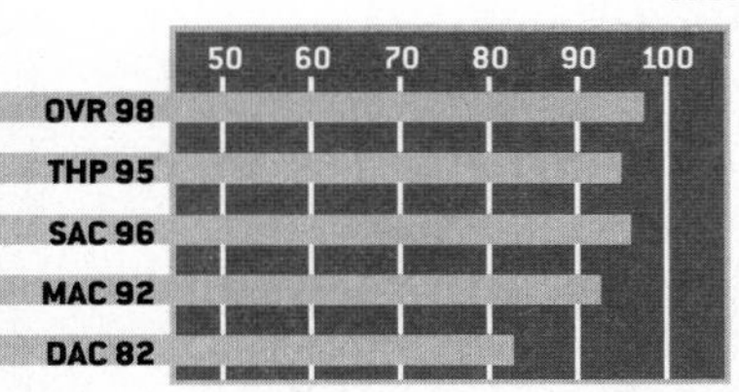

- > Brady is one of the greatest QBs to ever play the game. He can make any throw that is required.
- > Look to get the ball deep down the sideline to TE Rob Gronkowski.

ROLB #51

JEROD MAYO

KEY RATINGS

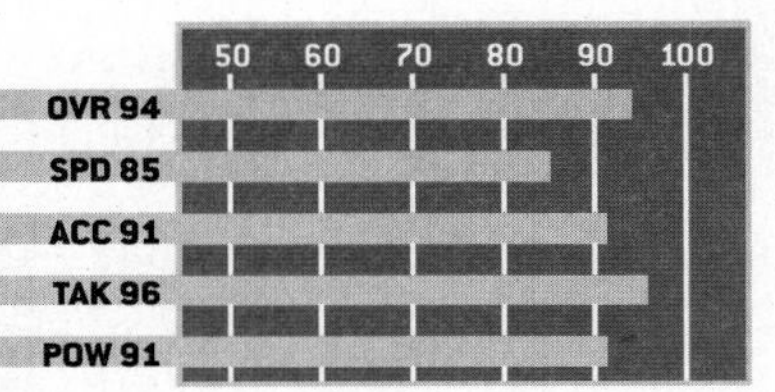

- > Mayo is the veteran of the Patriots defense, and he leads by example. He is the team's best overall tackler.
- > With his 91 POW rating, Mayo can cause fumbles when he hits ball carriers.

PRE-GAME SETUP

KEY RUNNING SUBSTITUTION

Who: HB Shane Vereen

Where: Backup HB

Why: Vereen needs to see the field on third downs. Vereen has a much better CTH rating for third down situations.

Key Stats: 83 CTH

KEY PASSING SUBSTITUTION

Who: WR Aaron Dobson

Where: #4 WR

Why: Dobson is only a rookie, but he has the potential to be a big target down the sideline and in the red zone.

Key Stats: 6'2", 87 CTH, 94 SPC

KEY RUN DEFENSE SUBSTITUTION

Who: SS Nate Ebner

Where: Starting FS

Why: Start Ebner for run situations only. He has 91 POW, which will force fumbles.

Key Stats: 91 POW

KEY PASS DEFENSE SUBSTITUTION

Who: CB Ras-I Dowling

Where: #3 CB

Why: Dowling is a big corner who plays a physical brand of football. Use him to press your opponents' big WRs.

Key Stats: 6'1" 85 PRS

OFFENSIVE DEPTH CHART

POS	FIRST NAME	LAST NAME	OVR
QB	Tom	Brady	97
QB	Ryan	Mallett	74
QB	Tim	Tebow	73
HB	Stevan	Ridley	85
HB	Shane	Vereen	78
HB	Leon	Washington	75
HB	LeGarrette	Blount	75
HB	Brandon	Bolden	72
FB	James	Develin	65
WR	Danny	Amendola	83
WR	Julian	Edelman	77
WR	Michael	Jenkins	77
WR	Aaron	Dobson	72
WR	Lavelle	Hawkins	71
WR	Matthew	Slater	70
WR	Josh	Boyce	67
WR	Kamar	Aiken	61
TE	Rob	Gronkowski	98
TE	Jake	Ballard	77
TE	Daniel	Fells	74
TE	Michael	Hoomanawanui	73
TE	Danny	Aiken	57
LT	Nate	Solder	85
LT	Will	Svitek	75
LG	Logan	Mankins	94
C	Ryan	Wendell	89
C	Nick	McDonald	65
RG	Dan	Connolly	81
RG	Marcus	Cannon	74
RT	Sebastian	Vollmer	91
RT	Markus	Zusevics	68

DEFENSIVE DEPTH CHART

POS	FIRST NAME	LAST NAME	OVR
LE	Rob	Ninkovich	85
LE	Justin	Francis	72
LE	Jermaine	Cunningham	68
LE	Michael	Buchanan	67
RE	Chandler	Jones	81
RE	Jake	Bequette	71
RE	Marcus	Benard	70
DT	Vince	Wilfork	93
DT	Tommy	Kelly	78
DT	Marcus	Forston	65
LOLB	Dont'a	Hightower	80
LOLB	A.J.	Edds	65
LOLB	Jeff	Tarpinian	63
MLB	Brandon	Spikes	86
MLB	Dane	Fletcher	70
MLB	Steve	Beauharnais	65
MLB	Mike	Rivera	63
ROLB	Jerod	Mayo	94
ROLB	Niko	Koutouvides	71
ROLB	Jamie	Collins	69
CB	Aqib	Talib	86
CB	Alfonzo	Dennard	81
CB	Kyle	Arrington	77
CB	Ras-I	Dowling	74
CB	Logan	Ryan	70
CB	Marquice	Cole	69
FS	Devin	McCourty	92
FS	Steve	Gregory	75
FS	Tavon	Wilson	72
SS	Adrian	Wilson	87
SS	Duron	Harmon	70
SS	Nate	Ebner	63

SPECIAL TEAMS DEPTH CHART

POS	FIRST NAME	LAST NAME	OVR
K	Stephen	Gostkowski	89
P	Zoltan	Mesko	84

New England Patriots

RECOMMENDED OFFENSIVE RUN FORMATION: SINGLEBACK NORMAL PATRIOTS (1 HB, 1 TE, 3 WR)

PRO TIPS

- > USE HB SHANE VEREEN FOR THIRD DOWN PASSING SITUATIONS.
- > TE ROB GRONKOWSKI IS ONE OF THE LEAGUE'S BEST RUN BLOCKING TIGHT ENDS.
- > LT NATE SOLDER CAN BE USED AT TE IN RED ZONE SITUATIONS.

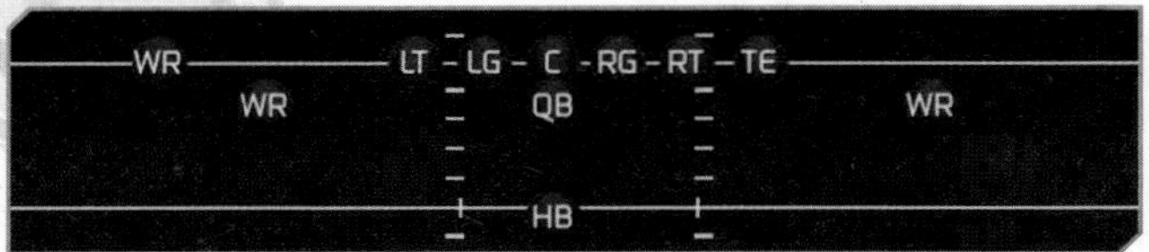

RUN LEFT

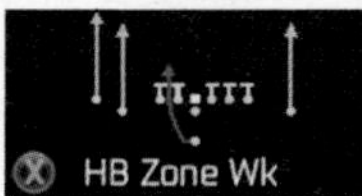

STEVAN RIDLEY IS A POWER BACK—KEEP THE RUNS OFF THE LEFT TACKLE.

RUN MIDDLE

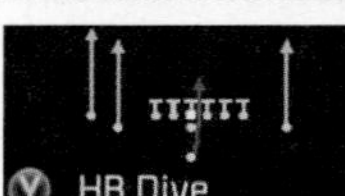

RIDLEY FIGHTS HARD FOR YARDS OVER THE MIDDLE.

RUN RIGHT

KEEP RIDLEY CLOSE TO THE OFFENSIVE LINEMEN AS YOU MOVE UPFIELD.

NEW ENGLAND PATRIOTS RUNNING PLAY CALL SHEET

LEGEND: Inside Run | Outside Run | Shotgun Run | QB Run

1ST DOWN RUNS	2ND AND SHORT	3RD AND SHORT	GOAL LINE RUNS	2ND AND LONG	3RD AND LONG
I-Form TE Flip—Pats Power O	I-Form TE Flip—FB Dive Strong	I-Form Tight Pair—HB Power	Goal Line Normal—QB Sneak	Gun Ace Pair Flex—45 Quick Base	Gun Bunch—HB Sweep
Singleback Ace Pair Twins—HB Dive	Singleback Ace Pair Twins—HB Slam	Strong Twins—Counter Weak	Goal Line Normal—HB Dive	Strong Pro—HB Dive	Gun Ace Tight Slots—HB Mid Draw
Singleback Deuce Wing—HB Toss	Singleback Normal Patriots—HB Power O	I-Form Tight Pair—HB Toss	Goal Line Normal—Power O	Gun Bunch—HB Mid Draw	Gun Ace Tight Slots—HB Sweep

NEW ENGLAND PATRIOTS PASSING PLAY CALL SHEET

LEGEND: Base Play | Man Beater | Zone Beater | Blitz Beater

1ST DOWN PLAY	2ND AND SHORT	3RD AND SHORT	GOAL LINE PASSING	2ND AND LONG	3RD AND LONG
Gun Ace Tight Slots—Pats Wheel Drag	Singleback Bunch—Y Trail	Gun Trips TE—Pats Slot Screen	Goal Line—PA Waggle	Gun Trips TE—Curl Flats	Gun Ace—Quick Slants
Gun Normal Flex Wk Pats—Patriots Spot	Singleback Normal Patriots—WR Drag	Gun Empty Y-Flex—Stutter Under	Goal Line—PA Spot	Gun Trups TE—HB Angle	Gun Ace—Hitch Corners
Gun Normal Y-Slot—Z Shallow Cross	Singleback Bunch—Flanker Drive	Gun Empty Y-Flex—Pats Y Shake	Goal Line—PA Power O	Gun Ace Wing TE—Inside Cross	Gun Ace Tight Slots—Mesh

In these play call sheets we picked the best plays for specific situations so that you will have a play for every down and distance.

OFFENSE

RECOMMENDED OFFENSIVE PASS FORMATION: GUN EMPTY ACE PATRIOT (1 HB, 2 TE, 2 WR)

PRO TIPS

> WR MIKE JENKINS IS 6'4" AND WILL BE A HUGE TARGET IN THE RED ZONE.

> TE JAKE BALLARD WILL SEE A TON OF PLAYING TIME THIS SEASON. GET HIM THE BALL EARLY AND OFTEN.

> HB SHANE VEREEN IS A GREAT OPTION FOR THIRD AND LONG PASSING SITUATIONS.

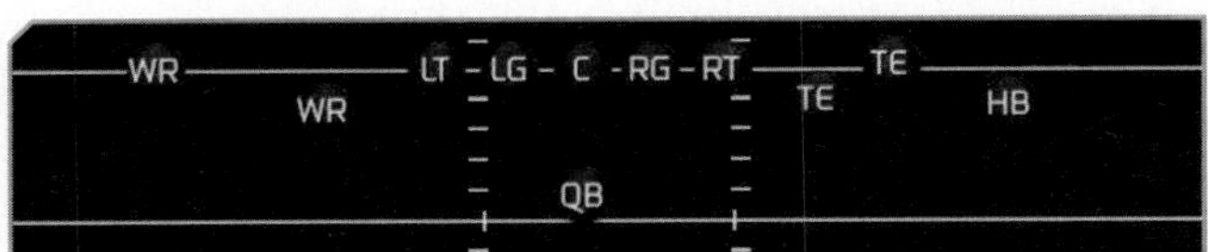

BASE PLAY

SETUP

> DRAG THE LEFT SLOT WR

> DRAG THE RIGHT SLOT WR

> Both outside WRs are unbumpable and will be great user-catch options down the sideline.

> The inside TE's double move is our favorite route on this play. It torches man-to-man coverage.

MAN BEATER

SETUP

> CURL THE FAR RIGHT HB

> DRAG THE FAR LEFT WR

> The TE running the shake route will beat man-to-man coverage inside.

> The slot TE running the fade is a user-catch option. Gronkowski can beat any defender running this route.

ZONE BEATER

SETUP

> NONE

> Against Cover 2 and Cover 3 zones look to the slot WRs and TEs.

> Against Cover 4 zones look to the outside WR and HB.

BLITZ BEATER

SETUP

> NONE

> The bubble screen on the left is great against man-to-man.

> The WR screen on the right is great against zone.

New England Patriots

RECOMMENDED DEFENSIVE RUN FORMATION: 4-3 OVER ODD

PRO TIPS

- MLB BRANDON SPIKES IS ONE OF THE BEST MIDDLE LINEBACKERS IN THE LEAGUE AT STOPPING THE RUN.
- PLACE DT VINCE WILFORK DIRECTLY OVER THE CENTER. HE WILL WIN THIS BATTLE ON MOST DOWNS.
- USER-CONTROL SS ADRIAN WILSON IN THE BOX FOR EXTRA RUN SUPPORT.

RUN DEFENSE

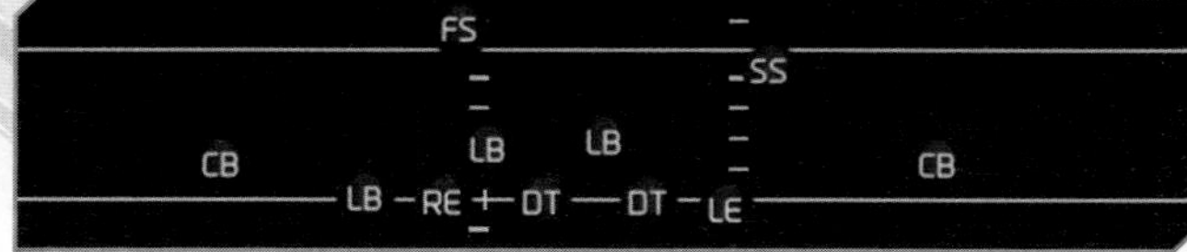

RUN DEFENSE LEFT

SETUP > SHIFT LINEBACKERS LEFT

RUN DEFENSE MIDDLE

SETUP > PINCH DEFENSIVE LINE

RUN DEFENSE RIGHT

SETUP > SHIFT LINEBACKERS RIGHT

NEW ENGLAND PATRIOTS DEFENSIVE RUN PLAY CALL SHEET

1ST DOWN RUN DEFENSE	2ND AND SHORT	3RD AND SHORT	GOAL LINE RUN DEFENSE	2ND AND LONG	3RD AND LONG
4-3 Over Odd—Cover 1 Robber	4-3 Over Plus—Saw 0 Blast	3-4 Odd—MLB Storm Blitz	Goal Line 5-3-3—Jam Cover 1	Dollar 3-2-6—Fire Dog 1	Nickel 3-3-5 Will—Dbl Safety Blitz
4-3 Over Odd—Cover 2	4-3 Over Plus—Cover 6	3-4 Odd—FS Zone Blitz	Goal Line 5-3-3—Flat Buzz	Dollar 3-2-6—Cross 3 Fire	Nickel 3-3-5 Will—Sugar Cover 3 Bluff

NEW ENGLAND PATRIOTS DEFENSIVE PASS PLAY CALL SHEET

1ST DOWN PLAY	2ND AND SHORT	3RD AND SHORT	GOAL LINE PASSING	2ND AND LONG	3RD AND LONG
4-3 Over Odd—2 Man Under	3-4 Solid—Cover 1 Robber	3-4 Odd—Storm Brave 1	Goal Line 6-3-2—GL Man	Dollar 3-2-6—Spinner Buck Dog 1	Nickel 3-3-5 Will—Cover 1 Spy
4-3 Over Odd—Cover 3 Buzz	3-4 Solid—Cover 6	3-4 Odd—Sam Mike 2 Sting	Goal Line 6-3-2—GL Zone	Dollar 3-2-6—Corner Fire 2 Roll	Nickel 3-3-5 Will—Overload 3 Seam

LEGEND: Man Coverage | Zone Coverage | Man Blitz | Zone Blitz

In these play call sheets we picked the best plays for specific situations so that you will have a play for every down and distance.

DEFENSE

RECOMMENDED DEFENSIVE PASS FORMATION: DOLLAR 3-2-6

PRO TIPS

> PLACE CB AQIB TALIB ON THE OPPOSING TEAM'S BEST WR.

> USE CB RAS-I DOWLING ON THE TEAM'S FASTEST RECEIVERS.

> USE CB ALFONZO DENNARD AS YOUR #2 CB.

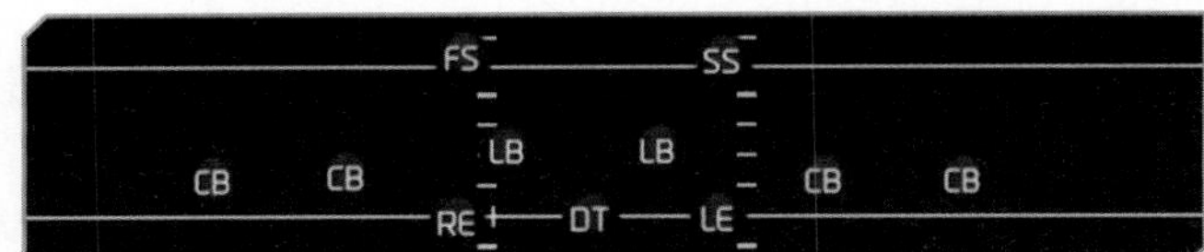

MAN COVERAGE

SETUP

> GLOBAL BLITZ THE ROLB

> MOVE HIM OUTSIDE THE RE

> This setup will send two of our best pass rushers off the left edge of the field.

> We are only rushing four defenders, but the pressure will be quick and the coverage will be tight.

ZONE COVERAGE

SETUP

> PUT THE ROLB ON GLOBAL BLITZ

> MOVE HIM OUTSIDE THE LE

> This setup is similar to our man coverage play.

> Our setup causes a stunt with the offensive line. This confusion helps our pass rush get after the QB.

MAN BLITZ

SETUP

> PRESS COVERAGE

> GLOBAL BLITZ LINEBACKERS

> Press coverage will slow down our opponent's reads.

> The Patriots have solid pressing CBs, so this play can be difficult for offenses to beat.

ZONE BLITZ

SETUP

> PRESS COVERAGE

> GLOBAL BLITZ THE LOLB

> This blitz sends six pass rushers after the QB.

> The goal here is to get two free pass rushers against the QB to force a throw into coverage.

Oakland Raiders

2012 TEAM RANKINGS

3rd AFC West (4-12-0)

PASSING OFFENSE: **8th**
RUSHING OFFENSE: **28th**
PASSING DEFENSE: **20th**
RUSHING DEFENSE: **18th**

2012 TEAM STAT LEADERS

PASSING: **Carson Palmer: 4,018**
RUSHING: **Darren McFadden: 707**
RECEIVING: **Brandon Myers: 806**
TACKLES: **Philip Wheeler: 109**
SACKS: **Lamarr Houston: 4**
INTS: **Matt Giordano: 2**

KEY ADDITIONS

QB Matt Flynn
FS Charles Woodson
FS Usama Young

KEY ROOKIES

CB D.J. Hayden
RT Menelik Watson
ROLB Sio Moore

CONNECTED FRANCHISE MODE STRATEGY

CFM TEAM RATING: **68**
OFFENSIVE SCHEME: **West Coast**
DEFENSIVE SCHEME: **Base 4-3**
STRENGTHS: **HB, FB, LT, LE, FS, SS, K**
WEAKNESSES: **QB, WR, TE, LOLB, MLB, CB**

SCHEDULE

Week	Date	Time		Opponent
1	Sep 8	1:00 PM ET	AT	COLTS
2	Sep 15	4:25 PM ET		JAGUARS
3	Sep 23	8:40 PM ET	AT	BRONCOS
4	Sep 29	4:25 PM ET		REDSKINS
5	Oct 6	4:25 PM ET		CHARGERS
6	Oct 13	1:00 PM ET	AT	CHIEFS
7	BYE			
8	Oct 27	4:05 PM ET		STEELERS
9	Nov 3	4:05 PM ET		EAGLES
10	Nov 10	1:00 PM ET	AT	GIANTS
11	Nov 17	1:00 PM ET	AT	TEXANS
12	Nov 24	4:05 PM ET		TITANS
13	Nov 28	4:30 PM ET	AT	COWBOYS
14	Dec 8	1:00 PM ET	AT	JETS
15	Dec 15	4:05 PM ET		CHIEFS
16	Dec 22	4:25 PM ET	AT	CHARGERS
17	Dec 29	4:25 PM ET		BRONCOS

FRANCHISE OVERVIEW

RAIDERS GAMEPLAY RATING

72

> See the inside back cover for a quick reference to the game abbreviations used throughout this guide.

> Improve with your team by visiting PrimaGames.com/MaddenNFL25 for more information and how-to videos.

OFFENSIVE SCOUTING REPORT

- Start QB Terrelle Pryor and try to upgrade him enough so that he can be a viable option for the short term. Moving forward, look to the draft to solve this situation.
- HB Darren McFadden has had injury concerns over the course of his career, and this is cause for concern. He is in the final year of his contract, and there is a star in the making waiting to fill his shoes. HB Taiwan Jones has all the tools needed to be a special player in this league.
- FB Marcel Reece's contract expires at the end of the season. Bring him back at all costs.

DEFENSIVE SCOUTING REPORT

- LE Lamarr Houston will need to be re-signed at the end of the season. Bring him back for at least three seasons.
- The Raiders' linebackers need to be rebuilt from the ground up. Look to the draft and free agency to strengthen this unit.
- FS Charles Woodson has been reunited with his former team and will be needed to control the secondary for the Raiders. He brings experience to a young group and will need to be the signal caller. We like keeping Woodson on for a few seasons.

OWNER & COACH PROFILES

MARK DAVIS
LEGACY SCORE: 0
OFF. SCHEME: West Coast
DEF. SCHEME: Base 4-3

DENNIS ALLEN
LEVEL: 1
LEGACY SCORE: 0
OFF. SCHEME: West Coast
DEF. SCHEME: Base 4-3

TEAM OVERVIEW

KEY PLAYERS

FB #45

MARCEL REECE

KEY RATINGS

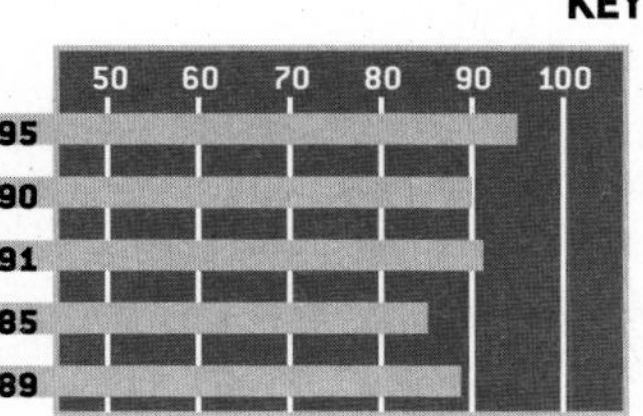

> Reece is the best FB in *Madden NFl 25*. He is one of the most versatile players in the game.

> Use him to run the ball, catch passes out of the backfield, and lead block for McFadden.

SS #33

TYVON BRANCH

KEY RATINGS

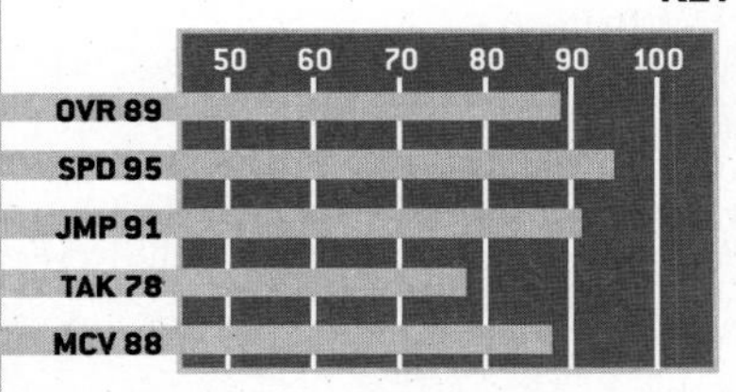

> Branch is one of the game's fastest strong safeties. With 95 SPD he can play sideline to sideline.

> Branch will be great in one-on-one man-to-man situations. This will allow you to be aggressive with the Raiders defense.

PRE-GAME SETUP

KEY RUNNING SUBSTITUTION

Who: HB Taiwan Jones

Where: Backup HB

Why: Jones is our favorite sleeper HB in *Madden NFL 25*. He has the speed and hands to be an elite HB.

Key Stats: 97 SPD, 92 AGI, 95 ACC, 73 CTH

KEY PASSING SUBSTITUTION

Who: WR Juron Criner

Where: #2 WR

Why: Criner is the Raiders' best jump-ball WR. Split him out wide and look for him down the sideline.

Key Stats: 6'3", 81 CTH, 91 JMP

KEY RUN DEFENSE SUBSTITUTION

Who: DT Pat Sims

Where: #2 DT

Why: Use Sims for running situations only. He has 91 STR and the ability to disrupt offensive run schemes.

Key Stats: 91 STR

KEY PASS DEFENSE SUBSTITUTION

Who: CB Chimdi Chekwa

Where: #3 Nickel CB

Why: Chekwa has straight-line speed as well as great agility and acceleration.

Key Stats: 94 SPD, 93 AGI, 90 ACC

OFFENSIVE DEPTH CHART

POS	FIRST NAME	LAST NAME	OVR
QB	Matt	Flynn	78
QB	Terrelle	Pryor	70
QB	Tyler	Wilson	69
HB	Darren	McFadden	87
HB	Rashad	Jennings	73
HB	Taiwan	Jones	68
HB	Jeremy	Stewart	68
HB	Latavius	Murray	67
FB	Marcel	Reece	95
FB	Jamize	Olawale	65
FB	Jon	Hoese	63
WR	Denarius	Moore	82
WR	Jacoby	Ford	74
WR	Rod	Streater	73
WR	Josh	Cribbs	72
WR	Juron	Criner	69
WR	Andre	Holmes	66
WR	Conner	Vernon	64
WR	Isaiah	Williams	62
WR	Brice	Butler	59
TE	Richard	Gordon	73
TE	David	Ausberry	71
TE	Mychal	Rivera	68
TE	Nick	Kasa	67
TE	Jeron	Mastrud	67
TE	Jon	Condo	44
LT	Jared	Veldheer	90
LT	Willie	Smith	60
LG	Tony	Bergstrom	71
C	Stefen	Wisniewski	85
C	Alex	Parsons	65
RG	Mike	Brisiel	79
RG	Lucas	Nix	64
RT	Alex	Barron	76
RT	Khalif	Barnes	76
RT	Menelik	Watson	72

DEFENSIVE DEPTH CHART

POS	FIRST NAME	LAST NAME	OVR
LE	Lamarr	Houston	89
LE	Andre	Carter	80
LE	Brandon	Bair	68
RE	Jason	Hunter	74
RE	Jack	Crawford	64
DT	Vance	Walker	81
DT	Pat	Sims	77
DT	Christo	Bilukidi	66
DT	Johnny	Jones	64
DT	Stacy	McGee	63
LOLB	Nick	Roach	78
LOLB	Miles	Burris	70
LOLB	Kaelin	Burnett	61
MLB	Kaluka	Maiava	75
MLB	Travis	Goethel	63
ROLB	Kevin	Burnett	83
ROLB	Sio	Moore	71
ROLB	Keenan	Clayton	67
CB	D.J.	Hayden	78
CB	Tracy	Porter	78
CB	Mike	Jenkins	77
CB	Joselio	Hanson	76
CB	Phillip	Adams	73
CB	Chimdi	Chekwa	68
CB	Coye	Francies	67
CB	Brandian	Ross	66
FS	Charles	Woodson	85
FS	Usama	Young	78
FS	Cory	Nelms	65
SS	Tyvon	Branch	89
SS	Reggie	Smith	74

SPECIAL TEAMS DEPTH CHART

POS	FIRST NAME	LAST NAME	OVR
K	Sebastian	Janikowski	94
P	Chris	Kluwe	79

Oakland Raiders

RECOMMENDED OFFENSIVE RUN FORMATION: I FORM TE FLIP (2 HB, 1 TE, 2 WR)

PRO TIPS

> HB TAIWAN JONES NEEDS TO GET AT LEAST FIVE TOUCHES EVERY GAME.

> WR JACOBY FORD IS ONE OF THE LEAGUE'S BEST KICK AND PUNT RETURNERS.

> FB MARCEL REECE CAN BE USED AS AN HB, FB, OR TE.

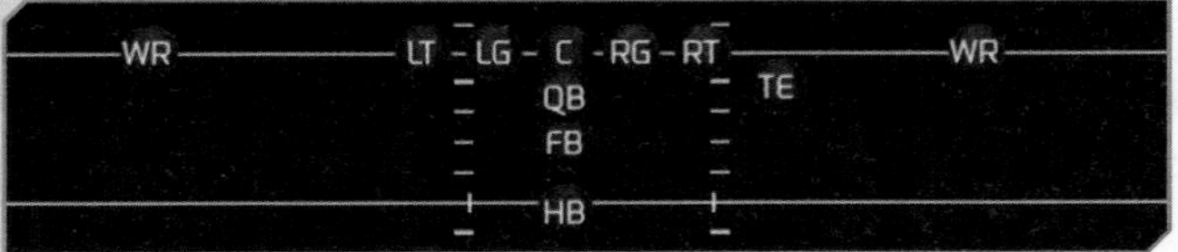

RUN LEFT

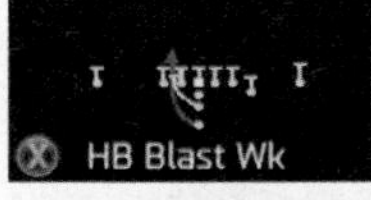

MCFADDEN BURSTS OFF THE LEFT EDGE.

RUN MIDDLE

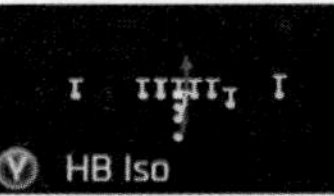

POWER THROUGH THE LINE OF SCRIMMAGE WITH MCFADDEN.

RUN RIGHT

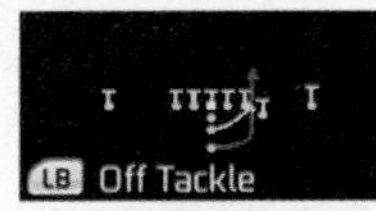

MCFADDEN CAN GET TO THE EDGE QUICKLY.

OAKLAND RAIDERS RUNNING PLAY CALL SHEET

LEGEND: Inside Run | Outside Run | Shotgun Run | QB Run

1ST DOWN RUNS	2ND AND SHORT	3RD AND SHORT	GOAL LINE RUNS	2ND AND LONG	3RD AND LONG
Singleback Ace—Off Tackle	Weak Twins—HB Gut	I-Form Pro—FB Dive	Singleback Wing Trio—Mtn Lead Dive	Gun Trey Open—HB Base	Gun Trio Offset—0 1 Trap
I-Form Pro Twins—HB Blast	I-Form Pro Twins Pair—OAK Dive Wk	I-Form Pro—FB Fake HB Flip	Singleback Ace Pair Slot—Power O	Singleback Tight Doubles—HB Draw	Gun Trey Open—Read Option
Strong H Pro—Counter Weak	Weak Twins—Toss Weak	Singleback Ace Pair Slot—HB Zone Wk	Singleback Doubles—Inside Zone	Gun Doubles On—HB Off Tackle	Gun Spread Y-Flex—HB Draw

OAKLAND RAIDERS PASSING PLAY CALL SHEET

LEGEND: Base Play | Man Beater | Zone Beater | Blitz Beater

1ST DOWN PLAY	2ND AND SHORT	3RD AND SHORT	GOAL LINE PASSING	2ND AND LONG	3RD AND LONG
Gun Trey Open—Four Verticals	Singleback Doubles—Flanker Drive	Singleback Tight Doubles—PA WR Cross	Gun Trio Offset—HB Slip Screen	Gun Trio Offset—Flood	Gun Spread Y-Flex—Deep Attack
Gun Spread Y-Flex—OAK Seam Comebacks	Singleback Ace—Quick Slants	I-Form TE Flip—PA FB Flat	Singleback Tight Doubles—Slot Fade	Gun Y-Trips Wk—Y Trail	Gun Empty Trey—Smash
Gun Doubles On—Curl Flats	Gun Trio Offset—Stick	Gun Y-Trips Wk—HB Slip Screen	Gun Empty Spread—Spacing	Gun Split Y-Flex—OAK Y-Cross	Singleback Bunch Base—Z Spot

In these play call sheets we picked the best plays for specific situations so that you will have a play for every down and distance.

OFFENSE

RECOMMENDED OFFENSIVE PASS FORMATION: SHOTGUN 5WR HB (1 RB, 1 TE, 3 WR)

PRO TIPS

- USE FB MARCEL REECE AT TE.
- WR JACOBY FORD CAN TURN ANY RECEPTION INTO A TOUCHDOWN WITH HIS SPEED.
- USE QB TERRELLE PRYOR FOR READ OPTIONS BECAUSE OF HIS 90 SPD.

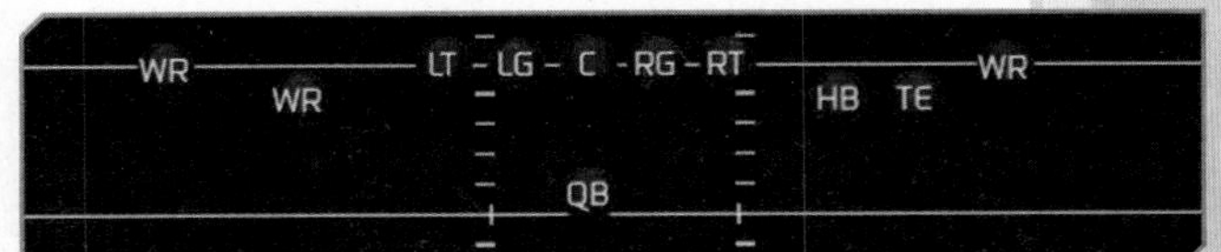

BASE PLAY

SETUP

- OUT ROUTE THE FAR LEFT WR
- OUT ROUTE THE FAR RIGHT WR

- Look to McFadden over the middle of the field. Against man-to-man coverage he gets great separation.
- Against zone look to the sideline out routes.

MAN BEATER

SETUP

- DRAG THE LEFT SLOT WR
- OUT ROUTE THE FAR LEFT WR

- The WR running the inside zig route gets separation as he cuts back inside.
- The double move route by the HB will be open downfield, but it needs extra time in the pocket to develop.

ZONE BEATER

SETUP

- NONE

- Against Cover 2 and Cover 3 zones look to the slot WRs.
- Against Cover 4 zones look to the outside WRs.

BLITZ BEATER

SETUP

- NONE

- Key in on your opponent's user defender and throw where he isn't covering.
- This play is extremely dangerous against the blitz because we have two screen options on both sides of the field.

Oakland Raiders

RECOMMENDED DEFENSIVE RUN FORMATION: 46 NORMAL

PRO TIPS

> DT PAT SIMS SHOULD BE USED DURING RUNNING SITUATIONS.

> LOLB MILES BURRIS IS AN UP-AND-COMING TACKLING MACHINE FOR THE RAIDERS.

> SS TYVON BRANCH WILL PROVIDE GREAT RUN SUPPORT IN THE BOX.

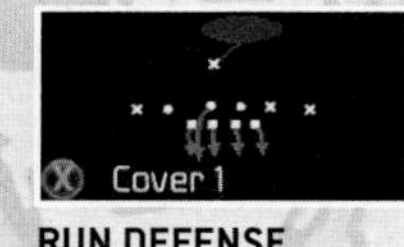

RUN DEFENSE

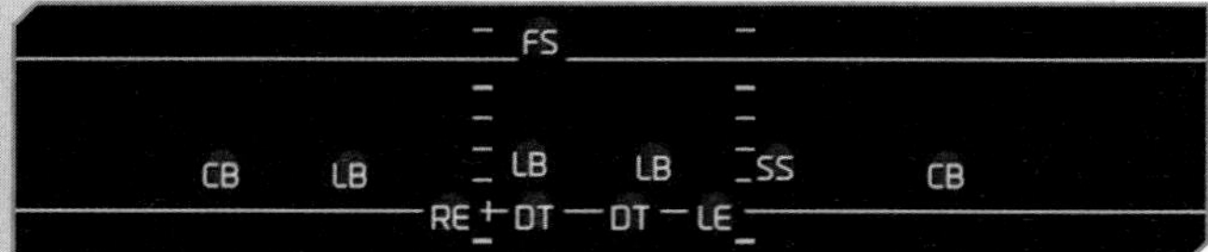

RUN DEFENSE LEFT

SETUP > SHIFT LINEBACKERS LEFT

RUN DEFENSE MIDDLE

SETUP > PINCH DEFENSIVE LINE

RUN DEFENSE RIGHT

SETUP > SHIFT LINEBACKERS RIGHT

OAKLAND RAIDERS DEFENSIVE RUN PLAY CALL SHEET

1ST DOWN RUN DEFENSE	2ND AND SHORT	3RD AND SHORT	GOAL LINE RUN DEFENSE	2ND AND LONG	3RD AND LONG
46 Normal—Cover 1	Dime—Cover 1 Press	46 Normal—Inside Blitz	Goal Line 5-3-3—Jam Cover 1	Dollar 3-2-6—Cover 1 LB Spy	Quarter 3 Deep—Man Up 3 Deep
4-3 Under—Cover 3 Buzz	4-3 Over—Cover 6	4-3 Stack—Will 2 Fire	Goal Line 5-3-3—Flat Buzz	Dollar 3-2-6—Okie Roll 2	Nickel Normal—Sugar Cover 3 Bluff

OAKLAND RAIDERS DEFENSIVE PASS PLAY CALL SHEET

1ST DOWN PLAY	2ND AND SHORT	3RD AND SHORT	GOAL LINE PASSING	2ND AND LONG	3RD AND LONG
Dime—2 Man Under	Nickel Wide 9—Cover 1 Robber	Nickel—Sugar Blitz	Goal Line 6-3-2—GL Man	Dime Normal—MLB Blitz	Nickel Normal—Over Storm Brave
Dime—Cover 4	4-3 Over—Cover 2 Buc	Nickel—Sugar 3 Seam	Goal Line 6-3-2—GL Zone	4-3 Under—Mike Will Cross 3	Quarter Normal—Fire Zone 3

LEGEND: Man Coverage | Zone Coverage | Man Blitz | Zone Blitz

In these play call sheets we picked the best plays for specific situations so that you will have a play for every down and distance.

DEFENSE

RECOMMENDED DEFENSIVE PASS FORMATION: NICKEL NORMAL

PRO TIPS

- PLACE CB D.J. HAYDEN ON YOUR OPPONENT'S BEST WR.
- USE CB CHIMDI CHEKWA TO COVER YOUR OPPONENT'S FASTEST WR.
- CB MIKE JENKINS SHOULD BE USED AS YOUR #2 CB.

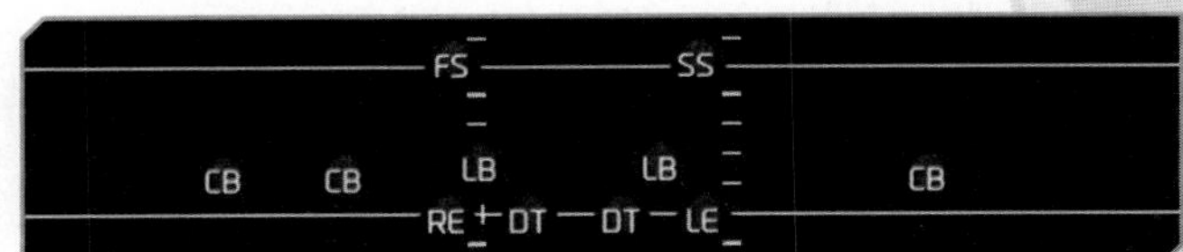

MAN COVERAGE

SETUP

- SPREAD DEFENSIVE LINE
- CRASH DEFENSIVE LINE DOWN

- SS Tyvon Branch has the speed to play near the line of scrimmage at the snap of the ball and recover deep to help in pass support.
- User-control the FS and let Branch patrol the deep portion of the field.

ZONE COVERAGE

SETUP

- FLAT ZONE THE RE
- BUZZ ZONE THE LE

- The press on the right side of the field will make our opponent think the flat is open.
- The flat defender will be in perfect position to make a play on any pass to the flat.

MAN BLITZ

SETUP

- PRESS COVERAGE
- GLOBAL BLITZ LINEBACKERS

- Pressure will come from our blitzing linebackers through the A gaps.
- If the opposing receivers don't get a beat press animation it will be difficult for the QB to find anyone to throw to.

ZONE BLITZ

SETUP

- HOOK ZONE THE NICKEL CB
- GLOBAL BLITZ THE LINEBACKERS

- Pressure will once again come from our blitzing linebackers through the A gaps.
- User-control the nickel CB over the middle of the field to take away any quick pass.
- We like to mix this setup in to confuse our opponents and throw off their timing.

St. Louis Rams

2012 TEAM RANKINGS

3rd NFC West (7-8-1)

PASSING OFFENSE: **18th**
RUSHING OFFENSE: **19th**
PASSING DEFENSE: **15th**
RUSHING DEFENSE: **15th**

2012 TEAM LEADERS

PASSING: **Sam Bradford: 3,702**
RUSHING: **Steven Jackson: 1,042**
RECEIVING: **Chris Givens: 698**
TACKLES: **James Laurinaitis: 142**
SACKS: **Chris Long: 11.5**
INTS: **Janoris Jenkins: 4**

KEY ADDITIONS

QB Kellen Clemens
TE Jared Cook
TE Zach Potter

KEY ROOKIES

WR Tavon Austin
ROLB Alex Ogletree
FS T.J. McDonald

CONNECTED FRANCHISE MODE STRATEGY

CFM TEAM RATING: **73**
OFFENSIVE SCHEME: **Power Run**
DEFENSIVE SCHEME: **Base 4-3**
STRENGTHS: **QB, TE, LT, LE, CB**
WEAKNESSES: **HB, WR, FS, SS**

SCHEDULE

1	Sep 8	4:25 PM ET		CARDINALS
2	Sep 15	1:00 PM ET	AT	FALCONS
3	Sep 22	1:00 PM ET	AT	COWBOYS
4	Sep 26	8:25 PM ET		49ERS
5	Oct 6	1:00 PM ET		JAGUARS
6	Oct 13	1:00 PM ET	AT	TEXANS
7	Oct 20	1:00 PM ET	AT	PANTHERS
8	Oct 28	8:40 PM ET		SEAHAWKS
9	Nov 3	1:00 PM ET		TITANS
10	Nov 10	1:00 PM ET	AT	COLTS
11	BYE			
12	Nov 24	1:00 PM ET		BEARS
13	Dec 1	4:05 PM ET	AT	49ERS
14	Dec 8	4:25 PM ET	AT	CARDINALS
15	Dec 15	1:00 PM ET		SAINTS
16	Dec 22	1:00 PM ET		BUCCANEERS
17	Dec 29	4:25 PM ET	AT	SEAHAWKS

FRANCHISE OVERVIEW

RAMS GAMEPLAY RATING

> SEE THE INSIDE BACK COVER FOR A QUICK REFERENCE TO THE GAME ABBREVIATIONS USED THROUGHOUT THIS GUIDE.

> IMPROVE WITH YOUR TEAM BY VISITING PRIMAGAMES.COM/MADDENNFL25 FOR MORE INFORMATION AND HOW-TO VIDEOS.

OFFENSIVE SCOUTING REPORT

- Is Sam Bradford the QB of the future? A lot will depend on how he performs over the course of his contract. He has three years left and will need to play at a much higher level in order to remain a Ram.
- The Rams have two young HBs in need of upgrades. We like Daryl Richardson over Isaiah Pead.
- Rookie WR Tavon Austin brings speed and excitement to a receiving unit that hasn't seen it since the "Greatest Show on Turf" days.

DEFENSIVE SCOUTING REPORT

- The combination of RE Robert Quinn and LE Chris Long is one you want to keep together over the next few seasons. Quinn needs upgrades to his STR rating so that he can develop into a star player.
- Rookie ROLB Alec Ogletree and MLB James Laurinaitis will carry this defense over the course of the next few years. Build your defense around their strengths—tackling and speed.
- CBs Cortland Finnegan and Janoris Jenkins have 85-plus MCV ratings, so play a good amount of man coverage with this defense.

OWNER & COACH PROFILES

STAN KROENKE

LEGACY SCORE: 0
OFF. SCHEME: Power Run
DEF. SCHEME: Base 4-3

JEFF FISHER

LEVEL: 23
LEGACY SCORE: 2050
OFF. SCHEME: Power Run
DEF. SCHEME: Base 4-3

TEAM OVERVIEW

KEY PLAYERS

QB #8

SAM BRADFORD

KEY RATINGS

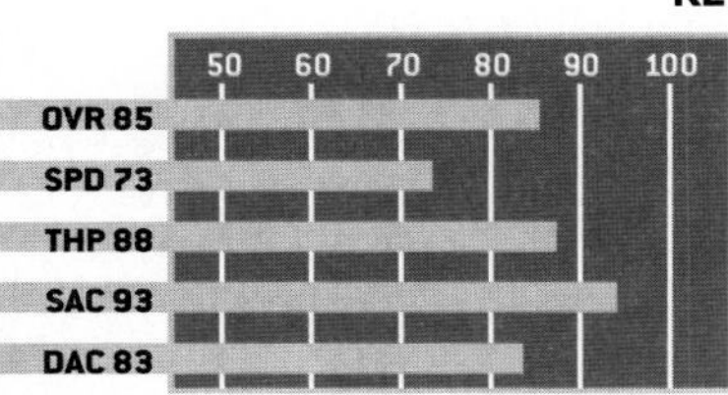

> Bradford is one of the best QBs in the game at attacking the short part of the field.

> Run a lot of crossing patterns over the middle of the field to take advantage of Bradford's SAC rating.

CB #31

CORTLAND FINNEGAN

KEY RATINGS

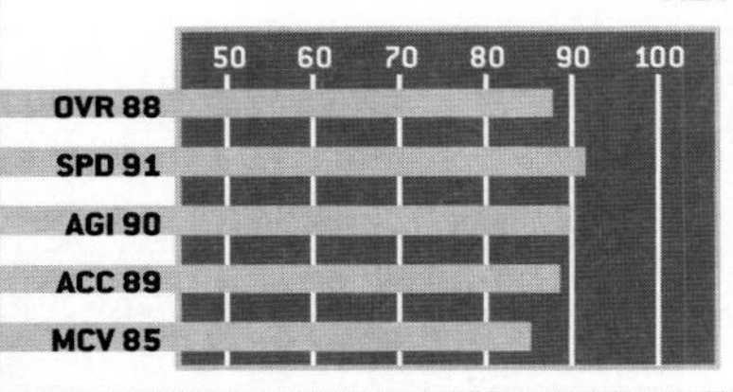

> Finnegan is a tough CB for most WRs to go up against. The physicality of his game allows him to win the battle at the line of scrimmage.

> Finnegan has enough speed to make him one of the game's elite CBs.

PRE-GAME SETUP

KEY RUNNING SUBSTITUTION

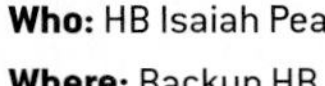

Who: HB Isaiah Pead

Where: Backup HB

Why: Pead has the skill set to be the Rams' feature HB.

Key Stats: 93 SPD, 90 AGI

KEY PASSING SUBSTITUTION

Who: WR Raymond Radway

Where: #4 WR

Why: Radway should be used as a deep-threat WR only. He has big-play potential.

Key Stats: 6'3", 94 SPD

KEY RUN DEFENSE SUBSTITUTION

Who: SS Matthew Daniels

Where: Starting FS

Why: Use Daniels for running situations only. His 89 POW rating will cause fumbles.

Key Stats: 89 POW

KEY PASS DEFENSE SUBSTITUTION

Who: CB Brandon McGee

Where: #3 CB

Why: Use McGee to blitz from the nickel, and also use him to cover your opponent's faster WRs.

Key Stats: 93 SPD

OFFENSIVE DEPTH CHART

POS	FIRST NAME	LAST NAME	OVR
QB	Sam	Bradford	85
QB	Kellen	Clemens	72
QB	Austin	Davis	68
HB	Daryl	Richardson	74
HB	Isaiah	Pead	74
HB	Zac	Stacy	70
HB	Chase	Reynolds	65
HB	Terrance	Ganaway	63
FB	Lance	Kendricks	78
FB	Mike	McNeill	63
WR	Tavon	Austin	76
WR	Chris	Givens	75
WR	Brian	Quick	73
WR	Austin	Pettis	73
WR	Stedman	Bailey	71
WR	Raymond	Radway	62
WR	Nick	Johnson	54
TE	Jared	Cook	87
TE	Cory	Harkey	69
TE	Zach	Potter	66
TE	Cameron	Graham	62
TE	Jake	McQuaide	49
LT	Jake	Long	88
LT	Ty	Nsekhe	57
LG	Shelley	Smith	74
LG	Rokevious	Watkins	67
C	Scott	Wells	80
C	Barrett	Jones	71
C	Tim	Barnes	63
RG	Harvey	Dahl	89
RG	Chris	Williams	76
RG	Brandon	Washington	61
RT	Rodger	Saffold	84
RT	Joe	Barksdale	69

DEFENSIVE DEPTH CHART

POS	FIRST NAME	LAST NAME	OVR
LE	Chris	Long	88
LE	William	Hayes	81
LE	Mason	Brodine	60
RE	Robert	Quinn	78
RE	Eugene	Sims	71
DT	Michael	Brockers	82
DT	Kendall	Langford	81
DT	Jermelle	Cudjo	68
DT	Matthew	Conrath	66
LOLB	Jo-Lonn	Dunbar	80
LOLB	Sammy	Brown	67
MLB	James	Laurinaitis	86
MLB	Josh	Hull	66
MLB	Jabara	Williams	60
ROLB	Alec	Ogletree	77
ROLB	Jonathan	Stewart	61
CB	Cortland	Finnegan	88
CB	Janoris	Jenkins	82
CB	Trumaine	Johnson	74
CB	Brandon	McGee	67
CB	Robert	Steeples	65
FS	T.J.	McDonald	71
FS	Rodney	McLeod	70
FS	Quinton	Pointer	67
SS	Darian	Stewart	77
SS	Matt	Giordano	73
SS	Matthew	Daniels	72

SPECIAL TEAMS DEPTH CHART

POS	FIRST NAME	LAST NAME	OVR
K	Greg	Zuerlein	79
P	John	Hekker	73

St. Louis Rams

RECOMMENDED OFFENSIVE RUN FORMATION: I-FORM TACKLE OVER (2 HB, 2 TE, 1 WR)

PRO TIPS

> HB ISAIAH PEAD SHOULD SEE PLAYING TIME. SPLIT CARRIES BETWEEN HIM AND DARYL RICHARDSON.

> TE ZACH POTTER IS A GREAT RUN-BLOCKING TE WITH 76 IBL.

> FB LANCE KENDRICKS WILL BE VITAL TO THE SUCCESS OF THE RAMS' RUN GAME.

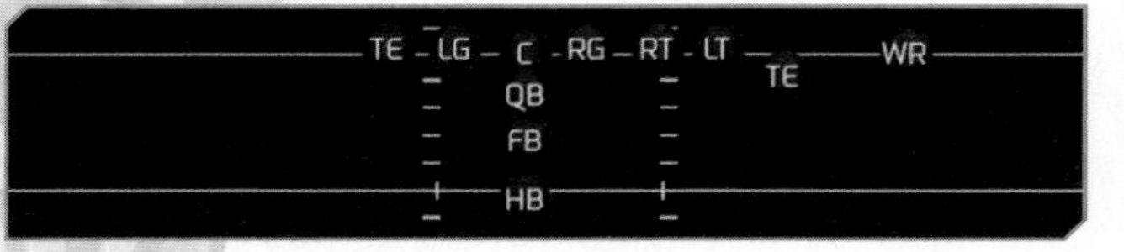

RUN LEFT

LANCE KENDRICKS IS A GREAT OPTION ON THE FB DIVE.

RUN MIDDLE

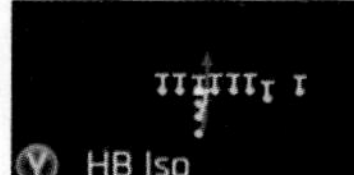

DARYL RICHARDSON HAS THE SPEED TO FIND HOLES UP THE MIDDLE.

RUN RIGHT

RICHARDSON GETS TO THE EDGE EXTREMELY QUICKLY.

ST. LOUIS RAMS RUNNING PLAY CALL SHEET

LEGEND: Inside Run | Outside Run | Shotgun Run | QB Run

1ST DOWN RUNS	2ND AND SHORT	3RD AND SHORT	GOAL LINE RUNS	2ND AND LONG	3RD AND LONG
I-Form Pro—Stretch	I-Form Tight Pair—HB Lead Dive	Weak Tight Pair—HB Gut	I-Form Tackle Over—HB Slam	Gun Trips TE—HB Mid Draw	Gun Doubles On—HB Draw
Singleback Jumbo—HB Dive	Singleback Ace Pair Twins—HB Slam	Singleback Jumbo—HB Toss	I-Form Tackle Over—FB Dive Strong	Singleback Y-Trips—HB Draw	Gun Double Flex—HB Mid Draw
Strong Close—Quick Toss	I-Form Tackle Over—HB Iso	Strong Y-Flex—Off Tackle	I-Form Tackle Over—Power O	Gun Bunch Wk—HB Mid Draw	Gun Double Flex—HB Counter

ST. LOUIS RAMS PASSING PLAY CALL SHEET

LEGEND: Base Play | Man Beater | Zone Beater | Blitz Beater

1ST DOWN PLAY	2ND AND SHORT	3RD AND SHORT	GOAL LINE PASSING	2ND AND LONG	3RD AND LONG
Gun Snugs Flip—Mesh	Gun Split Offset—X Dig Wheel	Singleback Ace Pair Twins—Y Stick	Weak Pro Twins—HB Slip Screen	Singleback Tight Doubles On—Rams Dig N Up	Gun Empty Trey—Stick
Gun Bunch Wk—Rams DBL Trail	Gun Trey Open—Fk WR Screen	Singleback Tight Doubles On—HB Slip Screen	Strong Close—Y-Trail	Gun Wing Trips Wk—WR Corners	Gun Double Flex—Rams Seams
Gun Doubles On—HB Delay Out	Singleback Jumbo—Verts Drag	Gun Split Offset—HB Slip Screen	Strong Close—TE Option	Gun Wing Trips Wk—TE Deep Option	Gun Bunch Wk—Bunch Curl Flat

In these play call sheets we picked the best plays for specific situations so that you will have a play for every down and distance.

OFFENSE

RECOMMENDED OFFENSIVE PASS FORMATION: SINGLEBACK TIGHT DOUBLES ON (1 HB, 1 TE, 3 WR)

PRO TIPS

- WR RAYMOND RADWAY IS YOUR DEEP-THREAT WR.
- TE ZACH POTTER IS 6'7" AND WILL BE A DANGEROUS TARGET IN THE RED ZONE.
- HB ISAIAH PEAD IS AN EXCELLENT PASS-CATCHING HB OUT OF THE BACKFIELD.

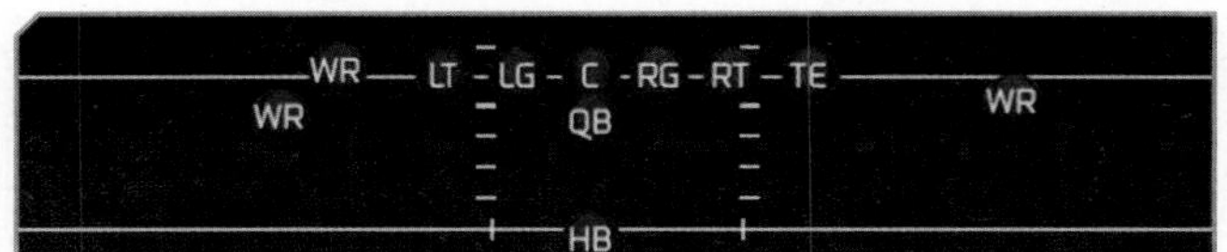

BASE PLAY

SETUP

- MOTION THE FAR LEFT WR OUTSIDE
- SNAP THE BALL AFTER HE TAKES THREE STEPS

- Throw a high bullet pass once the WR breaks back inside.
- The TE drag is a nice option against the blitz, and so is the HB out of the backfield.

MAN BEATER

SETUP

- DRAG THE FAR RIGHT WR
- ZIG THE TE

- If the TE gets separation at the snap of the ball, throw to him as he breaks to the sideline.
- The left slot WR will get inside position down the field.

ZONE BEATER

SETUP

- STREAK THE TE
- STREAK THE FAR LEFT WR

- Against Cover 2 and Cover 3 look to the sideline corner.
- Against Cover 4 zones look to the TE at the snap of the ball.

BLITZ BEATER

SETUP

- BLOCK THE TE
- MOTION THE FAR LEFT WR OUTSIDE

- We use the same motion as with our base play to confuse our opponent.
- Follow your blockers and get upfield as quickly as possible.

St. Louis Rams

RECOMMENDED DEFENSIVE RUN FORMATION: 4-3 UNDER

PRO TIPS

> LE CHRIS LONG WILL CONTROL THE RIGHT SIDE OF THE DEFENSIVE LINE.
> MLB JAMES LAURINAITIS SHOULD BE USER-CONTROLLED ON RUNNING PLAYS.

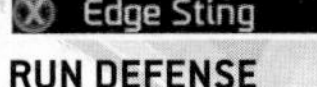
RUN DEFENSE

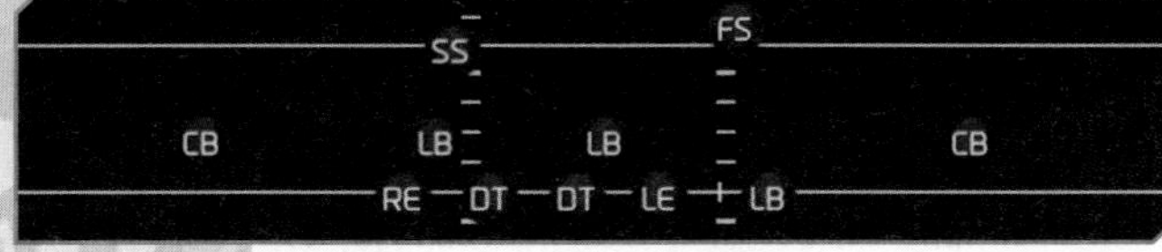

RUN DEFENSE LEFT

SETUP > SHIFT LINEBACKERS LEFT

RUN DEFENSE MIDDLE

SETUP > PINCH DEFENSIVE LINE

RUN DEFENSE RIGHT

SETUP > SHIFT LINEBACKERS RIGHT

ST. LOUIS RAMS DEFENSIVE RUN PLAY CALL SHEET

1ST DOWN RUN DEFENSE	2ND AND SHORT	3RD AND SHORT	GOAL LINE RUN DEFENSE	2ND AND LONG	3RD AND LONG
4-6 Bear Under—Cover 1	4-3 Under—Cover 1 Press	4-3 Stack—Engage Eight	Goal Line 5-3-3—Jam Cover 1	4-3 Over—2 Man Under	Nickel 3 D Ends—Cover 1 Robber
4-6 Bear Under—Cover 2	4-3 Over—Cover 2 Buc	4-3 Stack—Zip Shoot Gut	Goal Line 5-3-3—Flat Buzz	4-3 Stack—Cover 4	Nickel 3 D Ends—Cover 2 Sink

ST. LOUIS RAMS DEFENSIVE PASS PLAY CALL SHEET

1ST DOWN PLAY	2ND AND SHORT	3RD AND SHORT	GOAL LINE PASSING	2ND AND LONG	3RD AND LONG
Nickel Normal—Cover 1	Nickel Normal—2 Man Under	4-6 Bear Under—Gap Press	Goal Line 6-3-2—GL Man	4-6 Bear Under—LB Dogs	Dollar 3-2-6—Zero Blitz
Nickel Normal—Cover 6	4-6 Bear Under Cover 3	Nickel 3 D Ends—Odd Overload 3	Goal Line 6-3-2—GL Zone	4-6 Bear Under—LB Dogs 3	Dollar 3-2-6—Fire Zone 3

LEGEND: Man Coverage | Zone Coverage | Man Blitz | Zone Blitz

In these play call sheets we picked the best plays for specific situations so that you will have a play for every down and distance.

DEFENSE

RECOMMENDED DEFENSIVE PASS FORMATION: 46 BEAR UNDER

PRO TIPS

> PLACE CB CORTLAND FINNEGAN ON YOUR OPPONENT'S BEST WR.

> USE CB BRANDON MCGEE ON YOUR OPPONENT'S FASTEST WR.

> CB JANORIS JENKINS SHOULD BE YOUR #2 CB.

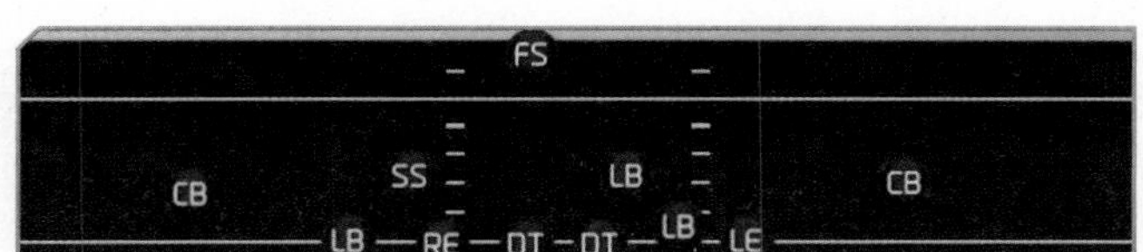

MAN COVERAGE

SETUP

- CRASH DEFENSIVE LINE OUT
- SHADE SECONDARY COVERAGE IN

> Our defense will be playing tight man-to-man coverage with press at the line.

> Crashing the defensive line out will result in a better pass rush against the QB.

ZONE COVERAGE

SETUP

- DEEP ZONE THE SS
- BUZZ ZONE THE RE

> With the setup of this play we have created a Cover 4 zone while showing man-to-man press coverage.

> This will lead to incorrect reads and bad decisions by opposing QBs.

MAN BLITZ

SETUP

- PRESS COVERAGE
- CRASH DEFENSIVE LINE DOWN

> User-control the MLB covering the HB.

> If the HB runs a route, follow him. If the HB stays in to block, drop into coverage with the MLB.

ZONE BLITZ

SETUP

- PRESS COVERAGE
- SHADE SECONDARY COVERAGE IN

> You can run the same pressure from Cover 2 but protect the flats.

> Having a Cover 3 and Cover 2 option will be vital to your defense's success.

Baltimore Ravens

2012 TEAM RANKINGS

1st AFC North (10-6-0)

PASSING OFFENSE: **15th**
RUSHING OFFENSE: **11th**
PASSING DEFENSE: **17th**
RUSHING DEFENSE: **20th**

2012 TEAM LEADERS

PASSING: **Joe Flacco: 3,817**
RUSHING: **Ray Rice: 1,143**
RECEIVING: **Anquan Boldin: 921**
TACKLES: **Bernard Pollard: 98**
SACKS: **Paul Kruger: 9**
INTS: **Ed Reed: 4**

KEY ADDITIONS

LE Chris Canty
ROLB Elvis Dumervil
FS Michael Huff

KEY ROOKIES

SS Matt Elam
MLB Arthur Brown
DT Brandon Williams

CONNECTED FRANCHISE MODE STRATEGY

CFM TEAM RATING: **78**
OFFENSIVE SCHEME: **Power Run**
DEFENSIVE SCHEME: **Hybrid Multiple Front**
STRENGTHS: **QB, HB, TE, RG, RE, LOLB, CB**
WEAKNESSES: **C, DT, MLB, SS**

SCHEDULE

1	Sep 5	8:30 PM ET	AT	BRONCOS
2	Sep 15	1:00 PM ET		BROWNS
3	Sep 22	1:00 PM ET		TEXANS
4	Sep 29	1:00 PM ET	AT	BILLS
5	Oct 6	1:00 PM ET	AT	DOLPHINS
6	Oct 13	1:00 PM ET		PACKERS
7	Oct 20	4:25 PM ET	AT	STEELERS
8	BYE			
9	Nov 3	4:25 PM ET	AT	BROWNS
10	Nov 10	1:00 PM ET		BENGALS
11	Nov 17	1:00 PM ET	AT	BEARS
12	Nov 24	1:00 PM ET		JETS
13	Nov 28	8:30 PM ET		STEELERS
14	Dec 8	1:00 PM ET		VIKINGS
15	Dec 16	8:40 PM ET	AT	LIONS
16	Dec 22	8:30 PM ET		PATRIOTS
17	Dec 29	1:00 PM ET	AT	BENGALS

FRANCHISE OVERVIEW

RAVENS GAMEPLAY RATING

87

> See the inside back cover for a quick reference to the game abbreviations used throughout this guide.

> Improve with your team by visiting PrimaGames.com/MaddenNFL25 for more information and how-to videos.

OFFENSIVE SCOUTING REPORT

> QB Joe Flacco is fresh off his first Super Bowl and no longer needs to prove he is a franchise QB. Surround him with downfield threat receivers and this offense has potential to be one of the best.

> HB Ray Rice is the workhorse of this offense. Make sure he touches the ball at least 20 times a game.

> The speed of WRs Torrey Smith and Jacoby Jones is needed for this offense and Joe Flacco to have success. Keep searching for speed in the draft as well as in free agency.

DEFENSIVE SCOUTING REPORT

> RE Haloti Ngata is the most dominant player in the league at his position. Look to upgrade DT Terrence Cody, who has potential to be a player like Ngata.

> LOLB Terrell Suggs is a premiere pass-rushing linebacker, but he's in the later stages of his career. Let him go after the final two seasons of his contract.

> CB Jimmy Smith is a very underrated player and is one of the better lower rated CBs in the game. Upgrade his stats during the season and sign him to a long-term deal.

OWNER & COACH PROFILES

STEVE BISCIOTTI

LEGACY SCORE: 3325 OFF. SCHEME: Power Run
DEF. SCHEME: Hybrid Multiple Front

JOHN HARBAUGH

LEVEL: 28 LEGACY SCORE: 1050
OFF. SCHEME: Power Run DEF. SCHEME: Hybrid Multiple Fro

TEAM OVERVIEW

KEY PLAYERS

HB #27

RAY RICE

KEY RATINGS

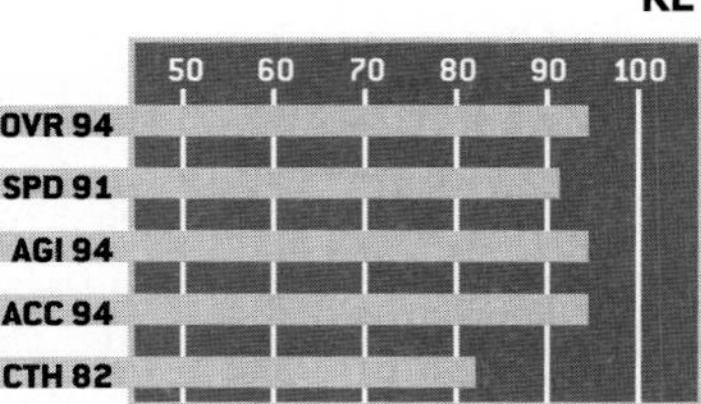

> Rice isn't the fastest HB in the game, but he is one of the quickest.

> Make Rice a vital part of your passing attack. He will catch everything thrown his way.

DT #92

HALOTI NGATA

KEY RATINGS

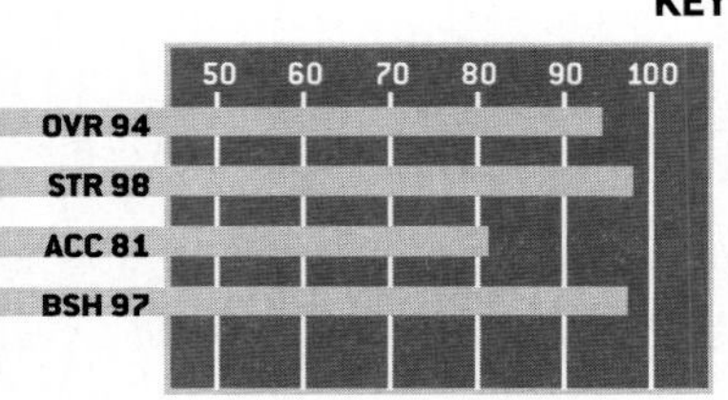

> Ngata is an immovable object on the defensive line. He will control the line of scrimmage.

> Blitz linebackers behind Ngata, as he will almost always demand a double team.

PRE-GAME SETUP

KEY RUNNING SUBSTITUTION

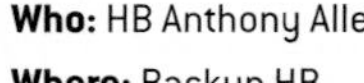

Who: HB Anthony Allen

Where: Backup HB

Why: Allen is the team's best trucking HB. He also has a 90 CAR rating.

Key Stats: 90 TRK, 90 CAR

KEY PASSING SUBSTITUTION

Who: WR Deonte Thompson

Where: #4 WR

Why: Thompson is strictly a deep-threat option. Use him only when attacking defenses deep.

Key Stats: 97 SPD

KEY RUN DEFENSE SUBSTITUTION

Who: DT Brandon Williams

Where: Backup #DT

Why: During running situations Williams will be one of three defenders on the line with 90-plus STR.

Key Stats: 90 STR

KEY PASS DEFENSE SUBSTITUTION

Who: CB Chris Johnson

Where: #3 CB

Why: Johnson is one of the best lower rated CBs in *Madden NFL 25*.

Key Stats: 6'1", 96 SPD

OFFENSIVE DEPTH CHART

POS	FIRST NAME	LAST NAME	OVR
QB	Joe	Flacco	93
QB	Tyrod	Taylor	73
QB	Caleb	Hanie	70
HB	Ray	Rice	94
HB	Bernard	Pierce	82
HB	Anthony	Allen	69
HB	Bobby	Rainey	68
HB	Damien	Berry	68
FB	Kyle	Juszczyk	74
WR	Torrey	Smith	85
WR	Jacoby	Jones	81
WR	Tandon	Doss	69
WR	David	Reed	67
WR	LaQuan	Williams	64
WR	Tommy	Streeter	63
WR	Aaron	Mellette	63
WR	Deonte	Thompson	61
TE	Dennis	Pitta	87
TE	Ed	Dickson	77
TE	Billy	Bajema	69
TE	Alex	Silvestro	52
TE	Morgan	Cox	44
LT	Bryant	McKinnie	81
LT	David	Mims	59
LG	Kelechi	Osemele	80
LG	Ramon	Harewood	74
C	Gino	Gradkowski	74
C	A.Q.	Shipley	73
C	Ryan	Jensen	67
C	Reggie	Stephens	65
RG	Marshal	Yanda	97
RG	Ricky	Wagner	67
RG	Antoine	McClain	64
RT	Michael	Oher	82
RT	Jah	Reid	76

DEFENSIVE DEPTH CHART

POS	FIRST NAME	LAST NAME	OVR
LE	Chris	Canty	85
LE	Arthur	Jones	77
LE	Kapron	Lewis-Moore	67
RE	Haloti	Ngata	94
RE	Marcus	Spears	73
RE	DeAngelo	Tyson	61
DT	Terrence	Cody	74
DT	Brandon	Williams	64
LOLB	Terrell	Suggs	89
LOLB	Pernell	McPhee	77
LOLB	John	Simon	69
LOLB	Adrian	Hamilton	57
MLB	Daryl	Smith	82
MLB	Jameel	McClain	78
MLB	Arthur	Brown	74
MLB	Albert	McClellan	69
MLB	Josh	Bynes	65
MLB	Bryan	Hall	56
ROLB	Elvis	Dumervil	83
ROLB	Courtney	Upshaw	79
ROLB	Spencer	Adkins	66
CB	Lardarius	Webb	90
CB	Corey	Graham	80
CB	Jimmy	Smith	76
CB	Chris	Johnson	72
CB	Chykie	Brown	66
CB	Asa	Jackson	66
CB	Marc	Anthony	66
FS	Michael	Huff	83
FS	Omar	Brown	73
FS	Anthony	Levine	64
SS	Matt	Elam	78
SS	James	Ihedigbo	74
SS	Christian	Thompson	67

SPECIAL TEAMS DEPTH CHART

POS	FIRST NAME	LAST NAME	OVR
K	Justin	Tucker	88
P	Sam	Koch	90

Baltimore Ravens

RECOMMENDED OFFENSIVE RUN FORMATION: WEAK H CLOSE FLIP (2 HB, 1 TE, 2 WR)

PRO TIPS

- HB RAY RICE SHOULD BE YOUR EVERY-DOWN HB.
- USE HB ANTHONY ALLEN FOR SHORT-YARD SITUATIONS BECAUSE OF HIS 90 TRK RATING.
- TE DENNIS PITTA IS YOUR TEAM'S BEST OPTION FOR RUN BLOCKING TIGHT ENDS.

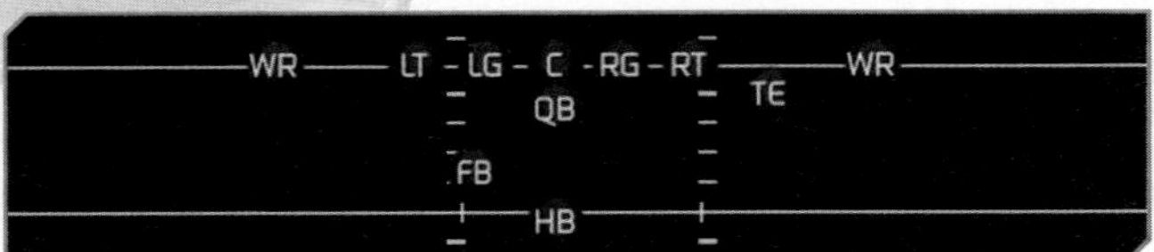

RUN LEFT

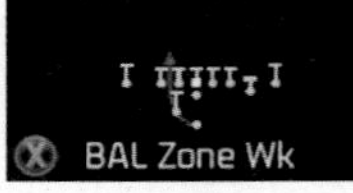

RAY RICE CAN EXPLODE OUT OF THE BACKFIELD.

RUN MIDDLE

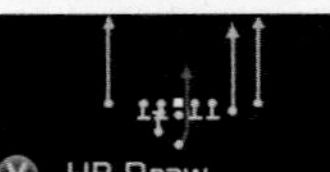

RICE IS ALSO A POWERFUL RUNNER UP THE MIDDLE.

RUN RIGHT

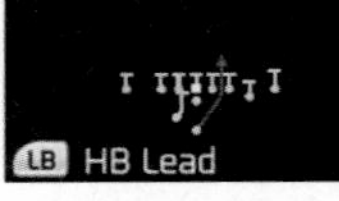

WAIT UNTIL YOU TURN UP THE SIDELINE TO USE YOUR ACCELERATION BURST.

BALTIMORE RAVENS RUNNING PLAY CALL SHEET

LEGEND: Inside Run | Outside Run | Shotgun Run | QB Run

1ST DOWN RUNS	2ND AND SHORT	3RD AND SHORT	GOAL LINE RUNS	2ND AND LONG	3RD AND LONG
Strong H Twins—Outside Zone	Weak H Pro—Inside Zone	Singleback Jumbo—Power O	Goal Line Normal—QB Sneak	Gun Split Raven—Power O	Gun Split Raven—HB Draw
Strong H Twins—HB Dive	Weak H Pro—HB Gut	Singleback F Pair Twins—HB Toss Strong	Goal Line Normal—HB Dive	Strong Pro—HB Blast	Gun Trey—HB Draw
Strong H Twins—Counter Weak	Singleback Jumbo—HB Plunge	I-Form Pro—HB Toss	Goal Line Normal—Power O	Gun Bunch Wk—HB Mid Draw	Gun Raven Trips—HB Off Tackle

BALTIMORE RAVENS PASSING PLAY CALL SHEET

LEGEND: Base Play | Man Beater | Zone Beater | Blitz Beater

1ST DOWN PLAY	2ND AND SHORT	3RD AND SHORT	GOAL LINE PASSING	2ND AND LONG	3RD AND LONG
Gun Raven Trips—Curls	Weak H Pro—Slants	Gun Ace Twins—HB Slip Screen	Goal Line—PA Waggle	Gun Trey Raven—Y-Sail	Gun Split Raven—WR Corners
Gun Raven Trips—Smash	Strong H Twins—Curl Flat	Gun Bunch Wk—Close Mesh	Goal Line—PA Spot	Gun Trey Raven—Stick N Nod	Gun Raven Empty—Ravens Wheels
Gun Raven Empty—Inside Cross	Singleback Y-Trips TE Slot—Four Verticals	Singleback Doubles Flex—HB Slip Screen	Goal Line—PA Power O	Gun Ace Twins—X Spot	Gun Trey Raven—Four Verticals

In these play call sheets we picked the best plays for specific situations so that you will have a play for every down and distance.

OFFENSE

RECOMMENDED OFFENSIVE PASS FORMATION: GUN TREY RAVEN (1 HB, 1 TE, 3 WR)

PRO TIPS

- TIGHT ENDS DENNIS PITTA AND ED DICKSON ARE TWO OF THE BEST PASS-CATCHING TIGHT ENDS IN THE LEAGUE.
- WR TANDON DOSS IS THE RAVENS' BEST CATCH-IN-TRAFFIC WR.
- WR TOMMY STREETER IS A MATCHUP NIGHTMARE BECAUSE OF HIS 6'5" HEIGHT.

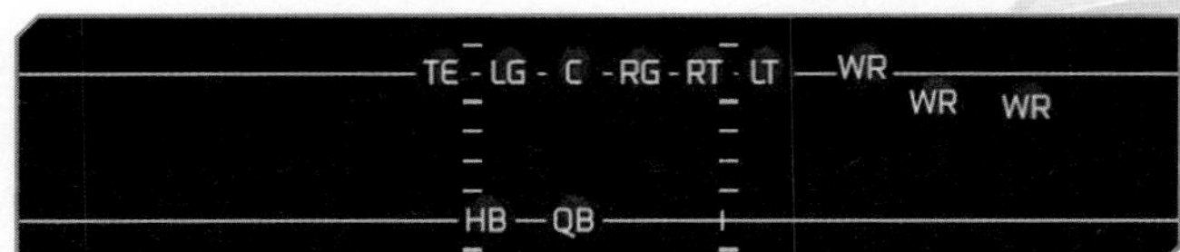

BASE PLAY

SETUP

- ZIG THE TE
- STREAK THE HB AND THE FAR LEFT WR

- Against man-to-man coverage look to the TE running the zig and the HB streak.
- Against zone coverage look to the deep post and the sideline curl.

MAN BEATER

SETUP

- BLOCK THE HB
- DRAG THE FAR RIGHT WR

- Look to either corner route when facing man-to-man coverage.
- Wait for the WR or TE to break to the sideline, then throw a high lead pass.

ZONE BEATER

SETUP

- STREAK THE HB
- DRAG THE TE

- Against Cover 2 and Cover 3 zones look to the angled slot streak or the sideline streak.
- Against Cover 4 zones look to the TE drag or the HB streak.

BLITZ BEATER

SETUP

- ZIG THE TE
- BLOCK THE HB

- You want to reblock the HB to change his blocking assignment.
- This play is designed for the QB to roll right. If you face a zone blitz hit the flat. If you face a man-to-man blitz look to the TE zig or the corner route.

Baltimore Ravens

RECOMMENDED DEFENSIVE RUN FORMATION: 3-4 OVER ED

PRO TIPS

- MOVE RE HALOTI NGATA INSIDE TO PLAY DT NEXT TO TERRENCE CODY.
- USE LOLB TERRELL SUGGS AS YOUR RE.
- USE ROLB ELVIS DUMERVIL AT LE.

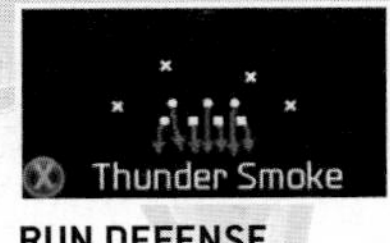

RUN DEFENSE

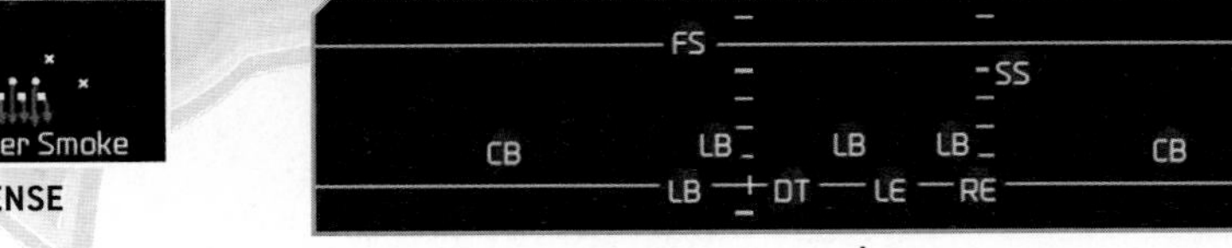

RUN DEFENSE LEFT

SETUP > SHIFT LINEBACKERS LEFT

RUN DEFENSE MIDDLE

SETUP > PINCH DEFENSIVE LINE

RUN DEFENSE RIGHT

SETUP > SHIFT LINEBACKERS RIGHT

BALTIMORE RAVENS DEFENSIVE RUN PLAY CALL SHEET

1ST DOWN RUN DEFENSE	2ND AND SHORT	3RD AND SHORT	GOAL LINE RUN DEFENSE	2ND AND LONG	3RD AND LONG
3-4 Even—MLB Cross Fire	4-3 Over—2 Man Under	3-4 Odd—Pinch Cover 0	Goal Line 5-3-3—Jam Cover 1	Nickel 2-4-5 Even—2 Man Under	Quarter Normal—Inside Blitz
3-4 Even MLB Cross Fire 3	4-3 Over—Cover 6	3-4 Odd—Sam Mike 3 Seam	Goal Line 5-3-3—Flat Buzz	Nickel 2-4-5 Even—Cover 3	Quarter Normal—Zone Blitz

BALTIMORE RAVENS DEFENSIVE PASS PLAY CALL SHEET

1ST DOWN PLAY	2ND AND SHORT	3RD AND SHORT	GOAL LINE PASSING	2ND AND LONG	3RD AND LONG
3-4 Predator—Cover 1 Lurk	3-4 Odd—SS Blitz	3-4 Predator—Pinch	Goal Line 6-3-2—GL Man	Sub 2-3-6—2 Over Storm Brave	Nickel 2-4-5 Even—Over Storm Brave
3-4 Predator—Cover 3	3-4 Odd—Cross 3 Fire	3-4 Predator—Weak Blitz 3	Goal Line 6-3-2—GL Zone	Sub 2-3-6—FS Middle 3	Nickel 2-4-5 Even—Sugar 3 Seam

LEGEND: Man Coverage | Zone Coverage | Man Blitz | Zone Blitz

In these play call sheets we picked the best plays for specific situations so that you will have a play for every down and distance.

DEFENSE

RECOMMENDED DEFENSIVE PASS FORMATION: NICKEL 2-4-5 EVEN

PRO TIPS

- PLACE CB LARDARIUS WEBB ON YOUR OPPONENT'S BEST WR.
- USE CB CHRIS JOHNSON ON YOUR OPPONENT'S FASTEST WR.
- CB COREY GRAHAM SHOULD BE YOUR #2 CB.

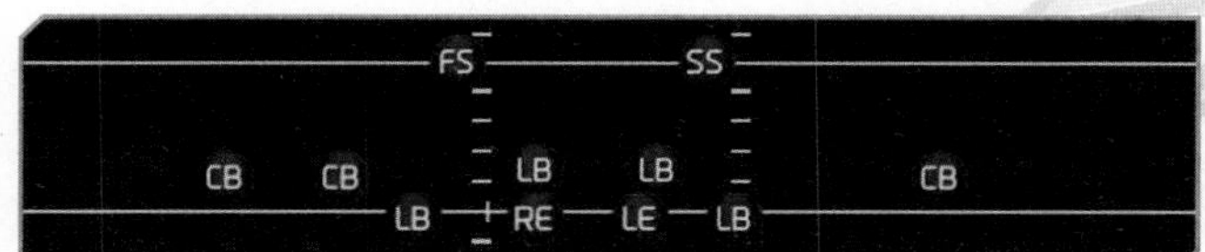

MAN COVERAGE

SETUP

- PUT THE LINEBACKERS ON A GLOBAL HOOK ZONE
- BASE ALIGN TWICE

- Our outside defenders will be in press coverage while the middle of the field will be flooded with zone defenders.
- This is a great setup if your opponent attempts to attack the middle of the field.

ZONE COVERAGE

SETUP

- SHADE THE DEFENSIVE SECONDARY COVERAGE IN
- FLAT ZONE BOTH OUTSIDE LINEBACKERS

- User-control the MLB over the middle of the field.
- The sidelines will be blanketed, so anticipate throws over the middle.

MAN BLITZ

SETUP

- PRESS COVERAGE
- GLOBAL BLITZ THE LINEBACKERS

- User-control the FS covering the HB.
- Watch for any CBs who get beaten off the line of scrimmage and look to protect deep.

ZONE BLITZ

SETUP

- PRESS COVERAGE
- GLOBAL BLITZ THE LINEBACKERS

- User-control the FS and look to play over the short middle.
- If there are any deep routes over the middle you must drop back and defend them.

Washington Redskins

2012 TEAM RANKINGS

1st NFC East (10-6-0)

PASSING OFFENSE: **20th**
RUSHING OFFENSE: **1st**
PASSING DEFENSE: **30th**
RUSHING DEFENSE: **5th**

2012 TEAM LEADERS

PASSING: **Robert Griffin III: 3,200**
RUSHING: **Alfred Morris: 1,613**
RECEIVING: **Pierre Garçon: 633**
TACKLES: **London Fletcher: 139**
SACKS: **Ryan Kerrigan: 8.5**
INTS: **London Fletcher: 5**

KEY ADDITIONS

QB Pat White
WR Donté Stallworth
WR Devery Henderson

KEY ROOKIES

CB David Amerson
TE Jordan Reed
SS Phillip Thomas

CONNECTED FRANCHISE MODE STRATEGY

CFM TEAM RATING: **77**
OFFENSIVE SCHEME: **West Coast**
DEFENSIVE SCHEME: **Base 3-4**
STRENGTHS: **QB, HB, FB, LT, C, ROLB**
WEAKNESSES: **RT, LE, RE, FS, SS**

SCHEDULE

1	Sep 9	7:10 PM ET		EAGLES
2	Sep 15	1:00 PM ET	AT	PACKERS
3	Sep 22	1:00 PM ET		LIONS
4	Sep 29	4:25 PM ET	AT	RAIDERS
5	BYE			
6	Oct 13	8:30 PM ET	AT	COWBOYS
7	Oct 20	1:00 PM ET		BEARS
8	Oct 27	4:25 PM ET	AT	BRONCOS
9	Nov 3	1:00 PM ET		CHARGERS
10	Nov 7	8:25 PM ET	AT	VIKINGS
11	Nov 17	1:00 PM ET	AT	EAGLES
12	Nov 25	8:40 PM ET		49ERS
13	Dec 1	8:30 PM ET		GIANTS
14	Dec 8	1:00 PM ET		CHIEFS
15	Dec 15	1:00 PM ET	AT	FALCONS
16	Dec 22	1:00 PM ET		COWBOYS
17	Dec 29	1:00 PM ET	AT	GIANTS

FRANCHISE OVERVIEW

REDSKINS GAMEPLAY RATING

86

> SEE THE INSIDE BACK COVER FOR A QUICK REFERENCE TO THE GAME ABBREVIATIONS USED THROUGHOUT THIS GUIDE.

> IMPROVE WITH YOUR TEAM BY VISITING PRIMAGAMES.COM/MADDENNFL25 FOR MORE INFORMATION AND HOW-TO VIDEOS.

OFFENSIVE SCOUTING REPORT

- With an 84 INJ rating, QB Robert Griffin III is the franchise for the Redskins. As he goes so does this team. Protect him at all costs and don't forget about upgrading QB Kirk Cousins, as he may have to fill in for RGIII every now and then.
- HB Alfred Morris is a load to take down when carrying the ball, but he needs major upgrades to his CTH rating. Focus on this during the season and off season.
- Your offense needs to funnel through Robert Griffin III's skill set. We recommend building your wide receivers around speed to complement RGIII and the option game.

DEFENSIVE SCOUTING REPORT

- One of our favorite under-the-radar players is LE Adam Carriker. With a 96 STR rating and standing 6'6", he is a rare player who can do a lot for this defense. We recommend signing him to a long-term deal right away.
- LOLB Ryan Kerrigan and ROLB Brian Orakpo are elite pass-rushing linebackers. Orakpo's contract is up at the end of the season, and we recommend signing him long-term. Kerrigan has two years remaining, but you should also lock him up for the long haul.
- In the draft and free agency focus on rebuilding the secondary.

OWNER & COACH PROFILES

DAN SNYDER
LEGACY SCORE: 150
OFF. SCHEME: West Coast
DEF. SCHEME: Base 3-4

MIKE SHANAHAN
LEVEL: 27
LEGACY SCORE: 8200
OFF. SCHEME: West Coast
DEF. SCHEME: Base 3-4

TEAM OVERVIEW

KEY PLAYERS

QB #10

ROBERT GRIFFIN III

KEY RATINGS

OVR 89
SPD 92
AGI 95
THP 95
DAC 85

- Griffin III is the fastest QB in the game, and he also has one of the best DAC ratings.
- A strong case can be made that Griffin III is the best QB in *Madden NFL 25*.

ROLB #98

BRIAN ORAKPO

KEY RATINGS

OVR 90
SPD 84
STR 91
POW 89
PMV 96

- What can't Orakpo do? He can rush the passer and he is a wrap-up tackling machine.
- Orakpo is one roster update away from having 90-plus TAK, 90-plus POW, and 90-plus PMV.

PRE-GAME SETUP

KEY RUNNING SUBSTITUTION

Who: HB Roy Helu Jr.

Where: Backup HB

Why: Use Helu when you are looking to add speed into your run game.

Key Stats: 93 SPD, 92 ACC

KEY PASSING SUBSTITUTION

Who: TE Niles Paul

Where: #3 WR

Why: Paul is a TE who has the skill set of a slot WR.

Key Stats: 85 SPD

KEY RUN DEFENSE SUBSTITUTION

Who: LE Adam Carriker

Where: #2 DT

Why: Carriker is similar to J.J Watt. They are both strong and athletic DEs.

Key Stats: 96 STR, 73 SPD.

KEY PASS DEFENSE SUBSTITUTION

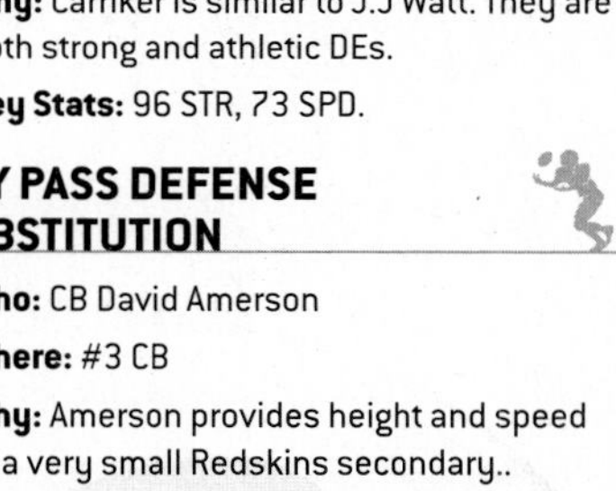

Who: CB David Amerson

Where: #3 CB

Why: Amerson provides height and speed to a very small Redskins secondary..

Key Stats: 6'1", 91 SPD

OFFENSIVE DEPTH CHART

POS	FIRST NAME	LAST NAME	OVR
QB	Robert	Griffin III	89
QB	Kirk	Cousins	75
QB	Rex	Grossman	72
QB	Pat	White	65
HB	Alfred	Morris	89
HB	Roy	Helu Jr.	74
HB	Evan	Royster	74
HB	Keiland	Williams	68
HB	Chris	Thompson	66
HB	Jawan	Jamison	66
FB	Darrel	Young	89
FB	Eric	Kettani	70
WR	Pierre	Garcon	87
WR	Santana	Moss	81
WR	Josh	Morgan	79
WR	Leonard	Hankerson	73
WR	Devery	Henderson	72
WR	Aldrick	Robinson	69
WR	Dezmon	Briscoe	68
TE	Fred	Davis	86
TE	Logan	Paulsen	75
TE	Niles	Paul	70
TE	Jordan	Reed	69
LT	Trent	Williams	89
LT	Xavier	Nixon	64
LT	Tom	Compton	63
LG	Kory	Lichtensteiger	80
LG	Maurice	Hurt	69
C	Will	Montgomery	90
C	Kevin	Matthews	66
C	Nick	Sundberg	57
RG	Chris	Chester	88
RG	Josh	LeRibeus	69
RG	Adam	Gettis	65
RT	Tyler	Polumbus	74
RT	Tony	Pashos	73
RT	Jeremy	Trueblood	73

DEFENSIVE DEPTH CHART

POS	FIRST NAME	LAST NAME	OVR
LE	Jarvis	Jenkins	79
LE	Adam	Carriker	78
RE	Stephen	Bowen	81
RE	Kedric	Golston	72
RE	Phillip	Merling	70
DT	Barry	Cofield	83
DT	Chris	Baker	74
DT	Chris	Neild	71
DT	Ron	Brace	70
LOLB	Ryan	Kerrigan	87
LOLB	Darryl	Tapp	69
LOLB	Vic	So'oto	66
MLB	London	Fletcher	82
MLB	Perry	Riley	78
MLB	Bryan	Kehl	66
MLB	Roddrick	Muckelroy	64
MLB	Keenan	Robinson	60
ROLB	Brian	Orakpo	90
ROLB	Rob	Jackson	77
ROLB	Brandon	Jenkins	64
ROLB	Ricky	Elmore	62
CB	Josh	Wilson	83
CB	DeAngelo	Hall	81
CB	E.J.	Biggers	74
CB	Jerome	Murphy	70
CB	Richard	Crawford	69
CB	David	Amerson	69
FS	Reed	Doughty	74
FS	Phillip	Thomas	72
FS	Jordan	Pugh	70
FS	Jordan	Bernstine	64
SS	Brandon	Meriweather	78
SS	DeJon	Gomes	72
SS	Bacarri	Rambo	71
SS	Devin	Holland	59

SPECIAL TEAMS DEPTH CHART

POS	FIRST NAME	LAST NAME	OVR
K	Kai	Forbath	81
P	Sav	Rocca	77

Washington Redskins

RECOMMENDED OFFENSIVE RUN FORMATION: PISTOL FULL HOUSE TIGHT (2 HB, 1 TE, 2 WR)

PRO TIPS

- > FB DARREL YOUNG IS A GREAT LEAD BLOCKER OUT OF THE BACKFIELD.
- > TE FRED DAVIS IS A GREAT RUN BLOCKER, BUT ALSO A NICE PASS CATCHING OPTION.
- > HB ROY HELU JR. WILL PROVIDE EXTRA SPEED TO YOUR BACKFIELD.

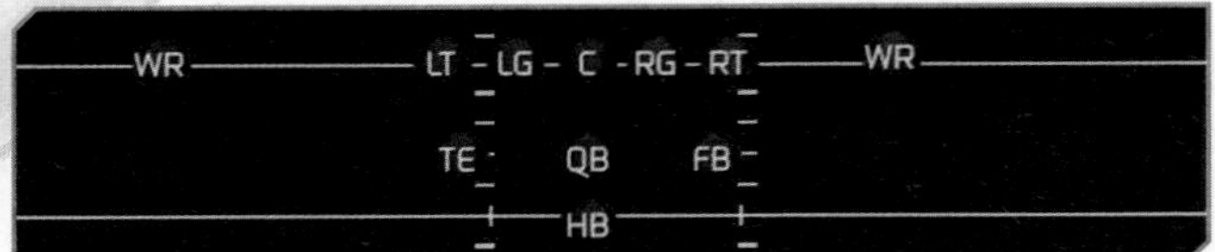

RUN LEFT

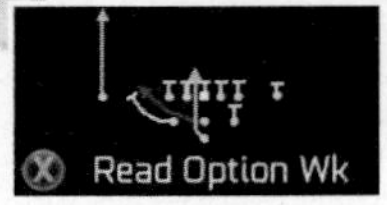

RG III KEEPS THE BALL FOR A BIG GAIN OFF THE LEFT EDGE.

RUN MIDDLE

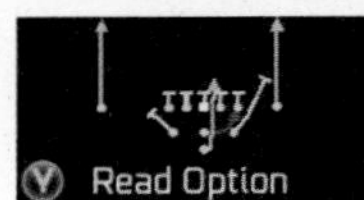

MORRIS FIGHTS FOR YARDS UP THE MIDDLE.

RUN RIGHT

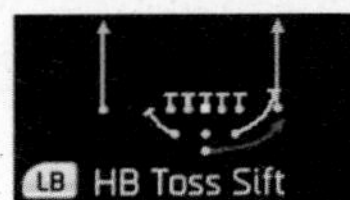

THIS TIME WE HAND OFF TO MORRIS TO FIGHT FOR YARDS OFF THE RIGHT EDGE.

WASHINGTON REDSKINS RUNNING PLAY CALL SHEET

LEGEND: Inside Run | Outside Run | Shotgun Run | QB Run

1ST DOWN RUNS	2ND AND SHORT	3RD AND SHORT	GOAL LINE RUNS	2ND AND LONG	3RD AND LONG
Strong Close—Quick Toss	Strong Close—HB Force	Pistol Weak—HB Zone Wk	Pistol Weak Twins Flex—HB Dive Wk	Pistol Y-Trips—HB Draw	Pistol Wing Trio—F Lead Read Option
Singleback Jumbo—HB Ace Power	Pistol Strong—Inside Zone Split	Pistol Full House Tight—Power Option	I-Form Twins Flex—HB Blast	Singleback Ace Pair Slot—HB Zone Wk Sift	Gun Split Redskin—Read Option
Singleback Ace—Stretch	Pistol Full House Tight—Read Option Wk	Pistol Weak—HB Stretch Sift	Pistol Strong—Tr Option Slip	Gun Snugs Flip—HB Mid Draw	Gun Split Redskin—HB Draw

WASHINGTON REDSKINS PASSING PLAY CALL SHEET

LEGEND: Base Play | Man Beater | Zone Beater | Blitz Beater

1ST DOWN PLAY	2ND AND SHORT	3RD AND SHORT	GOAL LINE PASSING	2ND AND LONG	3RD AND LONG
Pistol Strong—494 F Flat	Gun Doubles—Y-Sail	Gun Wing Trio Wk—HB Slip Screen	Full House Tight—PA Boot	Singleback Ace Pair Slot—PA Y-Drag Wheel	Gun Trey Open—Trail Shake
Singleback Tight Doubles—Close Skins Deep Cop	Gun Split Redskins—Close FB Trail	Pistol Strong—HB Slip Screen	Strong Close—TE Option	Singleback Tight Doubles—Close Skins Cross	Gun Wing Trio Wk—Four Verticals
Gun Bunch Offset—Y Trail	Gun Snugs Flip—Bench Switch	Pistol Full House Tight—Skins Curls	Singleback Jumbo—Quick Slant	Singleback Normal Skins—Whip Unders	Gun Bunch Offset—Verts HB Under

In these play call sheets we picked the best plays for specific situations so that you will have a play for every down and distance.

OFFENSE

RECOMMENDED OFFENSIVE PASS FORMATION: PISTOL WEAK TWINS FLEX (2 HB, 1 TE, 2 WR)

PRO TIPS

> GET TE FRED DAVIS INVOLVED IN THE PASSING GAME OVER THE MIDDLE OF THE FIELD.

> WR PIERRE GARÇON IS A GREAT OPTION DEEP.

> WR JOSH MORGAN IS THE REDSKINS' BEST CATCH-IN-TRAFFIC WR WITH AN 82 CIT RATING.

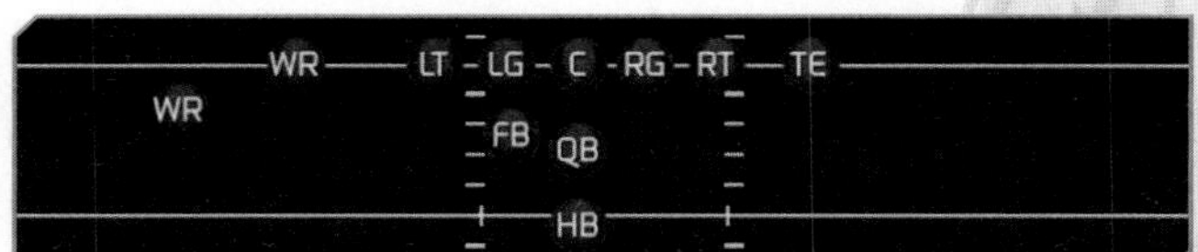

BASE PLAY

SETUP

> STREAK THE TE
> STREAK THE FB

> The TE is your first option with an inside pass lead. This route gets inside position against most defenses.

> Next look to the FB running the streak and then to either wheel route.

MAN BEATER

SETUP

> WHEEL THE HB
> DRAG THE FAR LEFT WR

> The FB's circle route can be thrown right at the snap of the ball, or you can wait for him to cut upfield.

> Next, wait for either corner route to break to the sideline and deliver a high lead pass.

ZONE BEATER

SETUP

> STREAK THE TE
> BLOCK THE HB

> Against Cover 2 and Cover 3 zones look to the TE streak and the sideline streak.

> Against Cover 4 zones look to the FB flat.

BLITZ BEATER

SETUP

> CREASE RIGHT THE FB
> WHEEL THE HB

> The HB is the decoy on this play. He will run his route to the right flat first, leaving the FB unguarded.

> As soon as the FB breaks past the TE get him the ball.

Washington Redskins

RECOMMENDED DEFENSIVE RUN FORMATION: 3-4 EVEN

PRO TIPS

- LE ADAM CARRIKER IS A TANK ON THE DEFENSIVE LINE. HE WILL BE A MATCHUP PROBLEM ALL SEASON LONG.
- DT RON BRACE IS A NICE OPTION ON RUNNING DOWNS. HIS 93 STR RATING MAKES HIM A TOUGH MATCHUP FOR MOST OFFENSIVE LINEMEN.
- MLB PERRY RILEY IS THE TEAM'S BEST TACKLER, WITH A 91 TAK RATING.

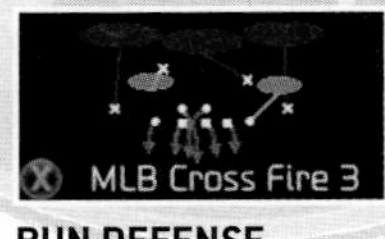

RUN DEFENSE

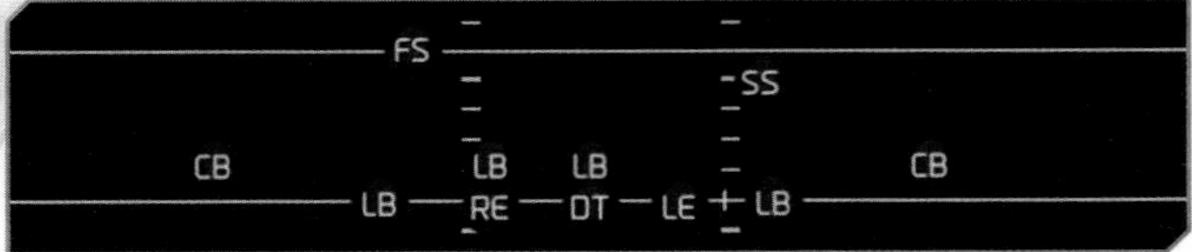

RUN DEFENSE LEFT

SETUP > SHIFT LINEBACKERS LEFT

RUN DEFENSE MIDDLE

SETUP > PINCH DEFENSIVE LINE

RUN DEFENSE RIGHT

SETUP > SHIFT LINEBACKERS RIGHT

WASHINGTON REDSKINS DEFENSIVE RUN PLAY CALL SHEET

1ST DOWN RUN DEFENSE	2ND AND SHORT	3RD AND SHORT	GOAL LINE RUN DEFENSE	2ND AND LONG	3RD AND LONG
3-4 Odd—2 Man Under	3-4 Under—Cover 1 Lurk	3-4 Under—Pinch	Goal Line 5-3-3—Jam Cover 1	Nickel 1-5-5 Prowl—2 Man Under	Nickel 2-4-5—2 Man Under
3-4 Odd—Cover 3	3-4 Under—Cover 6	3-4 Even—Trio Sky Zone	Goal Line 5-3-3—Flat Buzz	Nickel 1-5-5 Prowl—Cover 4	Nickel 2-4-5—Cover 2 Sink

WASHINGTON REDSKINS DEFENSIVE PASS PLAY CALL SHEET

1ST DOWN PLAY	2ND AND SHORT	3RD AND SHORT	GOAL LINE PASSING	2ND AND LONG	3RD AND LONG
Sub 2-3-6—Cover 1 Spy	Sub 1-4-6—2 Man LB Blitz	Nickel 1-5-5 Prowl—Dbl Loop	Goal Line 6-3-2—MLB Gap A Zone	Nickel 2-4-5—Overload 1 Roll	Nickel 1-5-5 Prowl—MLB Cross Fire
Sub 2-3-6—Sugar 2 Buzz	Sub 1-4-6—Cover 2 Sink	Nickel 1-5-5 Prowl—Dbl Loop 3	Goal Line 6-3-2—Pinch Zone	Nickel 2-4-5—Overload 3 Seam	Nickel 1-5-5 Prowl—Prowl Bear 2

LEGEND: Man Coverage | Zone Coverage | Man Blitz | Zone Blitz

In these play call sheets we picked the best plays for specific situations so that you will have a play for every down and distance.

DEFENSE

RECOMMENDED DEFENSIVE PASS FORMATION: SUB 1-4-6

PRO TIPS

> USE CB JOSH WILSON TO COVER THE OPPOSING TEAM'S BEST WR.
> CB DEANGELO HALL SHOULD COVER THE OPPOSING TEAM'S FASTEST WR.
> USE CB E.J. BIGGERS AS THE NICKEL CORNER.

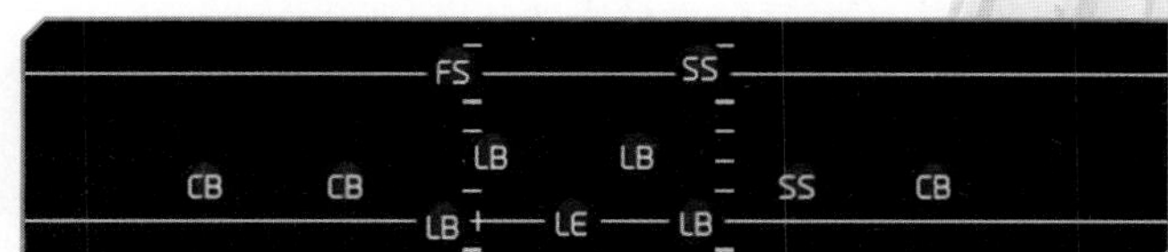

MAN COVERAGE

SETUP

- GLOBAL BLITZ BOTH OUTSIDE LINEBACKERS.
- HOOK ZONE THE BLITZING MLB

- User-control the hook zoned MLB over the middle of the field.
- Protect anything over the middle and make sure to use ballhawk to trigger interception animations!

ZONE COVERAGE

SETUP

- PUT BOTH OUTSIDE LINEBACKERS ON GLOBAL BLITZ
- QB SPY THE DT

- This setup has our defense only rushing two defenders.
- Luckily, the two defenders we are pass rushing are Brian Orakpo and Ryan Kerrigan, who will both provide pressure off the outside edge.

MAN BLITZ

SETUP

- PRESS COVERAGE
- USER-CONTROL THE MLB

- This defense is especially effective because of the speed the Redskins have in the secondary.
- In this example CB E.J. Biggers gets after the QB for the sack.

ZONE BLITZ

SETUP

- SHADE THE DEFENSIVE SECONDARY COVERAGE IN
- FLAT ZONE BOTH HOOK ZONES

- Pressure will once again fly in off the outside edge.
- This time the flats will be covered if your opponent looks to get rid of the ball quickly.

New Orleans Saints

2012 TEAM RANKINGS

3rd NFC South (7-9-0)

PASSING OFFENSE: **1st**
RUSHING OFFENSE: **25th**
PASSING DEFENSE: **31st**
RUSHING DEFENSE: **32nd**

2012 TEAM LEADERS

PASSING: **Drew Brees: 5,177**
RUSHING: **Mark Ingram: 602**
RECEIVING: **Marques Colston: 1,154**
TACKLES: **Curtis Lofton: 123**
SACKS: **Cameron Jordan: 8**
INTS: **Patrick Robinson: 3**

KEY ADDITIONS

QB Seneca Wallace
TE Benjamin Watson
LOLB Victor Butler

KEY ROOKIES

SS Kenny Vaccaro
LT Terron Armstead
DT John Jenkins

CONNECTED FRANCHISE MODE STRATEGY

CFM TEAM RATING: **72**
OFFENSIVE SCHEME: **Vertical Offense**
DEFENSIVE SCHEME: **Attacking 4-3**
STRENGTHS: **QB, HB, WR, LG, C, RG MLB, CB**
WEAKNESSES: **LT, LE, ROLB, FS**

SCHEDULE

1	Sep 8	1:00 PM ET		FALCONS
2	Sep 15	4:05 PM ET	AT	BUCCANEERS
3	Sep 22	1:00 PM ET		CARDINALS
4	Sep 30	8:40 PM ET		DOLPHINS
5	Oct 6	1:00 PM ET	AT	BEARS
6	Oct 13	4:25 PM ET	AT	PATRIOTS
7	BYE			
8	Oct 27	1:00 PM ET		BILLS
9	Nov 3	1:00 PM ET	AT	JETS
10	Nov 10	8:30 PM ET		COWBOYS
11	Nov 17	4:25 PM ET		49ERS
12	Nov 21	8:25 PM ET	AT	FALCONS
13	Dec 2	8:40 PM ET	AT	SEAHAWKS
14	Dec 8	1:00 PM ET		PANTHERS
15	Dec 15	1:00 PM ET	AT	RAMS
16	Dec 22	1:00 PM ET	AT	PANTHERS
17	Dec 29	1:00 PM ET		BUCCANEERS

FRANCHISE OVERVIEW

> SEE THE INSIDE BACK COVER FOR A QUICK REFERENCE TO THE GAME ABBREVIATIONS USED THROUGHOUT THIS GUIDE.

> IMPROVE WITH YOUR TEAM BY VISITING PRIMAGAMES.COM/MADDENNFL25 FOR MORE INFORMATION AND HOW-TO VIDEOS.

OFFENSIVE SCOUTING REPORT

> QB Drew Brees is 34 years old, but he's still playing at an elite level. Keep him around for as long as he is productive.

> HB Darren Sproles is the player who will help you win now, but HB Mark Ingram is the future. This is a problem that needs to be solved. Use Sproles in big situations, but give Ingram the bulk of the carries.

> After the year that WR Lance Moore had last season we think you should sell high on his stock. He is an 85 OVR WR, and we think you could bring in a younger, faster receiver to replace him.

DEFENSIVE SCOUTING REPORT

> The Saints defense needs work, and it starts with the defensive line. Rebuild the entire unit, but keep RE Cameron Jordan around for the future.

> The linebackers also need to be replaced for the Saints. Keep MLB Curtis Lofton and David Hawthorne, but everyone else needs to go. Rebuild from the draft and free agency.

> Rookie SS Kenny Vaccaro has the potential to be one of the best safeties in the game. Work on upgrading his speed and he will be a star in a few seasons.

OWNER & COACH PROFILES

TOM BENSON

LEGACY SCORE: 1550
DEF. SCHEME: Attacking 3-4
OFF. SCHEME: Vertical Offense

DUSTY MCDONALD

LEVEL: 13
OFF. SCHEME: Vertical Offense
LEGACY SCORE: 0
DEF. SCHEME: Attacking 3-4

TEAM OVERVIEW

KEY PLAYERS

QB #9
DREW BREES

KEY RATINGS

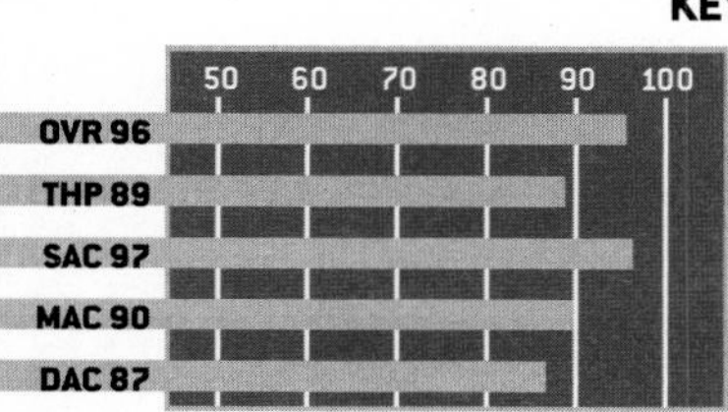

- While Brees doesn't have a laser rocket arm, he does have needle precision with all his throws.
- With the big targets that Brees throws to you should look to air it out deep down the sideline.

CB #33
JABARI GREER

KEY RATINGS

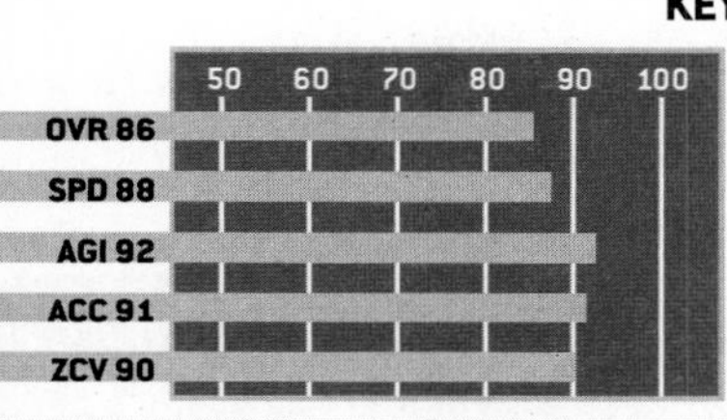

- Greer is a great zone defender and will be best used playing Cover 2 zone defenses.
- If you do play man-to-man with Greer, make sure to keep a safety over the top.

PRE-GAME SETUP

KEY RUNNING SUBSTITUTION

Who: HB Pierre Thomas

Where: Backup HB

Why: HB Darren Sproles isn't an every-down player. Thomas will fill in nicely when Sproles steps off the field.

Key Stats: 97 CAR

KEY PASSING SUBSTITUTION

Who: WR Nick Toon

Where: #4 WR

Why: Toon brings size to an already big lineup. With the focus on Colston and Graham expect Toon to get plenty of opportunities.

Key Stats: 6'4", 90 JMP

KEY RUN DEFENSE SUBSTITUTION

Who: DT John Jenkins

Where: #2 DT

Why: Jenkins is a rookie, but he has the strength of an NFL veteran.

Key Stats: 92 STR

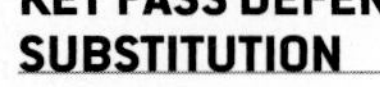

KEY PASS DEFENSE SUBSTITUTION

Who: CB Corey White

Where: #3 CB

Why: White brings much-needed height to the Saints secondary. Use him to cover opposing teams' taller WRs.

Key Stats: 6'1", 93 SPD

OFFENSIVE DEPTH CHART

POS	FIRST NAME	LAST NAME	OVR
QB	Drew	Brees	96
QB	Seneca	Wallace	72
QB	Luke	McCown	72
HB	Darren	Sproles	87
HB	Pierre	Thomas	82
HB	Mark	Ingram	81
HB	Travaris	Cadet	68
FB	Jed	Collins	90
WR	Marques	Colston	90
WR	Lance	Moore	85
WR	Joseph	Morgan	72
WR	Chris	Givens	71
WR	Preston	Parker	68
WR	Courtney	Roby	67
WR	Kenny	Stills	66
WR	Nick	Toon	65
WR	Andy	Tanner	57
WR	Jarred	Fayson	56
WR	Saalim	Hakim	52
TE	Jimmy	Graham	96
TE	Benjamin	Watson	82
TE	Michael	Higgins	66
TE	Justin	Drescher	45
LT	Charles	Brown	74
LT	Terron	Armstead	68
LT	Marcel	Jones	62
LG	Ben	Grubbs	95
LG	Eric	Olsen	70
C	Brian	De La Puente	91
RG	Jahri	Evans	95
RG	Ricky	Henry	66
RG	Andrew	Tiller	63
RT	Zach	Strief	77
RT	Jason	Smith	75
RT	Bryce	Harris	66

DEFENSIVE DEPTH CHART

POS	FIRST NAME	LAST NAME	OVR
LE	Akiem	Hicks	79
LE	Kenyon	Coleman	78
LE	Jay	Richardson	72
RE	Cameron	Jordan	81
RE	Tom	Johnson	70
DT	Brodrick	Bunkley	82
DT	John	Jenkins	70
DT	Tyrunn	Walker	66
DT	Isaako	Aaitui	63
LOLB	Victor	Butler	81
LOLB	Martez	Wilson	70
LOLB	Baraka	Atkins	60
MLB	Curtis	Lofton	82
MLB	David	Hawthorne	80
MLB	Jonathan	Vilma	78
MLB	Chris	Chamberlain	71
MLB	Will	Herring	70
MLB	Kevin	Reddick	64
MLB	Ramon	Humber	64
ROLB	Will	Smith	78
ROLB	Junior	Galette	77
ROLB	Chase	Thomas	69
CB	Jabari	Greer	86
CB	Keenan	Lewis	83
CB	Patrick	Robinson	78
CB	Corey	White	69
CB	Ryan	Steed	67
CB	Korey	Lindsey	63
CB	A.J.	Davis	60
FS	Malcolm	Jenkins	76
FS	Rafael	Bush	75
FS	Jim	Leonhard	75
FS	Jerico	Nelson	64
SS	Kenny	Vaccaro	80
SS	Roman	Harper	76
SS	Isa	Abdul-Quddus	72

SPECIAL TEAMS DEPTH CHART

POS	FIRST NAME	LAST NAME	OVR
K	Garrett	Hartley	76
P	Thomas	Morstead	94

New Orleans Saints

RECOMMENDED OFFENSIVE RUN FORMATION: I-FORM TWINS FLEX (2 HB, 1 TE, 2 WR)

PRO TIPS

> HB DARREN SPROLES SHOULD BE YOUR EVERY-DOWN HB.

> BACK UP SPROLES WITH HB PIERRE THOMAS.

> HB MARK INGRAM HAS MORE EXPLOSIVENESS THAN THOMAS, AND HIS 87 TRK RATING IS HIGHEST ON THE TEAM.

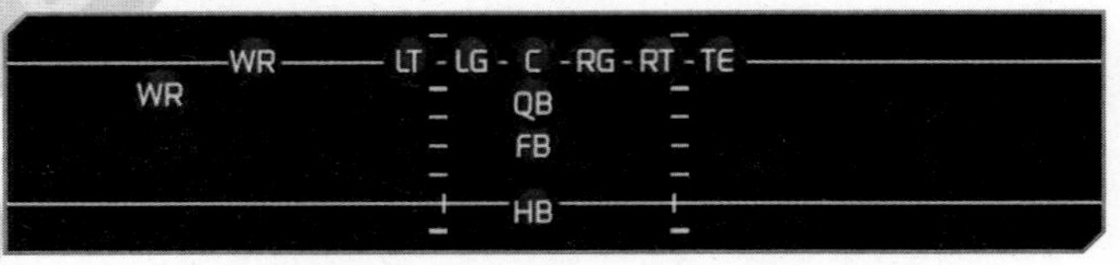

RUN LEFT

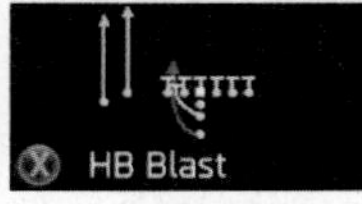

DARREN SPROLES IS QUICK AND FAST ENOUGH TO TURN ANY RUN INTO POSITIVE YARDS.

RUN MIDDLE

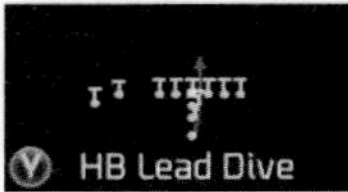

WE LIKE USING PIERRE THOMAS FOR RUNS UP THE MIDDLE.

RUN RIGHT

SPROLES IS DANGEROUS WHEN HE GETS INTO SPACE.

NEW ORLEANS SAINTS RUNNING PLAY CALL SHEET

LEGEND: Inside Run | Outside Run | Shotgun Run | QB Run

1ST DOWN RUNS	2ND AND SHORT	3RD AND SHORT	GOAL LINE RUNS	2ND AND LONG	3RD AND LONG
Singleback Jumbo—HB Sweep	Strong Close—Off Tackle	I-Form Twins Flex—HB Lead Dive	I-Form Tight—HB Iso	Gun Bunch Wk—HB Mid Draw	Gun Spread Y-Slot—HB Draw
Singleback Ace—HB Dive	Weak H Twins—HB Blast	I-Form Tight—Power O	Goal Line—FB Dive	Singleback Ace—HB Draw	Gun Spread Y-Slot HB Zone
Strong Close—Quick Toss	I-Form Tight—HB Blast	I-Form Twins Flex—Saints HB Power	Goal Line—Power O	Gun Snugs—HB Draw	Gun Trips Y Iso—HB Counter

NEW ORLEANS SAINTS PASSING PLAY CALL SHEET

LEGEND: Base Play | Man Beater | Zone Beater | Blitz Beater

1ST DOWN PLAY	2ND AND SHORT	3RD AND SHORT	GOAL LINE PASSING	2ND AND LONG	3RD AND LONG
Gun Snugs—Saints Spot Shake	Singleback Twin TE Flex—TE Spot	Singleback Doubles—Swing Screen	Goal Line—PA Spot	Gun Trey Open—HB Slip Screen	Gun Split Offset—Close HB Wheel
Gun Spread Y-Slot—Saints Y-Under	Singleback Bunch Base—FL Drive	Singleback Ace—HB Slip Screen	Singleback Y-Trips—Y Trail	Gun Trips Y Iso—Mesh Dig	Singleback Bunch Base—Seattle
Gun Wing Trio Wk—HB Drag	Singleback Doubles—Slants	Strong Close—Y Trail	I-Form Pro—Texas	Gun Empty Saint—Saints Flood	Gun Trey Open—Spacing HB Wheel

In these play call sheets we picked the best plays for specific situations so that you will have a play for every down and distance.

OFFENSE

RECOMMENDED OFFENSIVE PASS FORMATION: GUN SNUGS (1HB 0 TE 4 WR)

PRO TIPS

- WR MARQUES COLSTON HAS A 99 CIT RATING. GET HIM THE BALL IN CRUCIAL SITUATIONS.
- TE JIMMY GRAHAM SHOULD ALWAYS BE ON THE FIELD.
- WR JOSEPH MORGAN IS THE SAINTS' SPEED THREAT.

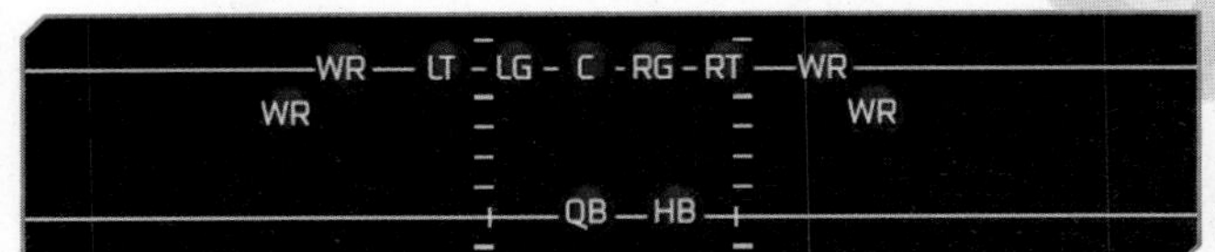

BASE PLAY

SETUP

- STREAK THE RIGHT SLOT WR
- MOTION THE FAR RIGHT WR OUTSIDE

- Against man-to-man coverage look to the left slot wheel as he cuts upfield.
- Against zone coverage look to the motioned WR on the curl-drag route as well as the deep post over the middle.

MAN BEATER

SETUP

- BLOCK THE HB
- STREAK THE FAR LEFT WR

- Look to the corner route as your first option against man-to-man coverage.
- The angled streak over the deep middle is also a nice user-catch option.

ZONE BEATER

SETUP

- STREAK BOTH OUTSIDE WIDE RECEIVERS
- WHEEL THE HB

- Against Cover 2 and Cover 3 zones look to the WRs running the corner routes.
- Against Cover 4 zones look to the HB on the wheel route.

BLITZ BEATER

SETUP

- DRAG THE LEFT SLOT WR
- DRAG THE FAR RIGHT WR

- First look to the HB out of the backfield. If you are facing a heavy blitz he will often catch the ball in wide-open space.
- Next look to the underneath drags, with your last read being to user-catch the far left fade.

New Orleans Saints

RECOMMENDED DEFENSIVE RUN FORMATION: 3-4 UNDER

PRO TIPS

- KEEP DEFENSIVE TACKLES JOHN JENKINS AND BRODRICK BUNKLEY ON THE FIELD AT ALL TIMES AGAINST THE RUN.
- USE ROLB WILL SMITH ON THE DEFENSIVE LINE FOR RUNNING SITUATIONS.
- SS KENNY VACCARO CAN HELP WITH RUN SUPPORT.

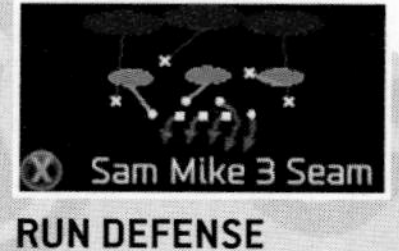

RUN DEFENSE

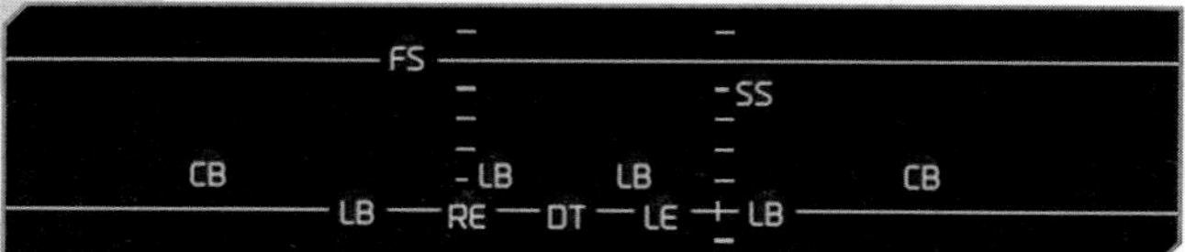

RUN DEFENSE LEFT

SETUP > SHIFT LINEBACKERS LEFT

RUN DEFENSE MIDDLE

SETUP > PINCH DEFENSIVE LINE

RUN DEFENSE RIGHT

SETUP > SHIFT LINEBACKERS RIGHT

NEW ORLEANS SAINTS DEFENSIVE RUN PLAY CALL SHEET

1ST DOWN RUN DEFENSE	2ND AND SHORT	3RD AND SHORT	GOAL LINE RUN DEFENSE	2ND AND LONG	3RD AND LONG
3-4 Odd—2 Deep MLB Spy	3-4 Solid—Cover 1 Robber	3-4 Odd—Storm Brave 1	Goal Line 5-3-3—Jam Cover 1	Nickel 2-4-5 Even—2 Man Under	Sub 1-4-6—2 Man MLB Blitz
3-4 Odd—Cover 2 Sink	3-4 Solid—Cover 4	3-4 Even— Strike OLB 2	Goal Line 5-3-3—Flat Buzz	Nickel 2-4-5—Cover 3	Sub 1-4-6—Cover 2 Sink

NEW ORLEANS SAINTS DEFENSIVE PASS PLAY CALL SHEET

1ST DOWN PLAY	2ND AND SHORT	3RD AND SHORT	GOAL LINE PASSING	2ND AND LONG	3RD AND LONG
Sub 1-4-6—Buck Dog 1	Nickel 2-4-5—Cover 1 Spy	Nickel 2-4-5—Over Storm Brave	Goal Line 6-3-2—GL Man	Sub 2-3-6 Will—Spinner	Sub 2-3-6—Silver Shoot Pinch
Sub 1-4-6—Cover 4	Nickel 2-4-5—Cover 2 Sink	Nickel 2-4-5—Sugar 3 Seam	Goal Line 6-3-2—GL Zone	Sub 2-3-6 Will—DB Fire 2	Nickel 2-4-5—Cover 3 Bluff

LEGEND: Man Coverage | Zone Coverage | Man Blitz | Zone Blitz

In these play call sheets we picked the best plays for specific situations so that you will have a play for every down and distance.

DEFENSE

RECOMMENDED DEFENSIVE PASS FORMATION: NICKEL 2-4-5

PRO TIPS

> PLACE CB JABARI GREER ON YOUR OPPONENT'S BEST WR.
> USE CB PATRICK ROBINSON ON YOUR OPPONENT'S FASTEST WR.
> CB KEENAN LEWIS SHOULD BE YOUR #2 CB.

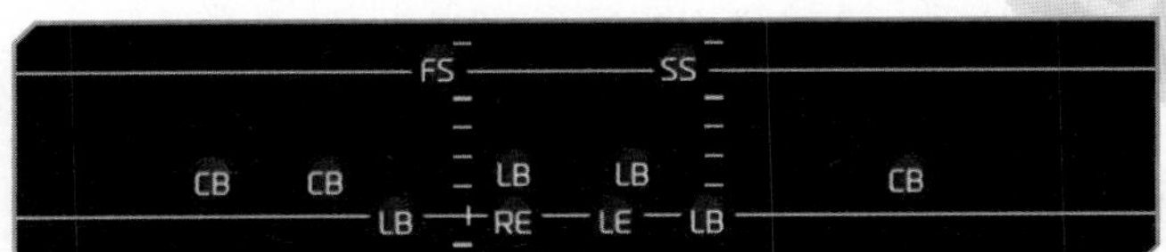

MAN COVERAGE

SETUP

> PUT THE LINEBACKERS IN A GLOBAL HOOK ZONE
> BASE ALIGN TWICE

> Our defense will be in press coverage, which will slow down reads on the outside.
> We will be rushing only our DTs on this play, but we'll have the middle of the field blanketed with defenders.

ZONE COVERAGE

SETUP

> FLAT ZONE THE RE
> BUZZ ZONE THE LE

> User-control the MLB and defend over the short middle.
> We will have zone defenders covering the field. Expect throws downfield to be batted down by the secondary.

MAN BLITZ

SETUP

> PRESS COVERAGE
> PUT THE LINEBACKERS ON A GLOBAL BLITZ

> As long as our CBs don't get beaten off the line of scrimmage the pressure should get to the QB before the WRs release on their routes.
> In our example you can see the pressure coming off the edge while our CB is still pressing the WR.

ZONE BLITZ

SETUP

> PRESS COVERAGE
> PUT THE LINEBACKERS ON A GLOBAL BLITZ

> User-control the Nickel CB and patrol over the middle.
> The hook zones on the outside will defend vertical patterns downfield and also protect everything in the flat.

Seattle Seahawks

2012 TEAM RANKINGS

2nd NFC West (11-5-0)

PASSING OFFENSE: **27th**
RUSHING OFFENSE: **3rd**
PASSING DEFENSE: **6th**
RUSHING DEFENSE: **10th**

2012 TEAM LEADERS

PASSING: **Russell Wilson: 3,118**
RUSHING: **Marshawn Lynch: 1,590**
RECEIVING: **Sidney Rice: 748**
TACKLES: **Bobby Wagner: 140**
SACKS: **Chris Clemons: 11.5**
INTS: **Richard Sherman: 8**

KEY ADDITIONS

CB Antoine Winfield
LE Michael Bennett
RE Cliff Avril

KEY ROOKIES

HB Christine Michael
DT Jordan Hill
WR Chris Harper

CONNECTED FRANCHISE MODE STRATEGY

CFM TEAM RATING: **75**
OFFENSIVE SCHEME: **Balanced Offense**
DEFENSIVE SCHEME: **Base 4-3**
STRENGTHS: **QB, HB, WR, C, RE, MLB, CB, FS, SS**
WEAKNESSES: **LG, RG, RT, ROLB**

SCHEDULE

1	Sep 8	1:00 PM ET	AT	PANTHERS
2	Sep 15	8:30 PM ET		49ERS
3	Sep 22	4:25 PM ET		JAGUARS
4	Sep 29	1:00 PM ET	AT	TEXANS
5	Oct 6	1:00 PM ET	AT	COLTS
6	Oct 13	4:05 PM ET		TITANS
7	Oct 17	8:25 PM ET	AT	CARDINALS
8	Oct 28	8:40 PM ET	AT	RAMS
9	Nov 3	4:05 PM ET		BUCCANEERS
10	Nov 10	1:00 PM ET	AT	FALCONS
11	Nov 17	4:25 PM ET		VIKINGS
12	BYE			
13	Dec 2	8:40 PM ET		SAINTS
14	Dec 8	4:25 PM ET	AT	49ERS
15	Dec 15	1:00 PM ET	AT	GIANTS
16	Dec 22	4:05 PM ET		CARDINALS
17	Dec 29	4:25 PM ET		RAMS

FRANCHISE OVERVIEW

SEAHAWKS GAMEPLAY RATING

90

> SEE THE INSIDE BACK COVER FOR A QUICK REFERENCE TO THE GAME ABBREVIATIONS USED THROUGHOUT THIS GUIDE.

> IMPROVE WITH YOUR TEAM BY VISITING PRIMAGAMES.COM/MADDENNFL25 FOR MORE INFORMATION AND HOW-TO VIDEOS.

OFFENSIVE SCOUTING REPORT

> QB Russell Wilson entered his rookie season as the backup in Seattle. He ended that same season as one of the best QBs in the league. Run an option offense with Wilson to take advantage of his skill set.

> Use HB Marshawn Lynch for every down. Use HB Robert Turbin for 3rd and long situations.

> WR Percy Harvin brings speed and a dynamic player to the Seahawks offense. Make sure to give rookie TE Luke Wilson touches, as he is a star in the making.

DEFENSIVE SCOUTING REPORT

> The defensive line for the Seahawks is stacked. There are so many good players that it will be difficult to play them all. When rushing the passer, start LE Michael Bennett, RE Chris Clemons, RE Bruce Irvin, and RE Cliff Avril. When stopping the run, start DT Brandon Mebane, LE Red Bryant, and DT Jesse Williams.

> MLB Bobby Wagner will often be the most dominant player on the field. He has the speed and power to change games. Build your outside linebackers around Wagner's skill set, speed, and power.

> The Seahawks have the best secondary in the league. Keep this entire unit intact for as long as possible: CB Richard Sherman, CB Brandon Browner, FS Earl Thomas, and SS Kam Chancellor.

OWNER & COACH PROFILES

PAUL ALLEN
LEGACY SCORE: 725
OFF. SCHEME: Balanced Offense
DEF. SCHEME: Base 4-3

PETE CARROLL
LEVEL: 12
LEGACY SCORE: 100
OFF. SCHEME: Balanced Offense
DEF. SCHEME: Base 4-3

TEAM OVERVIEW

KEY PLAYERS

QB #3

RUSSELL WILSON

KEY RATINGS

	50	60	70	80	90	100
OVR 89						
SPD 86						
ACC 92						
THP 93						
DAC 85						

> Use play action and get the ball deep to WR Percy Harvin.

> WR Sidney Rice is a great option for Wilson to target in the red zone.

CB #25

RICHARD SHERMAN

KEY RATINGS

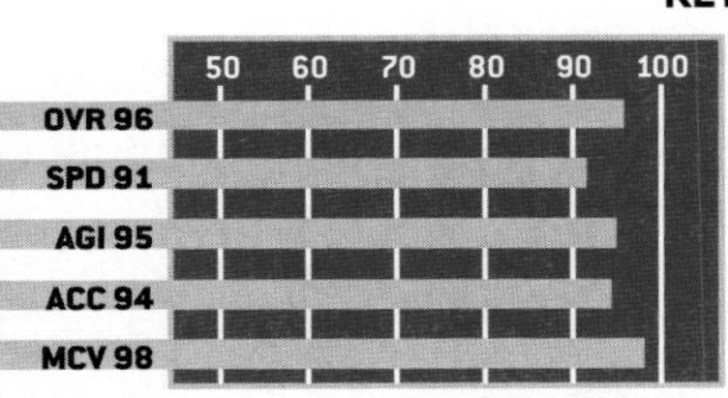

> It's almost impossible to find a CB with the size and speed that Sherman has. His 6'3" frame makes him one of the tallest CBs in the game.

> Sherman has no weakness. He can play man-to-man, zone, and even press at the line of scrimmage.

PRE-GAME SETUP

KEY RUNNING SUBSTITUTION

Who: HB Robert Turbin

Where: Backup HB

Why: Use Turbin on third downs when you plan on passing. He has the team's best hands out of the backfield.

Key Stats: 84 CAR, 76 CTH

KEY PASSING SUBSTITUTION

Who: TE Luke Wilson

Where: #4 WR

Why: Wilson is big and extremely fast for a TE. Use two-tight-end sets and take advantage of his athleticism.

Key Stats: 6'5", 88 SPD

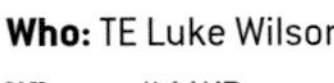

KEY RUN DEFENSE SUBSTITUTION

Who: LE Red Bryant

Where: #2 DT

Why: Bryant is so strong that opposing teams will have a very difficult time moving him out of the way on running downs.

Key Stats: 95 STR

KEY PASS DEFENSE SUBSTITUTION

Who: CB Tharold Simon

Where: #4 CB

Why: Simon is a great backup for the Seahawks secondary.

Key Stats: 6'2", 77 PRS

OFFENSIVE DEPTH CHART

POS	FIRST NAME	LAST NAME	OVR
QB	Russell	Wilson	89
QB	Tarvaris	Jackson	73
QB	Brady	Quinn	73
HB	Marshawn	Lynch	96
HB	Robert	Turbin	76
HB	Christine	Michael	70
FB	Michael	Robinson	87
FB	Spencer	Ware	65
WR	Percy	Harvin	92
WR	Sidney	Rice	86
WR	Golden	Tate	80
WR	Doug	Baldwin	74
WR	Chris	Harper	69
WR	Brett	Swain	66
WR	Jermaine	Kearse	64
WR	Stephen	Williams	62
WR	Phil	Bates	61
WR	Bryan	Walters	60
TE	Zach	Miller	83
TE	Anthony	McCoy	77
TE	Luke	Willson	63
TE	Sean	McGrath	61
TE	Clint	Gresham	49
TE	Kyle	Nelson	43
LT	Russell	Okung	88
LT	Mike	Person	63
LG	James	Carpenter	75
LG	John	Moffitt	71
LG	Alvin	Bailey	66
LG	Rishaw	Johnson	66
C	Max	Unger	92
C	Lemuel	Jeanpierre	67
RG	Paul	McQuistan	74
RG	J.R.	Sweezy	73
RT	Breno	Giacomini	77
RT	Michael	Bowie	64

DEFENSIVE DEPTH CHART

POS	FIRST NAME	LAST NAME	OVR
LE	Michael	Bennett	86
LE	Red	Bryant	80
LE	Greg	Scruggs	66
RE	Chris	Clemons	89
RE	Cliff	Avril	83
RE	Bruce	Irvin	79
DT	Brandon	Mebane	85
DT	Tony	McDaniel	77
DT	Clinton	McDonald	71
DT	Jesse	Williams	69
DT	Jaye	Howard	66
DT	Jordan	Hill	66
LOLB	K.J.	Wright	84
LOLB	Mike	Morgan	64
LOLB	Korey	Toomer	61
MLB	Bobby	Wagner	88
MLB	Ty	Powell	61
ROLB	Heath	Farwell	75
ROLB	Malcolm	Smith	67
ROLB	Allen	Bradford	56
CB	Richard	Sherman	96
CB	Antoine	Winfield	90
CB	Brandon	Browner	88
CB	Walter	Thurmond	72
CB	Jeremy	Lane	71
CB	Byron	Maxwell	70
CB	Tharold	Simon	67
CB	Will	Blackmon	65
CB	DeShawn	Shead	63
CB	Ron	Parker	62
FS	Earl	Thomas	91
FS	Chris	Maragos	65
SS	Kam	Chancellor	90
SS	Jeron	Johnson	74
SS	Winston	Guy	67

SPECIAL TEAMS DEPTH CHART

POS	FIRST NAME	LAST NAME	OVR
K	Steven	Hauschka	81
P	Jon	Ryan	86

Seattle Seahawks

RECOMMENDED OFFENSIVE RUN FORMATION: PISTOL JUMBO Z (1 HB, 3 TE, 1 WR)

PRO TIPS

> USE FB MICHAEL ROBINSON AS A LEAD BLOCKER FOR HB MARSHAWN LYNCH.

> HB ROBERT TURBIN SHOULD BE THE BACKUP HB.

> QB RUSSELL WILSON CAN BE AN EFFECTIVE RUSHING THREAT.

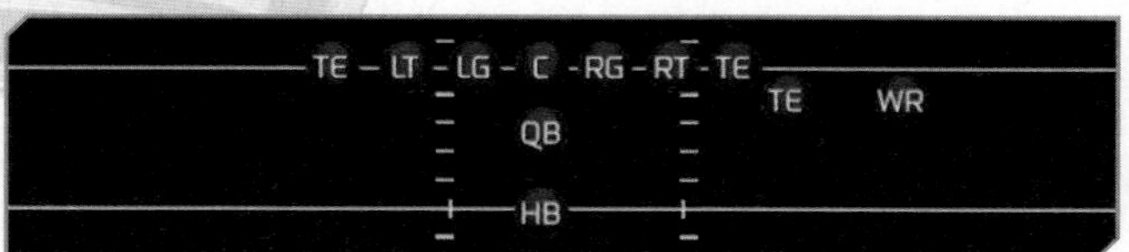

RUN LEFT

WE HAVE TO PULL GUARDS AS LEAD BLOCKERS.

RUN MIDDLE

GIVE THE BALL TO MARSHAWN LYNCH UP THE MIDDLE.

RUN RIGHT

HERE WE KEEP THE BALL WITH RUSSELL WILSON AS THE DEFENDER PLAYS THE HB.

SEATTLE SEAHAWKS RUNNING PLAY CALL SHEET

LEGEND: Inside Run | Outside Run | Shotgun Run | QB Run

1ST DOWN RUNS	2ND AND SHORT	3RD AND SHORT	GOAL LINE RUNS	2ND AND LONG	3RD AND LONG
Singleback Ace—HB Stretch	I-Form H Tight—FB Dive	I-Form H Slot—HB Iso	I-Form H Slot—FB Dive	Gun Tight Slots—HB Draw	Pistol Trips—Read Option
I-Form H Pro—Iso	Singleback Ace—HB Dive	Weak I H Pro—Toss Weak	Pistol Strong—Inside Zone Split	I-Form H Pro—HB Lead Draw	Pistol Trips—Lead Option
Singleback Ace Pair Flex—HB Toss Strong	I-Form H Twin Pair—HB Blast	I-Form H Slot—Power O	Pistol Strong—Power Option	Gun Trio 4 WR—QB Draw	Gun Spread—HB Draw

SEATTLE SEAHAWKS PASSING PLAY CALL SHEET

LEGEND: Base Play | Man Beater | Zone Beater | Blitz Beater

1ST DOWN PLAY	2ND AND SHORT	3RD AND SHORT	GOAL LINE PASSING	2ND AND LONG	3RD AND LONG
Singleback Snugs—Hawks HB Wheel	Gun Doubles On—Double Sluggo	I-Form H Slot—HB Slip Screen	Pistol Strong—Slants	Gun Empty Trey—Smash	Gun Trio Offset—Mesh
Singleback Doubles—Deep Attack	Pistol Twin TE—TE Stick	Pistol Strong—HB Slip Screen	Singleback Doubles—Goaline Fade	Gun Tight Slot—Hawks Drive Trail	Gun Spread—Four Verticals
Gun Trio Offset—TE In	Pistol Twin TE—WR Screen	Gun Split Hawk—Slants Middle	Singleback Ace Pair Flip—TE Out	Gun Y-Trips Wk—Y Trail	Gun Tight Slots—Bench

In these play call sheets we picked the best plays for specific situations so that you will have a play for every down and distance.

OFFENSE

RECOMMENDED OFFENSIVE PASS FORMATION: GUN TRIO OFFSET (1 HB, 1 TE, 3 WR)

PRO TIPS

- TE LUKE WILSON IS A GREAT PASS-RECEIVING TE AND HAS AN 88 SPD RATING, WHICH WILL CAUSE MATCHUP PROBLEMS FOR DEFENSES.
- TE ANTHONY MCCOY IS ALSO A GREAT PASS-RECEIVING TE. GET HIM THE BALL A FEW TIMES EACH GAME.
- GOLDEN TATE AND DOUG BALDWIN ARE BOTH SHIFTY RECEIVERS WHO WILL BE GREAT IN OPEN SPACE.

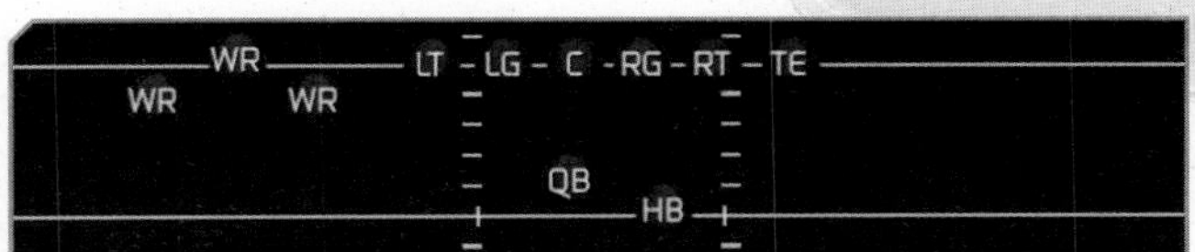

BASE PLAY

SETUP

- DRAG THE FAR LEFT WR
- BLOCK THE HB

- The deep post from this formation is one of the best in the entire game.
- It gets behind most defenses in the game, and if you have enough time in the pocket it will be a TD.

MAN BEATER

SETUP

- BLOCK THE HB
- ZIG THE TE

- The slot wheel route will get inside position down the left sideline.
- In our example you can see that we catch the ball just before the FS is able to make a play on the ball.

ZONE BEATER

SETUP

- STREAK THE TE
- STREAK THE INSIDE SLOT WR

- Against Cover 2 and Cover 3 zone look to the TE's streak and the sideline corner route.
- Against Cover 4 zone look to the sideline hitch and the HB's wheel.

BLITZ BEATER

SETUP

- SWING THE HB LEFT
- STREAK THE FAR LEFT WR

- This play is best used against zone blitzes.
- If you face a man-to-man blitz, the MLB covering the HB typically is able to defend him before he can get upfield towards his blockers.

Seattle Seahawks

RECOMMENDED DEFENSIVE RUN FORMATION: 4-3 UNDER

PRO TIPS

- > MOVE LE RED BRYANT INSIDE TO PLAY DT. HE IS BEST USED FOR RUNNING SITUATIONS.
- > LE MICHAEL BENNETT IS STRONG ENOUGH TO PLAY DT AND WILL PROVIDE ADDED SPEED TO THE DEFENSIVE LINE.
- > SS KAM CHANCELLOR IS ONE OF THE HARDEST-HITTING PLAYERS IN THE GAME.

RUN DEFENSE

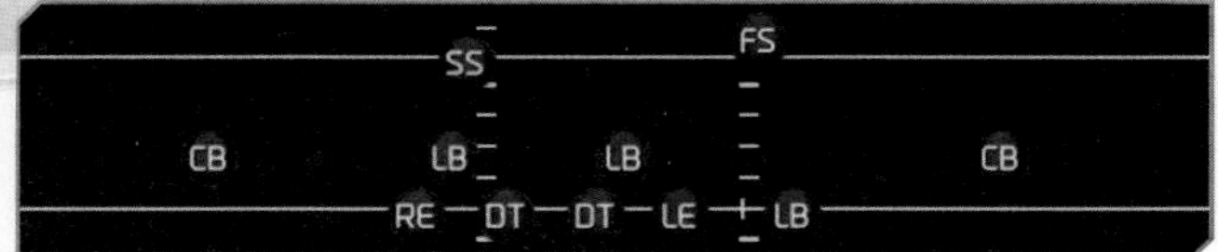

RUN DEFENSE LEFT

SETUP > SHIFT LINEBACKERS LEFT

RUN DEFENSE MIDDLE

SETUP > PINCH DEFENSIVE LINE

RUN DEFENSE RIGHT

SETUP > SHIFT LINEBACKERS RIGHT

SEATTLE SEAHAWKS DEFENSIVE RUN PLAY CALL SHEET

1ST DOWN RUN DEFENSE	2ND AND SHORT	3RD AND SHORT	GOAL LINE RUN DEFENSE	2ND AND LONG	3RD AND LONG
4-3 Over—Cover 1	4-3 Stack—2 Deep Gap Shoot	4-3 Stack—Free Fire	Goal Line 5-3-3—Jam Cover 1	Nickel Wide 9—Cover 1 Robber	Nickel Normal—2 Man Under
4-3 Over—Fire Zone 2	4-3 Stack—Cover 3 Buzz	4-3 Stack—Will 2 Fire	Goal Line 5-3-3—Flat Buzz	Nickel Wide 9—Cover 2	Nickel Normal—Cover 6

SEATTLE SEAHAWKS DEFENSIVE PASS PLAY CALL SHEET

1ST DOWN PLAY	2ND AND SHORT	3RD AND SHORT	GOAL LINE PASSING	2ND AND LONG	3RD AND LONG
Dime Normal—2 Man Under	Nickel Normal—Cover 1 Press	Dollar 3-2-6—Spinner	Goal Line 6-3-2—GL Man	Nickel Normal—Under Smoke	Dime Normal—All Out Blitz
Dime Normal—Cover 3	Nickel Normal—Cover 4	Dollar 3-2-6—Okie Roll 3	Goal Line 6-3-2—GL Zone	Nickel Normal—Mid Zone Blitz	Dime Normal—MLB Loop 2

LEGEND: Man Coverage | Zone Coverage | Man Blitz | Zone Blitz

In these play call sheets we picked the best plays for specific situations so that you will have a play for every down and distance.

DEFENSE

RECOMMENDED DEFENSIVE PASS FORMATION: 4-3 OVER PLUS

PRO TIPS

- MAKE SURE THAT YOU ALWAYS HAVE FS EARL THOMAS AND SS KAM CHANCELLOR IN THE GAME.
- CORNERBACKS RICHARD SHERMAN AND BRANDON BROWNER ARE THE TALLEST TANDEM IN THE GAME.
- THE SEAHAWKS DEFENSIVE SECONDARY IS THE BEST IN THE GAME.

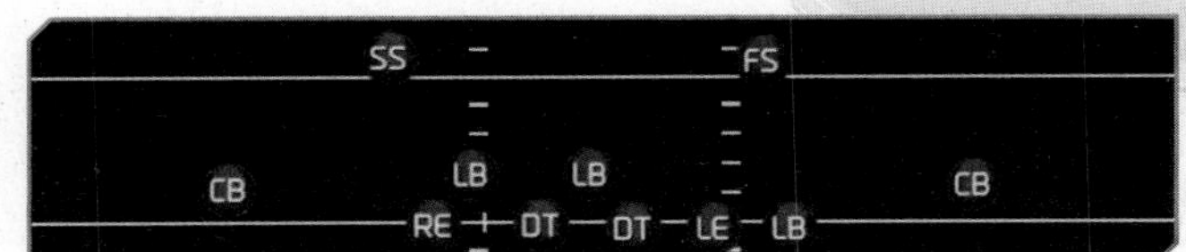

MAN COVERAGE

SETUP

- SEND THE LOLB ON A GLOBAL BLITZ
- CRASH THE DEFENSIVE LINE DOWN

- Pressure will come off the right edge.
- The TE will be uncovered, so watch out for quick passes to him.

ZONE COVERAGE

SETUP

- PRESS COVERAGE
- HOOK ZONE BOTH DEFENSIVE ENDS.

- This play is great at stopping opponents who like to let fly a quick pass to their TEs.
- The DE playing the hook zone will defend the TE streak for about 10 yards.

MAN BLITZ

SETUP

- SPREAD THE DEFENSIVE LINE AND CRASH DOWN
- PUT BOTH OUTSIDE LINEBACKERS ON GLOBAL BLITZ

- This pressure will send two free pass rushers after the QB.
- Your opponent needs to block seven players to pick this pressure up.

ZONE BLITZ

SETUP

- SPREAD THE DEFENSIVE LINE AND CRASH DOWN
- PUT BOTH OUTSIDE LINEBACKERS ON GLOBAL BLITZ

- We again are sending six pass rushers and will get two free after the QB.
- Anticipate a quick pass to the flat, where SS Kam Chancellor can lay the big hit to knock the ball free.

Pittsburgh Steelers

2012 TEAM RANKINGS

3rd AFC North (8-8-0)

PASSING OFFENSE: **14th**
RUSHING OFFENSE: **26th**
PASSING DEFENSE: **1st**
RUSHING DEFENSE: **2nd**

2012 TEAM LEADERS

PASSING: **Ben Roethlisberger: 3,265**
RUSHING: **Jonathan Dwyer: 623**
RECEIVING: **Mike Wallace: 836**
TACKLES: **Larry Foote: 113**
SACKS: **Lawrence Timmons: 6**
INTS: **Lawrence Timmons: 3**

KEY ADDITIONS

QB Bruce Gradkowski
HB LaRod Stephens-Howling
TE Matt Spaeth

KEY ROOKIES

ROLB Jarvis Jones
HB Le'Veon Bell
WR Markus Wheaton

CONNECTED FRANCHISE MODE STRATEGY

CFM TEAM RATING: **82**
OFFENSIVE SCHEME: **Balanced Offense**
DEFENSIVE SCHEME: **Zone Blitz 3-4**
STRENGTHS: **QB, TE, C, LOLB, MLB, CB, SS**
WEAKNESSES: **HB, LT, LE, DT, ROLB**

SCHEDULE

Week	Date	Time		Opponent
1	Sep 8	1:00 PM ET		TITANS
2	Sep 16	8:40 PM ET	AT	BENGALS
3	Sep 22	8:30 PM ET		BEARS
4	Sep 29	1:00 PM ET	AT	VIKINGS
5	BYE			
6	Oct 13	1:00 PM ET	AT	JETS
7	Oct 20	4:25 PM ET		RAVENS
8	Oct 27	4:05 PM ET	AT	RAIDERS
9	Nov 3	4:25 PM ET	AT	PATRIOTS
10	Nov 10	1:00 PM ET		BILLS
11	Nov 17	1:00 PM ET		LIONS
12	Nov 24	1:00 PM ET	AT	BROWNS
13	Nov 28	8:30 PM ET	AT	RAVENS
14	Dec 8	1:00 PM ET		DOLPHINS
15	Dec 15	8:30 PM ET		BENGALS
16	Dec 22	4:25 PM ET	AT	PACKERS
17	Dec 29	1:00 PM ET		BROWNS

FRANCHISE OVERVIEW

STEELERS GAMEPLAY RATING

80

> SEE THE INSIDE BACK COVER FOR A QUICK REFERENCE TO THE GAME ABBREVIATIONS USED THROUGHOUT THIS GUIDE.

> IMPROVE WITH YOUR TEAM BY VISITING PRIMAGAMES.COM/MADDENNFL25 FOR MORE INFORMATION AND HOW-TO VIDEOS.

OFFENSIVE SCOUTING REPORT

> QB Ben Roethlisberger has two Super Bowl rings. He is one of the greatest QBs to play the game. At age 31 he still has plenty of years left ahead of him. We think that you should spend your upgrades on rookie QB Landry Jones and groom him while Big Ben competes for another Super Bowl.

> Priority number one for the Steelers is to find a feature HB. Big Ben is aging and needs a complete team to have another chance at a Super Bowl. No HB on this roster is the long-term answer.

> WR Emmanuel Sanders will surprise people this season. After the departure of WR Mike Wallace he will see plenty of opportunities, and we think he has the talent to take advantage of it.

DEFENSIVE SCOUTING REPORT

> The Steelers defensive line was once the most dominant in all of football. It is a shell of its former self and needs to be rebuilt. Focus on this in the draft and in free agency.

> MLB Lawrence Timmons has big shoes to fill. The departure of James Harrison means more chances for Timmons to showcase his ability.

> SS Troy Polamalu is a hall of fame player and still has juice left in the tank. It is time, though, to start thinking about his replacement. Keep this thought on the back burner so that when he does retire you won't be surprised.

OWNER & COACH PROFILES

Steelers

DAN ROONEY

LEGACY SCORE: 6075
DEF. SCHEME: Zone Blitz 3-4
OFF. SCHEME: Balanced Offense

Steelers

MIKE TOMLIN

LEVEL: 29
OFF. SCHEME: Balanced Offense
LEGACY SCORE: 1550
DEF. SCHEME: Zone Blitz 3-4

TEAM OVERVIEW

KEY PLAYERS

Steelers

QB #7

BEN ROETHLISBERGER

KEY RATINGS

50 60 70 80 90 100

OVR 92
SPD 70
THP 94
SAC 91
MAC 86

> Roethlisberger is one of the hardest QBs to tackle in the game.

> He has just enough speed to escape the pocket and frustrate opposing pass rushers.

SS #43

TROY POLAMALU

KEY RATINGS

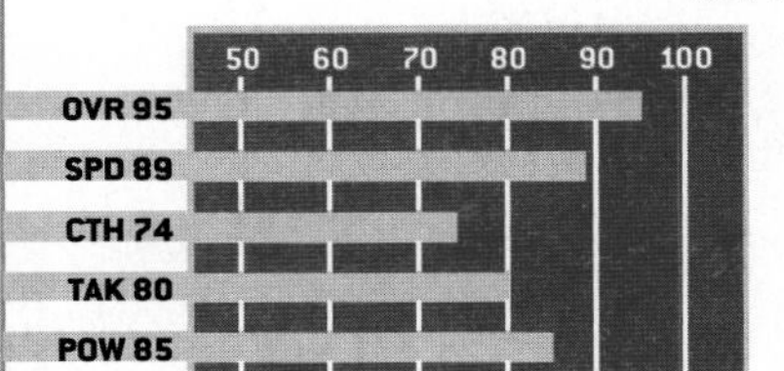

> Polamalu has been patrolling the deep secondary for the Steelers for a decade.

> He is one of our favorite user-controlled players because he does everything well.

PRE-GAME SETUP

KEY RUNNING SUBSTITUTION

Who: HB LaRod Stephens-Howling

Where: Starting HB

Why: We like more explosive HBs to see more playing time. That's why Stephens-Howling gets the start.

Key Stats: 93 SPD, 76 CTH

KEY PASSING SUBSTITUTION

Who: TE Matt Spaeth

Where: #2 TE

Why: Spaeth should be used almost always in the red zone. His 6'7" height makes him difficult to defend.

Key Stats: 6'7", 82 CIT, 86 JMP

KEY RUN DEFENSE SUBSTITUTION

Who: LE Al Woods

Where: #2 DT

Why: Woods will help the defensive line with his 94 STR rating during run situations.

Key Stats: 94 STR

KEY PASS DEFENSE SUBSTITUTION

Who: CB DeMarcus Van Dyke

Where: #1 CB

Why: Van Dyke is the game's fastest defender. He is the Steelers' best chance at defending opposing teams' best WRs.

Key Stats: 6'1", 98 SPD

OFFENSIVE DEPTH CHART

POS	FIRST NAME	LAST NAME	OVR
QB	Ben	Roethlisberger	92
QB	Bruce	Gradkowski	73
QB	Landry	Jones	67
QB	John Parker	Wilson	64
HB	Jonathan	Dwyer	76
HB	Isaac	Redman	74
HB	Le'Veon	Bell	73
HB	LaRod	Stephens-Howling	72
HB	Baron	Batch	67
FB	David	Johnson	76
FB	Will	Johnson	72
WR	Antonio	Brown	86
WR	Emmanuel	Sanders	76
WR	Jerricho	Cotchery	75
WR	Plaxico	Burress	74
WR	Markus	Wheaton	70
WR	Justin	Brown	62
WR	David	Gilreath	58
WR	Kashif	Moore	57
TE	Heath	Miller	88
TE	Matt	Spaeth	80
TE	David	Paulson	69
TE	Jamie	McCoy	66
LT	Mike	Adams	73
LT	Kelvin	Beachum	66
LG	Ramon	Foster	83
LG	John	Malecki	67
C	Maurkice	Pouncey	88
C	Joe	Madsen	73
C	Greg	Warren	71
RG	David	DeCastro	79
RT	Marcus	Gilbert	78
RT	Guy	Whimper	73
RT	Joe	Long	59

DEFENSIVE DEPTH CHART

POS	FIRST NAME	LAST NAME	OVR
LE	Ziggy	Hood	77
LE	Al	Woods	65
RE	Brett	Keisel	83
RE	Cameron	Heyward	77
RE	Nicholas	Williams	63
DT	Steve	McLendon	79
DT	Alameda	Ta'amu	74
DT	Hebron	Fangupo	63
LOLB	LaMarr	Woodley	87
LOLB	Chris	Carter	64
LOLB	Adrian	Robinson	60
MLB	Lawrence	Timmons	91
MLB	Larry	Foote	75
MLB	Stevenson	Sylvester	69
MLB	Brian	Rolle	68
MLB	Sean	Spence	66
MLB	Kion	Wilson	65
MLB	Vince	Williams	61
MLB	Marshall	McFadden	58
ROLB	Jason	Worilds	78
ROLB	Jarvis	Jones	76
CB	Ike	Taylor	89
CB	Cortez	Allen	80
CB	William	Gay	77
CB	DeMarcus	Van Dyke	69
CB	Curtis	Brown	69
CB	Terry	Hawthorne	67
CB	Justin	King	67
CB	Ross	Ventrone	64
CB	Josh	Victorian	62
FS	Ryan	Clark	85
FS	Robert	Golden	65
SS	Troy	Polamalu	95
SS	Shamarko	Thomas	72
SS	Da'Mon	Cromartie-Smith	65

SPECIAL TEAMS DEPTH CHART

POS	FIRST NAME	LAST NAME	OVR
K	Shaun	Suisham	86
P	Brian	Moorman	77
P	Drew	Butler	71

Steelers

Pittsburgh Steelers

RECOMMENDED OFFENSIVE RUN FORMATION: STRONG CLOSE (2 HB, 1 TE, 2 WR)

PRO TIPS

- > HB LAROD STEPHENS-HOWLING IS THE TEAM'S FASTEST HB.
- > ROOKIE LE'VEON BELL IS THE STEELERS' BEST HB.
- > HB JONATHAN DWYER'S 95 TRK RATING IS THE TEAM'S HIGHEST.

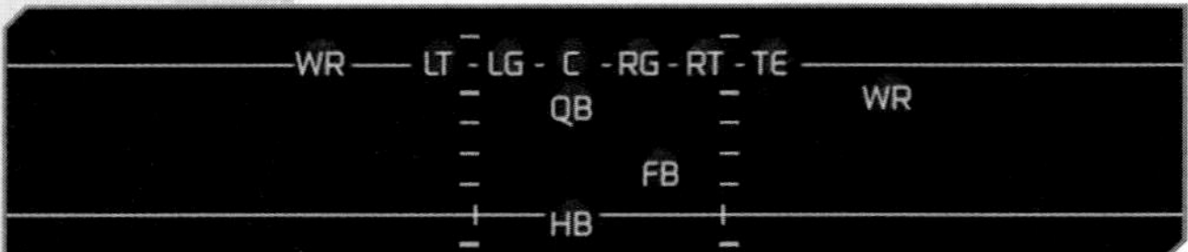

RUN LEFT

JONATHAN DWYER WILL RUN OVER SMALLER DEFENDERS.

RUN MIDDLE

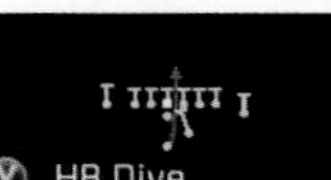

DWYER IS BEST USED FOR RUNS UP THE MIDDLE.

RUN RIGHT

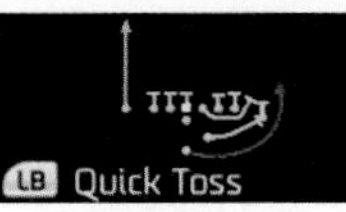

DON'T AVOID CONTACT WITH DWYER. INITIATE IT.

PITTSBURGH STEELERS RUNNING PLAY CALL SHEET

LEGEND: Inside Run | Outside Run | Shotgun Run | QB Run

1ST DOWN RUNS	2ND AND SHORT	3RD AND SHORT	GOAL LINE RUNS	2ND AND LONG	3RD AND LONG
Strong Twins—HB Sweep	Full House Normal Wide—Power O	I-Form Pro—Iso	Goal Line Normal—QB Sneak	Gun Trio—Off Tackle	Gun Bunch Wk—HB Mid Draw
Weak Pro—Misdirection	Singleback Ace Pair Flex—HB Slam	Singleback Y-Trips—HB Toss Strong	Goal Line Normal—HB Dive	Singleback Jumbo—Power O	Gun Y-Trips Wk—Steeler HB Base
Weak Pro—Toss Weak	Singleback Ace Pair Flex—HB Dive	Singleback Ace Close—HB Blunt Dive	Goal Line Normal—Power O	Gun Trips HB Wk—HB Base	Gun Wing Trips Wk—HB Mid Draw

PITTSBURGH STEELERS PASSING PLAY CALL SHEET

LEGEND: Base Play | Man Beater | Zone Beater | Blitz Beater

1ST DOWN PLAY	2ND AND SHORT	3RD AND SHORT	GOAL LINE PASSING	2ND AND LONG	3RD AND LONG
Gun Wing Trips Wk—Deep Slot Curl	Gun Spread Y-Slot—Hitch Seam	Gun Trips HB Wk—HB Slip Screen	Goal Line—PA Waggle	Gun Y-Trips Wk—Steeler Fade	Gun Trio—Pitt Smash
I-Form Twins—China Special	Singleback Ace Pair Flex—Steeler Drive	Singleback Pitt Doubles—Inside Cross	Goal Line—PA Spot	Singleback Jumbo—Mesh	Gun Split Close—Pitt DBL Ins
Gun Trio—Curl Flat	Singleback Bunch—Verticals	Singleback Bunch—Close Mesh Corner	Goal Line—PA Power O	Gun Snugs—Bench	Gun Empty Steeler—Verticals

In these play call sheets we picked the best plays for specific situations so that you will have a play for every down and distance.

OFFENSE

RECOMMENDED OFFENSIVE PASS FORMATION: SINGLEBACK ACE PAIR FLEX (1 HB, 2 TE, 2 WR)

PRO TIPS

> TE MATT SPAETH IS A BIG TARGET IN THE RED ZONE.

> TE HEATH MILLER IS ONE OF THE STEELERS' BEST RECEIVING OPTIONS.

> GET THE BALL TO RECEIVERS ANTONIO BROWN AND EMMANUEL SANDERS EARLY AND OFTEN.

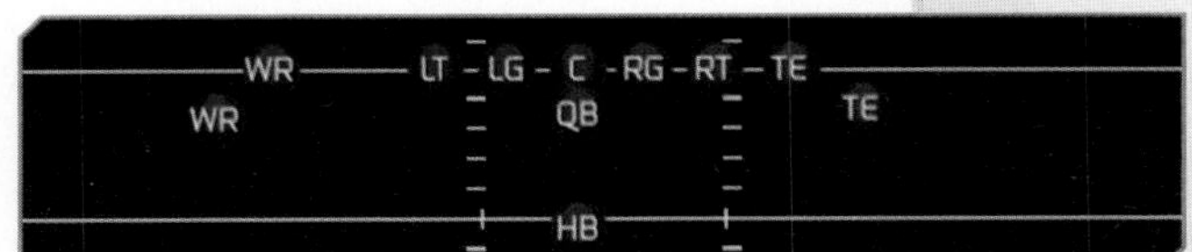

BASE PLAY

SETUP

> STREAK THE INSIDE TE

> ZIG THE OUTSIDE TE

> The main read on this play is to target the HB out of the backfield.

> Don't use lead pass, and throw the ball as soon as he moves upfield.

MAN BEATER

SETUP

> ZIG THE OUTSIDE TE

> MOTION THE FAR LEFT WR OUTSIDE

> At the snap of the ball the motioned WR will burst upfield, beating his defender inside.

> Throw an inside pass lead to the WR, which will lead him upfield for more yards after the catch.

ZONE BEATER

SETUP

> OPTION THE HB

> Against Cover 2 and Cover 3 look to any of the four vertical patterns.

> Against Cover 4 zones look to the HB option.

BLITZ BEATER

SETUP

> ZIG THE INSIDE TE

> DRAG THE OUTSIDE TE

> Our main target is the HB on the screen.

> The TEs running the zig and drag combo are also nice quick options against heavy pressure.

PITTSBURGH STEELERS

Pittsburgh Steelers

RECOMMENDED DEFENSIVE RUN FORMATION: 3-4 SOLID

PRO TIPS

> LE AL WOODS AND RE CAMERON HEYWARD NEED TO SEE THE FIELD WHEN FACING THE RUN.
> AGAINST THE RUN START TACKLES ALAMEDA TA'AMU AND HEBRON FANGUPO.
> FS RYAN CLARK CAN HELP IN RUN SUPPORT.

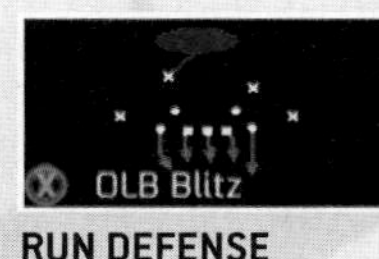

RUN DEFENSE

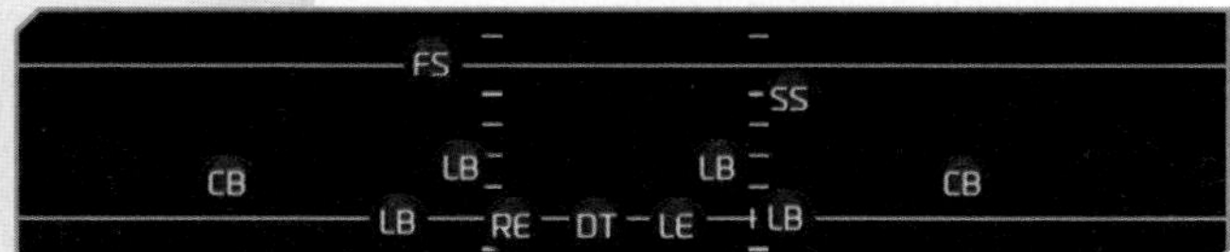

RUN DEFENSE LEFT

SETUP > SHIFT LINEBACKERS LEFT

RUN DEFENSE MIDDLE

SETUP > PINCH DEFENSIVE LINE

RUN DEFENSE RIGHT

SETUP > SHIFT LINEBACKERS RIGHT

PITTSBURGH STEELERS DEFENSIVE RUN PLAY CALL SHEET

1ST DOWN RUN DEFENSE	2ND AND SHORT	3RD AND SHORT	GOAL LINE RUN DEFENSE	2ND AND LONG	3RD AND LONG
3-4 Solid—Cover 1 Robber	3-4 Odd—Storm Brave 1	3-4 Under—Will Fire 1	Goal Line 5-3-3—Jam Cover 1	Nickel 1-5-5 Prowl—2 Man Under	Nickel 2-4-5—Overload 1 Roll
3-4 Solid—Cover 6	3-4 Odd—Zorro Will Jack 3	3-4 Under—OLB Strike 2	Goal Line 5-3-3—Flat Buzz	Nickel 1-5-5 Prowl—Cover 3	Nickel 2-4-5—Cover 6

PITTSBURGH STEELERS DEFENSIVE PASS PLAY CALL SHEET

1ST DOWN PLAY	2ND AND SHORT	3RD AND SHORT	GOAL LINE PASSING	2ND AND LONG	3RD AND LONG
3-4 Solid—2 Man Under	3-4 Odd—2 Man Under	3-4 Even—Strong Blitz	Goal Line Man	Nickel 2-4-5 Cross Fire 0	Nickel 2-4-5—Sugar Blitz
3-4 Solid—Cover 3 Buzz	3-4 Odd—Cover 3	3-4 Even—Trio Sky Zone	Goal Line 6-3-2—GL Zone	Nickel 2-4-5—Cross Fire 3 Seam	Nickel 2-4-5—Sugar Cover 3 Bluff

LEGEND: Man Coverage | Zone Coverage | Man Blitz | Zone Blitz

In these play call sheets we picked the best plays for specific situations so that you will have a play for every down and distance.

DEFENSE

RECOMMENDED DEFENSIVE PASS FORMATION: NICKEL 1-5-5 PROWL

PRO TIPS

> PLACE CB IKE TAYLOR ON YOUR OPPONENT'S BEST WR.
> USE CB DEMARCUS VAN DYKE ON YOUR OPPONENT'S FASTEST WR.
> CB CORTEZ ALLEN SHOULD BE YOUR #2 CB.

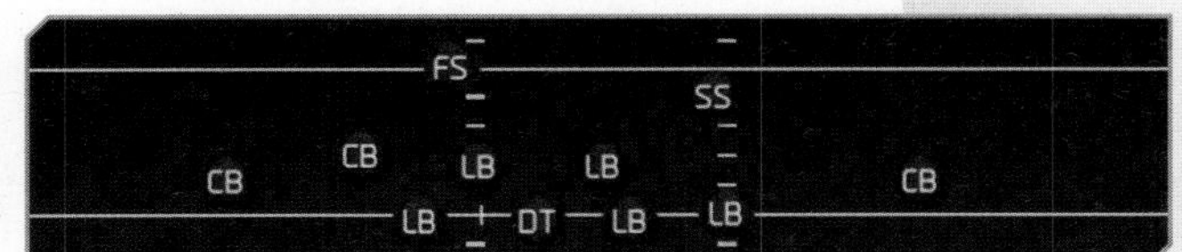

MAN COVERAGE

SETUP

> PUT BOTH OUTSIDE LINEBACKERS ON GLOBAL BLITZ
> USER-CONTROL THE SS

> User-defend the TE or the HB.
> Either the TE or the HB will be uncovered, but with this defense we are looking to play an aggressive brand of football. Make your opponent throw to the open player.

ZONE COVERAGE

SETUP

> DEEP ZONE THE DT
> QB SPY THE MLB

> With this setup we have created a Cover 5 zone.
> Opponents will find it nearly impossible to throw deep down the field.

MAN BLITZ

SETUP

> PRESS COVERAGE
> PUT THE LINEBACKERS ON GLOBAL BLITZ

> User-control the FS covering the HB.
> If the HB runs a route, you must cover him with the FS. If he stays in to block you can drop into coverage with him instead.

ZONE BLITZ

SETUP

> PUT THE LINEBACKERS ON GLOBAL BLITZ
> USER-CONTROL THE FS

> Play up in the box with the FS.
> If a slot WR or TE runs a deep vertical over the middle, you must drop back and defend with the FS.

PITTSBURGH STEELERS

Houston Texans

2012 TEAM RANKINGS

1st AFC South (12-4-0)

PASSING OFFENSE: **11th**
RUSHING OFFENSE: **8th**
PASSING DEFENSE: **16th**
RUSHING DEFENSE: **7th**

2012 TEAM LEADERS

PASSING: **Matt Schaub: 4,008**
RUSHING: **Arian Foster: 1,424**
RECEIVING: **Andre Johnson: 1,598**
TACKLES: **Glover Quin: 84**
SACKS: **J.J. Watt: 20.5**
INTS: **Kareem Jackson: 4**

KEY ADDITIONS

FS Ed Reed
FB Greg Jones
P Shane Lechler

KEY ROOKIES

WR DeAndre Hopkins
SS D.J. Swearinger
RT Brennan Williams

CONNECTED FRANCHISE MODE STRATEGY

CFM TEAM RATING: **79**
OFFENSIVE SCHEME: **Zone Run**
DEFENSIVE SCHEME: **Attacking 3-4**
STRENGTHS: **QB, HB, WR, TE, LT, C, LE, RE, MLB, CB, FS**
WEAKNESSES: **RG, RT, DT, ROLB**

SCHEDULE

1	Sep 9	10:20 PM ET	AT	CHARGERS
2	Sep 15	1:00 PM ET		TITANS
3	Sep 22	1:00 PM ET	AT	RAVENS
4	Sep 29	1:00 PM ET		SEAHAWKS
5	Oct 6	8:30 PM ET	AT	49ERS
6	Oct 13	1:00 PM ET		RAMS
7	Oct 20	1:00 PM ET	AT	CHIEFS
8	BYE			
9	Nov 3	8:30 PM ET		COLTS
10	Nov 10	4:25 PM ET	AT	CARDINALS
11	Nov 17	1:00 PM ET		RAIDERS
12	Nov 24	1:00 PM ET		JAGUARS
13	Dec 1	4:25 PM ET		PATRIOTS
14	Dec 5	8:25 PM ET	AT	JAGUARS
15	Dec 15	1:00 PM ET	AT	COLTS
16	Dec 22	1:00 PM ET		BRONCOS
17	Dec 29	1:00 PM ET	AT	TITANS

FRANCHISE OVERVIEW

TEXANS GAMEPLAY RATING

84

> SEE THE INSIDE BACK COVER FOR A QUICK REFERENCE TO THE GAME ABBREVIATIONS USED THROUGHOUT THIS GUIDE.

> IMPROVE WITH YOUR TEAM BY VISITING PRIMAGAMES.COM/MADDENNFL25 FOR MORE INFORMATION AND HOW-TO VIDEOS.

OFFENSIVE SCOUTING REPORT

- QB Matt Schaub has proven that he can put up big numbers throwing the ball around in Houston. What he hasn't proven is that he can win in the playoffs. He has four years remaining on his contract; you should give him one more year and then cut ties.
- HB Arian Foster started from the bottom and is now here to stay as one of the league's best HBs. We also like backup HB Ben Tate. His contract is up at the end of the season, and you should bring him back for a few more seasons.
- Outside of WR Andre Johnson, the Texans don't have much a receiving threat. Focus on this in the draft and find Johnson's future replacement.

DEFENSIVE SCOUTING REPORT

- LE J.J. Watt is the single most dominant defensive lineman in the game. His 77 SPD and 97 STR ratings are unheard of at his position. He is faster and stronger than every player he goes up against. He has two years remaining on his contract, and you should consider extending him to a max deal.
- MLB Brian Cushing and LOLB Brooks Reed are a duo that should remain together over the next few seasons. Cushing's contract expires at the end of the season, and you will want to bring him back for a max deal.
- The Texans added Super Bowl-winning FS Ed Reed to the roster to provide stability to a secondary in need of leadership.

OWNER & COACH PROFILES

BOB MCNAIR
LEGACY SCORE: 125
OFF. SCHEME: Zone Run
DEF. SCHEME: Attacking 3-4

GARY KUBIAK
LEVEL: 18
LEGACY SCORE: 0
OFF. SCHEME: Zone Run
DEF. SCHEME: Attacking 3-4

TEAM OVERVIEW

KEY PLAYERS

HB #23

ARIAN FOSTER

KEY RATINGS

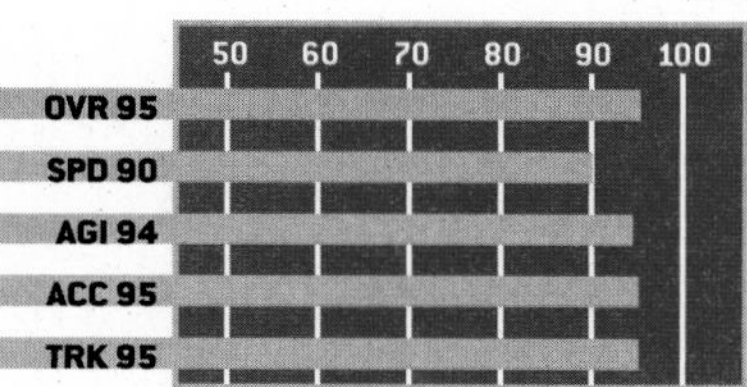

> Foster is an every-down HB for the Texans. He's especially good at catching passes out of the backfield.

> Foster is 6'1", so split outside as a WR he is a mismatch for most defenders.

LE #99

J.J. WATT

KEY RATINGS

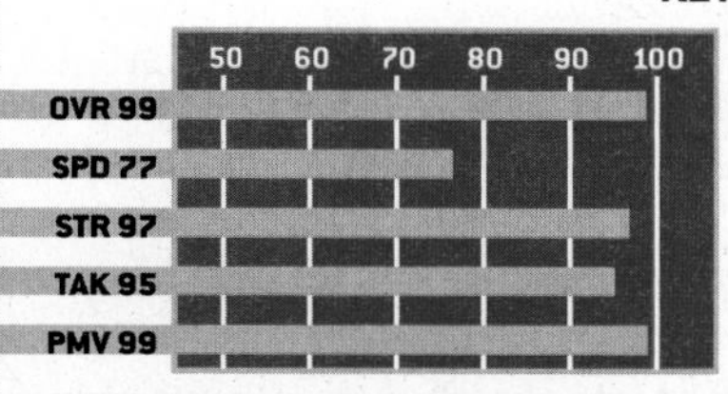

> Watt is literally the best rated player in *Madden NFL 25*.

> Watt is the perfect defender. He has not only the speed to play both LB and DE, but also the strength to dominate as a DT.

PRE-GAME SETUP

KEY RUNNING SUBSTITUTION

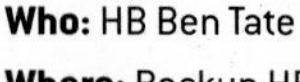

Who: HB Ben Tate

Where: Backup HB

Why: Foster should see the majority of carries, but Tate is one of the best backups in the league.

Key Stats: 90 SPD, 88 CAR

KEY PASSING SUBSTITUTION

Who: WR Keshawn Martin

Where: #2 WR

Why: Martin will have to get the job done for the Texans. His 94 SPD is why he plays opposite Andre Johnson.

Key Stats: 94 SPD.

KEY RUN DEFENSE SUBSTITUTION

Who: MLB Darryl Sharpton

Where: #2 MLB

Why: Sharpton is a wrap-up tackler who delivers the boom.

Key Stats: 92 POW

KEY PASS DEFENSE SUBSTITUTION

Who: CB Brice McCain

Where: #2 CB

Why: We like to use McCain to cover our opponent's fastest WR.

Key Stats: 95 SPD

OFFENSIVE DEPTH CHART

POS	FIRST NAME	LAST NAME	OVR
QB	Matt	Schaub	87
QB	T.J.	Yates	74
QB	Stephen	McGee	66
QB	Case	Keenum	65
HB	Arian	Foster	95
HB	Ben	Tate	81
HB	Deji	Karim	69
HB	Ray	Graham	68
HB	Cierre	Wood	67
HB	Dennis	Johnson	66
FB	Greg	Jones	89
FB	Tyler	Clutts	70
WR	Andre	Johnson	97
WR	DeAndre	Hopkins	74
WR	Lestar	Jean	68
WR	DeVier	Posey	67
WR	Keshawn	Martin	67
WR	Jeff	Maehl	62
WR	Alan	Bonner	62
TE	Owen	Daniels	87
TE	Garrett	Graham	78
TE	Ryan	Griffin	67
TE	Phillip	Supernaw	65
TE	Jonathan	Weeks	45
LT	Duane	Brown	96
LT	Ryan	Harris	70
LT	David	Quessenberry	62
LT	Nick	Mondek	57
LG	Wade	Smith	84
C	Chris	Myers	93
C	Cody	White	62
RG	Ben	Jones	74
RG	Brandon	Brooks	68
RT	Derek	Newton	73
RT	Brennan	Williams	71
RT	Andrew	Gardner	68

DEFENSIVE DEPTH CHART

POS	FIRST NAME	LAST NAME	OVR
LE	J.J.	Watt	99
LE	Tim	Jamison	76
LE	David	Hunter	65
LE	Ra'Shon	Harris	65
RE	Antonio	Smith	90
RE	Jared	Crick	69
DT	Earl	Mitchell	77
DT	Terrell	McClain	70
DT	Chris	Jones	66
LOLB	Brooks	Reed	79
LOLB	Bryan	Braman	68
LOLB	Sam	Montgomery	66
MLB	Brian	Cushing	90
MLB	Darryl	Sharpton	73
MLB	Tim	Dobbins	72
MLB	Mike	Mohamed	61
MLB	Cameron	Collins	58
ROLB	Whitney	Mercilus	77
ROLB	Trevardo	Williams	63
CB	Johnathan	Joseph	89
CB	Kareem	Jackson	85
CB	Brice	McCain	76
CB	Brandon	Harris	71
CB	Roc	Carmichael	65
FS	Ed	Reed	86
FS	D.J.	Swearinger	75
FS	Shiloh	Keo	67
SS	Danieal	Manning	84
SS	Eddie	Pleasant	68

SPECIAL TEAMS DEPTH CHART

POS	FIRST NAME	LAST NAME	OVR
K	Randy	Bullock	66
P	Shane	Lechler	89

Houston Texans

RECOMMENDED OFFENSIVE RUN FORMATION: I-FORM CLOSE (2 HB, 1 TE, 2 WR)

PRO TIPS

- > GIVE THE MAJORITY OF THE CARRIES TO HB ARIAN FOSTER.
- > MAKE SURE TO GIVE HB BEN TATE A FEW CARRIES A GAME.
- > FB GREG JONES IS A NICE OPTION IN SHORT-YARDAGE SITUATIONS.

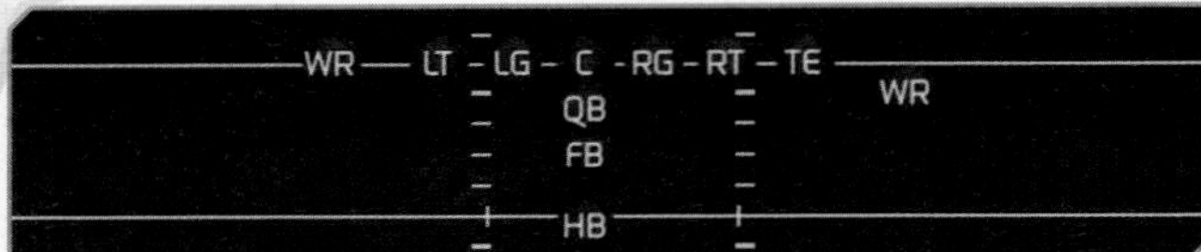

RUN LEFT

ARIAN FOSTER HAS THE SPEED TO RUN OUTSIDE.

RUN MIDDLE

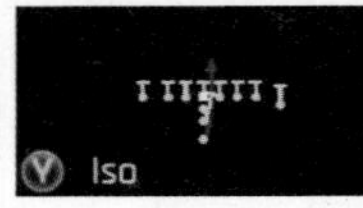

FOSTER ALSO HAS THE POWER TO RUN OVER DEFENDERS.

RUN RIGHT

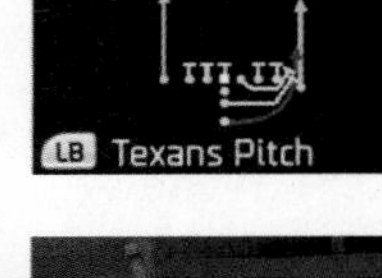

GET TO THE EDGE AND RUN PAST THE DEFENDERS.

HOUSTON TEXANS RUNNING PLAY CALL SHEET

LEGEND: Inside Run | Outside Run | Shotgun Run | QB Run

1ST DOWN RUNS	2ND AND SHORT	3RD AND SHORT	GOAL LINE RUNS	2ND AND LONG	3RD AND LONG
Singleback Ace Twins—Zone Weak	Singleback Tight Doubles—HB Dive	I-Form Pro—FB Dive	Goal Line Normal—QB Sneak	Gun Split Close—HB Power O	Gun Bunch Wk—HB Mid Draw
Strong Close—HB Dive Weak	Singleback Tight Doubles—HB Cutback	Singleback Ace Close—HB Sweep	Goal Line Normal—HB Dive	Singleback Bunch Base—HB Slash	Gun Snugs Flipped—HB Mid Draw
Strong Close—HB Off Tackle	Singleback Ace—HB Smash	Weak Twins—Toss Weak	Goal Line Normal—Power O	Gun Doubles—HB Mid Draw	Gun Split Texan—HB Draw

HOUSTON TEXANS PASSING PLAY CALL SHEET

LEGEND: Base Play | Man Beater | Zone Beater | Blitz Beater

1ST DOWN PLAY	2ND AND SHORT	3RD AND SHORT	GOAL LINE PASSING	2ND AND LONG	3RD AND LONG
Gun Split Texan—Mesh	Singleback Ace Twins—Slants	Gun Trips TE—HB Slip Screen	Goal Line—PA Waggle	Singleback Y-Trips Texan—Curls	Gun Bunch Wk—Texans Trail
Gun Bunch Wk—Z Spot Dig	Gun Doubles—Flanker Drive	Gun Split Close—HB Wheel	Goal Line—PA Spot	Gun Empty Y-Flex—Deep Dig	Gun Empty Y-Flex—Texans Short Posts
Gun Doubles—Texan Out N Up	I-Form Pro—PA Scissors	Gun Split Close—HB Slip Screen	Goal Line—PA Power O	Gun Trips TE—X Spot	Singleback Doubles—HB Slip Screen

In these play call sheets we picked the best plays for specific situations so that you will have a play for every down and distance.

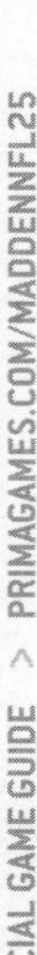

OFFENSE

RECOMMENDED OFFENSIVE PASS FORMATION: GUN TIGHT DOUBLES ON (1 HB, 1 TE, 3 WR)

PRO TIPS

- > WR KESHAWN MARTIN IS THE TEXANS' ONLY SPEED WR.
- > INVOLVE TE OWEN DANIELS IN THE PASSING GAME.
- > HB ARIAN FOSTER HAS THE SIZE TO BE SPLIT OUT WIDE AND CREATE MATCHUP PROBLEMS.

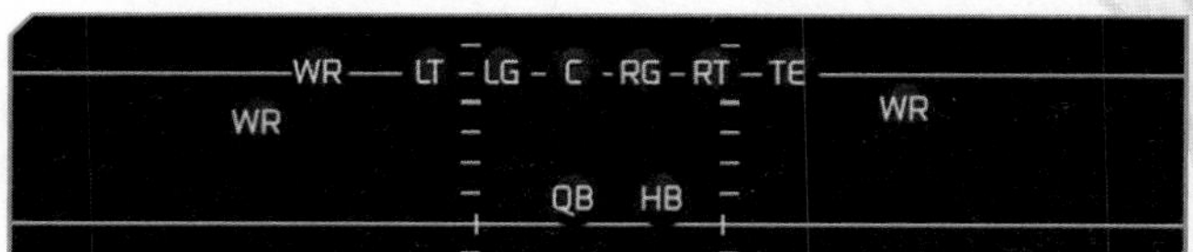

BASE PLAY

SETUP

> MOTION THE FAR RIGHT WR OUTSIDE

> The HB is your first read on this play. His route explodes to the flat and is our favorite route on this play.

> Next look to the crossing patterns underneath and then to the deep post and sideline wheel.

MAN BEATER

SETUP

> STREAK THE LEFT SLOT WR

> MOTION THE FAR RIGHT WR OUTSIDE

> The motioned WR will get inside position on his man-to-man defender. Throw a high inside pass lead.

> Next look to the TE and throw the ball as soon as he breaks to the sideline.

ZONE BEATER

SETUP

> STREAK BOTH OUTSIDE WIDE RECEIVERS

> WHEEL THE HB

> Against Cover 2 and Cover 3 look to the corner routes.

> Against Cover 4 zones look to the HB wheel.

BLITZ BEATER

SETUP

> STREAK BOTH OUTSIDE RECEIVERS

> BLOCK THE HB

> You will have eight pass blockers on this play.

> Virtually no blitz will get you in. Lob it deep to Andre Johnson for the easy score!

Houston Texans

RECOMMENDED DEFENSIVE RUN FORMATION: 3-4 OVER STACK

PRO TIPS

- MANY TIMES WE LIKE TO USE LE J.J. WATT AS OUR DT. HIS SIZE AND STRENGTH DEMANDS DOUBLE TEAMS.
- USE DT TERRELL MCCLAIN FOR RUNNING SITUATIONS.
- MLB DARRYL SHARPTON IS A BIG TIME HITTER. GET HIM IN THE GAME DURING RUNNING SITUATIONS.

RUN DEFENSE

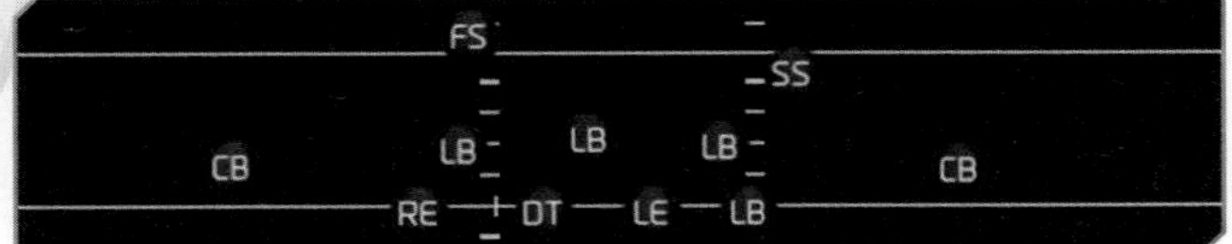

RUN DEFENSE LEFT

SETUP > SHIFT LINEBACKERS LEFT

RUN DEFENSE MIDDLE

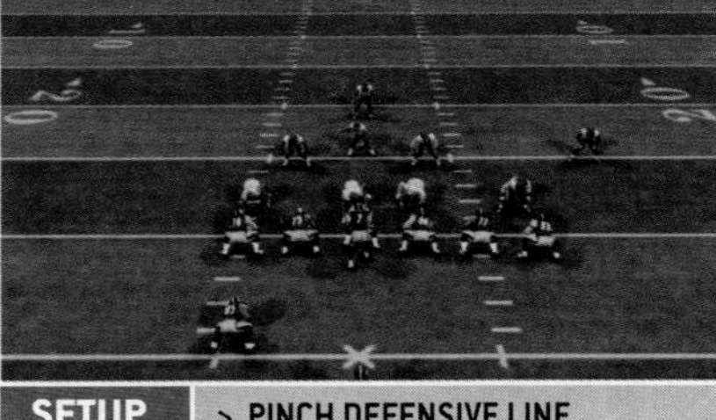

SETUP > PINCH DEFENSIVE LINE

RUN DEFENSE RIGHT

SETUP > SHIFT LINEBACKERS RIGHT

HOUSTON TEXANS DEFENSIVE RUN PLAY CALL SHEET

1ST DOWN RUN DEFENSE	2ND AND SHORT	3RD AND SHORT	GOAL LINE RUN DEFENSE	2ND AND LONG	3RD AND LONG
3-4 Odd—2 Man Under	3-4 Under—Cover 1 Lurk	3-4 Over Stack—OLB Fire Man	Goal Line 5-3-3—Jam Cover 1	Nickel 2-4-5 Even—Overload 1 Roll	Sub 1-4-6—2 Man LB Blitz
3-4 Odd—Cover 3	3-4 Under—Will Fire 3 Seam	3-4 Over Stack—Roll Eagle 2 Invert	Goal Line 5-3-3—Flat Buzz	Nickel 2-4-5 Even—Sugar Cover 3 Bluff	Sub 1-4-6—Okie Roll 2

HOUSTON TEXANS DEFENSIVE PASS PLAY CALL SHEET

1ST DOWN PLAY	2ND AND SHORT	3RD AND SHORT	GOAL LINE PASSING	2ND AND LONG	3RD AND LONG
3-4 Over Stack—Cover 1 Lurk	3-4 Even—MLB Cross Fire	3-4 Even—Strong Blitz	Goal Line 6-3-2—GL Man	Sub 2-3-6 Even—Overload 1 Roll	Nickel 2-4-5—Sugar Blitz
3-4 Over Stack—Cover 3	3-4 Even—Cover 2	3-4 Even—Trio Sky Zone	Goal Line 6-3-2—GL Zone	Sub 2-3-6 Even—FS Middle 3	Nickel 2-4-5—Sugar Cover 3 Bluff

LEGEND: Man Coverage | Zone Coverage | Man Blitz | Zone Blitz

In these play call sheets we picked the best plays for specific situations so that you will have a play for every down and distance.

DEFENSE

RECOMMENDED DEFENSIVE PASS FORMATION: DIME NORMAL

PRO TIPS

> PLACE CB JOHNATHAN JOSEPH ON YOUR OPPONENT'S BEST WR.

> USE CB BRICE MCCAIN ON YOUR OPPONENT'S FASTEST WR.

> KAREEM JACKSON SHOULD BE YOUR #2 CB.

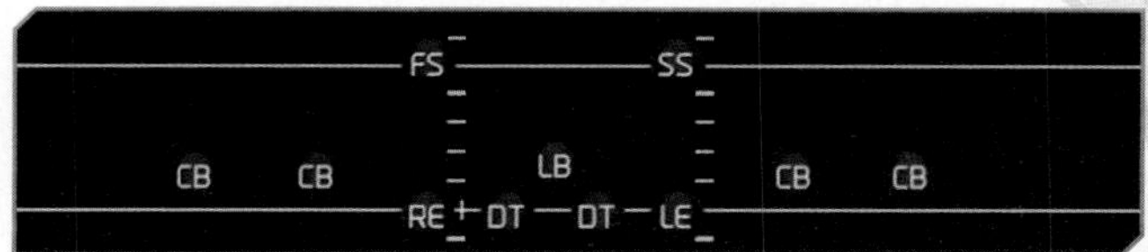

MAN COVERAGE

SETUP

- > SPREAD THE DEFENSIVE LINE AND CRASH DOWN
- > BLITZ THE FS AND SLIDE OUTSIDE THE RE

> Pressure will come off the left edge.

> This setup is great for the Texans defense, as pressure will force a roll-out towards DE J.J. Watt.

ZONE COVERAGE

SETUP

- > PINCH THE DEFENSIVE LINE AND CRASH OUT
- > USER-CONTROL THE FS AND WATCH THE SEAM

> The double buzz by the safeties is unique, and most opponents won't expect both safeties playing hook zones.

> In our example FS Ed Reed is able to go up for the ballhawk interception.

MAN BLITZ

SETUP

- > PRESS COVERAGE
- > USER-CONTROL THE MLB

> Drop into coverage with the MLB, but leave him on his blitz assignment.

> Watch out for routes over the middle and HB screens.

ZONE BLITZ

SETUP

- > SPREAD THE DEFENSIVE LINE AND CRASH DOWN
- > USER-CONTROL THE MLB

> Sit directly over the middle of the field, and if there are no routes over the middle of the field drop over the deep middle.

> Opposing offenses will likely make you defend a TE streak and have an underneath crossing pattern to beat this defense.

Tennessee Titans

2012 TEAM RANKINGS

3rd AFC South (6-10-0)

PASSING OFFENSE: **22nd**
RUSHING OFFENSE: **21st**
PASSING DEFENSE: **26th**
RUSHING DEFENSE: **24th**

2012 TEAM LEADERS

PASSING: **Jake Locker: 2,176**
RUSHING: **Chris Johnson: 1,243**
RECEIVING: **Nate Washington: 746**
TACKLES: **Akeem Ayers: 104**
SACKS: **Derrick Morgan: 6.5**
INTS: **Jason McCourty: 4**

KEY ADDITIONS

QB Ryan Fitzpatrick
HB Shonn Greene
TE Delanie Walker

KEY ROOKIES

RG Chance Warmack
WR Justin Hunter
CB Blidi Wreh-Wilson

CONNECTED FRANCHISE MODE STRATEGY

CFM TEAM RATING: **70**
OFFENSIVE SCHEME: **Balanced Offense**
DEFENSIVE SCHEME: **Base 4-3**
STRENGTHS: **HB, LT, LG, RT, DT, CB**
WEAKNESSES: **QB, LOLB, MLB, ROLB, FS**

SCHEDULE

1	Sep 8	1:00 PM ET	AT	STEELERS
2	Sep 15	1:00 PM ET	AT	TEXANS
3	Sep 22	1:00 PM ET		CHARGERS
4	Sep 29	4:05 PM ET		JETS
5	Oct 6	1:00 PM ET		CHIEFS
6	Oct 13	4:05 PM ET	AT	SEAHAWKS
7	Oct 20	4:05 PM ET		49ERS
8	BYE			
9	Nov 3	1:00 PM ET	AT	RAMS
10	Nov 10	1:00 PM ET		JAGUARS
11	Nov 14	8:25 PM ET		COLTS
12	Nov 24	4:05 PM ET	AT	RAIDERS
13	Dec 1	1:00 PM ET	AT	COLTS
14	Dec 8	4:05 PM ET	AT	BRONCOS
15	Dec 15	1:00 PM ET		CARDINALS
16	Dec 22	1:00 PM ET	AT	JAGUARS
17	Dec 29	1:00 PM ET		TEXANS

FRANCHISE OVERVIEW

TITANS GAMEPLAY RATING

> See the inside back cover for a quick reference to the game abbreviations used throughout this guide.

> Improve with your team by visiting PrimaGames.com/MaddenNFL25 for more information and how-to videos.

OFFENSIVE SCOUTING REPORT

> QB Jake Locker still has yet to prove he is a starting NFL quarterback. We think that he has what it takes to be the future QB for Tennessee. Upgrade his SAC rating and you will see instant results.

> HB Chris Johnson is the fastest player in the game. Every time he touches the ball he is a threat to score a touchdown. Make sure he gets 30-plus touches in this offense. He is the franchise.

> WR Kenny Britt has the potential to be a dominating receiver in this league. He is a big-bodied player who is a force in the red zone and in jump ball situations. His contract expires at the end of this season, but we think it's worth bringing him back for two more seasons.

DEFENSIVE SCOUTING REPORT

> LE Derrick Morgan surpassed people's expectations last season and looks to rebound again in 2013. If Morgan has another big year, extend his contract and get him at a cheap price.

> Rookie ROLB Zaviar Gooden has the speed of a CB. With 90 SPD he can cover any player on the field. Make sure to upgrade his TAK and POW ratings in the off-season.

> CB Jason McCourty had a breakout year last season and is one of the league's top cover corners. Put him on an island and roll coverage to your other CBs..

OWNER & COACH PROFILES

BUD ADAMS

LEGACY SCORE: 1475
DEF. SCHEME: Base 4-3
OFF. SCHEME: Balanced Offense

MIKE MUNCHAK

LEVEL: 1
OFF. SCHEME: Balanced Offense
LEGACY SCORE: 0
DEF. SCHEME: Base 4-3

TEAM OVERVIEW

KEY PLAYERS

HB #28

CHRIS JOHNSON

KEY RATINGS

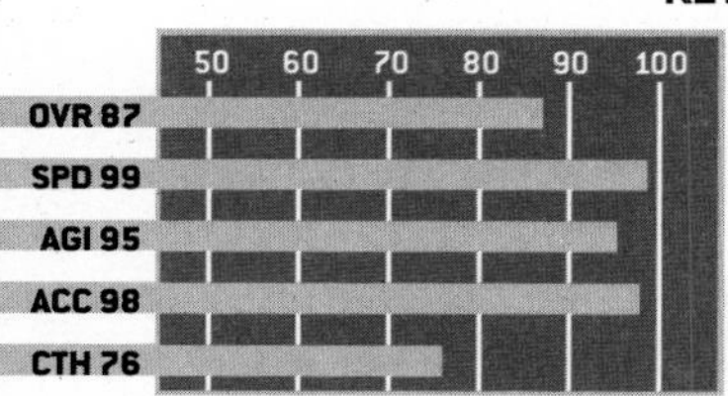

- Johnson is the fastest player in *Madden NFL 25* with 99 SPD.
- If you play with the Titans get Johnson at least 20 touches a game.

CB #30

JASON MCCOURTY

KEY RATINGS

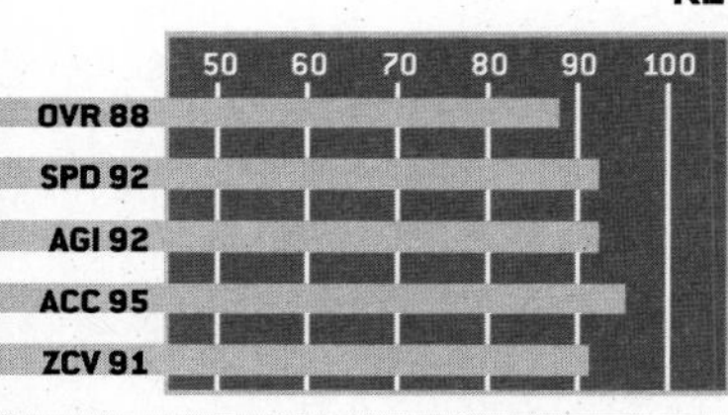

- McCourty has speed that will make you want to play man-to-man coverage, but his coverage skills are best when playing zone.
- McCourty can also press, as he has an 81 PRS rating.

PRE-GAME SETUP

KEY RUNNING SUBSTITUTION

Who: HB Shonn Greene

Where: Backup HB

Why: Greene is fresh off his second consecutive 1,000-rushing-yards season. Get him the ball in short-yardage situations.

Key Stats: 89 TRK

KEY PASSING SUBSTITUTION

Who: WR Justin Hunter

Where: #2 WR

Why: Hunter is a 69 OVR, but he is a dominant WR in *Madden NFL 25*.

Key Stats: 6'4", 92 SPD, 95 JMP

KEY RUN DEFENSE SUBSTITUTION

Who: DT Sammie Hill

Where: #2 DT

Why: Hill provides added strength to the defensive line during run situations.

Key Stats: 90 STR

KEY PASS DEFENSE SUBSTITUTION

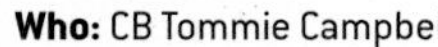

Who: CB Tommie Campbell

Where: #2 CB

Why: Campbell is the best CB that no one uses in *Madden NFL 25*. Get him on the field.

Key Stats: 6'3", 95 SPD, 77 POW

OFFENSIVE DEPTH CHART

POS	FIRST NAME	LAST NAME	OVR
QB	Jake	Locker	77
QB	Ryan	Fitzpatrick	76
QB	Rusty	Smith	65
QB	Nathan	Enderle	65
HB	Chris	Johnson	87
HB	Shonn	Greene	79
HB	Darius	Reynaud	74
HB	Jalen	Parmele	69
FB	Craig	Stevens	79
FB	Quinn	Johnson	68
WR	Kenny	Britt	83
WR	Nate	Washington	78
WR	Kendall	Wright	78
WR	Kevin	Walter	74
WR	Damian	Williams	72
WR	Justin	Hunter	71
WR	Marc	Mariani	69
WR	Roberto	Wallace	66
WR	Diondre	Borel	65
WR	Michael	Preston	61
TE	Delanie	Walker	83
TE	Taylor	Thompson	71
TE	Brandon	Barden	62
TE	Beau	Brinkley	53
LT	Michael	Roos	91
LT	Michael	Otto	70
LT	Barry	Richardson	69
LG	Andy	Levitre	96
LG	Chris	Spencer	75
LG	Kasey	Studdard	74
C	Fernando	Velasco	82
C	Brian	Schwenke	71
RG	Chance	Warmack	84
RG	Robert	Turner	73
RT	David	Stewart	90
RT	Byron	Stingily	69
RT	Daniel	Baldridge	68

DEFENSIVE DEPTH CHART

POS	FIRST NAME	LAST NAME	OVR
LE	Derrick	Morgan	88
LE	Thaddeus	Gibson	69
LE	Lavar	Edwards	68
RE	Kamerion	Wimbley	82
RE	Keyunta	Dawson	67
RE	Scott	Solomon	66
DT	Jurrell	Casey	88
DT	Mike	Martin	82
DT	Sammie	Hill	79
DT	Karl	Klug	77
DT	Ropati	Pitoitua	76
DT	Antonio	Johnson	73
DT	Zach	Clayton	66
DT	DaJohn	Harris	64
LOLB	Akeem	Ayers	79
LOLB	Tim	Shaw	69
LOLB	Patrick	Bailey	67
MLB	Colin	McCarthy	74
MLB	Moise	Fokou	73
MLB	Greg	Jones	66
ROLB	Zach	Brown	79
ROLB	Zaviar	Gooden	65
CB	Jason	McCourty	88
CB	Alterraun	Verner	83
CB	Blidi	Wreh-Wilson	73
CB	Coty	Sensabaugh	71
CB	Tommie	Campbell	70
CB	Khalid	Wooten	68
FS	Michael	Griffin	78
FS	Robert	Johnson	69
FS	Tracy	Wilson	67
SS	George	Wilson	85
SS	Bernard	Pollard	85
SS	Al	Afalava	73
SS	Markelle	Martin	67

SPECIAL TEAMS DEPTH CHART

POS	FIRST NAME	LAST NAME	OVR
Rob	Bironas	88	81
Brett	Kern	82	63

Tennessee Titans

RECOMMENDED OFFENSIVE RUN FORMATION: I-FORM TIGHT (2 HB, 2 TE, 1 WR)

PRO TIPS

- HB CHRIS JOHNSON SHOULD GET THE MAJORITY OF TOUCHES FOR THE TITANS.
- USE HB SHONN GREENE FOR SHORT-YARDAGE SITUATIONS.
- TE DELANIE WALKER IS A SOLID RUN-BLOCKING TE.

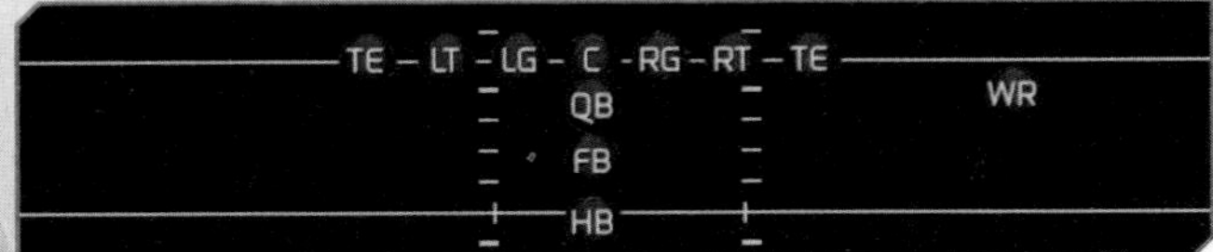

RUN LEFT

CHRIS JOHNSON GETS TO THE EDGE FASTER THAN ANY OTHER HB IN THE GAME.

RUN MIDDLE

BE PATIENT WITH JOHNSON WHEN RUNNING UP THE MIDDLE.

RUN RIGHT

AT THE SNAP OF THE BALL USE ACCELERATION BURST. YOU WANT TO GET OUTSIDE QUICKLY WITH JOHNSON.

TENNESSEE TITANS RUNNING PLAY CALL SHEET

LEGEND: Inside Run | Outside Run | Shotgun Run | QB Run

1ST DOWN RUNS	2ND AND SHORT	3RD AND SHORT	GOAL LINE RUNS	2ND AND LONG	3RD AND LONG
I-Form Pro—HB Toss	I-Form Tight—FB Dive	I-Form Tight Pair—Iso	Goal Line Normal—QB Sneak	Gun Dbls Y-Flex Tight—HB Draw	Gun Doubles Wk—HB Counter
I-Form Pro—Iso	I-Form Tight—Strong Stretch	Strong Pro Twins—HB Sweep	Goal Line Normal—HB Dive	Singleback Y-Trips—HB Stretch	Gun Y-Trips Wk—HB Mid Draw
I-Form Tight—Power O	Singleback Doubles—Inside Zone	Singleback Jumbo Pair—HB Sweep	Goal Line Normal—Power O	Gun Trey Open—HB Draw	Gun Split Slot—FB Inside

TENNESSEE TITANS PASSING PLAY CALL SHEET

LEGEND: Base Play | Man Beater | Zone Beater | Blitz Beater

1ST DOWN PLAY	2ND AND SHORT	3RD AND SHORT	GOAL LINE PASSING	2ND AND LONG	3RD AND LONG
Gun Split Slot—Slants	Singleback Bunch—Slants Slot Flat	Gun Dbls Y-Flex Tight—HB Slip Screen	Goal Line—PA Waggle	Gun Normal Y-Slot—Corner Strike	Gun Doubles Wk—Slot Post
Gun Empty Spread—Quick Slant	I-Form Tight—PA HB Wheel	Singleback Bunch—Flanker Drive	Goal Line—PA Spot	Gun Trey Open—Deep Post	Gun Doubles Wk—Corner Strike
Gun Ace Twins—Posts	Gun Y-Trips Wk—Four Verticals	Full House Normal Wide—PA Power O	Goal Line—PA Power O	Gun Dbls Y-Flex Tight—Y-Sail	Gun Split Slot—689 Hook

In these play call sheets we picked the best plays for specific situations so that you will have a play for every down and distance.

OFFENSE

RECOMMENDED OFFENSIVE PASS FORMATION: GUN ACE TWINS (1 HB, 2 TE, 2 WR)

PRO TIPS

- WR KENDALL WRIGHT WILL BE EXTREMELY EFFECTIVE ON DRAG AND SLANT ROUTES.
- MAKE SURE TO TAKE YOUR CHANCES DOWN THE SIDELINE TO ROOKIE WR JUSTIN HUNTER.
- TE TAYLOR THOMPSON IS 6'6" AND HAS 84 SPD. HE IS A MATCHUP PROBLEM FOR MOST DEFENSES.

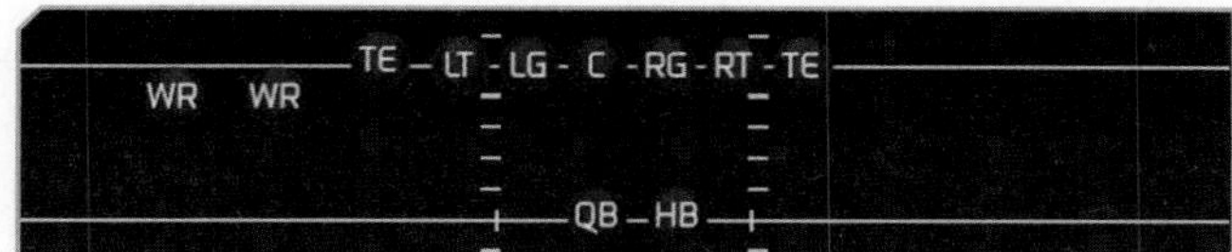

BASE PLAY

SETUP

- ZIG THE LEFT TE
- ZIG THE RIGHT TE

- Against man-to-man both TEs are great options as they break towards the sideline.
- The HB out of the backfield is our favorite route on this play and works especially well because of HB Chris Johnson.

MAN BEATER

SETUP

- SMART ROUTE THE RIGHT TE
- WHEEL THE HB

- The HB wheel will be a nice option if you face a man-to-man blitz.
- The TE running the double move is one of the best man-beating routes in the game.

ZONE BEATER

SETUP

- STREAK BOTH TIGHT ENDS
- WHEEL THE HB

- Against Cover 2 and Cover 3 zones look to the sideline corner route.
- Against Cover 4 zones look to the sideline hitch and the HB wheel.

BLITZ BEATER

SETUP

- DRAG BOTH TIGHT ENDS
- STREAK THE SLOT WR

- If you face a zone blitz, the left TE running the drag will act as an extra blocker for the HB screen.
- Johnson is lethal on screens. He has the speed to take it the distance every play.

Tennessee Titans

RECOMMENDED DEFENSIVE RUN FORMATION: 46 BEAR

PRO TIPS

- > RE SCOTT SOLOMON CAN BE USED DURING RUN SITUATIONS TO HELP STOP THE RUN.
- > MLB MOISE FOKOU IS THE TEAM'S BEST TACKLING MLB AND HAS 87 POW.
- > SS BERNARD POLLARD IS ONE OF THE HARDEST-HITTING SAFETIES IN THE GAME.

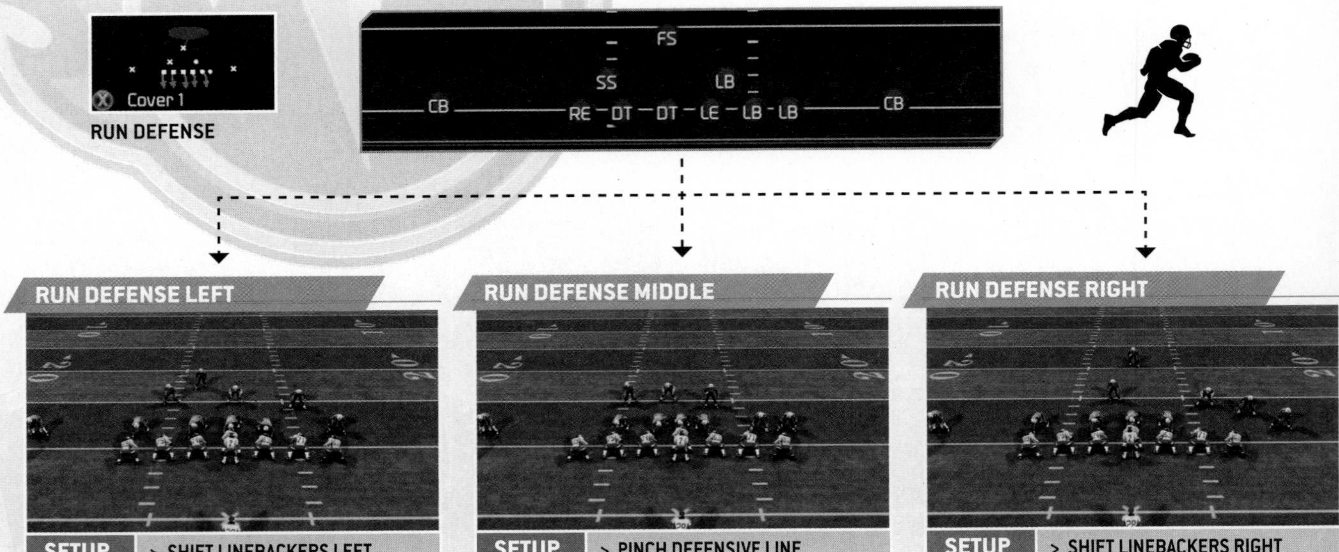

TENNESSEE TITANS DEFENSIVE RUN PLAY CALL SHEET

1ST DOWN RUN DEFENSE	2ND AND SHORT	3RD AND SHORT	GOAL LINE RUN DEFENSE	2ND AND LONG	3RD AND LONG
4-3 Over—2 Man Under	4-3 Over Plus—Cover 1	4-3 Under—Free Fire	Goal Line 5-3-3—Jam Cover 1	Dime Normal—2 Man Under	Dollar 3-2-6—2 Man Under
4-3 Over—Cover 2 Buc	4-3 Over Plus—Cover 2	4-3 Under—Sam Blitz 2	Goal Line 5-3-3—Flat Buzz	Dime Normal—Cover 2 Sink	Dollar 3-2-6—Cover 2 Spy

TENNESSEE TITANS DEFENSIVE PASS PLAY CALL SHEET

1ST DOWN PLAY	2ND AND SHORT	3RD AND SHORT	GOAL LINE PASSING	2ND AND LONG	3RD AND LONG
46 Bear—Cover 1	4-3 Over—Man QB Spy	4-3 Stack—Free Fire	Goal Line 6-3-2—GL Man	Dollar 3-2-6—Fire Dog 1	Nickel Wide 9—Dbl Safety Blitz
46 Bear—Cover 2	4-3 Over—Cover 4	4-3 Stack—2 Deep Gap Shoot	Goal Line 6-3-2—GL Zone	Dollar 3-2-6—DB Fire 2	Nickel Wide 9—Sugar 3 DB Fire

LEGEND: Man Coverage | Zone Coverage | Man Blitz | Zone Blitz

In these play call sheets we picked the best plays for specific situations so that you will have a play for every down and distance.

DEFENSE

RECOMMENDED DEFENSIVE PASS FORMATION: 46 BEAR

PRO TIPS

- PLACE CB JASON MCCOURTY ON YOUR OPPONENT'S BEST WR.
- USE CB COTY SENSABAUGH ON YOUR OPPONENT'S FASTEST WR.
- CB TOMMIE CAMPBELL SHOULD BE YOUR #2 CB.

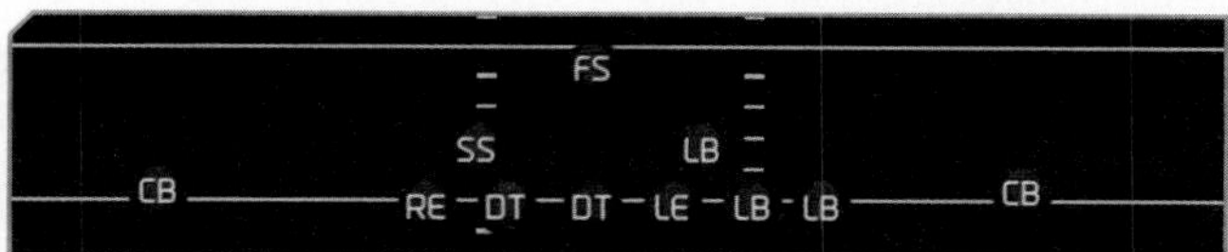

MAN COVERAGE

SETUP

- CRASH THE DEFENSIVE LINE DOWN
- BLITZ THE SS AND MOVE HIM OFF THE EDGE OF THE RE

- Pressure is going to come off the left edge.
- Expect a roll-out to the right, and if the QB starts escaping the pocket look to QB contain the LE.

ZONE COVERAGE

SETUP

- FLAT ZONE THE LE
- FLAT ZONE THE RE

- User-control the SS and drop over the deep middle.
- You want to user-control the SS near the line of scrimmage and then drop over the middle and towards the TE. This will be a delayed read for opposing QBs.

MAN BLITZ

SETUP

- PRESS COVERAGE
- BLITZ THE DT OVER THE CENTER.

- Pressure will come through the A gap from the blitzing MLB.
- The Titans CBs aren't the best press corners in the league, so watch for "beat press" animations at the snap.

ZONE BLITZ

SETUP

- PRESS COVERAGE
- BLITZ THE RE

- You can also QB contain the RE, but the pressure won't be as quick.
- The QB contain will help delay any type of throw to the short flat because the QB contain defender will react to the throw.

Minnesota Vikings

2012 TEAM RANKINGS

2nd NFC North (10-6-0)

PASSING OFFENSE: **31st**
RUSHING OFFENSE: **2nd**
PASSING DEFENSE: **24th**
RUSHING DEFENSE: **11th**

2012 TEAM LEADERS

PASSING: **Christian Ponder: 2,935**
RUSHING: **Adrian Peterson: 2,097**
RECEIVING: **Percy Harvin: 677**
TACKLES: **Chad Greenway: 148**
SACKS: **Jared Allen: 12**
INTS: **Harrison Smith: 3**

KEY ADDITIONS

QB Matt Cassel
WR Greg Jennings
CB Jacob Lacey

KEY ROOKIES

DT Sharrif Floyd
CB Xavier Rhodes
WR Cordarrelle Patterson

CONNECTED FRANCHISE MODE STRATEGY

CFM TEAM RATING: **73**
OFFENSIVE SCHEME: **West Coast**
DEFENSIVE SCHEME: **Tampa 2**
STRENGTHS: **HB, WR, TE, C, RE, DT**
WEAKNESSES: **QB, RG, ROLB, CB, SS**

SCHEDULE

Week	Date	Time		Opponent
1	Sep 8	1:00 PM ET	AT	LIONS
2	Sep 15	1:00 PM ET	AT	BEARS
3	Sep 22	1:00 PM ET		BROWNS
4	Sep 29	1:00 PM ET		STEELERS
5	BYE			
6	Oct 13	1:00 PM ET		PANTHERS
7	Oct 21	8:40 PM ET	AT	GIANTS
8	Oct 27	8:30 PM ET		PACKERS
9	Nov 3	1:00 PM ET	AT	COWBOYS
10	Nov 7	8:25 PM ET		REDSKINS
11	Nov 17	4:25 PM ET	AT	SEAHAWKS
12	Nov 24	1:00 PM ET	AT	PACKERS
13	Dec 1	1:00 PM ET		BEARS
14	Dec 8	1:00 PM ET	AT	RAVENS
15	Dec 15	1:00 PM ET		EAGLES
16	Dec 22	1:00 PM ET	AT	BENGALS
17	Dec 29	1:00 PM ET		LIONS

FRANCHISE OVERVIEW

VIKINGS GAMEPLAY RATING

81

> SEE THE INSIDE BACK COVER FOR A QUICK REFERENCE TO THE GAME ABBREVIATIONS USED THROUGHOUT THIS GUIDE.

> IMPROVE WITH YOUR TEAM BY VISITING PRIMAGAMES.COM/MADDENNFL25 FOR MORE INFORMATION AND HOW-TO VIDEOS.

OFFENSIVE SCOUTING REPORT

- QB Christian Ponder showed flashes of brilliance last season, especially in the red zone. If you can upgrade his DAC rating he will be a solid start for the Vikings.
- HB Adrian Peterson is the best player in this game.
- The Vikings have three TEs with 80-plus OVR ratings. Use a lot of jumbo packages and pound the rock with Peterson. Then use play action and target your talented TEs.

DEFENSIVE SCOUTING REPORT

- RE Jared Allen is the premiere pass rusher for the Vikings. Look to match him up on the blind side of QBs and try to generate as many one-on-one situations as possible for him.
- MLB Erin Henderson is the team's best tackler, but that doesn't mean you will re-sign him in two years when his contract ends. The Vikings' entire secondary needs to be rebuilt from top to bottom, starting with the CBs, FSs, and SSs.

OWNER & COACH PROFILES

ZYGI WILF
LEGACY SCORE: 175 | OFF. SCHEME: West Coast
DEF. SCHEME: Tampa 2

LESLIE FRAZIER
LEVEL: 9 | LEGACY SCORE: 0
OFF. SCHEME: West Coast | DEF. SCHEME: Tampa 2

TEAM OVERVIEW

KEY PLAYERS

HB #28

ADRIAN PETERSON

KEY RATINGS

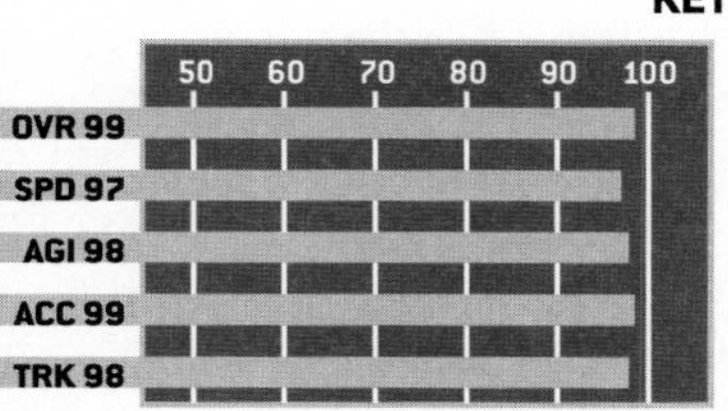

- Peterson is the best overall HB in *Madden NFL 25*. He is also one of the fastest.
- If you play with the Vikings make sure to get Peterson 20-plus touches a game.

RE #69

JARED ALLEN

KEY RATINGS

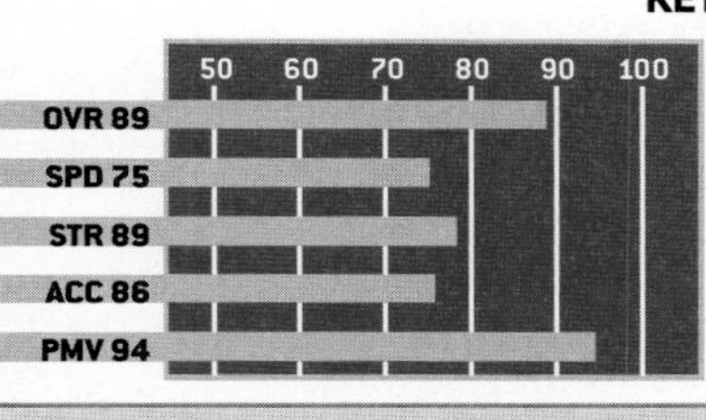

- Allen has been causing havoc in the opposing team's backfield for the past nine seasons.
- Allen is best when he is isolated off the edge in a pure pass-rush situation.

PRE-GAME SETUP

KEY RUNNING SUBSTITUTION

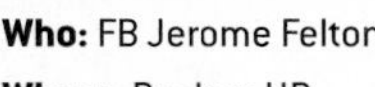

Who: FB Jerome Felton

Where: Backup HB

Why: Only use Felton on crucial third down passing situations. He has the team's best backfield hands.

Key Stats: 73 CTH

KEY PASSING SUBSTITUTION

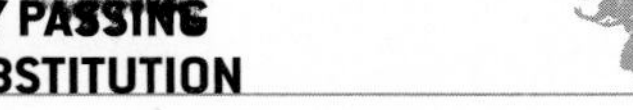

Who: WR Cordarrelle Patterson

Where: #2 WR

Why: Patterson is a star in the making for the Vikings.

Key Stats: 6'1", 93 SPD, 83 CIT

KEY RUN DEFENSE SUBSTITUTION

Who: MLB Michael Mauti

Where: #2 MLB

Why: Rookie MLB Mauti will provide extra tackling to take down ball carriers.

Key Stats: 85 TAK

KEY PASS DEFENSE SUBSTITUTION

Who: CB Josh Robinson

Where: #2 CB

Why: Robinson has speed for days. Get him on the field to lock down opposing team's fastest WRs.

Key Stats: 97 SPD

OFFENSIVE DEPTH CHART

POS	FIRST NAME	LAST NAME	OVR
QB	Christian	Ponder	78
QB	Matt	Cassel	76
QB	McLeod	Bethel-Thompson	64
HB	Adrian	Peterson	99
HB	Toby	Gerhart	74
HB	Joe	Banyard	70
FB	Jerome	Felton	88
FB	Matt	Asiata	61
WR	Greg	Jennings	88
WR	Jerome	Simpson	74
WR	Cordarrelle	Patterson	73
WR	Jarius	Wright	68
WR	Stephen	Burton	66
WR	Greg	Childs	65
WR	Joe	Webb	64
TE	Kyle	Rudolph	86
TE	John	Carlson	81
TE	Rhett	Ellison	80
TE	Cullen	Loeffler	67
LT	Matt	Kalil	87
LT	DeMarcus	Love	63
LG	Charlie	Johnson	79
LG	Troy	Kropog	74
LG	Jeff	Baca	71
C	John	Sullivan	95
C	Joe	Berger	74
RG	Brandon	Fusco	76
RG	Seth	Olsen	66
RG	Travis	Bond	66
RT	Phil	Loadholt	86
RT	Brandon	Keith	74

DEFENSIVE DEPTH CHART

POS	FIRST NAME	LAST NAME	OVR
LE	Brian	Robison	87
LE	Lawrence	Jackson	75
LE	D'Aundre	Reed	67
RE	Jared	Allen	89
RE	Everson	Griffen	78
RE	George	Johnson	66
DT	Kevin	Williams	90
DT	Sharrif	Floyd	78
DT	Fred	Evans	76
DT	Letroy	Guion	75
DT	Christian	Ballard	73
DT	Everett	Dawkins	66
LOLB	Chad	Greenway	87
LOLB	Marvin	Mitchell	69
LOLB	Audie	Cole	67
MLB	Desmond	Bishop	83
MLB	Erin	Henderson	80
MLB	Michael	Mauti	66
MLB	Tyrone	McKenzie	65
ROLB	Gerald	Hodges	70
ROLB	Larry	Dean	62
CB	Chris	Cook	79
CB	Xavier	Rhodes	74
CB	Jacob	Lacey	73
CB	Josh	Robinson	73
CB	A.J.	Jefferson	71
CB	Brandon	Burton	68
CB	Marcus	Sherels	67
CB	Greg	McCoy	59
FS	Harrison	Smith	84
FS	Jamarca	Sanford	77
FS	Andrew	Sendejo	65
SS	Mistral	Raymond	76
SS	Robert	Blanton	71

SPECIAL TEAMS DEPTH CHART

POS	FIRST NAME	LAST NAME	OVR
K	Blair	Walsh	92
P	Jeff	Locke	68

Minnesota Vikings

RECOMMENDED OFFENSIVE RUN FORMATION: I-FORM TWINS FLEX (2 HB, 1 TE, 2 WR)

PRO TIPS

> HB ADRIAN PETERSON SHOULD NEVER COME OFF THE FIELD.

> FB JEROME FELTON HAS 93 IBL AND IS ONE OF THE BEST LEAD-BLOCKING FULLBACKS IN THE GAME.

> TE KYLE RUDOLPH IS BIG AND STRONG AND WILL HELP IN THE RUN-BLOCKING DEPARTMENT.

WR — LT - LG - C - RG - RT - TE
WR
QB
FB
HB

RUN LEFT

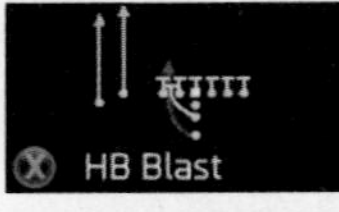

ADRIAN PETERSON TURNS ANY RUN INTO A TOUCHDOWN WAITING TO HAPPEN.

RUN MIDDLE

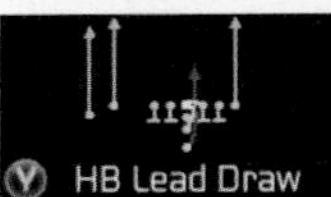

PETERSON WILL RUN OVER DEFENDERS UP THE MIDDLE.

RUN RIGHT

PETERSON IS GOOD IN SPACE AND IN TRAFFIC.

MINNESOTA VIKINGS RUNNING PLAY CALL SHEET

LEGEND: Inside Run | Outside Run | Shotgun Run | QB Run

1ST DOWN RUNS	2ND AND SHORT	3RD AND SHORT	GOAL LINE RUNS	2ND AND LONG	3RD AND LONG
Singleback Ace—Outside Zone	I-Form Pro—Inside Zone	Full House Normal Wide—HB Slam	I-Form Pro—Iso	Gun Doubles On—HB Mid Draw	Gun Empty Bunch—Mtn Read Option
Singleback Ace—HB Zone Wk	Strong Pro—HB Blast	Strong Close—Quick Toss	I-Form Twins Flex—HB Power O	Singleback Ace—Pump HB Draw	Gun Empty Trey—Jet Sweep
Singleback Ace Twins—Vikes Toss	Strong Close—HB Dive	I-Form Tight Pair—Power O	Singleback Ace—HB Dive	Gun Double Flex—HB Mid Draw	Gun Double Flex—HB Quick Base

MINNESOTA VIKINGS PASSING PLAY CALL SHEET

LEGEND: Base Play | Man Beater | Zone Beater | Blitz Beater

1ST DOWN PLAY	2ND AND SHORT	3RD AND SHORT	GOAL LINE PASSING	2ND AND LONG	3RD AND LONG
Gun Y-Trips Wk—Y Trail	Strong Pro—F Angle	Gun Split Viking—HB Slip Screen	Goal Line—PA Spot	Singleback Bunch—Seattle	Gun Empty Bunch—Vikes Trail
Gun Split Viking—Vikes Drive	Strong Close—Mesh	Gun Trips TE—Slot Swing	Full House Normal Wide—WR DBL Shake	Singleback Bunch—Flanker Drive	Gun Empty Trey—Vikes Y-Shake
Singleback Bunch—Close Mesh Post	Gun Split Viking—Slot Post	Gun Double Flex—HB Slip Screen	Full House Normal Wide—Slants	Singleback Bunch—Vikes HB Angle	Gun Snugs Flip—Bench

In these play call sheets we picked the best plays for specific situations so that you will have a play for every down and distance.

OFFENSE

RECOMMENDED OFFENSIVE PASS FORMATION: GUN EMPTY BUNCH (1 HB, 1 TE, 3 WR)

PRO TIPS

- WR GREG JENNINGS WILL BE VITAL TO THE SUCCESS OF THE VIKINGS' PASSING GAME.
- TAKE CHANCES DEEP TO ROOKIE WR CORDARRELLE PATTERSON.
- WR JEROME SIMPSON IS 6'2" AND HAS A 98 JMP RATING.

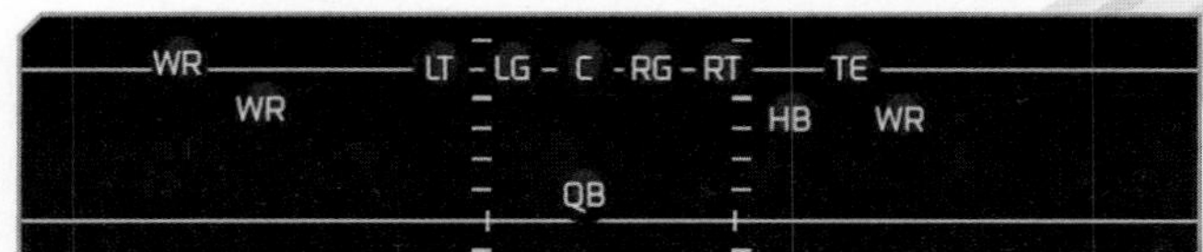

BASE PLAY

Divide Wheel

SETUP

- STREAK THE FAR RIGHT WR
- DRAG THE TE

- Against man-to-man coverage look to the wheel on the left and crossing patterns over the middle of the field.
- Against zone coverage look to the HB running the vertical on the right.

MAN BEATER

Vikes Trail

SETUP

- STREAK THE FAR RIGHT WR
- DRAG THE FAR LEFT WR

- The HB's angle route destroys man-to-man coverage over the middle.
- HB Adrian Peterson makes this route even better.

ZONE BEATER

Z Spot

SETUP

- STREAK THE FAR RIGHT WR
- PUT THE FAR LEFT WR ON A SMOKE SCREEN

- Against Cover 2 and Cover 3 zones look to the TE running the corner route.
- Against Cover 4 zones look to the WR on the smoke screen and the HB in the flat.

BLITZ BEATER

Curl Flats

SETUP

- STREAK THE FAR RIGHT WR
- DRAG THE FAR LEFT WR

- Against zone blitzes look to either flat.
- Against man-to-man blitzes look to the drag over the middle of the field.

Minnesota Vikings

RECOMMENDED DEFENSIVE RUN FORMATION: 46 NORMAL

PRO TIPS

> DT KEVIN WILLIAMS WILL CONTROL THE MIDDLE OF THE FIELD.

> MLB ERIN HENDERSON IS THE TEAM'S BEST TACKLING LINEBACKER.

> FS HARRISON SMITH CAN BE USED FOR RUN SUPPORT.

RUN DEFENSE

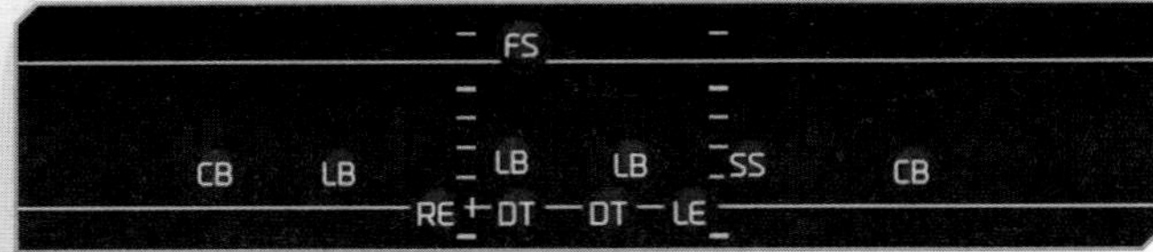

RUN DEFENSE LEFT

SETUP > SHIFT LINEBACKERS LEFT

RUN DEFENSE MIDDLE

SETUP > PINCH DEFENSIVE LINE

RUN DEFENSE RIGHT

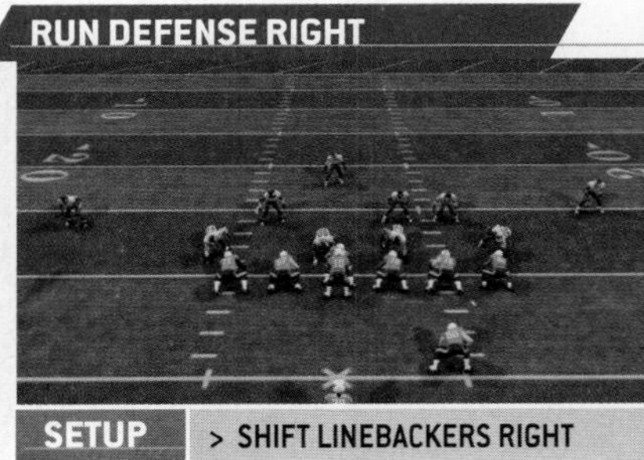

SETUP > SHIFT LINEBACKERS RIGHT

MINNESOTA VIKINGS DEFENSIVE RUN PLAY CALL SHEET

1ST DOWN RUN DEFENSE	2ND AND SHORT	3RD AND SHORT	GOAL LINE RUN DEFENSE	2ND AND LONG	3RD AND LONG
4-3 Stack—Man QB Spy	4-6 Normal—Man QB Spy	4-6 Normal—Rush Outside	Goal Line 5-3-3—Jam Cover 1	4-6 Normal— 2 Man Under	Nickel 3-3-5—2 Man Under
4-3 Stack—Cover 3 Buzz	4-6 Normal—Cover 3	4-6 Normal—Fire Zone 3	Goal Line 5-3-3—Flat Buzz	4-6 Normal—Cover 4	Nickel 3-3-5—Cover 2

MINNESOTA VIKINGS DEFENSIVE PASS PLAY CALL SHEET

1ST DOWN PLAY	2ND AND SHORT	3RD AND SHORT	GOAL LINE PASSING	2ND AND LONG	3RD AND LONG
Nickel 3-3-5—2 Man Under	Nickel Normal—Cover 1	Nickel Normal—Over Storm Brave	Goal Line 6-3-2—GL Man	Nickel 3-3-5—Dogs All Go	Nickel 3 D Ends—Odd LB Dogs
Nickel 3-3-5—Cover 2 Sink	Nickel Normal—Cover 6	Nickel 3 D Ends—Odd Overload 2	Goal Line 6-3-2—GL Zone	Nickel 3-3-5—LB Cross 3	Nickel 3 D Ends—Odd Overload 4

LEGEND: Man Coverage | Zone Coverage | Man Blitz | Zone Blitz

In these play call sheets we picked the best plays for specific situations so that you will have a play for every down and distance.

DEFENSE

RECOMMENDED DEFENSIVE PASS FORMATION: 46 NORMAL

PRO TIPS

> PLACE CB CHRIS COOK ON YOUR OPPONENT'S BEST WR.
> USE CB JOSH ROBINSON ON YOUR OPPONENT'S FASTEST WR.
> CB XAVIER RHODES SHOULD BE YOUR #2 CB.

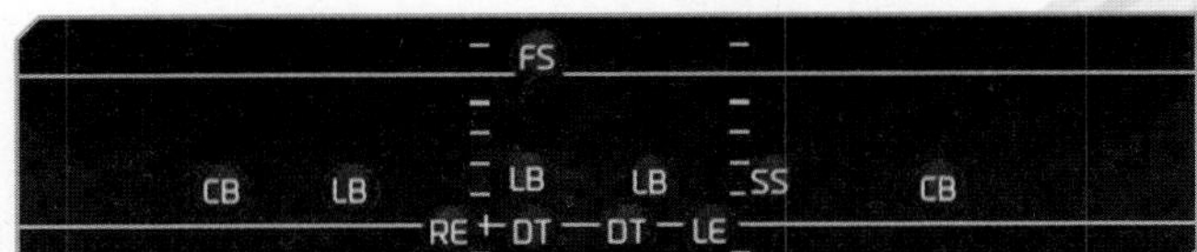

MAN COVERAGE

SETUP

> BLITZ THE SS AND MOVE HIM OFF THE RIGHT EDGE OF THE DEFENSIVE LINE
> SHIFT THE DEFENSIVE LINE RIGHT

> Pressure will come off the right edge.
> Be ready for the pressure to force throws towards the left side of the field.

ZONE COVERAGE

SETUP

> FLAT ZONE THE LE
> FLAT ZONE THE RE

> User-control the MLB and defend over the short middle.
> The extra protection on the field will force opposing QBs to roll out of the pocket, causing coverage sacks.

MAN BLITZ

SETUP

> PRESS COVERAGE
> USER-CONTROL THE FS

> The HB is uncovered, so be ready for HB screens and passes to the flat.
> Against Gun Empty sets this defense will struggle.

ZONE BLITZ

SETUP

> PRESS COVERAGE
> GLOBAL BLITZ THE ROLB

> User-control the FS and play up near the line of scrimmage.
> This defense is weak against deep sideline patterns.

Playbook
Riddell

NOTE: The following section is intended for tournament level players and may use more technical terms, formations, and strategies. If this is the type of content you're looking for you should visit MaddenTips.com for more options and playbooks. As a bonus for purchasing this strategy guide you'll get 30% any purchase from MaddenTips.com be using the following coupon code at checkout – **SCORE**

MINNESOTA VIKINGS OFFENSIVE TOURNAMENT GUIDE

The Minnesota Vikings playbook will be one of the most used playbooks in *Madden NFL 25*. In this tournament-approved offensive guide we break down plays and formations to give you the tools to never lose to friends and family members again! The plays, tips, and strategies you are about to master will take your game to new heights.

WITH US, WINNING IS EASY

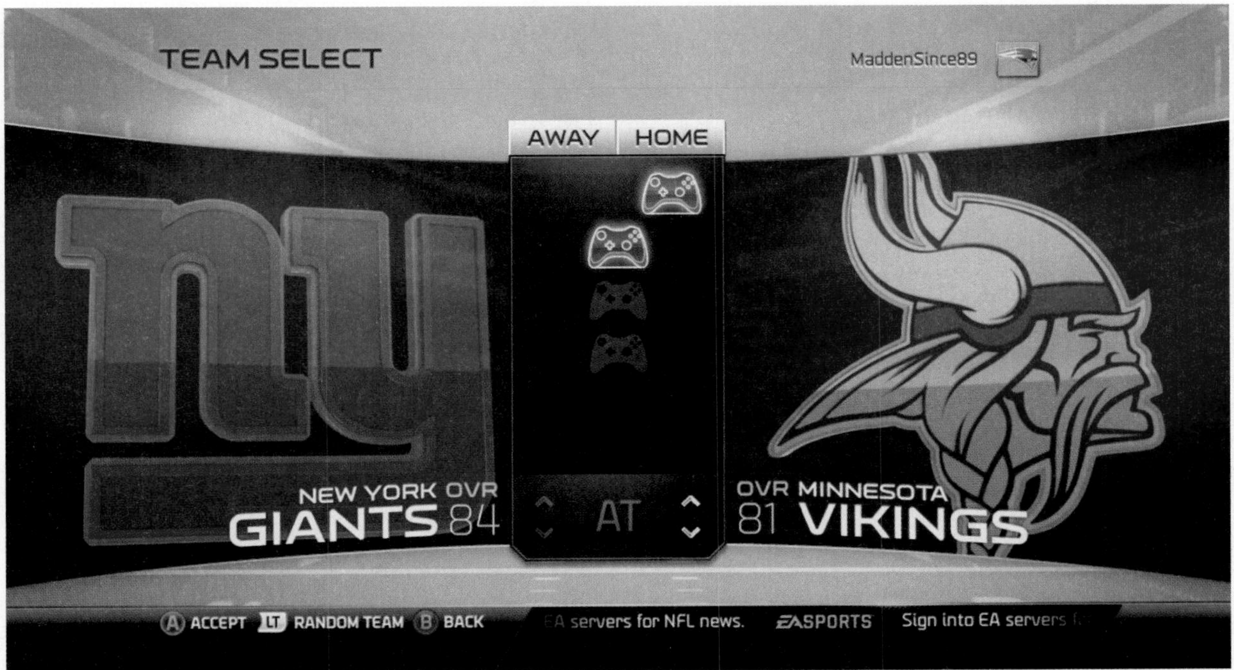

3-HEADED RUSHING ATTACK

Dominate the ground.

BASE PASSING PLAYS

Dominate the air.

QUICK PASSING

Dominate the blitz.

MAN BEATERS

Torch man coverage.

ZONE BEATERS

Destroy zone coverage.

FORMATIONS AND PLAYS

We use six formations and 24 plays from the Minnesota Vikings playbook. Each play is broken down step by step to teach you how to use it most effectively. We also break down your secondary reads and what you should do against the most popular defensive coverages in *Madden NFL 25*. These are the formations and plays that we break down in this guide.

GUN EMPTY BUNCH

The Gun Empty Bunch is new to *Madden NFL 25* and is one of the most dangerous formations in the game. Aligned to the right of the formation is a three-receiver bunch, which is great for attacking zone. The left side of the field is split with two receivers spread out, which is effective for isolating man-to-man coverages. What makes this formation so great is that you can run the Read Option from it. When run correctly this formation is unstoppable.

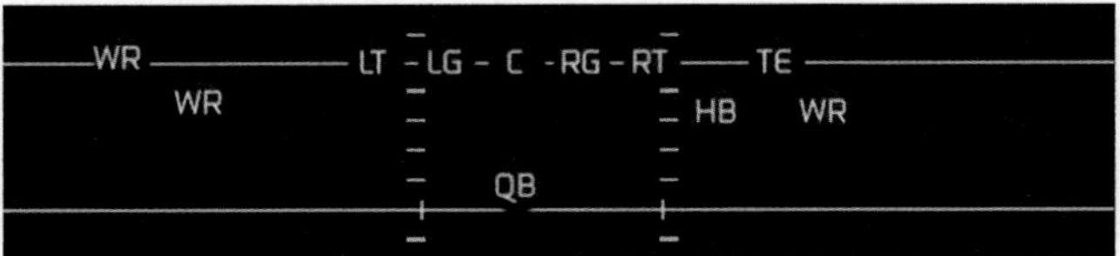

- Vikes Trail
- Mtn Read Option
- Divide Wheel
- Z Spot

SINGLEBACK BUNCH

The combination of plays in the Singleback Bunch makes it a formation that could be used all game. We show you our favorite plays to attack any coverage and show why it's one of the best short-yardage passing formations in *Madden NFL 25*.

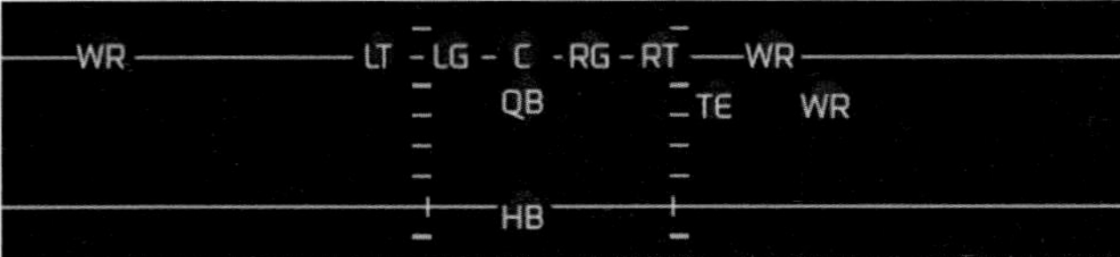

- HB Draw
- HB Slash
- Y Trail
- Vikes HB Angle

GUN TREY OPEN

The Gun Trey Open formation is used to isolate our best offensive WR and to get our HB involved heavily in the passing game. We teach you how to use this formation to attack all areas of the field, and we give you one of the most effective screens in the game.

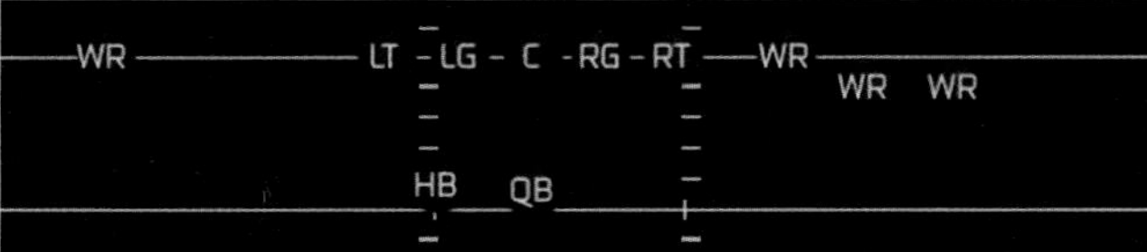

- Stick N Nod
- HB Mid Draw
- WR Screen
- Vikes Dig

FULL HOUSE NORMAL WIDE

When you want to pound the rock you will use the Full House Normal Wide formation. We also show you how to effectively quick pass form this formation so that when defenses load up the box to stop the run you will beat them with the pass!

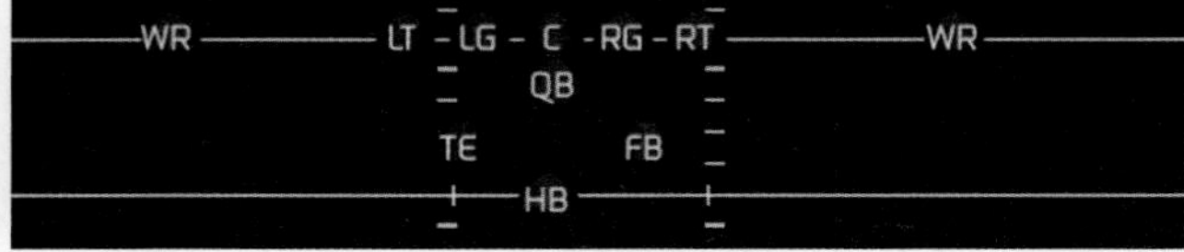

- HB Slam
- HB Draw
- HB Sweep
- WR DBL Shake

GUN TRIPS TE

We want to set the pace for the defense, and by using the Gun Trips TE formation we force the defense to adjust to an unbalanced formation. This can often result in defenses that are slow to adjust to what we are doing offensively. Did we mention that within this formation you get the best deep ball route in the game?

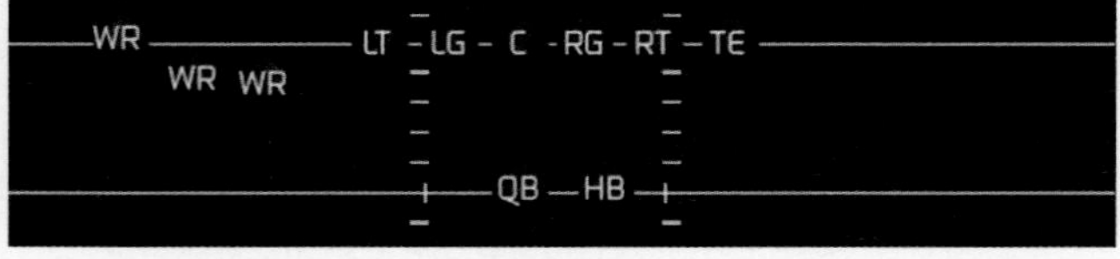

- HB Counter
- Slot Screen
- WR Deep In
- HB Wheel

GOAL LINE

Goal Line is an unconventional formation, but we show you why it's one of the best formations to use to attack man-to-man coverage. We show you how to get inside position against 2 Man Under coverage every snap of the ball!

- QB Sneak
- PA Spot
- PA Waggle
- Power O

TEAM SELECTION

The team you use is almost as important as the plays. For the Minnesota Vikings playbook we need specific players at specific positions for the offensive system to work perfectly. The first thing we look for is a QB who has at least an 80 Speed rating. A major focus of this offense is for our QB to have mobility. Next we are looking for an HB who has 90-plus speed so that we can maximize the success of the Gun Empty Bunch—Read Option. Size in the passing game is our next requirement, and we are looking for starting receivers who are at least 6'1" and have at least 85 CIT. Being able to throw the ball downfield and have confidence in your receiver's abilities to go up and get it is one of the most important factors in this year's game. The final two things we look for are 6'4" or taller TEs and backup HBs with 90-plus Speed ratings. This offensive scheme uses multiple TEs and HBs, so it's important we have a surplus of these players.

> **No team in the game will meet all the requirements, but it's important to try fulfill them.**

Team Checklist

- ☐ 80+ SPD QBs
- ☐ 90+ SPD HBs
- ☐ 80+ CIT WRs
- ☐ 6'1" WRs
- ☐ 6'4" TEs
- ☐ 90+ SPD backup HB

TOP 5 TEAMS TO USE

5 WASHINGTON REDSKINS
4 PHILADELPHIA EAGLES
3 GREEN BAY PACKERS
2 SEATTLE SEAHAWKS
1 SAN FRANCISCO 49ERS

HONORABLE MENTION: **BUFFALO BILLS, CAROLINA PANTHERS, OAKLAND RAIDERS**

5 WASHINGTON REDSKINS

QB Robert Griffin III fits our scheme perfectly. His 92 SPD, 95 AGI, and 90 ACC ratings make him one of the best QBs to run the read option with. He also can throw the ball all over the field with accuracy and power. His 95 THP and 87 THA make him the ideal QB for this offense. HB Alfred Morris doesn't have the 90+ SPD we are looking for, but he does have a 98 TRK rating, which will allow him to run over defenders. WR Pierre Garçon is 6'0" and will be our feature WR in this scheme because of his 80 CIT and 95 SPD. Starting TE Fred Davis is 6'4", and he has the athleticism we are looking for in a big body. Backing up Alfred Morris will be HB Roy Helu Jr., who will bring speed to this offense with his 93 SPD rating.

4 PHILADELPHIA EAGLES

Starting QB Michael Vick is one of the best mobile QBs in the game. He can take over games with both his legs and arm. He has 92 SPD, 96 THP, and 74 THA, which makes him ideal for this scheme. In the backfield the Eagles have three HBs that we can utilize: LeSean McCoy, Bryce Brown, and Felix Jones. McCoy is the best of the bunch, so give him the most touches. WR DeSean Jackson has 98 SPD and will be a great target downfield, while WR Jason Avant stands 6'0" and has 95 CIT. TEs Brent Celek and rookie Zach Ertz give you the flexibility of pass-catching TEs that can block during running situations.

3 GREEN BAY PACKERS

QB Aaron Rodgers is perfect for the Minnesota Vikings playbook. His 80 SPD, 95 THP, and 89 THA make him the prototypical QB for this scheme. Sub in HB DuJuan Harris as your feature back because of his 94 SPD. To back him up use rookie HB Johnathan Franklin, who has 90 SPD. Rely on WRs Jordy Nelson and Randall Cobb to make big plays in the passing game and for WR James Jones to be your target on third downs. The last piece of the puzzle for the Packers is TE Jermichael Finley, who is 6'5" and has 95 JMP.

2 SEATTLE SEAHAWKS

Seahawks QB Russell Wilson has 86 SPD and 92 ACC, which means he will be a threat with his legs on every play. The gamechanger for this offense is HB Marshawn Lynch, who has 91 SPD, 88 STR, and 99 TRK. He is one of the best HBs in *Madden NFL 25*. Spell him with HB Robert Turbin, who has 87 SPD and 90 ACC. The receiving corps for the Seahawks is dangerous because of WR Sidney Rice's ability to go up for jump balls. Look to get WR Percy Harvin in the mix with his 96 SPD and ability to turn short plays into touchdowns. TE Zach Miller provides a reliable receiving option who can make plays over the middle. TE Luke Wilson is a bonus for the Seahawks. He is 6'5" and has 88 SPD, which will make him a valuable backup to Miller.

1 SAN FRANCISCO 49ERS

There is no better team in Madden NFL 25 than the San Francisco 49ers. QB Colin Kaepernick can do it all at the quarterback position. He has 88 SPD, 91 AGI, and 92 ACC ratings. He also has 96 THP and 84 THA. If you are looking for a QB to lead your offensive success then this is your team. Look to give HB Frank Gore the majority of carries, but back him up with HB LaMichael James because of his 93 ELU. The 49ers WRs will make your life easier because of their CIT ratings. WR Anquan Boldin has 98 CIT, and WR Michael Crabtree has 92 CIT. Rounding out this offense you have TE Vernon Davis, who is one of the fastest TEs in the game.

GUN EMPTY BUNCH

VIKES TRAIL

Vikes Trail is one of the best plays in the game because it is set up to attack man-to-man coverage on the right side of the field and zone coverage on the left. Our favorite route on this play is the HB's trail route. If you are facing the blitz you can throw the ball right away for an easy gain or you can wait for the HB to break back over the middle. Against zone the left side of the field has a corner route to beat Cover 2 and 3 zones and a quick hitch route for Cover 4.

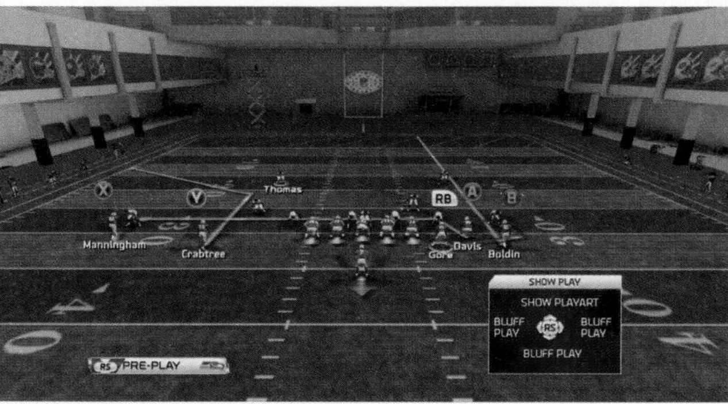

Hot route the far left WR to a smoke screen and streak the far right WR.

Gore catches the ball for a short gain but has room to run.

OPTIONAL PACKAGES

- Backup QB—If you have a faster backup QB this is a good package to use.
- TE Sub—Use this if you have a better receiving or blocking option.

KEY ADJUSTMENTS

- Streak the far right WR.

WHAT TO LOOK FOR

- The HB is your primary target; be ready to get him the ball at the snap.
- The corner route is an option against man-to-man. Wait for the route to break towards the sideline, then throw a high lead pass.

MTN READ OPTION

The Mtn Read Option requires you to read the defense and key in on the *read man*. This defender can be seen by viewing the coach cam on-field. This defender will have a "read" symbol labeled above him. At the snap of the ball key in on him. If he crashes down towards the HB keep the ball with the QB. If he drops into containment of the QB then give the ball to the HB by holding down the Snap button.

The read man is containing the QB. Give the ball to the HB.

The defender is crashing on the HB. Keep the ball with the QB.

OPTIONAL PACKAGES

- Backup QB—If you have a faster backup QB this is a good package to use.
- TE Sub—Use this if you have a better receiving or blocking option.

KEY ADJUSTMENTS

- None

WHAT TO LOOK FOR

- Savvy user defenders will user-blitz off the right edge when they expect the Mtn Read Option.
- Mix up your play calls so they can't anticipate the read option.

DIVIDE WHEEL

The Divide Wheel is our favorite play in this playbook. There is a route to beat every defense on this play. We focus on the HB's vertical route and the left slot WR's sideline wheel route. Both destroy man-to-man coverage and will force your opponent to start playing zone coverage!

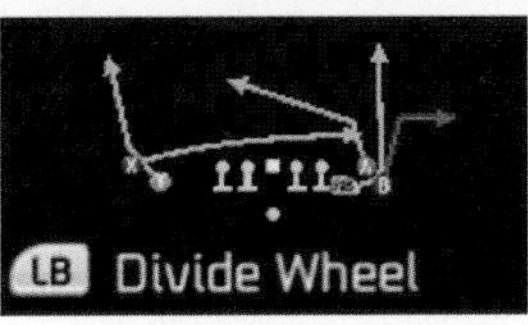

Our HB catches the ball with no one around him.

Crabtree goes up for the ball down the left sideline.

OPTIONAL PACKAGES

- > Backup QB—If you have a faster backup QB this is a good package to use.
- > TE Sub—Use this if you have a better receiving or blocking option.

KEY ADJUSTMENTS

- > Drag the far right WR.

WHAT TO LOOK FOR

- > The wheel routes are effective, but they do take time to develop.
- > The underneath drag routes are your next best option. If they get open throw them the ball.

Z SPOT

Z Spot is our primary zone-beating play from the Gun Empty Bunch. Both sides of the field are set up to attack zone coverage. If you face Cover 4 zones look to the smoke screen on the far left and the flat route to the HB on the right. If you face Cover 2 and Cover 3 zones attack the slot streaks and the TE corner route.

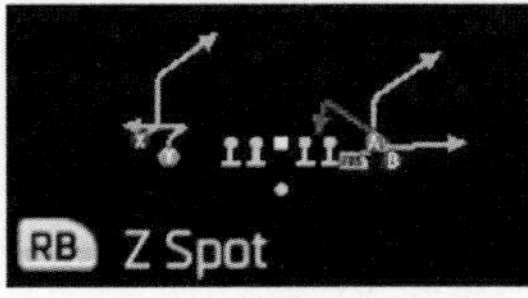

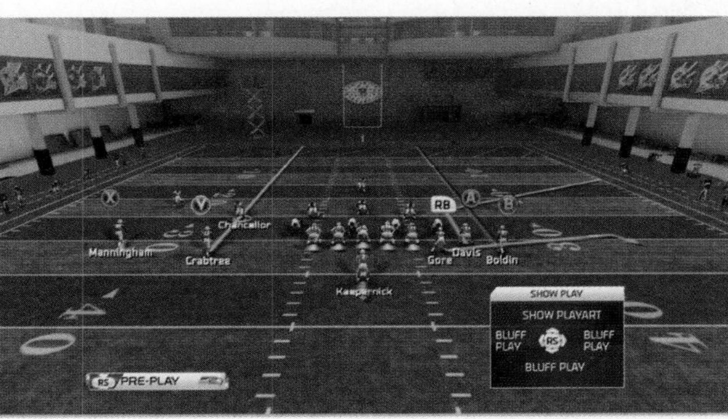

Smoke screen the far left WR, streak the left slot, and streak the far right WR.

The defense is playing Cover 3 zone. We throw to our TE for the big completion.

OPTIONAL PACKAGES

- > Backup QB—If you have a faster backup QB this is a good package to use.
- > TE Sub—Use this if you have a better receiving or blocking option.

KEY ADJUSTMENTS

- > Smoke screen the far left WR.
- > Streak the left slot.

WHAT TO LOOK FOR

- > Defenses will naturally gravitate towards the bunch on the right side of the field. This leaves the smoke screen and streak route combination on the right wide open against blitzing zone defenses. This is one of our favorite ways in this year's game to attack opponents that blitz heavily.

TO LEARN MORE TIPS ABOUT HOW TO USER CATCH IN *MADDEN NFL 25*, VISIT WWW.MADDENTIPS.COM.

GUN TREY OPEN

STICK N NOD

Stick N Nod has two unique routes that destroy man coverage, so it is one of the best ways to attack man-to-man setups. It's difficult for defenses to defend this play because they can often stop only one of the routes.

The inside zig gets crazy separation against man-to-man.

The double move gets open downfield for big gains.

OPTIONAL PACKAGES

> TE Slot—If you want to, package your TE in the slot for a mismatch.

> TE Wide—This package isolates your big TE outside.

KEY ADJUSTMENTS

> Streak the HB.

WHAT TO LOOK FOR

> The HB can be a quick pass option if you face heavy pressure.

> The right slot WR will beat his defender by about 5 yards. The double-move WR doesn't get open as often, but when he does it's for big yards.

HB MID DRAW

A popular defensive strategy gamers use online is to play max coverage defense. This is when they pass rush two or fewer defenders after the QB. When they do this, be ready and call the Gun Trey Open—HB Mid Draw.

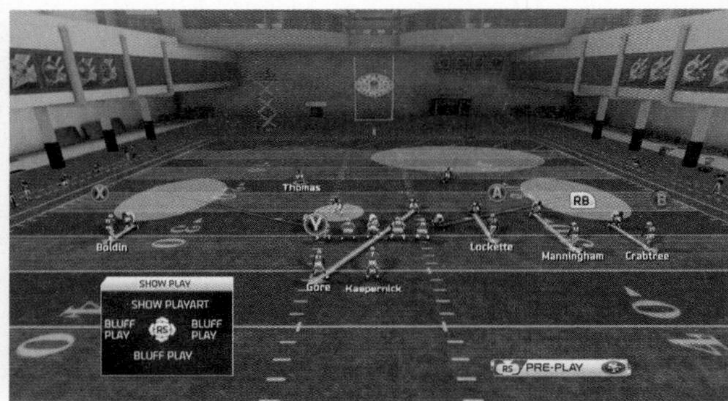

The defense is rushing only one defender.

The HB Draw is extremely effective against max coverage defense.

OPTIONAL PACKAGES

> TE Slot—If you want to, package your TE in the slot for a mismatch.

> TE Wide—This package isolates your big TE outside.

KEY ADJUSTMENTS

> Slide protect in any direction.

WHAT TO LOOK FOR

> Using slide protection on an HB Draw shifts your offensive line to block in the direction you choose. This helps you determine where you want to run the ball before the snap of the ball.

WR SCREEN

The WR Screen from the Gun Trey Open is one of the best screens in the game—only we won't be targeting the WR on this play. We will get the ball to our HB and let him do the dirty work for our offense. This play is unique, and your opponent won't see it coming!

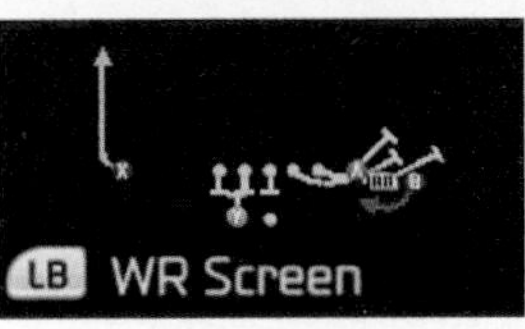

Throw to the HB earlier rather than later.

There will be four blockers leading the way upfield.

OPTIONAL PACKAGES

- TE Slot—Use this if you want to package your TE in the slot for a mismatch.
- TE Wide—This package isolates your big TE outside.

KEY ADJUSTMENTS

- Streak the far right HB.
- Swing the HB right.

WHAT TO LOOK FOR

- The far left WR is completely isolated from the rest of the defense. If you see a one-on-one matchup you like take a chance and lob it deep!
- Watch out for user defenders jumping the HB and trying to make a big play.

VIKES DIG

This play has a ton of options against any defense you will face. You need to get into practice mode and work on all the reads. This is one of the best plays in the game if you use it correctly. The corner route is the primary route on this play, but the HB's route is also a great option to beat the blitz.

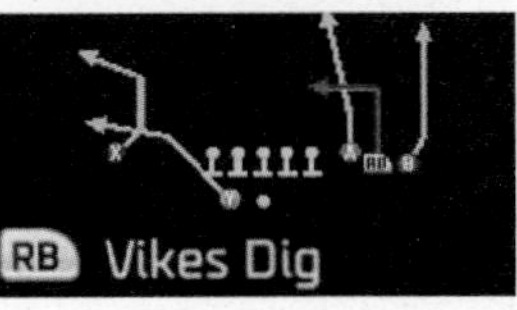

User-catch the far right fade against man-to-man defenses.

When facing the blitz, look to the angled streak over the deep middle.

OPTIONAL PACKAGES

- TE Slot—You can package your TE in the slot for a mismatch.
- TE Wide—This isolates your big TE outside.

KEY ADJUSTMENTS

- Drag the right slot WR.

WHAT TO LOOK FOR

- The angled streak is one of the best ways to attack the deep part of the field this year. If you see the blitz, take a chance and air it out deep.
- If you face a zone blitz, the HB to the left flat will be wide open. Throw a high lead pass and you will lead him upfield for positive yards.

GUN TRIPS TE

HB COUNTER

HB Counters from Gun formations can result in huge gains on the ground. When in the Gun Trips TE formation you want to focus on one key area of the field. Look towards the right flat, and if you see a defender in that area you shouldn't run the HB Counter. This is because the defense has one extra defender on the side of the field that we are running towards. If you see no defender in the right flat that is your signal to run the HB Counter. These images show you what to look for.

Don't run the HB Counter.

Run the HB Counter.

OPTIONAL PACKAGES

- HB Slot—This places your starting HB in the left slot.
- Spell HB—Sub out your starting HB for your backup.

KEY ADJUSTMENTS

- Read the right flat.

WHAT TO LOOK FOR

- If you see a defender in the right flat, audible out to a passing play and target the left side of the field.
- When running this formation you will always have the numbers advantage in the passing game or run game.

SLOT SCREEN

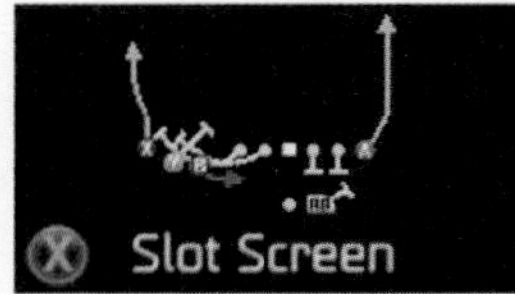

Use this screen specifically against zone defenses. The play is designed to go to the slot WR, but we change things up and look to target the HB out of the backfield. When used against man-to-man coverage the defender covering the HB tends not to get picked up by the screen blocking, so make sure to use this specifically against zone coverage.

Our blockers are in place to lead our HB upfield.

Get upfield as quickly as possible and follow your blockers!

OPTIONAL PACKAGES

- HB Slot—This places your starting HB in the left slot.
- Spell HB—Sub out your starting HB for your backup.

KEY ADJUSTMENTS

- Swing the HB left.

WHAT TO LOOK FOR

- The more you run this play, the more your opponents will be able to key in on it and stop it. You want them to respect this play every snap, but use it only occasionally.
- Screens can be the ultimate determining factor for any offense and can often be the difference between a drive stalling and scoring a touchdown.

WR DEEP IN

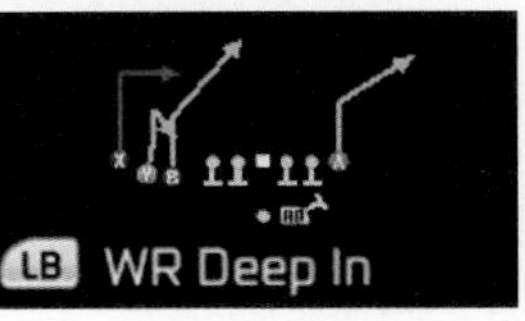

There hasn't been a deep ball route that has been this good since *Madden NFL 2008* and the play Trips Attack. The route we are talking about is the inside slot WR's deep post. This route is hands down the best deep route in the game. If you can get time in the pocket this can be a touchdown. It's also a great user-catch option as soon as it cuts over the middle of the field.

Throw a deep lob leading the WR upfield.

We also have underneath options in case we don't have the time in the pocket.

OPTIONAL PACKAGES

- HB Slot—This places your starting HB in the left slot.
- Spell HB—Sub out your starting HB for your backup.

KEY ADJUSTMENTS

- Streak the middle slot WR.
- Drag the far left WR.

WHAT TO LOOK FOR

- If you don't have time in the pocket you should check down to the drag over the middle or the TE running the corner route.
- If you get a one-on-one situation this play will result in a touchdown almost every time.

HB WHEEL

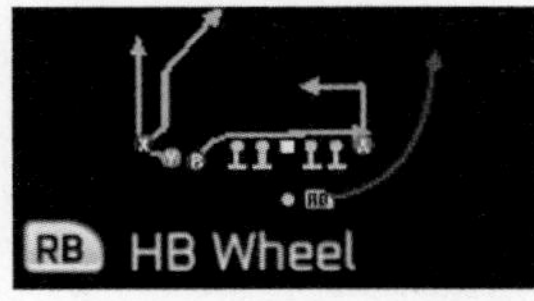

This is the play that we call upon the most from the Gun Trips TE formation. The wheel route on the left side of the field crushes both man-to-man coverage and zone blitzes. This one route makes this entire play effective. The HB out of the backfield is also a great option against zone blitzes and becomes a user-catch option as the play develops.

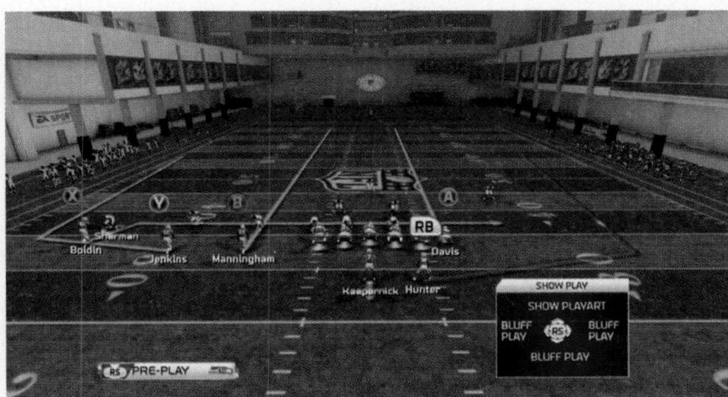

Drag the far left WR, streak the inside slot WR, and streak the TE.

We user-catch the TE streak right in front of the safety.

OPTIONAL PACKAGES

- HB Slot—This places your starting HB in the left slot.
- Spell HB—Sub out your starting HB for your backup.

KEY ADJUSTMENTS

- Streak the TE.
- Drag the far left WR.

WHAT TO LOOK FOR

- Target the left sideline wheel until your opponents take it away from you. They will spend so much time trying to slow down that one route that they will not be able to defend all the other options on this play.
- The two streaks over the middle of the field absolutely torch zone coverage when user-caught.

SINGLEBACK BUNCH

HB DRAW

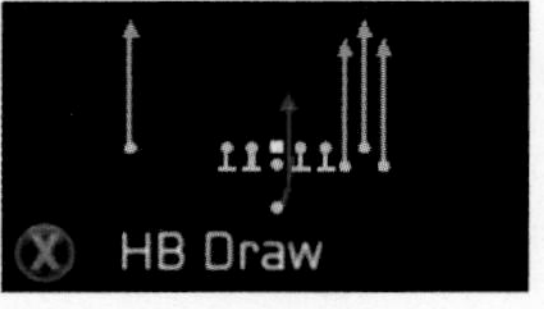

The Singleback Bunch—HB Draw is extremely effective because of the bunch on the right side of the field. Defenses have to realign their defenders to stop this formation, and much of the attention goes to stopping the pass. The WRs and TEs in the bunch alignment push upfield and give the HB a running lane to pick up yards.

The defense is set up to stop the pass.

We slide protect right and pick up big yards off the right edge.

OPTIONAL PACKAGES

- Twin TE—This places another TE on the field to create a 1 HB, 2 TE, 2 WR formation.
- HB Wideout—Isolate your HB outside near the left sideline.

KEY ADJUSTMENTS

- Slide protect down.

WHAT TO LOOK FOR

- Be precise with your cuts at the snap of the ball. Don't run into offensive linemen!
- If your opponent starts overloading the offensive line with blitzers don't call the HB Draw.

HB SLASH

Against four-down defensive lines you will get double-team blocks on the interior of the offensive line. The double teams mean fewer block sheds by defensive linemen and more yards for your HB. This is one of the most consistent runs in the game and will be the staple of your offense.

Our offensive line doubles down on the defensive line.

Get upfield and follow your blockers.

OPTIONAL PACKAGES

- Twin TE—This places another TE on the field to create a 1 HB, 2 TE, 2 WR formation.
- HB Wideout—Isolate your HB outside near the left sideline.

KEY ADJUSTMENTS

- None.
- Drag the far left WR.

WHAT TO LOOK FOR

- Your TE blocking off the right edge of the offensive line needs to be able to hold his block consistently. Make sure you have a solid blocking TE for key running situations.
- The double teams are great, but they do open up lanes for user defenders to shoot.

Y TRAIL

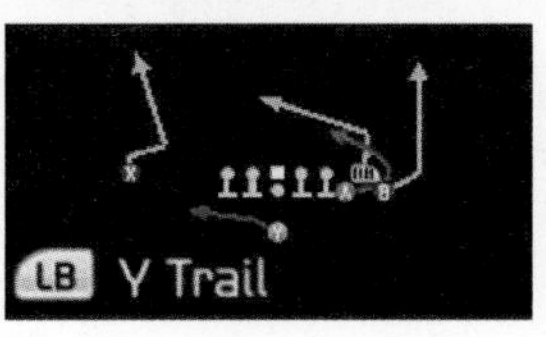

Y Trail has three routes that are unique to it and are very difficult for defenses to stop. The far right wheel route gets inside position against man-to-man defense, the angle route to the TE beats man coverage over the middle, and the deep slant gets to a spot on the field that most routes don't. All things considered, this is one of the best plays in *Madden NFL 25*.

Throw a high inside pass lead against man coverage.

Throw a high pass lead when targeting the deep slant.

OPTIONAL PACKAGES

- Twin TE—This places another TE on the field to create a 1 HB, 2 TE, 2 WR formation.
- HB Wideout—Isolate your HB outside near the left sideline.

KEY ADJUSTMENTS

- Streak the far left WR.
- Block the HB.

WHAT TO LOOK FOR

- If you are facing an opponent who calls a lot of zone coverage, consider hot routing the far left WR to a drag.
- Force the issue with the wheel on the right side. This route is difficult to stop, and your opponents will need to spend all their resources to stop it.

VIKES HB ANGLE

Vikes HB Angle is one of our favorite plays in this playbook. It has been an effective play for many years in Madden and is once again a difficult play to stop in *Madden NFL 25*. The play is built around the HB's angle route out of the backfield. This is one of the best routes in the game and is our primary target.

We wait for the HB to cut back towards the middle of the field.

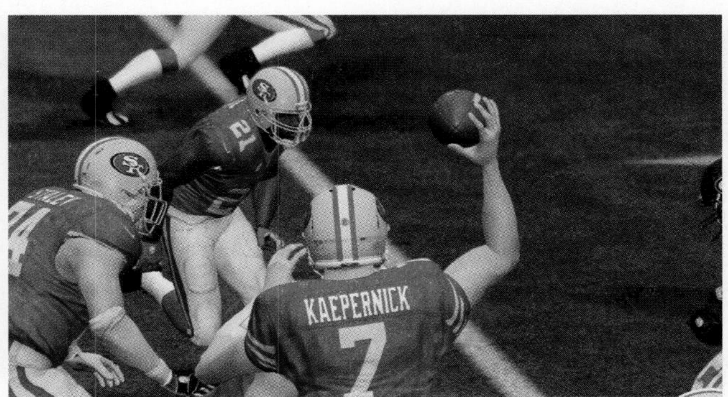

We motion the HB to the left and throw the ball immediately at the snap of the ball.

OPTIONAL PACKAGES

- Twin TE—This places another TE on the field to create a 1 HB, 2 TE, 2 WR formation.
- HB Wideout—Isolate your HB outside near the left sideline.

KEY ADJUSTMENTS

- Streak the far left WR.
- Streak the far right WR.

WHAT TO LOOK FOR

- The TE over the middle is a nice option when defenses aren't protecting he short middle, and the TE corner route destroys man-to-man coverage.
- The outside streaks are user-catch options against zone coverages, and the HB's route can be used as a quick pass to the left and right.

FULL HOUSE NORMAL WIDE

HB SLAM

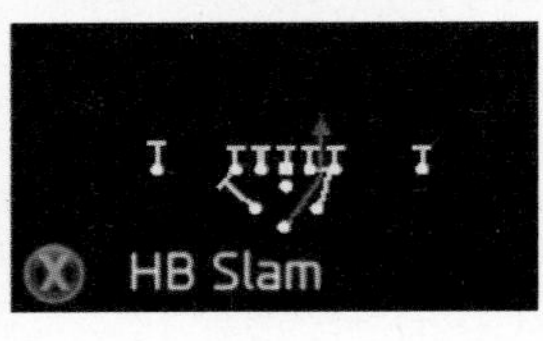

The Full House Normal Wide is our primary running formation in this playbook. We use it when we plan on pounding the rock on our opponent, and it's also extremely effective inside the red zone. The HB Slam is the most consistent run from this formation and is what we call upon most often.

Our lead blocking FB will seal the edge.

We flip the play and run off the left edge.

OPTIONAL PACKAGES

> Twin FB—This package has two lead FBs for your starting HB.

> Jumbo—Sub out your HB for another FB. This provides great pass protection.

KEY ADJUSTMENTS

> Motion the weak-side FB/TE towards the strong side.

WHAT TO LOOK FOR

> The motioned FB/TE will cut back across the formation and will pick up defenders who shoot through the A gaps.

> You have the ability to flip this formation without your opponent knowing. This means you can run towards the right one play and then run towards the left the next.

HB DRAW

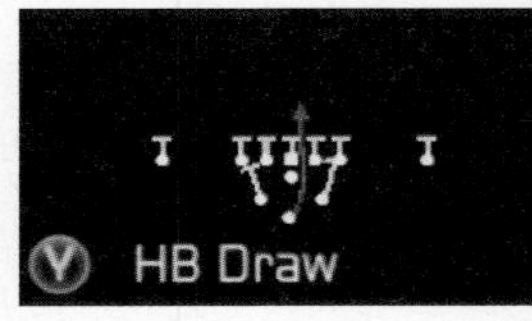

The Full House Normal Wide—HB Draw is the best draw in the game because it has two lead blockers in the backfield paving the way for the HB. This makes it extremely difficult to call the typical HB Draw defense, which is to send six pass rushers after the QB. That usually floods the offensive line and blows the run up in the backfield, but that tactic won't work against this play.

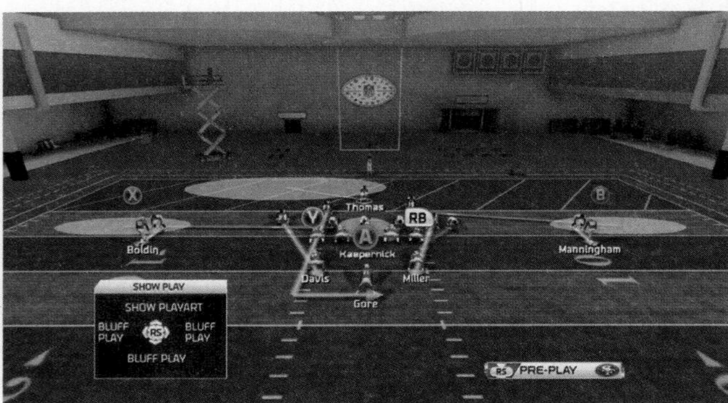

A typical defense in the red zone is to use max coverage.

Notice that all seven of our blockers are pushing upfield.

OPTIONAL PACKAGES

> Twin FB—This package has two lead FBs for your starting HB.

> Jumbo—Sub out your HB for another FB. This provides great pass protection.

KEY ADJUSTMENTS

> Slide protect.

WHAT TO LOOK FOR

> Use slide protection if you are looking to run towards a certain area of the field. For example, if you see pressure set up to come off the left edge, we recommend you slide protect right.

> Patience is most important when running draws. Don't out-run your blockers!

HB SWEEP

A great change-of-pace run is the HB Sweep. The Full House is built to run up the middle and off tackle. When you call upon the HB Sweep you will catch your opponent off-guard. This run can pick up big yards for your offense.

Motion the TE/FB towards the strong side.

Follow your blocks and get to the end zone!

OPTIONAL PACKAGES

> Twin FB—This package has two lead FBs for your starting HB.

> Jumbo—Sub out your HB for another FB. This provides great pass protection.

KEY ADJUSTMENTS

> Motion the weak-side FB/TE towards the strong side.

WHAT TO LOOK FOR

> Motioning the TE/FB is important to the success of this play. He adds an extra blocker on the run side and helps to seal the edge against would-be defenders.

> An elite FB is key for the HB Sweep. FB Bruce Miller does an excellent job taking on defenders and clearing a path for our HB.

WR DBL SHAKE

WR DBL Shake has been one of our favorite plays for years. It's also been the staple of our red zone offense. This play has a lot of options that you can use to attack in the red zone. The main focus is on the TE's route out of the backfield. You want to snap the ball and throw to the TE, then click onto him so that he will catch the ball.

You must click onto the TE after the throw for him to catch the ball.

Block both the FB and TE and the HB will release nicely!

OPTIONAL PACKAGES

> Twin FB—This package has two lead FBs for your starting HB.

> Jumbo—Sub out your HB for another FB. This provides great pass protection.

KEY ADJUSTMENTS

> Block the TE and FB.

WHAT TO LOOK FOR

> If you block both the FB and TE place both outside WRs on fades. This will give you a jump ball option in the event that the HB is covered.

GOAL LINE

QB SNEAK

QB Sneak is the best run in the game with inches and one yard to go for a first down. It's also not the most conventional play that you see online. That's exactly why we like it. When we want to grind out games we call upon the Goal Line formation and will run the ball down our opponents' throat. The QB Sneak forces them to pinch their defensive line, which opens up running lanes outside.

We have picked up 2 yards before Kaepernick has even been touched!

At the snap of the ball look to juke to avoid the auto QB breakdown.

OPTIONAL PACKAGES

- WR Wing—This package places your #1 WR at #3 TE.
- Heavy—This package places an offensive tackle at #1 TE.

KEY ADJUSTMENTS

- Motion the far right TE to the left.
- Snap the ball once he reaches the right A gap.

WHAT TO LOOK FOR

- The motioned TE will fire through the A gap and will be a lead blocker for our QB.
- This is a very effective strategy that you should use whenever you are in a pinch. This will frustrate your opponent beyond belief.

POWER O

The Power O is the most consistent run from the Goal Line formation. With defenses stacking the box and middle of the field to stop the QB Sneak we will have running lanes outside for the Power O. We like to use motion that mimics the QB Sneak when we run the Power O.

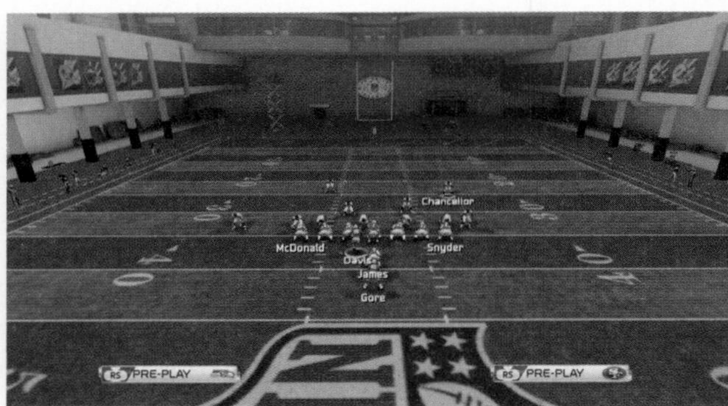

We motion the far right TE to the left and snap once he's in the A gap.

We follow our lead blockers for a big gain.

OPTIONAL PACKAGES

- WR Wing—This package places your #1 WR at #3 TE.
- Heavy—This package places an offensive tackle at #1 TE.

KEY ADJUSTMENTS

- Motion the TE.
- Playmaker the run left.

WHAT TO LOOK FOR

- Do a fake playmaker every once in a while. This means to motion the TE left and playmaker to the right. Snap the ball once the TE reaches the A gap.
- Your opponent will think the run is going to the left, which will give you the advantage during the play.

PA WAGGLE

With all the running we will be doing from the Goal Line formation we can catch our opponent off guard by passing. We like the PA Waggle because of the crossing patterns by the TEs. The TE on the right runs a delayed drag, which you can throw to at the snap of the ball as a quick pass or wait and let it develop. We will also target the far right TE on a streak as a user-catch option.

This is a great quick pass that is difficult to defend.

The streak gets inside position for the easy catch.

OPTIONAL PACKAGES

- WR Wing—This package places your #1 WR at #3 TE.
- Heavy—This package places an offensive tackle at #1 TE.

KEY ADJUSTMENTS

- Streak the far right TE.
- Block the TE.

WHAT TO LOOK FOR

- The crossing patterns will get great separation over the middle of the field.
- The TE streaks out of the Goal Line formation will be one of the toughest tactics to stop this year in *Madden NFL 25*.

PA SPOT

PA Spot has one unique route that we want to take advantage of. The inside TE on the right side of the field runs a slant out. This route is only in a few plays in the entire game. It's one of the best man-beating routes in the game. It's also great for beating zone in combination with the flat route.

The flat route will pull down, flat zones leaving the slant out open.

We can also hit our TE on a streak.

OPTIONAL PACKAGES

- WR Wing—This package places your #1 WR at #3 TE.
- Heavy—This package places an offensive tackle at #1 TE.

KEY ADJUSTMENTS

- Streak both outside TEs.

WHAT TO LOOK FOR

- The far left TE is a safety valve route. Check down to this streak if your reads on the right aren't open.
- The PA Spot is one of the best plays in the game for 2-point conversions. Look to the slant first and then to the spot curl.

Fantasy Football
Riddell
DETROIT 60 LIONS
Wilson

FOREWORD

MICHAEL FABIANO, FANTASY EDITOR – NFL.COM

Fantasy football has changed the way NFL fans watch the game that has become the passion of this nation—but did you know it's been around for over 50 years? That's right—fantasy football started in 1962 at the Milford Plaza (New York City). The basis for what we now know as fantasy football is attributed to Wilfred "Bill" Winkenbach, a one-time limited partner with the Oakland Raiders, who together with former Raiders public relations manager Bill Tunnell and reporter Scotty Stirling created the first set of rules and guidelines.

The first fantasy football league, the GOPPPL (Greater Oakland Professional Pigskin Prognosticators Leagues), included eight separate "owners." Because players played multiple positions in the 1960s, two different fantasy teams could own the same player at different positions. For example, superstar George Blanda could have been picked as a quarterback by one team and as a kicker by another squad!

Each roster was made up of two quarterbacks, four halfbacks, two fullbacks, four offensive ends, two kick and/or punt returners, two field goal kickers, two defensive backs/linebackers, and two defensive linemen. That's right, the GOPPPL was quite nontraditional in current terms, as it used individual defensive players. Furthermore, the scoring system was based on touchdowns, field goals, and extra points alone.

The next step in the slow rise in popularity of fantasy football came in 1969, when Oakland restaurateur and original GOPPPL member Andy Mousalimas opened the first "public" league at the Kings X Sports Bar. It was at that time that the scoring system was "expanded" to include yardage in addition to touchdowns.

Ironically, several members of the Raiders were among the top-scoring players (based on fantasy points) in the AFL that season, including quarterback Daryl Lamonica and his dynamic duo of wide receivers, Warren Wells and Hall of Famer Fred Biletnikoff. On the NFL side, Hall of Fame stars Sonny Jurgensen, Fran Tarkenton (then with the Giants), and Gale Sayers were among the highest-scoring fantasy players.

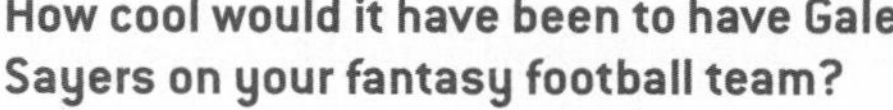

How cool would it have been to have Gale Sayers on your fantasy football team?

Of course, the biggest innovation in the development and eventual widespread popularity of fantasy football came several decades later with the dawn of the Internet. No longer did owners have to calculate points with a pen and paper while sifting through countless box scores (something I did quite a bit during the mid- 1990s), as sports websites built services that ran leagues and tracked rosters, scoring, and matchups.

Now, more than a decade and a half later, fantasy football is a lucrative business that includes millions of participants. Furthermore, it's been estimated that around three-fourths of the estimated 30-plus million people who play fantasy sports participate in fantasy football leagues. Not only are people playing online, but you can even manage your fantasy team(s) via your Madden game console and **NFL.com**.

Oh, and how's this for a real-game fantasy football experience—the Jacksonville Jaguars are planning to turn their Sky Patio at EverBank Field into a high-tech fantasy football lounge. The San Francisco 49ers have also unveiled a plan for a similar experience at their new stadium, which is slated to open in 2014. Teams are also streaming the NFL Network's RedZone Channel on stadium video boards so fantasy enthusiasts can keep tabs on how their players are performing during live in-stadium action.

Little did Mr. Winkenbach and his cohorts know that what was first created as a way "to bring together some of Oakland's finest Saturday morning gridiron forecasters to pit their respective brains against each other" would turn into one of the most wildly popular hobbies in the history of professional sports.

So whether you have been a part of the fantasy life for many years or are just now getting into fantasy football, NFL.com has all the tools, expert advice, and the best game in the business to help you not only have fun, but succeed on the virtual gridiron. And over the next several pages, you'll learn a few tricks of the trade that I've been able to compile over my close to 15 years in the business (wow, time flies)!

Yes, it truly has become a fantasy world in the National Football League.

FANTASY FOOTBALL

WHAT IS FANTASY FOOTBALL?

Do you have what it takes to put together a winning football franchise? NFL.com Fantasy Football gives you the perfect chance to find out. Fantasy football, like other fantasy games, puts you in the front office and on the sidelines as general manager and coach of your team. You select from a list of the best players in the NFL, and they compete on a weekly basis for your team. Their on-field performance drives your fantasy point total and overall success.

Specifically, fantasy football works like this: You decide what type of league you want to participate in, acquire a roster of players (either through a draft or through autopick assignment), then set your lineup each week during the season and watch as touchdowns, field goals, yards gained, sacks, interceptions, and much, much more generate fantasy points for or against your team. Whether you win or lose and climb or fall on the leaderboard all depends on how well you maximize the talent on your roster each week. Will you make a risky move to start that backup running back, or will you play it safe and keep your starting lineup consistent?

From prize-eligible NFL-Managed Leagues to fully customizable Custom Leagues, NFL.com provides ample options to start your fantasy season. Want to compete to win official NFL prizes, including trips to the Pro Bowl and Super Bowl XLVIII? Join an NFL-Managed League, where you will go head-to-head against other NFL fans across the country for the right to be called a league champion. Or are you looking to fully customize your fantasy experience, from the league and scoring settings to the users you will compete with on a weekly basis? Create your Custom League today and invite friends, family, coworkers, and anyone else to compete in a season-long fantasy battle on NFL.com. Exclusive NFL.com Fantasy Football features including instant video highlights and free Fantasy Game Center Live Scoring await in all NFL.com fantasy leagues.

Will your team earn the title of NFL.com Fantasy Football Champion this season? Find the right settings to suit your interests and start building your winning franchise today!

New and Upgraded Features

- Redesigned Mobile Apps
- All-New Player Cards
- Matchup Previews and Recaps
- Improved Site Performance
- More Research Stats and Data

Exclusive Features

- Free Live Scoring with Instant Video Highlights
- Free, All-New Mobile Apps
- Ultimate Experience Prize Leagues
- Upgraded Draft Client with iPad Support
- Advanced Fantasy Football Stats and Data
- 200+ Custom League and Scoring Settings

WHY CHOOSE NFL.COM FANTASY?

If you want football, then go to the NFL. You will experience the *only* fantasy football game with exclusive NFL access through Instant Video Highlights, player projections from EA SPORTS' *Madden NFL 25,* and more. NFL.com Fantasy Football brings you closer to the sport you love, because here at the NFL, football is all we do.

Completely redesigned, the new NFL.com Fantasy Football experience was built from the ground up to suit all types of fantasy players, regardless of experience or skill. Fantasy rookies will enjoy the user-friendly experience, and fantasy football fanatics will enjoy ground-breaking features. Signup is easy, and NFL.com Fantasy Football is absolutely *free* to play.

Head over to NFL.com today to create a customized NFL.com Fantasy Football league to play with your friends, or start your fantasy football dynasty on **NFL.com** today with a prize-eligible NFL-Managed league.

SCORING SETTINGS (NFL-MANAGED)

These are the default scoring settings used in all NFL-Managed Leagues.

OFFENSE

Passing Yards: 1 point per 25 yards passing

Passing Touchdowns: 4 points

Interceptions: -2 points

Rushing Yards: 1 point per 10 yards

Rushing Touchdowns: 6 points

Receiving Yards: 1 point per 10 yards

Receiving Touchdowns: 6 points

Fumble Recovered for a Touchdown: 6 points

2-Point Conversions: 2 points

Fumbles Lost: -2 points

KICKING

PAT Made: 1 point

FG Made (0-49 yards): 3 points

FG Made (50+ yards): 5 points

DEFENSE

Sacks: 1 point

Interceptions: 2 points

Fumbles Recovered: 2 points

Safeties: 2 points

Defensive Touchdowns: 6 points

Kick and Punt Return Touchdowns: 6 points

Points Allowed (0): 10 points

Points Allowed (1–6): 7 points

Points Allowed (7–13): 4 points

Points Allowed (14–20): 1 points

Points Allowed (21–27): 0 points

Points Allowed (28–34): -1 points

Points Allowed (35+): -4 points

GENERAL

Use Fractional Points: Yes

Use Negative Points: Yes

HEAD-TO-HEAD SCORING FORMAT

All NFL.com Fantasy Football leagues feature head-to-head scoring. Much as in the games that take place across the NFL each Sunday, your team will be matched up against another team within your league. Similar to an NFL game being decided on the field with the team scoring the most points earning a win, your fantasy matchup behaves accordingly.

Based on your NFL-Managed League scoring settings, your team will earn points based on the actual statistics and results played out in the NFL that week. If your team earns more points than your opponent's team, you earn a win in the league standings. Fewer points? Take a loss. And if your game ends in a tie—you guessed it—it's a tie in the overall standings.

LEAGUE SETTINGS

These default league settings are used in all NFL-Managed Leagues.

Teams: 10

Divisions: None

League Viewable by Public: No

Undroppable List: NFL.com Fantasy Default List

Maximum Acquisitions per Season: No Maximum

Maximum Acquisitions per Week: No Maximum

Trade Limit per Season: No Limit

Trade Review Type: League Votes

Waiver Period: 1 Day

Waiver Type: Weekly Reset, Inverse Order of Standings

Post-Draft Players: Follow Waiver Rules

Roster Lock Type: Players Lock at Individual Game Time

2014 Keeper Settings: None

Starting Positions and Roster Size: 9 starters (QB, RB, RB, WR, WR, W/R Flex, TE, K, DEF) and 6 bench

NFL-MANAGED DRAFT TYPES

Live Online Draft and Autopick Draft are the only draft types used in NFL-Managed Leagues.

LIVE DRAFT

The Live Online Draft feature allows you to select a full fantasy team, *live*, round-by-round in an interactive environment. The draft client features comprehensive stats, analysis, and chat functionality, all packaged in a user-friendly interface. In this draft application you can rank your players in real time, adding them to a queue that will update as players are taken by other teams in the league. You can search for players or filter the available players by position so that you can make fast, easy, and informed decisions to fill out your roster. When you have found the perfect selection, click "Draft Now" and the player you selected will be assigned to your team. You can track all of the action by round and by individual team, all in one place inside the draft application.

AUTOPICK

The Autopick Draft operates based on NFL.com fantasy experts' default rankings or a team owner's established pre-rankings. This draft type is an excellent choice for beginners as well as leagues that can't agree on a live draft time. In an Autopick Draft, players are assigned to your team automatically. NFL.com helps you fill your roster, either by going strictly off your Pre-Rank Draft list and Excluded Players list or by selecting the best available player at an open position of need on your roster. Select a day and time for your Autopick Draft and that is all you need to produce a league full of fantasy teams for each owner to manage as they see fit.

Draft Formats

STANDARD

Leagues with a standard draft format rely on a draft order with a specified time limit per pick to draft a team of players.

AUCTION

Leagues with an auction draft format rely on player nominations and an open bidding system to draft a team of players.

Head over to NFL.com to sign up today!

FANTASY FOOTBALL EXPERT TIPS WITH NFL.COM'S MICHAEL FABIANO

Michael Fabiano is an award-winning fantasy football author for NFL.com

TOP 5 MUST-HAVE PLAYERS

5 RANDALL COBB (WR), GREEN BAY PACKERS
4 PERCY HARVIN (WR), SEATTLE SEAHAWKS
3 C.J. SPILLER (RB), BUFFALO BILLS
2 TRENT RICHARDSON (RB), CLEVELAND BROWNS
1 ANDREW LUCK (QB), INDIANAPOLIS COLTS

5 RANDALL COBB (WR), GREEN BAY PACKERS

With Greg Jennings now a member of the Minnesota Vikings and superstar quarterback Aaron Rodgers slinging him the football, Cobb is in line to reach the next level of fantasy stardom this season. In fact, I have Cobb ranked in the top 10 at his position for the 2013 campaign. Don't be surprised to see the upstart receiver out of Kentucky come off the board in the second or third round of drafts as a borderline number one or two fantasy wideout.

4 PERCY HARVIN (WR), SEATTLE SEAHAWKS

One of the most versatile wide receivers in the league, Harvin has the tools and potential to develop into one of the top fantasy players at his position in 2013. Now a member of the Seahawks and joining what is already a prolific offensive attack, he'll be in a great position to succeed with the talented Wilson under center. The Florida product will be worth as much as a second- or third-round selection in all standard leagues this upcoming season.

3 C.J. SPILLER (RB), BUFFALO BILLS

Spiller made an impact for fantasy leaguers in 2012, posting career-best totals across the board despite starting just nine games. The Clemson product will be in a position to improve on those totals this season, as he'll see more touches out of the backfield under new coach Doug Marrone. Like Richardson, Spiller has the tools to finish among the five best running backs in fantasy land. He won't make it out of the first 10–12 overall picks in 2013.

2 TRENT RICHARDSON (RB), CLEVELAND BROWNS

Richardson was a member of my "Fantasy Man Crush" list last season, and he promptly went out and posted solid rookie totals. That was just the tip of the iceberg for this fantasy monster, though, as the Browns' offensive centerpiece is a great bet to improve on his yardage totals while also finding the end zone 10–12 times. Richardson could easily be a top-five fantasy runner this season, making him worth a first-round selection.

1 ANDREW LUCK (QB), INDIANAPOLIS COLTS

Luck finished ninth in fantasy points among quarterbacks in 2012, but he wasn't at all consistent. In fact, he failed to score at least 16 fantasy points in seven of his 16 starts. I think that percentage will improve in 2013, as Luck is an intelligent and accurate signal-caller who now has one full season of NFL experience under his belt. He's a virtual lock to become a fantasy superstar and could be a top-five quarterback in 2013.

TOP 5 SLEEPERS

5 KENDALL WRIGHT (WR), TENNESSEE TITANS
4 DANARIO ALEXANDER (WR), SAN DIEGO CHARGERS
3 DENNIS PITTA (TE), BALTIMORE RAVENS
2 DAVID WILSON (RB), NEW YORK GIANTS
1 LAMAR MILLER (RB), MIAMI DOLPHINS

5 KENDALL WRIGHT (WR), TENNESSEE TITANS

Wright finished just 55th among wide receivers based on fantasy points in standard leagues last year, but his 64 receptions were tied for the most among all rookie wideouts. With a full pro season and five starts on his NFL résumé, the Baylor product will now be in line to see additional work in the Titans passing attack moving forward. Aside from Kenny Britt, there won't be a better option in the pass attack for quarterback Jake Locker in 2013.

4 DANARIO ALEXANDER (WR), SAN DIEGO CHARGERS

Alexander recorded 37 catches, 658 yards and seven touchdowns during a nine-game stretch as a member of the Chargers last season. Project those totals over a full 16 games, and Alexander would have ranked among the top 15 players at his position based on fantasy points. While he has had multiple knee injuries during his young career, the Missouri product clearly has a rapport with Philip Rivers and some upside for fantasy leaguers.

3 DENNIS PITTA (TE), BALTIMORE RAVENS

Pitta wasn't at all consistent in the stat sheets last season, but he finished on a high note with four touchdowns in the final five games of the fantasy season. He was also a superstar during the Ravens run to the Super Bowl, finding the end zone in three of the team's four postseason contests. With Anquan Boldin now out of the picture, look for Pitta to see an even greater role in the offensive attack. He's a viable No. 1 fantasy tight end.

2 DAVID WILSON (RB), NEW YORK GIANTS

Wilson became an instant sleeper this off-season when the Giants decided to part ways with veteran starter Ahmad Bradshaw. The move left Wilson, a second-year runner out of Virginia Tech, as the top runner on the depth chart for coach Tom Coughlin. While he will lose some work to Andre Brown, Wilson should still lead the team in backfield touches. The explosive runner has 1,000-yard potential and is a potential number two fantasy running back.

1 LAMAR MILLER (RB), MIAMI DOLPHINS

Miller carried the football a mere 51 times as a rookie, but he showed some flashes of potential with a solid 4.9-yards-per-carry average. With Reggie Bush now in Detroit, the Miami (FL) product is in a great spot to take over the number one role in the backfield for coach Joe Philbin. He also has the best schedule among running backs based on fantasy points for 2013. In a best-case scenario, Miller could turn into a legitimate number two fantasy runner.

TOP 5 OVERRATED PLAYERS

5 BENJARVUS GREEN-ELLIS (RB), CINCINNATI BENGALS
4 JOE FLACCO (QB), BALTIMORE RAVENS
3 GREG JENNINGS (WR), MINNESOTA VIKINGS
2 RYAN MATHEWS (RB), SAN DIEGO CHARGERS
1 DESEAN JACKSON (WR), PHILADELPHIA EAGLES

5 BENJARVUS GREEN-ELLIS (RB), CINCINNATI BENGALS

Green-Ellis finished among the 20 best running backs in fantasy football last season, rushing for 1,094 yards and six touchdowns. Unfortunately, the addition of rookie runner Giovani Bernard means that a decrease in his overall touches could be imminent. In fact, the Law Firm is almost certain to lose work on third downs and in passing situations. Bernard is talented enough to see some time in early-down situations as well.

4 JOE FLACCO (QB), BALTIMORE RAVENS

Flacco was outstanding in the 2012 postseason and earned Super Bowl XLVII MVP honors for his impressive performance against the San Francisco 49ers. That will prompt countless fantasy football owners to reach for him in 2013 drafts. Just keep in mind that during the regular season, the veteran was just 14th in fantasy points at his position and was awful on the road. Don't be fooled—he's still a fantasy reserve at a very deep position.

3 GREG JENNINGS (WR), MINNESOTA VIKINGS

Jennings is going to get more than his share of targets in Minnesota's passing game, but the downgrade from Aaron Rodgers to Christian Ponder at the quarterback position is enormous. In fact, it's hard to see him finishing anywhere near the top 12 wideouts based on fantasy points—that's something he did quite often in Green Bay. Jennings should now be seen as a number three fantasy wideout in drafts, so make sure not to reach for him before Round 5.

2 RYAN MATHEWS (RB), SAN DIEGO CHARGERS

I have been on the Mathews bandwagon ever since he entered the NFL, and he's been a major disappointment in two of his first three pro seasons. He's had problems with injuries—he had more broken collarbones (2) than touchdowns (1) last season—and the addition of Danny Woodhead is a virtual guarantee that he won't be on the field on third downs. While the addition of new coach Mike McCoy could be a positive, Mathews is still only a flex starter now.

1 DESEAN JACKSON (WR), PHILADELPHIA EAGLES

The presence of new coach Chip Kelly and his dynamic offensive attack could help Jackson reclaim his role as a viable fantasy starter, but I'm still pretty skeptical. His yardage and touchdown totals have dropped in each of the last three seasons, and Jackson hasn't played in a full 16 games since his rookie campaign. Simply put, Jackson shouldn't be reached for in drafts based on his name alone—he's just a number three wide receiver.

TOP 5 ROOKIES

5 GIOVANI BERNARD (RB), CINCINNATI BENGALS
4 TAVON AUSTIN (WR), ST. LOUIS RAMS
3 EDDIE LACY (RB), GREEN BAY PACKERS
2 LE'VEON BELL (RB), PITTSBURGH STEELERS
1 MONTEE BALL (RB), DENVER BRONCOS

5 GIOVANI BERNARD (RB), CINCINNATI BENGALS

Bernard isn't in the best position to succeed on a statistical level, as the Bengals still have BenJarvus Green-Ellis as the incumbent starter in their backfield mix. However, the North Carolina product should still get enough work to warrant fantasy draft consideration. An explosive runner with terrific skills as a pass catcher, Bernard will be the lightning to Green-Ellis's thunder in what looks like a committee situation. He'll be worth a look in the late rounds.

4 TAVON AUSTIN (WR), ST. LOUIS RAMS

Despite his small stature (5'8", 174 pounds), Austin proved to be a major playmaker at the collegiate level. Compared to Percy Harvin for his versatile skill set, he'll have a chance to start right out of the gate with Danny Amendola (Patriots) and Brandon Gibson (Dolphins) no longer in the pass attack. Fantasy leaguers shouldn't expect him to make an enormous impact as a rookie, but he's certainly worth a look as a number four or five fantasy wideout in most standard leagues.

3 EDDIE LACY (RB), GREEN BAY PACKERS

Lacy has the tools to be the top-scoring rookie in 2013, and he'll be drafted as a borderline number two or three fantasy runner in most leagues. There are some red flags to consider, though. First, a lot of teams passed on him in the draft due to his health and a questionable work ethic. Second, the Packers also drafted Johnathan Franklin—that could signal a potential committee situation. Third, this offense will continue to be a pass-first unit with Aaron Rodgers at the helm.

2 LE'VEON BELL (RB), PITTSBURGH STEELERS

Bell isn't the most talented running back in the 2013 class, but no other player at his position has a better chance to produce right out of the gate. He's a nice fit for the offensive attack of coordinator Todd Haley, as Bell is a strong pass catcher despite his bruising frame. With little competition at the position—Jonathan Dwyer and Isaac Redman are more suitable for lesser roles—Bell should start in Week 1. He has the upside to be a solid number two fantasy runner.

1 MONTEE BALL (RB), DENVER BRONCOS

Ball has entered what could be a tremendous situation in Denver. With Knowshon Moreno coming off an injury, the rookie will be in a great position to start in an offense that has a ton of firepower.

Last season, we saw an emergence of rookie HB's who performed well when given a chance like the Redskins Alfred Morris. Defenses will keep a special eye on QB Peyton Manning, so ball should get plenty of runs if the defense is too focused on the pass. Ball is a special runner with upside on the field and in fantasy land.

TOP 5 WAIVER SECRETS

- 5 PLAY THE DEFENSIVE MATCHUPS
- 4 HOARD RBS
- 3 LOOK AHEAD AND PROJECT VALUES
- 2 BE QUICK BUT NOT HASTY
- 1 CHECK THE WAIVER WIRE DAILY

5 PLAY THE DEFENSIVE MATCHUPS

Just because you drafted a defense doesn't mean you need to stick with that unit all season long—especially if it's not performing up to par. In fact, it makes sense to play the matchups on a week-to-week basis if you aren't lucky enough to land one of the better defensive units in fantasy football. Case in point: There was a stretch last season when, no matter the defense, fantasy points were being scored in abundance when facing the Arizona Cardinals.

4 HOARD RBS

Running backs come at a premium—that's why you see so many of them picked in the first round and over the first five rounds. In an effort to gain an edge over the competition—and valuable bargaining chips for potential trades—don't be afraid to grab runners with upside coming off good performances—even if you don't have a need at the position. I'd rather carry five backs than have a second tight end, kicker, or defense sitting on my fantasy bench.

3 LOOK AHEAD AND PROJECT VALUES

You always want to be one step ahead of the competition, right? Well, part of that includes looking ahead to what might happen or is likely to happen based on current events. If Eddie Lacy is struggling to make plays in the backfield for the Packers, well, it makes sense to go out and grab Johnathan Franklin if he's a free agent. Are the targets of Jon Baldwin starting to increase in Kansas City? Make a waiver claim for him if you need a wide receiver.

2 BE QUICK BUT NOT HASTY

If a player comes out of nowhere to produce a nice stat line in the first few weeks of the season, it makes sense to put in a waiver claim—as long as you think it wasn't a one-time performance. However, you never want to add a player in favor of dropping a struggling player you drafted in the early to middle rounds. If you think someone else will immediately put in a claim for a player you're considering dropping, find someone else to release.

1 CHECK THE WAIVER WIRE DAILY

A lot of people have busy lives and might not have time to go online each day, but checking the transactions wire often is good fantasy business. You never know when one of your fellow owners might make a quick move to drop an underachieving player who has no business being a free agent. I can't tell you the number of times I've looked at the wire and was shocked to see a free agent who could help me win a championship sitting there unclaimed.

TOP 5 DRAFT DAY TIPS

5 GO WITH UPSIDE RATHER THAN "NAME VALUE"
4 FILL YOUR OFFENSIVE SKILL POSITIONS FIRST
3 FOLLOW THE FLOW OF THE DRAFT
2 FOCUS ON HBS AND WRS EARLY
1 WAIT TO DRAFT YOUR STARTING QB

5 GO WITH UPSIDE RATHER THAN "NAME VALUE"

It was nice to have guys like Philip Rivers, DeAngelo Williams, and Anquan Boldin in your starting fantasy lineup a few years back, but that was then and this is now. And if you want to win now, you need to focus on players with upside instead those who have already reached their statistical ceiling. Players like Andy Dalton, Chris Ivory, Lamar Miller, Emmanuel Sanders, Antonio Brown, and Tavon Austin, all fit the bill heading into the 2013 season.

4 FILL YOUR OFFENSIVE SKILL POSITIONS FIRST

It happens all the time—someone in your league takes a defense in the middle rounds and starts an almost inevitable run at the position. A lot of defenses (and kickers for that matter) can be interchangeable, though, so it makes more sense to focus on the important offensive skill position players. Go ahead and grab some potential sleepers and deep sleepers that could bear fantasy fruit during the course of the regular season.

3 FOLLOW THE FLOW OF THE DRAFT

You should always try to stick with your draft strategy, but there will be times when you'll have to call an audible. If you decide to wait on a quarterback until Round 8, for example, but your fellow owners are picking signal-callers fast and furious, well, maybe you'll have to target the position in Round 6 or 7. On the flip side, you should wait to grab a quarterback until after Round 8 if your fellow owners are waiting on the position too.

2 FOCUS ON HBS AND WRS EARLY

The running back and wide receiver spots have definitely increased in terms of depth after the 2012 campaign, but it's still not on the same level as the quarterbacks. As a result, it's a good idea to focus on backs and wideouts early and often in an effort to gain depth at each of those positions. In fact, it makes a lot of sense to draft at least two or even three players from each position before you even consider picking up a quarterback.

1 WAIT TO DRAFT YOUR STARTING QB

Nine of the top 10 fantasy scorers last season were quarterbacks, so you will not be short on a viable starter at what is a ridiculously deep position. In fact, I can almost guarantee you that signal-callers like Matt Ryan, Tony Romo, and Matthew Stafford will be on the board after Round 8. You might even be able to get someone like Andrew Luck, Colin Kaepernick, or Robert Griffin III in the fifth or sixth round. There are plenty of good options.

TOP 5 AUCTION DRAFT TIPS

5 DON'T NOMINATE SOMEONE YOU DON'T WANT
4 WAIT ISN'T JUST A WHITE LION SONG FROM THE '80S
3 HAVE A POSITIONAL AUCTION BUDGET IN PLACE
2 DON'T BE AFRAID TO SET THE MARKET QUICKLY
1 HAVE A LIST OF PLAYERS AND DOLLAR VALUES

5 DON'T NOMINATE SOMEONE YOU DON'T WANT

If you absolutely believe that Alfred Morris is going to be a bust this season, don't nominate him—at least not for any real portion of your budget. Some owners try to get too clever and nominate a player they're down on hoping that the rest of the league will bid him up for big bucks. However, I can't tell you how many times I've seen that owner get stuck with that player in the end. Don't over-think things—be smart and always make sensible bids.

4 WAIT ISN'T JUST A WHITE LION SONG FROM THE '80S

OK, I admit to being a fan of the glam bands from back in my youth. But you shou learn Patience (Guns 'N' Roses) when it comes to auction drafts. While you want to be aggressive in trying to add the players you have targeted, it also makes a lo of sense to hold back part of your funds to land the inevitable bargains that will b Free (Stryper) at the auction's end when the rest of the owners have blown much their budget.

3 HAVE A POSITIONAL AUCTION BUDGET IN PLACE

You need to have a sense of what kind of fantasy dollars you're going to spend per position. To start, you should have no more than a few dollars ($2–5) allotted to a kicker and defense. Of course, the two positions you'll spend the most on are running backs and wide receivers—just be sure you don't blow a huge part of your budget on one or two players at those positions and leave yourself with little money to fill out your entire roster.

2 DON'T BE AFRAID TO SET THE MARKET QUICKLY

Remember the days when auction draft advice began with "nominate players you *don't* want first"? It seems like everyone enters an auction with that philosophy, so go against the grain and put a player out there you're actually willing to own for the right price. If you think Matt Ryan could be a steal for $15, nominate him at that price. Who knows—the other owners in your league might have tight purse strings at the start of the auction.

1 HAVE A LIST OF PLAYERS AND DOLLAR VALUES

You can't go into an auction blind—you need to have a cheat sheet with tiers of players you like/dislike along with the amount you're willing to spend to acquire them. NFL.com auction values are based on a $200 cap and can be a useful guide, but there are leagues that have different cap numbers and, of course, different starting lineup requirements. You should also have a side list of "preferred" players that you're willing to spend a little more to acquire.

FANTASY FOOTBALL 2013 DRAFT GUIDE

QUARTERBACK

QB	PLAYER	TEAM	BYE WEEK	PROJ POINTS
	LOCKS			
1	Drew Brees	Saints	7	341
2	Peyton Manning	Broncos	9	334
3	Aaron Rodgers	Packers	4	341
4	Andrew Luck	Colts	8	329
5	Tom Brady	Patriots	10	318
	OVERVALUED			
1	Colin Kaepernick	49ers	9	302
2	Robert Griffin III	Redskins	5	290
3	Cam Newton	Panthers	4	307
4	Josh Freeman	Buccaneers	5	255
5	Joe Flacco	Ravens	8	223
	UNDERVALUED			
1	Matt Ryan	Eagles	6	277
2	Tony Romo	Cowboys	11	260
3	Russell Wilson	Seahawks	12	283
4	Ben Roethlisberger	Steelers	5	329
5	Eli Manning	Giants	9	244
	SLEEPERS			
1	Andy Dalton	Bengals	12	254
2	Matt Flynn	Raiders	7	121
3	Carson Palmer	Cardinals	9	225
4	Matt Schaub	Texans	8	206
5	Alex Smith	Cheifs	10	203

HALFBACK

HB	PLAYER	TEAM	BYE WEEK	PROJ POINTS
	LOCKS			
1	Adrian Peterson	Vikings	5	288
2	Arian Foster	Texans	8	310
3	Doug Martin	Buccaneers	5	248
4	Marshawn Lynch	Seahawks	12	248
5	Ray Rice	Ravens	8	226
	OVERVALUED			
1	Jamaal Charles	Chiefs	10	242
2	C.J. Spiller	Bills	12	236
3	Alfred Morris	Redskins	5	223
4	Darren McFadden	Raiders	7	207
5	DeMarco Murray	Cowboys	11	207
	UNDERVALUED			
1	Trent Richardson	Browns	10	212
2	LeSean McCoy	Eagles	12	212
3	Stevan Ridley	Patriots	10	208
4	Reggie Bush	Lions	9	207
5	Maurice Jones-Drew	Jaguars	9	190
	SLEEPERS			
1	Steven Jackson	Falcons	6	187
2	Ahmad Bradshaw	Colts	8	171
3	Eddie Lacy	Packers	4	163
4	Chris Johnson	Titans	8	189
5	Matt Forte	Bears	8	189

WIDE RECEIVER

WR	PLAYER	TEAM	BYE WEEK	PROJ POINTS
	LOCKS			
1	Calvin Johnson	Lions	9	207
2	Brandon Marshall	Bears	8	201
3	A.J. Green	Bengals	12	194
4	Julio Jones	Falcons	6	184
5	Andre Johnson	Texans	8	169
	OVERVALUED			
1	Dez Bryant	Cowboys	11	187
2	Demaryius Thomas	Broncos	9	176
3	Vincent Jackson	Buccaneers	5	170
4	Roddy White	Falcons	6	160
5	Percy Harvin	Seahawks	12	161
	UNDERVALUED			
1	Jordy Nelson	Packers	4	149
2	Torrey Smith	Ravens	8	155
3	Antonio Brown	Steelers	5	152
4	Cecil Shorts	Jaguars	9	146
5	Eric Decker	Broncos	9	143
	SLEEPERS			
1	T.Y. Hilton	Colts	8	133
2	Mike Wallace	Dolphins	6	137
3	Emmanuel Sanders	Steelers	5	119
4	Greg Little	Browns	10	109
5	Darrius Heyward-Bey	Colts	8	102

TIGHT END

TE	PLAYER	TEAM	BYE WEEK	PROJ POINTS
	LOCKS			
1	Jimmy Graham	Saints	7	179
2	Dennis Pitta	Ravens	8	121
3	Jason Witten	Cowboys	11	115
4	Tony Gonzalez	Falcons	6	126
5	Rob Gronkowski	Patriots	10	153
	OVERVALUED			
1	Martellus Bennett	Bears	8	73
2	Fred Davis	Redskins	5	83
3	Jermichael Finley	Packers	4	96
4	Owen Daniels	Texans	8	95
5	Vernon Davis	49ers	9	107
	UNDERVALUED			
1	Brandon Myers	Giants	9	100
2	Jordan Cameron	Browns	10	81
3	Scott Chandler	Bills	12	71
4	Brent Celek	Eagles	12	69
5	Tyler Eifert	Bengals	12	53
	SLEEPERS			
1	Jake Ballard	Patriots	10	60
2	Delanie Walker	Titans	8	70
3	Tony Moeaki	Chiefs	10	45
4	Mercedes Lewis	Jaguars	9	78
5	Joel Dreessen	Broncos	9	39

DEFENSE

DEF	PLAYER	TEAM	BYE WEEK	PROJ POINTS
	DEFENSIVE LOCKS			
1	Houston Texans		8	194
2	Chicago Bears		8	179
3	New England Patriots		10	171
4	Seattle Seahawks		12	170
5	San Francisco 49ers		9	169
	DEFENSIVE SPOTS STARTERS			
1	Dallas Cowboys		11	115
2	Buffalo Bills		12	113
3	Philadelphia Eagles		12	96
4	New York Jets		10	108
5	Miami Dolphins		6	111

DEFENSE

DEF	PLAYER	TEAM	BYE WEEK	PROJ POINTS
	KICKER LOCKS			
1	Justin Tucker	Ravens	8	153
2	Matt Prater	Broncos	9	152
3	Stephen Gostkowski	Patriots	10	149
4	Steven Hauschka	Seahawks	12	148
5	Greg Zuerlein	Rams	11	145
	KICK SPOT STARTERS			
1	Alex Henery	Eagles	12	133
2	Rob Bironas	Titans	8	104
3	Nick Novak	Chargers	8	113
4	Nick Folk	Jets	10	119
5	Ryan Succop	Chiefs	10	109

Appendix

LEGEND									
ACC	Acceleration	ELU	Elusiveness	OVR	Overall	RBF	Run Block Footwork	STR	Strength
AGI	Agility	FMV	Finesse Moves	PAC	Play Action	RBS	Run Block Strength	TAK	Tackle
AWR	Awareness	IBL	Impact Blocking	PBF	Pass Block Footwork	RTE	Route Running	THA	Throw Accuracy
BCV	Call Carrier Vision	INJ	Injury	PBS	Pass Block Strength	RUN	Throwing On The Run	THP	Throw Power
BPR	Beat Press	JKM	Juke Move	PMV	Power Moves	SAC	Short Throw Accuracy	TRK	Trucking
BSH	Block Shedding	JMP	Jump	POS	Position	SFA	Stiff Arm	ZCV	Zone Coverage
CAR	Carry	KAC	Kick Accuracy	POW	Hit Power	SPC	Spectacular Catch		
CIT	Catch In Traffic	KPW	Kick Power	PRC	Play Recognition	SPD	Speed		
CTH	Catch	MAC	Medium Throw Accuracy	PRS	Press	SPM	Spin Move		
DAC	Deep Throw Accuracy	MCV	Man Coverage	PUR	Pursuit	STA	Stamina		

QUARTERBACKS

TEAM	FIRST NAME	LAST NAME	POS	OVR	SPD	AWR	THP	THA
Greats	Steve	Young	QB	99	87	95	90	97
Greats	Troy	Aikman	QB	99	74	96	94	95
Greats	Warren	Moon	QB	99	71	97	96	97
Greats	Joe	Montana	QB	99	79	99	87	99
Greats	John	Elway	QB	99	80	97	99	96
Greats	Dan	Marino	QB	99	57	99	98	98
Greats	Otto	Graham	QB	99	83	99	94	98
All-25	Tom	Brady	QB	99	62	99	99	98
Packers	Aaron	Rodgers	QB	98	80	92	95	90
Broncos	Peyton	Manning	QB	97	60	99	89	95
Patriots	Tom	Brady	QB	97	57	99	95	93
Greats	Sammy	Baugh	QB	97	75	97	92	88
All-25	Kurt	Warner	QB	97	57	97	90	98
Saints	Drew	Brees	QB	96	65	97	89	96
Falcons	Matt	Ryan	QB	94	65	92	89	92
All-25	Randall	Cunningham	QB	94	90	87	97	86
Ravens	Joe	Flacco	QB	93	69	89	98	87
Steelers	Ben	Roethlisberger	QB	92	70	91	94	87
Giants	Eli	Manning	QB	91	65	92	90	89
All-25	Michael	Vick	QB	90	95	77	98	84
49ers	Colin	Kaepernick	QB	89	88	75	96	84
Panthers	Cam	Newton	QB	89	85	75	97	84
Redskins	Robert	Griffin III	QB	89	92	70	95	87
Seahawks	Russell	Wilson	QB	89	86	76	93	86
Colts	Andrew	Luck	QB	88	82	74	92	86
Cowboys	Tony	Romo	QB	88	73	84	90	87
Chiefs	Alex	Smith	QB	87	77	87	85	93
Texans	Matt	Schaub	QB	87	61	90	86	89
Bears	Jay	Cutler	QB	86	70	78	98	81
Lions	Matthew	Stafford	QB	85	70	77	99	80
Rams	Sam	Bradford	QB	85	73	79	88	87
Bengals	Andy	Dalton	QB	84	69	80	86	85
Cardinals	Carson	Palmer	QB	84	52	87	91	83
Chargers	Philip	Rivers	QB	84	63	88	85	88
Buccaneers	Josh	Freeman	QB	82	74	73	97	79
Dolphins	Ryan	Tannehill	QB	81	83	69	90	81
Eagles	Michael	Vick	QB	81	92	71	96	74
Colts	Matt	Hasselbeck	QB	79	66	87	83	82
Raiders	Matt	Flynn	QB	78	76	76	82	84
Vikings	Christian	Ponder	QB	78	77	72	85	78
Cowboys	Kyle	Orton	QB	77	64	78	84	81
Titans	Jake	Locker	QB	77	83	65	95	73
Bills	Kevin	Kolb	QB	76	74	73	85	78
Browns	Brandon	Weeden	QB	76	64	66	92	78
Lions	Shaun	Hill	QB	76	69	79	79	85
Titans	Ryan	Fitzpatrick	QB	76	72	81	80	82
Vikings	Matt	Cassel	QB	76	69	79	83	76
Browns	Jason	Campbell	QB	75	72	68	90	73
Chiefs	Chase	Daniel	QB	75	72	71	83	78
Dolphins	Matt	Moore	QB	75	69	71	84	79
Eagles	Nick	Foles	QB	75	57	67	92	76
Redskins	Kirk	Cousins	QB	75	63	65	85	82
Bills	E.J.	Manuel	QB	74	83	53	94	77
Giants	David	Carr	QB	74	68	74	88	76
Jaguars	Blaine	Gabbert	QB	74	75	67	89	76
Jaguars	Chad	Henne	QB	74	67	69	93	74
Patriots	Ryan	Mallett	QB	74	51	50	98	79
Texans	T.J.	Yates	QB	74	64	67	87	75
Broncos	Brock	Osweiler	QB	73	69	52	96	79
Cardinals	Drew	Stanton	QB	73	71	68	87	76
Chargers	Charlie	Whitehurst	QB	73	65	68	88	76
Eagles	Matt	Barkley	QB	73	65	54	84	84
49ers	Colt	McCoy	QB	73	74	73	81	82
Jets	Geno	Smith	QB	73	85	40	92	82
Jets	Mark	Sanchez	QB	73	69	68	88	75
Panthers	Derek	Anderson	QB	73	56	70	95	75
Patriots	Tim	Tebow	QB	73	81	72	86	71
Ravens	Tyrod	Taylor	QB	73	87	65	92	68
Seahawks	Tarvaris	Jackson	QB	73	83	66	93	74
Seahawks	Brady	Quinn	QB	73	70	71	86	76
Steelers	Bruce	Gradkowski	QB	73	70	74	78	82
Giants	Ryan	Nassib	QB	72	67	48	88	78
Jets	Greg	McElroy	QB	72	64	73	79	81
Rams	Kellen	Clemens	QB	72	66	72	87	74
Redskins	Rex	Grossman	QB	72	60	72	89	73
Saints	Seneca	Wallace	QB	72	83	72	79	73
Saints	Luke	McCown	QB	72	74	76	85	73
Bears	Josh	McCown	QB	71	77	74	78	79
Browns	Brian	Hoyer	QB	71	65	70	84	76
Jaguars	Mike	Kafka	QB	71	63	66	84	78
Bengals	Josh	Johnson	QB	70	88	63	89	70
Buccaneers	Dan	Orlovsky	QB	70	65	70	79	79
Falcons	Sean	Renfree	QB	70	73	55	84	76
Raiders	Terrelle	Pryor	QB	70	90	52	92	72
Ravens	Caleb	Hanie	QB	70	69	67	90	72
Raiders	Tyler	Wilson	QB	69	65	46	88	79
Free Agents	Tyler	Thigpen	QB	69	75	62	82	75
Broncos	Zac	Dysert	QB	68	73	50	89	81
Eagles	Dennis	Dixon	QB	68	84	60	84	70
Falcons	Dominique	Davis	QB	68	83	59	86	71
Lions	Kellen	Moore	QB	68	56	59	75	85
Panthers	Jimmy	Clausen	QB	68	57	57	88	72
Rams	Austin	Davis	QB	68	75	50	82	77
Free Agents	Trent	Edwards	QB	68	63	70	81	79
Free Agents	Thaddeus	Lewis	QB	68	65	68	89	75
Bengals	John	Skelton	QB	67	72	63	95	67
Steelers	Landry	Jones	QB	67	55	53	92	77
Buccaneers	Adam	Weber	QB	66	76	58	82	74
Buccaneers	Mike	Glennon	QB	66	54	46	95	76
Colts	Chandler	Harnish	QB	66	77	55	84	76
Packers	Graham	Harrell	QB	66	56	70	78	85
Texans	Stephen	McGee	QB	66	75	57	83	67
Cardinals	Ryan	Lindley	QB	65	56	54	93	71
Chiefs	Ricky	Stanzi	QB	65	62	49	85	76
Dolphins	Pat	Devlin	QB	65	68	50	80	79
49ers	Scott	Tolzien	QB	65	66	50	82	77
Redskins	Pat	White	QB	65	87	54	84	69
Titans	Rusty	Smith	QB	65	62	57	89	74
Titans	Nathan	Enderle	QB	65	50	50	90	72
Texans	Case	Keenum	QB	65	70	55	81	82
Bears	Matt	Blanchard	QB	64	78	48	84	75
Bengals	Zac	Robinson	QB	64	72	55	82	73
Bills	Jeff	Tuel	QB	64	81	48	84	73
Chargers	Brad	Sorensen	QB	64	68	41	91	74
Chiefs	Tyler	Bray	QB	64	56	47	96	75
Jaguars	Matt	Scott	QB	64	82	42	88	73
Jaguars	Jordan	Rodgers	QB	64	78	39	82	76
Steelers	John Parker	Wilson	QB	64	70	69	80	78
Vikings	McLeod	Bethel-Thompson	QB	64	71	45	92	76
Free Agents	Jack	Klein	QB	64	76	49	84	75
Free Agents	Jerrod	Johnson	QB	64	75	44	94	72
Eagles	G.J.	Kinne	QB	63	81	49	83	74
49ers	B.J.	Daniels	QB	63	84	39	84	68
Packers	B.J.	Coleman	QB	63	67	46	93	72
Free Agents	Jordan	Palmer	QB	63	52	54	87	76
Dolphins	Aaron	Corp	QB	62	78	40	78	82
Jets	Matt	Simms	QB	61	76	35	87	72

FULLBACKS

TEAM	FIRST NAME	LAST NAME	POS	OVR	SPD	STR	CTH	CAR
Greats	Mike	Alstott	FB	99	83	85	78	94
All-25	Mike	Alstott	FB	99	83	85	78	94
Raiders	Marcel	Reece	FB	95	90	78	85	84
Free Agents	Vonta	Leach	FB	94	69	84	69	75
Panthers	Mike	Tolbert	FB	92	83	83	77	88
Saints	Jed	Collins	FB	90	75	74	74	78
Redskins	Darrel	Young	FB	89	73	77	71	79
Texans	Greg	Jones	FB	89	77	82	62	87
49ers	Bruce	Miller	FB	88	75	78	69	69
Packers	John	Kuhn	FB	88	79	77	70	83
Vikings	Jerome	Felton	FB	88	73	80	73	75
Greats	Franco	Harris	FB	88	90	85	84	90
Seahawks	Michael	Robinson	FB	87	79	79	76	83
Giants	Henry	Hynoski	FB	85	69	84	72	68
Eagles	James	Casey	FB	82	82	68	87	72
Chargers	Le'Ron	McClain	FB	81	78	79	67	85
Bengals	Chris	Pressley	FB	79	70	77	64	74
Broncos	Jacob	Hester	FB	79	83	70	77	84
Cowboys	Lawrence	Vickers	FB	79	73	81	63	81
Titans	Craig	Stevens	FB	79	72	79	74	70
Rams	Lance	Kendricks	FB	78	79	67	81	67
Dolphins	Charles	Clay	FB	77	81	68	84	76
Dolphins	Jorvorskie	Lane	FB	77	70	85	60	78
Free Agents	Spencer	Larsen	FB	77	72	78	61	69
Buccaneers	Erik	Lorig	FB	76	69	81	51	66
Falcons	Patrick	DiMarco	FB	76	74	73	65	73
Steelers	David	Johnson	FB	76	75	81	64	68
Browns	Owen	Marecic	FB	75	73	76	48	73
Jets	Lex	Hilliard	FB	75	80	82	72	80
Free Agents	Mike	Cox	FB	75	70	85	60	69
Bears	Harvey	Unga	FB	74	74	76	64	78
Bengals	John	Conner	FB	74	72	77	52	72

TEAM	FIRST NAME	LAST NAME	POS	OVR	SPD	AWR	THP	THA
Ravens	Kyle	Juszczyk	FB	74	77	75	78	77
Free Agents	Brit	Miller	FB	74	75	75	61	72
Browns	Brad	Smelley	FB	73	73	75	77	80
Chiefs	Anthony	Sherman	FB	73	80	78	72	67
Colts	Stanley	Havili	FB	73	80	68	82	81
Free Agents	Corey	McIntyre	FB	73	75	85	67	66
Bills	Dorin	Dickerson	FB	72	90	64	70	76
Jets	Tommy	Bohanon	FB	72	73	89	74	75
Steelers	Will	Johnson	FB	72	76	78	61	72
Cardinals	Jim	Dray	FB	71	72	70	66	65
Chiefs	Braden	Wilson	FB	71	76	74	59	74
Lions	Shaun	Chapas	FB	71	69	78	68	77
Jaguars	Will	Ta'ufo'ou	FB	70	69	83	61	71
Redskins	Eric	Kettani	FB	70	82	68	62	73
Texans	Tyler	Clutts	FB	70	69	76	58	72
Free Agents	Nate	Eachus	FB	70	84	75	70	77
Bears	Tony	Fiammetta	FB	69	81	77	55	78
Panthers	Richie	Brockel	FB	69	67	72	70	72
Titans	Quinn	Johnson	FB	68	70	67	49	66
Bills	Frank	Summers	FB	67	75	74	58	80
Jaguars	Lonnie	Pryor	FB	67	80	66	73	79
Chargers	Chris	Gronkowski	FB	65	73	67	69	73
Falcons	Bradie	Ewing	FB	65	76	59	70	75
49ers	Will	Tukuafu	FB	65	67	83	54	66
Patriots	James	Develin	FB	65	73	76	59	70
Raiders	Jamize	Olawale	FB	65	75	72	61	71
Seahawks	Spencer	Ware	FB	65	85	73	67	95
Browns	Dan	Gronkowski	FB	64	72	69	70	65
Raiders	Jon	Hoese	FB	63	72	69	70	79
Rams	Mike	McNeill	FB	63	77	60	75	67
Eagles	Emil	Igwenagu	FB	62	75	69	73	68
Vikings	Matt	Asiata	FB	61	77	69	59	83

APPENDIX

HALFBACKS

TEAM	FIRST NAME	LAST NAME	POS	OVR	SPD	ACC	AGI	CAR
Vikings	Adrian	Peterson	HB	99	97	99	98	90
Greats	Barry	Sanders	HB	99	97	99	99	93
Greats	Emmitt	Smith	HB	99	88	95	90	97
Greats	Walter	Payton	HB	99	98	99	98	97
All-25	Barry	Sanders	HB	99	97	99	99	95
All-25	Adrian	Peterson	HB	99	97	99	98	90
All-25	Marshall	Faulk	HB	99	93	99	99	88
Seahawks	Marshawn	Lynch	HB	96	90	91	88	97
All-25	Curtis	Martin	HB	96	90	92	90	98
Texans	Arian	Foster	HB	95	90	95	94	93
Chiefs	Jamaal	Charles	HB	94	98	97	97	85
Ravens	Ray	Rice	HB	94	91	94	94	95
Eagles	LeSean	McCoy	HB	93	91	98	98	93
49ers	Frank	Gore	HB	93	90	90	91	90
Bills	C.J.	Spiller	HB	92	96	96	98	88
Bears	Matt	Forte	HB	91	91	93	92	89
Jaguars	Maurice	Jones-Drew	HB	91	92	93	95	91
Buccaneers	Doug	Martin	HB	90	91	96	92	93
Falcons	Steven	Jackson	HB	89	86	88	83	96
Redskins	Alfred	Morris	HB	89	87	92	84	95
Browns	Trent	Richardson	HB	87	90	94	90	91
Raiders	Darren	McFadden	HB	87	97	94	87	81
Saints	Darren	Sproles	HB	87	93	96	98	97
Titans	Chris	Johnson	HB	87	99	98	95	85
Patriots	Stevan	Ridley	HB	85	87	91	83	79
Cowboys	DeMarco	Murray	HB	84	94	91	85	89
Bills	Fred	Jackson	HB	83	87	88	87	75
Colts	Ahmad	Bradshaw	HB	83	90	93	91	77
Lions	Reggie	Bush	HB	83	95	96	97	76
Bengals	BenJarvus	Green-Ellis	HB	82	83	86	78	96

TEAM	FIRST NAME	LAST NAME	POS	OVR	SPD	ACC	AGI	CAR
Chargers	Ryan	Mathews	HB	82	91	90	90	73
Chargers	Danny	Woodhead	HB	82	91	95	95	88
Panthers	DeAngelo	Williams	HB	82	93	92	92	93
Panthers	Jonathan	Stewart	HB	82	90	89	83	90
Ravens	Bernard	Pierce	HB	82	90	95	88	88
Saints	Pierre	Thomas	HB	82	86	87	82	97
Free Agents	Michael	Turner	HB	82	83	85	77	95
Free Agents	Willis	McGahee	HB	82	85	87	85	77
Bears	Michael	Bush	HB	81	85	86	80	95
Falcons	Jacquizz	Rodgers	HB	81	87	96	94	83
Saints	Mark	Ingram	HB	81	87	94	88	89
Texans	Ben	Tate	HB	81	90	91	86	88
Cardinals	Rashard	Mendenhall	HB	80	86	87	81	88
Jets	Chris	Ivory	HB	80	88	85	77	94
49ers	Kendall	Hunter	HB	79	91	96	94	80
Lions	Mikel	Leshoure	HB	79	86	87	83	95
Titans	Shonn	Greene	HB	79	85	87	81	90
Chargers	Ronnie	Brown	HB	78	87	87	85	93
Giants	David	Wilson	HB	78	95	94	93	74
Patriots	Shane	Vereen	HB	78	91	93	93	75
Free Agents	Peyton	Hillis	HB	78	83	85	80	78
Colts	Vick	Ballard	HB	77	84	88	80	91
Eagles	Bryce	Brown	HB	77	93	93	92	66
Jaguars	Justin	Forsett	HB	77	91	94	94	77
Jets	Mike	Goodson	HB	77	94	95	93	68
Free Agents	Beanie	Wells	HB	77	86	84	79	87
Free Agents	Brandon	Jacobs	HB	77	84	79	76	87
Broncos	Knowshon	Moreno	HB	76	86	91	90	86
Eagles	Felix	Jones	HB	76	94	92	86	76
Giants	Andre	Brown	HB	76	88	83	84	87

HALFBACKS CONTINUED

TEAM	FIRST NAME	LAST NAME	POS	OVR	SPD	ACC	AGI	CAR
Lions	Joique	Bell	HB	76	85	88	84	82
Packers	Eddie	Lacy	HB	76	87	86	88	89
Seahawks	Robert	Turbin	HB	76	93	92	80	84
Steelers	Jonathan	Dwyer	HB	76	88	84	82	86
Bengals	Giovani	Bernard	HB	75	89	94	94	82
Broncos	Montee	Ball	HB	75	86	90	86	96
Dolphins	Lamar	Miller	HB	75	95	96	93	86
Patriots	Leon	Washington	HB	75	94	94	91	69
Patriots	LeGarrette	Blount	HB	75	85	83	79	75
Free Agents	Jackie	Battle	HB	75	82	86	78	89
Free Agents	Ryan	Grant	HB	75	82	82	77	84
Bengals	Bernard	Scott	HB	74	92	91	86	73
Cardinals	Ryan	Williams	HB	74	87	93	91	72
Colts	Donald	Brown	HB	74	89	83	79	88
Dolphins	Daniel	Thomas	HB	74	86	87	80	72
Falcons	Jason	Snelling	HB	74	81	84	78	86
49ers	LaMichael	James	HB	74	93	97	96	73
Jets	Bilal	Powell	HB	74	86	89	86	81
Lions	Montell	Owens	HB	74	84	87	79	86
Rams	Daryl	Richardson	HB	74	90	94	93	72
Rams	Isaiah	Pead	HB	74	92	95	92	70
Redskins	Roy	Helu Jr.	HB	74	93	92	85	80
Redskins	Evan	Royster	HB	74	82	88	86	88
Steelers	Isaac	Redman	HB	74	82	85	78	87
Titans	Darius	Reynaud	HB	74	91	92	94	75
Vikings	Toby	Gerhart	HB	74	85	81	86	77
Bills	Tashard	Choice	HB	73	87	89	84	85
Buccaneers	Brian	Leonard	HB	73	80	84	81	85
Packers	Johnathan	Franklin	HB	73	90	88	91	78
Raiders	Rashad	Jennings	HB	73	85	86	80	83
Steelers	Le'Veon	Bell	HB	73	85	87	87	81
Free Agents	Javon	Ringer	HB	73	87	94	88	79
Broncos	Ronnie	Hillman	HB	72	91	93	94	74
Browns	Montario	Hardesty	HB	72	84	86	82	85
Colts	Delone	Carter	HB	72	85	88	83	75
Packers	James	Starks	HB	72	89	85	85	75
Packers	DuJuan	Harris	HB	72	94	96	93	74
Patriots	Brandon	Bolden	HB	72	87	84	88	83
Steelers	LaRod	Stephens-Howling	HB	72	93	93	92	72
Browns	Brandon	Jackson	HB	71	88	91	90	74
Browns	Dion	Lewis	HB	71	85	91	93	72
Giants	Ryan	Torain	HB	71	83	84	75	86
Lions	Jahvid	Best	HB	71	95	94	92	75
Packers	Alex	Green	HB	71	88	91	89	77
Bengals	Cedric	Peerman	HB	70	92	90	89	73
Broncos	Lance	Ball	HB	70	85	86	83	79
Browns	Chris	Ogbonnaya	HB	70	85	88	83	76
Dolphins	Mike	Gillislee	HB	70	87	89	91	88
49ers	Marcus	Lattimore	HB	70	86	89	83	84
Rams	Zac	Stacy	HB	70	87	89	93	77
Seahawks	Christine	Michael	HB	70	92	87	82	71
Vikings	Joe	Banyard	HB	70	91	85	88	75
Cardinals	William	Powell	HB	69	85	90	88	75
Chiefs	Shaun	Draughn	HB	69	81	87	87	77
Cowboys	Joseph	Randle	HB	69	88	90	87	79
Cowboys	Phillip	Tanner	HB	69	86	90	85	80
Giants	Da'Rel	Scott	HB	69	96	94	87	71
Jets	Joe	McKnight	HB	69	93	94	94	65
Panthers	Kenjon	Barner	HB	69	93	95	92	73
Ravens	Anthony	Allen	HB	69	84	82	78	90
Titans	Jalen	Parmele	HB	69	84	89	83	83
Texans	Deji	Karim	HB	69	90	93	92	74
Free Agents	Curtis	Brinkley	HB	69	87	91	89	76
Bengals	Rex	Burkhead	HB	68	80	86	87	79
Bengals	Daniel	Herron	HB	68	83	89	85	82
Buccaneers	Mike	James	HB	68	87	84	89	83
Cardinals	Stepfan	Taylor	HB	68	82	85	81	86
Dolphins	Marcus	Thigpen	HB	68	92	94	92	71
49ers	Anthony	Dixon	HB	68	81	82	77	86
Panthers	Tauren	Poole	HB	68	85	90	80	75
Raiders	Taiwan	Jones	HB	68	97	95	92	69
Raiders	Jeremy	Stewart	HB	68	84	87	88	83
Ravens	Bobby	Rainey	HB	68	86	91	92	77
Ravens	Damien	Berry	HB	68	83	87	86	92
Redskins	Keiland	Williams	HB	68	82	84	83	76
Saints	Travaris	Cadet	HB	68	85	91	90	75
Texans	Ray	Graham	HB	68	84	93	96	87
Free Agents	Jamie	Harper	HB	68	85	91	84	81
Bears	Armando	Allen	HB	67	84	91	87	75
Cardinals	Alfonso	Smith	HB	67	93	87	85	75
Cardinals	Andre	Ellington	HB	67	91	93	92	73
Eagles	Chris	Polk	HB	67	88	77	84	86
Jaguars	Denard	Robinson	HB	67	92	96	95	73
Raiders	Latavius	Murray	HB	67	93	87	84	95
Steelers	Baron	Batch	HB	67	86	85	85	73
Texans	Cierre	Wood	HB	67	89	90	87	76
Free Agents	Kregg	Lumpkin	HB	67	87	89	87	69
Free Agents	Kahlil	Bell	HB	67	85	87	83	73
Bills	Zach	Brown	HB	66	79	86	78	84
Buccaneers	Michael	Smith	HB	66	95	94	91	75
Chiefs	Knile	Davis	HB	66	94	88	83	67
Chiefs	Cyrus	Gray	HB	66	92	93	84	74
Jaguars	Jonathan	Grimes	HB	66	86	92	85	76
Jaguars	Jordan	Todman	HB	66	94	91	90	73
Lions	Theo	Riddick	HB	66	83	94	88	74
Redskins	Chris	Thompson	HB	66	93	97	86	82
Redskins	Jawan	Jamison	HB	66	84	88	91	93
Texans	Dennis	Johnson	HB	66	90	86	88	69
Free Agents	D.J.	Ware	HB	66	84	86	81	69
Free Agents	Johnny	White	HB	66	86	89	92	76
Broncos	Jeremiah	Johnson	HB	65	86	92	90	72
Cowboys	Lance	Dunbar	HB	65	87	92	92	77
Falcons	Antone	Smith	HB	65	92	94	93	69
49ers	Jewel	Hampton	HB	65	85	87	81	79
Rams	Chase	Reynolds	HB	65	84	79	86	77
Free Agents	David	Blumberg	HB	65	93	89	83	73
Browns	Miguel	Maysonet	HB	64	87	90	91	77
Colts	Kerwynn	Williams	HB	64	92	87	88	74
Falcons	Josh	Vaughan	HB	64	82	86	79	83
49ers	D.J.	Harper	HB	64	89	91	92	82
Giants	Michael	Cox	HB	64	86	88	85	81
Buccaneers	Jeff	Demps	HB	63	98	98	95	67
Panthers	Armond	Smith	HB	63	94	95	87	75
Rams	Terrance	Ganaway	HB	63	84	86	76	82
Chargers	Edwin	Baker	HB	62	88	82	84	76
Free Agents	Brandon	Saine	HB	62	93	95	83	74
Free Agents	Chris	Rainey	HB	62	94	97	99	62
Free Agents	Mario	Fannin	HB	61	94	86	78	73

WIDE RECEIVERS

TEAM	FIRST NAME	LAST NAME	POS	OVR	SPD	AWR	THP	THA
Lions	Calvin	Johnson Jr.	WR	99	95	94	97	98
Greats	Michael	Irvin	WR	99	93	96	97	92
Greats	Jerry	Rice	WR	99	96	99	100	95
All-25	Calvin	Johnson Jr.	WR	99	95	94	97	98
All-25	Randy	Moss	WR	98	99	93	97	100
Texans	Andre	Johnson	WR	97	91	90	97	91
Greats	Fred	Biletnikoff	WR	97	87	88	99	97
Greats	Cris	Carter	WR	97	86	88	98	98
All-25	Cris	Carter	WR	97	86	88	98	98
All-25	Larry	Fitzgerald	WR	96	89	90	98	98
Bears	Brandon	Marshall	WR	95	88	87	94	92
Greats	Reggie	Wayne	WR	95	88	93	98	87
Bengals	A.J.	Green	WR	94	90	92	96	97
Broncos	Wes	Welker	WR	93	85	98	96	74
Falcons	Roddy	White	WR	93	89	90	96	92
Buccaneers	Vincent	Jackson	WR	92	90	87	94	95
Cardinals	Larry	Fitzgerald	WR	92	87	88	94	98
Cowboys	Dez	Bryant	WR	92	92	94	97	98
Falcons	Julio	Jones	WR	92	95	91	90	96
Seahawks	Percy	Harvin	WR	92	96	98	91	90
Colts	Reggie	Wayne	WR	91	86	87	97	85
All-25	Isaac	Bruce	WR	91	94	96	95	88
Broncos	Demaryius	Thomas	WR	90	96	92	92	95
49ers	Michael	Crabtree	WR	90	88	87	91	92
Giants	Victor	Cruz	WR	90	95	94	90	93
Panthers	Steve	Smith	WR	90	92	91	91	90
Saints	Marques	Colston	WR	90	86	87	96	92
Bills	Stevie	Johnson	WR	89	85	92	90	91
Giants	Hakeem	Nicks	WR	89	91	86	89	95
Packers	Jordy	Nelson	WR	89	90	87	93	84
Chiefs	Dwayne	Bowe	WR	88	88	87	88	97
49ers	Anquan	Boldin	WR	88	85	86	87	86
Packers	Randall	Cobb	WR	88	92	95	93	86
Vikings	Greg	Jennings	WR	88	93	91	89	90
All-25	DeSean	Jackson	WR	88	99	98	89	87
Broncos	Eric	Decker	WR	87	87	85	88	82
Dolphins	Mike	Wallace	WR	87	98	99	86	90
Packers	James	Jones	WR	87	86	87	92	86
Redskins	Pierre	Garcon	WR	87	95	94	88	91
All-25	Brian	Finneran	WR	87	85	87	90	99
Seahawks	Sidney	Rice	WR	86	89	86	88	95
Steelers	Antonio	Brown	WR	86	93	95	90	85
Buccaneers	Mike	Williams	WR	85	87	88	88	94
Eagles	DeSean	Jackson	WR	85	98	97	84	87
Ravens	Torrey	Smith	WR	85	95	97	87	92
Saints	Lance	Moore	WR	85	89	95	92	82
Cowboys	Miles	Austin	WR	84	88	87	89	89
Jets	Santonio	Holmes	WR	84	95	94	85	88
Eagles	Jeremy	Maclin	WR	83	93	92	87	87
Jaguars	Cecil	Shorts III	WR	83	94	96	88	91
Patriots	Danny	Amendola	WR	83	85	96	95	76
Titans	Kenny	Britt	WR	83	88	86	85	91
Greats	Devin	Hester	WR	83	99	99	80	92
All-25	Devin	Hester	WR	83	100	99	80	92
Free Agents	Brandon	Lloyd	WR	83	89	91	88	92
Chargers	Danario	Alexander	WR	82	89	85	85	97
Raiders	Denarius	Moore	WR	82	94	95	84	96
All-25	Josh	Cribbs	WR	82	92	97	75	90
Browns	Josh	Gordon	WR	81	92	91	84	89
Chargers	Malcom	Floyd	WR	81	87	82	87	96
Dolphins	Brian	Hartline	WR	81	87	88	88	79
49ers	Mario	Manningham	WR	81	93	89	83	94
Jaguars	Justin	Blackmon	WR	81	87	91	90	88
Ravens	Jacoby	Jones	WR	81	94	96	79	88
Redskins	Santana	Moss	WR	81	94	93	87	87
Seahawks	Golden	Tate	WR	80	93	91	83	91
Colts	T.Y.	Hilton	WR	79	95	96	85	86

TEAM	FIRST NAME	LAST NAME	POS	OVR	SPD	AWR	THP	THA
Colts	Darrius	Heyward-Bey	WR	79	97	92	76	92
Dolphins	Brandon	Gibson	WR	79	86	89	85	86
Eagles	Jason	Avant	WR	79	82	83	86	82
Redskins	Josh	Morgan	WR	79	87	88	80	90
Free Agents	Randy	Moss	WR	79	90	83	85	94
Cardinals	Andre	Roberts	WR	78	92	91	83	85
Titans	Nate	Washington	WR	78	93	89	82	92
Titans	Kendall	Wright	WR	78	92	95	85	90
Bears	Earl	Bennett	WR	77	86	88	88	80
Panthers	Brandon	LaFell	WR	77	86	87	83	87
Patriots	Julian	Edelman	WR	77	87	91	83	84
Patriots	Donald	Jones	WR	77	90	88	80	92
Patriots	Michael	Jenkins	WR	77	85	78	82	91
Browns	Davone	Bess	WR	76	85	94	90	77
Browns	Greg	Little	WR	76	87	87	76	95
Chiefs	Donnie	Avery	WR	76	94	95	79	85
Falcons	Harry	Douglas	WR	76	93	96	80	89
Giants	Rueben	Randle	WR	76	90	84	83	82
Lions	Nate	Burleson	WR	76	92	90	82	90
Panthers	Domenik	Hixon	WR	76	91	93	82	86
Rams	Tavon	Austin	WR	76	95	97	82	85
Steelers	Emmanuel	Sanders	WR	76	94	95	83	92
Free Agents	Jabar	Gaffney	WR	76	83	87	89	82
Bears	Alshon	Jeffery	WR	75	88	83	88	91
Cardinals	Michael	Floyd	WR	75	89	84	79	89
Rams	Chris	Givens	WR	75	95	94	81	85
Steelers	Jerricho	Cotchery	WR	75	82	85	84	83
Free Agents	Austin	Collie	WR	75	87	86	87	80
Bengals	Mohamed	Sanu	WR	74	86	84	85	88
Broncos	Andre	Caldwell	WR	74	92	90	75	90
Browns	David	Nelson	WR	74	84	87	80	88
Buccaneers	Kevin	Ogletree	WR	74	95	92	78	89
Chargers	Vincent	Brown	WR	74	85	92	84	91
Chargers	Keenan	Allen	WR	74	84	90	86	90
Chargers	Eddie	Royal	WR	74	94	95	77	87
Chiefs	Dexter	McCluster	WR	74	92	95	80	80
Jaguars	Mohamed	Massaquoi	WR	74	88	88	78	90
Jets	Stephen	Hill	WR	74	96	93	76	93
Panthers	Ted	Ginn	WR	74	97	96	69	88
Raiders	Jacoby	Ford	WR	74	98	97	76	88
Seahawks	Doug	Baldwin	WR	74	92	94	80	89
Steelers	Plaxico	Burress	WR	74	85	81	78	93
Titans	Kevin	Walter	WR	74	83	82	82	82
Vikings	Jerome	Simpson	WR	74	91	93	75	98
Texans	DeAndre	Hopkins	WR	74	89	87	87	91
Free Agents	Braylon	Edwards	WR	74	87	84	73	96
Free Agents	Laurent	Robinson	WR	74	91	92	78	89
Bears	Devin	Hester	WR	73	98	95	69	90
Bears	Eric	Weems	WR	73	91	94	76	82
Bills	Brad	Smith	WR	73	91	87	73	87
Chargers	Robert	Meachem	WR	73	92	87	73	88
Chiefs	Jonathan	Baldwin	WR	73	91	85	76	97
Eagles	Arrelious	Benn	WR	73	89	84	74	89
Giants	Louis	Murphy	WR	73	93	92	74	93
Jaguars	Jordan	Shipley	WR	73	87	91	89	77
Jets	Ben	Obomanu	WR	73	87	90	81	86
Jets	Jeremy	Kerley	WR	73	87	94	84	82
Lions	Ryan	Broyles	WR	73	87	94	87	78
Lions	Mike	Thomas	WR	73	93	94	80	92
Raiders	Rod	Streater	WR	73	93	87	79	90
Rams	Brian	Quick	WR	73	87	91	77	88
Rams	Austin	Pettis	WR	73	84	89	82	88
Redskins	Leonard	Hankerson	WR	73	91	85	80	90
Vikings	Cordarrelle	Patterson	WR	73	93	95	81	93
Free Agents	Legedu	Naanee	WR	73	84	85	83	80
Free Agents	Steve	Breaston	WR	73	91	92	77	91
Bengals	Andrew	Hawkins	WR	72	94	96	79	91

WIDE RECEIVERS CONTINUED

TEAM	FIRST NAME	LAST NAME	POS	OVR	SPD	AWR	THP	THA
Buccaneers	Derek	Hagan	WR	72	82	87	81	82
49ers	Kyle	Williams	WR	72	92	94	77	88
Giants	Ramses	Barden	WR	72	85	88	77	95
Patriots	Aaron	Dobson	WR	72	87	87	87	91
Raiders	Josh	Cribbs	WR	72	90	95	71	90
Redskins	Devery	Henderson	WR	72	97	92	75	83
Saints	Joseph	Morgan	WR	72	96	94	75	87
Titans	Damian	Williams	WR	72	87	83	81	84
Cowboys	Dwayne	Harris	WR	71	89	94	82	81
49ers	A.J.	Jenkins	WR	71	93	91	81	91
Patriots	Lavelle	Hawkins	WR	71	92	94	75	90
Rams	Stedman	Bailey	WR	71	89	88	84	86
Saints	Chris	Givens	WR	71	85	89	77	90
Titans	Justin	Hunter	WR	71	92	88	78	95
Free Agents	Johnny	Knox	WR	71	91	91	75	89
Free Agents	Jason	Hill	WR	71	88	86	76	87
Bengals	Brandon	Tate	WR	70	95	92	69	91
Bengals	Marvin	Jones	WR	70	88	87	82	87
Bills	Robert	Woods	WR	70	89	92	81	86
Bills	T.J.	Graham	WR	70	96	94	78	84
Chargers	Deon	Butler	WR	70	95	93	80	88
Eagles	Riley	Cooper	WR	70	86	77	78	87
Panthers	David	Gettis	WR	70	93	90	74	88
Patriots	Matthew	Slater	WR	70	90	94	74	85
Steelers	Markus	Wheaton	WR	70	93	95	79	90
Free Agents	Early	Doucet	WR	70	86	87	75	82
Free Agents	Micheal	Spurlock	WR	70	89	93	75	84
Free Agents	Greg	Camarillo	WR	70	82	84	83	82
Buccaneers	Tiquan	Underwood	WR	69	95	92	75	91
49ers	Quinton	Patton	WR	69	89	93	83	84
Raiders	Juron	Criner	WR	69	83	84	81	91
Ravens	Tandon	Doss	WR	69	85	88	85	87
Redskins	Aldrick	Robinson	WR	69	93	95	77	87
Seahawks	Chris	Harper	WR	69	88	85	82	88
Titans	Marc	Mariani	WR	69	91	92	72	82
Free Agents	Sammie	Stroughter	WR	69	86	93	81	82
Bengals	Ryan	Whalen	WR	68	84	83	79	75
Browns	Travis	Benjamin	WR	68	96	95	74	90
Jets	Clyde	Gates	WR	68	96	97	71	90
Panthers	Kealoha	Pilares	WR	68	91	87	81	78
Redskins	Dezmon	Briscoe	WR	68	82	86	79	91
Saints	Preston	Parker	WR	68	87	91	73	86
Vikings	Jarius	Wright	WR	68	91	94	77	90
Texans	Lestar	Jean	WR	68	88	87	75	87
Greats	Steve	Largent	WR	68	88	95	99	88
Free Agents	Matthew	Willis	WR	68	88	90	74	85
Bengals	Cobi	Hamilton	WR	67	87	92	80	78
Broncos	Trindon	Holliday	WR	67	98	97	70	88
Colts	LaVon	Brazill	WR	67	89	91	78	87
Colts	Griff	Whalen	WR	67	85	91	80	88
Cowboys	Terrance	Williams	WR	67	91	90	84	83
Cowboys	Carlton	Mitchell	WR	67	89	82	74	86
Cowboys	Anthony	Armstrong	WR	67	94	93	69	93
Dolphins	Armon	Binns	WR	67	87	82	75	83
Eagles	Damaris	Johnson	WR	67	92	95	75	80
49ers	Kassim	Osgood	WR	67	81	83	69	87
Lions	Chastin	West	WR	67	87	91	74	88
Packers	Jarrett	Boykin	WR	67	84	87	76	87
Patriots	Josh	Boyce	WR	67	93	92	74	85
Ravens	David	Reed	WR	67	90	94	73	85
Saints	Courtney	Roby	WR	67	90	91	74	84
Texans	DeVier	Posey	WR	67	90	87	74	89
Texans	Keshawn	Martin	WR	67	94	96	76	92
Free Agents	Ruvell	Martin	WR	67	79	84	74	87
Bears	Marquess	Wilson	WR	66	89	87	83	93
Bills	Marcus	Easley	WR	66	91	86	76	88
Bills	Da'Rick	Rogers	WR	66	89	87	75	94

TEAM	FIRST NAME	LAST NAME	POS	OVR	SPD	AWR	THP	THA
Browns	Jordan	Norwood	WR	66	88	94	75	79
Chargers	Richard	Goodman	WR	66	87	91	71	86
Falcons	Drew	Davis	WR	66	87	89	74	83
49ers	Marlon	Moore	WR	66	89	91	73	85
Giants	Jerrel	Jernigan	WR	66	90	94	72	83
Lions	Devin	Thomas	WR	66	91	90	67	88
Panthers	Armanti	Edwards	WR	66	91	95	73	87
Raiders	Andre	Holmes	WR	66	90	84	72	86
Saints	Kenny	Stills	WR	66	93	93	75	86
Seahawks	Brett	Swain	WR	66	86	88	75	74
Titans	Roberto	Wallace	WR	66	88	81	75	93
Vikings	Stephen	Burton	WR	66	90	85	73	88
Free Agents	Brian	Robiskie	WR	66	88	85	79	85
Bengals	Dane	Sanzenbacher	WR	65	85	79	81	75
Broncos	Tavarres	King	WR	65	92	94	73	89
Cardinals	Ryan	Swope	WR	65	94	95	81	90
Cardinals	Jarett	Dillard	WR	65	84	85	80	97
Chiefs	Terrance	Copper	WR	65	84	90	74	80
Cowboys	Cole	Beasley	WR	65	88	91	78	90
Dolphins	Rishard	Matthews	WR	65	86	84	77	87
Eagles	Greg	Salas	WR	65	85	85	81	88
49ers	Ricardo	Lockette	WR	65	96	93	71	94
49ers	Chad	Hall	WR	65	86	91	74	80
Lions	Kris	Durham	WR	65	87	80	82	84
Packers	Charles	Johnson	WR	65	93	91	77	94
Saints	Nick	Toon	WR	65	87	83	79	90
Seahawks	Charly	Martin	WR	65	85	86	75	82
Titans	Diondre	Borel	WR	65	88	85	74	82
Vikings	Greg	Childs	WR	65	93	91	75	94
Bills	Marquise	Goodwin	WR	64	98	96	74	88
Browns	Josh	Cooper	WR	64	83	87	76	81
Chiefs	Devon	Wylie	WR	64	94	96	73	92
Dolphins	Marvin	McNutt	WR	64	85	83	73	89
Eagles	B.J.	Cunningham	WR	64	84	79	76	82
Giants	Kris	Adams	WR	64	91	86	75	92
Giants	Jeremy	Horne	WR	64	87	86	73	86
Jaguars	Taylor	Price	WR	64	95	93	73	91
Packers	Jeremy	Ross	WR	64	91	95	69	95
Panthers	Joe	Adams	WR	64	90	94	69	90
Raiders	Conner	Vernon	WR	64	83	87	83	82
Ravens	LaQuan	Williams	WR	64	87	88	73	87
Seahawks	Jermaine	Kearse	WR	64	90	84	77	86
Vikings	Joe	Webb	WR	64	88	93	69	95
Free Agents	Brandon	Banks	WR	64	97	98	69	84
Free Agents	Seyi	Ajirotutu	WR	64	88	82	73	85
Bills	Chris	Hogan	WR	63	86	87	72	89
Browns	Tori	Gurley	WR	63	83	79	77	90
Buccaneers	Eric	Page	WR	63	87	93	84	80
Cardinals	LaRon	Byrd	WR	63	91	85	72	87
Chiefs	Mardy	Gilyard	WR	63	87	93	73	85
Colts	Nathan	Palmer	WR	63	94	93	74	89
Cowboys	Danny	Coale	WR	63	94	89	78	88
Dolphins	Jeff	Fuller	WR	63	84	78	78	88
Falcons	Kevin	Cone	WR	63	92	89	72	90
Jaguars	Ace	Sanders	WR	63	88	93	76	81
Jets	Jordan	White	WR	63	82	89	80	87
Lions	Corey	Fuller	WR	63	94	94	73	82
Packers	Kevin	Dorsey	WR	63	90	90	72	91
Ravens	Tommy	Streeter	WR	63	93	82	72	85
Ravens	Aaron	Mellette	WR	63	87	85	79	83
Free Agents	Quan	Cosby	WR	63	85	95	72	88
Bills	DeMarco	Sampson	WR	62	88	76	69	88
Broncos	Gerell	Robinson	WR	62	84	86	78	87
Buccaneers	David	Douglas	WR	62	89	91	73	88
Buccaneers	Chris	Owusu	WR	62	96	92	75	95
Chiefs	Junior	Hemingway	WR	62	85	90	74	87
Dolphins	Joe	Hastings	WR	62	88	86	74	86

WIDE RECEIVERS CONTINUED

TEAM	FIRST NAME	LAST NAME	POS	OVR	SPD	AWR	THP	THA
Raiders	Isaiah	Williams	WR	62	91	84	68	88
Rams	Raymond	Radway	WR	62	94	95	72	90
Seahawks	Stephen	Williams	WR	62	88	83	74	93
Steelers	Justin	Brown	WR	62	88	86	78	79
Texans	Jeff	Maehl	WR	62	84	89	81	75
Texans	Alan	Bonner	WR	62	91	92	74	82
Free Agents	Jeremy	Ebert	WR	62	94	87	74	84
Free Agents	Kerry	Meier	WR	62	82	75	86	86
Bears	Terrence	Toliver	WR	61	85	82	68	92
Bears	Joe	Anderson	WR	61	89	91	72	87
Broncos	Greg	Orton	WR	61	84	81	72	89
Falcons	James	Rodgers	WR	61	83	91	74	89
Jaguars	Toney	Clemons	WR	61	93	91	71	88
Patriots	Kamar	Aiken	WR	61	91	87	69	89
Ravens	Deonte	Thompson	WR	61	97	96	69	88
Seahawks	Phil	Bates	WR	61	90	85	69	93
Titans	Michael	Preston	WR	61	86	85	74	84
Free Agents	Lance	Long	WR	61	92	95	68	78
Free Agents	J.T.	Conheeney	WR	61	92	88	78	91
Bills	Kevin	Elliott	WR	60	86	88	70	86
Chiefs	Jamar	Newsome	WR	60	90	88	68	91
Cowboys	Tim	Benford	WR	60	86	85	76	86
Jets	Thomas	Mayo	WR	60	87	82	73	91
Lions	Terrence	Austin	WR	60	93	89	69	87
Seahawks	Bryan	Walters	WR	60	84	90	76	76
Falcons	Tim	Toone	WR	59	90	86	71	82
Raiders	Brice	Butler	WR	59	94	90	71	92
Cardinals	Kerry	Taylor	WR	58	87	89	73	92
Steelers	David	Gilreath	WR	58	92	94	65	87
Free Agents	Dale	Moss	WR	58	87	88	70	94
Dolphins	Brian	Tyms	WR	57	88	89	72	84
Jets	Vidal	Hazelton	WR	57	83	86	72	85
Saints	Andy	Tanner	WR	57	84	87	74	75
Steelers	Kashif	Moore	WR	57	95	95	65	97
Chargers	Mike	Willie	WR	56	79	82	72	86
Eagles	Nick	Miller	WR	56	94	93	67	85
Jaguars	Tobais	Palmer	WR	56	93	95	70	83
Lions	Patrick	Edwards	WR	56	87	93	72	82
Saints	Jarred	Fayson	WR	56	93	87	71	93
Jets	Titus	Ryan	WR	54	97	98	66	92
Rams	Nick	Johnson	WR	54	93	96	65	88
Saints	Saalim	Hakim	WR	52	95	94	66	88

TIGHT ENDS

TEAM	FIRST NAME	LAST NAME	POS	OVR	SPD	ACC	CTH	CIT
Greats	Dave	Casper	TE	99	85	87	93	97
Greats	Kellen	Winslow	TE	99	86	85	97	93
Greats	Mike	Ditka	TE	99	83	90	94	99
Greats	John	Mackey	TE	99	88	94	94	94
All-25	Shannon	Sharpe	TE	99	88	92	96	97
All-25	Antonio	Gates	TE	99	86	90	97	96
Patriots	Rob	Gronkowski	TE	98	83	87	90	97
All-25	Rob	Gronkowski	TE	98	83	87	90	97
Cowboys	Jason	Witten	TE	96	75	81	96	96
Saints	Jimmy	Graham	TE	96	85	88	90	95
Falcons	Tony	Gonzalez	TE	95	78	79	96	94
Greats	Tony	Gonzalez	TE	95	84	86	97	88
49ers	Vernon	Davis	TE	94	90	91	78	75
Bears	Martellus	Bennett	TE	88	78	82	78	78
Jaguars	Marcedes	Lewis	TE	88	73	76	80	86
Panthers	Greg	Olsen	TE	88	87	86	88	88
Steelers	Heath	Miller	TE	88	75	77	90	92
Chargers	Antonio	Gates	TE	87	81	79	87	81
Rams	Jared	Cook	TE	87	90	88	82	79
Ravens	Dennis	Pitta	TE	87	81	83	90	88
Texans	Owen	Daniels	TE	87	82	83	88	88
Redskins	Fred	Davis	TE	86	84	89	86	84
Vikings	Kyle	Rudolph	TE	86	81	84	85	77
Eagles	Brent	Celek	TE	85	77	82	87	85
Packers	Jermichael	Finley	TE	85	85	86	82	74
Colts	Dwayne	Allen	TE	84	73	83	84	76
Dolphins	Dustin	Keller	TE	84	86	85	83	83
Bills	Scott	Chandler	TE	83	72	78	83	87
Broncos	Joel	Dreessen	TE	83	78	82	86	82
Seahawks	Zach	Miller	TE	83	81	82	83	86
Titans	Delanie	Walker	TE	83	85	86	72	74
Saints	Benjamin	Watson	TE	82	82	83	78	74
Giants	Brandon	Myers	TE	81	74	77	90	95
Vikings	John	Carlson	TE	81	73	72	79	80
Bengals	Tyler	Eifert	TE	80	82	83	88	84
Bengals	Jermaine	Gresham	TE	80	83	84	79	83
Broncos	Jacob	Tamme	TE	80	82	83	84	82
Chiefs	Tony	Moeaki	TE	80	81	76	83	82
Chiefs	Anthony	Fasano	TE	80	73	76	81	84
Steelers	Matt	Spaeth	TE	80	65	74	73	82
Vikings	Rhett	Ellison	TE	80	74	78	72	75
Jets	Kellen	Winslow	TE	79	82	80	77	74
Lions	Brandon	Pettigrew	TE	79	73	77	73	78
Free Agents	Dallas	Clark	TE	79	82	79	84	74
Lions	Tony	Scheffler	TE	78	83	86	87	72
Texans	Garrett	Graham	TE	78	75	78	81	83
Free Agents	David	Thomas	TE	78	76	83	77	82
Free Agents	Todd	Heap	TE	78	80	78	85	65
Bengals	Alex	Smith	TE	77	74	73	72	75
Browns	Jordan	Cameron	TE	77	84	88	77	78
Browns	Kellen	Davis	TE	77	74	77	72	77
Buccaneers	Luke	Stocker	TE	77	74	76	72	78
Colts	Coby	Fleener	TE	77	87	85	83	83
Patriots	Jake	Ballard	TE	77	74	79	78	74
Ravens	Ed	Dickson	TE	77	83	84	79	79
Seahawks	Anthony	McCoy	TE	77	80	87	77	75
Chargers	John	Phillips	TE	76	74	80	74	75
Jets	Jeff	Cumberland	TE	76	85	79	74	72
Free Agents	Visanthe	Shiancoe	TE	76	77	80	79	82
Cardinals	Jeff	King	TE	75	69	79	75	76
Eagles	Zach	Ertz	TE	75	77	81	88	74
Packers	Andrew	Quarless	TE	75	79	81	76	67
Panthers	Ben	Hartsock	TE	75	63	73	74	72
Redskins	Logan	Paulsen	TE	75	74	82	67	72
Free Agents	Leonard	Pope	TE	75	75	74	71	72
Browns	Gary	Barnidge	TE	74	81	82	74	79
Buccaneers	Tom	Crabtree	TE	74	76	84	75	76
Cardinals	Rob	Housler	TE	74	85	89	79	81
Eagles	Clay	Harbor	TE	74	84	87	75	71
Packers	D.J.	Williams	TE	74	83	88	79	68
Patriots	Daniel	Fells	TE	74	75	77	69	73
Free Agents	Travis	Beckum	TE	74	83	85	84	77
Free Agents	Donald	Lee	TE	74	74	76	74	80
Free Agents	Evan	Moore	TE	74	78	83	80	73
Bills	Lee	Smith	TE	73	68	76	64	75
Chiefs	Travis	Kelce	TE	73	83	84	74	78
Colts	Weslye	Saunders	TE	73	73	80	76	80
Dolphins	Evan	Rodriguez	TE	73	83	75	79	79
Giants	Bear	Pascoe	TE	73	65	72	69	72
Patriots	Michael	Hoomanawanui	TE	73	67	74	74	80
Raiders	Richard	Gordon	TE	73	79	84	65	69
Free Agents	Dante	Rosario	TE	73	73	76	82	79

TIGHT ENDS CONTINUED

TEAM	FIRST NAME	LAST NAME	POS	OVR	SPD	ACC	CTH	CIT
Cowboys	James	Hanna	TE	72	88	88	73	77
Cowboys	Gavin	Escobar	TE	72	75	80	85	87
Packers	Matthew	Mulligan	TE	72	66	75	69	64
Bengals	Orson	Charles	TE	71	75	86	75	78
Broncos	Virgil	Green	TE	71	81	84	76	76
Cardinals	Mike	Leach	TE	71	71	72	62	72
Cardinals	D.C.	Jefferson	TE	71	70	76	76	78
49ers	Vance	McDonald	TE	71	84	74	79	68
Raiders	David	Ausberry	TE	71	86	82	74	72
Titans	Taylor	Thompson	TE	71	84	87	67	64
Bengals	Richard	Quinn	TE	70	69	74	65	72
Buccaneers	Zach	Miller	TE	70	82	83	72	72
Dolphins	Dion	Sims	TE	70	77	81	73	82
Dolphins	Michael	Egnew	TE	70	84	82	81	82
Jaguars	Allen	Reisner	TE	70	68	76	76	75
Lions	Michael	Williams	TE	70	69	74	75	75
Redskins	Niles	Paul	TE	70	85	82	73	81
Free Agents	Michael	Palmer	TE	70	69	77	68	71
Free Agents	Cameron	Morrah	TE	70	84	86	75	74
Bears	Steve	Maneri	TE	69	65	75	69	73
Bills	Chris	Gragg	TE	69	88	85	74	79
Chiefs	Thomas	Gafford	TE	69	72	74	57	68
Colts	Justice	Cunningham	TE	69	73	84	75	76
Cowboys	Colin	Cochart	TE	69	78	81	76	71
Giants	Adrien	Robinson	TE	69	84	86	74	67
Jets	Konrad	Reuland	TE	69	67	74	71	68
Rams	Cory	Harkey	TE	69	69	76	73	73
Ravens	Billy	Bajema	TE	69	68	76	72	70
Redskins	Jordan	Reed	TE	69	79	86	80	84
Steelers	David	Paulson	TE	69	82	74	81	74
Buccaneers	Nate	Byham	TE	68	65	70	68	74
Chargers	Ladarius	Green	TE	68	87	83	78	74
Cowboys	Andre	Smith	TE	68	71	76	66	75
Falcons	Chase	Coffman	TE	68	71	77	85	90
Raiders	Mychal	Rivera	TE	68	79	84	77	78
Cardinals	Kory	Sperry	TE	67	74	78	75	75
49ers	Garrett	Celek	TE	67	75	83	71	70
Jaguars	Isaiah	Stanback	TE	67	87	85	72	60
Jets	Hayden	Smith	TE	67	79	82	69	69
Packers	Ryan	Taylor	TE	67	76	81	72	74
Raiders	Nick	Kasa	TE	67	80	78	72	74
Raiders	Jeron	Mastrud	TE	67	70	72	68	64
Vikings	Cullen	Loeffler	TE	67	67	66	60	66
Texans	Ryan	Griffin	TE	67	73	84	76	67
Free Agents	Jake	O'Connell	TE	67	72	75	63	55
Bears	Kyle	Adams	TE	66	73	72	72	76
Bills	Mike	Caussin	TE	66	73	74	68	73
Jaguars	Ryan	Otten	TE	66	81	82	77	77
Rams	Zach	Potter	TE	66	72	82	69	59
Saints	Michael	Higgins	TE	66	75	84	73	80
Steelers	Jamie	McCoy	TE	66	76	74	69	75

TEAM	FIRST NAME	LAST NAME	POS	OVR	SPD	ACC	CTH	CIT
Free Agents	Will	Heller	TE	66	60	70	74	62
Bears	Brody	Eldridge	TE	65	69	75	60	67
Broncos	Julius	Thomas	TE	65	83	88	79	77
Chiefs	Kevin	Brock	TE	65	76	82	73	65
Falcons	Levine	Toilolo	TE	65	75	77	73	76
Lions	Joseph	Fauria	TE	65	75	73	75	76
Lions	Nathan	Overbay	TE	65	75	77	71	71
Panthers	Nelson	Rosario	TE	65	83	79	74	71
Texans	Phillip	Supernaw	TE	65	80	84	74	67
Falcons	Tommy	Gallarda	TE	64	66	73	73	68
49ers	Brian	Jennings	TE	64	69	72	55	62
Free Agents	Adam	Nissley	TE	64	73	67	67	67
Bengals	Clark	Harris	TE	63	73	74	67	66
Buccaneers	Danny	Noble	TE	63	79	77	71	67
Dolphins	Kyle	Miller	TE	63	76	74	64	67
Lions	Matt	Veldman	TE	63	75	69	74	66
Seahawks	Luke	Willson	TE	63	88	85	74	69
Steelers	Zack	Pianalto	TE	63	73	83	68	69
Bears	Fendi	Onobun	TE	62	84	86	69	69
Bills	Mickey	Shuler	TE	62	71	74	68	72
Eagles	Derek	Carrier	TE	62	89	94	73	72
Rams	Cameron	Graham	TE	62	67	72	74	77
Titans	Brandon	Barden	TE	62	77	75	72	69
Free Agents	Colin	Cloherty	TE	62	75	72	72	69
49ers	Demarcus	Dobbs	TE	61	66	76	65	57
Seahawks	Sean	McGrath	TE	61	76	84	72	66
Free Agents	Dominique	Curry	TE	61	86	89	74	54
Jaguars	Brett	Brackett	TE	60	80	77	72	64
Lions	Don	Muhlbach	TE	58	65	67	49	49
Falcons	Josh	Harris	TE	57	74	83	53	62
Patriots	Danny	Aiken	TE	57	69	72	60	50
Jets	Tanner	Purdum	TE	54	66	69	58	52
Titans	Beau	Brinkley	TE	53	76	72	58	65
Cowboys	L.P.	Ladouceur	TE	52	72	67	54	49
Ravens	Alex	Silvestro	TE	52	75	82	64	66
Colts	Matt	Overton	TE	50	70	72	46	55
Giants	Zak	DeOssie	TE	50	75	82	45	45
Chargers	Mike	Windt	TE	49	70	72	60	55
Panthers	J.J.	Jansen	TE	49	63	70	55	51
Rams	Jake	McQuaide	TE	49	70	72	59	58
Seahawks	Clint	Gresham	TE	49	65	74	60	55
Dolphins	John	Denney	TE	48	66	71	48	55
Eagles	Jon	Dorenbos	TE	45	66	72	46	52
Jaguars	Jeremy	Cain	TE	45	73	79	54	43
Saints	Justin	Drescher	TE	45	70	72	55	45
Texans	Jonathan	Weeks	TE	45	69	71	60	47
Raiders	Jon	Condo	TE	44	66	72	49	49
Ravens	Morgan	Cox	TE	44	73	74	50	44
Chargers	Kyle	Nelson	TE	43	68	70	58	40
Broncos	Aaron	Brewer	TE	39	70	66	53	10

LEFT TACKLES

TEAM	FIRST NAME	LAST NAME	POS	OVR	STR	AWR	RBS	PBS
Browns	Joe	Thomas	LT	97	94	90	91	97
Greats	Walter	Jones	LT	97	97	97	99	94
All-25	Walter	Jones	LT	97	97	97	99	94
49ers	Joe	Staley	LT	96	88	97	97	85
Texans	Duane	Brown	LT	96	91	92	95	97
Greats	Orlando	Pace	LT	96	95	92	88	95
All-25	Orlando	Pace	LT	96	95	92	88	95
Broncos	Ryan	Clady	LT	94	89	93	73	90
Jets	D'Brickashaw	Ferguson	LT	91	88	91	83	92
Titans	Michael	Roos	LT	91	94	92	85	93

TEAM	FIRST NAME	LAST NAME	POS	OVR	STR	AWR	RBS	PBS
Bengals	Andrew	Whitworth	LT	90	94	90	90	99
Giants	Will	Beatty	LT	90	88	82	86	92
Raiders	Jared	Veldheer	LT	90	96	82	88	94
Chiefs	Branden	Albert	LT	89	91	84	83	94
Jaguars	Eugene	Monroe	LT	89	90	85	89	90
Redskins	Trent	Williams	LT	89	91	80	85	89
Eagles	Jason	Peters	LT	88	96	89	96	93
Panthers	Jordan	Gross	LT	88	88	94	92	87
Rams	Jake	Long	LT	88	96	88	93	96
Seahawks	Russell	Okung	LT	88	88	81	81	86

LEFT TACKLES CONTINUED

TEAM	FIRST NAME	LAST NAME	POS	OVR	STR	AWR	RBS	PBS
Buccaneers	Donald	Penn	LT	87	95	90	95	92
Cowboys	Tyron	Smith	LT	87	88	75	90	94
Vikings	Matt	Kalil	LT	87	91	74	82	87
Bears	Jermon	Bushrod	LT	86	92	85	89	90
Patriots	Nate	Solder	LT	85	85	76	85	89
Packers	Bryan	Bulaga	LT	82	88	73	96	91
Ravens	Bryant	McKinnie	LT	81	96	92	82	92
Falcons	Sam	Baker	LT	80	86	85	85	83
Colts	Anthony	Castonzo	LT	79	89	74	75	85
Chargers	King	Dunlap	LT	78	91	77	76	85
Bills	Cordy	Glenn	LT	77	93	72	88	75
Lions	Riley	Reiff	LT	77	86	67	82	84
Free Agents	Jared	Gaither	LT	77	94	74	90	93
Chargers	Max	Starks	LT	75	92	86	93	91
Giants	David	Diehl	LT	75	87	96	87	79
Patriots	Will	Svitek	LT	75	88	77	86	87
Bills	Chris	Hairston	LT	74	87	74	85	79
Cardinals	Levi	Brown	LT	74	89	79	88	84
Saints	Charles	Brown	LT	74	84	74	86	88
Steelers	Mike	Adams	LT	73	84	70	83	88
Bears	Eben	Britton	LT	70	90	77	88	82
Titans	Michael	Otto	LT	70	86	74	74	80
Texans	Ryan	Harris	LT	70	85	75	79	76
Bengals	Dennis	Roland	LT	69	87	71	88	85
Panthers	Bruce	Campbell	LT	69	89	50	84	81
Titans	Barry	Richardson	LT	69	90	78	87	77
Dolphins	Jonathan	Martin	LT	68	84	73	79	72
Saints	Terron	Armstead	LT	68	83	46	76	85
Cardinals	Nate	Potter	LT	67	82	61	72	65
Dolphins	Will	Yeatman	LT	67	73	65	74	74
Eagles	Ed	Wang	LT	67	85	59	84	78
Bengals	Tanner	Hawkinson	LT	66	79	63	71	82
Browns	Oniel	Cousins	LT	66	88	72	85	79

TEAM	FIRST NAME	LAST NAME	POS	OVR	STR	AWR	RBS	PBS
Dolphins	Andrew	McDonald	LT	66	82	66	74	78
Packers	David	Bakhtiari	LT	66	83	51	81	85
Steelers	Kelvin	Beachum	LT	66	77	69	82	76
Free Agents	Demetress	Bell	LT	66	85	70	82	85
Panthers	Patrick	Brown	LT	65	86	55	87	84
Broncos	Chris	Clark	LT	64	86	69	85	81
Buccaneers	Mike	Remmers	LT	64	79	64	73	77
Redskins	Xavier	Nixon	LT	64	82	45	75	86
Jets	Oday	Aboushi	LT	63	78	59	73	85
Redskins	Tom	Compton	LT	63	90	61	81	76
Seahawks	Mike	Person	LT	63	79	65	74	74
Vikings	DeMarcus	Love	LT	63	90	48	87	85
Colts	Bradley	Sowell	LT	62	78	62	72	77
Giants	Matthew	McCants	LT	62	84	51	84	91
Packers	Andrew	Datko	LT	62	82	58	66	74
Saints	Marcel	Jones	LT	62	88	60	63	85
Texans	David	Quessenberry	LT	62	80	53	82	73
Bills	Thomas	Welch	LT	60	84	55	83	79
Browns	Chris	Faulk	LT	60	83	47	80	85
Cowboys	Darrion	Weems	LT	60	85	54	77	73
Raiders	Willie	Smith	LT	60	87	64	85	76
Bears	Cory	Brandon	LT	59	83	52	72	75
Colts	Justin	Anderson	LT	59	87	59	85	79
Falcons	Alec	Savoie	LT	59	79	55	81	75
Jaguars	Mark	Asper	LT	59	84	51	82	77
Ravens	David	Mims	LT	59	93	53	85	77
Eagles	Matt	Kopa	LT	58	88	52	82	78
Chargers	Mike	Harris	LT	57	82	65	75	73
Rams	Ty	Nsekhe	LT	57	85	49	76	74
Texans	Nick	Mondek	LT	57	83	39	71	75
Chiefs	Steven	Baker	LT	56	77	47	75	82
49ers	Kenny	Wiggins	LT	56	84	60	82	74

LEFT GUARDS

TEAM	FIRST NAME	LAST NAME	POS	OVR	STR	AWR	RBS	PBS
Greats	Gene	Upshaw	LG	99	95	99	99	98
All-25	Steve	Hutchinson	LG	99	95	96	97	96
Eagles	Evan	Mathis	LG	98	85	91	89	84
Greats	Steve	Hutchinson	LG	98	94	99	97	94
All-25	Logan	Mankins	LG	97	92	93	96	86
Packers	Josh	Sitton	LG	96	93	88	95	93
Titans	Andy	Levitre	LG	96	88	92	84	88
Buccaneers	Carl	Nicks	LG	95	96	86	96	92
49ers	Mike	Iupati	LG	95	97	82	99	86
Saints	Ben	Grubbs	LG	95	93	87	93	92
Patriots	Logan	Mankins	LG	94	92	93	96	86
Lions	Rob	Sims	LG	89	91	90	87	94
Texans	Wade	Smith	LG	84	85	87	86	81
Cardinals	Jonathan	Cooper	LG	83	90	58	85	87
Dolphins	Richie	Incognito	LG	83	93	76	91	84
Steelers	Ramon	Foster	LG	83	88	79	87	89
Bengals	Travelle	Wharton	LG	82	85	77	85	80
Falcons	Justin	Blalock	LG	82	91	84	87	90
Giants	Kevin	Boothe	LG	82	91	79	89	85
Broncos	Zane	Beadles	LG	81	84	74	80	79
Colts	Donald	Thomas	LG	81	87	73	88	77
Cardinals	Daryn	Colledge	LG	80	81	80	74	77
Jets	Willie	Colon	LG	80	88	78	89	87
Ravens	Kelechi	Osemele	LG	80	92	73	90	81
Redskins	Kory	Lichtensteiger	LG	80	83	77	77	72
Bears	Matt	Slauson	LG	79	90	79	86	85
Vikings	Charlie	Johnson	LG	79	85	82	76	83
Bengals	Clint	Boling	LG	78	82	73	75	81

TEAM	FIRST NAME	LAST NAME	POS	OVR	STR	AWR	RBS	PBS
Cowboys	Nate	Livings	LG	78	92	79	91	83
Browns	John	Greco	LG	77	83	72	84	79
Chiefs	Geoff	Schwartz	LG	77	92	73	89	85
Broncos	Manny	Ramirez	LG	76	93	74	90	78
Chargers	Chad	Rinehart	LG	76	87	72	85	86
Seahawks	James	Carpenter	LG	75	90	71	90	79
Titans	Chris	Spencer	LG	75	86	73	85	73
Browns	Jason	Pinkston	LG	74	90	68	85	83
Dolphins	Dallas	Thomas	LG	74	84	53	77	83
Panthers	Amini	Silatolu	LG	74	87	71	85	85
Rams	Shelley	Smith	LG	74	80	70	75	72
Ravens	Ramon	Harewood	LG	74	92	66	84	78
Titans	Kasey	Studdard	LG	74	91	72	89	81
Vikings	Troy	Kropog	LG	74	78	64	74	77
Bears	Edwin	Williams	LG	73	83	66	88	82
Eagles	Danny	Watkins	LG	73	88	50	80	83
Bills	Sam	Young	LG	72	83	72	75	80
Jaguars	Will	Rackley	LG	72	89	68	87	79
Jets	Brian	Winters	LG	72	85	61	85	82
Cardinals	Chilo	Rachal	LG	71	90	67	91	75
Falcons	Jacques	McClendon	LG	71	87	55	86	82
Giants	Selvish	Capers	LG	71	81	43	73	78
Raiders	Tony	Bergstrom	LG	71	85	64	83	81
Seahawks	John	Moffitt	LG	71	86	69	91	79
Vikings	Jeff	Baca	LG	71	85	56	81	81
Free Agents	Rex	Hadnot	LG	71	88	73	86	82
Chargers	Rich	Ohrnberger	LG	70	82	68	77	70
Colts	Jeff	Linkenbach	LG	70	85	72	77	81

LEFT GUARDS CONTINUED

TEAM	FIRST NAME	LAST NAME	POS	OVR	STR	AWR	RBS	PBS
Giants	Chris	DeGeare	LG	70	90	68	85	82
Saints	Eric	Olsen	LG	70	83	60	76	84
Chiefs	Jeff	Allen	LG	69	83	56	80	75
Colts	Joe	Reitz	LG	69	87	69	86	81
Eagles	Allen	Barbre	LG	69	84	65	74	67
Lions	Rodney	Austin	LG	69	86	63	79	74
Redskins	Maurice	Hurt	LG	69	88	68	86	84
Bills	Chris	Scott	LG	68	92	58	88	86
Lions	Derek	Hardman	LG	68	85	52	82	84
Free Agents	Mitch	Petrus	LG	68	92	48	72	70
Rams	Rokevious	Watkins	LG	67	87	48	84	83
Steelers	John	Malecki	LG	67	82	61	78	76
Panthers	Edmund	Kugbila	LG	66	86	47	87	81

TEAM	FIRST NAME	LAST NAME	POS	OVR	STR	AWR	RBS	PBS
Seahawks	Alvin	Bailey	LG	66	90	39	88	83
Seahawks	Rishaw	Johnson	LG	66	83	52	84	74
Bears	James	Brown	LG	65	85	56	77	80
Jets	Dennis	Landolt	LG	64	83	58	72	70
Packers	Greg	Van Roten	LG	64	84	48	78	75
49ers	Joe	Looney	LG	63	82	47	85	78
Jaguars	Austin	Pasztor	LG	63	79	61	81	72
Free Agents	Kevin	Haslam	LG	63	84	53	84	78
Free Agents	Desmond	Wynn	LG	63	85	49	65	60
Bills	Colin	Brown	LG	62	88	60	87	75
Cowboys	Ronald	Leary	LG	62	87	48	85	83
Panthers	Hayworth	Hicks	LG	62	83	52	81	76

CENTERS

TEAM	FIRST NAME	LAST NAME	POS	OVR	STR	AWR	RBS	PBS
Greats	Mike	Webster	C	99	88	99	94	93
All-25	Dermontti	Dawson	C	97	92	95	96	91
All-25	Nick	Mangold	C	96	92	93	95	87
Vikings	John	Sullivan	C	95	87	95	95	84
Jets	Nick	Mangold	C	94	92	96	95	87
Texans	Chris	Myers	C	93	85	92	91	83
Seahawks	Max	Unger	C	92	84	90	92	88
Browns	Alex	Mack	C	91	91	83	90	94
Saints	Brian	De La Puente	C	91	88	82	83	89
Redskins	Will	Montgomery	C	90	94	85	93	88
Dolphins	Mike	Pouncey	C	89	88	77	87	77
Patriots	Ryan	Wendell	C	89	87	89	96	78
Steelers	Maurkice	Pouncey	C	88	92	79	92	89
49ers	Jonathan	Goodwin	C	85	85	84	91	82
Panthers	Ryan	Kalil	C	85	89	88	89	85
Raiders	Stefen	Wisniewski	C	85	86	79	84	80
Lions	Dominic	Raiola	C	83	84	90	74	82
Bills	Eric	Wood	C	82	89	80	90	85
Titans	Fernando	Velasco	C	82	87	82	95	78
Rams	Scott	Wells	C	80	86	88	91	91
Broncos	J.D.	Walton	C	79	79	82	76	73
Eagles	Jason	Kelce	C	79	77	74	77	80
Chargers	Nick	Hardwick	C	78	86	88	82	85
Colts	Samson	Satele	C	78	83	79	89	83
Giants	David	Baas	C	78	85	81	82	82
Jaguars	Brad	Meester	C	78	85	96	89	86
Buccaneers	Jeremy	Zuttah	C	77	84	77	84	82
Cardinals	Lyle	Sendlein	C	77	81	82	83	83
Bears	Roberto	Garza	C	76	87	85	82	77
Bengals	Trevor	Robinson	C	76	90	75	82	79
Chiefs	Rodney	Hudson	C	76	82	72	75	82
Bengals	Kyle	Cook	C	75	87	80	87	86
Packers	Evan	Dietrich-Smith	C	75	84	75	75	73
Cowboys	Phil	Costa	C	74	89	74	79	83
Ravens	Gino	Gradkowski	C	74	85	70	75	73
Vikings	Joe	Berger	C	74	86	72	86	81
Bills	Doug	Legursky	C	73	87	72	89	83
Buccaneers	Ted	Larsen	C	73	78	68	77	74
Cowboys	Travis	Frederick	C	73	84	65	91	85
Ravens	A.Q.	Shipley	C	73	86	67	81	86
Steelers	Joe	Madsen	C	73	84	54	81	76
Free Agents	Eugene	Amano	C	73	84	74	78	84
Cowboys	Ryan	Cook	C	72	85	69	86	79
Falcons	Peter	Konz	C	72	80	70	80	74
Lions	Dylan	Gandy	C	71	85	69	75	78

TEAM	FIRST NAME	LAST NAME	POS	OVR	STR	AWR	RBS	PBS
Rams	Barrett	Jones	C	71	79	69	74	81
Steelers	Greg	Warren	C	71	76	80	74	78
Titans	Brian	Schwenke	C	71	91	60	87	83
Falcons	Joe	Hawley	C	70	83	69	81	79
Bills	David	Snow	C	69	82	64	71	70
Buccaneers	Cody	Wallace	C	69	85	66	82	79
Colts	Khaled	Holmes	C	69	77	66	76	74
Free Agents	Jeff	Faine	C	69	84	80	83	82
Broncos	Philip	Blake	C	68	86	52	82	88
Chargers	David	Molk	C	68	97	57	78	82
Chargers	Colin	Baxter	C	68	88	67	83	80
Eagles	Dallas	Reynolds	C	68	88	70	80	76
Panthers	Jeff	Byers	C	67	75	67	74	75
Ravens	Ryan	Jensen	C	67	90	52	86	78
Seahawks	Lemuel	Jeanpierre	C	67	83	64	83	77
Bears	Patrick	Mannelly	C	66	84	75	76	74
Giants	Jim	Cordle	C	66	82	66	81	75
Jaguars	Mike	Brewster	C	66	90	62	82	80
Jets	Caleb	Schlauderaff	C	66	85	66	85	75
Packers	Garth	Gerhart	C	66	85	66	76	71
Redskins	Kevin	Matthews	C	66	87	64	83	78
Free Agents	Jason	Slowey	C	66	91	50	75	78
Broncos	C.J.	Davis	C	65	90	55	93	81
Dolphins	Josh	Samuda	C	65	90	58	78	75
Eagles	Matt	Tennant	C	65	87	59	83	86
Patriots	Nick	McDonald	C	65	85	61	84	79
Raiders	Alex	Parsons	C	65	78	59	78	72
Ravens	Reggie	Stephens	C	65	89	65	87	77
Broncos	Quentin	Saulsberry	C	64	86	50	73	80
Browns	Braxston	Cave	C	64	88	63	77	86
49ers	Daniel	Kilgore	C	64	89	51	86	85
Free Agents	Ryan	Bartholomew	C	64	92	50	74	75
Cowboys	Kevin	Kowalski	C	63	83	63	82	76
Packers	Brett	Goode	C	63	73	78	69	67
Rams	Tim	Barnes	C	63	80	54	70	76
Buccaneers	Andrew	Economos	C	62	73	73	72	67
Chiefs	Eric	Kush	C	62	79	49	77	76
Jaguars	Dan	Gerberry	C	62	84	56	83	79
Texans	Cody	White	C	62	84	58	79	74
Bears	Taylor	Boggs	C	61	86	57	81	74
Broncos	Justin	Boren	C	61	90	50	85	78
Cardinals	Scott	Wedige	C	61	83	51	77	74
Bills	Garrison	Sanborn	C	57	77	64	72	68
Browns	Christian	Yount	C	57	69	62	69	67
Redskins	Nick	Sundberg	C	57	69	62	69	65

RIGHT GUARDS

TEAM	FIRST NAME	LAST NAME	POS	OVR	STR	AWR	RBS	PBS
Greats	Larry	Allen	RG	98	99	96	99	95
All-25	Larry	Allen	RG	98	99	98	99	95
Ravens	Marshal	Yanda	RG	97	91	87	95	87
All-25	Jahri	Evans	RG	97	97	88	94	97
Saints	Jahri	Evans	RG	95	96	88	94	97
Greats	Logan	Mankins	RG	95	89	92	96	87
Giants	Chris	Snee	RG	90	92	95	90	88
Broncos	Louis	Vasquez	RG	89	96	87	91	93
49ers	Alex	Boone	RG	89	89	79	97	79
Rams	Harvey	Dahl	RG	89	90	85	94	94
Buccaneers	Davin	Joseph	RG	88	92	82	91	89
Chiefs	Jon	Asamoah	RG	88	89	75	80	85
Redskins	Chris	Chester	RG	88	84	81	77	84
Free Agents	Brandon	Moore	RG	88	90	86	89	91
Bengals	Kevin	Zeitler	RG	87	91	74	86	81
Eagles	Todd	Herremans	RG	87	92	87	90	89
Packers	T.J.	Lang	RG	85	88	82	84	92
Titans	Chance	Warmack	RG	84	92	64	95	89
Bills	Kraig	Urbik	RG	81	96	78	95	90
Broncos	Chris	Kuper	RG	81	84	83	74	85
Patriots	Dan	Connolly	RG	81	86	79	87	87
Jaguars	Uche	Nwaneri	RG	80	94	83	95	86
Jets	Stephen	Peterman	RG	79	94	85	85	94
Raiders	Mike	Brisiel	RG	79	87	77	87	83
Steelers	David	DeCastro	RG	79	94	67	92	84
Bengals	Mike	Pollak	RG	77	81	69	74	81
Panthers	Geoff	Hangartner	RG	77	85	76	86	79
Cowboys	Mackenzy	Bernadeau	RG	76	98	75	95	87
Jaguars	Jason	Spitz	RG	76	86	73	82	75
Rams	Chris	Williams	RG	76	85	72	80	82
Vikings	Brandon	Fusco	RG	76	88	73	79	81
Free Agents	Leroy	Harris	RG	76	88	77	85	91
Bears	Kyle	Long	RG	75	80	49	81	83
Browns	Shawn	Lauvao	RG	75	89	75	82	79
Dolphins	John	Jerry	RG	75	92	76	93	84
Dolphins	Lance	Louis	RG	75	86	72	85	77
Falcons	Garrett	Reynolds	RG	74	85	73	81	67
Panthers	Garry	Williams	RG	74	91	71	78	74
Patriots	Marcus	Cannon	RG	74	91	60	91	86
Seahawks	Paul	McQuistan	RG	74	90	78	84	88
Texans	Ben	Jones	RG	74	89	67	85	82
Free Agents	Tyronne	Green	RG	74	85	70	78	74
Chargers	Jeromey	Clary	RG	73	88	83	87	77
49ers	Adam	Snyder	RG	73	92	77	85	75
Seahawks	J.R.	Sweezy	RG	73	80	62	75	71

TEAM	FIRST NAME	LAST NAME	POS	OVR	STR	AWR	RBS	PBS
Titans	Robert	Turner	RG	73	85	71	81	79
Free Agents	Antoine	Caldwell	RG	73	83	66	89	77
Colts	Mike	McGlynn	RG	72	88	74	81	82
Lions	Larry	Warford	RG	72	88	59	85	91
Free Agents	Jamey	Richard	RG	72	86	65	82	80
Buccaneers	Jamon	Meredith	RG	71	87	61	83	86
Jets	Vladimir	Ducasse	RG	71	93	64	91	88
Lions	Bill	Nagy	RG	71	84	62	85	77
Cardinals	Earl	Watford	RG	70	85	45	85	80
Cardinals	Mike	Gibson	RG	70	84	65	84	81
Chargers	Stephen	Schilling	RG	70	78	59	72	79
Free Agents	Tony	Hills	RG	70	85	56	75	76
Chiefs	Ryan	Durand	RG	69	87	55	82	84
Colts	Hugh	Thornton	RG	69	91	45	88	85
Cowboys	David	Arkin	RG	69	91	46	89	88
Packers	J.C.	Tretter	RG	69	89	42	75	76
Redskins	Josh	LeRibeus	RG	69	88	60	76	79
Texans	Brandon	Brooks	RG	68	94	50	90	83
Giants	Brandon	Mosley	RG	67	93	52	85	77
Ravens	Ricky	Wagner	RG	67	82	57	88	74
Saints	Ricky	Henry	RG	66	89	56	86	75
Vikings	Seth	Olsen	RG	66	85	67	83	76
Vikings	Travis	Bond	RG	66	83	54	76	82
Packers	Kevin	Hughes	RG	65	85	54	76	74
Redskins	Adam	Gettis	RG	65	78	47	78	70
Browns	Jarrod	Shaw	RG	64	86	56	85	76
Cardinals	Senio	Kelemete	RG	64	86	52	82	74
Chargers	Johnnie	Troutman	RG	64	92	58	75	79
Cowboys	Ray	Dominguez	RG	64	86	60	88	76
Eagles	Julian	Vandervelde	RG	64	82	53	82	73
Falcons	Phillipkeith	Manley	RG	64	82	54	75	72
Jets	William	Campbell	RG	64	90	49	85	79
Raiders	Lucas	Nix	RG	64	82	54	82	77
Ravens	Antoine	McClain	RG	64	81	60	81	70
Free Agents	Zack	Williams	RG	64	86	50	82	85
Bills	Zack	Chibane	RG	63	83	48	84	74
Giants	Bryant	Browning	RG	63	88	51	88	85
Saints	Andrew	Tiller	RG	63	79	55	83	76
Falcons	Harland	Gunn	RG	62	85	49	79	75
Giants	Michael	Jasper	RG	62	94	49	84	76
Bills	Keith	Williams	RG	61	93	46	92	84
Colts	Robert	Griffin	RG	61	90	49	86	83
Rams	Brandon	Washington	RG	61	85	49	77	65
Bears	Derek	Dennis	RG	60	86	45	75	66
Browns	Dominic	Alford	RG	60	88	60	86	77

RIGHT TACKLES

TEAM	FIRST NAME	LAST NAME	POS	OVR	STR	AWR	RBS	PBS
Greats	Dan	Dierdorf	RT	99	94	98	96	97
Greats	Jonathan	Ogden	RT	98	98	97	97	94
All-25	Jonathan	Ogden	RT	98	98	97	97	94
All-25	David	Stewart	RT	96	95	92	87	97
Bengals	Andre	Smith	RT	92	96	78	94	92
Patriots	Sebastian	Vollmer	RT	91	92	81	93	91
Colts	Gosder	Cherilus	RT	90	93	86	85	87
49ers	Anthony	Davis	RT	90	93	79	93	82
Titans	David	Stewart	RT	90	94	88	87	97
Dolphins	Tyson	Clabo	RT	89	91	87	91	94
Free Agents	Eric	Winston	RT	88	84	85	85	82
Broncos	Orlando	Franklin	RT	86	92	78	85	94
Vikings	Phil	Loadholt	RT	86	96	77	99	85
Chiefs	Eric	Fisher	RT	84	86	65	82	87
Rams	Rodger	Saffold	RT	84	87	79	79	75
Browns	Mitchell	Schwartz	RT	83	85	76	85	83

TEAM	FIRST NAME	LAST NAME	POS	OVR	STR	AWR	RBS	PBS
Jaguars	Luke	Joeckel	RT	83	87	64	84	87
Ravens	Michael	Oher	RT	82	98	76	95	86
Jets	Austin	Howard	RT	80	89	73	95	77
Buccaneers	Demar	Dotson	RT	79	87	74	80	76
Eagles	Lane	Johnson	RT	79	86	54	79	85
Bengals	Anthony	Collins	RT	78	90	70	89	87
Bills	Erik	Pears	RT	78	92	74	81	92
Chargers	D.J.	Fluker	RT	78	89	58	94	85
Steelers	Marcus	Gilbert	RT	78	93	69	83	91
Bears	J'Marcus	Webb	RT	77	90	74	86	80
Cowboys	Doug	Free	RT	77	82	78	82	82
Giants	Justin	Pugh	RT	77	82	60	81	83
Saints	Zach	Strief	RT	77	92	78	93	90
Seahawks	Breno	Giacomini	RT	77	83	75	85	78
Cardinals	Bobby	Massie	RT	76	83	66	87	83
Cowboys	Jermey	Parnell	RT	76	84	70	79	79

RIGHT TACKLES CONTINUED

TEAM	FIRST NAME	LAST NAME	POS	OVR	STR	AWR	RBS	PBS
Dolphins	Nate	Garner	RT	76	88	70	90	74
Giants	James	Brewer	RT	76	88	65	92	79
Raiders	Alex	Barron	RT	76	88	73	81	80
Raiders	Khalif	Barnes	RT	76	91	82	92	76
Ravens	Jah	Reid	RT	76	91	65	92	85
Free Agents	Sean	Locklear	RT	76	85	76	73	72
Free Agents	Jammal	Brown	RT	76	89	75	88	81
Buccaneers	Gabe	Carimi	RT	75	92	67	95	85
Jaguars	Cameron	Bradfield	RT	75	84	68	79	75
Lions	Corey	Hilliard	RT	75	91	72	87	84
Packers	Derek	Sherrod	RT	75	84	55	79	83
Packers	Marshall	Newhouse	RT	75	90	76	83	79
Saints	Jason	Smith	RT	75	89	71	82	76
Free Agents	Winston	Justice	RT	75	89	74	84	83
Browns	Rashad	Butler	RT	74	83	70	75	79
Redskins	Tyler	Polumbus	RT	74	85	81	75	81
Vikings	Brandon	Keith	RT	74	85	66	79	74
Free Agents	Wayne	Hunter	RT	74	88	74	86	81
Panthers	Byron	Bell	RT	73	90	72	90	79
Redskins	Tony	Pashos	RT	73	89	73	85	90
Redskins	Jeremy	Trueblood	RT	73	92	74	91	77
Steelers	Guy	Whimper	RT	73	87	72	85	70
Texans	Derek	Newton	RT	73	83	68	73	74
Bears	Jonathan	Scott	RT	72	84	71	82	82
Chargers	Brandyn	Dombrowski	RT	72	88	66	88	80
Chiefs	Donald	Stephenson	RT	72	85	59	76	72
Colts	Ben	Ijalana	RT	72	87	54	83	89
Falcons	Lamar	Holmes	RT	72	83	68	69	83
Packers	Don	Barclay	RT	72	81	65	79	76
Raiders	Menelik	Watson	RT	72	84	45	83	87
49ers	Al	Netter	RT	71	81	66	78	76
Texans	Brennan	Williams	RT	71	88	50	91	83
Bears	Jordan	Mills	RT	70	81	60	84	82
Cardinals	Paul	Fanaika	RT	70	87	68	82	85
Eagles	Dennis	Kelly	RT	70	86	68	70	75
Free Agents	William	Robinson	RT	70	83	65	74	74
Bengals	Reid	Fragel	RT	69	91	44	85	82
Lions	Jason	Fox	RT	69	78	59	69	76
Rams	Joe	Barksdale	RT	69	87	58	88	81
Titans	Byron	Stingily	RT	69	82	54	73	78
Falcons	Mike	Johnson	RT	68	82	58	82	71
Patriots	Markus	Zusevics	RT	68	80	62	73	71
Titans	Daniel	Baldridge	RT	68	86	61	83	77
Texans	Andrew	Gardner	RT	68	87	55	90	80
Bills	Zebrie	Sanders	RT	66	84	50	74	69
Panthers	Thomas	Austin	RT	66	78	62	71	74
Saints	Bryce	Harris	RT	66	82	52	75	69
Browns	Ryan	Miller	RT	65	90	49	83	80
Eagles	Nate	Menkin	RT	65	95	45	81	74
Jets	Mark	Popek	RT	65	84	55	79	77
Free Agents	Johnny	Culbreath	RT	65	80	49	74	77
Broncos	Vinston	Painter	RT	64	85	45	84	76
Colts	Lee	Ziemba	RT	64	89	50	89	82
Dolphins	Jeff	Adams	RT	64	75	60	68	75
Seahawks	Michael	Bowie	RT	64	79	52	77	73
Buccaneers	Jason	Weaver	RT	61	88	45	83	85
Chiefs	Matt	Reynolds	RT	59	85	45	78	70
Steelers	Joe	Long	RT	59	75	49	71	81

DEFENSIVE TACKLES

TEAM	FIRST NAME	LAST NAME	POS	OVR	ACC	STR	AWR	TKL
Greats	Mean Joe	Greene	DT	99	94	97	98	95
Greats	Warren	Sapp	DT	99	93	94	94	90
Greats	John	Randle	DT	99	94	92	95	91
All-25	Warren	Sapp	DT	99	93	94	94	90
Bengals	Geno	Atkins	DT	97	94	91	85	90
All-25	Vince	Wilfork	DT	95	79	98	94	98
All-25	Kevin	Williams	DT	95	85	92	95	91
Lions	Ndamukong	Suh	DT	93	87	96	83	74
Patriots	Vince	Wilfork	DT	93	79	96	94	94
Greats	William	Perry	DT	93	85	97	90	94
All-25	Albert	Haynesworth	DT	93	82	98	93	95
Buccaneers	Gerald	McCoy	DT	91	93	90	78	91
Bears	Henry	Melton	DT	90	86	85	81	79
Lions	Nick	Fairley	DT	90	92	88	71	90
Vikings	Kevin	Williams	DT	90	83	89	95	81
Free Agents	Richard	Seymour	DT	89	76	90	96	82
Bills	Marcell	Dareus	DT	88	82	94	75	82
Dolphins	Randy	Starks	DT	88	75	95	90	79
Titans	Jurrell	Casey	DT	88	84	90	83	97
Cowboys	Jason	Hatcher	DT	87	81	83	81	88
Packers	Ryan	Pickett	DT	86	76	94	87	90
Dolphins	Paul	Soliai	DT	85	76	94	85	84
Falcons	Jonathan	Babineaux	DT	85	81	89	85	76
Seahawks	Brandon	Mebane	DT	85	79	91	86	94
Free Agents	Sione	Pouha	DT	85	81	96	85	91
Cowboys	Jay	Ratliff	DT	84	82	84	87	73
Giants	Linval	Joseph	DT	84	84	95	74	92
Browns	Phil	Taylor	DT	83	72	93	75	86
Giants	Cullen	Jenkins	DT	83	83	87	85	75
Redskins	Barry	Cofield	DT	83	76	89	84	82
Colts	Aubrayo	Franklin	DT	82	74	95	83	85
Rams	Michael	Brockers	DT	82	82	84	71	93
Saints	Brodrick	Bunkley	DT	82	74	95	84	87
Titans	Mike	Martin	DT	82	80	88	69	84
Bengals	Domata	Peko	DT	81	77	90	85	78
Cardinals	Dan	Williams	DT	81	71	95	79	94
Panthers	Star	Lotulelei	DT	81	79	96	65	91
Raiders	Vance	Walker	DT	81	87	80	80	83
Rams	Kendall	Langford	DT	81	74	87	85	74
Free Agents	Casey	Hampton	DT	81	68	96	94	87
Broncos	Terrance	Knighton	DT	80	74	93	75	78
Eagles	Isaac	Sopoaga	DT	80	73	94	85	83
Dolphins	Vaughn	Martin	DT	79	85	91	73	83
Panthers	Dwan	Edwards	DT	79	76	85	83	74
Steelers	Steve	McLendon	DT	79	76	83	77	86
Titans	Sammie	Hill	DT	79	81	90	79	83
Broncos	Kevin	Vickerson	DT	78	72	88	77	82
Chiefs	Dontari	Poe	DT	78	85	96	61	86
Patriots	Tommy	Kelly	DT	78	73	93	72	75
Vikings	Sharrif	Floyd	DT	78	87	84	56	84
Free Agents	Shaun	Cody	DT	78	82	84	81	87
Bears	Sedrick	Ellis	DT	77	78	88	76	84
Falcons	Peria	Jerry	DT	77	83	82	74	71
Jaguars	Sen'Derrick	Marks	DT	77	83	78	76	78
Raiders	Pat	Sims	DT	77	83	91	73	83
Seahawks	Tony	McDaniel	DT	77	72	90	72	77
Titans	Karl	Klug	DT	77	83	82	72	73
Texans	Earl	Mitchell	DT	77	87	77	75	76
Bears	Stephen	Paea	DT	76	77	98	67	86
Broncos	Sylvester	Williams	DT	76	88	85	54	86
Chargers	Cam	Thomas	DT	76	78	96	71	84
Cowboys	Sean	Lissemore	DT	76	83	86	72	84
Titans	Ropati	Pitoitua	DT	76	74	88	70	80
Vikings	Fred	Evans	DT	76	76	88	73	89

DEFENSIVE TACKLES CONTINUED

TEAM	FIRST NAME	LAST NAME	POS	OVR	ACC	STR	AWR	TKL
Free Agents	Spencer	Johnson	DT	76	73	88	75	81
Giants	Shaun	Rogers	DT	75	62	94	77	81
Giants	Mike	Patterson	DT	75	79	77	79	75
Jaguars	Roy	Miller	DT	75	74	88	74	87
Jaguars	Kyle	Love	DT	75	74	86	73	79
Lions	C.J.	Mosley	DT	75	75	89	75	87
Panthers	Colin	Cole	DT	75	73	87	75	80
Vikings	Letroy	Guion	DT	75	83	85	77	65
Free Agents	Amobi	Okoye	DT	75	81	85	75	72
Bengals	Devon	Still	DT	74	84	82	58	84
Buccaneers	Derek	Landri	DT	74	79	85	74	79
Buccaneers	Gary	Gibson	DT	74	78	85	73	74
Cowboys	Josh	Brent	DT	74	81	87	69	77
Falcons	Corey	Peters	DT	74	86	79	72	65
Packers	Johnny	Jolly	DT	74	85	90	74	75
Ravens	Terrence	Cody	DT	74	70	97	72	83
Redskins	Chris	Baker	DT	74	72	87	67	80
Steelers	Alameda	Ta'amu	DT	74	72	93	57	84
Free Agents	Anthony	Hargrove	DT	74	81	77	75	72
49ers	Ian	Williams	DT	73	69	93	71	82
Jaguars	Brandon	Deaderick	DT	73	72	87	72	81
Jets	Kenrick	Ellis	DT	73	85	93	63	83
Panthers	Sione	Fua	DT	73	69	91	66	76
Panthers	Frank	Kearse	DT	73	78	90	63	72
Panthers	Kawann	Short	DT	73	85	85	54	78
Titans	Antonio	Johnson	DT	73	78	82	73	75
Vikings	Christian	Ballard	DT	73	88	82	56	78
Free Agents	Matt	Toeaina	DT	73	74	92	73	78
Cardinals	David	Carter	DT	72	84	82	65	79
Free Agents	Leger	Douzable	DT	72	75	83	68	82
Free Agents	Ma'ake	Kemoeatu	DT	72	53	94	81	79
Buccaneers	Akeem	Spence	DT	71	76	94	45	85
Chiefs	Anthony	Toribio	DT	71	74	85	70	72
Colts	Brandon	McKinney	DT	71	74	89	70	82
Giants	Marvin	Austin	DT	71	92	81	51	74
Redskins	Chris	Neild	DT	71	71	86	72	76
Seahawks	Clinton	McDonald	DT	71	78	83	69	81
Free Agents	Trevor	Laws	DT	71	81	85	67	78
Chiefs	Jerrell	Powe	DT	70	73	92	64	79
Eagles	Antonio	Dixon	DT	70	80	88	64	76
Giants	Johnathan	Hankins	DT	70	81	92	49	85
Lions	Ogemdi	Nwagbuo	DT	70	68	88	70	75
Redskins	Ron	Brace	DT	70	66	93	71	78
Saints	John	Jenkins	DT	70	70	92	54	91
Texans	Terrell	McClain	DT	70	79	92	58	78
Eagles	Bennie	Logan	DT	69	83	87	52	80
Seahawks	Jesse	Williams	DT	69	74	95	49	88
Free Agents	Daniel	Muir	DT	69	72	86	67	71
Bills	Torell	Troup	DT	68	68	93	61	84
Packers	Jordan	Miller	DT	68	84	85	65	79
Rams	Jermelle	Cudjo	DT	68	75	82	65	72
Bears	Nate	Collins	DT	67	71	77	66	70
Bears	Corvey	Irvin	DT	67	87	77	63	76
Browns	Ishmaa'ily	Kitchen	DT	67	74	92	63	80
Colts	Josh	Chapman	DT	67	69	89	59	76
Cowboys	Nick	Hayden	DT	67	70	88	69	78
49ers	Lamar	Divens	DT	67	70	92	58	70
Bengals	Brandon	Thompson	DT	66	83	90	48	83
Bills	Corbin	Bryant	DT	66	72	88	52	75
Broncos	Mitch	Unrein	DT	66	66	85	61	77
Colts	Martin	Tevaseu	DT	66	70	90	58	82
Falcons	Travian	Robertson	DT	66	63	93	57	76
Giants	Frank	Okam	DT	66	76	91	66	72
Jets	Damon	Harrison	DT	66	71	89	61	82
Raiders	Christo	Bilukidi	DT	66	82	85	55	77
Rams	Matthew	Conrath	DT	66	74	76	60	75
Saints	Tyrunn	Walker	DT	66	79	82	61	69
Seahawks	Jaye	Howard	DT	66	87	76	54	71
Seahawks	Jordan	Hill	DT	66	80	84	48	77
Titans	Zach	Clayton	DT	66	84	77	59	74
Vikings	Everett	Dawkins	DT	66	85	78	45	74
Texans	Chris	Jones	DT	66	72	88	52	74
Free Agents	Andre	Fluellen	DT	66	82	87	51	70
Broncos	Sealver	Siliga	DT	65	66	89	63	81
Buccaneers	Andre	Neblett	DT	65	81	78	64	64
Jaguars	D'Anthony	Smith	DT	65	84	77	55	77
Patriots	Marcus	Forston	DT	65	78	89	54	82
Buccaneers	Lazarius	Levingston	DT	64	74	87	56	78
Cowboys	Jeris	Pendleton	DT	64	76	79	52	83
Dolphins	Kheeston	Randall	DT	64	78	82	51	78
49ers	Quinton	Dial	DT	64	73	87	44	86
Giants	Markus	Kuhn	DT	64	82	86	49	73
Raiders	Johnny	Jones	DT	64	77	85	57	74
Ravens	Brandon	Williams	DT	64	76	90	41	75
Titans	DaJohn	Harris	DT	64	82	79	49	83
Colts	Montori	Hughes	DT	63	76	85	43	82
Falcons	Micanor	Regis	DT	63	76	80	49	72
Panthers	Nate	Chandler	DT	63	79	78	54	77
Raiders	Stacy	McGee	DT	63	75	86	45	68
Saints	Isaako	Aaitui	DT	63	72	88	56	77
Steelers	Hebron	Fangupo	DT	63	74	93	51	77
Lions	Jimmy	Saddler-McQueen	DT	62	74	83	51	73
Chargers	Kwame	Geathers	DT	61	72	89	46	87
Cowboys	Ben	Bass	DT	61	74	78	54	75
Buccaneers	Matthew	Masifilo	DT	60	74	93	53	67
Cardinals	Ricky	Lumpkin	DT	60	66	88	51	74
Dolphins	Chas	Alecxih	DT	60	72	71	62	69
Jets	Lanier	Coleman	DT	60	76	76	48	74
Browns	Nicolas	Jean-Baptiste	DT	58	62	81	52	84
Free Agents	Robert	Callaway	DT	58	72	85	56	71

LEFT ENDS

TEAM	FIRST NAME	LAST NAME	POS	OVR	SPD	STR	PMV	FMV
Colts	Kellen	Heard	LE	59	55	91	81	44
Rams	Mason	Brodine	LE	60	69	76	74	55
Cardinals	Ronald	Talley	LE	63	67	84	79	54
Colts	Lawrence	Guy	LE	63	68	84	74	42
49ers	Tony	Jerod-Eddie	LE	63	64	84	80	55
Free Agents	Doug	Worthington	LE	63	63	85	81	49
Bears	Cheta	Ozougwu	LE	64	74	65	74	76
Browns	Hall	Davis	LE	64	74	77	70	65
Browns	Brian	Sanford	LE	64	68	79	76	54
Broncos	Malik	Jackson	LE	65	71	78	84	48
Steelers	Al	Woods	LE	65	54	94	78	65
Texans	David	Hunter	LE	65	66	87	76	56
Texans	Ra'Shon	Harris	LE	65	69	77	79	45
Broncos	Jeremy	Beal	LE	66	65	82	85	38
Dolphins	Derrick	Shelby	LE	66	72	75	81	66
Eagles	Clifton	Geathers	LE	66	67	81	82	46
Jets	Tevita	Finau	LE	66	62	77	74	59
Seahawks	Greg	Scruggs	LE	66	74	81	81	57
Buccaneers	Aaron	Morgan	LE	67	77	68	76	64
Buccaneers	William	Gholston	LE	67	71	77	85	61
Falcons	Malliciah	Goodman	LE	67	75	84	79	53
Panthers	Frank	Alexander	LE	67	74	74	62	83

LEFT ENDS CONTINUED

TEAM	FIRST NAME	LAST NAME	POS	OVR	SPD	STR	PMV	FMV
Patriots	Michael	Buchanan	LE	67	79	75	83	68
Ravens	Kapron	Lewis-Moore	LE	67	70	89	82	50
Vikings	D'Aundre	Reed	LE	67	72	83	84	47
Falcons	Cliff	Matthews	LE	68	75	76	73	82
Giants	Adrian	Tracy	LE	68	76	69	61	79
Patriots	Jermaine	Cunningham	LE	68	81	73	82	58
Raiders	Brandon	Bair	LE	68	71	77	76	62
Titans	Lavar	Edwards	LE	68	76	72	80	52
Free Agents	George	Selvie	LE	68	75	64	64	82
Bears	Cornelius	Washington	LE	69	85	91	86	52
Bills	Jarron	Gilbert	LE	69	67	80	76	85
Titans	Thaddeus	Gibson	LE	69	82	71	72	83
Free Agents	John	Chick	LE	69	74	80	84	66
Bengals	Margus	Hunt	LE	70	85	88	66	79
Bengals	Wallace	Gilberry	LE	70	74	71	84	65
Jaguars	Pannel	Egboh	LE	70	70	78	82	64
Eagles	Cedric	Thornton	LE	71	64	90	75	52
Packers	Mike	Daniels	LE	71	70	74	66	84
Bears	Turk	McBride	LE	72	66	84	62	73
Chiefs	Austen	Lane	LE	72	74	73	62	81
Cowboys	Tyrone	Crawford	LE	72	74	80	86	57
Patriots	Justin	Francis	LE	72	73	75	84	69
Saints	Jay	Richardson	LE	72	74	82	68	55
Free Agents	Dave	Tollefson	LE	72	69	75	81	57
Chargers	Jarius	Wynn	LE	73	69	83	84	59
Chiefs	Marcus	Dixon	LE	73	64	85	75	65
Colts	Ricardo	Mathews	LE	73	71	84	82	65
Bengals	Jamaal	Anderson	LE	74	71	84	70	52
Broncos	Derek	Wolfe	LE	74	68	89	81	48
Falcons	Kroy	Biermann	LE	74	75	80	54	78
Lions	Willie	Young	LE	74	74	79	61	85
Packers	Mike	Neal	LE	74	69	89	84	54
Browns	Billy	Winn	LE	75	73	77	54	82
Chiefs	Tyson	Jackson	LE	75	67	87	75	54
49ers	Tank	Carradine	LE	75	79	83	92	65
Vikings	Lawrence	Jackson	LE	75	78	77	85	57
Jaguars	Jeremy	Mincey	LE	76	68	87	79	53
Texans	Tim	Jamison	LE	76	74	81	74	54
Free Agents	Juqua	Parker	LE	76	74	78	82	60
Buccaneers	Da'Quan	Bowers	LE	77	78	83	87	54
Cardinals	Matt	Shaughnessy	LE	77	73	84	80	51

TEAM	FIRST NAME	LAST NAME	POS	OVR	SPD	STR	PMV	FMV
Ravens	Arthur	Jones	LE	77	67	90	85	51
Steelers	Ziggy	Hood	LE	77	66	85	66	76
Bears	Corey	Wootton	LE	78	74	84	85	55
Jaguars	Tyson	Alualu	LE	78	69	88	81	45
Redskins	Adam	Carriker	LE	78	73	96	74	52
Saints	Kenyon	Coleman	LE	78	66	85	76	55
Free Agents	Ray	Edwards	LE	78	75	83	79	54
Dolphins	Jared	Odrick	LE	79	68	85	88	57
Redskins	Jarvis	Jenkins	LE	79	66	92	83	53
Saints	Akiem	Hicks	LE	79	63	82	87	68
Raiders	Andre	Carter	LE	80	76	78	56	82
Seahawks	Red	Bryant	LE	80	68	95	77	44
Lions	Israel	Idonije	LE	81	73	87	84	45
Lions	Jason	Jones	LE	81	73	86	89	65
Rams	William	Hayes	LE	81	80	73	79	63
Colts	Cory	Redding	LE	83	70	87	79	55
Giants	Mathias	Kiwanuka	LE	83	74	79	73	83
Packers	B.J.	Raji	LE	83	64	94	92	61
Browns	Ahtyba	Rubin	LE	84	59	95	85	49
Chargers	Corey	Liuget	LE	84	68	92	86	55
Patriots	Rob	Ninkovich	LE	85	74	75	83	62
Ravens	Chris	Canty	LE	85	66	86	86	68
Seahawks	Michael	Bennett	LE	86	74	87	87	55
Giants	Justin	Tuck	LE	87	82	85	66	85
Vikings	Brian	Robison	LE	87	76	81	65	92
Rams	Chris	Long	LE	88	75	90	95	74
Titans	Derrick	Morgan	LE	88	75	83	96	74
Bengals	Carlos	Dunlap	LE	89	84	81	71	94
Cowboys	Anthony	Spencer	LE	89	80	77	72	92
49ers	Ray	McDonald	LE	89	69	88	85	67
Raiders	Lamarr	Houston	LE	89	74	88	85	65
Panthers	Greg	Hardy	LE	90	76	84	95	73
Bills	Mario	Williams	LE	92	83	88	68	83
Cardinals	Calais	Campbell	LE	93	74	86	74	91
Jets	Muhammad	Wilkerson	LE	94	72	94	89	64
Dolphins	Cameron	Wake	LE	97	84	79	69	97
All-25	Justin	Smith	LE	97	73	96	84	54
Greats	Jared	Allen	LE	98	77	88	97	76
Texans	J.J.	Watt	LE	99	77	97	99	67
Greats	Reggie	White	LE	99	78	99	99	97
All-25	J.J.	Watt	LE	99	77	97	99	67

RIGHT ENDS

TEAM	FIRST NAME	LAST NAME	POS	OVR	SPD	STR	PMV	FMV
Bills	Jay	Ross	RE	57	63	82	74	48
Bengals	DeQuin	Evans	RE	60	69	74	74	55
Ravens	DeAngelo	Tyson	RE	61	69	86	76	49
Giants	Adewale	Ojomo	RE	63	74	76	79	67
Packers	Josh	Boyd	RE	63	64	91	77	49
Steelers	Nicholas	Williams	RE	63	75	83	83	57
Free Agents	Auston	English	RE	63	77	78	75	66
Browns	Armonty	Bryant	RE	64	75	67	71	81
Buccaneers	Markus	White	RE	64	74	68	63	82
Chargers	Damik	Scafe	RE	64	64	84	76	52
Cowboys	DeVonte	Holloman	RE	64	77	64	71	62
Falcons	Stansly	Maponga	RE	64	77	83	66	84
Giants	Justin	Trattou	RE	64	80	75	76	62
Jaguars	Ryan	Davis	RE	64	76	74	65	84
Raiders	Jack	Crawford	RE	64	73	68	76	44
Bengals	Dontay	Moch	RE	65	90	65	78	52
Falcons	Jonathan	Massaquoi	RE	65	74	71	87	60
Lions	Devin	Taylor	RE	66	79	67	83	55
Saints	Greg	Romeus	RE	66	75	84	85	48
Titans	Scott	Solomon	RE	66	71	89	82	56

TEAM	FIRST NAME	LAST NAME	POS	OVR	SPD	STR	PMV	FMV
Vikings	George	Johnson	RE	66	74	66	65	79
Buccaneers	Steven	Means	RE	67	81	69	82	66
Titans	Keyunta	Dawson	RE	67	74	77	69	79
Broncos	Quanterus	Smith	RE	68	78	66	88	72
Browns	John	Hughes	RE	68	63	82	67	79
Buccaneers	Daniel	Te'o-Nesheim	RE	68	75	80	80	60
Dolphins	Olivier	Vernon	RE	69	83	82	85	67
Giants	Damontre	Moore	RE	69	73	65	87	67
Lions	Ronnell	Lewis	RE	69	79	85	84	63
Texans	Jared	Crick	RE	69	68	78	81	44
Chiefs	Allen	Bailey	RE	70	75	91	87	55
Eagles	Vinny	Curry	RE	70	78	78	74	88
Packers	Jerel	Worthy	RE	70	68	82	86	49
Patriots	Marcus	Benard	RE	70	80	69	67	82
Redskins	Phillip	Merling	RE	70	71	82	76	60
Saints	Tom	Johnson	RE	70	67	81	84	64
Bills	Alex	Carrington	RE	71	72	85	85	64
Cowboys	Kyle	Wilber	RE	71	77	73	62	84
Jaguars	Andre	Branch	RE	71	81	70	86	57
Patriots	Jake	Bequette	RE	71	75	69	84	60

RIGHT ENDS CONTINUED

TEAM	FIRST NAME	LAST NAME	POS	OVR	SPD	STR	PMV	FMV
Rams	Eugene	Sims	RE	71	75	78	66	85
Bears	Kyle	Moore	RE	72	69	82	83	62
Packers	C.J.	Wilson	RE	72	74	90	79	45
Panthers	Mario	Addison	RE	72	80	73	66	83
Redskins	Kedric	Golston	RE	72	63	85	79	49
Bears	Shea	McClellin	RE	73	83	67	64	87
Colts	Drake	Nevis	RE	73	66	76	62	83
Colts	Fili	Moala	RE	73	60	82	65	74
Ravens	Marcus	Spears	RE	73	65	84	76	54
Packers	Datone	Jones	RE	74	76	77	73	84
Raiders	Jason	Hunter	RE	74	77	69	63	80
Bills	Alan	Branch	RE	75	60	94	87	54
Colts	Ricky	Jean Francois	RE	75	68	82	77	52
Bengals	Robert	Geathers	RE	76	78	75	49	83
Jets	Antonio	Garay	RE	76	60	89	88	54
Cardinals	Frostee	Rucker	RE	77	68	82	78	55
Steelers	Cameron	Heyward	RE	77	73	91	79	48
Lions	Ezekiel	Ansah	RE	78	83	84	88	82
Rams	Robert	Quinn	RE	78	83	78	90	64
Vikings	Everson	Griffen	RE	78	83	77	93	69
Broncos	Shaun	Phillips	RE	79	81	79	86	65
Cardinals	Darnell	Dockett	RE	79	72	90	85	71
Eagles	Fletcher	Cox	RE	79	76	84	86	59
Jaguars	Jason	Babin	RE	79	74	83	86	59
Jets	Sheldon	Richardson	RE	79	72	81	74	80
Seahawks	Bruce	Irvin	RE	79	90	70	95	67
Buccaneers	Adrian	Clayborn	RE	80	76	89	93	64
Chargers	Kendall	Reyes	RE	80	75	92	88	58
Chiefs	Mike	Devito	RE	80	63	88	76	49
Broncos	Robert	Ayers	RE	81	78	81	88	69
Patriots	Chandler	Jones	RE	81	75	75	92	65
Redskins	Stephen	Bowen	RE	81	69	86	85	55
Saints	Cameron	Jordan	RE	81	75	88	86	63
49ers	Glenn	Dorsey	RE	82	69	89	71	77
Titans	Kamerion	Wimbley	RE	82	80	78	67	90
Dolphins	Dion	Jordan	RE	83	85	67	64	93
Seahawks	Cliff	Avril	RE	83	81	73	65	88
Steelers	Brett	Keisel	RE	83	72	88	76	45
Falcons	Osi	Umenyiora	RE	84	83	73	66	94
Browns	Desmond	Bryant	RE	88	67	87	93	72
Bengals	Michael	Johnson	RE	89	84	72	69	91
Seahawks	Chris	Clemons	RE	89	80	75	66	95
Vikings	Jared	Allen	RE	89	75	89	94	67
Free Agents	John	Abraham	RE	89	81	85	94	64
Texans	Antonio	Smith	RE	90	73	88	96	79
Bills	Kyle	Williams	RE	91	62	89	91	61
Bears	Julius	Peppers	RE	92	84	85	79	93
Panthers	Charles	Johnson	RE	93	78	87	97	78
Cowboys	DeMarcus	Ware	RE	94	84	86	93	83
49ers	Justin	Smith	RE	94	73	94	84	54
Giants	Jason	Pierre-Paul	RE	94	85	82	75	94
Ravens	Haloti	Ngata	RE	94	68	98	88	55
All-25	Julius	Peppers	RE	97	85	85	79	98
Greats	Deacon	Jones	RE	99	77	93	99	78
Greats	Dwight	Freeney	RE	99	88	79	82	99
All-25	Dwight	Freeney	RE	99	88	79	82	99

LEFT OUTSIDE LINEBACKERS

TEAM	FIRST NAME	LAST NAME	POS	OVR	SPD	ACC	AWR	TKL
Greats	Jack	Ham	LOLB	99	76	88	99	97
Broncos	Von	Miller	LOLB	97	88	94	86	95
Greats	Derrick	Brooks	LOLB	97	87	90	99	96
All-25	Derrick	Brooks	LOLB	97	87	90	99	96
All-25	Terrell	Suggs	LOLB	92	83	94	90	90
Chiefs	Justin	Houston	LOLB	91	81	91	81	93
49ers	Ahmad	Brooks	LOLB	89	76	84	84	96
Ravens	Terrell	Suggs	LOLB	89	82	90	86	85
Browns	Paul	Kruger	LOLB	87	78	86	86	84
Redskins	Ryan	Kerrigan	LOLB	87	81	86	78	89
Steelers	LaMarr	Woodley	LOLB	87	82	86	87	87
Vikings	Chad	Greenway	LOLB	87	79	83	88	87
Bengals	James	Harrison	LOLB	86	83	82	90	86
Seahawks	K.J.	Wright	LOLB	84	81	87	78	93
Eagles	Connor	Barwin	LOLB	83	83	87	83	84
Bears	James	Anderson	LOLB	82	85	89	82	81
Chargers	Jarret	Johnson	LOLB	82	72	84	84	86
Dolphins	Koa	Misi	LOLB	82	82	87	79	88
49ers	Parys	Haralson	LOLB	82	81	91	82	80
Cowboys	Justin	Durant	LOLB	81	85	85	82	89
Jaguars	Russell	Allen	LOLB	81	79	85	81	93
Saints	Victor	Butler	LOLB	81	79	86	78	85
Panthers	Thomas	Davis	LOLB	80	87	88	77	77
Patriots	Dont'a	Hightower	LOLB	80	80	83	71	90
Rams	Jo-Lonn	Dunbar	LOLB	80	78	85	78	90
Titans	Akeem	Ayers	LOLB	79	74	86	71	82
Texans	Brooks	Reed	LOLB	79	81	87	74	88
Cardinals	Lorenzo	Alexander	LOLB	78	75	85	78	81
Falcons	Stephen	Nicholas	LOLB	78	78	86	79	84
Raiders	Nick	Roach	LOLB	78	83	85	78	84
Chargers	Melvin	Ingram	LOLB	77	82	89	66	80
Giants	Keith	Rivers	LOLB	77	84	86	78	78
Ravens	Pernell	McPhee	LOLB	77	72	78	76	79
Browns	Quentin	Groves	LOLB	76	83	88	70	76
Cardinals	O'Brien	Schofield	LOLB	76	79	87	74	75
Eagles	Brandon	Graham	LOLB	76	80	82	72	77
Giants	Aaron	Curry	LOLB	76	83	85	75	81
Packers	Nick	Perry	LOLB	76	86	91	61	81
Jets	Calvin	Pace	LOLB	75	77	82	84	78
Jets	Quinton	Coples	LOLB	75	80	82	68	84
Free Agents	Scott	Shanle	LOLB	75	78	84	85	83
Bengals	Aaron	Maybin	LOLB	74	83	91	71	72
Colts	Erik	Walden	LOLB	74	76	85	74	75
Lions	Ashlee	Palmer	LOLB	74	79	86	74	80
Free Agents	Rocky	McIntosh	LOLB	74	82	85	76	83
Bills	Mark	Anderson	LOLB	73	80	85	77	70
Dolphins	Jason	Trusnik	LOLB	73	75	83	70	71
Bills	Jerry	Hughes	LOLB	72	85	93	70	74
Broncos	Stewart	Bradley	LOLB	72	75	82	75	79
Buccaneers	Adam	Hayward	LOLB	72	83	88	75	79
Free Agents	Quincy	Black	LOLB	71	85	87	69	74
Buccaneers	Dekoda	Watson	LOLB	70	86	87	60	79
Raiders	Miles	Burris	LOLB	70	83	89	66	78
Saints	Martez	Wilson	LOLB	70	87	90	66	73
Free Agents	Sergio	Kindle	LOLB	70	82	93	45	75
Lions	Cory	Greenwood	LOLB	69	85	82	69	74
Ravens	John	Simon	LOLB	69	83	78	55	82
Redskins	Darryl	Tapp	LOLB	69	78	84	73	73
Titans	Tim	Shaw	LOLB	69	79	84	68	71
Vikings	Marvin	Mitchell	LOLB	69	78	84	72	75
Cardinals	Alex	Okafor	LOLB	68	73	81	60	79
Panthers	Jason	Williams	LOLB	68	86	85	64	72
Texans	Bryan	Braman	LOLB	68	79	83	70	76
Browns	James-Michael	Johnson	LOLB	67	81	77	60	79
Jets	Garrett	McIntyre	LOLB	67	76	81	67	79
Panthers	A.J.	Klein	LOLB	67	82	85	57	82
Rams	Sammy	Brown	LOLB	67	82	86	54	74

LEFT OUTSIDE LINEBACKERS CONTINUED

TEAM	FIRST NAME	LAST NAME	POS	OVR	SPD	ACC	AWR	TKL
Titans	Patrick	Bailey	LOLB	67	77	82	68	78
Vikings	Audie	Cole	LOLB	67	74	76	66	81
Buccaneers	Jacob	Cutrera	LOLB	66	77	75	68	78
Chargers	Thomas	Keiser	LOLB	66	74	81	65	76
Colts	Justin	Hickman	LOLB	66	78	82	58	77
Eagles	Joe	Kruger	LOLB	66	77	79	49	79
49ers	Darius	Fleming	LOLB	66	84	86	49	73
Lions	Tahir	Whitehead	LOLB	66	81	84	59	78
Redskins	Vic	So'oto	LOLB	66	82	78	55	74
Texans	Sam	Montgomery	LOLB	66	76	78	54	84
Chiefs	Edgar	Jones	LOLB	65	78	84	63	72
Jaguars	Julian	Stanford	LOLB	65	85	91	62	73
Patriots	A.J.	Edds	LOLB	65	73	67	72	83
Bears	J.T.	Thomas	LOLB	64	80	81	60	76
Seahawks	Mike	Morgan	LOLB	64	77	84	65	78
Steelers	Chris	Carter	LOLB	64	82	85	53	73
Cowboys	Alex	Albright	LOLB	63	73	83	60	74
Packers	Nate	Palmer	LOLB	63	79	87	52	77
Patriots	Jeff	Tarpinian	LOLB	63	83	79	68	79
Bears	Patrick	Trahan	LOLB	62	79	86	63	70
Falcons	Nick	Clancy	LOLB	61	74	79	45	77
Raiders	Kaelin	Burnett	LOLB	61	82	86	52	73
Seahawks	Korey	Toomer	LOLB	61	87	88	51	73
Free Agents	Eric	Bakhtiari	LOLB	61	75	78	59	74
Colts	Quinton	Spears	LOLB	60	78	84	61	71
Saints	Baraka	Atkins	LOLB	60	70	78	64	72
Steelers	Adrian	Robinson	LOLB	60	79	81	51	69
Cowboys	Caleb	McSurdy	LOLB	58	73	76	48	83
Ravens	Adrian	Hamilton	LOLB	57	74	78	51	67
Bills	Kourtnei	Brown	LOLB	56	78	82	44	68

MIDDLE LINEBACKERS

TEAM	FIRST NAME	LAST NAME	POS	OVR	SPD	ACC	AWR	TKL
Greats	Ray	Lewis	MLB	99	85	88	99	99
All-25	Ray	Lewis	MLB	99	85	91	99	99
All-25	Patrick	Willis	MLB	98	90	93	95	97
49ers	Patrick	Willis	MLB	97	90	93	95	96
Greats	London	Fletcher	MLB	94	83	86	99	99
Chiefs	Derrick	Johnson	MLB	93	85	90	93	96
49ers	NaVorro	Bowman	MLB	93	83	91	84	99
Steelers	Lawrence	Timmons	MLB	91	85	91	88	93
Cardinals	Daryl	Washington	MLB	90	86	93	83	93
Cowboys	Sean	Lee	MLB	90	83	81	88	97
Texans	Brian	Cushing	MLB	90	83	89	87	93
Panthers	Luke	Kuechly	MLB	89	86	84	81	99
Lions	Stephen	Tulloch	MLB	88	80	85	88	89
Seahawks	Bobby	Wagner	MLB	88	89	86	80	97
Browns	D'Qwell	Jackson	MLB	87	77	83	88	89
Patriots	Brandon	Spikes	MLB	86	75	87	78	92
Rams	James	Laurinaitis	MLB	86	76	85	91	85
Chargers	Donald	Butler	MLB	85	84	93	77	95
Eagles	DeMeco	Ryans	MLB	85	77	84	88	90
Dolphins	Dannell	Ellerbe	MLB	84	83	88	82	93
Packers	A.J.	Hawk	MLB	84	82	85	86	88
Cardinals	Karlos	Dansby	MLB	83	78	83	87	88
Jaguars	Paul	Posluszny	MLB	83	76	84	89	87
Vikings	Desmond	Bishop	MLB	83	78	84	81	90
Ravens	Daryl	Smith	MLB	82	78	84	88	89
Redskins	London	Fletcher	MLB	82	80	82	97	82
Saints	Curtis	Lofton	MLB	82	78	84	87	87
Free Agents	Bart	Scott	MLB	82	75	79	90	82
Jets	David	Harris	MLB	81	79	84	88	82
Bears	D.J.	Williams	MLB	80	83	86	86	83
Saints	David	Hawthorne	MLB	80	79	82	85	86
Vikings	Erin	Henderson	MLB	80	77	85	82	88
Free Agents	Takeo	Spikes	MLB	80	74	79	95	81
Broncos	Joe	Mays	MLB	79	78	85	73	97
Packers	Brad	Jones	MLB	78	81	86	77	87
Ravens	Jameel	McClain	MLB	78	81	83	77	86
Redskins	Perry	Riley	MLB	78	83	78	75	91
Saints	Jonathan	Vilma	MLB	78	83	85	87	80
Colts	Pat	Angerer	MLB	77	78	83	81	85
Falcons	Akeem	Dent	MLB	77	75	79	75	91
Panthers	Chase	Blackburn	MLB	77	73	81	81	87
Bengals	Rey	Maualuga	MLB	76	80	86	79	86
Colts	Kelvin	Sheppard	MLB	76	78	83	74	88
Giants	Dan	Connor	MLB	76	74	82	82	86
Buccaneers	Mason	Foster	MLB	75	77	85	74	86
Cardinals	Jasper	Brinkley	MLB	75	73	76	74	90
Raiders	Kaluka	Maiava	MLB	75	80	85	79	85
Steelers	Larry	Foote	MLB	75	73	79	77	82
Free Agents	Brandon	Siler	MLB	75	77	87	72	82
Free Agents	Paris	Lenon	MLB	75	77	81	85	78
Chargers	Manti	Te'o	MLB	74	77	82	66	88
Colts	Jerrell	Freeman	MLB	74	82	78	69	84
Ravens	Arthur	Brown	MLB	74	82	86	62	87
Titans	Colin	McCarthy	MLB	74	84	82	75	83
Free Agents	Larry	Grant	MLB	74	79	87	76	84
Bills	Nigel	Bradham	MLB	73	84	88	67	86
Browns	Craig	Robertson	MLB	73	78	84	74	86
Chargers	D.J.	Smith	MLB	73	76	80	69	85
Colts	Kavell	Conner	MLB	73	82	88	76	87
Titans	Moise	Fokou	MLB	73	79	84	75	85
Texans	Darryl	Sharpton	MLB	73	77	87	72	82
Eagles	Mychal	Kendricks	MLB	72	90	92	72	78
Texans	Tim	Dobbins	MLB	72	78	80	74	83
Cardinals	Kevin	Minter	MLB	71	80	82	63	87
Chiefs	Akeem	Jordan	MLB	71	84	85	76	78
Jets	Demario	Davis	MLB	71	87	92	67	78
Saints	Chris	Chamberlain	MLB	71	81	82	73	77
Bills	Arthur	Moats	MLB	70	82	87	62	77
Bills	Kiko	Alonso	MLB	70	77	85	58	85
Cardinals	Reggie	Walker	MLB	70	77	80	73	84
Eagles	Jason	Phillips	MLB	70	76	72	71	86
Eagles	Jamar	Chaney	MLB	70	86	83	69	79
Patriots	Dane	Fletcher	MLB	70	79	84	73	80
Saints	Will	Herring	MLB	70	79	85	74	79
Bears	Blake	Costanzo	MLB	69	77	78	73	81
Chargers	Jonas	Mouton	MLB	69	77	84	64	87
Ravens	Albert	McClellan	MLB	69	79	84	71	79
Steelers	Stevenson	Sylvester	MLB	69	82	77	69	83
Chiefs	Zac	Diles	MLB	68	75	85	73	81
49ers	Dan	Skuta	MLB	68	74	78	74	81
Steelers	Brian	Rolle	MLB	68	84	87	73	72
Bears	Jon	Bostic	MLB	67	83	79	54	83
Jets	Josh	Mauga	MLB	67	76	82	70	76
Free Agents	Brendon	Ayanbadejo	MLB	67	79	78	75	81
Broncos	Nate	Irving	MLB	66	77	82	52	79
Browns	Tank	Carder	MLB	66	82	77	66	83
Browns	L.J.	Fort	MLB	66	80	75	61	84
Dolphins	Jelani	Jenkins	MLB	66	82	86	53	83
Dolphins	Austin	Spitler	MLB	66	76	80	71	77
Giants	Mark	Herzlich	MLB	66	74	78	67	82
Lions	Travis	Lewis	MLB	66	74	88	60	85
Rams	Josh	Hull	MLB	66	74	76	72	82

MIDDLE LINEBACKERS CONTINUED

TEAM	FIRST NAME	LAST NAME	POS	OVR	SPD	ACC	AWR	TKL
Redskins	Bryan	Kehl	MLB	66	74	83	74	78
Steelers	Sean	Spence	MLB	66	79	86	59	74
Titans	Greg	Jones	MLB	66	75	84	65	84
Vikings	Michael	Mauti	MLB	66	77	81	63	85
Chiefs	Nico	Johnson	MLB	65	77	81	54	88
Eagles	Emmanuel	Acho	MLB	65	73	79	66	84
Jets	Nick	Bellore	MLB	65	73	76	66	84
Packers	Robert	Francois	MLB	65	75	82	70	80
Patriots	Steve	Beauharnais	MLB	65	75	82	56	83
Ravens	Josh	Bynes	MLB	65	71	79	64	80
Steelers	Kion	Wilson	MLB	65	74	81	68	85
Vikings	Tyrone	McKenzie	MLB	65	83	86	69	79
Chargers	Andrew	Gachkar	MLB	64	82	85	64	75
Chargers	Phillip	Dillard	MLB	64	82	77	55	81
Packers	Terrell	Manning	MLB	64	76	83	64	79
Redskins	Roddrick	Muckelroy	MLB	64	77	88	68	78
Saints	Kevin	Reddick	MLB	64	78	85	50	79
Saints	Ramon	Humber	MLB	64	79	83	69	75
Colts	Mario	Harvey	MLB	63	89	85	62	75
Cowboys	Cameron	Sheffield	MLB	63	74	87	62	75
Patriots	Mike	Rivera	MLB	63	74	78	70	77
Raiders	Travis	Goethel	MLB	63	77	82	68	77
Free Agents	Greg	Lloyd	MLB	63	73	75	54	75
Chargers	Bront	Bird	MLB	62	73	79	65	77
Eagles	Casey	Matthews	MLB	62	74	76	68	78
49ers	Michael	Wilhoite	MLB	62	78	84	65	77

TEAM	FIRST NAME	LAST NAME	POS	OVR	SPD	ACC	AWR	TKL
Bills	Brian	Smith	MLB	61	75	79	60	77
Packers	Sam	Barrington	MLB	61	76	84	49	82
Seahawks	Ty	Powell	MLB	61	85	91	49	76
Steelers	Vince	Williams	MLB	61	80	82	50	81
Texans	Mike	Mohamed	MLB	61	76	85	64	74
Broncos	Steven	Johnson	MLB	60	75	81	59	75
Falcons	Pat	Schiller	MLB	60	74	78	65	77
49ers	Nathan	Stupar	MLB	60	82	86	55	73
Panthers	Ben	Jacobs	MLB	60	73	80	61	74
Rams	Jabara	Williams	MLB	60	82	86	64	76
Redskins	Keenan	Robinson	MLB	60	74	84	65	77
Buccaneers	Najee	Goode	MLB	59	82	80	64	74
Colts	Scott	Lutrus	MLB	59	79	72	61	73
Bengals	J.K.	Schaffer	MLB	58	74	77	61	81
Jaguars	Michael	Zimmer	MLB	58	77	81	53	74
Steelers	Marshall	McFadden	MLB	58	77	84	57	73
Texans	Cameron	Collins	MLB	58	80	79	60	71
Chiefs	Orie	Lemon	MLB	57	69	79	64	79
Falcons	Brian	Banks	MLB	57	76	85	46	76
Free Agents	Ryan	Rau	MLB	57	80	77	60	78
Packers	Jamari	Lattimore	MLB	56	79	87	58	74
Ravens	Bryan	Hall	MLB	56	67	82	66	70
Browns	Adrian	Moten	MLB	55	82	76	59	74
Buccaneers	Joe	Holland	MLB	55	87	86	55	73
Bills	Marcus	Dowtin	MLB	52	85	82	41	67
Cardinals	Zack	Nash	MLB	52	73	84	48	71

RIGHT OUTSIDE LINEBACKERS

TEAM	FIRST NAME	LAST NAME	POS	OVR	SPD	ACC	AWR	TKL
Greats	Lawrence	Taylor	ROLB	99	89	97	96	95
Greats	Derrick	Thomas	ROLB	99	88	94	90	93
All-25	Derrick	Thomas	ROLB	99	88	94	90	93
All-25	James	Harrison	ROLB	98	85	88	99	91
49ers	Aldon	Smith	ROLB	95	84	97	83	90
Packers	Clay	Matthews	ROLB	95	86	94	86	90
Bears	Lance	Briggs	ROLB	94	79	84	94	95
Patriots	Jerod	Mayo	ROLB	94	85	91	88	96
Redskins	Brian	Orakpo	ROLB	90	84	92	79	88
Buccaneers	Lavonte	David	ROLB	89	85	88	85	98
Chiefs	Tamba	Hali	ROLB	89	77	89	91	75
Chargers	Dwight	Freeney	ROLB	88	87	94	92	77
Panthers	Jon	Beason	ROLB	88	85	91	90	88
Dolphins	Philip	Wheeler	ROLB	87	79	86	84	87
Colts	Robert	Mathis	ROLB	86	86	96	92	75
Eagles	Trent	Cole	ROLB	84	83	91	90	72
Free Agents	Nick	Barnett	ROLB	84	78	83	85	88
Falcons	Sean	Weatherspoon	ROLB	83	83	88	78	76
Raiders	Kevin	Burnett	ROLB	83	77	84	86	89
Ravens	Elvis	Dumervil	ROLB	83	83	92	88	76
Bills	Manny	Lawson	ROLB	82	88	93	80	77
Browns	Jabaal	Sheard	ROLB	82	81	87	79	87
Cowboys	Bruce	Carter	ROLB	81	88	91	73	86
Free Agents	Thomas	Howard	ROLB	81	87	86	79	79
Broncos	Wesley	Woodyard	ROLB	80	85	88	78	90
Lions	DeAndre	Levy	ROLB	79	84	86	85	78
Ravens	Courtney	Upshaw	ROLB	79	79	82	70	90
Titans	Zach	Brown	ROLB	79	88	91	69	88
Free Agents	LeRoy	Hill	ROLB	79	79	84	80	81
Free Agents	Chris	Gocong	ROLB	79	78	86	78	83
Saints	Will	Smith	ROLB	78	73	82	88	80
Steelers	Jason	Worilds	ROLB	78	80	90	71	77
Bengals	Vontaze	Burfict	ROLB	77	74	82	71	89
Chargers	Larry	English	ROLB	77	79	87	74	79
Jets	Antwan	Barnes	ROLB	77	85	92	75	68
Rams	Alec	Ogletree	ROLB	77	83	90	64	79

TEAM	FIRST NAME	LAST NAME	POS	OVR	SPD	ACC	AWR	TKL
Redskins	Rob	Jackson	ROLB	77	77	83	75	77
Saints	Junior	Galette	ROLB	77	78	92	76	76
Texans	Whitney	Mercilus	ROLB	77	84	89	64	82
Browns	Barkevious	Mingo	ROLB	76	87	95	60	80
Giants	Jacquian	Williams	ROLB	76	85	89	74	80
Steelers	Jarvis	Jones	ROLB	76	77	89	62	81
Seahawks	Heath	Farwell	ROLB	75	76	80	77	82
Cardinals	Sam	Acho	ROLB	74	82	84	69	74
Colts	Bjoern	Werner	ROLB	74	75	87	63	81
Jaguars	Geno	Hayes	ROLB	74	84	88	73	78
Bills	Bryan	Scott	ROLB	73	79	83	76	69
Buccaneers	Jonathan	Casillas	ROLB	73	87	87	73	76
Panthers	Jordan	Senn	ROLB	72	83	85	72	80
Bears	Khaseem	Greene	ROLB	71	79	83	59	85
Cowboys	Ernie	Sims	ROLB	71	85	86	69	77
Patriots	Niko	Koutouvides	ROLB	71	70	85	74	82
Raiders	Sio	Moore	ROLB	71	82	86	54	77
Bengals	Sean	Porter	ROLB	70	78	89	60	77
Chiefs	Frank	Zombo	ROLB	70	81	78	71	78
Lions	Carmen	Messina	ROLB	70	73	83	65	80
Vikings	Gerald	Hodges	ROLB	70	77	83	63	80
Free Agents	Justin	Cole	ROLB	70	73	69	67	78
Patriots	Jamie	Collins	ROLB	69	83	88	55	84
Saints	Chase	Thomas	ROLB	69	72	78	56	82
Broncos	Danny	Trevathan	ROLB	68	79	85	56	83
49ers	Corey	Lemonier	ROLB	68	85	90	54	74
Falcons	Robert	James	ROLB	67	75	85	69	77
Raiders	Keenan	Clayton	ROLB	67	79	84	64	76
Seahawks	Malcolm	Smith	ROLB	67	86	84	65	76
Free Agents	Jamaal	Westerman	ROLB	67	75	80	65	77
Bears	Lawrence	Wilson	ROLB	66	75	78	51	89
Bengals	Vincent	Rey	ROLB	66	80	79	64	74
Colts	Lawrence	Sidbury	ROLB	66	84	88	68	67
Giants	Spencer	Paysinger	ROLB	66	79	85	63	77
Panthers	Doug	Hogue	ROLB	66	82	88	66	76
Ravens	Spencer	Adkins	ROLB	66	82	85	55	72

RIGHT OUTSIDE LINEBACKERS

TEAM	FIRST NAME	LAST NAME	POS	OVR	SPD	ACC	AWR	TKL
Free Agents	Kyle	Bosworth	ROLB	66	77	83	65	76
Eagles	Phillip	Hunt	ROLB	65	74	81	66	75
49ers	Nick	Moody	ROLB	65	79	83	52	75
49ers	Cam	Johnson	ROLB	65	73	90	55	78
Jaguars	Brandon	Marshall	ROLB	65	80	74	61	74
Jets	Ricky	Sapp	ROLB	65	84	91	64	60
Packers	Dezman	Moses	ROLB	65	77	87	55	73
Titans	Zaviar	Gooden	ROLB	65	90	91	51	69
Bengals	Emmanuel	Lamur	ROLB	64	82	84	50	73
Redskins	Brandon	Jenkins	ROLB	64	74	88	49	74
Chargers	Tourek	Williams	ROLB	63	79	77	48	78
Texans	Trevardo	Williams	ROLB	63	86	92	43	81

TEAM	FIRST NAME	LAST NAME	POS	OVR	SPD	ACC	AWR	TKL
Cardinals	Tim	Fugger	ROLB	62	82	78	48	68
Dolphins	Jonathan	Freeny	ROLB	62	81	86	61	69
Redskins	Ricky	Elmore	ROLB	62	73	82	59	81
Vikings	Larry	Dean	ROLB	62	84	88	64	74
Free Agents	Darryl	Gamble	ROLB	62	74	84	60	73
Bills	Chris	White	ROLB	61	81	83	55	75
Dolphins	Josh	Kaddu	ROLB	61	81	83	52	76
Rams	Jonathan	Stewart	ROLB	61	81	79	53	75
Bears	Jerry	Franklin	ROLB	60	74	74	56	82
Jets	Jacquies	Smith	ROLB	56	84	81	48	64
Seahawks	Allen	Bradford	ROLB	56	83	84	62	72
Free Agents	Stephen	Franklin	ROLB	51	81	83	35	66

CORNERBACKS

TEAM	FIRST NAME	LAST NAME	POS	OVR	SPD	ACC	MCV	ZCV
Greats	Night Train	Lane	CB	99	95	96	95	99
Greats	Deion	Sanders	CB	99	99	99	99	98
All-25	Deion	Sanders	CB	99	99	99	99	98
All-25	Darrelle	Revis	CB	98	93	96	98	94
Buccaneers	Darrelle	Revis	CB	97	93	95	99	93
Greats	Champ	Bailey	CB	97	95	93	97	90
All-25	Champ	Bailey	CB	97	95	95	97	90
Seahawks	Richard	Sherman	CB	96	91	94	98	92
Greats	Charles	Woodson	CB	96	91	93	90	97
Bears	Charles	Tillman	CB	95	88	92	92	90
All-25	Nnamdi	Asomugha	CB	95	93	92	97	92
Chiefs	Brandon	Flowers	CB	94	90	94	96	92
Greats	Antoine	Winfield	CB	94	87	92	83	96
All-25	Charles	Woodson	CB	94	91	93	85	93
Broncos	Champ	Bailey	CB	93	92	90	92	89
Jets	Antonio	Cromartie	CB	92	96	95	98	88
Browns	Joe	Haden	CB	91	91	96	95	89
Bears	Tim	Jennings	CB	90	94	95	92	91
Bengals	Leon	Hall	CB	90	88	89	87	93
49ers	Carlos	Rogers	CB	90	88	91	86	93
Ravens	Lardarius	Webb	CB	90	93	94	96	87
Seahawks	Antoine	Winfield	CB	90	86	88	78	91
Cardinals	Patrick	Peterson	CB	89	98	96	91	85
Dolphins	Brent	Grimes	CB	89	87	95	93	88
Falcons	Asante	Samuel	CB	89	91	93	86	96
Steelers	Ike	Taylor	CB	89	95	92	87	92
Texans	Johnathan	Joseph	CB	89	94	91	92	86
Cowboys	Brandon	Carr	CB	88	88	92	90	87
49ers	Tarell	Brown	CB	88	90	95	93	90
Rams	Cortland	Finnegan	CB	88	91	89	85	88
Seahawks	Brandon	Browner	CB	88	88	87	87	94
Titans	Jason	McCourty	CB	88	92	95	86	91
Colts	Vontae	Davis	CB	87	93	95	92	82
Packers	Tramon	Williams	CB	86	92	94	91	85
Packers	Casey	Hayward	CB	86	87	94	93	96
Patriots	Aqib	Talib	CB	86	88	93	91	87
Saints	Jabari	Greer	CB	86	88	91	87	90
Bengals	Terence	Newman	CB	85	96	91	89	82
Lions	Chris	Houston	CB	85	92	94	89	77
Texans	Kareem	Jackson	CB	85	90	88	89	90
Chargers	Derek	Cox	CB	84	92	91	86	87
Packers	Sam	Shields	CB	84	97	95	92	84
Eagles	Cary	Williams	CB	83	89	87	84	89
49ers	Nnamdi	Asomugha	CB	83	89	86	85	83
Redskins	Josh	Wilson	CB	83	95	94	88	77
Saints	Keenan	Lewis	CB	83	86	90	86	89
Titans	Alterraun	Verner	CB	83	87	91	88	83
Free Agents	Sheldon	Brown	CB	83	86	87	82	88
Bills	Stephon	Gilmore	CB	82	94	93	85	89
Broncos	Chris	Harris	CB	82	91	93	92	81

TEAM	FIRST NAME	LAST NAME	POS	OVR	SPD	ACC	MCV	ZCV
Chiefs	Dunta	Robinson	CB	82	93	92	84	76
Chiefs	Sean	Smith	CB	82	89	91	87	77
Cowboys	Morris	Claiborne	CB	82	91	92	93	85
Eagles	Bradley	Fletcher	CB	82	87	90	94	84
Rams	Janoris	Jenkins	CB	82	92	96	91	83
Free Agents	Nate	Clements	CB	82	86	89	79	84
Free Agents	Rashean	Mathis	CB	82	88	87	82	88
Cardinals	Antoine	Cason	CB	81	89	92	86	82
Giants	Corey	Webster	CB	81	87	89	73	85
Jaguars	Marcus	Trufant	CB	81	87	92	85	75
Jets	Dee	Milliner	CB	81	94	92	88	86
Patriots	Alfonzo	Dennard	CB	81	87	88	87	84
Redskins	DeAngelo	Hall	CB	81	97	95	82	86
Giants	Prince	Amukamara	CB	80	93	92	85	82
Ravens	Corey	Graham	CB	80	91	88	83	86
Steelers	Cortez	Allen	CB	80	88	93	87	85
Bengals	Adam	Jones	CB	79	92	94	91	78
Broncos	Dominique	Rodgers-Cromartie	CB	79	98	95	88	74
Buccaneers	Eric	Wright	CB	79	89	90	76	87
Dolphins	Richard	Marshall	CB	79	93	90	83	76
Vikings	Chris	Cook	CB	79	90	85	83	87
Cardinals	Jerraud	Powers	CB	78	88	90	81	87
49ers	Chris	Culliver	CB	78	95	90	85	76
Jets	Kyle	Wilson	CB	78	89	92	81	75
Raiders	D.J.	Hayden	CB	78	93	91	86	88
Raiders	Tracy	Porter	CB	78	93	94	84	75
Saints	Patrick	Robinson	CB	78	92	92	85	77
Free Agents	Terrence	McGee	CB	78	90	92	82	85
Bills	Leodis	McKelvin	CB	77	93	94	80	77
Colts	Greg	Toler	CB	77	93	89	83	78
Falcons	Desmond	Trufant	CB	77	93	94	87	84
Giants	Terrell	Thomas	CB	77	85	87	78	84
Patriots	Kyle	Arrington	CB	77	89	93	79	85
Raiders	Mike	Jenkins	CB	77	92	91	81	74
Steelers	William	Gay	CB	77	85	87	75	83
Free Agents	Stanford	Routt	CB	77	95	92	85	76
Bengals	Dre	Kirkpatrick	CB	76	89	88	77	92
Cardinals	Javier	Arenas	CB	76	88	92	79	84
Cowboys	Orlando	Scandrick	CB	76	95	97	81	76
Dolphins	Jamar	Taylor	CB	76	93	95	83	85
Giants	Aaron	Ross	CB	76	87	91	77	74
Panthers	Captain	Munnerlyn	CB	76	90	93	78	82
Raiders	Joselio	Hanson	CB	76	87	88	79	84
Ravens	Jimmy	Smith	CB	76	90	89	83	77
Texans	Brice	McCain	CB	76	95	93	82	76
Bears	Kelvin	Hayden	CB	75	87	85	74	80
Chargers	Shareece	Wright	CB	75	89	87	86	77
49ers	Tramaine	Brock	CB	75	93	91	82	73
Lions	Ron	Bartell	CB	75	86	87	79	74

CORNERBACKS CONTINUED

TEAM	FIRST NAME	LAST NAME	POS	OVR	SPD	ACC	MCV	ZCV
Bears	Zack	Bowman	CB	74	90	91	84	73
Broncos	Tony	Carter	CB	74	92	95	81	82
Browns	Buster	Skrine	CB	74	96	95	78	82
Colts	Darius	Butler	CB	74	91	93	80	76
Packers	Davon	House	CB	74	90	86	84	77
Panthers	Josh	Norman	CB	74	86	92	82	75
Patriots	Ras-I	Dowling	CB	74	90	85	84	89
Rams	Trumaine	Johnson	CB	74	86	93	86	76
Redskins	E.J.	Biggers	CB	74	94	92	77	80
Vikings	Xavier	Rhodes	CB	74	92	88	84	88
Browns	Christopher	Owens	CB	73	88	92	82	76
Falcons	Robert	McClain	CB	73	92	94	81	72
Packers	Jarrett	Bush	CB	73	85	87	75	81
Raiders	Phillip	Adams	CB	73	92	93	80	74
Titans	Blidi	Wreh-Wilson	CB	73	90	91	84	86
Vikings	Jacob	Lacey	CB	73	87	85	75	84
Vikings	Josh	Robinson	CB	73	97	97	79	81
Free Agents	Chris	Carr	CB	73	91	92	80	74
Buccaneers	Johnthan	Banks	CB	72	86	87	84	80
Colts	Cassius	Vaughn	CB	72	95	91	79	76
Dolphins	Nolan	Carroll	CB	72	93	91	77	69
Eagles	Brandon	Boykin	CB	72	90	94	84	78
Falcons	Dominique	Franks	CB	72	89	91	78	84
Falcons	Robert	Alford	CB	72	93	95	87	77
Giants	Jayron	Hosley	CB	72	92	91	73	85
Lions	Bill	Bentley	CB	72	92	94	78	86
Panthers	D.J.	Moore	CB	72	88	91	74	83
Ravens	Chris	Johnson	CB	72	96	93	77	68
Seahawks	Walter	Thurmond	CB	72	90	94	86	78
Free Agents	Pat	Lee	CB	72	87	92	80	73
Broncos	Omar	Bolden	CB	71	87	92	79	73
Browns	Leon	McFadden	CB	71	88	90	86	80
49ers	Perrish	Cox	CB	71	90	93	73	82
Jaguars	Alan	Ball	CB	71	87	90	70	78
Jaguars	Dwayne	Gratz	CB	71	90	88	83	80
Jets	Ellis	Lankster	CB	71	86	91	72	78
Lions	Darius	Slay	CB	71	95	93	84	79
Seahawks	Jeremy	Lane	CB	71	90	92	80	75
Titans	Coty	Sensabaugh	CB	71	95	96	74	79
Vikings	A.J.	Jefferson	CB	71	90	92	74	72
Texans	Brandon	Harris	CB	71	88	90	82	75
Free Agents	William	Middleton	CB	71	88	87	76	81
Buccaneers	Anthony	Gaitor	CB	70	87	92	75	82
Buccaneers	Leonard	Johnson	CB	70	86	87	73	81
Chargers	Johnny	Patrick	CB	70	87	93	81	73
Chiefs	Sanders	Commings	CB	70	92	90	83	77
Dolphins	Dimitri	Patterson	CB	70	87	89	73	75
Giants	Trumaine	McBride	CB	70	86	90	78	73
Jets	Aaron	Berry	CB	70	88	90	73	80
Lions	Jonte	Green	CB	70	94	90	75	83
Panthers	Drayton	Florence	CB	70	87	87	73	69
Patriots	Logan	Ryan	CB	70	87	91	79	87
Redskins	Jerome	Murphy	CB	70	87	92	84	75
Seahawks	Byron	Maxwell	CB	70	91	89	72	77
Titans	Tommie	Campbell	CB	70	95	92	77	72
Broncos	Kayvon	Webster	CB	69	91	92	82	75
Chargers	Steve	Williams	CB	69	91	95	83	73
Colts	Josh	Gordy	CB	69	92	94	77	75
Eagles	Brandon	Hughes	CB	69	87	91	79	74
Jaguars	Demetrius	McCray	CB	69	91	93	79	77
Jets	Isaiah	Trufant	CB	69	92	94	78	73
Panthers	James	Dockery	CB	69	89	92	71	77
Panthers	Josh	Thomas	CB	69	88	91	72	79
Patriots	Marquice	Cole	CB	69	88	90	77	72
Redskins	Richard	Crawford	CB	69	91	87	75	80
Redskins	David	Amerson	CB	69	91	88	76	86
Saints	Corey	White	CB	69	93	93	74	76

TEAM	FIRST NAME	LAST NAME	POS	OVR	SPD	ACC	MCV	ZCV
Steelers	DeMarcus	Van Dyke	CB	69	98	96	74	69
Steelers	Curtis	Brown	CB	69	88	87	81	74
Free Agents	Kevin	Barnes	CB	69	89	86	72	76
Free Agents	Michael	Coe	CB	69	84	89	72	78
Bengals	Brandon	Ghee	CB	68	91	93	84	70
Bills	Ron	Brooks	CB	68	95	90	75	72
Cowboys	Sterling	Moore	CB	68	87	91	75	82
Cowboys	B.W.	Webb	CB	68	89	92	85	74
Dolphins	Will	Davis	CB	68	89	93	85	73
Eagles	Jordan	Poyer	CB	68	89	87	73	85
Jaguars	Mike	Harris	CB	68	86	87	80	75
Raiders	Chimdi	Chekwa	CB	68	94	90	80	77
Titans	Khalid	Wooten	CB	68	89	93	73	82
Vikings	Brandon	Burton	CB	68	87	85	85	68
Free Agents	Reggie	Corner	CB	68	84	92	74	78
Bengals	Shaun	Prater	CB	67	87	86	68	84
Bills	Justin	Rogers	CB	67	93	90	74	79
Bills	Crezdon	Butler	CB	67	92	87	69	79
Buccaneers	Myron	Lewis	CB	67	87	88	70	82
Cardinals	Jamell	Fleming	CB	67	90	93	74	83
Eagles	Curtis	Marsh	CB	67	89	90	74	85
Jaguars	Kevin	Rutland	CB	67	89	88	75	71
Packers	Micah	Hyde	CB	67	86	88	73	81
Raiders	Coye	Francies	CB	67	85	90	70	80
Rams	Brandon	McGee	CB	67	92	94	75	82
Saints	Ryan	Steed	CB	67	85	87	75	79
Seahawks	Tharold	Simon	CB	67	88	87	76	83
Steelers	Terry	Hawthorne	CB	67	90	92	82	74
Steelers	Justin	King	CB	67	94	95	72	65
Vikings	Marcus	Sherels	CB	67	96	94	78	69
Bears	Sherrick	McManis	CB	66	89	86	63	84
Broncos	Mario	Butler	CB	66	82	87	75	74
Cardinals	Bryan	McCann	CB	66	96	98	74	69
Chiefs	Jalil	Brown	CB	66	87	88	78	73
Lions	Chris	Greenwood	CB	66	96	94	74	65
Raiders	Brandian	Ross	CB	66	88	91	81	75
Ravens	Chykie	Brown	CB	66	89	92	81	66
Ravens	Asa	Jackson	CB	66	89	94	79	72
Ravens	Marc	Anthony	CB	66	86	91	76	77
Browns	Trevin	Wade	CB	65	86	92	77	74
Rams	Robert	Steeples	CB	65	92	94	74	75
Seahawks	Will	Blackmon	CB	65	91	93	71	66
Texans	Roc	Carmichael	CB	65	88	88	69	84
Buccaneers	Danny	Gorrer	CB	64	88	91	73	67
Dolphins	R.J.	Stanford	CB	64	89	92	78	72
Jets	Darrin	Walls	CB	64	90	87	68	75
Lions	DeQuan	Menzie	CB	64	83	85	66	75
Lions	Domonique	Johnson	CB	64	87	86	64	71
Steelers	Ross	Ventrone	CB	64	86	88	73	65
Eagles	Trevard	Lindley	CB	63	87	84	82	64
Falcons	Terrence	Johnson	CB	63	87	92	74	76
Falcons	Peyton	Thompson	CB	63	92	86	74	70
Giants	Terrence	Frederick	CB	63	89	83	67	74
Jaguars	Jeremy	Harris	CB	63	90	89	72	76
Saints	Korey	Lindsey	CB	63	89	92	73	79
Seahawks	DeShawn	Shead	CB	63	86	89	68	74
Chargers	Gregory	Gatson	CB	62	87	90	76	70
Dolphins	Julian	Posey	CB	62	90	87	70	80
Seahawks	Ron	Parker	CB	62	95	91	73	66
Steelers	Josh	Victorian	CB	62	87	90	67	74
Colts	Marshay	Green	CB	61	85	90	76	69
Lions	Ross	Weaver	CB	61	86	90	67	73
Bears	Isaiah	Frey	CB	60	90	84	71	82
Bills	T.J.	Heath	CB	60	93	94	76	68
Chargers	Cornelius	Brown	CB	60	86	91	71	76
Giants	Laron	Scott	CB	60	91	88	74	69
Saints	A.J.	Davis	CB	60	91	93	68	74

CORNERBACKS CONTINUED

TEAM	FIRST NAME	LAST NAME	POS	OVR	SPD	ACC	MCV	ZCV
Browns	Prince	Miller	CB	59	90	88	70	66
Colts	Teddy	Williams	CB	59	97	96	69	67
Jets	Donnie	Fletcher	CB	59	87	86	68	77
Vikings	Greg	McCoy	CB	59	92	87	72	73
Bengals	Onterio	McCalebb	CB	58	97	91	74	67
Chiefs	Neiko	Thorpe	CB	57	90	93	71	64
Dolphins	De'Andre	Presley	CB	57	88	87	72	71

FREE SAFETIES

TEAM	FIRST NAME	LAST NAME	POS	OVR	SPD	AGI	AWR	HPW
Greats	Rod	Woodson	FS	99	93	95	97	93
All-25	Sean	Taylor	FS	99	93	93	85	98
All-25	Ed	Reed	FS	99	92	94	98	75
Greats	Ed	Reed	FS	98	92	94	98	75
Chargers	Eric	Weddle	FS	96	84	91	93	77
Bills	Jairus	Byrd	FS	95	87	93	84	60
Patriots	Devin	McCourty	FS	92	93	93	83	64
Seahawks	Earl	Thomas	FS	91	93	93	78	74
Buccaneers	Dashon	Goldson	FS	90	87	88	82	96
Bengals	Reggie	Nelson	FS	88	92	94	82	76
Colts	Antoine	Bethea	FS	87	89	87	87	81
Free Agents	Kerry	Rhodes	FS	87	84	85	87	78
Texans	Ed	Reed	FS	86	88	89	90	72
Free Agents	Quintin	Mikell	FS	86	88	83	85	75
Eagles	Kenny	Phillips	FS	85	88	90	73	83
Packers	Morgan	Burnett	FS	85	87	86	75	88
Raiders	Charles	Woodson	FS	85	85	87	87	57
Steelers	Ryan	Clark	FS	85	82	81	87	93
Falcons	Thomas	DeCoud	FS	84	86	85	84	72
Vikings	Harrison	Smith	FS	84	86	87	74	82
Giants	Antrel	Rolle	FS	83	85	91	86	50
Lions	Glover	Quin	FS	83	85	86	78	74
Ravens	Michael	Huff	FS	83	93	93	82	54
Broncos	Rahim	Moore	FS	82	84	90	75	83
Jaguars	Dwight	Lowery	FS	81	85	91	78	54
Broncos	Quentin	Jammer	FS	79	87	85	76	62
Chiefs	Kendrick	Lewis	FS	79	83	85	71	87
Dolphins	Chris	Clemons	FS	79	92	86	71	83
Raiders	Usama	Young	FS	78	90	95	73	47
Titans	Michael	Griffin	FS	78	87	87	76	74
Vikings	Jamarca	Sanford	FS	77	83	77	76	88
49ers	Eric	Reid	FS	76	88	86	53	93
Lions	Amari	Spievey	FS	76	86	89	71	65
Saints	Malcolm	Jenkins	FS	76	87	87	71	75
Free Agents	Madieu	Williams	FS	76	84	87	76	69
Bills	Aaron	Williams	FS	75	87	89	69	68
Buccaneers	Ahmad	Black	FS	75	78	92	63	82
Patriots	Steve	Gregory	FS	75	85	85	78	65
Saints	Rafael	Bush	FS	75	91	88	67	60
Saints	Jim	Leonhard	FS	75	83	83	78	66
Texans	D.J.	Swearinger	FS	75	82	84	50	89
Bears	Chris	Conte	FS	74	89	77	66	71
Cardinals	Yeremiah	Bell	FS	74	83	79	73	88
Chargers	Darrell	Stuckey	FS	74	89	88	62	64
49ers	Craig	Dahl	FS	74	85	83	74	75
Panthers	Haruki	Nakamura	FS	74	84	80	75	76
Redskins	Reed	Doughty	FS	74	79	78	78	74
Free Agents	Eric	Hagg	FS	74	80	83	69	64
Free Agents	James	Sanders	FS	74	78	78	76	83
Free Agents	Sherrod	Martin	FS	74	88	90	70	74
Ravens	Omar	Brown	FS	73	82	86	64	64
Free Agents	Chris	Sentef	FS	73	90	91	46	91
Broncos	Quinton	Carter	FS	72	84	78	64	92
Cardinals	Tyrann	Mathieu	FS	72	90	94	40	83
Jets	Josh	Bush	FS	72	88	84	64	61
Patriots	Tavon	Wilson	FS	72	86	88	61	69
Redskins	Phillip	Thomas	FS	72	84	90	44	64
Browns	Tashaun	Gipson	FS	71	84	87	64	70
Cardinals	Justin	Bethel	FS	71	87	93	47	65
Cowboys	Matt	Johnson	FS	71	85	77	58	62
Lions	Tyrell	Johnson	FS	71	87	84	65	74
Packers	Jerron	McMillian	FS	71	93	91	54	83
Rams	T.J.	McDonald	FS	71	85	82	54	86
Bears	Brandon	Hardin	FS	70	91	85	42	87
Colts	John	Boyett	FS	70	84	79	45	71
Eagles	Kurt	Coleman	FS	70	84	81	72	64
Rams	Rodney	McLeod	FS	70	83	89	60	69
Redskins	Jordan	Pugh	FS	70	87	87	63	60
Buccaneers	Keith	Tandy	FS	69	85	90	55	70
Falcons	Charles	Mitchell	FS	69	82	89	55	64
49ers	C.J.	Spillman	FS	69	86	84	65	83
Panthers	Colin	Jones	FS	69	93	85	65	70
Titans	Robert	Johnson	FS	69	86	79	65	63
Bears	Anthony	Walters	FS	68	87	84	55	72
Colts	Larry	Asante	FS	68	84	77	55	79
Cowboys	J.J.	Wilcox	FS	68	86	89	45	87
Dolphins	Jimmy	Wilson	FS	68	88	89	57	62
Falcons	Kemal	Ishmael	FS	68	84	82	44	78
Browns	Johnson	Bademosi	FS	67	91	88	55	65
Cowboys	Brandon	Underwood	FS	67	84	86	52	68
Giants	Will	Hill	FS	67	82	88	54	87
Jaguars	Josh	Evans	FS	67	86	88	44	87
Jets	Antonio	Allen	FS	67	82	80	53	71
Rams	Quinton	Pointer	FS	67	91	90	47	49
Titans	Tracy	Wilson	FS	67	85	84	64	77
Texans	Shiloh	Keo	FS	67	74	75	55	95
Colts	Delano	Howell	FS	66	86	82	52	74
Jets	Bret	Lockett	FS	66	83	82	65	74
Bengals	George	Iloka	FS	65	82	86	52	84
Chiefs	Tysyn	Hartman	FS	65	79	87	55	54
Jaguars	Antwon	Blake	FS	65	95	87	43	63
Raiders	Cory	Nelms	FS	65	93	80	50	75
Seahawks	Chris	Maragos	FS	65	81	81	65	71
Steelers	Robert	Golden	FS	65	85	83	53	66
Vikings	Andrew	Sendejo	FS	65	81	79	60	80
Ravens	Anthony	Levine	FS	64	91	88	53	67
Redskins	Jordan	Bernstine	FS	64	93	86	51	78
Saints	Jerico	Nelson	FS	64	84	82	54	68
Free Agents	Robert	Sands	FS	64	84	85	45	88
Bears	Tom	Nelson	FS	63	92	84	56	52
Eagles	David	Sims	FS	63	87	79	44	82
Dolphins	Kelcie	McCray	FS	62	86	92	54	52

STRONG SAFETIES

TEAM	FIRST NAME	LAST NAME	POS	OVR	SPD	AGI	AWR	HPW
Greats	Brian	Dawkins	SS	99	88	91	95	95
Greats	Ronnie	Lott	SS	99	93	95	99	99
All-25	Brian	Dawkins	SS	99	88	91	95	95
All-25	Troy	Polamalu	SS	98	92	95	88	88
Steelers	Troy	Polamalu	SS	95	89	92	88	85
Dolphins	Reshad	Jones	SS	92	86	85	75	88
Browns	T.J.	Ward	SS	90	86	84	79	92
Seahawks	Kam	Chancellor	SS	90	84	85	78	93
Raiders	Tyvon	Branch	SS	89	95	86	81	74
Chiefs	Eric	Berry	SS	88	92	90	74	88
Falcons	William	Moore	SS	87	86	87	76	90
Patriots	Adrian	Wilson	SS	87	83	83	87	88
Colts	LaRon	Landry	SS	86	91	83	76	98
49ers	Donte	Whitner	SS	86	88	87	77	89
Titans	George	Wilson	SS	85	84	86	76	74
Titans	Bernard	Pollard	SS	85	81	82	86	89
Lions	Louis	Delmas	SS	84	87	90	69	82
Texans	Danieal	Manning	SS	84	96	93	80	67
Giants	Stevie	Brown	SS	83	85	82	72	77
Eagles	Patrick	Chung	SS	82	86	87	72	87
Bears	Major	Wright	SS	81	85	87	72	90
Buccaneers	Mark	Barron	SS	80	85	83	60	94
Panthers	Charles	Godfrey	SS	80	90	86	78	69
Saints	Kenny	Vaccaro	SS	80	83	91	58	86
Bears	Tom	Zbikowski	SS	79	88	86	75	78
Jets	Dawan	Landry	SS	79	82	79	76	86
Free Agents	Jordan	Babineaux	SS	79	85	83	77	67
Broncos	Mike	Adams	SS	78	87	84	76	64
Chiefs	Husain	Abdullah	SS	78	86	85	73	75
Ravens	Matt	Elam	SS	78	88	92	48	90
Redskins	Brandon	Meriweather	SS	78	91	91	74	70
Rams	Darian	Stewart	SS	77	86	91	67	90
Free Agents	Abram	Elam	SS	77	83	82	72	75
Cardinals	Rashad	Johnson	SS	76	85	84	72	82
Jaguars	Johnathan	Cyprien	SS	76	82	85	52	91
Lions	Don	Carey	SS	76	88	87	68	74
Packers	M.D.	Jennings	SS	76	87	83	69	71
Saints	Roman	Harper	SS	76	81	77	73	87
Vikings	Mistral	Raymond	SS	76	82	83	72	80
Bills	Da'Norris	Searcy	SS	75	84	82	65	75
Cowboys	Barry	Church	SS	75	84	82	71	88
Panthers	Mike	Mitchell	SS	75	87	87	70	91
Free Agents	Erik	Coleman	SS	75	81	79	75	74
Bengals	Taylor	Mays	SS	74	94	93	62	86
Colts	Joe	Lefeged	SS	74	91	86	66	71
Giants	Ryan	Mundy	SS	74	83	84	64	87
Raiders	Reggie	Smith	SS	74	88	87	67	69
Ravens	James	Ihedigbo	SS	74	83	84	72	75
Seahawks	Jeron	Johnson	SS	74	86	81	64	87
Rams	Matt	Giordano	SS	73	91	84	76	60
Titans	Al	Afalava	SS	73	80	83	66	83
Free Agents	Troy	Nolan	SS	73	87	87	62	66
Bears	Craig	Steltz	SS	72	79	75	70	84
Bengals	Shawn	Williams	SS	72	91	83	46	85
Chargers	Marcus	Gilchrist	SS	72	88	91	57	55
49ers	Darcel	McBath	SS	72	85	91	60	66
Rams	Matthew	Daniels	SS	72	88	76	65	89
Redskins	DeJon	Gomes	SS	72	85	78	55	80
Saints	Isa	Abdul-Quddus	SS	72	92	84	61	74
Steelers	Shamarko	Thomas	SS	72	91	91	46	90
Bengals	Jeromy	Miles	SS	71	87	85	54	84
Broncos	David	Bruton	SS	71	88	78	65	65
Buccaneers	Cody	Grimm	SS	71	79	84	66	77
Eagles	Earl	Wolff	SS	71	90	84	52	73
Falcons	Zeke	Motta	SS	71	78	85	51	77
Giants	David	Caldwell	SS	71	86	81	63	69
Jets	Jaiquawn	Jarrett	SS	71	81	82	52	87
Redskins	Bacarri	Rambo	SS	71	83	86	39	89
Vikings	Robert	Blanton	SS	71	84	84	53	67
Bills	Duke	Williams	SS	70	91	89	44	82
Browns	Jamoris	Slaughter	SS	70	86	84	52	73
Chargers	Brandon	Taylor	SS	70	85	78	54	73
Colts	Sergio	Brown	SS	70	83	83	61	76
Eagles	Colt	Anderson	SS	70	82	82	64	68
Lions	John	Wendling	SS	70	80	83	65	60
Patriots	Duron	Harmon	SS	70	88	85	46	75
Cowboys	Will	Allen	SS	69	79	77	65	50
Eagles	Nate	Allen	SS	69	88	86	66	59
49ers	Trenton	Robinson	SS	69	89	84	52	65
Cardinals	Jonathon	Amaya	SS	68	87	84	65	71
Giants	Cooper	Taylor	SS	68	89	80	38	73
Texans	Eddie	Pleasant	SS	68	85	78	54	80
Cowboys	Eric	Frampton	SS	67	82	85	62	82
Falcons	Shann	Schillinger	SS	67	82	79	58	72
Panthers	Anderson	Russell	SS	67	83	85	65	66
Ravens	Christian	Thompson	SS	67	90	88	51	82
Seahawks	Winston	Guy	SS	67	84	83	49	83
Titans	Markelle	Martin	SS	67	89	82	51	80
Cowboys	Danny	McCray	SS	66	87	84	57	73
Jaguars	Chris	Prosinski	SS	66	93	81	61	67
Lions	Ricardo	Silva	SS	66	83	85	51	77
Panthers	D.J.	Campbell	SS	66	87	85	54	74
Bills	Mana	Silva	SS	65	92	85	56	70
Packers	Sean	Richardson	SS	65	88	86	54	74
Steelers	Da'Mon	Cromartie-Smith	SS	65	88	85	48	73
Bills	Jonathan	Meeks	SS	64	87	90	43	72
Cardinals	Curtis	Taylor	SS	63	85	79	48	88
Dolphins	Don	Jones	SS	63	93	90	48	85
Giants	Tyler	Sash	SS	63	84	75	49	53
Patriots	Nate	Ebner	SS	63	87	86	45	91
Chargers	Sean	Cattouse	SS	62	81	85	47	86
Broncos	Duke	Ihenacho	SS	61	87	88	43	85
Redskins	Devin	Holland	SS	59	92	85	50	71
Bears	Cyhl	Quarles	SS	57	85	79	48	71
Cowboys	Micah	Pellerin	SS	51	85	93	41	44

PUNTERS

TEAM	FIRST NAME	LAST NAME	POS	OVR	KPW	KAC
Greats	Shane	Lechler	P	99	99	97
All-25	Shane	Lechler	P	99	99	97
49ers	Andy	Lee	P	95	98	92
Colts	Pat	McAfee	P	94	97	94
Saints	Thomas	Morstead	P	94	99	93
Dolphins	Brandon	Fields	P	92	97	94
Cardinals	Dave	Zastudil	P	91	92	96
Eagles	Donnie	Jones	P	91	96	92
Ravens	Sam	Koch	P	90	87	97
Chargers	Mike	Scifres	P	89	94	93
Texans	Shane	Lechler	P	89	92	87
Chiefs	Dustin	Colquitt	P	88	89	96
Seahawks	Jon	Ryan	P	86	95	92
Bengals	Kevin	Huber	P	84	90	94
Patriots	Zoltan	Mesko	P	84	94	93
Buccaneers	Michael	Koenen	P	82	96	84
Titans	Brett	Kern	P	82	94	90
Broncos	Britton	Colquitt	P	81	94	92
Falcons	Matt	Bosher	P	81	97	89
Giants	Steve	Weatherford	P	81	88	94
Free Agents	Mat	McBriar	P	81	90	87
Raiders	Chris	Kluwe	P	79	90	87
Jaguars	Bryan	Anger	P	78	96	90
Packers	Tim	Masthay	P	78	95	88
Redskins	Sav	Rocca	P	77	91	88
Steelers	Brian	Moorman	P	77	85	84
Free Agents	Nick	Harris	P	75	88	88
Free Agents	Jeremy	Kapinos	P	74	92	87
Bears	Adam	Podlesh	P	73	89	86
Rams	John	Hekker	P	73	95	89
Jets	Robert	Malone	P	71	91	88
Steelers	Drew	Butler	P	71	94	88

TEAM	FIRST NAME	LAST NAME	POS	OVR	KPW	KAC
Browns	Spencer	Lanning	P	69	95	84
Panthers	Brad	Nortman	P	69	90	88
Buccaneers	Chas	Henry	P	68	94	85
Vikings	Jeff	Locke	P	68	90	92
Browns	T.J.	Conley	P	67	92	86
Cowboys	Chris	Jones	P	67	92	86
Bills	Shawn	Powell	P	65	87	89
Free Agents	Reggie	Hodges	P	65	88	86
Lions	Sam	Martin	P	63	94	86
Cardinals	Jim	Dray	FB	71	72	70
Chiefs	Braden	Wilson	FB	71	76	74
Lions	Shaun	Chapas	FB	71	69	78
Jaguars	Will	Ta'ufo'ou	FB	70	69	83
Redskins	Eric	Kettani	FB	70	82	68
Texans	Tyler	Clutts	FB	70	69	76
Free Agents	Nate	Eachus	FB	70	84	75
Bears	Tony	Fiammetta	FB	69	81	77
Panthers	Richie	Brockel	FB	69	67	72
Titans	Quinn	Johnson	FB	68	70	67
Bills	Frank	Summers	FB	67	75	74
Jaguars	Lonnie	Pryor	FB	67	80	66
Chargers	Chris	Gronkowski	FB	65	73	67
Falcons	Bradie	Ewing	FB	65	76	59
49ers	Will	Tukuafu	FB	65	67	83
Patriots	James	Develin	FB	65	73	76
Raiders	Jamize	Olawale	FB	65	75	72
Seahawks	Spencer	Ware	FB	65	85	73
Browns	Dan	Gronkowski	FB	64	72	69
Raiders	Jon	Hoese	FB	63	72	69
Rams	Mike	McNeill	FB	63	77	60
Eagles	Emil	Igwenagu	FB	62	75	69
Vikings	Matt	Asiata	FB	61	77	69

KICKERS

TEAM	FIRST NAME	LAST NAME	POS	OVR	KPW	KAC
All-25	Adam	Vinatieri	K	99	94	99
Greats	George	Blanda	K	98	96	91
Raiders	Sebastian	Janikowski	K	94	98	90
Bears	Robbie	Gould	K	93	92	93
Vikings	Blair	Walsh	K	92	96	98
49ers	Phil	Dawson	K	89	87	90
Patriots	Stephen	Gostkowski	K	89	92	92
Ravens	Justin	Tucker	K	88	95	96
Titans	Rob	Bironas	K	88	92	88
Colts	Adam	Vinatieri	K	87	87	89
Falcons	Matt	Bryant	K	87	87	93
Steelers	Shaun	Suisham	K	86	89	95
Buccaneers	Connor	Barth	K	85	90	95
Cardinals	Jay	Feely	K	85	91	88
Jaguars	Josh	Scobee	K	85	94	88
Bills	Rian	Lindell	K	84	86	89
Broncos	Matt	Prater	K	84	99	86
Bengals	Mike	Nugent	K	83	91	91
Browns	Shayne	Graham	K	83	86	90
Cowboys	Dan	Bailey	K	83	88	96
Giants	Josh	Brown	K	82	92	87

TEAM	FIRST NAME	LAST NAME	POS	OVR	KPW	KAC
Free Agents	Lawrence	Tynes	K	82	90	89
Lions	David	Akers	K	81	96	75
Redskins	Kai	Forbath	K	81	88	96
Seahawks	Steven	Hauschka	K	81	94	90
Eagles	Alex	Henery	K	80	91	93
Free Agents	Olindo	Mare	K	80	91	82
Chargers	Nick	Novak	K	79	92	88
Rams	Greg	Zuerlein	K	79	99	87
Chiefs	Ryan	Succop	K	78	91	88
Dolphins	Dan	Carpenter	K	78	96	86
Jets	Nick	Folk	K	76	88	87
Panthers	Graham	Gano	K	76	95	86
Saints	Garrett	Hartley	K	76	93	87
Free Agents	Billy	Cundiff	K	75	95	78
Packers	Mason	Crosby	K	73	98	78
Bills	Dustin	Hopkins	K	71	95	86
Dolphins	Caleb	Sturgis	K	71	90	90
Giants	David	Buehler	K	67	97	79
Texans	Randy	Bullock	K	66	89	91
Free Agents	Justin	Medlock	K	63	90	85
Free Agents	John	Potter	K	60	95	84

ACHIEVEMENTS

ACHIEVEMENT NAME	DESCRIPTION	XBOX POINTS	PLAYSTATION TROPHY	PLAYSTATION POINTS
Beginning the Journey	Win a Madden Ultimate Team Seasons game.	10	Bronze	15
The Playoffs?!	Make the playoffs.	15	Bronze	15
Well Rested	Earn a first-round bye.	20	Bronze	15
Complete the Journey	Win a Madden Ultimate Team Seasons Super Bowl.	35	Silver	30
Mr. Suitcase	Complete a Madden Ultimate Team collection.	20	Bronze	15
You Know the Business	Build a Madden Ultimate Team with a team chemistry of 30.	25	Silver	30
Really Clicking	Build a Madden Ultimate Team with a team chemistry of 70.	35	Silver	30
Completely Gelled	Build a Madden Ultimate Team with two team chemistry ratings of 60.	50	Gold	90
The Mogul	Win a Madden Ultimate Team auction.	15	Bronze	15
Flying Solo	Win a Madden Ultimate Team Solo Challenge.	20	Bronze	15
This One Is Hard 3.0	Build an 85 rated Madden Ultimate Team.	50	Gold	90
It's Still Easy	Create a Madden Ultimate Team.	5	Bronze	15
Giver	Post a piece of content to Madden Share.	10	Bronze	15
Taker	Download a piece of content from Madden Share.	10	Bronze	15
Quality Gift	Download three pieces of content from Madden Share	20	Bronze	15
Feedback	Rate a piece of content you've downloaded from Madden Share.	10	Bronze	15
Get Your Feet Wet	Complete an online ranked head-to-head game.	20	Bronze	15
Only Seventeen	Score 17 total points in online ranked head-to-head games.	10	Bronze	15
Nice Round Number	Score 34 total points in online ranked head-to-head games.	20	Bronze	15
Arm's Length Away	Stiff arm a defender during a single run (no SuperSim, OTP, or Co-op).	25	Silver	30
College Influence	Score a TD on a read option play (no SuperSim, OTP, or Co-op).	25	Bronze	15
Defense Wins Championships	Achieve 100% completion of all defensive tutorials (all gold medals).	30	Silver	30
Going for Gold	Earn gold in a tutorial.	15	Bronze	15
Happy 25th Madden!	Score 25+ points and celebrate 25 years of Madden Football (no SuperSim, OTP, or Co-Op)	25	Bronze	15
Knowledge Is Power	Achieve 100% completion of all pre-play tutorials (all gold medals).	30	Silver	30
On the Ball	Enter the no huddle offense by using Kinect (no SuperSim, OTP, or Co-op).	15	Xbox Only	
QB Camp	Achieve 100% completion of all passing tutorials (all gold medals).	30	Silver	30
Stick Skills	Achieve 100% completion of all rushing tutorials (all gold medals).	30	Silver	30
The New Breed	Score a rushing and passing TD with the same QB in a single game (no SuperSim, OTP, or Co-op).	25	Silver	30
Unstoppable	Truck a defender during a single run (no SuperSim, OTP, or Co-op).	25	Silver	30
Verizon MVP	Combine for 75 points total, with your opponent (no SuperSim, OTP, or Co-op).	25	Silver	30
Blaine Gabbert Legacy Award	Using a created player, coach, or owner, surpass a legacy score of 25.	10	Bronze	15
James Laurinaitis Legacy Award	Using a created player, coach, or owner, surpass a legacy score of 280.	15	Bronze	15
Jermichael Finley Legacy Award	Using a created player, coach, or owner, surpass a legacy score of 645.	20	Bronze	15
Marvin Lewis Legacy Award	Using a created player, coach, or owner, surpass a legacy score of 1,250.	25	Bronze	15
Drew Brees Legacy Award	Using a created player, coach, or owner, surpass a legacy score of 4,805.	30	Bronze	15
John Elway Legacy Award	Using a created player, coach, or owner, surpass a legacy score of 11,745.	50	Silver	30
Cortland Finnegan Legacy Award	Using a created player, coach, or owner, surpass a legacy score of 500.	15	Bronze	15
Matt Forte Legacy Award	Using a created player, coach, or owner, surpass a legacy score of 726.	20	Bronze	15
Walter Payton Legacy Award	Using a created player, coach, or owner, surpass a legacy score of 14,035.	100	Gold	90
Ron Rivera Legacy Award	Using a created player, coach, or owner, surpass a legacy score of 100.	15	Bronze	15

MADDEN ALL-25 TEAM

During 25 years of the Madden NFL franchise, gamers have developed favorite players. This team celebrates the best players in the entire history of the series! This team will allow you to relive the glory days and bring your favorite players back to the virtual gridiron to dominate once again!

REFER TO PAGE 327 OR THE INSIDE OF THE BACK COVER FOR AN EXPLANATION OF THE ABBREVIATIONS

FIRST NAME	LAST NAME	POSITION	OVR	SPD	ACC	STR	AGI	AWR	CTH	CAR	THP	THA	KPW	KAC	RBK	PBK	TKL	JMP	TRK	ELU	SFA	SPM	JKM	PMV	FMV	BSH	PUR	MCV	ZCV	HPW
Tom	Brady	QB	99	62	63	65	55	99	43	62	99	98	18	17	34	19	33	47	20	20	25	35	54	10	10	33	30	11	19	12
Kurt	Warner	QB	97	57	54	54	55	97	21	49	90	98	23	26	11	10	9	57	19	13	10	25	30	10	10	10	26	25	26	12
Randall	Cunningham	QB	94	90	87	67	97	87	70	68	97	86	26	27	28	32	40	92	45	90	69	94	96	10	10	41	52	11	30	12
Michael	Vick	QB	90	95	97	62	97	77	70	64	98	84	19	22	24	19	31	87	35	92	64	93	96	10	10	31	40	18	16	12
Barry	Sanders	HB	99	97	99	82	99	99	73	95	39	28	37	35	55	60	40	75	75	99	90	100	99	35	22	30	35	35	36	35
Adrian	Peterson	HB	99	97	99	89	98	93	65	90	35	40	25	26	43	55	42	90	98	97	97	95	97	10	10	35	40	12	12	15
Marshall	Faulk	HB	99	93	99	69	99	99	90	88	45	35	36	25	35	45	35	82	77	97	68	96	98	10	10	21	29	13	16	25
Curtis	Martin	HB	96	90	92	84	90	95	78	98	46	44	26	15	54	66	35	82	96	74	95	92	88	10	10	25	14	30	19	25
Mike	Alstott	FB	99	83	86	85	81	92	78	94	39	34	19	19	77	76	35	90	98	44	94	84	82	10	10	35	45	10	25	45
Calvin	Johnson Jr.	WR	99	95	94	78	96	91	97	65	35	33	14	11	65	35	28	98	72	88	82	87	91	10	10	45	47	12	22	15
Randy	Moss	WR	98	99	93	64	97	95	97	55	64	49	19	15	48	44	33	100	45	91	75	90	92	10	10	30	40	13	27	15
Cris	Carter	WR	97	86	88	73	93	96	98	76	39	35	27	19	60	50	29	98	50	84	75	85	90	10	10	10	10	38	38	12
Larry	Fitzgerald	WR	96	89	90	76	93	95	98	74	26	29	18	19	60	40	30	98	73	54	75	85	87	10	10	40	42	18	14	12
Isaac	Bruce	WR	91	94	96	49	97	93	95	71	39	35	24	16	52	45	25	88	35	93	40	88	97	10	10	14	35	17	17	15
DeSean	Jackson	WR	88	99	98	43	98	84	89	64	40	35	30	30	46	30	22	87	44	99	45	95	98	10	10	35	35	15	35	12
Brian	Finneran	WR	87	85	87	74	87	82	90	75	30	31	15	19	63	48	31	99	60	59	67	84	82	10	10	41	35	15	18	15
Devin	Hester	WR	83	100	99	55	99	85	80	69	35	40	22	18	30	20	40	92	36	99	45	97	99	20	25	44	64	61	62	30
Josh	Cribbs	WR	82	92	97	64	98	86	75	84	78	63	21	25	36	26	29	90	49	98	55	98	99	10	10	16	40	12	16	12
Shannon	Sharpe	TE	99	88	92	92	88	95	96	86	25	25	15	19	68	67	45	88	87	77	93	78	82	10	10	44	35	10	24	12
Antonio	Gates	TE	99	86	90	78	88	95	97	75	25	25	15	19	58	48	44	92	75	75	78	82	85	10	10	44	35	10	24	12
Rob	Gronkowski	TE	98	83	87	88	86	80	90	67	27	22	21	20	80	62	20	84	91	50	75	74	75	10	10	43	40	12	17	25
Walter	Jones	LT	97	64	78	97	63	97	28	40	34	27	19	17	98	93	12	46	30	17	10	10	10	30	30	12	21	17	17	20
Orlando	Pace	LT	96	66	89	95	73	92	25	40	30	34	15	32	90	97	29	70	25	18	10	10	10	10	10	26	25	22	21	35
Steve	Hutchinson	LG	99	59	75	95	64	96	35	40	28	22	25	20	97	95	25	39	10	35	10	10	10	10	10	25	33	14	19	20
Logan	Mankins	LG	97	62	79	92	62	93	14	40	15	16	14	17	96	88	36	40	10	19	10	10	10	10	10	36	41	11	13	20
Dermontti	Dawson	C	97	69	85	92	64	95	30	40	26	26	22	22	95	89	10	55	25	10	10	10	10	10	10	10	23	15	9	20
Nick	Mangold	C	96	63	85	92	57	93	25	40	14	25	27	28	97	90	44	64	10	19	10	10	10	10	10	44	29	13	14	20
Larry	Allen	RG	98	52	67	99	54	98	30	40	25	21	32	35	99	91	28	45	22	15	25	10	10	25	10	17	12	17	18	20
Jahri	Evans	RG	97	56	75	97	65	88	22	40	26	21	14	15	88	97	30	48	10	21	10	10	10	10	10	30	19	12	12	20
Jonathan	Ogden	RT	98	53	74	98	62	97	19	40	15	19	26	31	97	95	26	45	25	17	10	10	10	10	10	26	25	28	12	20
David	Stewart	RT	96	53	66	95	55	92	25	40	12	13	14	13	90	98	25	30	10	18	10	10	10	10	10	25	23	9	14	20
J.J.	Watt	LE	99	77	90	97	75	85	72	55	20	19	10	10	45	45	95	82	47	32	35	33	35	99	67	98	96	24	35	84
Justin	Smith	LE	97	73	83	96	68	97	23	40	26	25	16	24	45	45	95	68	30	25	10	10	10	84	54	96	95	17	21	75
Dwight	Freeney	RE	99	88	97	79	87	90	48	40	19	16	15	10	45	45	75	72	25	39	10	85	55	82	99	69	97	55	60	81
Julius	Peppers	RE	97	85	95	85	87	88	68	60	25	24	16	11	45	45	76	87	10	40	70	65	65	79	98	69	95	40	62	88
Warren	Sapp	DT	99	72	93	94	70	94	62	40	17	19	17	24	45	45	90	65	25	45	45	40	25	94	98	88	96	25	35	88
Vince	Wilfork	DT	95	61	79	98	64	94	60	54	56	44	11	10	45	45	98	65	35	13	10	10	10	88	47	98	91	28	24	68
Kevin	Williams	DT	95	68	85	92	67	95	16	40	28	16	24	18	45	45	91	48	10	29	10	10	10	96	67	82	85	19	25	66
Albert	Haynesworth	DT	93	65	82	98	63	93	21	40	15	15	21	19	45	45	95	64	25	10	10	10	10	93	49	95	77	15	25	80
Derrick	Brooks	LOLB	97	87	90	74	87	99	82	75	19	37	15	36	45	45	96	75	10	48	55	70	67	55	75	82	97	80	95	88
Terrell	Suggs	LOLB	92	83	94	93	76	90	51	65	19	18	26	17	45	45	90	80	10	45	10	55	45	97	78	83	95	51	60	84
Ray	Lewis	MLB	99	85	91	95	87	99	65	60	14	15	17	23	45	45	99	74	50	36	75	40	50	80	69	94	99	74	84	99
Patrick	Willis	MLB	98	90	93	88	88	95	64	63	30	35	20	21	45	45	97	75	30	31	60	30	35	70	60	90	98	75	82	98
Derrick	Thomas	ROLB	99	88	94	92	85	90	40	55	28	14	23	30	45	45	93	81	74	39	55	55	60	93	99	95	99	60	75	95
James	Harrison	ROLB	98	85	88	88	79	99	44	55	28	14	23	30	45	45	91	70	44	29	15	35	25	98	88	97	95	45	60	100
Deion	Sanders	CB	99	99	99	44	99	99	90	55	55	45	25	10	45	45	40	97	10	98	35	92	99	25	35	40	75	99	98	49
Darrelle	Revis	CB	98	93	96	64	96	94	70	70	30	32	22	15	45	45	64	92	36	70	30	84	90	45	54	60	85	98	94	66
Champ	Bailey	CB	97	95	95	55	97	95	84	64	29	17	19	19	45	45	66	91	48	75	45	90	95	35	55	43	79	97	90	50
Nnamdi	Asomugha	CB	95	93	92	69	94	91	69	65	14	21	14	16	45	45	57	94	10	37	26	65	65	48	60	52	84	97	92	60
Charles	Woodson	CB	94	91	93	68	95	97	83	80	22	19	24	19	45	45	66	93	54	70	52	82	87	60	78	64	88	85	93	48
Sean	Taylor	FS	99	93	96	80	93	85	82	76	32	25	18	12	45	45	85	96	35	60	75	84	85	75	87	84	94	70	94	98
Ed	Reed	FS	99	92	93	62	94	98	85	60	20	14	22	12	45	45	65	90	56	93	40	88	90	45	75	52	82	77	96	75
Brian	Dawkins	SS	99	88	90	69	91	95	74	70	15	22	23	22	45	45	83	91	25	65	55	82	84	65	82	74	94	75	97	95
Troy	Polamalu	SS	98	92	94	69	95	88	77	65	9	14	11	12	45	45	76	93	62	75	50	56	85	70	80	75	98	61	83	88
Adam	Vinatieri	K	99	59	60	40	58	97	29	40	29	15	94	99	18	22	32	29	10	25	10	10	10	10	10	32	19	14	16	12
Shane	Lechler	P	99	60	62	33	52	95	28	40	57	50	99	97	22	25	18	31	10	19	10	10	10	10	10	18	14	10	23	12

MADDEN NFL 1989 25 2014

WRITTEN BY

ZACH "ZFARLS" FARLEY AND STEVE "SGIBS" GIBBONS

PRIMA OFFICIAL GAME GUIDE

PRODUCT MANAGER: **Paul Giacomotto**
COPYEDITOR: **Deana Shields**
DESIGN & LAYOUT: **In Color Design**
TECH EDITOR: **Josef Frech**
VIDEO EDITOR: **Julian Ogans**

PRIMA GAMES

An Imprint of Random House LLC,
a Penguin Random House Company

3000 Lava Ridge Ct, Suite 100
Roseville, CA. 95661

PrimaGames.com/MaddenNFL25 and MaddenTips.com

ISBN: 978-0-804-16127-5
ISBN: 978-0-804-16258-6
Printed in the United States of America

SPECIAL THANKS

Prima Games would like to thank: Moya Dacey, Jennica Pearson, Anthony Stevenson, Larry Richart, Clint Oldenburg, Mike Scantlebury, Anthony White, Donny Moore, Mike Young, Victor Lugo, Tom Lischke, Joe Alread, Ryan Simmons, Chuck Kallenbach, Mike Christman, Seann Graddy, Thomas Singleton, Jake Stein, Danny Doeberling, Matt Bialosuknia, Justin Dewiel, Markus Frieske, Brad Hilderbrand, Andrew Johnson, Cam Weber, Roy Harvey, Alexander Lee, Eric "PROBLEM" Wright, Daniel Shlossman, Evan Singer, Shaun McPartlin and Michael Fabiano. Last but not least... the amazing tandem of ZFARLS and SGIBS!

ZFarls (Zach) and SGibs (Steve) would like to thank: Their friends and family for supporting them during the writing of this guide. As we headed down to Florida, you were fully behind our effort and it made a world of difference in the final version.

The team was also heavily supported by the employees of EA SPORTS. The gameplay team was extremely supportive and stayed late on multiple nights to further break down the sport of football and game of Madden NFL. This insight and passion proved to us a great level of commitment to Madden NFL and furthered our love for the game.

Special thanks to Prima Games for sharing in the full vision of a guide with a new format. We are so thankful for a company that truly offers full support by continually delivering passionate people and resources to get the job done.

Lastly, to our fans who continue to support the dream that Steve and I started in 2007 in our dorm room, we thank you. We seek to improve the game of Madden NFL players everywhere, and increase the enjoyment we all share when we pick up the stick. Thank you!